PENGUIN BOO

THE PENGUIN F
MODERN SPE

Brian MacArthur was founder editor of *Today* and *The Times Higher Education Supplement*, and editor of the *Western Morning News*. He was deputy editor of the *Sunday Times* and executive editor of *The Times*. He has written *Surviving the Sword: Prisoners of the Japanese 1942–1945*. He has been interested in the power of oratory since first hearing Aneurin Bevan on the hustings in 1956 and has edited *The Penguin Book of Historic Speeches* and *The Penguin Book of Twentieth-Century Protest*.

Brian MacArthur lives in Norfolk and London and has two daughters.

# THE PENGUIN BOOK OF
# MODERN SPEECHES

EDITED BY BRIAN MacARTHUR

PENGUIN BOOKS

PENGUIN BOOKS

UK | USA | Canada | Ireland | Australia
India | New Zealand | South Africa

Penguin Books is part of the Penguin Random House group of companies
whose addresses can be found at global.penguinrandomhouse.com.

Penguin
Random House
UK

First published as *The Penguin Book of Twentieth-Century Speeches* by Viking 1992
Published with revisions in Penguin Books 1993
Second revised edition published 1999
Third revised edition published as *The Penguin Book of Modern Speeches* 2012
Fourth revised edition published 2017

007

The acknowledgements on pp. xxvii–xxix constitute an extension of this copyright page

Typeset by Jouve (UK), Milton Keynes

Printed and bound in Great Britain by Clays Ltd, Elcograf S.p.A.

A CIP catalogue record for this book is available from the British Library

ISBN: 978–0–241–98230–3

www.greenpenguin.co.uk

For Maureen Waller

Each time a man stands up for an ideal,
or acts to improve the lot of others,
or strikes out against injustice,
he sends forth a tiny ripple of hope,
and crossing each other from a million
different centres of energy and daring,
those ripples build a current that can
sweep down the mightiest walls of
oppression and resistance.

Robert Kennedy, 1966

# CONTENTS

# Contents

# INTRODUCTION

Oratory is always a declining art. Every generation judges contemporary speakers unfavourably against the giants of the past. At the end of the twentieth century, the speeches of the British prime minister Tony Blair were criticized (by the Tory *Daily Telegraph*) as being like the voice-overs in advertisements, depending on beguiling images rather than having coherent meaning in their own right. It accused Blair of using phrases not sentences. Matthew Parris, the outstanding parliamentary reporter of his generation, asked in *The Times* if there was no way of steering Blair clear of visionary, salvationist nouns.

Similar complaints were made eighty years earlier about Lloyd George who now stands out as one of the greatest of lyrical orators. Yet an Everyman anthology of oratory published in the 1920s complained that oratory had given way to 'talk'. The change, according to the editor, could be seen in the natural colloquial style of Lloyd George compared with the oratorical styles of Lord Rosebery or Winston Churchill. That allegedly colloquial style, with which Lloyd George summoned the nation to 'the great pinnacle of sacrifice pointing like a rugged finger to heaven', now strikes us not as talk but as magnificent oratory and we complain about the dull, colloquial style of George Bush or John Major or the often messianic style of Blair.

Lloyd George himself made the same complaint when he wrote a short introduction to a collection of his speeches in 1929, arguing that the conditions of modern speaking were not conducive to the preparation of speeches that survived the controversy to which they were addressed. He was, nevertheless, an optimist. Acknowledging that first the school boards and the popular press and then the cheap entertainment offered by film, gramophone and broadcasting had been accused of destroying oratory, he pointed out that the Labour Party, the most powerful party in the state, had been created by spoken appeals from myriads of platforms.

'Broadcasting will give new life and sway to speech-making. Controversy may be ruled out yet awhile by timid counsels. In the end it will force its way to the disc. A sporting nation, which is also a political people, will insist on seeing the ball kicked in one of its favourite games. When that time comes, the style of oratory may be altered to the exigencies of the machine; but the true orator will adapt his art to the occasion, and the spoken word will be more potent than ever.'

As Franklin D. Roosevelt and Winston Churchill were to show by their mastery of the wireless, Lloyd George was right. Since then, orators have adapted not only to radio but also to the very different demands of television – which has magnified the power of oratory. Speeches can now be broadcast live round the world, as on such memorable occasions as John F. Kennedy during the Cuban missile crisis, Nelson Mandela on leaving jail after twenty-seven years or Earl Spencer delivering his philippic over the catafalque of his sister, Diana, Princess of Wales, a speech that probably had the largest audience in history. Yet still the complaint is made that oratory is a declining art. According to Peggy Noonan, author of some of Ronald Reagan's most memorable oratory, the irony of modern speeches is that as our ability to disseminate them has exploded their quality has declined.

'Why? Lots of reasons, including that we as a nation no longer learn the rhythms of public utterance from Shakespeare and the Bible. When young Lincoln was sprawled in front of the fireplace reading *Julius Caesar* – "The abuse of greatness is, when it disjoins remorse from power" – he was, unconsciously, learning to be a poet. You say, "That was Lincoln, not the common man." But the common man was flocking to the docks to get the latest instalment of Dickens off the ship from England.

'The modern egalitarian impulse has made politicians leery of flaunting high rhetoric; attempts to reach, to find the right if esoteric quote or allusion seem pretentious. They don't really know what "the common man" thinks any more; they forget that we've all had at least some education and a number of us read on our own and read certain classics in junior high and high school. The guy at the gas station read *Call of the Wild* when he was fourteen, and sometimes thinks about it. Moreover, he has imagination. Politicians forget. They go in for the lowest common denominator – like a newscaster.'

Any contemporary observer who relishes great oratory and who observes American presidential elections or British general elections cannot but agree with Noonan's thesis. Where are the visions and where the words that inspire men and women to greater things and make them vote with enthusiasm, even passion? Both President Clinton and Tony Blair were significant improvements on their immediate predecessors but the verdict still seems to stand. The springs of oratory are drying up, it seems, as churches become deserted, the study of Latin and Greek declines, and schools fail to give students the thorough grounding in their literary and religious heritage that was once taken for granted and which inspired the great orators.

Or are they? Perhaps Noonan despairs too soon – and also ignores the evidence of her own work, shown in this anthology by her speeches for Reagan after the *Challenger* disaster and at Pointe du Hoc in Normandy. She herself, moreover, supplies the answer to the complaint that speeches today are prepared only for the 'sound bites' demanded by television. Speeches have always had sound bites or memorable phrases. 'With malice towards none. With charity towards all' (Lincoln); 'You shall not crucify mankind upon a cross of gold' (Bryan); 'He has not a single redeeming defect' (Disraeli on Gladstone) – all were nineteenth-century sound bites as surely as 'The only thing we have to fear is fear itself' or 'Ask not what your country can do for you' were memorable sound bites from the twentieth century.

Even as Noonan was writing her book, moreover, Vaclav Havel, the playwright-president of Czechoslovakia, was eloquently celebrating the joy of a nation freed from Soviet tyranny – and without the help of a speechwriter. Whether it is Nelson Mandela in South Africa, Ronald Reagan or Margaret Thatcher, Edward Kennedy or

Jesse Jackson, Boris Yeltsin or Elie Wiesel, Neil Kinnock or Tony Blair, the speeches made over the past thirty years collected in this anthology demonstrate that oratory still helps to overcome tyranny, defy despair, or to articulate the hopes and dreams of millions and change the world. Global television meanwhile ensures that speeches are heard by millions rather than the hundreds or thousands of the early twentieth century.

Oratory still flourishes but the style of oratory is always changing. Nineteenth-century orators might speak on only three great occasions a year. They would think about a speech for a fortnight and then spend several days polishing its phrases and committing the speech to memory (as Churchill often did a century later). Gladstone was the first British speaker to break with that tradition. During the Midlothian campaign he addressed several audiences at great length in less than a fortnight – and was attacked for departing from the dignity and decorum appropriate to a former prime minister.

When Lloyd George was at his peak, and speakers made at least a score of speeches a year outside parliament, he noted that addresses had become as a matter of course largely improvisations: 'The meticulous care with which words were chosen and sentences were framed and adorned and afterwards rooted in the memory has thus necessarily become a thing of the past.' That change was an undoubted advantage for audiences, Lloyd George thought. In ninety-nine cases out of a hundred, lengthy prepared orations were 'boring, dreary, and wholly ineffective'. A perfectly phrased but badly delivered speech might be a dazzling essay, but it was not oratory.

So what is oratory? Quoting approvingly the maxim that oratory was the harlot of the arts, the British prime minister Stanley Baldwin pointed out that to tell the truth needed no art at all. God help the man who tries to think on it, he said. The gift of rhetoric had been responsible for more bloodshed than all the guns and explosives ever invented:

'If we look back only over the last century, was there anything more responsible for the French Revolution than the literary rhetoric of Rousseau, fanned by the verbal rhetoric of Robespierre and others, just as the Russian Revolution was due to the rhetoric of

Kerensky – flatulent rhetoric which filled the bellies of his people with the east wind? That appalling twopenny-ha'penny gift of fluency, with the addition of a certain amount of training and of imagination in word-spinning, is the kind of rhetoric which stirs the emotions of the ignorant mob and sets it moving. It is because such forces can be set in motion by rhetoric that I have no regard for it but a positive horror.'

When circumstances required, Baldwin was himself capable of the telling, destructive phrase, as he showed when he condemned Britain's two main press proprietors for 'seeking power without responsibility, the prerogative of the harlot throughout the ages'. That positive horror nevertheless inspired Baldwin's own prosaic speaking style (which was unequally matched to the oratorical power of his German adversary Adolf Hitler). As seen by their opponents (if not by their followers, who were obviously uplifted by their speeches), the Baldwin thesis of the orator's destructive power is notably demonstrated within this anthology by Lenin, Stalin, Fidel Castro and Joseph McCarthy. Yet no orator of the twentieth century better illustrates that destructive power of oratory against which Baldwin warned than Hitler, undoubtedly the greatest speaker of the century. Churchill, the other main contender, roused a willing nation to war. Hitler changed a nation by his oratory.

As his biographer Alan Bullock explains, speech was the essential medium of Hitler's power not only over his audiences but his own temperament. He set out his creed in *Mein Kampf*. 'The force which ever set in motion the great historical avalanches of religious and political movements is the magic power of the spoken word. The broad masses of a population are more amenable to the appeal of rhetoric than to any other force.' As for the orator: 'He will always follow the lead of the great mass in such a way that from the living emotion of his hearers the apt word that he needs will be suggested to him and in its turn this will go straight to the hearts of his hearers.'

That magic, hypnotic power is shown at its most effective in this anthology by Hitler's speech to the Düsseldorf Industry Club in 1932. When Hitler arrived, his reception from the West German industrialists was cool and reserved. Yet he spoke for two and a half hours without pause and made one of the best speeches of his life, setting out all his stock ideas brilliantly dressed up for his audience of businessmen. At the end they rose and cheered him wildly. Contributions from German industry started flowing into the Nazi treasury. Hitler by that one speech had won an important victory. That was the (relatively) emollient Hitler. The frightening and destructive power of his oratory, palpable even in translation, is shown in the extracts from the two other speeches in this collection.

Yet although the power of Hitler's speeches roused Germany to barbarity, and made Baldwin's case, most of the speeches in this anthology demonstrate the power of oratory for good rather than evil. They articulate dreams, offer hope, stir hearts and minds, and offer their audiences visions of a better world. The phrases by which they are remembered, whether the summons to the 'strenuous life' of Theodore Roosevelt or to the 'new frontier' of John F. Kennedy or the 'I have a dream' of Martin Luther King, sounded the trumpet for constructive action; and the defining principle of this anthology, beyond significance or eloquence, is that it selects speeches that sent forth the 'ripples of hope' that Robert Kennedy so memorably offered to South African students in 1966.

Those ripples of hope were sent forth by Emmeline Pankhurst and Betty Friedan for women's freedom; by Patrick Pearse, Roger Casement, Mahatma Gandhi, Fidel Castro and Nelson Mandela to nations and races that were oppressed; by John F. Kennedy and Harold Wilson and Margaret Thatcher and Ronald Reagan – in their different causes – to dispossessed constituencies that yearned for power. Few speeches sent forth more ripples of hope than those of Franklin D. Roosevelt – or of Winston Churchill when he mobilized the English language for war.

There are also destructive speeches. Leo Amery and Lloyd George destroyed Neville Chamberlain by their speeches in the Norway debate in the House of Commons in 1940. By his speech on race (the most elegantly constructed and most difficult to edit in this anthology), Enoch Powell barred his path to the highest office of state which, if that speech had not been made, would sooner or later have been his to command. On paper, Sir Geoffrey Howe made a rather plodding speech when he resigned as foreign secretary, but its very restraint, only barely concealing the inner fury and frustration of a man who had been so often slighted, initiated the downfall of Margaret Thatcher.

So much care is still given to speeches by contemporary politicians, moreover, that it is obvious that they still think oratory matters. An individual politician like Roy Jenkins spent as much time in solitary preparation of a speech as Lloyd George. That care was put into Jenkins's Dimbleby Lecture and that lecture led to the creation of a new British political party, the Social Democrats. As Peggy Noonan explains, hours and often weeks were spent preparing major speeches by Ronald Reagan. Draft after draft of a speech would be submitted to Mrs Thatcher into the early hours of the morning until she was satisfied that every nuance of what she wanted to say was covered.

If any vindication of the power of modern oratory is required, there is a splendid account by Noonan of the making of Reagan's Pointe du Hoc speech in Normandy in 1984. The speech was important for Reagan. Not only was he addressing the citizens of Europe, but the speech was being broadcast live by all the American networks and an extract was wanted for the Reagan film at the Republican convention. Make it like the Gettysburg Address, she was told. Make people cry.

Noonan describes how she constructed the speech – first the big, emotional words and images, then the placing of Pointe du Hoc in time and space, then what happened in 1944 (mostly to stop the children chewing their Rice Krispies and make them reflect on the greatness of their grandfathers) and so on. As the speech was prepared, there was a White House battle between literature (Noonan) and the National Security Council which wanted a statement about the Soviets. Noonan held her ground, reasoning that if she held off the bureaucrats they would have to scribble in their insert about the Soviets on the plane and they wouldn't have time to take something out. That was what happened.

The main question posed by the moving Pointe du Hoc speech is whether it was a speech by Ronald Reagan or by Peggy Noonan. It was, obviously, written by Noonan. But it was delivered by Reagan and it was his characteristic delivery of the words she wrote that worked the alchemy on the speech and made people weep. However brilliant the words, it is also the manner of delivery, the sincerity of the speaker, that makes a speech great.

Although many of the speeches in this anthology – for instance, Sir Roger Casement and Churchill – read as well as great literature, one objection to an anthology of speeches is that it inevitably presents oratory as literature, when in fact speeches are made to be heard. Speeches succeed, according to Lloyd George, by a combination of word, voice and gesture in moving their audiences to the action the orator desires. The nobler the action, the more exalted the orator. Yet many of the most effective speeches are quite unreadable in cold print and certainly unsuitable for an anthology. What Lord Morley said, in a discussion of Gladstone's Midlothian speeches, still rings true today: 'The statesman who makes or dominates a crisis, who has to rouse and mould the mind of senate or nation, has something else to think about than the production of literary masterpieces.'

That is particularly true of the British House of Commons where the outstanding speakers rarely use notes except for their perorations, and explains why several brilliant oratorical triumphs – Iain Macleod forging his reputation by demolishing Aneurin Bevan, Michael Foot at bay before the barracking Tories as he defended the Callaghan government against the no-confidence motion that brought Thatcher to power, John Biffen on monetary policy or Margaret Thatcher on her resignation – make no appearance in this anthology. Many British MPs remember those speeches as the best they ever heard in the Commons but the interruptions to Commons speeches destroys their flow. They do not read as well as they were heard. Most speeches in translation suffer from the same defect, which is why both Chairman Mao and Mikhail Gorbachev are absent from this anthology. Communist-speak was also deeply uneloquent.

Nor can an anthology capture the spell cast at the moment of delivery by the greatest speakers. That must be left to the imagination, though we can still capture some of their magic from contemporary accounts of their varying styles.

There is Patrick Pearse, speaking for Ireland: 'Calm and deliberate, in soft yet thrilling accents, his oration was almost sublime. Here was no rhetoric, no mathematical oratory; it was the soul of a patriot breathing words of love and devotion, of hope and truth and cour-age, no threnody but a paean of triumph such as might have come from out of the tomb by which we were.'

There is Lloyd George, as described by A. J. P. Taylor: 'Lloyd George spoke with his audience, not to them, and snapped up phrases as they were thrown at him. "Ninepence for fourpence" was the result of one such interruption; making Germany pay to the last farthing, the less happy result of another. Lloyd George gave a music hall turn, worthy of Harry Lauder or George Robey, the prime minister of mirth.'

There is Stalin: 'When Stalin speaks with his knowing, comfort-able smile, pointing with his forefinger, he does not, like other orators, make a breach between himself and his audience; he does not stand commandingly on the platform while they sit below him, but very soon an alliance, an intimacy is established between him and his listeners. They, being made of the same stuff, are susceptible to the arguments, and both laugh merrily at the same simple stories.'

There is Hitler: 'He would lash himself to a pitch of near hysteria in which he would scream and spit out his resentment – men groaned or hissed, women sobbed involuntarily, caught up in the spell of powerful emotions of hatred and exaltation, from which all restraint had been removed.'

There is Bevan, as described by Michael Foot. 'Bevan wrought an alchemy before our eyes. He could mix fire with ice. He could evoke dreams and the boldest aspirations, yet the purpose always was to use the motive force thus generated to help forward the business in hand. He unleashed the imagination yet still wanted it tethered to the earth where the immediate enemy must be fought. "Oh! the brave music of a distant drum!" was a quotation he scornfully applied to those who wanted to escape from awkward present con-flicts altogether . . . Few speakers who have been called orators have indulged less in rhetoric and rodomontade. At his best he was never strident . . . He hated grandiloquence; instead the bulk of his speeches was an intricate, intellectual elaboration, interspersed with paradox and irony ... He presented arguments emotionally and emotions argumentatively.'

More recently there is Neil Kinnock, who was described as daring to believe that oratory still had a part to play in British politics. 'Mr Kinnock does not just deliver a speech with his voice: he dances it with his feet and choreographs it with his body ... His timing is as good as that of any stand-up comic; he uses gesture as well as any serious actor; and, seldom still for a moment, his whole mobile demeanour suggests someone whose natural allegiance is just as much to the sports field as to the public platform.'

Kinnock also had the ability to ignore his speechwriters. His 'Why am I the first Kinnock in a thousand generations' speech of 1987 was a series of notes jotted down in the back of his car. When he rose to speak, he glanced at his notes and extemporized the words. Clinton did the same with his powerful Memphis speech in 1994. Clinton and Blair used speechwriters but still wrote many sections of their speeches themselves. Where Blair represented a new phenomenon, as did Lloyd George earlier in the century, was that his speeches were written primarily not for his immediate audience but for the millions who would watch the sound bites deliberately crafted for the television news bulletins.

The sense of drama that still attends a major speech is captured well by Peggy Noonan. 'A speech is a soliloquy,' she says, 'one man on a bare stage with a big spotlight. He will tell us who he is and what he wants and how he will get it and what it means that he wants it and what it will mean when he does or does not get it, and ...

'He looks up at us in the balconies and clears his throat. "Ladies and gentlemen . . ." We lean forward, hungry to hear. Now it will be said, now we will hear the thing we long for. A speech is part theatre and part political declaration; it is personal communication between a leader and his people; it is art, and all art is a paradox, being at once a thing of great power and great delicacy. A speech is poetry: cadence, rhythm, imagery, sweep! A speech reminds us that words, like children, have the power to make dance the dullest beanbag of a heart ... Speeches are important because they are one of the great constants of our political history. They have been not only the way we measure

public men, they have been how we tell each other who we are . . .
They count. They more than count, they shape what happens.'

The drama that Noonan describes still attends the great political
set-piece speeches and shows that oratory is not a declining art, even
though some of the political leaders of the West are not natural orators, even though television places more emphasis on moving images
than moving words.

Amidst the lazy illiteracy of so much modern speech, eloquent
words still have power to pierce through all the banal platitudes and
make audiences stop and think and sometimes even wonder. Our
political leaders still search for the writers who can gild their prosaic
visions (as was shown in 1992 again when Bush summoned Noonan
back to add to his speeches the eloquence he so signally lacked himself). Political leaders still achieve power by the quality of their
speeches; and we still need heroes who can articulate our hopes and
dreams and who can say what in our hearts we want to hear.

My own introduction to great oratory occurred when Aneurin
Bevan addressed a by-election meeting in Chester Corn Exchange
after the Suez crisis. He wielded wit, invective and sarcasm against
hecklers, as did Quintin Hogg (later Lord Hailsham) the following
night. I was hooked. That style may seem to have passed in an era
when audiences prefer their politics on television rather than the
hustings, but it has been kept alive by the speakers represented in
this anthology. The drama of Earl Spencer's speech at Princess
Diana's funeral was so palpable that the listeners outside Westmin
ster Abbey started to applaud, prompting the mourners within the
Abbey to join in – and that sense of drama arose when Tony Blair or
Bill Clinton stepped up to make great speeches and still arises today
when Barack Obama rises to speak. In the twenty-first century it is
drama that television covets and therefore nourishes. A good speech
still makes headlines; and memorable speeches are posted on the
Internet for all to read.

My hope is that this anthology will be an inspiration to those in
politics who seek to change the world and who wish to speak with
the eloquence displayed throughout this book.

# ACKNOWLEDGEMENTS

An anthology requires detailed reading and research and I gratefully acknowledge my debt to the following who helped with advice: Juliet Annan, Charles Anson, Roberto de Armas of the Cuban Embassy, Timothy Garton Ash, Sally Baker, Jonathan Bastable, Tony Benn, Alan Bennett, Hugh Brogan, Stephen Brooks, Sir Alan Bullock, Brigid Callaghan, Lord Callaghan of Cardiff, Alastair Campbell, Professor Colin Campbell, Charles Clarke, Brian Collett, Philip Collins, the former Czechoslovakian Embassy, Lord Dainton, Beryl Drinkwater, Margarette Driscoll, Alan Evans, Harold Evans, Daniel Finkelstein, Lord Fitt, Gillian Fryer, Martyn Goff, Alan Golding, Roy Greenslade, John Grigg, A. H. Halsey, Nigel Hamilton, Denis Healey, Sir Edward Heath, Peter Hennessy, Louis Heren, Michael Heseltine, Anthony Howard, the Indian High Commission, Martin Jacques, Lord Jenkins of Putney, Canon Graham James, Monty Johnstone, Trevor Kavanagh, Frank Keating, Maurice Kogan, Magnus Linklater, Tom McNally, Brenda and John Maddox, Anne Manson, David Marquand, T. W. Roberts of Merthyr Tydfil Trades Council, Rosalind Miles, Peter Millar, Bryan Moynahan, Novosti Press Agency, David Owen, Edward Pearce, Richard Peel, Penny Perrick, Ben Pimlott, Ben Pogrund, Enoch Powell, Nigel Rees, Peter Riddell, David Rogers, Lord Runcie, Ruth Salazar, Mike Smith, Lord Soper, the South African Embassy, Hugh Skillen, Sir David Steel, Andrew J. Taylor, James Taylor, Andrew Thomas, Barry Turner, Charles Webster, Giles Whittell, John Whittingdale and Lord Wilson of Rievaulx.

Many speeches would be lost for ever unless they were kept in libraries and I acknowledge a profound debt to the London Library, the *Times* library, the Library of Congress, and the librarians of the National Museum of Labour History, the Imperial War Museum, the Institute of Jewish Affairs, the Weizmann Institute, the Campaign for Nuclear Disarmament, the Institute of Commonwealth Studies, the European Economic Commission and the German Historical Institute.

John Biffen, Michael Foot and Lord Jenkins of Hillhead were especially helpful.

My greatest debts are to Jackson Boggs, Daria Antonucci, Peter Rose and Toby Bourne for research in America and Britain; to Lynn Moorlen, Tony Lacey, Ellen Levine and Hilary Rubinstein; and Bridget, Tessa and Georgie MacArthur.

For this edition, I acknowledge gratefully the help of Philip Bassett, Paul Bew, Philip Breeden, George Bridges, Alastair Campbell, Lynette Carr, Matthew d'Ancona, Michael Gove, Peter Kellner, the Labour Party, John Lloyd, Robert Low, Manuella Pavlidou of the Melina Mercouri Foundation, Michael Portillo, Michael Shea and Isabel Wall.

## Sources

Several books have been particularly helpful and I acknowledge a sincere debt to their authors: Robert Blake (*The Conservative Party from Peel to Thatcher*), Hugh Brogan (*The Penguin History of the United States of America*), Roy Foster (*Modern Ireland 1600–1972*), Roy Jenkins (*Baldwin* and *A Life at the Centre*), Kenneth O. Morgan (*The People's Peace: British History 1945–1989* and *Labour People*), Peggy Noonan (*What I Saw at the Revolution*), Alan Palmer (*The Penguin Dictionary of Twentieth-century History*), A. J. P. Taylor (*English History, 1914–1945*) and William Safire (*Lend Me Your Ears*). Grateful thanks are also due to the following for permission to reprint copyright material: Aneurin Bevan: to Labour Party Library; Sir Winston S. Churchill: to Curtis Brown Ltd, London, on behalf of the Estate of Sir Winston S. Churchill; copyright the Estate of Sir Winston S. Churchill; Éamon de Valera: to Radio Telefis Eireann; William Faulkner: to Random House UK Ltd and Random House Inc. (reprinted from *Essays, Speeches and Public Letters*, ed. James Meriwether; copyright © 1965 by Random House Inc.); Betty Friedan: to Curtis Brown Ltd, New York (reprinted from *It Changed My Life* (Dell, 1991)); Hugh Gaitskell: to Labour Party Library; David Lloyd George: to Express Newspapers plc and Macmillan Publishing Company (reprinted from *Slings and Arrows* (Cassell, 1929)); David Grossman; Gideon Hausner: to Longman Group UK (reprinted from *Keesings*); Martin Luther King:

to Joan Daves Literary Agency; Douglas MacArthur: to Time Warner Inc./Katz (reprinted from *Reminiscences* (De Capo, 1985; copyright © Time Warner Inc./Katz)); Iain Macleod: to Rt. Hon. Baroness Macleod of Borve; Nelson Mandela: to Penguin Books Ltd and Anthony Sheil Associates (reprinted from *Higher Than Hope: The Authorised Biography* by Fatima Meer); General Bernard Montgomery: to Public Record Office and Controller of Her Majesty's Stationery Office; Oswald Mosley: to Lady Mosley (reprinted from *My Life* (Nelson, 1968)); Richard Nixon: to the Office of Richard M. Nixon; Kwame Nkrumah: to Zed Books (Panaf Books division, 1973; reprinted from *I Speak of Freedom*); J. Robert Oppenheimer: to Harvard University Press (reprinted from *Robert Oppenheimer: Letters and Recollections*, eds. Alice Kimball Smith and Charles Weiner; copyright © Alice Kimball Smith and Charles Weiner); Pope John Paul: to Incorporated Catholic Truth Society; Ronald Reagan: to Random House UK Ltd and Simon & Schuster Inc. (reprinted from *Speaking My Mind*; copyright © 1989 by Ronald Reagan); Chaim Rumkowski: to Penguin Books Ltd and Ellen Levine Literary Agency Inc. (reprinted from *Łódź Ghetto*, compiled and edited by Alan Adelson and Robert Lapides (Penguin Books, 1991; copyright © The Jewish Heritage Writing Project Inc., 1989)); Salman Rushdie: to Aitken & Stone Ltd and Wylie, Aitken & Stone Inc. on behalf of the author; Bertrand Russell: to British Broadcasting Corporation and The Bertrand Russell Peace Foundation Ltd; Alexander Solzhenitsyn: to Random House UK Ltd and Hanover Trust Company on behalf of the author. Report of the House of Lords and House of Commons Debates (Hansard): to Controller of Her Majesty's Stationery Office; 'Freedom from Fear' from *Freedom from Fear and Other Writings*, Revised Edn, by Aung San Suu Kyi, edited by Michael Aris, foreword by Václav Havel, copyright © 1991, 1995 Aung San Suu Kyi and Michael Aris. Used by permission of Viking Penguin, a division of Penguin Group (USA) Inc. and by Penguin Books UK.

Every effort has been made to contact copyright holders. The publishers will be glad to rectify, in future editions, any errors or omissions brought to their notice.

# THEODORE ROOSEVELT
## Chicago, 10 April 1899

*'The doctrine of the strenuous life'*

*Theodore Roosevelt (1856–1919) was still a child growing up in a philistine society when he decided to turn himself into a man of action. He built up his skinny body by dogged exercise and sought continually to prove his manliness. After Harvard he spent two tough years on a cattle ranch in Dakota. He boxed, wrestled and swam, and always carried a revolver.*

*At the turn of the century he was an influential Republican in New York and he became assistant secretary to the navy in 1897. He first won national fame as a colonel of the 'Rough Riders' in Cuba during the Spanish–American war of 1898. A year later, when this speech was given at the Appomattox Day celebration of the Hamilton Club, he became governor of New York.*

*This speech, made (as he put it) as 'the twentieth century looms before us big with the fate of many nations' and preaching the virtues of the 'strenuous life' of action, swelled the reputation that swept him into the vice-presidency in the election of 1900 and then, after the assassination of President McKinley, into the presidency.*

I wish to preach not the doctrine of ignoble ease but the doctrine of the strenuous life; the life of toil and effort; of labour and strife; to preach that highest form of success which comes not to the man who desires mere easy peace but to the man who does not shrink from danger, from hardship, or from bitter toil, and who out of these wins the splendid ultimate triumph.

A life of ignoble ease, a life of that peace which springs merely from lack either of desire or of power to strive after great things, is as little worthy of a nation as of an individual . . .

We do not admire the man of timid peace. We admire the man who embodies victorious effort; the man who never wrongs his neighbour; who is prompt to help a friend; but who has those virile qualities necessary to win in the stern strife of actual life. It is hard to fail; but it is worse never to have tried to succeed. In this life we get nothing save by effort. Freedom from effort in the present, merely means that there has been stored up effort in the past. A man can be freed from the necessity of work only by the fact that he or his fathers before him have worked to good purpose. If the freedom thus purchased is used aright, and the man still does actual work, though of a different kind, whether as a writer or a General, whether in the field of politics or in the field of exploration and adventure, he shows he deserves his good fortune. But if he treats this period of freedom from the need of actual labour as a period not of preparation but of mere enjoyment, he shows that he is simply a cumberer on the earth's surface; and he surely unfits himself to hold his own with his fellows if the need to do so should again arise. A mere life of ease is not in the end a satisfactory life, and above all it is a life which ultimately unfits those who follow it for serious work in the world.

As it is with the individual so it is with the nation. It is a base untruth to say that happy is the nation that has no history. Thrice happy is the nation that has a glorious history. Far better it is to dare mighty things, to win glorious triumphs, even though chequered by failure, than to take rank with those poor spirits who neither enjoy much nor suffer much because they live in the grey twilight that knows neither victory nor defeat. If in 1861 the men who loved the Union had believed that peace was the end of all things and war and strife a worst of all things, and had acted up to their belief, we would have saved hundreds of thousands of lives, we would have saved hundreds of millions of dollars. Moreover, besides saving all the blood and treasure we then lavished, we would have prevented the heartbreak of many women, the dissolution of many homes; and we would have spared the country those months of gloom and shame when it seemed as if our armies marched only to defeat We could have avoided all this suffering, simply by shrinking from strife. And if we had thus avoided it we would have shown that we were weaklings and that we were unfit to stand among the great nations of the earth. Thank God for the iron in the blood of our fathers, the men who upheld the wisdom of Lincoln and bore sword or rifle in the armies of Grant! Let us, the children of the men who proved themselves equal to the mighty days – let us, the children of the men who carried the great Civil War to a triumphant conclusion, praise the God of our fathers that the ignoble counsels of peace were rejected, that the suffering and loss, the blackness of sorrow and despair, were unflinchingly faced, and the years of strife endured; for in the end the slave was freed, the Union restored, and the mighty American Republic placed once more as a helmeted queen among nations . . .

The timid man, the lazy man, the man who distrusts his country, the overcivilized man, who has lost the great fighting, masterful virtues, the ignorant man and the man of dull mind, whose soul is incapable of feeling the mighty lift that thrills 'stern men with empires in their brains' – all these, of course, shrink from seeing the nation undertake its new duties; shrink from seeing us build a navy and army adequate to our needs; shrink from seeing us do our share of the world's work by bringing order out of chaos in the great, fair tropic islands from which the valour of our soldiers and sailors has driven the Spanish flag. These are the men who fear the strenuous life, who fear the only national life which is really worth leading. They believe in that cloistered life which saps the hardy virtues in a nation, as it saps them in the individual; or else they are wedded to that base spirit of gain and greed which recognizes in commercialism the be-all and end-all of national life, instead of realizing that, though an indispensable element, it is after all but one of the many elements that go to make up true national greatness. No country can long endure if its foundations are not laid deep in the material prosperity which comes from thrift, from business energy and enterprise, from hard, unsparing effort in the fields of industrial activity; but neither was any nation ever yet truly great if it relied upon material prosperity alone.

I preach to you, then, my countrymen, that our country calls not for the life of ease, but for the life of strenuous endeavour. The twentieth century looms before us big with the fate of many nations. If we stand idly by, if we seek merely swollen, slothful ease, and ignoble peace, if we shrink from the hard contests where men must win at hazard of their lives and at the risk of all they hold dear, then the bolder and stronger peoples will pass us by and will win for themselves the domination of the world. Let us therefore boldly face the life of strife, resolute to do our duty well and manfully; resolute to uphold righteousness by deed and by word; resolute to be both honest and brave, to serve high ideals, yet to use practical methods. Above all, let us shrink from no strife, moral or physical, within or without the nation, provided we are certain that the strife is justified; for it is only through strife, through hard and dangerous endeavour, that we shall ultimately win the goal of true national greatness.

.

# SIR HENRY CAMPBELL-BANNERMAN
## Stirling, 26 October 1901

### *'Methods of barbarism'*

*The leader of the Liberal Party, Sir Henry Campbell-Bannerman (1836–1908), who had represented Stirling since 1868 and served in Gladstone's Cabinet, was denounced as a traitor when he condemned the setting up of Boer concentration camps as 'methods of barbarism' during Britain's war with the Boers.*

The cardinal fact upon which the whole problem turns is that this is of the nature of a civil war. We are not fighting with a foreign foe whom we are to thrash and overcome and vanquish and punish, and then abandon him and turn our back upon him. These men are to be our neighbours – nay, they are to be our fellow-citizens. Whatever be their faults, whatever be their offences in the present or in the past against us, if we are to stay in South Africa at all, they will be there; and not only so, but they are indistinguishable from the great majority of our own citizens in our own colonies . . . Now anyone who rightly appreciates these facts, what will he say are to be our objects in the war which we have undertaken in South Africa? The first ought to be to impose upon our antagonists our military superiority. But the second is to impress upon them our ultimate and essential friendliness towards them . . .

Are the elements to be found for a settlement in the conditions to which you have now reduced South Africa?

The whole country in the two belligerent States outside the mining towns is a howling wilderness. The farms are burned, the country is wasted; the flocks and herds are either butchered or driven off; the mills are destroyed; furniture and implements of agriculture are smashed. These things are what I have termed methods of barbarism. I adhere to the phrase. I cannot improve upon it. If these are not the methods of barbarism, what methods does barbarism employ? . . . In time of war, things are not done in a rosewater sort of way; but the universal treatment of a whole country in this way, and the sweeping of women and children into camps is a process for which I venture to say nothing can furnish justification. When the war is happily ended and we set about the Constitution of this Arcadia, the fifty thousand prisoners of war will, of course, return to what by some sort of irony we may perhaps be permitted to call their home. These are the materials for your new self-government. They will meet the hundred thousand women and children or the survivors of them. There will not be many children at the present rate. They will meet them, and in what sort of mind towards the British Empire will these men be when the husband meets the wife and hears her story, when the brother meets the sister, when the father asks in vain for his child? . . .

Hitherto I have spoken of the belligerent States. Now, what of the old Colony of the Cape? To what condition has the statesmanship of the Government brought it? . . . The Constitution is suspended . . . Martial law, which is in other words no law, nothing but the arbitrary rule of soldiers, who know nothing of law, prevails from end to end of the country. We have reason to fear that martial law is but a form of undeclared war upon the Dutch population. With all the ordinary guarantees of civil rights suspended, no man is safe in property, in liberty or in life. The independent Press is silenced. So severe are the restrictions on news, that we have only partial information; but we have enough to know that hundreds of men, not Dutch only, but many British, have been arrested, thrown into gaol, deported to a distance from their homes, tried and condemned by these military tribunals on the evidence, it may be, of spiteful neighbours or political opponents. Why, with what indignation would we denounce such proceedings in other countries . . . Have these Ministers of ours not learned that it is not by the suppression of civil rights, not by harshness, not by coercion and force in any form, that a free people can be kept quiet and contented? . . .

The Government . . . have revived old enmities and created new ones, they have sown seeds of lasting discord, and when they, by-and-by, lay down in discredit their responsibilities, they will leave a new Ireland in the Southern Seas to be a weakness and a difficulty to the Empire . . . How true are the words of Mr Burke in his famous speech on the conciliation of the American colonies . . . Mr Burke in this great speech urged a further objection to force – he was objecting to applying force in any case of this kind – and that was that you impair the object by your very endeavour to preserve it. The thing you fought for is not the thing you recover, but depreciated, small, wasted and consumed in the contest. You may preserve your authority in South Africa, but it will be depreciated, and lessened, and wasted, and consumed. Is it too late even now to hope for counsels of moderation and a statesmanship which shall revert to the great traditions which have bound Great Britain and her Colonies together?

*Campbell-Bannerman's phrase 'methods of barbarism' went round the world and reached the Boers on the battlefield. When he became prime minister in 1906, the Boers trusted him and agreed to work in a spirit of reconciliation with Britain when he conferred self-government on the Transvaal and the Orange River Colony.*

•

## KEIR HARDIE
House of Commons, 23 April 1901

### 'Socialism'

*James Keir Hardie (1856–1915), who began work at the age of seven, became the first Independent Labour MP when he was elected for West Ham in 1892. A century later, he remains Labour's acknowledged folk hero. Hardie, a pacifist, supporter of the temperance movement and a fierce champion of the miners, went down the mines himself when he was only ten. He was the first (defeated) Labour candidate in Mid-Lanark in 1888, the main inspiration of the Independent Labour Party and, in 1900, the Labour Representation Committee, which became the Labour Party in 1906.*

*When he delivered this protest against capitalism, he had become MP for Merthyr Tydfil, a mining community in South Wales. It was the first complete socialist speech made in the House of Commons.*

I make no apology for bringing the question of Socialism before the House of Commons. It has long commanded the attention of the best minds in the country. It is a growing force in the thought of the world, and whether men agree or disagree with it, they have to reckon with it, and may as well begin by understanding it.

I begin by pointing out that the growth of our national wealth instead of bringing comfort to the masses of the people is imposing additional burdens on them. We are told on high authority that some 300 years ago the total wealth of the English nation was 100 millions sterling. At the beginning of the last century it had increased to 2,000 millions, and this year it is estimated to be 13,000 millions. While our population during the last century increased three and a half times, the wealth of the community increased over six times. But one factor in our national life remained with us all through the century, and is with us still, and that is that at the bottom of the social scale there is a mass of poverty and misery equal in magnitude to that which obtained 100 years ago. I submit that the true test of progress is not the accumulation of wealth in the hands of a few, but the elevation of a people as a whole. I admit frankly that a considerable improvement was made in the condition of the working people during the last century. At the beginning of the nineteenth century the nation industrially was sick almost unto death. It was at that time passing from the old system of handicraft, under which every man was his own employer and his own capitalist, and traded direct with his customer, to the factory system which the introduction of machinery brought into existence. During these 100 years the wealth of the nation accumulated, and the condition of the working classes as compared with the early years of the century improved, but I respectfully submit to the House that there was more happiness, more comfort and more independence before machinery began to accumulate wealth.

The high standard of comfort reached by the labouring classes at the end of the last century has not brought them that happiness which obtained in England 300 years ago, when there was no machinery, no large capitalists, no private property in land, as we know it today, and when every person had the right to use the land for the purpose of producing food for himself and his family. I said that an improvement was made during the last century, but I would qualify that statement in this respect – that practically the whole of that improvement was made during the first seventy-five years. During the last quarter of the century the condition of the working classes has been practically stationary. There have been slight increases of wages here and reductions of hours there, but the landlord with his increased rent has more than absorbed any advantage that may have been gained.

We are rapidly approaching a point when the nation will be called upon to decide between an uncontrolled monopoly, conducted for the benefit and in the interests of its principal shareholders, and a monopoly owned, controlled and manipulated by the state in the interests of the nation as a whole. I do not require to go far afield for arguments to support that part of my statement concerning the danger which the aggregation of wealth in a few hands is bringing upon us. This House and the British nation know to their cost the danger which comes from allowing men to grow rich and permitting them to use their wealth to corrupt the press, to silence the pulpit, to degrade our national life, and to bring reproach and shame upon a great people, in order that a few unscrupulous scoundrels might be able to add to their ill-gotten gains. The war in South Africa is a millionaires' war. Our troubles in China are due to the desire of the capitalists to exploit the people of that country as they would fain exploit the people of South Africa. Much of the jealousy and bad blood existing between this country and France is traceable to the fact that we went to war in Egypt to suppress a popular uprising, seeking freedom for the people, in order that the interest of our bondholders might be secured. Socialism, by placing land and the instruments of production in the hands of the community, eliminates only the idle, useless class at both ends of the scale. Half a million of the people of this country benefit by the present system; the remaining millions of toilers and business men do not. The pursuit of wealth corrupts the manhood of men. We are called upon at the beginning of the twentieth century to decide the question propounded in the Sermon on the Mount as to whether we will worship God or Mammon. The present day is a Mammon-worshipping age. Socialism proposes to dethrone the brute-god Mammon and to lift humanity into its place. I beg to submit in this very imperfect fashion the resolution on the Paper, merely promising that the last has not been heard of the Socialist movement either in the country or on the floor of this House, but that, just as sure as Radicalism democratized the system of government politically in the last century, so will Socialism democratize the country industrially during the century upon which we have just entered.

*Hardie lost his seat in 1915 after opposing Britain's involvement in the First World War, and died the same year. It was his relentless campaigns which forced the government to admit its responsibility for the unemployed.*

•

## JOSEPH CHAMBERLAIN
### Birmingham, 15 May 1903

*'I believe in a British Empire and I do not believe in a Little England'*

*The campaign for tariff reform, memorably advocated by Joseph Chamberlain (1836–1914) in this speech at Birmingham, split the Conservative Party, convulsed the country and eventually handed power for nearly two decades to the Liberals, led by Asquith and Lloyd George.*

*Chamberlain, at first a radical Liberal whose opposition to Irish Home Rule in 1886 had split the party and brought down the government, had joined the Tories and now proposed protection, renamed tariff reform, in order to unite the Dominions (such as Canada and South Africa) to the Empire by preferential tariffs.*

*He provoked a great sensation. 'The Birmingham speech,' wrote Leo Amery, the Tory politician, was 'a challenge to free trade as direct and provocative as the theses which Luther nailed to the church door at Wittenberg. To many of the younger generation, passionately imperialist by conviction, beginning to be intellectually sceptical about free trade, the speech was a sudden crystallization of all their ideals in an imperious call to action.'*

I cannot look forward without dread to handing over the security and existence of this great Empire to the hands of those who have made common cause with its enemies, who have charged their own countrymen with methods of barbarism, and who apparently have been untouched by that pervading sentiment which I found everywhere where the British flag floats, and which has done so much in recent years to draw us together. I should not require to go to South Africa in order to be convinced that this feeling has obtained deep hold on the minds and hearts of our children beyond the seas. It has had a hard life of it, this feeling of Imperial patriotism. It was checked for a generation by the apathy and the indifference which were the characteristics of our former relations with our Colonies, but it was never extinguished. The embers were still alight, and when in the late war this old country of ours showed that it was still possessed by the spirit of our ancestors, and that it was still prepared to count no sacrifice that was necessary in order to maintain the honour and the interests of the Empire, then you found a response from your children across the seas that astonished the whole world by a proof, an undeniable proof, of affection and regard.

Is it to end there? Are we to sink back into the old policy of selfish isolation which went very far to dry and even to sap the loyalty of our colonial brethren? I do not think so. I think these larger issues touch the people of this country. I think they have awakened to the enormous importance of a creative time like the present, and of taking advantage of the opportunities offered in order to make permanent what has begun so well. Remember, we are a kingdom, an old country. We proceed here on settled lines. We have our quarrels and our disputes, and we pass legislation which may be good or bad; but we know that, whatever changes there may be, at all events the main stream will ultimately reach its appointed destination. That is the result of centuries of constitutional progress and freedom.

But the Empire is not old. The Empire is new – the Empire is in its infancy. Now is the time when we can mould that Empire and when we and those who live with us can decide its future destinies. Just let us consider what that Empire is; I am not going tonight to speak of those hundreds of millions of our Indian and native fellow subjects for whom we have become responsible. I consider for the moment only our relations to that white British population that constitutes the majority in the great self-governing colonies of the Empire. Here in the United Kingdom there are some forty millions of us. Outside there are ten millions of men either directly descended from ancestors who left this country or more probably men who themselves in their youth left this country in order to find their fortunes in our possessions abroad. How long do you suppose that this proportion of population is going to endure? The development of those colonies has been delayed by many reasons – but mainly probably by a more material reason – by the fact that the United States of America has offered a greater attraction to British emigration.

But that has changed. The United States, with all their vast territory, are filling up; and even now we hear of tens of thousands of emigrants leaving the United States in order to take up the fresh and rich lands of our colony in Canada. It seems to me not at all an impossible assumption that before the end of this present century we may find our fellow subjects beyond the seas as numerous as we are at home. I want you to look forward. I want you to consider the infinite importance of this not only to yourselves but to your descendants. Now is the time when you can exert influence. Do you wish that if these ten millions become forty millions they shall still be closely, intimately, affectionately united to you, or do you contemplate the possibility of their being separated, going off each in his own direction, under a separate flag? Think what it means to your power and influence as a country; think what it means to your position among the nations of the world; think what it means to your trade and commerce – I put that last.

What is the meaning of an Empire? What does it mean to us? We have had a little experience. We have had a war, a war in which the majority of our children abroad had no apparent direct interest. We had no hold over them of any kind, and yet at one time during this war, by the voluntary decision of these people, at least 50,000 Colonial soldiers were standing shoulder to shoulder with British troops, displaying a gallantry equal to their own and the keenest intelligence. It is something for a beginning, and if this country were in danger, I mean if we were, as our forefathers were, face to face some day – Heaven forfend – with some great coalition of hostile nations, when we had with our backs to the wall to struggle for our very lives, it is my firm conviction there is nothing within the power of these self-governing colonies they would not do to come to our aid. I believe their whole resources in men and in money would be at the disposal of the Mother Country in such an event. That is something – something which it is wonderful to have achieved, and which it is worth almost any sacrifice to maintain . . .

I believe in a British Empire, in an Empire which, though it should be its first duty to cultivate friendship with all the nations of the world, should yet, even if alone, be self-sustaining and self-sufficient, able to maintain itself against the competition of all its rivals. And I do not believe in a Little England which shall be separated from all those to whom it would in the natural course look for support and affection, a Little England which would then be dependent absolutely on the mercy of those who envy its present prosperity, and who have shown they are ready to do all in their power to prevent its future union with the British races throughout the world.

*The tariff reform campaign was a disaster for the Conservative Party. It united the Liberals, lost the Tories the general election of 1906, put the Liberals into power for nearly twenty years, and was a major factor in pushing the Tories into rejecting Lloyd George's 1909 'People's Budget'.*

*Chamberlain was struck down by paralysis in 1906 and played no further part in politics.*

•

## F. E. SMITH (LORD BIRKENHEAD)
House of Commons, 11 March 1906

### *'I warn the Government'*

*More than a hundred years later, the maiden speech in 1906 by the English barrister F. E. Smith (1872–1930), Conservative MP for Liverpool, Walton (and subsequently Lord Birkenhead), is still considered the most famous ever made in the House of Commons. The main reason was its sheer audacity – Smith, the new MP, dared to tweak the tails of such lions as Lloyd George and Winston Churchill. As his latest biographer, John Campbell, writes: 'He gambled for the highest stake; and won . . . and in this one dazzling hour wrote his name more indelibly than by any other of his more solemn later actions into the history of Parliament.'*

*The Tories had been routed by the Liberals in the 1906 general election. One reason was the tariff reform campaign espoused by Joseph Chamberlain. Smith was speaking against a Liberal resolution stating that the people of the United Kingdom had demonstrated their 'unqualified fidelity' to the principles and practice of free trade and recording its determination to resist any proposal to create a system of protection.*

Unemployment yearly grows chronic over a larger area, while a Parliament of Free Importers celebrates in academic resolutions the economic system which has depopulated rural England, has filled the emigrant steamers with fugitives from these happy shores, and has aggravated the evils of the most revolting slums in Christendom. The progress of tonight's debate makes one profoundly conscious of the constructive shortcomings of the Cobdenism of today. I myself am a perfectly unrepentant member of the Tariff Reform League. I do not know how many members of the league there may be in the House; it may be that a division would show that they are not more numerous than the representatives of the Liberal League. I have, at least, the satisfaction of reflecting that, if tariff reform is found not to be a winning horse, I have not necessarily compromised my political future. I have in hon. and right hon. gentlemen opposite an admirable example of how to cut the painter of a similar league, with the maximum of political advancement, and the minimum of fidelity to a founder. Such a model of chivalrous loyalty is of great value to a young member of Parliament . . .

The resolution before the House consists of two parts. In the first, we are asked to recognize the merits of what is described on an obscure prescriptive principle as free trade, and, in the second, we are invited to register the proposition that the country gave an unqualified verdict in its favour. The word 'unqualified' is in itself ambiguous, and may have more than one meaning. If we say that a man is an unqualified slave, we mean that his condition can be honestly described as completely servile, and not, merely, as semi-servile. If, on the other hand, we say that a man is an unqualified medical practitioner, or an unqualified under-secretary, we mean that he is not entitled to any particular respect, because he has not passed through the normal period of training, or preparation. It is, on the whole, probable that the word is used in the first sense in the present motion.

But, perhaps, it is necessary to distinguish even further. When hon. gentlemen opposite are successful at the polls, it is probably used in the first sense. In the comparatively few cases in which I and my friends were successful, it is used in the second. Birmingham, under circumstances which will never be effaced from the memory of hon. gentlemen, on whichever side of the House they sit, displayed the rare and beautiful quality of political constancy, and voted in all its divisions for tariff reform. [Laughter.] The result is sneered at, in the spirit of the laughter which we have just heard, as a triumph for Tammanyism, or, more profoundly analysed by an eminent Nonconformist divine, as an instance of that mysterious dispensation, which occasionally permits the ungodly to triumph. Hon. gentlemen opposite are, in fact, very much more successful controversialists than hon. members on this side of the House.

It is far easier, if one is a master of scholarly irony, and of a charming literary style, to describe protection as a 'stinking rotten carcase' than to discuss scientifically whether certain limited proposals are likely to prove protective in their incidence. It is far easier, if one has a strong stomach, to suggest to simple rustics, as the President of the Board of Trade did, that, if the Tories came into power, they would introduce slavery on the hills of Wales. [Mr LLOYD GEORGE: 'I did not say that.']

The right hon. gentleman would, no doubt, be extremely anxious to forget it, if he could; but, anticipating a temporary lapse of memory, I have in my hand the *Manchester Guardian* of 16 January 1906, which contains a report of his speech. The right hon. gentleman said: 'What would they say to introducing Chinamen at 1s. a day into the Welsh quarries? Slavery on the hills of Wales! Heaven forgive me for the suggestion!' I have no means of judging how heaven will deal with persons who think it decent to make such suggestions. The distinction drawn by the right hon. gentleman is more worthy of the county court than of the Treasury Bench. I express a doubt whether any honest politician will ever acquit the right hon. gentleman of having deliberately given the impression to those he thus addressed that, if the Conservative Party were returned, the hills of Wales would be polluted by conditions of industrial slavery. The alternative construction is that the right hon. gentleman thought it worth his while, in addressing ignorant men ['No'] – in relation to the right hon. gentleman they are ignorant; is that disputed? – to put before ignorant men an abstract and academic statement as to Chinese labour on the hills of Wales. If he did not mean his hearers to draw the false but natural inference, why make any reference to Chinese slavery as a conceivable prospect on the hills of Wales?

Since this House of Commons met, we have heard a great deal about the war. I would suggest to hon. gentlemen, as a humble admirer of their methods, that, if they wish for targets in that matter, they ought to aim, not at the Opposition Benches, but at right hon. gentlemen who sit on the Front Government Bench. Hon. gentlemen opposite should remember that the present Secretary of State for War [Lord (then Mr) Haldane] justly observed that the Boers waged the war, not only with the object of maintaining their independence, but also to undermine our authority in South Africa; and the present Attorney-General [Sir John Lawson Walton] said that the war could be shown to be as just, as it was inevitable, and to have been defensible on the grounds of freedom. The circumstances of which you complain were anterior to the war. While the only panacea which hon. gentlemen opposite can suggest is the employment of broken down artisans in planting trees, and constructing dams against the encroachment of the sea, the Unionist Party need not be discouraged by their reverses at the polls. We will say of the goddess who presides over the polls, as Dryden said of Fortune in general:

> I can enjoy her while she's kind;
> But when she dances in the wind,
> And shakes her wings, and will not stay,
> I puff the prostitute away.

Was the verdict unqualified, having regard to the aggregate number of votes polled on behalf of Liberal members? The votes polled at the last election for Liberal, Labour, and Nationalist candidates were 3,300,000, while those polled for tariff reform candidates and other gentlemen sitting around me were 2,500,000. ['No! Not true!'] I gather that it is suggested that my figures are wrong. ['Yes.'] They very probably are. I took them from the *Liberal Magazine*.

Perhaps the Minister of Education [Mr Birrell] was responsible for them, before he gave up the hecatomb line of business for the

Christian toleration and charity department. I venture to suggest to hon. gentlemen opposite, that the figures I have quoted, so far as they are accurate, are not altogether discouraging to those who, for the first time after so many years of blind dogma, have challenged the verdict of the country on the issue of tariff reform. What would hon. gentlemen who represent Ireland say, if it was suggested that they were Cobdenites? Will one of them get up to say that Cobdenism has brought prosperity or success to Ireland, or to guarantee that a representative Irish Parliament would not introduce a general tariff on foreign manufactured articles? The jury who gave this unqualified verdict is unaccountably silent. The spectacle of the Cobdenite hen cackling over a protectionist duckling of her own hatching in Ireland would add a partially compensating element of humour even to the prospect of Home Rule.

The Irish and – I may add – the Indian case for tariff reform were both once and for all conceded by the 'infant community' admission of Adam Smith. Why do we force upon India and Ireland alike a system, of which every honest man knows that – whether it be good or bad for us – it denies to them the right to develop and mature their nascent industries upon the lines in which they themselves most earnestly believe, and in which every country in the world except Great Britain believes? The answer is as short as it is discreditable. We perpetuate this tyranny in order that our Indian and Irish fellow-subjects may be forced to buy from our manufacturers articles which they would otherwise attempt to manufacture for themselves. In other words, we perpetuate in these two cases a compulsory and unilateral trade preference – demonstrably the fruit of selfishness – at the sacrifice of a voluntary and bilateral preference, based deep and strong upon mutual interest and mutual affection.

I have heard the majority on the other side of the House described as the pure fruit of the Cobdenite tree. I should rather say that they were begotten by Chinese slavery out of passive resistance, by a rogue sire out of a dam that roared. I read a short time ago that the Free Church Council claimed among its members as many as two hundred of hon. gentlemen opposite.

The Free Church Council gave thanks publicly for the fact that

Providence had inspired the electors with discrimination to vote on the right side. Mr Speaker, I do not, more than another man, mind being cheated at cards; but I find it a little nauseating if my opponent then publicly ascribes his success to the partnership of the Most High. What the future of this Parliament has in store for right hon. and hon. gentlemen opposite I do not know, but I hear that the Government will deny to the Colonial Conference of 1907 free discussion on the subject which the House is now debating, so as to prevent the statement of unpalatable truths. I know that I am the insignificant representative of an insignificant numerical minority in this House, but I venture to warn the Government that the people of this country will neither forget nor forgive a party which, in the heyday of its triumph, denies to the infant Parliament of the Empire one jot or tittle of that ancient liberty of speech which our predecessors in this House vindicated for themselves at the point of the sword.

*Smith became Attorney-General in 1915 and Lord Chancellor at the age of forty-seven. He appeared for the Crown in the prosecution of Roger Casement and played a major role in the Irish settlement of 1921. He coined the phrase, 'The world continues to offer glittering prizes to those who have stout hearts and sharp swords.'*

•

THEODORE ROOSEVELT
Washington, DC, 14 April 1906

*'The men with the muck-rakes'*

*The strenuous life. Ignoble ease. Theodore Roosevelt had a gift for the striking oratorical phrase. One of his maxims was speak softly and carry a big stick. He also gave a new word to the language when he compared investigative journalists to Bunyan's man with a muck-rake in this speech at the laying of the cornerstone of the office building of the House of Representatives.*

We now administer the affairs of a nation in which the extraordinary growth of population has been outstripped by the growth of wealth and the growth in complex interests. The material problems that face us today are not such as they were in Washington's time, but the underlying facts of human nature are the same now as they were then. Under altered external form we war with the same tendencies towards evil that were evident in Washington's time, and are helped by the same tendencies for good.

In Bunyan's *Pilgrim's Progress* you may recall the description of the Man with the Muck-rake, the man who could look no way but downward, with the muck-rake in his hand; who was offered a celestial crown for his muck-rake, but who would neither look up nor regard the crown he was offered, but continued to rake to himself the filth of the floor.

In *Pilgrim's Progress* the Man with the Muck-rake is set forth as the example of him whose vision is fixed on carnal instead of on spiritual things. Yet he also typifies the man who in this life consistently refuses to see aught that is lofty, and fixes his eyes with solemn intentness only on that which is vile and debasing. Now, it is very necessary that we should not flinch from seeing what is vile and debasing. There is filth on the floor, and it must be scraped up with the muck-rake; and there are times and places where this service is the most needed of all the services that can be performed. But the man who never does anything else, who never thinks or speaks or writes save of his deeds with the muck-rake, speedily becomes, not a help to society, not an incitement to good, but one of the most potent forces for evil.

There are, in the body politic, economic and social, many and grave evils, and there is urgent necessity for the sternest war upon them. There should be relentless exposure of and attack upon every evil man whether politician or business man, every evil practice, whether in politics, in business, or in social life. I hail as a benefactor every writer or speaker, every man who, on the platform, or in book, magazine, or newspaper, with merciless severity makes such attack, provided always that he in his turn remembers that the attack is of use only if it is absolutely truthful. The liar is no whit better than the thief, and if his mendacity takes the form of slander, he may be worse than most thieves. It puts a premium upon knavery untruthfully to attack an honest man, or even with hysterical exaggeration to assail a bad man with untruth. An epidemic of indiscriminate assault upon character does not good, but very great harm. The soul of every scoundrel is gladdened whenever an honest man is assailed, or even when a scoundrel is untruthfully assailed . . .

My plea is, not for immunity to but for the most unsparing exposure of the politician who betrays his trust, of the big business man who makes or spends his fortune in illegitimate or corrupt ways. There should be a resolute effort to hunt every such man out of the position he has disgraced. Expose the crime, and hunt down the criminal; but remember that even in the case of crime, if it is attacked in sensational, lurid, and untruthful fashion, the attack may do more damage to the public mind than the crime itself. It is because I feel that there should be no rest in the endless war against the forces of evil that I ask that the war be conducted with sanity as well as with resolution. The men with the muck-rakes are often indispensable to the well-being of society; but only if they know when to stop raking the muck, and to look upward to the celestial crown above them, to the crown of worthy endeavour. There are beautiful things above and round about them; and if they gradually grow to feel that the whole world is nothing but muck, their power of usefulness is gone. If the whole picture is painted black there remains no hue whereby to single out the rascals for distinction from their fellows. Such painting finally induces a kind of moral colour-blindness; and people affected by it come to the conclusion that no man is really black, and no man really white, but they are all grey. In other words, they neither believe in the truth of the attack, nor in the honesty of the man who is attacked; they grow as suspicious of the accusation as of the offence; it becomes well-nigh hopeless to stir them either to wrath against wrong-doing or to enthusiasm for what is right; and such a mental attitude in the public gives hope to every knave, and is the despair of honest men.

# EMMELINE PANKHURST
London, 24 March 1908

### 'The plight of women'

*Emmeline Pankhurst (1858–1928), leader of the British suffragettes, formed the Women's Franchise League in 1889, but it was not until 1903 that she was persuaded by her daughter Christabel (1880–1958) to found the more militant Women's Social and Political Union. After meeting Herbert Asquith, the Liberal prime minister, in 1906, she despaired of winning the vote from a Liberal government and began to resort to militant tactics.*

*She made this speech at the Portman Rooms in London. A few months later she was arrested after suffragettes tried to 'rush' the House of Commons.*

Men politicians are in the habit of talking to women as if there were no issues that affect women. 'The fact is,' they say, 'the home is the place for women. Their interests are the rearing and training of children. These are the things that interest women. Politics have nothing to do with these things, and therefore politics do not concern women.' Yet the laws decide how women are to live in marriage, how their children are to be trained and educated, and what the future of their children is to be. All that is decided by Act of Parliament. Let us take a few of the laws, and see what there is to say about them from the women's point of view.

First of all, let us take the marriage laws. They are made by men for women. Let us consider whether they are equal, whether they are just, whether they are wise. What security of maintenance has the married woman? Many a married woman having given up her economic independence in order to marry, how is she compensated for that loss? What security does she get in that marriage for which she gave up economic independence? Take the case of a woman who has been earning a good income. She is told that she ought to give up her employment when she becomes a wife and a mother. What does she get in return? All that a married man is obliged by law to do for his wife is to provide for her shelter of some kind, food of some kind, and clothing of some kind. It is left to his good pleasure to decide what the shelter shall be, what the food shall be, what the clothing shall be. It is left to him to decide what money shall be spent on the home, and how it shall be spent; the wife has no voice legally in deciding any of these things. She has no legal claim upon any definite portion of his income. If he is a good man, a conscientious man, he does the right thing. If he is not, if he chooses almost to starve his wife, she has no remedy. What he thinks sufficient is what she has to be content with.

I quite agree, in all these illustrations, that the majority of men are considerably better than the law compels them to be, so the majority of women do not suffer as much as they might suffer if men were all as bad as they might be, but since there are some bad men, some unjust men, don't you agree with me that the law ought to be altered so that those men could be dealt with? . . .

Now let us look at [the woman's] position if she had been very unfortunate in marriage, so unfortunate as to get a bad husband, an immoral husband, a vicious husband, a husband unfit to be the father of little children. We turn to the Divine Court. How is she to get rid of such a man? If a man has got married to a bad wife, and he wants to be rid of her, he has but to prove against her one act of infidelity. But if a woman who is married to a vicious husband wants to get rid of him, not one act nor a thousand acts of infidelity entitle her to a divorce; she must prove either bigamy, desertion, or gross cruelty, in addition to immorality before she can get rid of that man.

Let us consider her position as a mother. We have repeated this so often at our meetings that I think the echo of what we have said must have reached many. By English law no married woman exists as the mother of the child she brings into the world. In the eyes of the law she is not the parent of her child. The child, according to our marriage laws, has only one parent, who can decide the future of the child, who can decide where it shall live, how it shall live, how much shall be spent upon it, how it shall be educated, and what religion it shall profess. That parent is the father.

These are examples of some of the laws that men have made, laws that concern women. I ask you, if women had had the vote, should we have had such laws? If women had had the vote, as men have the vote, we should have had equal laws. We should have had equal laws for divorce, and the law would have said that as nature has given to children two parents, so the law should recognize that they have two parents.

I have spoken to you about the position of the married woman who does not exist legally as a parent, the parent of her own child. In marriage, children have one parent. Out of marriage children have also one parent. That parent is the mother – the unfortunate mother. She alone is responsible for the future of her child; she alone is punished if her child is neglected and suffers from neglect. But let me give you one illustration. I was in Herefordshire during the by-election. While I was there, an unmarried mother was brought before the bench of magistrates charged with having neglected her illegitimate child. She was a domestic servant, and had put the child out to nurse. The magistrates – there were colonels and landowners on that bench – did not ask what wages the mother got; they did not ask who the father was or whether he contributed to the support of the child. They sent that woman to prison for three months for having neglected her child. I ask you women here tonight, if women had had some share in the making of the laws, don't you think they would have found a way of making all fathers of such children equally responsible with the mothers for the welfare of those children?

*Pankhurst was arrested again in 1909 (when forcible feeding was introduced to deal with the hunger strikes of the suffragettes) at the door of the Commons.*

•

## DAVID LLOYD GEORGE
London, 30 July 1909

### 'The People's Budget'

*The historic budget introduced in 1909 by David Lloyd George (1863–1945) proposed a modest supertax on the very rich and new taxes on land. Its aim, he said, was to wage implacable warfare against poverty and squalor. After the first national pension scheme of 1908, he had to provide for old-age pensions and to meet a heavy demand for naval construction. The budget was thrown out by the House of Lords after a momentous national controversy – an action which provoked the conflict between Lords and Commons that eventually led to the Parliament Act of 1911 and curbed the power of the hereditary lords.*

*Lloyd George's first full-scale defence of his budget was at Limehouse in London where he addressed an audience of 4,000 at the Edinburgh Castle. The speech provoked tumultuous applause from the audience of cockneys. It also provoked King Edward VII, who dispatched a message to Lloyd George from the royal yacht saying his speech was 'calculated to set class against class and to inflame the passions of the working and lower orders against people who happened to be owners of property'.*

*A master of improvised speech, Lloyd George, with his seductive, vibrant voice, was the greatest natural orator in an age of great orators. He spoke with his audiences and not to them. 'My platform is the country,' he said, and he gave his audiences a music-hall turn.*

*He mobilized the forces of change outside parliament as only a very few, such as Cobden, Gladstone and Joseph Chamberlain, had done before – but his driving passion was to action more than speech, to put far-reaching measures on the Statute Book and to root out the palpable injustices he saw all around him. He was the true founder of the Welfare State.*

A few months ago a meeting was held not far from this hall, in the heart of the city of London, demanding that the government should launch out and run into enormous expenditure on the navy. That meeting ended up with a resolution promising that those who passed that resolution would give financial support to the government in their undertaking. There have been two or three meetings held in the City of London since, attended by the same class of people, but not ending up with a resolution promising to pay. On the contrary, we are spending the money, but they don't pay. What has happened since to alter their tone? Simply that we have sent in the bill. We started our four Dreadnoughts. They cost eight millions of money. We promised them four more; they cost another eight millions. Somebody has got to pay, and these gentlemen say, 'Perfectly true; somebody has got to pay, but we would rather that somebody were somebody else.' We started building; we wanted money to pay for the building; so we sent the hat round. We sent it round amongst the workmen and the miners of Derbyshire and Yorkshire, the weavers of Dumfries, who, like all their countrymen, know the value of money. They all brought in their coppers. We went round Belgravia, but there has been such a howl ever since that it has completely deafened us.

But they say, 'It is not so much the Dreadnoughts we object to, it is the pensions.' If they object to pensions, why did they promise them? They won elections on the strength of their promises. It is true they never carried them out. Deception is always a pretty contemptible vice, but to deceive the poor is the meanest of all crimes. But they say, 'When we promised pensions we meant pensions at the expense of the people for whom they were provided. We simply meant to bring in a bill to compel workmen to contribute to their own pensions.' If that is what they meant, why did they not say so? The budget is introduced not merely for the purpose of raising barren taxes, but taxes that are fertile taxes, taxes that will bring forth fruit – the security of the country which is paramount in the midst of all. The provision for the aged and deserving poor – it was time it was done. It is rather a shame for a rich country like ours – probably the richest country in the world, if not the richest the world has ever seen – that it should allow those who have toiled all their days to end in penury and possibly starvation. It is rather hard that an old workman should have to find his way to the gates of the tomb, bleeding and footsore, through the brambles and thorns of poverty. We cut a new path through it, an easier one, a pleasanter one, through fields of waving corn. We are raising money to pay for the new road, aye, and to widen it, so that 200,000 paupers shall be able to join in the march. There are many in the country blessed by Providence with great wealth, and if there are amongst them men who grudge out of their riches a fair contribution toward the less fortunate of their fellow countrymen, they are shabby rich men. We propose to do more by means of the budget. We are raising money to provide against the evils and the sufferings that follow from unemployment. We are raising money for the purpose of assisting our great friendly societies to provide for the sick and the widows and orphans. We are providing money to enable us to develop the resources of our own land. I do not believe any fair-minded man would challenge the justice and the fairness of the objects which we have in view in raising this money . . .

Have you been down a coal-mine? I was telling you I went down one the other day. We sank down into a pit half a mile deep. We then walked underneath the mountain, and we did about three-quarters of a mile with rock and shale above us. The earth seemed to be straining – around us and above us – to crush us in. You could see the pit-props bent and twisted and sundered until you saw their fibres split. Sometimes they give way, and then there is mutilation and death. Often a spark ignites, the whole pit is deluged in fire, and the breath of life is scorched out of hundreds of breasts by the consuming fire.

In the very next colliery to the one I descended, just three years ago, three hundred people lost their lives in that way, and yet when the Prime Minister and I knock at the door of these great landlords and say to them, 'Here, you know these poor fellows who have been digging up royalties at the risk of their lives, some of them are old, they have survived the perils of their trade, they are broken, they can earn no more. Won't you give something towards keeping them out of the workhouse?' – they scowl at you. And we say, 'Only a ha'penny, just a copper!' They say, 'You thieves!' And they turn their dogs on to us, and every day you can hear their bark. If this is an indication of the view taken by these great landlords of their responsibility to the people who, at the risk of life, create their wealth, then I say their day of reckoning is at hand.

The other day, at the great Tory meeting held at the Cannon Street Hotel, they had blazoned on the walls, 'We protest against the budget in the name of democracy, liberty, and justice.' Where does the democracy come in this landed system? Where is the justice in all these transactions? We claim that the tax we impose on land is fair, just, and moderate. They go on threatening that if we proceed they will cut down their benefactions and discharge labour. What kind of labour? What is the labour they are going to choose for dismissal? Are they going to threaten to devastate rural England, while feeding themselves and dressing themselves? Are they going to reduce their gamekeepers? That would be sad! The agricultural labourer and the farmer might then have some part of the game which they fatten with their labour. But what would happen to you in the season? No week-end shooting with the Duke of Norfolk for any of us! But that is not the kind of labour that they are going to cut down. They are going to cut down productive labour – builders and gardeners – and they are going to ruin their property so that it shall not be taxed. All I can say is this – the ownership of land is not merely an enjoyment, it is a stewardship. It has been reckoned as such in the past, and if they cease to discharge their functions, the security and defence of the country, looking after the broken in their villages and neighbourhoods – then those functions which are part of the traditional duties attached to the ownership of land and which have given to it its title – if they cease to discharge those functions, the time will come to reconsider the conditions under which land is held in this country. No country, however rich, can permanently afford to have quartered upon its revenue a class which declines to do the duty which it was called upon to perform. And, therefore, it is one of the prime duties of statesmanship to investigate those conditions.

But I do not believe it. They have threatened and menaced like that before. They have seen it is not to their interest to carry out these futile menaces. They are now protesting against paying their fair share of the taxation of the land, and they are doing so by saying, 'You are burdening the community; you are putting burdens upon the people which they cannot bear.' Ah! they are not thinking of themselves. Noble souls! It is not the great dukes they are feeling for; it is the market gardener, it is the builder, and it was, until recently, the small holder. In every debate in the House of Commons they said: 'We are not worrying for ourselves. We can afford it with our broad acres; but just think of the little man who has got a few acres,' and we were so very impressed with this tearful appeal that at last we said, 'We will leave him out.' And I almost expected to see Mr Prettyman jump over the table and say, 'Fall on my neck and embrace me.' Instead of that, he stiffened up, his face wreathed with anger, and he said, 'The budget is more unjust than ever.'

Oh! no. We are placing the burdens on the broad shoulders. Why should I put burdens on the people? I am one of the children of the people. I was brought up amongst them. I know their trials; and God forbid that I should add one grain of trouble to the anxiety which they bear with such patience and fortitude. When the Prime Minister did me the honour of inviting me to take charge of the national exchequer at a time of great difficulty, I made up my mind in framing the budget which was in front of me that at any rate no cupboard should be bared, no lot would be harder to bear. By that test, I challenge them to judge the budget.

•

## DAVID LLOYD GEORGE
### Caernarvon, 9 December 1909

### 'We are in for rough weather'

*Lloyd George made many speeches on his People's Budget. After Limehouse, where he attacked dukes with their leaseholds of ever-increasing value, he spoke in Newcastle, where he said that fully equipped dukes, who cost as much to keep up as two Dreadnoughts, were just as great a terror and lasted longer. 'The question will be asked: "Should 500 men, ordinary men, chosen accidentally from among the unemployed, override the judgement, the deliberate judgement, of millions of people who are engaged in the industry which makes the wealth of the country?"' At Wolverhampton, he again attacked the hereditary principle.*

*At Caernarvon in Wales at the end of the year, there was a superb peroration to his speech, in which he set out his case for the betterment of the people.*

These are the taxes, these are our proposals. What do our opponents object to? Where is the Socialism, injustice and wrong? Where is the oppression; where is the unfairness of it? Do they object to what we are spending the money for? They do not complain about our building Dreadnoughts; they want more, except that they want someone else to pay for them. Do they object to pensions? What do they object to? Is it unfair to raise money for these purposes? We are imposing no burdens upon the earnings of any working man. The vast majority – I am sure whole – of the middle class of this country escape additional burdens. We put no burden upon the necessities of life of anyone. We are taxing the surplus. We are taxing the luxuries. If a man has enough after maintaining his wife and family, and can spare something upon whisky and tobacco, why should he not afterwards contribute towards the pensions and defences of the country? No; we are raising money by means that make it no more difficult for men to live, we are raising it for making provision for hundreds of thousands of workmen in the country who have nothing between them and starvation in old age except the charity of the parish. We propose a great scheme in order to set up a fund in this country that will see that no man suffers hunger in the dark days of sickness, breakdown in health, and unemployment which visit so many of us. That is what we are going to do. These schemes for the betterment of the people, we shall get them some day. We cannot get them without effort, and they will not be worth getting without effort. Freedom does not descend like manna from Heaven. It has been won step by step, by tramping the wilderness, fighting enemies, crossing Jordan, and clearing Jebusites out of the land. I do not regret that we cannot obtain these blessings except by fighting. The common people have taken no step that was worth taking without effort, sacrifice and suffering.

I cannot pretend to regret this conflict with which we are now confronted. It is well that democracies should now and again engage in these great struggles for a wider freedom and a higher life. They represent stages in the advance of the people from the bondage of the past to the blessings of the future. Those who dread these political convulsions, who apprehend from them nothing but destruction and danger, have read their history in vain. The race has nothing to fear except from stagnation. Against our will we have been precipitated into this tumult. For all that, we mean to win our way through it to a better time. The people may not secure all they seek, but if they bear themselves manfully they will achieve other ends they dare not even hope for now. Yesterday I visited the old village where I was brought up. I wandered through the woods familiar to my boyhood. There I saw a child gathering sticks for firewood, and I thought of

the hours which I spent in the same pleasant and profitable occupation, for I also have been something of a 'backwoodsman'. And there
is one experience taught me then which is of use to me today. I learnt
as a child that it was little use going into the woods after a period of
calm and fine weather, for I generally returned empty-handed; but
after a great storm I always came back with an armful. We are in for
rough weather. We may be even in for a winter of storms which will
rock the forest, break many a withered branch, and leave many a rotten tree torn up by the roots. But when the weather clears, you may
depend upon it that there will be something brought within the reach
of the people that will give warmth and glow to their grey lives,
something that will help to dispel the hunger, the despair, the oppression, and the wrong which now chill so many of their hearts.

•

## THEODORE ROOSEVELT
### Osawatomie, Kansas, 1910

*'The new nationalism'*

*After becoming president of the United States on the assassination of President
McKinley in 1901, Theodore Roosevelt won the election of 1904 with an overwhelming majority, but withdrew from politics in 1908 for a two-year world tour
and went big-game hunting in Africa.*

*On his return he tried to re-enter politics. The 'New Nationalism' he now
preached not only embraced most of the political and social reforms of the
moment but also accepted as both 'inevitable and necessary' the concentration of
economic power in big corporations. Roosevelt would regulate rather than dissolve
them, maintaining instead of destroying their contributions to America's wealth.
Big business would be matched by big government.*

*This was the programme that he presented in his speech at Osawatomie,
Kansas, in August 1910.*

We come here today to commemorate one of the epoch-making
events of the long struggle for the rights of man, the long struggle

for the uplift of humanity. Our country – this great republic – means nothing unless it means the triumph of a real democracy, the triumph of popular government, and, in the long run, of an economic system under which each man shall be guaranteed the opportunity to show the best that there is in him. That is why the history of America is now the central feature of the history of the world; for the world has set its face hopefully towards our democracy; and, O my fellow citizens, each one of you carries on your shoulders not only the burden of doing well for the sake of your own country, but the burden of doing well and seeing that this nation does well for the sake of mankind . . .

At many stages in the advance of humanity, conflict between the men who possess more than they have earned and the men who have earned more than they possess is the central condition of progress. In our day it appears as the struggle of free men to gain and hold the right of self-government as against the special interests, who twist the methods of free government into machinery for defeating the popular will. At every stage, and under all circumstances, the essence of the struggle is to equalize opportunity, destroy privilege, and give to the life and citizenship of every individual the highest possible value both to himself and to the commonwealth . . .

Practical equality of opportunity for all citizens, when we achieve it, will have two great results. First, every man will have a fair chance to make of himself all that in him lies; to reach the highest point to which his capacities, unassisted by special privilege of his own and unhampered by the special privilege of others, can carry him, and to get for himself and his family substantially what he has earned. Second, equality of opportunity means that the commonwealth will get from every citizen the highest service of which he is capable. No man who carries the burden of the special privileges of another can give to the commonwealth that service to which it is fairly entitled . . .

National efficiency has many factors. It is a necessary result of the principle of conservation widely applied. In the end it will determine our failure or success as a Nation. National efficiency has to do, not only with natural resources and with men, but it is equally concerned with institutions. The State must be made efficient for the work which concerns only the people of the State; and the Nation for that which concerns all the people. There must remain no neutral ground to serve as a refuge for lawbreakers, and especially for lawbreakers of great wealth, who can hire the vulpine legal cunning which will teach them how to avoid both jurisdictions. It is a misfortune when the national legislature fails to do its duty in providing a national remedy, so that the only national activity is the purely negative activity of the judiciary in forbidding the state to exercise power in the premises . . .

The American people are right in demanding that New Nationalism, without which we cannot hope to deal with new problems. The New Nationalism puts the national need before sectional or personal advantage. It is impatient of the utter confusion that results from local legislatures attempting to treat national issues as local issues. It is still more impatient of the impotence which springs from overdivision of governmental powers, the impotence which makes it possible for local selfishness or for legal cunning, hired by wealthy special interests, to bring national activities to a deadlock. This New Nationalism regards the executive power as the steward of the public welfare. It demands of the judiciary that it shall be interested primarily in human welfare rather than in property, just as it demands that the representative body shall represent all the people rather than any one class or section of the people . . .

The object of government is the welfare of the people. The material progress and prosperity of a nation are desirable chiefly so far as they lead to the moral and material welfare of all citizens. Just in proportion as the average man and woman are honest, capable of sound judgement and high ideals, active in public affairs – but, first of all, sound in their home life, and the father and mother of healthy children whom they bring up well – just so far, and no further, we may count our civilization a success. We must have – I believe we have already – a genuine and permanent moral awakening, without which no wisdom of legislation or administration really means anything; and, on the other hand, we must try to secure the social and economic legislation without which any improvement due to purely moral agitation is necessarily evanescent . . . No matter how honest and decent we are in our private lives, if we do not have the right kind of law and the right kind of administration of the law, we cannot go forward as a nation. That is imperative; but it must be an addition to, and not a substitution for, the qualities that make up good citizens. In the last analysis, the most important elements in any man's career must be the sum of those qualities which, in the aggregate, we speak of as character. If he has not got it, then no law that the wit of man can devise, no administration of the law by the boldest and strongest executive, will avail to help him. We must have the right kind of character – character that makes a man, first of all, a good man in the home, a good father, a good husband – that makes a man a good neighbour. You must have that, and, then, in addition, you must have the kind of law and the kind of administration of the law which will give to those qualities in the private citizen the best possible chance for development. The prime problem of our nation, is to get the right type of good citizenship, and, to get it, we must have progress, and our public men must be genuinely progressive.

*After failing to win the Republican nomination against William Taft, the incumbent president, in 1912, Roosevelt stood as an independent progressive candidate. He polled more votes than Taft but split the vote and allowed Woodrow Wilson to win.*

•

# EMMELINE PANKHURST
## Hartford, Connecticut, 13 November 1913

### *'Freedom or death'*

*Emmeline Pankhurst was convicted of conspiracy in 1912. After her release she and her daughter Christabel assumed full control of the Women's Social and Political Union. She was rearrested in 1913 for incitement to violence and sent to prison under the 'Cat and Mouse Act'. She went on hunger and thirst strike and was released only when her condition became critical. She was then rearrested twelve times but appeared on public platforms on a stretcher.*

*On a visit to the United States, where she had made fund-raising tours in 1909 and 1911, she explained in this speech why she was a 'dangerous person' under sentence of penal servitude in a convict prison.*

I do not come here as an advocate, because whatever position the suffrage movement may occupy in the United States of America, in England it has passed beyond the realm of advocacy and it has entered into the sphere of practical politics. It has become the subject of revolution and civil war, and so tonight I am not here to advocate woman suffrage. American suffragists can do that very well for themselves. I am here as a soldier who has temporarily left the field of battle in order to explain – it seems strange it should have to be explained – what civil war is like when civil war is waged by women. I am not only here as a soldier temporarily absent from the field of battle; I am here – and that, I think, is the strangest part of my coming – I am here as a person who, according to the law courts of my country, it has been decided, is of no value to the community at all; and I am adjudged because of my life to be a dangerous person, under sentence of penal servitude in a convict prison. So you see there is some special interest in hearing so unusual a person address you. I dare say, in the minds of many of you – you will perhaps forgive me this personal touch – that I do not look either very like a soldier or very like a convict, and yet I am both.

It would take too long to trace the course of militant methods as adopted by women, because it is about eight years since the word militant was first used to describe what we were doing; it is about eight years since the first militant action was taken by women. It was not militant at all, except that it provoked militancy on the part of those who were opposed to it. When women asked questions in political meetings and failed to get answers, they were not doing anything militant. To ask questions at political meetings is an acknowledged right of all people who attend public meetings; certainly in my country, men have always done it, and I hope they do it in America, because it seems to me that if you allow people to enter your legislatures without asking them any questions as to what they are going to do when they get there you are not exercising your citizen rights and your citizen duties as you ought. At any rate in Great Britain it is a custom, a time-honoured one, to ask questions of candidates for Parliament, and ask questions of members of the government. No man was ever put out of a public meeting for asking a question until Votes for Women came on to the political horizon. The first people who were put out of a political meeting for asking questions were women; they were brutally ill-used; they found themselves in jail before twenty-four hours had expired. But instead of the newspapers, which are largely inspired by the politicians, putting militancy and the reproach of militancy, if reproach there is, on the people who had assaulted the women, they actually said it was the women who were militant and very much to blame.

It was not the speakers on the platform who would not answer them who were to blame, or the ushers at the meeting; it was the poor women who had had their bruises and their knocks and scratches, and who were put into prison for doing precisely nothing but holding a protest meeting in the street after it was all over. However, we were called militant for doing that, and we were quite willing to accept the name, because militancy for us is time-honoured; you have the church militant and in the sense of spiritual militancy we were very militant indeed. We were determined to press this question of the enfranchisement of the women to the point where we were no longer to be ignored by the politicians as had been the case for about fifty years, during which time women had patiently used every means open to them to win their political enfranchisement.

Experience will show you that if you really want to get anything done, it is not so much a matter of whether you alienate sympathy; sympathy is a very unsatisfactory thing if it is not practical sympathy. It does not matter to the practical suffragist whether she alienates sympathy that was never of any use to her. What she wants is to get something practical done, and whether it is done out of sympathy or whether it is done out of fear, or whether it is done because you want to be comfortable again and not be worried in this way, doesn't particularly matter so long as you get it. We had enough of sympathy for fifty years; it never brought us anything; and we would rather have an angry man going to the government and saying, my business is interfered with and I won't submit to its being interfered with any longer because you won't give women the vote, than to have a gentleman come on to our platforms year in and year out and talk about his ardent sympathy with woman suffrage.

'Put them in prison,' they said; 'that will stop it.' But it didn't stop it. They put women in prison for long terms of imprisonment, for making a nuisance of themselves – that was the expression when they took petitions in their hands to the door of the House of Commons; and they thought that sending them to prison, giving them a day's imprisonment, would cause them to all settle down again and there would be no further trouble. But it didn't happen so at all: instead of the women giving it up, more women did it, and more and more and more women did it until there were three hundred women at a time, who had not broken a single law, only 'made a nuisance of themselves' as the politicians say.

The whole argument with the anti-suffragists, or even the critical suffragist man, is this: that you can govern human beings without their consent. They have said to us, 'Government rests upon force; the women haven't force, so they must submit.' Well, we are showing them that government does not rest upon force at all; it rests upon consent. As long as women consent to be unjustly governed, they can be; but directly women say: 'We withhold our consent, we will not be governed any longer so long as that government is unjust,' not by the forces of civil war can you govern the very weakest woman. You can kill that woman, but she escapes you then; you cannot govern her. And that is, I think, a most valuable demonstration we have been making to the world.

Now, I want to say to you who think women cannot succeed, we have brought the government of England to this position, that it has to face this alternative; either women are to be killed or women are to have the vote. I ask American men in this meeting, what would you say if in your State you were faced with that alternative, that you must either kill them or give them their citizenship – women, many of whom you respect, women whom you know have lived useful lives, women whom you know, even if you do not know them personally, are animated with the highest motives, women who are in pursuit of liberty and the power to do useful public service? Well, there is only one answer to that alternative; there is only one way out of it, unless you are prepared to put back civilization two or three generations; you must give those women the vote. Now that is the outcome of our civil war.

You won your freedom in America when you had the Revolution, by bloodshed, by sacrificing human life. You won the Civil War by the sacrifice of human life when you decided to emancipate the negro. You have left it to the women in your land, the men of all civilized countries have left it to women, to work out their own salvation. That is the way in which we women of England are doing. Human life for us is sacred, but we say if any life is to be sacrificed it shall be ours; we won't do it ourselves, but we will put the enemy in the position where they will have to choose between giving us freedom or giving us death.

*During the tour, Emmeline was detained on Ellis Island. On the outbreak of war, the WSPU stopped campaigning. Women secured the vote in 1918, and full suffrage in 1928. Emmeline lived in Canada from 1919 to 1926 when she returned to England, joined the Conservative Party and stood for Whitechapel.*

• 

## EDWARD CARSON
### London, 11 February 1914

*'Ulster is asking to be let alone'*

*Edward Carson, born and educated in Dublin, was Unionist MP for Dublin for twenty-six years before becoming MP for a Belfast seat, 1918–21. He was Solicitor-General in the administrations of Salisbury and Balfour. In 1910 he organized British resistance to Irish Home Rule and set up an Ulster Unionist Council in 1911. A year later he established the Ulster Volunteers, a private army of 80,000 men pledged to resist Home Rule.*

*He was the most powerful defender of the interests of Ulster in the British House of Commons. As Asquith wrestled with the issue of Home Rule in*

*1914, he had come to accept in some form the temporary exclusion of Ulster. He used the King's speech and the debate on the address to create a conciliatory atmosphere.*

*'The event of the afternoon', Asquith wrote on 11 February, 'was Carson's speech. He followed a somewhat arid display by the Impeccable and was really very impressive. I wrote him a line of congratulation.'*

Ulster is not asking for concessions. Ulster is asking to be let alone. When you talk of concessions, what you really mean is, 'We want to lay down what is the minimum of wrong we can do to Ulster.' Let me tell you that the results of two years' delay and the treatment we have received during these two years have made your task and made our task far more difficult. You have driven these men to enter into a covenant for their mutual protection. No doubt you have laughed at their covenant. Have a good laugh at it now. Well, so far as I am concerned, I am not the kind of man who will go over to Ulster one day and say, 'Enter into a covenant', and go over next day and say, 'Break it.' But there is something more. You have insulted them. I do not say the Prime Minister has done so. I would be wrong if I were to say that he has done so. He has treated them seriously, but the large body of his colleagues in the rank and file of his party have taken every opportunity of jeering at these men, of branding them as braggarts and bluffers and cowards, and all the rest of it. Well, do not you see that having done that, these men can never go back, and never will go back, and allow these gibes and insults and sneers to prove true.

The Speech from the Throne talks of the fears of these men. Yes, they have, I think, genuine fears for their civil and religious liberty under the Bill, but do not imagine that that is all that these men are fighting for. They are fighting for a great principle, and a great ideal. They are fighting to stay under the Government which they were invited to come under, under which they have flourished, and under which they are content, and to refuse to come under a Government which they loathe and detest. Men do not make sacrifices or take up the attitude these men in Ulster have taken up on a question of detail or paper safeguards. I am not going to argue whether they are right or wrong in resisting. It would be useless to argue it, because they have thoroughly made up their minds, but I say this: If these men are not morally justified when they are attempted to be driven out of one Government with which they are satisfied, and put under another which they loathe, I do not see how resistance ever can be justified in history at all . . .

Believe me, whatever way you settle the Irish question, there are only two ways to deal with Ulster. It is for statesmen to say which is the best and right one. She is not a part of the community which can be bought. She will not allow herself to be sold. You must therefore either coerce her if you go on, or you must, in the long run, by showing that good government can come under the Home Rule Bill, try and win her over to the case of the rest of Ireland. You probably can coerce her – though I doubt it. If you do, what will be the disastrous consequences not only to Ulster, but to this country and the Empire? Will my fellow countryman, the Leader of the Nationalist party, have gained anything? I will agree with him – I do not believe he wants to triumph any more than I do. But will he have gained anything if he takes over these people and then applies for what he used to call – at all events his party used to call – the enemies of the people to come in and coerce them into obedience? No, Sir, one false step taken in relation to Ulster will, in my opinion, render for ever impossible a solution of the Irish question. I say this to my Nationalist fellow countrymen, and, indeed, also to the Government: you have never tried to win over Ulster. You have never tried to understand her position. You have never alleged, and can never allege, that this Bill gives her one atom of advantage. Nay, you cannot deny that it takes away many advantages that she has as a constituent part of the United Kingdom. You cannot deny that in the past she had produced the most loyal and law-abiding part of the citizens of Ireland. After all that, for these two years, every time we came before you your only answer to us – the majority of you, at all events – was to insult us, and to make little of us. I say to the leader of the Nationalist party, if you want Ulster, go and take her, or go and win her. You have never wanted her affections; you have wanted her taxes . . .

•

## DAVID LLOYD GEORGE
London, 21 September 1914

*'The great pinnacle of sacrifice'*

*Many speeches were made in the autumn of 1914 rallying the British for the war with Germany – but none matched in sheer poetic eloquence this address by Lloyd George, whose war speeches were described as sounding like 'superannuated spells'.*

*Although there was a broad consensus about the justice of the war, the one element required to make it acceptable to a liberal society was some kind of broad, humane justification to explain what the war was really about.*

*'Lloyd George remained suspiciously silent during the early weeks,' says the British historian Kenneth O. Morgan. 'But in an eloquent address to a massed audience of his Welsh fellow-countrymen at the Queen's Hall, London, he committed himself without reserve to a fight to the finish. He occupied, or claimed to occupy, the highest moral ground. It was, he declared, a war on behalf of liberal principles, a crusade on behalf of the "little five-foot-five nations" . . .*

*'It was not surprising that a claim that the war was a holy cause, backed up not only by the leaders of all the Christian churches but by all the Liberal pantheon of heroes from Fox to Gladstone, met with an instant response, not least in the smaller nations of Scotland and Wales within Britain itself.'*

This is the story of two little nations. The world owes much to little nations . . . The greatest art in the world was the work of little nations; the most enduring literature of the world came from little nations; the greatest literature of England came when she was a nation of the size of Belgium fighting a great Empire. The heroic deeds that thrill humanity through generations were the deeds of little nations fighting for their freedom. Yes, and the salvation of mankind came through a little nation. God has chosen little nations as the vessels by which He carries His choicest wines to the lips of humanity, to rejoice their hearts, to exalt their vision, to stimulate and strengthen their faith; and if we had stood by when two little nations were being crushed and broken by the brutal hands of barbarism, our shame would have rung down the everlasting ages.

But Germany insists that this is an attack by a lower civilization upon a higher one. As a matter of fact, the attack was begun by the civilization which calls itself the higher one. I am no apologist for Russia; she has perpetrated deeds of which I have no doubt her best sons are ashamed. What Empire has not? But Germany is the last Empire to point the finger of reproach at Russia. Russia has made sacrifices for freedom – great sacrifices. Do you remember the cry of Bulgaria when she was torn by the most insensate tyranny that Europe has ever seen? Who listened to that cry? The only answer of the 'higher civilization' was that the liberty of the Bulgarian peasants was not worth the life of a single Pomeranian soldier. But the 'rude barbarians' of the North sent their sons by the thousand to die for Bulgarian freedom. What about England? Go to Greece, the Netherlands, Italy, Germany, France – in all those lands I could point out places where the sons of Britain have died for the freedom of those peoples. France has made sacrifices for the freedom of other lands than her own. Can you name a single country in the world for the freedom of which modern Prussia has ever sacrificed a single life? By the test of our faith the highest standard of civilization is the readiness to sacrifice for others.

Have you read the Kaiser's speeches? They are full of the glitter and bluster of German militarism – 'mailed fist' and 'shining armour'. Poor old mailed fist! Its knuckles are getting a little bruised. Poor shining armour! The shine is being knocked out of it. There is the same swagger and boastfulness running through the whole of the speeches. The extract which was given in the *British Weekly* this week is a very remarkable product as an illustration of the spirit we have to fight. It is the Kaiser's speech to his soldiers on the way to the front:

Remember that the German people are the chosen of God. On me, the German Emperor, the Spirit of God has descended. I am His sword, His weapon and His Vicegerent. Woe to the disobedient, and death to cowards and unbelievers.

Lunacy is always distressing, but sometimes it is dangerous; and when you get it manifested in the head of the State, and it has become the policy of a great Empire, it is about time that it should be ruthlessly put away. I do not believe he meant all these speeches; it was simply the martial straddle he had acquired. But there were men around him who meant every word of them. This was their religion. Treaties? They tangle the feet of Germany in her advance. Cut them with the sword! Little nations? They hinder the advance of Germany. Trample them in the mire under the German heel. The Russian Slav? He challenges the supremacy of Germany in Europe. Hurl your legions at him and massacre him! Britain? She is a constant menace to the predominance of Germany in the world. Wrest the trident out of her hand. Christianity? Sickly sentimentalism about sacrifice for others! Poor pap for German digestion! We will have a new diet. We will force it upon the world. It will be made in Germany – the diet of blood and iron. What remains? Treaties have gone. The honour of nations has gone. Liberty has gone. What is left? Germany. Germany is left! *'Deutschland über Alles!'*

That is what we are fighting – that claim to predominance of a material, hard civilization which, if it once rules and sways the world, liberty goes, democracy vanishes. And unless Britain and her sons come to the rescue it will be a dark day for humanity.

Have you followed the Prussian Junker and his doings? We are not fighting the German people. The German people are under the heel of this military caste, and it will be a day of rejoicing for the German peasant, artisan and trader when the military caste is broken. You know its pretensions. They give themselves the air of demigods. They walk the pavements, and civilians and their wives are swept into the gutter; they have no right to stand in the way of a great Prussian soldier. Men, women, nations – they all have to go. He thinks all he has to say is, 'We are in a hurry.' That is the answer he gave to Belgium – 'Rapidity of action is Germany's greatest asset,' which means, 'I am in a hurry; clear out of my way.' You know the type of motorist, the terror of the roads, with a sixty-horse-power car, who thinks the roads are made for him, and knocks down anybody who impedes the action of his car by a single mile an hour. The Prussian Junker is the road-hog of Europe. Small nationalities in his way are hurled to the roadside, bleeding and broken. Women and children are crushed under the wheels of his cruel car, and Britain is ordered out of his road. All I can say is this: if the old British spirit is alive in British hearts, that bully will be torn from his seat. Were he to win, it would be the greatest catastrophe that has befallen democracy since the day of the Holy Alliance and its ascendancy.

They think we cannot beat them. It will not be easy. It will be a long job; it will be a terrible war; but in the end we shall march through terror to triumph. We shall need all our qualities – every quality that Britain and its people possess – prudence in counsel, daring in action, tenacity in purpose, courage in defeat, moderation in victory; in all things faith.

It has pleased them to believe and to preach the belief that we are a decadent and degenerate people. They proclaim to the world through their professors that we are a non-heroic nation skulking behind our mahogany counters, whilst we egg on more gallant races to their destruction. This is a description given of us in Germany – 'a timorous, craven nation, trusting to its Fleet'. I think they are beginning to find their mistake out already – and there are half a million young men of Britain who have already registered a vow to their King that they will cross the seas and hurl that insult to British courage against its perpetrators on the battlefields of France and Germany. We want half a million more; and we shall get them.

I envy you young people your opportunity. They have put up the age limit for the Army, but I am sorry to say I have marched a good many years even beyond that. It is a great opportunity, an opportunity that only comes once in many centuries to the children of men. For most generations sacrifice comes in drab and weariness of spirit. It comes to you today, and it comes today to us all, in the form of the glow and thrill of a great movement for liberty, that impels millions throughout Europe to the same noble end. It is a great war for the emancipation of Europe from the thraldom of a military caste which has thrown its shadows upon two generations of men, and is now plunging the world into a welter of bloodshed and death. Some have already given their lives. There are some who have given more than their own lives; they have given the lives of those who are dear to them. I honour their courage, and may God be their comfort and their strength. But their reward is at hand; those who have fallen have died consecrated deaths. They have taken their part in the making of a new Europe – a new world. I can see signs of its coming in the glare of the battlefield.

The people will gain more by this struggle in all lands than they comprehend at the present moment. It is true they will be free of the greatest menace to their freedom. That is not all. There is something infinitely greater and more enduring which is emerging already out of this great conflict – a new patriotism, richer, nobler, and more exalted than the old. I see amongst all classes, high and low, shedding themselves of selfishness, a new recognition that the honour of the country does not depend merely on the maintenance of its glory in the stricken field, but also in protecting its homes from distress. It is bringing a new outlook for all classes. The great flood of luxury and sloth which had submerged the land is receding, and a new Britain is appearing. We can see for the first time the fundamental things that matter in life, and that have been obscured from our vision by the tropical growth of prosperity.

May I tell you in a simple parable what I think this war is doing for us? I know a valley in North Wales, between the mountains and the sea. It is a beautiful valley, snug, comfortable, sheltered by the mountains from all the bitter blasts. But it is very enervating, and I remember how the boys were in the habit of climbing the hill above the village to have a glimpse of the great mountains in the distance, and to be stimulated and freshened by the breezes which came from the hilltops, and by the great spectacle of their grandeur. We have been living in a sheltered valley for generations. We have been too comfortable and too indulgent – many, perhaps, too selfish – and the stem hand of fate has scourged us to an elevation where we can see the great everlasting things that matter for a nation – the great peaks we had forgotten, of Honour, Duty, Patriotism, and, clad in glittering white, the great pinnacle of Sacrifice pointing like a rugged finger to Heaven. We shall descend into the valleys again; but as long as the men and women of this generation last, they will carry in their hearts the image of those great mountain peaks whose foundations are not shaken, though Europe rock and sway in the convulsions of a great war.

*From the moment of his Queen's Hall speech, Lloyd George challenged Asquith, the prime minister. 'Unconsciously, perhaps even unwillingly, he was offering himself as the man who could run the war better,' says A. J. P. Taylor. Lloyd George became prime minister in 1916 and led Britain to victory.*

•

## PATRICK PEARSE
### Dublin, 1 August 1915

*'Ireland unfree shall never be at peace'*

*Patrick Pearse (1879–1916) was a founder member of the Irish Volunteers and was inducted into the Irish Republican Brotherhood in 1913. His panegyric at the graveside of O'Donovan Rossa was the apogee of his oratorical career and part of a carefully prepared campaign in the year leading up to the Easter Rising. Rossa, one of the most bitter but also most courageous of the old Fenians, had died after a long illness in America and was to be buried at Glasnevin Cemetery in Dublin. The funeral was arranged as a propaganda exercise and there were hundreds of thousands at Glasnevin.*

*It was Pearse's greatest test and he rose to the occasion with a speech which was his masterpiece. In his idealization of Rossa, Pearse sketched himself and heralded the approaching revolution. His peroration was open defiance of the British in Dublin Castle.*

*The souvenir of the funeral said: 'Cold, lifeless print cannot convey even an idea of the depth and intensity of feeling in which his words were couched. Calm and deliberate, in soft yet thrilling accents, his oration was almost sublime. Here was no rhetoric, no mathematical oratory; it was the soul of a patriot breathing words of love and devotion, of hope and truth and courage, no threnody, but a paean of triumph such as might have come from out of the tomb by which we were . . .'*

It has seemed right, before we turn away from this place in which we have laid the mortal remains of O'Donovan Rossa, that one among us should, in the name of all, speak the praise of that valiant man, and endeavour to formulate the thought and the hope that are in us as we stand around his grave. And if there is anything that makes it fitting that I, rather than some other, I rather than one of the grey-haired men who were young with him and shared in his labour and in his suffering, should speak here, it is perhaps that I may be taken as speaking on behalf of a new generation that has been rebaptized in the Fenian faith, and that has accepted the responsibility of carrying out the Fenian programme. I propose to you then that, here by the grave of this unrepentant Fenian, we renew our baptismal vows; that, here by the grave of this unconquered and unconquerable man, we ask of God, each one for himself, such unshakable purpose, such high and gallant courage, such unbreakable strength of soul as belonged to O'Donovan Rossa.

Deliberately here we avow ourselves, as he avowed himself in the dock, Irishmen of one allegiance only. We of the Irish Volunteers, and you others who are associated with us in today's task and duty, are bound together and must stand together henceforth in brotherly union for the achievement of the freedom of Ireland. And we know only one definition of freedom: it is Tone's definition, it is Mitchel's definition, it is Rossa's definition. Let no man blaspheme the cause that the dead generations of Ireland served by giving it any other name and definition than their name and their definition.

We stand at Rossa's grave not in sadness but rather in exaltation of spirit that it has been given to us to come thus into so close a communion with that brave and splendid Gael. Splendid and holy causes are served by men who are themselves splendid and holy. O'Donovan Rossa was splendid in the proud manhood of him, splendid in the heroic grace of him, splendid in the Gaelic strength and clarity and truth of him. And all that splendour and pride and strength was compatible with a humility and a simplicity of devotion to Ireland, to all that was olden and beautiful and Gaelic in Ireland, the holiness and simplicity of patriotism of a Michael O'Clery or of an Eoghan O'Growney. The clear true eyes of this man almost alone in his day visioned Ireland as we of today would surely have her: not free merely, but Gaelic as well; not Gaelic merely, but free as well.

In a closer spiritual communion with him now than ever before or perhaps ever again, in a spiritual communion with those of his day, living and dead, who suffered with him in English prisons, in communion of spirit too with our own dear comrades who suffer in English prisons today, and speaking on their behalf as well as our own, we pledge to Ireland our love, and we pledge to English rule in Ireland our hate. This is a place of peace, sacred to the dead, where men should speak with all charity and with all restraint; but I hold it a Christian thing, as O'Donovan Rossa held it, to hate evil, to hate untruth, to hate oppression, and, hating them, to strive to overthrow them. Our foes are strong and wise and wary but, strong and wise and wary as they are, they cannot undo the miracles of God who ripens in the hearts of young men the seeds sown by the young men of a former generation. And the seeds sown by the young men of '65 and '67 are coming to their miraculous ripening today. Rulers and Defenders of Realms had need to be wary if they would guard against such processes. Life springs from death; and from the graves of patriot men and women spring living nations. The Defenders of this Realm have worked well in secret and in the open. They think that they have pacified Ireland. They think that they have purchased half of us and intimidated the other half. They think that they have foreseen everything, think that they have provided against everything; but the fools, the fools, the fools! – they have left us our Fenian dead, and while Ireland holds these graves, Ireland unfree shall never be at peace.

•

## MAHATMA GANDHI
### Benares, 4 February 1916

*'There is no salvation for India'*

*As a barrister in South Africa from 1907 to 1914, Mohandas Gandhi conducted passive-resistance campaigns of protest at the Transvaal government's discrimination against its Indian minority settlers. He returned to India in 1915 and gradually emerged as leader of the Congress movement.*

*In September 1915, Mrs Annie Besant, a remarkable Englishwoman who had made India her home, announced the formation of a Home Rule League. Earlier, in 1892, she started a school in Benares which was expanded into the Hindu University Central College in 1916. An illustrious gathering of notables was there for the opening ceremonies, including the Viceroy and many bejewelled maharajas, maharanis, rajas and high officials in all their dazzling panoply.*

*Gandhi addressed the meeting on 4 February. As the audience grew unruly and arguments broke out, it broke up before he could finish. 'India had never heard such a forthright, unvarnished speech,' says Louis Fisher, Gandhi's biographer. 'Gandhi spared no one, least of all those present. In 1916 the ear [of India] began to catch the voice of a man who was courageous and indiscreet, a little man who lived like a poor man and defended the poor to the face of the rich, a holy man in an ashram.'*

Our language is the reflection of ourselves, and if you tell me that our languages are too poor to express the best thought, then I say that the sooner we are wiped out of existence the better for us. Is there a man who dreams that English can ever become the national language of India? (*Cries of 'Never'.*) Why this handicap on the nation? Just consider for one moment what an unequal race our lads have to run with every English lad. I had the privilege of a close conversation with some Poona professors. They assured me that every Indian youth, because he reached his knowledge through the English language, lost at least six precious years of life. Multiply that by the number of students turned out by our schools and colleges, and find out for yourselves how many thousand years have been lost to the nation. The charge against us is that we have no initiative. How can we have any if we are to devote the precious years of our life to the mastery of a foreign tongue? . . .

The only education we receive is English education. Surely we must show something for it. But suppose that we had been receiving during the past fifty years education through our vernaculars, what should we have today? We should have today a free India, we should have our educated men, not as if they were foreigners in their own land but speaking to the heart of the nation; they would be working amongst the poorest of the poor, and whatever they would have gained during the past fifty years would be a heritage for the nation. (*Applause . . .*)

His Highness the Maharajah who presided yesterday over our deliberations spoke about the poverty of India . . . But what did we witness in the great pandal in which the foundation ceremony was performed by the Viceroy. Certainly a most gorgeous show, an exhibition of jewellery which made a splendid feast for the eyes of the greatest jeweller who chose to come from Paris. I compare with the richly bedecked noblemen the millions of the poor. And I feel like saying to these noblemen, 'There is no salvation for India unless you strip yourselves of this jewellery and hold it in trust for your countrymen in India.' ('Hear, hear' and applause.)

Sir, whenever I hear of a great palace rising in any great city of India, be it in British India or be it in India which is ruled by our great chiefs, I become jealous at once, and I say, 'Oh, it is the money that has come from the agriculturists.' Over seventy-five per cent of the population are agriculturists and Mr Higginbotham told us last night in his own felicitous language that they are the men who grow two blades of grass in the place of one. But there cannot be much spirit of self-government about us if we take away or allow others to take away from them almost the whole of the results of their labour. Our salvation can only come through the farmer. Neither the lawyers, nor the doctors, not the rich landlords are going to secure it . . .

I was talking the other day to a member of the much-abused civil service. I have not very much in common with the members of that service, but I could not help admiring the manner in which he was speaking to me. He said: 'Mr Gandhi, do you for one moment suppose that all we, civil servants, are a bad lot, that we want to oppress the people whom we have come to govern?' 'No,' I said. 'Then if you get an opportunity put in a word for the much-abused civil service?' And I am here to put in that word. Yes, many members of the Indian civil service are most decidedly overbearing; they are tyrannical, at times thoughtless . . .

But what does that signify? They were gentlemen before they came here, and if they have lost some of the moral fibre, it is a reflection upon ourselves. (Cries of 'No'.) Just think out for yourselves, if a man who was good yesterday has become bad after having come in contact with me, is he responsible that he has deteriorated or am I? The atmosphere of sycophancy and falsity that surrounds them on their coming to India demoralizes them, as it would many of us. It is well to take the blame sometimes. If we are to receive self-government, we shall have to take it. We shall never be granted self-government. Look at the history of the British Empire and the British nation; freedom-loving as it is, it will not be a party to give freedom to a people who will not take it themselves.

•

## PROCLAMATION OF THE IRISH REPUBLIC
*The Provisional Government of the Irish Republic
to the People of Ireland*
Dublin, 24 April 1916

*'Ireland summons her children to the flag'*

*The Easter Rising, a rebellion in Dublin on 24–29 April 1916 seeking imme-
diate independence for Ireland, was led by Patrick Pearse and James Connolly of
Sinn Féin. The proclamation was mainly the work of Pearse, who proclaimed a
provisional government of the Irish Republic, as its president, from the General
Post Office which served as the rebel headquarters.*

Irishmen and Irishwomen: In the name of God and of the dead generations from which she receives her old tradition of nation-hood, Ireland, through us, summons her children to her flag and strikes for her freedom.

Having organized and trained her manhood through her secret revolutionary organization, the Irish Republican Brotherhood, and through her open military organizations, the Irish Volunteers, and the Irish Citizen Army, having patiently perfected her discipline, having resolutely waited for the right moment to reveal itself, she now seizes that moment, and, supported by her exiled children in America and by gallant allies in Europe, but relying in the first on her own strength, she strikes in full confidence of victory.

We declare the right of the people of Ireland to the ownership of Ireland, and to the unfettered control of Irish destinies, to be sovereign and indefeasible. The long usurpation of that right by a foreign people and government has not extinguished the right, nor can it ever be extinguished except by the destruction of the Irish people. In every generation the Irish people have asserted their right to national freedom and sovereignty, six times during the past three hundred years they have asserted it in arms. Standing on that fundamental right and again asserting it in arms in the face of the world, we hereby proclaim the Irish republic as a sovereign independent state, and we pledge our lives and the lives of our comrades-in-arms to the cause of its freedom, of its welfare, and of its exaltation among the nations.

The Irish republic is entitled to, and hereby claims, the allegiance of every Irishman and Irishwoman. The republic guarantees religious and civil liberty, equal rights and equal opportunities to all its citizens, and declares its resolve to pursue the happiness and prosperity of the whole nation and of all its parts, cherishing all the children of the nation equally, and oblivious of the differences carefully fostered by an alien government, which have divided a minority from the majority in the past.

Until our arms have brought the opportune moment for the establishment of a permanent national government, representative of the whole people of Ireland, and elected by the suffrages of all her men and women, the Provisional Government, hereby constituted, will administer the civil and military affairs of the republic in trust for the people. We place the cause of the Irish republic under the protection of the Most High God, whose blessing we invoke upon our arms, and we pray that no one who serves that cause will dishonour it by cowardice, inhumanity, or rapine. In this supreme hour the Irish nation must, by its valour and discipline, and by the readiness of its children to sacrifice themselves for the common good, prove itself worthy of the august destiny to which it is called.

Signed on behalf of the provisional government,

Thomas J. Clarke, Sean MacDiarmada, Thomas MacDonagh,
P. H. Pearse, Eamonn Ceannt, James Connolly, Joseph Plunkett

*Pearse, Connolly and twelve other rebel leaders were court-martialled and exe-
cuted. Pearse was shot at 3.30 a.m. on 3 May. In his speech from the dock,
eloquent even in the face of death, Pearse told his captors: 'We seem to have lost.
We have not lost. To refuse to fight would have been to lose; to fight is to win. We
have kept faith with the past and handed on a tradition to the future . . . You
cannot conquer Ireland. You cannot extinguish the Irish passion for freedom. If
our deed has not been sufficient to win freedom, then our children will win it by a
better deed.'*

•

# ROGER CASEMENT
## London, 1916

*'In Ireland alone, in this twentieth century, is loyalty held to be a crime'*

*On his retirement from the British consular service in 1911, Roger Casement
became a fervent Irish nationalist. At the outbreak of the First World War, he
sought to recruit Irish prisoners of war for the German army. He went to Berlin
to secure German aid for Irish independence but the Germans preferred the British Empire to a free Ireland and considered Casement a nuisance.*

*On the eve of the Easter Rising, he travelled to Ireland in a German U-boat
to warn that there would be no German aid and that a rising would not succeed.
He landed near Tralee but was quickly arrested by the British. He was taken to
London and tried for high treason at the Old Bailey by an English Lord Chief
Justice and an English jury. He was refused permission to conduct his own case
and was allowed to speak only after the jury found him guilty.*

*His defiance in the dock and the powerful oratory of his defence explains why,
for the Irish, he remains a patriot martyr. The speech has been described (by William Blunt) as the finest document in patriotic literature, finer than anything in
Plutarch or elsewhere in Pagan literature. Years later Jawaharlal Nehru, leader*

*of the Indian movement for independence from the British, said it seemed to point out exactly how a subject nation should feel.*

My Lord Chief Justice, as I wish my words to reach a much wider audience than I see before me here, I intend to read all that I propose to say. What I shall read now is something I wrote more than twenty days ago. I may say, my lord, at once, that I protest against the jurisdiction of this court in my case on this charge, and the argument, that I am now going to read, is addressed not to this court, but to my own countrymen.

There is an objection, possibly not good in law, but surely good on moral grounds, against the application to me here of this old English statute, 565 years old, that seeks to deprive an Irishman today of life and honour, not for 'adhering to the King's enemies', but for adhering to his own people.

When this statute was passed, in 1351, what was the state of men's minds on the question of a far higher allegiance – that of a man to God and His kingdom? The law of that day did not permit a man to forsake his Church, or deny his God, save with his life. The 'heretic', then, had the same doom as the 'traitor'.

Today a man may forswear God and His heavenly kingdom, without fear or penalty – all earlier statutes having gone the way of Nero's edicts against the Christians, but that constitutional phantom 'the king' can still dig up from the dungeons and torture-chambers of the Dark Ages a law that takes a man's life and limb for an exercise of conscience.

If true religion rests on love, it is equally true that loyalty rests on love. The law that I am charged under has no parentage in love, and claims the allegiance of today on the ignorance and blindness of the past.

I am being tried, in truth, not by my peers of the live present, but by the fears of the dead past; not by the civilization of the twentieth century, but by the brutality of the fourteenth; not even by a statute framed in the language of the land that tries me, but emitted in the language of an enemy land – so antiquated is the law that must be sought today to slay an Irishman, whose offence is that he puts Ireland first.

Loyalty is a sentiment, not a law. It rests on love, not on restraint. The government of Ireland by England rests on restraint, and not on law; and since it demands no love, it can evoke no loyalty . . .

Judicial assassination today is reserved only for one race of the king's subjects – for Irishmen, for those who cannot forget their allegiance to the realm of Ireland. The kings of England, as such, had no rights in Ireland up to the time of Henry VIII, save such as rested on compact and mutual obligation entered into between them and certain princes, chiefs, and lords of Ireland. This form of legal right, such as it was, gave no king of England lawful power to impeach an Irishman for high treason under this statute of King Edward III of England until an Irish Act, known as Poyning's Law, the tenth of Henry VII, was passed in 1494 at Drogheda, by the Parliament of the Pale in Ireland, and enacted as law in that part of Ireland. But, if by Poyning's Law an Irishman of the Pale could be indicted for high treason under this Act, he could be indicted in only one way, and before one tribunal – by the laws of the Realm of Ireland and in Ireland. The very law of Poyning, which, I believe, applies this statute of Edward III to Ireland, enacts also for the Irishman's defence 'all these laws by which England claims her liberty'.

And what is the fundamental charter of an Englishman's liberty? That he shall be tried by his peers. With all respect, I assert this court is to me, an Irishman, charged with this offence, a foreign court – this jury is for me, an Irishman, not a jury of my peers to try me on this vital issue, for it is patent to every man of conscience that I have a right, an indefeasible right, if tried at all, under this statute of high treason, to be tried in Ireland, before an Irish court and by an Irish jury. This court, this jury, the public opinion of this country, England, cannot but be prejudiced in varying degrees against me, most of all in time of war. I did not land in England. I landed in Ireland. It was to Ireland I came; to Ireland I wanted to come; and the last place I desired to land was in England.

But for the Attorney-General of England there is only 'England';

there is no Ireland; there is only the law of England, no right of Ireland; the liberty of Ireland and of an Irishman is to be judged by the power of England. Yet for me, the Irish outlaw, there is a land of Ireland, a right of Ireland, and a charter for all Irishmen to appeal to, in the last resort, a charter that even the very statutes of England itself cannot deprive us of – nay more, a charter that Englishmen themselves assert as the fundamental bond of law that connects the two kingdoms. This charge of high treason involves a moral responsibility, as the very terms of the indictment against myself recite, inasmuch as I committed the acts I am charged with to the 'evil example of others in like case'. What was the evil example I set to others in the like case, and who were these others? The 'evil example' charged is that I asserted the right of my own country and the 'others' I appealed to, to aid my endeavour, were my own countrymen. The example was given, not to Englishmen, but to Irishmen, and the 'like case' can never arise in England, but only in Ireland. To Englishmen I set no evil example, for I made no appeal to them. I asked no Englishman to help me. I asked Irishmen to fight for their rights. The 'evil example' was only to other Irishmen, who might come after me, and in 'like case' seek to do as I did. How, then, since neither my example, nor my appeal was addressed to Englishmen, can I be rightfully tried by them?

If I did wrong in making that appeal to Irishmen to join with me in an effort to fight for Ireland, it is by Irishmen, and by them alone, I can be rightfully judged. From this court and its jurisdiction I appeal to those I am alleged to have wronged, and to those I am alleged to have injured by my 'evil example' and claim that they alone are competent to decide my guilt or innocence. If they find me guilty, the statute may affix the penalty, but the statute does not override or annul my right to seek judgement at their hands.

This is so fundamental a right, so natural a right, so obvious a right, that it is clear that the Crown were aware of it when they brought me by force and by stealth from Ireland to this country. It was not I who landed in England, but the Crown who dragged me here, away from my own country to which I had returned with a price upon my head, away from my own countrymen whose loyalty is not in doubt, and safe from the judgement of my peers whose judgement I do not shrink from. I admit no other judgement but theirs. I accept no verdict save at their hands.

I assert from this dock that I am being tried here, not because it is just, but because it is unjust. Place me before a jury of my own countrymen, be it Protestant or Catholic, Unionist or Nationalist, Sinn Féineach or Orangemen, and I shall accept the verdict, and bow to the statute and all its penalties. But I shall accept no meaner finding against me, than that of those, whose loyalty I have endangered by my example, and to whom alone I made appeal. If they adjudge me guilty, then guilty I am. It is not I who am afraid of their verdict – it is the Crown. If this is not so, why fear the test? I fear it not. I demand it as my right.

This is the condemnation of English rule, of English-made law, of English government in Ireland, that it dare not rest on the will of the Irish people, but exists in defiance of their will: that it is a rule, derived not from right, but from conquest.

Conquest, my Lord, gives no title; and, if it exists over the body, it fails over the mind. It can exert no empire over men's reason and judgement and affections; and it is from this law of conquest without title to the reason, judgement, and affection of my own countrymen that I appeal.

I can answer for my own acts and speeches. While one English party was responsible for preaching a doctrine of hatred, designed to bring about civil war in Ireland, the other, and that the party in power, took no active steps to restrain a propaganda that found its advocates in the Army, Navy, and Privy Council – in the House of Parliament, and in the State Church – a propaganda the methods of whose expression were so 'grossly illegal and utterly unconstitutional' that even the Lord Chancellor of England could find only words and no repressive action to apply to them. Since lawlessness sat in high places in England, and laughed at the law as at the custodians of the law, what wonder was it that Irishmen should refuse to accept the verbal protestations of an English Lord Chancellor as a sufficient safeguard for their lives and liberties? I know not how all my colleagues on the Volunteer Committee in Dublin reviewed the growing menace, but those with whom I was in closest cooperation redoubled, in face of these threats from without, our efforts to unite all Irishmen from within. Our appeals were made to Protestant and Unionist as much almost as to Catholic and Nationalist Irishmen. We hoped that, by the exhibition of affection and goodwill on our part toward our political opponents in Ireland, we should yet succeed in winning them from the side of an English party whose sole interest in our country lay in its oppression in the past, and in the present in its degradation to the mean and narrow needs of their political animosities. It is true that they based their actions, so they averred, on 'ears for the empire', and on a very diffuse loyalty that took in all the peoples of the empire, save only the Irish. That blessed word *empire* that bears so paradoxical resemblance to charity! For if charity begins at home, *empire* begins in other men's homes, and both may cover a multitude of sins. I, for one, was determined that Ireland was much more to me than *empire*, and, if charity begins at home, so must loyalty. Since arms were so necessary to make our organization a reality, and to give to the minds of Irishmen, menaced with the most outrageous threats, a sense of security, it was our bounden duty to get arms before all else. I decided, with this end in view, to go to America, with surely a better right to appeal to Irishmen there for help in an hour of great national trial, than those envoys of *empire* could assert for their weekend descents on Ireland, or their appeals to Germany.

If, as the right honourable gentleman, the present Attorney-General, asserted in a speech at Manchester, Nationalists would neither fight for Home Rule nor pay for it, it was our duty to show him that we knew how to do both. Within a few weeks of my arrival in the United States, the fund that had been opened to secure arms for the Volunteers of Ireland amounted to many thousands of pounds. In every case the money subscribed, whether it came from the purse of the wealthy man, or from the still readier pocket of the poor man, was Irish gold.

We have been told, we have been asked to hope, that after this war Ireland will get Home Rule, as a reward for the lifeblood shed in a cause which, whomever else its success may benefit, can surely not benefit Ireland. And what will Home Rule be in return for what its vague promise has taken, and still hopes to take away from Ireland? It is not necessary to climb the painful stairs of Irish History – that treadmill of a nation, whose labours are as vain for her own uplifting as the convict's exertions are for his redemption, to review the long list of British promises made only to be broken – of Irish hopes, raised only to be dashed to the ground. Home Rule, when it comes, if come it does, will find an Ireland drained of all that is vital to its very existence unless it be that unquenchable hope we build on the graves of the dead. We are told that if Irishmen go by the thousand to die, not for Ireland, but for Flanders, for Belgium, for a patch of sand in the deserts of Mesopotamia, or a rocky trench on the heights of Gallipoli, they are winning self-government for Ireland. But if they dare to lay down their lives on their native soil, if they dare to dream even that freedom can be won only at home by men resolved to fight for it there, then they are traitors to their country, and their dream and their deaths are phases of a dishonourable phantasy.

But history is not so recorded in other lands. In Ireland alone, in this twentieth century, is loyalty held to be a crime. If loyalty be something less than love and more than law, then we have had enough of such loyalty for Ireland and Irishmen. If we are to be indicted as criminals, to be shot as murderers, to be imprisoned as convicts, because our offence is that we love Ireland more than we value our lives, then I do not know what virtue resides in any offer of self-government held out to brave men on such terms. Self-government is our right, a thing born in us at birth, a thing no more to be doled out to us, or withheld from us, by another people than the right to life itself – than the right to feel the sun, or smell the flowers, or to love our kind. It is only from the convict these things are withheld, for crime committed and proven – and Ireland, that has wronged no man, has injured no land, that has sought no dominion over others – Ireland is being treated today among the nations of the world as if she were a convicted criminal. If it be treason to fight against such an unnatural fate as this, then I am proud to be a rebel, and shall cling to my 'rebellion' with the last drop of my blood. If there be no right of rebellion against the state of things that no savage tribe would endure without resistance, then I am sure that it is better for men to fight and die without right than to live in such a state of right as this. Where all your rights have become only an accumulated wrong, where men must beg with bated breath for leave to subsist in their own land, to think their own thoughts, to sing their own songs, to gather the fruits of their own labours, and, even while they beg, to see things inexorably withdrawn from them – then, surely, it is a braver, a saner and truer thing to be a rebel, in act and in deed, against such circumstances as these, than to tamely accept it, as the natural lot of men.

*Casement was condemned to death and hanged. His so-called Black Diaries containing homosexual passages were circulated by British agents to discredit him and discourage any movement for a reprieve. Thanks to Casement, Sinn Féin got the credit for the Easter Rising – and the independence of Ireland triumphed when he was hanged.*

•

## WOODROW WILSON
### Washington, DC, 2 April 1917

*'The world must be made safe for democracy'*

*When the First World War broke out, Woodrow Wilson immediately issued a proclamation of neutrality. Yet real neutrality was impossible for a nation so powerful as America, especially after the* Lusitania *with her 1,198 passengers, including 128 Americans, was sunk by a German torpedo in 1915. American opinion was appalled.*

*Wilson sent strong notes of protest to Berlin and made a memorable speech in which he proclaimed: 'There is no such thing as a man being too proud to fight. There is no such thing as a nation being so right that it does not need to convince others by force that it is right.'*

*In 1916 Wilson was re-elected president by a slender majority. He directed a note to the belligerent governments offering an honourable excuse to start negotiations. After this tactic failed, he delivered an address to Congress on 'Peace without victory'. The announcement that Germany was resorting to unrestricted submarine warfare – that all Allied or neutral vessels in the Atlantic would be torpedoed without warning – abruptly destroyed Wilson's dream.*

*One month after his second inaugural address, he went before a joint session of Congress to ask for a declaration that a state of war existed between Germany and the United States – and got what he wanted by a nearly unanimous vote on 6 April, Good Friday.*

With a profound sense of the solemn and even tragical character of the step I am taking and of the grave responsibilities which it involves, but in unhesitating obedience to what I deem my constitutional duty, I advise that the Congress declare the recent course of the imperial German government to be in fact nothing less than war against the government and people of the United States; that it formally accept the status of belligerent which has thus been thrust upon it; and that it take immediate steps not only to put the country in a more thorough state of defence, but also to exert all its power and employ all its resources to bring the government of the German Empire to terms and end the war . . .

We are accepting this challenge of hostile purpose because we know that in such a government, following such methods, we can never have a friend; and that in the presence of its organized power, always lying in wait to accomplish we know not what purpose, there can be no assured security for the democratic governments of the world. We are now about to accept the gage of battle with this natural foe to liberty and shall, if necessary, spend the whole force of the nation to check and nullify its pretensions and its power. We are glad, now that we see the facts with no veil of false pretence about them, to fight thus for the ultimate peace of the world and for the liberation of its peoples, the German peoples included: for the rights of nations great and small and the privilege of men everywhere to choose their way of life and of obedience. The world must be made safe for democracy. Its peace must be planted upon the tested foundations of political liberty. We have no selfish ends to serve. We desire no conquest, no dominion. We seek no indemnities for ourselves, no material compensation for the sacrifices we shall freely make. We are but one of the champions of the rights of mankind. We shall be satisfied when those rights have been made as secure as the faith and the freedom of nations can make them.

Just because we fight without rancour and without selfish object, seeking nothing for ourselves but what we shall wish to share with all free peoples, we shall, I feel confident, conduct our operations as belligerents without passion and ourselves observe with proud punctilio the principles of right and of fair play we profess to be fighting for . . .

It will be all the easier for us to conduct ourselves as belligerents in a high spirit of right and fairness because we act without animus, not in enmity toward a people or with the desire to bring any injury or disadvantage upon them, but only in armed opposition to an irresponsible government which has thrown aside all considerations of humanity and of right and is running amuck. We are, let me say again, the sincere friends of the German people, and shall desire nothing so much as the early re-establishment of intimate relations of mutual advantage between us – however hard it may be for them, for the time being, to believe that this is spoken from our hearts. We have borne with their present government through all these bitter months because of that friendship – exercising a patience and forbearance which would otherwise have been impossible. We shall, happily, still have an opportunity to prove that friendship in our daily attitude and actions toward the millions of men and women of German birth and native sympathy who live amongst us and share our life, and we shall be proud to prove it toward all who are in fact loyal to their neighbours and to the government in the hour of test. They are, most of them, as true and loyal Americans as if they had never known any other fealty or allegiance. They will be prompt to stand with us in rebuking and restraining the few who may be of a different mind and purpose. If there should be disloyalty, it will be dealt with with a firm hand of stern repression; but, if it lifts its head at all, it will lift it only here and there and without countenance except from a lawless and malignant few.

It is a distressing and oppressive duty, gentlemen of the Congress, which I have performed in thus addressing you. There are, it may be, many months of fiery trial and sacrifice ahead of us. It is a fearful thing to lead this great peaceful people into war, into the most terrible and disastrous of all wars, civilization itself seeming to be in the balance. But the right is more precious than peace, and we shall fight for the things which we have always carried nearest our hearts – for democracy, for the right of those who submit to authority to have a voice in their own governments, for the dominion of right by such a concert of free peoples as shall bring peace and safety to all nations and make the world itself at last free. To such a task we can dedicate our lives and our fortunes, everything that we are and everything that we have, with the pride of those who know that the day has come when America is privileged to spend her blood and her might for the principles that gave her birth and happiness and the peace which she has treasured. God helping her, she can do no other.

*Wilson's address set the United States on a new course; armed neutrality was impracticable and the world must be made safe for democracy. He was rewarded with tumultuous cheers. They were no comfort. 'My message today was a message of death for our young men,' he said afterwards. 'How strange it seems to applaud that.'*

•

## V. I. LENIN
### Petrograd, 15 April 1917

### 'A new phase in the history of Russia begins'

*After the Russian Revolution of March 1917, Lenin travelled back to Petrograd from Switzerland, passing through Germany in a sealed train provided by the German general staff, who counted on the Bolsheviks spreading disaffection among the Russian soldiers.*

*An honour guard of Kronstadt sailors in striped jerseys and red pompon hats met Lenin at the Finland Station. A brass band played the 'Marseillaise'. Lenin was taken to the imperial waiting-room where he addressed a dense crowd and immediately snubbed any hope that the Bolsheviks would close democratic ranks with the Mensheviks. He appealed directly for civil war and international revolution.*

Dear comrades, soldiers, sailors and workers! I am happy to greet in your persons the victorious Russian revolution, and greet you as the vanguard of the worldwide proletarian army ... The piratical imperialist war is the beginning of civil war throughout Europe ... The hour is not far distant when the peoples will turn their arms against their own capitalist exploiters ... The worldwide socialist revolution has already dawned ... Germany is seething ... Any day now the whole of European capitalism may crash. The Russian revolution accomplished by you has prepared the way and opened a new epoch. Long live the worldwide socialist revolution!

*As Lenin left the room, an officer on the platform outside saluted him and a detachment of soldiers with bayonets stood to attention. A great roar of a cheer went up from the revolutionary workers and sailors of Petrograd who had come to greet him. The sailors presented arms and their commander reported to Lenin for duty. They wanted him to speak, it was whispered. Lenin walked a few paces and took off his bowler hat.*

I don't know yet whether you agree with the Provisional Government. But I know very well that when they give you sweet speeches and make many promises they are deceiving you and the whole Russian people. The people need peace. The people need bread and land. And they give you war, hunger, no food, and the land remains with the landowners. Sailors, comrades, you must fight for the revolution, fight to the end.

*Lenin remained in Petrograd until 18 July, when the failure of an abortive Soviet coup d'état forced him to escape again to Finland. He returned to Petrograd on 23 October and from his headquarters in the Smolny Institute led the rising which captured the government offices. The Bolshevik forces went into action on 25 October. The key points in the city were occupied. Members of the provisional government were prisoners or fugitives. That afternoon, Lenin announced to a meeting of the Petrograd Soviet the triumph of 'the workers' and peasants' revolution'.*

Comrades, the workers' and peasants' revolution, about the necessity of which the Bolsheviks have always spoken, has been accomplished.

What is the significance of this workers' and peasants' revolution? Its significance is, first of all, that we shall have a Soviet government, our own organ of power, in which the bourgeoisie will have no share whatsoever. The oppressed masses will themselves create a power. The old state apparatus will be shattered to its foundations and a new administrative apparatus set up in the form of the Soviet organizations.

From now on, a new phase in the history of Russia begins, and this, the third Russian revolution, should in the end lead to the victory of socialism.

One of our urgent tasks is to put an immediate end to the war. It is clear to everybody that in order to end this war, which is closely bound up with the present capitalist system, capital itself must be fought.

We shall be helped in this by the world working-class movement, which is already beginning to develop in Italy, Britain and Germany.

The proposal we make to international democracy for a just and immediate peace will everywhere awaken an ardent response among the international proletarian masses. All the secret treaties must be immediately published in order to strengthen the confidence of the proletariat.

Within Russia a huge section of the peasantry have said that they have played long enough with the capitalists, and will now march with the workers. A single decree putting an end to landed proprietorship will win us the confidence of the peasants. The peasants will understand that the salvation of the peasantry lies only in an alliance with the workers. We shall institute genuine workers' control over production.

We have now learned to make a concerted effort. The revolution that has just been accomplished is evidence of this. We possess the strength of mass organization, which will overcome everything and lead the proletariat to the world revolution.

We must now set about building a proletarian socialist state in Russia.

Long live the world socialist revolution! (*Stormy applause.*)

*That evening the second All-Russian Congress of Soviets proclaimed the transfer of all power throughout Russia to Soviets of Workers', Soldiers' and Peasants' Deputies. As Lenin stood at the reading-stand, he was greeted by a long-rolling ovation. When it finished, he said simply: 'We shall now proceed to construct the socialist order.' Again there was an overwhelming human roar. The congress adopted decrees on peace and on the land and approved the composition of the Council of People's Commissars – the first workers' and peasants' government.*

*Yet the Bolsheviks were massively defeated in the elections that followed. When the Constituent Assembly, the dream of Russia's revolutionaries and liberals for nearly a century, met in January 1918, it was dissolved by force.*

*The Bolsheviks seized power and went on, particularly under Lenin's successor Joseph Stalin, to construct one of the worst tyrannies of the twentieth century. 'Lenin and the party, the man and the instrument, were now indissolubly one,' says E. H. Carr. 'The foundations had been laid of the ascendancy in the party of the single leader.'*

•

## LEON TROTSKY
### St Petersburg, 25 October 1917

#### 'The dustbin of history'

*Trotsky (1879–1940) was arrested as a revolutionary at the age of eighteen and sent to Siberia, where he escaped to join Lenin in London in 1902. He was back in St Petersburg in 1905, organizing the First Soviet. Again arrested and sent to Siberia, he escaped and spent several years as a revolutionary organizer in central Europe and beyond.*

*He returned to Petrograd (ex-St Petersburg) from America in May 1917 and was chairman of the Petrograd Soviet during the October revolution. Trotsky made this speech at the meeting of the Soviet Congress, one of the most often-quoted speeches of the century, when he denounced a resolution for a coalition government of all the Soviet parties, led by the Menshevik leader, Yuli Martov.*

What has taken place, is an insurrection, not a conspiracy. An insurrection of the popular masses needs no justification. We have tempered and hardened the revolutionary energy of the Petrograd workers and soldiers. We have openly forged the will of the masses to insurrection, and not conspiracy . . . Our insurrection has conquered, and now we are told: Renounce your victory; make concessions, compromise. With whom? I ask: With whom ought we to make a compromise? With that pitiful handful who just went out? . . . Haven't we seen them through and through? There is no longer anybody in Russia who is for them. Are the millions of workers and peasants represented in this Congress, whom they are ready now as always to turn over for a price to the mercies of the bourgeoisie, are they to enter a compromise with these men? No, a compromise is no good here. To those who have left, and to all who tell us to do this, we must say, 'You are pitiful isolated individuals; you are miserable bankrupts; your role is played out. Go where you belong from now on – into the dustbin of history!'

*In his award-winning account of the Russian Revolution,* A People's Tragedy, *Orlando Figes describes what happened next: 'In a moment of rage which he must have agonized over for the rest of his life, Martov, an old comrade of Lenin's, shouted: "Then we'll leave!" and walked in silence towards the exit without looking back – into the political wilderness.'*

•

## LEON TROTSKY
### Moscow, 19 March 1918

### 'We need an army'

*On the outbreak of civil war, Trotsky became Commissar for War and created the Red Army, even though he had no military experience. He wrote in* My Life: *'The problem was to make a clean sweep of the remains of the old army and in its place to build, under fire, a new army whose plan was not to be discovered in any books.'*

*Trotsky lived for almost two years in an armoured train which served as a mobile headquarters of the new army. By his ferocious energy, his insistence on military authority, his personal exposure in crucial battles and, above all, by stirring his followers to fight by the exaltation of his speeches and manifestos he created an army that finally defeated the Whites.*

*One of those speeches was given to the Moscow Soviet of Workers', Soldiers' and Peasants' Deputies.*

Comrades! Our Soviet Socialist Republic needs a well-organized army.

In the world situation in which it has been the will of history to place us, amid the conditions of unprecedented difficulty that surround us, conditions that, again, are not of our making, we need to be strong . . . We say, comrades, that Russia, exhausted and unarmed, will inevitably become the slave of international imperialism united against her if the international proletariat does not save her in time by its support, and if we ourselves do not organize our own defence . . .

We must arm and fight, so as to ensure the mere possibility of carrying out our programme; and that, if the European proletariat fails to come to our aid in the fatal moment of our tragic lonely struggle, then, by remaining unarmed, we may perish altogether. We were the first to raise the flag of revolt amid this bloody and black night of imperialist war, and it is hard for us, sometimes almost beyond our strength, to fight against the iron ring of enemies that surrounds us. Is it surprising if we are not accomplishing all that we wanted to accomplish?

We need an army, which would give us powerful strength for the inevitable coming struggle with international imperialism. With the aid of this army we shall not only defend ourselves but shall be in a position to help the struggle of the international proletariat.

For there can be no doubt that, the more international imperialism grabs and strangles, the more passionate and terrible will be the wrath of the European worker–soldier who, emerging from the trenches, will find at home, as the result of his inhuman sufferings, his family reduced to poverty and hunger, and his country in a state of economic collapse.

Let those of little faith, yielding to weariness, no longer wish to hear of the revolutionary movement of the proletariat of other countries, of the victory of the world revolution: we declare that the moment of social explosion in all states is inevitably approaching, and we, to whom history has given victory sooner than the rest, with all the possibilities that follow from this, must be ready, at the first thunderclap of the world revolution, to bring armed help to our foreign brothers in revolt.

For proper organization of the army and, in particular for expedient utilization of the specialists, we need revolutionary discipline. We are introducing this with determination at the top, but we need with no less vigour to introduce it down below, arousing a sense of responsibility among the masses. When the people realize that discipline is being introduced now not in order to defend the moneybags of the bourgeoisie, not to restore the land to the landlords, but, on the contrary, in order to consolidate and defend all the conquests made by the revolution, they will approve even the strictest of measures aimed at the establishment of discipline. We must at all costs and at any price implant discipline in the Red Army – not the previous sort, the automatic discipline of the rod, but conscious, collective discipline, based on revolutionary enthusiasm and clear understanding by the workers and peasants of their duty to their own classes.

We shall not be halted by any difficulties. It may be that, in order to bring our cause to triumph and accomplish our great tasks, we shall have for a time to work not eight hours but ten and twelve hours a day. So what? We shall work twice as hard, we shall harness ourselves together, we shall go forward along the road of labour discipline and creative work. We did not say, and we do not say now, that everything will come by itself. No, the difficulties that face us are beyond counting. But we have proved to be richer in spirit, resources and forces than we ourselves had thought we were: and that is no small thing, that is the pledge of victory.

Let us work tirelessly, so that at the moment when the European proletariat rise up, we shall be able to go fully armed to their aid and, together with them, in a combined effort, overthrow for ever the power of capital! . . .

The Soviet Republic needs an army that will be able to fight and conquer.

It is the responsibility of the Soviet power to make sure that none of the separate institutions or units of the people's army are transformed into centres of counter-revolution, into instruments directed against the workers and peasants. Political control over the entire organization and life of the army will be entrusted to military commissars. The post of military commissar is one of the most responsible and most honourable in the Soviet Republic. The commissar will safeguard the closest internal bond between the Army and the Soviet regime as a whole. The commissar will incarnate the principle of revolutionary duty and indestructible discipline. The commissar will ensure, with the full force of his authority and power, immediate and unquestioning fulfilment of the operational and combat instructions issued by the military leaders.

These are the principles which the Government lays down as the basis for creating the Army: universal and obligatory military training in schools, factories and villages; immediate formation of firm cadres from the most self-sacrificing fighters; bringing in military commissars as guardians of the highest interests of the revolution and of socialism.

In the name of the Socialist Republic, the Council of People's Commissars calls upon all Soviets, all conscious workers and peasants, all honest citizens who are devoted to the people's cause, to redouble their efforts in the great work of safeguarding the independence and freedom of our country.

Liberated Russia will not be enslaved. It will arise and grow strong, it will cast out the beasts of prey, it will live in fraternal unity with the liberated peoples of all lands.

All that is needed is that, in these dark days of calamity affecting the whole people, all true sons of revolutionary Russia shall have no thought, no desire, no commitment but the salvation of our blood-drained homeland.

Let there be no wavering, no doubts! Work, order, perseverance, discipline, self-sacrifice – and we shall triumph!

•

## EUGENE V. DEBS
Cleveland, Ohio, 14 September 1918

*'While there is a lower class, I am in it'*

*Eugene Victor Debs (1855–1926), founder of the American Railway Union, was one of the most attractive men thrown up by the American labour movement. When the ARU instituted a boycott of Pullman trains, the Attorney-General accused the union of acting in restraint of trade and sent troops against its strikers. The strike and boycott collapsed and Debs served six months in prison, where he was converted to socialism.*

*He formed the Socialist Party of America in 1900 and stood as a candidate in the presidential elections of 1904, 1908 and 1912 when he polled 900,000 votes in the contest with Wilson, Roosevelt and Taft.*

*A bitter opponent of what he thought was a bloody war of the plutocracies in 1914–18, appalled by the campaign against freedom of speech which had shut down the German-language as well as the socialist press and determined to demonstrate what was happening to the constitutional guarantee of free speech, Debs made a speech in Canton denouncing the war.*

*At the federal court in Cleveland, he was found guilty of trying to obstruct the Conscription Act. The Wilson administration made sure that such wickedness would never go unpunished by pushing through Espionage and Sedition Acts. Debs remained in prison until Wilson left office, when he was pardoned by President Harding.*

*Before sentence was passed, Debs addressed the judge.*

Your Honour, years ago I recognized my kinship with all living beings, and I made up my mind that I was not one bit better than the meanest on earth. I said then, and I say now, that while there is a lower class, I am in it, while there is a criminal element, I am of it, and while there is a soul in prison, I am not free . . .

Standing here this morning, I recall my boyhood. At fourteen I went to work in a railroad shop; at sixteen I was firing a freight engine on a railroad. I remember all the hardships and privations of that earlier day, and from that time until now my heart has been with the working class. I could have been in Congress long ago. I have preferred to go to prison . . .

I am thinking this morning of the men in the mills and factories; of the men in the mines and on the railroads. I am thinking of the women who for a paltry wage are compelled to work out their barren lives; of the little children who in this system are robbed of their childhood and in their tender years are seized in the remorseless grasp of Mammon and forced into the industrial dungeons, there to feed the monster machines while they themselves are being starved and stunted, body and soul. I see them dwarfed and diseased and their little lives broken and blasted because in this high noon of our twentieth-century Christian civilization money is still so much more important than the flesh and blood of childhood. In very truth gold is god today and rules with pitiless sway in the affairs of men.

In this country – the most favoured beneath the bending skies – we have vast areas of the richest and most fertile soil, material resources in inexhaustible abundance, the most marvellous productive machinery on earth, and millions of eager workers ready to apply their labour to that machinery to produce in abundance for every man, woman, and child – and if there are still vast numbers of our people who are the victims of poverty and whose lives are an unceasing struggle all the way from youth to old age, until at last death comes to their rescue and stills their aching hearts and lulls these hapless victims to dreamless sleep, it is not the fault of the Almighty: it cannot be charged to nature, but it is due entirely to the outgrown social system in which we live, that ought to be abolished not only in the interest of the toiling masses but in the higher interest of all humanity . . .

I believe, Your Honour, in common with all Socialists, that this nation ought to own and control its own industries. I believe, as all

Socialists do, that all things that are jointly needed and used ought to be jointly owned – that industry, the basis of our social life, instead of being the private property of the few and operated for their enrichment, ought to be the common property of all, democratically administered in the interest of all . . .

I am opposing a social order in which it is possible for one man who does absolutely nothing that is useful to amass a fortune of hundreds of millions of dollars, while millions of men and women who work all the days of their lives secure barely enough for a wretched existence.

This order of things cannot always endure. I have registered my protest against it. I recognize the feebleness of my effort, but fortunately I am not alone. There are multiplied thousands of others who, like myself, have come to realize that before we may truly enjoy the blessings of civilized life, we must reorganize society upon a mutual and cooperative basis; and to this end we have organized a great economic and political movement that spreads over the face of all the earth.

There are today upwards of sixty millions of Socialists, loyal, devoted adherents to this cause, regardless of nationality, race, creed, colour, or sex. They are all making common cause. They are spreading with tireless energy the propaganda of the new social order. They are waiting, watching, and working hopefully through all the hours of the day and the night. They are still in a minority. But they have learned how to be patient and to bide their time. They feel – they know, indeed – that the time is coming, in spite of all opposition, all persecution, when this emancipating gospel will spread among all the peoples, and when this minority will become the triumphant majority and, sweeping into power, inaugurate the greatest social and economic change in history.

In that day we shall have the universal commonwealth – the harmonious cooperation of every nation with every other nation on earth . . .

Your Honour, I ask no mercy and I plead for no immunity. I realize that finally the right must prevail. I never so clearly comprehended as now the great struggle between the powers of greed and exploitation on the one hand and upon the other the rising hosts of industrial freedom and social justice.

I can see the dawn of the better day for humanity. The people are awakening. In due time they will and must come to their own . . .

I am now prepared to receive your sentence.

•

## DAVID LLOYD GEORGE
### Wolverhampton, 24 November 1918

*'A fit country for heroes to live in'*

*When the war ended on 11 November 1918, Lloyd George assumed total command. Acclaimed as 'the man who won the war', he was the most dominant British political leader since Cromwell and won an overwhelming triumph at the general election in December 1918.*

*Britain had just emerged from a great peril, Lloyd George said in this speech at Wolverhampton within two weeks of the war's ending. But it was not an hour for boasting.*

There is, as I never witnessed before, a new comradeship of classes, and I am glad, as an old political fighter – who has been hard hit and has been able to return the blows, always in a spirit of meekness – that we are approaching the new problems in a spirit of comradeship. Let us keep it as long as we can. I have no doubt human nature will prevail yet, but for the moment let us finish the task together, and when we have finished it, then let us play political football. You can afford to do it then. But the work is not over yet – the work of the nation, the work of the people, the work of those who have sacrificed. Let us work together first.

What is our task? To make Britain a fit country for heroes to live in. I am not using the word 'heroes' in any spirit of boastfulness, but in the spirit of humble recognition of the fact. I cannot think what these men have gone through. I have been there at the door of the furnace and witnessed it, but that is not being in it, and I saw them march into the furnace. There are millions of men who will come back. Let us make this a land fit for such men to live in. There is no time to lose. I want us to take advantage of this new spirit. Don't let us waste this victory merely in ringing joybells. Let us make victory the motive power to link the old land up in such measure that it will be nearer the sunshine than ever before, and that at any rate it will lift those who have been living in the dark places to a plateau where they will get the rays of the sun. We cannot undertake that without a new Parliament. Those of you who have been at the front have seen the star shells, how they light up the darkness and illuminate all the obscure places. The Great War has been like a gigantic star shell, flashing all over the land, illuminating the country and showing up the dark, deep places. We have seen places that we have never noticed before, and we mean to put these things right.

What is the first thing the Great War has shown us? The appalling waste of human material in the country. There is hardly any material placed by Providence in this country which is so much wasted as human life and human strength and human intellect – the most precious and irreplaceable material of all. I have previously said something about the figures of the recruiting officers. Those who were in charge of recruiting came to the conclusion that if the people of this country had lived under proper conditions, were properly fed and housed, had lived under healthy conditions – had lived their lives in their full vigour – you could have had a million more men available and fit to put into the army. It is not merely that. When life has not been lost, its vitality has been depressed. There are millions who are below par. You cannot keep even animals in their full vigour unless you give them good conditions. You cannot do it with men and women, and you cannot bring up children under bad conditions. There are millions of men's lives which have been lost as a result of the war, but there are millions more of maimed lives in the sense of undermined constitutions through atrocious social conditions in consequence of the terrors of this Great War. You must put that right. Put it at its lowest – trade, commerce and industry all suffer through it. A vigorous community of strong, healthy men and women is more valuable even from the commercial and industrial point of view than a community which is below par in consequence of bad conditions. Treat it if you like not as a human proposition, but as a business proposition. It is good business to see that the men, the women and the children of this country are brought up and sustained under conditions that will give strength and vigour to their frames, more penetration and endurance to their intelligence, and more spirit and heart than ever to face the problems of life which will always be problems that will require fighting right from the cradle to the tomb. That is the first problem. One of the ways of dealing with that is, of course, to deal with housing conditions. Slums are not fit homes for the men who have won this war or for their children. They are not fit nurseries for the children who are to make an Imperial race, and there must be no patching up. This problem has got to be undertaken in a way never undertaken before, as a great national charge and duty. The housing of the people must be a national concern.

•

## HENRY CABOT LODGE
### Washington, DC, 12 August 1919

#### 'American I was born'

*Senator Lodge, Senate majority leader and chairman of the Foreign Relations Committee, was the principal critic of Woodrow Wilson as he attempted to sell the League of Nations to Americans reared on George Washington's warning that the United States should stand aloof from permanent alliances.*

*He disliked Wilson, believed that America should play an important role in world affairs, and needed to shape a strategy that all Republicans – both isolationists and internationalists – could accept. He argued, therefore, that the League should be accepted with 'reservations' which, by limiting American obligations, would make it impossible for the League or any of its members to involve the nation in important international commitments without the consent of Congress.*

*Lodge's arguments in 1919, particularly about national sovereignty, were persuasive twenty-five years later when the United Nations was established. His influence can be especially detected in the veto granted to the great powers in the UN Security Council.*

*His speech on 12 August 1919 was Lodge's first statement of his position in the Senate. He prepared for the occasion with great care, delivered the speech devoid of emphasis or accentuation, rarely raised his eyes from his manuscript – but his words unleashed a storm of applause from the galleries and it was minutes before order was restored.*

The independence of the United States is not only more precious to ourselves but to the world than any single possession. Look at the United States today. We have made mistakes in the past. We have had shortcomings. We shall make mistakes in the future and fall short of our own best hopes. But none the less is there any country today on the face of the earth which can compare with this in ordered liberty, in peace, and in the largest freedom? I feel that I can say this without being accused of undue boastfulness, for it is the simple fact, and in making this treaty and taking on these obligations all that we do is in a spirit of unselfishness and in a desire for the good of mankind. But it is well to remember that we are dealing with nations every one of which has a direct individual interest to serve, and there is grave danger in an unshared idealism. Contrast the United States with any country on the face of the earth today and ask yourself whether the situation of the United States is not the best to be found. I will go as far as anyone in world service, but the first step to world service is the maintenance of the United States.

You may call me selfish if you will, conservative or reactionary, or use any other harsh adjective you see fit to apply, but an American I was born, an American I have remained all my life. I can never be anything else but an American, and I must think of the United States first, and when I think of the United States first in an arrangement like this I am thinking of what is best for the world, for if the United States fails the best hopes of mankind fail with it. I have never had but one allegiance – I cannot divide it now. I have loved but one flag and I cannot share that devotion and give affection to the mongrel banner invented for a league. Internationalism, illustrated by the Bolshevik and by the men to whom all countries are alike provided they can make money out of them, is to me repulsive. National I must remain, and in that way I like all other Americans can render the amplest service to the world. The United States is the world's best hope, but if you fetter her in the interests and quarrels of other nations, if you tangle her in the intrigues of Europe, you will destroy her power for good and endanger her very existence. Leave her to march freely through the centuries to come as in the years that have gone. Strong, generous, and confident, she has nobly served mankind. Beware how you trifle with your marvellous inheritance, this great land of ordered liberty, for if we stumble and fall freedom and civilization everywhere will go down in ruin.

We are told that we shall 'break the heart of the world' if we do not take this league just as it stands. I fear that the hearts of the vast majority of mankind would beat on strongly and steadily and without any quickening if the league were to perish altogether. If it should be effectively and beneficiently changed the people who would lie awake in sorrow for a single night could be easily gathered in one not very large room but those who would draw a long breath of relief would reach to millions.

We hear much of visions and I trust we shall continue to have visions and dream dreams of a fairer future for the race. But visions are one thing and visionaries are another, and the mechanical appliances of the rhetorician designed to give a picture of a present which does not exist and of a future which no man can predict are as unreal and shortlived as the steam or canvas clouds, the angels suspended on wires and the artificial lights of the stage. They pass with the moment of effect and are shabby and tawdry in the daylight. Let us at least be real. Washington's entire honesty of mind and his fearless look into the face of all facts are qualities which can never go out of fashion and which we should all do well to imitate.

Ideals have been thrust upon us as an argument for the league until the healthy mind which rejects cant revolts from them. Are ideals confined to this deformed experiment upon a noble purpose, tainted, as it is, with bargains and tied to a peace treaty which might have been disposed of long ago to the great benefit of the world if it had not been compelled to carry this rider on its back? 'Post equitem sedet atra cura,' Horace tells us, but no blacker care ever sat behind any rider than we shall find in this covenant of doubtful and disputed interpretation as it now perches upon the treaty of peace.

No doubt many excellent and patriotic people see a coming fulfilment of noble ideals in the words 'league for peace'. We all respect and share these aspirations and desires, but some of us see no hope, but rather defeat, for them in this murky covenant. For we, too, have our ideals, even if we differ from those who have tried to establish a monopoly of idealism. Our first ideal is our country, and we see her in the future, as in the past, giving service to all her people and to the world. Our ideal of the future is that she should continue to render that service of her own free will. She has great problems of her own to solve, very grim and perilous problems, and a right solution, if we can attain to it, would largely benefit mankind. We would have our country strong to resist a peril from the West, as she has flung back the German menace from the East. We would not have our politics distracted and embittered by the dissensions of other lands. We would not have our country's vigour exhausted or her moral force abated, by everlasting meddling and muddling in every quarrel, great and small, which afflicts the world. Our ideal is to make her ever stronger and better and finer, because in that way alone, as we believe, can she be of the greatest service to the world's peace and to the welfare of mankind.

•

## WOODROW WILSON
### Pueblo, Colorado, 25 September 1919

*'Man will see the truth'*

*When the Senate baulked at the League of Nations covenant, which he had negotiated with the Allied leaders in Paris, Wilson, aged sixty-three, set out on a great speaking tour through the West to rally the people to him and overcome Senator Lodge. Thirty speeches were planned in twenty days.*

*'Worn out by his labours; appalled at what might flow from the repudiation of his handiwork; filled with a prophet's vision and also, unfortunately, with the vanity of Jonah, he refused all compromise,' says Hugh Brogan. 'His eloquence was never greater. He defended the treaty with a passion worthy of a better cause . . . The choice, he assured them again and again, trying to press home the lessons of his own education, lay between peace with the treaty, faults and all, or war without it.'*

*At Pueblo, Colorado, where this speech was made, he suffered complete nervous exhaustion and collapsed. The tour was cancelled and Wilson returned to the White House, where he suffered a massive stroke. The treaty was defeated in the Senate by a small margin. For the fifteen remaining months of his presidency, Wilson lay inert in the White House, doing nothing, saying nothing.*

Again and again, my fellow citizens, mothers who lost their sons in France have come to me and, taking my hand, have shed tears upon it not only, but they had added, 'God bless you, Mr President!' Why, my fellow citizens, should they pray God to bless me? I advised the Congress of the United States to create the situation that led to the death of their sons. I ordered their sons oversea. I consented to their sons being put in the most difficult parts of the battle line, where death was certain, as in the impenetrable difficulties of the forest of Argonne. Why should they weep upon my hand and call down the blessings of God upon me? Because they believe that their boys died for something that vastly transcends any of the immediate and palpable objects of the war. They believe, and they rightly believe, that their sons saved the liberty of the world. They believe that wrapped up with the liberty of the world is the continuous protection of that liberty by the concerted powers of all civilized people. They believe that this sacrifice was made in order that other sons should not be called upon for a similar gift – the gift of life, the gift of all that died – and if we did not see this thing through, if we fulfilled the dearest present wish of Germany and now dissociated ourselves from those alongside whom we fought in the war, would not something of the halo go away from the gun over the mantelpiece, or the sword? Would not the old uniform lose something of its significance? These men were crusaders. They were not going forth to prove the might of the United States. They were going forth to prove the might of justice and right, and all the world accepted them as crusaders, and their transcendent achievement has made all the world believe in America as it believes in no other nation organized in the modern world. There seems to me to stand between us and the rejection or qualification of this treaty the serried ranks of those boys in khaki, not only these boys who came home, but those dear ghosts that still deploy upon the fields of France.

My friends, on last Decoration Day I went to a beautiful hillside near Paris, where was located the cemetery of Suresnes, a cemetery given over to the burial of the American dead. Behind me on the slopes was rank upon rank of living American soldiers, and lying before me upon the levels of the plain was rank upon rank of departed American soldiers. Right by the side of the stand where I spoke there was a little group of French women who had adopted those graves, had made themselves mothers of those dear ghosts by putting flowers every day upon those graves, taking them as their own sons, their own beloved, because they had died in the same cause – France was free and the world was free because America had come! I wish some men in public life who are now opposing the settlement for which these men died could visit such a spot as that. I wish that the thought that comes out of those graves could penetrate their consciousness. I wish that they could feel the moral obligation that rests upon us not to go back on those boys, but to see the thing through, to see it through to the end and make good their redemption of the world. For nothing less depends upon this decision, nothing less than the liberation and salvation of the world . . .

You will say, 'Is the League an absolute guarantee against war?' No; I do not know any absolute guarantee against the errors of human judgement or the violence of human passion, but I ask you this: if it is not an absolute insurance against war, do you want no insurance at all? Do you want nothing? Do you want not only no probability that war will not recur, but the probability that it will recur? The arrangements of justice do not stand of themselves, my fellow citizens. The arrangements of this treaty are just, but they need the support of the combined power of the great nations of the world. And they will have that support. Now that the mists of this great question have cleared away, I believe that men will see the truth, eye to eye and face to face. There is one thing that the American people always rise to and extend their hand to, and that is the truth of justice and of liberty and of peace. We have accepted that truth and we are going to be led by it, and it is going to lead us, and through us the world, out into pastures of quietness and peace such as the world never dreamed of before.

•

## ALFRED E. SMITH
New York, 29 October 1919

### *'A man as low and mean as I can picture'*

*Al Smith, a Roman Catholic who left school at fourteen, was a New York Democrat politician who became governor in 1919. At Tammany Hall he gathered round him a generation of equally remarkable younger men and women, including Harry Hopkins, Frances Perkins, Robert Moses and Franklin Delano Roosevelt, and instituted honest government.*

*At the mass meeting in Carnegie Hall at which this speech was made, Smith (1873–1944) made an irreparable break with William Randolph Hearst, the powerful owner of a newspaper chain extending from New York to California and the newspaper baron on whom Citizen Kane was based. Hearst had combined with Tammany Hall to elect the local administration but had been scurrilously attacking the governor for 'starving' children because he refused to reduce the price of milk.*

*Smith had expected to debate with Hearst at the meeting called by a citizens' committee but Hearst refused to meet him. Smith's speech therefore meant that he had decided to fight the influence of one of the richest of men, who used his newspapers to wield power.*

*He asked for absolute silence and attention. 'I feel that I am here tonight upon a mission as important not only to myself but to this city, to this state and to this country as I could possibly perform.' As he reached his peroration, he*

*declared that nearly every paper had commended his administration except the*
*paper that belonged to the man who wanted to tell him what he ought to do. Then*
*he launched his assault on America's most powerful newspaper mogul.*

I cannot think of a more contemptible man – my power of imagination fails me to bring into my mind's eye a more despicable man
than the man that exploits the poor. Any man that leads you to
believe that your lot in life is not all right, any man that conjures up
for you a fancied grievance against your government or against the
man at the head of it, to help himself, is breeding the seeds of an
anarchy and a dissatisfaction more disastrous to the welfare of the
community than any other teaching that I can think of, because, at
least, the wildest anarchist, the most extreme Socialist, the wildest
radical that you can think of, may at least be sincere in his own heart.
He may think that it is right when he preaches it. But the man that
preaches to the poor of this or of any other community discontent
and dissatisfaction to help himself and to make good his side of the
argument, and to destroy, as he said himself he would, the Governor
of the State, is a man as low and as mean as I can picture . . . Follow
back the history of this man's newspapers since he came to this part
of the country, and you will have to read out of his newspapers this
remarkable fact: that in this great democracy, in this land of the free
and in this home of the brave, there has never been a man elected to
office yet that has not been tainted in some way. If the Hearst newspapers were the text books for the children of our schools, they
would have to spell out of its every line that no man can be trusted
in this country after he is put into public office; that no man thinks
enough about it; no man has enough of regard for it; no man has
enough of real Christian charity to do the thing right; no man that
ever held great public office had enough of respect and regard for
his mother and his wife and his children and his friends to be right in
office. About that there can be no question, because no public man
in this State, from Grover Cleveland right down to today, has ever
escaped this fellow. We all know that. The children on the street
know it.

Nobody that ever went to the Governor's office went there with a graver sense of the responsibility of that office than I did. What could there possibly be about me that I should be assailed in this reckless manner by this man? I have more reason probably than any man I will meet tonight to have a strong love and a strong devotion for this country, for this State, and for this city. Look at what I have received at its hands: I left school and went to work before I was fifteen years of age. I worked hard, night and day; I worked honestly and conscientiously at every job that I was ever put at, until I went to the Governor's chair in Albany. What can it be? It has got to be jealousy, it has got to be envy, it has got to be hatred, or it has to be something that nobody understands, that makes me come down here, into the city of New York, before this audience, and urge them to organize in this city to stay the danger that comes from these papers, to the end that the health, and welfare, and the comfort of this people, of the people of this State, may be promoted, and we may get rid of this pestilence that walks in the darkness.

*Smith was governor of New York for a second term from 1923 to 1929. At the 1924 Democratic convention he was beaten for the presidential nomination after 103 ballots. He gained the nomination in 1928 but was beaten by Herbert Hoover.*

•

# GEORGE V
## Belfast, 22 June 1921

### 'The eyes of the whole Empire are on Ireland today'

*Under the 1920 Government of Ireland Act there were to be two Home Rule parliaments: one for most of Ireland at Dublin (which Sinn Féin refused to recognize), the other for the six counties of Ulster at Belfast. The act secured the Ulster Unionists from Dublin rule and they grudgingly accepted their own parliament and their own government.*

*King George V resolved to open the first North of Ireland parliament himself, in spite of the risk of assassination. Jan Smuts, the South African statesman, drafted a warm plea for civil peace which was accepted by Lloyd George, who was looking for a way out of the Irish imbroglio.*

*According to A. J. P. Taylor, George V's initiative 'was perhaps the greatest service performed by a British monarch in modern times'. That view is considered 'sentimental' by the Irish historian R. F. Foster, who argues that Lloyd George's hand was forced by the unpalatable alternative of governing the sixteen counties as a Crown colony under martial law.*

Members of the Senate and of the House of Commons – for all who love Ireland, as I do with all my heart, this is a profoundly moving occasion in Irish history. My memories of the Irish people date back to the time when I spent many happy days in Ireland as a midshipman. My affection for the Irish people has been deepened by successive visits since that time, and I have watched with constant sympathy the course of their affairs. I could not have allowed myself to give Ireland by deputy alone my earnest prayers and good wishes in the new era which opens with this ceremony, and I have therefore come in person, as the Head of the Empire, to inaugurate this Parliament on Irish soil. I inaugurate it with deep-felt hope, and I feel assured that you will do your utmost to make it an instrument of happiness and good government for all parts of the community which you represent.

This is a great and critical occasion in the history of the six counties, but not for the six counties alone, for everything which interests them touches Ireland, and everything which touches Ireland finds an echo in the remotest parts of the Empire. Few things are more earnestly desired throughout the English-speaking world than a satisfactory solution of the age-long Irish problems which for generations embarrassed our forefathers, as they now weigh heavily upon us. Most certainly there is no wish nearer my own heart than that every man of Irish birth, whatever be his creed and wherever be his home, should work in loyal cooperation with the free communities on which the British Empire is based.

I am confident that the important matters entrusted to the control and guidance of the Northern Parliament will be managed with wisdom and with moderation, with fairness and due regard to every faith and interest, and with no abatement of that patriotic devotion to the Empire which you proved so gallantly in the Great War. Full partnership in the United Kingdom and religious freedom Ireland has long enjoyed. She now has conferred upon her the duty of dealing with all the essential tasks of domestic legislation and government; and I feel no misgiving as to the spirit in which you who stand here today will carry out the all-important functions entrusted to your care.

My hope is broader still. The eyes of the whole Empire are on Ireland today – that Empire in which so many nations and races have come together in spite of ancient feuds, and in which new nations have come to birth within the lifetime of the youngest in this hall. I am emboldened by that thought to look beyond the sorrow and the anxiety which have clouded of late my vision of Irish affairs. I speak from a full heart when I pray that my coming to Ireland today may prove to be the first step towards an end of strife amongst her people, whatever their race or creed. In that hope I appeal to all Irishmen to pause, to stretch out the hand of forbearance and conciliation, to forgive and to forget, and to join in making for the land which they love a new era of peace, contentment and good will. It is my earnest desire that in Southern Ireland too there may ere long take place a parallel to what is now passing in this hall; that there a similar occasion may present itself and a similar ceremony be performed.

For this the Parliament of the United Kingdom has in the fullest measure provided the powers; for this the Parliament of Ulster is pointing the way. The future lies in the hands of my Irish people themselves. May this historic gathering be the prelude of a day in which the Irish people, North and South, under one Parliament or two, as those Parliaments may themselves decide, shall work together in common love for Ireland upon the sure foundation of mutual justice and respect.

*The response to the king's speech was immediate. Éamon de Valera, president of the Irish republic, agreed to negotiate and a truce followed on 8 July. Fighting*

*ended three days later. Civil war followed in Ireland but the Irish Free State was*
*approved by the British parliament on 5 December 1922.*

•

## MAHATMA GANDHI
### Ahmadabad, 23 March 1922

### *'Non-violence is the first article of my faith'*

*Gandhi became leader of the Indian National Congress in 1920 and the con-*
*gress adopted his programme of Satyagraha, non-violent non-cooperation, which*
*he had earlier practised in South Africa. 'I discovered that pursuit of truth did*
*not admit of violence being inflicted on one's opponent,' Gandhi wrote, 'but that*
*he must be weaned from error by patience and sympathy. For what appears to be*
*truth to one may appear to be error to the other. And patience means self-suffering.*
*So the doctrine came to mean vindication of truth, not by the infliction of suffering*
*on the opponent but on one's self.'*

*Supporting the Satyagraha campaign, Gandhi travelled throughout India,*
*often speaking to meetings of more than 100,000 Indians. He was constantly*
*shadowed by the police but it was not until 1922 that he was arrested and*
*charged with sedition for three articles in his magazine* Young India. *The great*
*trial at Ahmadabad, at which Gandhi pleaded guilty, followed.*

*'Men's minds involuntarily turned to another great trial 1,900 years ago*
*when Jesus stood before Pontius Pilate,' said a contemporary Indian account.*
*'Mr Gandhi's statement was in his best form, terse and lucid, courageous and*
*uncompromising, with just that touch of greatness which elevates it to the level of*
*a masterpiece. Never before was such a prisoner arraigned before a British Court*
*of Justice. Never before were the laws of an all-powerful government so defiantly,*
*yet with such humility, challenged.'*

Non-violence is the first article of my faith. It is the last article of my
faith. But I had to make my choice. I had either to submit to a system
which I considered has done an irreparable harm to my country or
incur the risk of the mad fury of my people bursting forth when

they understood the truth from my lips. I know that my people have sometimes gone mad. I am deeply sorry for it; and I am therefore, here, to submit not to a light penalty but to the highest penalty. I do not ask for mercy. I do not plead any extenuating act. I am here, therefore, to invite and submit to the highest penalty that can be inflicted upon me for what in law is a deliberate crime and what appears to me to be the highest duty of a citizen. The only course open to you, Mr Judge, is, as I am just going to say in my statement, either to resign your post or inflict on me the severest penalty if you believe that the system and law you are assisting to administer are good for the people. I do not expect that kind of conversion. But by the time I have finished with my statement you will, perhaps, have a glimpse of what is raging within my breast to run this maddest risk which a sane man can run.

*Gandhi then read his statement to the court.*

I owe it perhaps to the Indian public and to the public in England, to placate which this prosecution is mainly taken up, that I should explain why from a staunch loyalist and cooperator I have become an uncompromising disaffectionist and non-cooperator. To the court too I should say why I plead guilty to the charge of promoting disaffection towards the Government established by law in India.

My public life began in 1893 in South Africa in troubled weather. My first contact with British authority in that country was not of a happy character. I discovered that as a man and an Indian I had no rights. On the contrary I discovered that I had no rights as a man because I was an Indian.

But I was not baffled. I thought that this treatment of Indians was an excrescence upon a system that was intrinsically and mainly good. I gave the Government my voluntary and hearty cooperation, criticizing it fully where I felt it was faulty but never wishing its destruction.

Consequently when the existence of the Empire was threatened in 1899 by the Boer challenge, I offered my services to it, raised a volunteer ambulance corps and served at several actions that took place for the relief of Ladysmith. Similarly in 1906 at the time of the Zulu revolt I raised a stretcher-bearer party and served till the end of the 'rebellion'. On both these occasions I received medals and was even mentioned in despatches. For my work in South Africa I was given by Lord Hardinge a Kaiser-i-Hind Gold Medal. When the war broke out in 1914 between England and Germany I raised a volunteer ambulance corps in London consisting of the then resident Indians in London, chiefly students. Its work was acknowledged by the authorities to be valuable. Lastly in India when a special appeal was made at the War Conference in Delhi in 1917 by Lord Chelmsford for recruits, I struggled at the cost of my health to raise a corps in Kheda and the response was being made when the hostilities ceased and orders were received that no more recruits were wanted. In all these efforts at service I was actuated by the belief that it was possible by such services to gain a status of full equality in the Empire for my countrymen.

The first shock came in the shape of the Rowlatt Act, a law designed to rob the people of all real freedom. I felt called upon to lead an intensive agitation against it. Then followed the Punjab horrors beginning with the massacre at Jallianwala Bagh and culminating in crawling orders, public floggings and other indescribable humiliations. The Punjab crime was white-washed and most culprits went not only unpunished but remained in service and some continued to draw pensions from the Indian revenue, and in some cases were even rewarded. I saw too that not only did the reforms not mark a change of heart, but they were only a method of further draining India of her wealth and of prolonging her servitude.

I came reluctantly to the conclusion that the British connection had made India more helpless than she ever was before, politically and economically. A disarmed India has no power of resistance against any aggressor if she wanted to engage in an armed conflict with him. So much is this the case that some of our best men consider that India must take generations before she can achieve the Dominion status. She has become so poor that she has little power of resisting famines. Before the British advent, India spun and wove in her millions of cottages just the supplement she needed for adding to her meagre agricultural resources. The cottage industry, so vital for India's existence, has been ruined by incredibly heartless and inhuman processes as described by English witnesses.

Little do town-dwellers know how the semi-starved masses of Indians are slowly sinking to lifelessness. Little do they know that their miserable comfort represents the brokerage they get for the work they do for the foreign exploiter, that the profits and the brokerage are sucked from the masses. Little do they realize that the Government established by law in British India is carried on for this exploitation of the masses. No sophistry, no jugglery in figures can explain away the evidence the skeletons in many villages present to the naked eye. I have no doubt whatsoever that both England and the town-dwellers of India will have to answer, if there is a God above, for this crime against humanity which is perhaps unequalled in history. The law itself in this country has been used to serve the foreign exploiter. My unbiased examination of the Punjab Martial Law cases has led me to believe that at least ninety-five per cent of convictions were wholly bad. My experience of political cases in India leads me to the conclusion that in nine out of every ten the condemned men were totally innocent. Their crime consisted in love of their country. In ninety-nine cases out of a hundred, justice has been denied to Indians as against Europeans in the Courts of India. This is not an exaggerated picture. It is the experience of almost every Indian who has had anything to do with such cases. In my opinion the administration of the law is thus prostituted consciously or unconsciously for the benefit of the exploiter.

The greatest misfortune is that Englishmen and their Indian associates in the administration of the country do not know that they are engaged in the crime I have attempted to describe. I am satisfied that many English and Indian officials honestly believe that they are administering one of the best systems devised in the world and that India is making steady though slow progress. They do not know that a subtle but effective system of terrorism and an organized display of force on the one hand and the deprivation of all powers of retaliation or self-defence on the other have emasculated the people and induced in them the habit of simulation. This awful habit has added to the ignorance and the self-deception of the administrators. Section 124-A under which I am happily charged is perhaps the prince among the political sections of the Indian Penal Code designed to suppress the liberty of the citizen. Affection cannot be manufactured or regulated by law. If one has no affection for a person or thing one should be free to give the fullest expression to his disaffection so long as he does not contemplate, promote or incite to violence. But the section under which Mr Banker and I are charged is one under which mere promotion of disaffection is a crime. I have studied some of the cases tried under it, and I know that some of the most loved of India's patriots have been convicted under it. I consider it a privilege, therefore, to be charged under it. I have endeavoured to give in their briefest outline the reasons for my disaffection. I have no personal ill-will against any single administrator, much less can I have any disaffection towards the King's person. But I hold it to be a virtue to be disaffected towards a Government which in its totality has done more harm to India than any previous system. India is less manly under the British rule than she ever was before. Holding such a belief, I consider it to be a sin to have affection for the system. And it has been a precious privilege for me to be able to write what I have in the various articles tendered in evidence against me.

In fact I believe that I have rendered a service to India and England by showing in non-cooperation the way out of the unnatural state in which both are living. In my humble opinion, non-cooperation with evil is as much a duty as is cooperation with good. But in the past, non-cooperation has been deliberately expressed in violence to the evildoer. I am endeavouring to show to my countrymen that violent non-cooperation only multiplies evil and that as evil can only be sustained by violence, withdrawal of support of evil requires complete abstention from violence. Non-violence implies voluntary submission to the penalty for non-cooperation with evil. I am here, therefore, to invite and submit cheerfully to the highest penalty that can be inflicted upon me for what in law is deliberate crime and what appears to me to be the highest duty of a citizen. The only course open to you, the Judge and the Assessors, is either to resign your posts and thus dissociate yourselves from evil if you feel that the law you are called upon to administer is an evil and that in reality I am innocent, or to inflict on me the severest penalty if you believe that the system and the law you are assisting to administer are good for the people of this country and that my activity is therefore injurious to the public weal.

*After his statement before the court, Gandhi was sentenced to six years' impris-onment and thanked the judge for his courtesy. He was imprisoned again in 1930, 1933 and 1942 when he went on hunger strike as part of his campaign of civil disobedience. He eventually collaborated with the English to gain inde-pendence for India which was proclaimed twenty-five years later. A saint to many Hindus, he was assassinated in 1948.*

•

## A. J. BALFOUR
London, 21 June 1922

*'A message to every land where the Jewish race is scattered'*

*Arthur Balfour (1848–1930), Conservative prime minister from 1902 to 1906 and Foreign Secretary in the wartime coalitions, considered the Balfour Declaration of 1917 the most worthwhile act of his long political career. Balfour had been interested in the Jewish national movement since his first meeting with Chaim Weizmann, the leader of British Zionism, in 1906. The declaration affirmed British support for the establishment of a Jewish national home in Palestine provided that safeguards could be reached for the rights of its non-Jewish communities. The declaration formed the basis for the League of Nations mandate for Palestine.*

*Balfour, according to his niece Blanche Dugdale, thought of the Zionists as guardians of a continuity of religious and racial tradition that made the unas-similated Jew a great conservative force in world politics. He felt strongly about the way the Jewish contribution to culture and religion had for the most part been requited by the Christian world:*

*That moral indignation was never put more clearly than to the House of*

*Lords in 1922 after Lord Islington had attacked the acceptance of the mandate by Britain.*

My noble friend told us in his speech, and I believe him absolutely, that he has no prejudice against the Jews. I think I may say that I have no prejudice in their favour. But their position and their history, their connection with world religion and with world politics, is absolutely unique. There is no parallel to it, there is nothing approaching to a parallel to it, in any other branch of human history. Here you have a small race originally inhabiting a small country, I think of about the size of Wales or Belgium, at any rate of comparable size to those two, at no time in its history wielding anything that can be described as material power, sometimes crushed in between great Oriental monarchies, its inhabitants deported, then scattered, then driven out of the country altogether into every part of the world, and yet maintaining a continuity of religious and racial tradition of which we have no parallel elsewhere.

That, itself, is sufficiently remarkable, but consider – it is not a pleasant consideration, but it is one that we cannot forget – how they have been treated during long centuries, during centuries which in some parts of the world extend to the minute and the hour in which I am speaking; consider how they have been subjected to tyranny and persecution; consider whether the whole culture of Europe, the whole religious organization of Europe, has not from time to time proved itself guilty of great crimes against this race. I quite understand that some members of the race may have given, doubtless did give, occasion for much ill-will, and I do not know how it could be otherwise, treated as they were; but, if you are going to lay stress on that, do not forget what part they have played in the intellectual, the artistic, the philosophic and scientific development of the world. I say nothing of the economic side of their energies, for on that Christian attention has always been concentrated.

I ask your Lordships to consider the other side of their activities. Nobody who knows what he is talking about will deny that they have at least – and I am putting it more moderately than I could do – rowed all their weight in the boat of scientific, intellectual and artistic progress, and they are doing so to this day. You will find them in every University, in every centre of learning; and at the very moment when they were being persecuted, when some of them, at all events, were being persecuted by the Church, their philosophers were developing thoughts which the great doctors of the Church embodied in their religious system. As it was in the Middle Ages, as it was in earlier times, so it is now. And yet, is there anyone here who feels content with the position of the Jews? They have been able, by this extraordinary tenacity of their race, to maintain this continuity, and they have maintained it without having any Jewish Home.

What has been the result? The result has been that they have been described as parasites on every civilization in whose affairs they have mixed themselves – very useful parasites at times I venture to say. But however that may be, do not your Lordships think that if Christendom, not oblivious of all the wrong it has done, can give a chance, without injury to others, to this race of showing whether it can organize a culture in a Home where it will be secured from oppression, that it is not well to say, if we can do it, that we will do it. And, if we can do it, should we not be doing something material to wash out an ancient stain upon our own civilization if we absorb the Jewish race in friendly and effective fashion in those countries in which they are the citizens? We should then have given them what every other nation has, some place, some local habitation, where they can develop the culture and the traditions which are peculiarly their own.

I could defend – I have endeavoured, and I hope not unsucessfully, to defend – this scheme of the Palestine Mandate from the most material economic view, and from that point of view it is capable of defence. I have endeavoured to defend it from the point of view of the existing population, and I have shown – I hope with some effect – that their prosperity also is intimately bound up with the success of Zionism. But having endeavoured to the best of my ability to maintain those two propositions, I should, indeed, give an inadequate view to your Lordships of my opinions if I sat down without insisting to the utmost of my ability that, beyond and above all this, there is this great ideal at which those who think with me are aiming, and which, I believe, it is within their power to reach.

It may fail. I do not deny that this is an adventure. Are we never to have adventures? Are we never to try new experiments? I hope your Lordships will never sink to that unimaginative depth, and that experiment and adventure will be justified if there is any case or cause for their justification. Surely, it is in order that we may send a message to every land where the Jewish race has been scattered, a message which will tell them that Christendom is not oblivious of their faith, is not unmindful of the service they have rendered to the great religions of the world, and, most of all, to the religion that the majority of your Lordships' House profess, and that we desire to the best of our ability to give them that opportunity of developing, in peace and quietness under British rule, those great gifts which hitherto they have been compelled from the very nature of the case only to bring to fruition in countries which know not their language, and belong not to their race. That is the ideal which I desire to see accomplished, that is the aim which lay at the root of the policy I am trying to defend; and, though it be defensible indeed on every ground, that is the ground which chiefly moves me.

•

## STANLEY BALDWIN
### London, 6 May 1924

### *'The sounds of England'*

*After serving in the governments of Lloyd George and Bonar Law, Stanley Baldwin (1867–1947) succeeded Law as prime minister in May 1923. He resigned when he failed to get a clear majority in the 1923 election but became prime minister again in 1924.*

*Baldwin was the most self-conscious countryman among British prime ministers of the century, according to his biographer Roy Jenkins. The unchanging nature of English rural life was one of his more effective and frequently recurring oratorical themes, reaching its apogee in this speech to the Royal Society of St George.*

*This, like many of his other speeches, was prose of a high evocative quality, even though its prophecy was inaccurate in both letter and spirit. 'His romantic nostalgia was wholly genuine, although his dislike of change from the countryside of his boyhood was probably more acute than that of those whose origins and lives were more deeply rooted in it.'*

To me, England is the country, and the country is England. And when I ask myself what I mean by England, when I think of England when I am abroad, England comes to me through my various senses – through the ear, through the eye, and through certain imperishable scents. I will tell you what they are, and there may be those among you who feel as I do.

The sounds of England, the tinkle of the hammer on the anvil in the country smithy, the corncrake on a dewy morning, the sound of the scythe against the whetstone, and the sight of a plough team coming over the brow of a hill, the sight that has been seen in England since England was a land, and may be seen in England long after the Empire has perished and every works in England has ceased to function, for centuries the one eternal sight of England. The wild anemones in the woods in April, the last load at night of hay being drawn down a lane as the twilight comes on, when you can scarcely distinguish the figures of the horses as they take it home to the farm, and above all, most subtle, most penetrating and most moving, the smell of wood smoke coming up in an autumn evening, or the smell of the scutch fires: that wood smoke that our ancestors, tens of thousands of years ago, must have caught on the air when they were coming home with the results of the day's forage, when they were still nomads, and when they were still roaming the forests and the plains of the continent of Europe. These things strike down into the very depths of our nature, and touch chords that go back to the beginning of time and the human race, but they are chords that with every year of our life sound a deeper note in our innermost being.

These are the things that make England, and I grieve for it that they are not the childish inheritance of the majority of the people today in our country. They ought to be the inheritance of every child born into this country, but nothing can be more touching than to see how the working man and woman after generations in the towns will have their tiny bit of garden if they can, will go to gardens if they can, to look at something they have never seen as children, but which their ancestors knew and loved. The love of these things is innate and inherent in our people. It makes for that love of home, one of the strongest features of our race, and it is that that makes our race seek its new home in the Dominions overseas, where they have room to see things like this that they can no more see at home. It is that power of making homes, almost peculiar to our people, and it is one of the sources of their greatness. They go overseas, and they take with them what they learned at home: love of justice, love of truth, and the broad humanity that are so characteristic of English people. It may well be that these traits on which we pride ourselves, which we hope to show and try to show in our own lives, may survive – survive among our people so long as they are a people – and I hope and believe this, that just as today more than fifteen centuries since the last of those great Roman legionaries left England, we still speak of the Roman strength, and the Roman work, and the Roman character, so perhaps in the ten thousandth century, long after the Empires of this world as we know them have fallen and others have risen and fallen, and risen and fallen again, the men who are then on this earth may yet speak of those characteristics which we prize as the characteristics of the English, and that long after, maybe, the name of the country has passed away, wherever men are honourable and upright and persevering, lovers of home, of their brethren, of justice and of humanity, the men in the world of that day may say, 'We still have among us the gifts of that great English race.'

•

## CLARENCE DARROW
Detroit, 19 May 1926

*'The life of the Negro race has been a life of tragedy'*

*More than a hundred clients of Clarence Darrow (1857–1938) were accused of murder but none was executed. For forty years, the Chicago attorney, a militant agnostic, fanatical humanitarian and spokesman for the underdog, dominated hundreds of courtrooms.*

*He resigned as general counsel for the Chicago and Northwestern Railway in 1894 to defend Eugene Debs during the Pullman strike. Debs was acquitted and Darrow subsequently became involved in a series of important or sensational cases.*

*In 1926 some 60,000 blacks in Chicago lived in overcrowded quarters. They were so crowded that some families had moved to the white districts but were regularly driven out. One was Dr Ossian Sweet, who provided himself with guns and ammunition and fired a volley into the street when a big crowd attacked his home. One white man was killed. Sweet and eleven blacks were arrested and Darrow became lawyer for the defence. The jurors could not agree and were dismissed.*

*A month later the state ordered a retrial, making Henry Sweet, the doctor's brother, who had apparently fired the fatal shot, the sole defendant. Darrow's final plea for Sweet, which lasted eight hours, was perhaps the best appeal to a jury of a brilliant career. Sweet was acquitted.*

*For Darrow the verdict meant simply that the doctrine that a man's house is his castle applied to blacks as well as whites – probably the first occasion on which that principle had been upheld by a white jury.*

We come now to lay this man's case in the hands of a jury of our peers – the first defence and the last defence is the protection of home and life as provided by our law. We are willing to leave it here. I feel, as I look at you, that we will be treated fairly and decently, even understandingly and kindly. You know what this case is. You know why it is. You know that if white men had been fighting their way against coloured men, nobody would ever have dreamed of a prosecution. And you know that from the beginning of this case to the end, up to the time you write your verdict, the prosecution is based on race prejudice and nothing else.

Gentlemen, I feel deeply on this subject; I cannot help it. Let us take a little glance at the history of the Negro race. It seems to me that the story would melt hearts of stone. I was born in America. I could have left it if I had wanted to go away. Some other men, reading about this land of freedom that we brag about on the Fourth of July, came voluntarily to America. These men, the defendants, are here because they could not help it. Their ancestors were captured in the jungles and on the plains of Africa, captured as you capture wild beasts, torn from their homes and their kindred; loaded into slave ships, packed like sardines in a box, half of them dying on the ocean passage; some jumping into the sea in their frenzy, when they had a chance to choose death in place of slavery. They were captured and brought there. They could not help it. They were bought and sold as slaves, to work without pay, because they were black. They were subject to all of this for generations, until finally they were given their liberty, so far as the law goes – and that is only a little way, because, after all, every human being's life in this world is inevitably mixed with every other life and, no matter what laws we pass, no matter what precautions we take, unless the people we meet are kindly and decent and human and liberty-loving then there is no liberty. Freedom comes from human beings, rather than from laws and institutions.

Now, that is their history. These people are the children of slavery. If the race that we belong to owes anything to any human being, or to any power in the universe, they owe it to these black men. Above all other men, they owe an obligation and a duty to these black men that can never be repaid. I never see one of them that I do not feel I ought to pay part of the debt of my race – and if you gentlemen feel as you should feel in this case, your emotions will be like mine.

Gentlemen, you are called into this case by chance. It took us a week to find you, a week of culling out prejudice and hatred. Probably we did not cull it all out at that; but we took the best and the fairest that we could find. It is up to you.

Your verdict means something in this case. It means something more than the fate of this boy. It is not often that a case is submitted to twelve men where the decision may mean a milestone in the history of the human race. But this case does. And I hope and I trust that you have a feeling of responsibility that will make you take it and do your duty as citizens of a great nation, and as members of the human family, which is better still.

Let me say just a parting word for Henry Sweet, who has well-nigh been forgotten. I am serious, but it seems almost like a reflection upon this jury to talk as if I doubted your verdict. What has this boy done? This one boy now that I am culling out from all of the rest, and whose fate is in your hands – can you tell me what he has done? Can I believe myself? Am I standing in a court of justice where twelve men on their oaths are asked to take away the liberty of a boy twenty-one years of age, who has done nothing more than what Henry Sweet has done?

Gentlemen, you may think he shot too quick; you may think he erred in judgement; you may think that Dr Sweet should not have gone there prepared to defend his home. But, what of this case of Henry Sweet? What has he done? I want to put it up to you, each one of you, individually. Dr Sweet was his elder brother. He had helped Henry through school. He loved him. He had taken him into his home. Henry had lived with him and his wife; he had fondled his baby. The doctor had promised Henry the money to go through school. Henry was getting his education, to take his place in the world, gentlemen – and this is a hard job. With his brother's help he has worked his way through college up to the last year. The doctor had bought a home. He feared danger. He moved in with his wife and he asked this boy to go with him. And this boy went to defend his brother, and his brother's wife and his child and his home.

Do you think more of him or less of him for that? I never saw twelve men in my life – and I have looked at a good many faces of a good many juries – I never saw twelve men in my life that, if you could get them to understand a human case, were not true and right.

Should this boy have gone along and helped his brother? Or, should he have stayed away? What would you have done? And yet, gentlemen, here is a boy, and the president of his college came all the way from Ohio to tell you what he thinks of him. His teachers have come here, from Ohio, to tell you what they think of him. The Methodist bishop has come here to tell you what he thinks of him.

So, gentlemen, I am justified in saying that this boy is as kindly, as well disposed, as decent a man as one of you twelve. Do you think he ought to be taken out of his school and sent to the penitentiary? All right, gentlemen, if you think so, do it. It's your job, not mine. If you think so, do it. But if you do, gentlemen, if you should ever look into the face of your own boy, or your own brother, or look into your own heart, you will regret it in sackcloth and ashes. You know, if he committed any offence, it was being loyal and true to his brother whom he loved. I know where you will send him and it will not be to a penitentiary.

I do not believe in the law of hate. I may not be true to my ideals always, but I believe in the law of love, and I believe you can do nothing with hatred. I would like to see a time when man loves his fellow man and forgets his colour or his creed. We will never be civilized until that time comes. I know the Negro race has a long road to go. I believe that the life of the Negro race has been a life of tragedy, of injustice, of oppression. The law has made him equal, but man has not. And, after all, the last analysis is: what has man done? – and not what has the law done? I know there is a long road ahead of him before he can take the place which I believe he should take. I know that before him there is sorrow, tribulation, and death among the blacks, and perhaps the whites. I am sorry. I would do what I could to avert it. I would advise patience; I would advise tolerance; I would advise understanding; I would advise all those things which are necessary for men who live together.

Gentlemen, what do you think of your duty in this case? I have watched day after day these black, tense faces that have crowded this court. These black faces that now are looking to you twelve whites, feeling that the hopes and fears of a race are in your keeping.

This case is about to end, gentlemen. To them, it is life. Not one of their colour sits on this jury. Their fate is in the hands of twelve whites. Their eyes are fixed on you, their hearts go out to you, and their hopes hang on your verdict.

This is all. I ask you, on behalf of this defendant, on behalf of these helpless ones who turn to you, and more than that – on behalf of this great state, and this great city, which must face this problem and face it fairly – I ask you in the name of progress and of the human race, to return a verdict of not guilty in this case!

•

# NICOLA SACCO and BARTOLOMEO VANZETTI
Dedham, Massachusetts, 19 April 1927

*'I am never be guilty, never'*

*The United States in 1920 was suffering a violent 'Red scare' and organized labour was protesting at the importation of cheap labour from overseas. On 15 April 1920, the paymaster and the guard of a shoe factory at Milford, Massachusetts, were shot dead and robbed. Nicola Sacco (1891–1927) and Bartolomeo Vanzetti (1888–1927), two Italian immigrants who had become anarchists and also dodged the draft, were arrested and charged with the murders.*

*The trial was held in Dedham and they were found guilty. Associates of Sacco and Vanzetti alerted the left throughout the world to what seemed a perversion of justice, especially because of the prejudice of the judge who described them as 'anarchist bastards'. After the men had been in prison for seven years, they were finally told they were to be executed. Their last speeches to Judge Webster Thayer were movingly dignified, perhaps because their English was so imperfect.*

[*Sacco:*] I am not an orator. It is not very familiar with me the English language, and, as I know, as my friend has told me, my comrade Vanzetti will speak more long, so I thought to give him the chance.

I never know, never heard, even read in history anything so cruel as this court. After seven years prosecuting they still consider us guilty. And these gentle people here are arrayed with us in this court today.

I know the sentence will be between two class, the oppressed class and the rich class, and there will be always collision between one and the other. We fraternize the people with the books, with the literature. You persecute the people, tyrannize over them, and kill them. We try the education of people always. You try to put a path between us and some other nationality that hates each other. That is why I am here today on this bench, for having been the oppressed class. Well, you are the oppressor.

You know it, Judge Thayer – you know all my life, you know why I have been here, and after seven years that you have been persecuting me and my poor wife, and you still today abuse us to death. I would like to tell you my life, but what is the use? You know all about what I say before, and my friend – that is, my comrade – will be talking, because he is more familiar with the language, and I will give him a chance. My comrade, the man kind, the kind man to all the children, you sentence him two times, in the Bridgewater case and the Dedham case, connected with me, and you know he is innocent. You forget all the population that has been with us for seven years, to sympathize and give us all their energy and all their kindness. You do not care for them. Among that peoples and the comrades and the working class there is a big legion of intellectual people which have been with us for seven years, but to not commit the iniquitous sentence, but still the court goes ahead. And I think I thank you all, you peoples, my comrades who have been with me for seven years, with the Sacco–Vanzetti case, and I will give my friend a chance.

I forget one thing which my comrade remember me. As I said before, Judge Thayer know all my life, and he know that I am never be guilty, never – not yesterday nor today nor for ever.

*

[*Vanzetti*:] What I say is that I am innocent, not only of the Braintree crime, but also of the Bridgewater crime. That I am not only innocent of these two crimes, but in all my life I have never stole and I have never killed and I have never spilled blood. That is what I want to say. And it is not all. Not only am I innocent of these two crimes, not only in all my life I have never stole, never killed, never spilled blood, but I have struggled all my life, since I began to reason, to eliminate crime from the earth.

Everybody that knows these two arms knows very well that I did not need to go in between the streets and kill a man to make the money. I can live with my two arms, and live well. But besides that, I can live even without work with my arm for other people. I have had plenty of chance to live independently and to live what the world conceives to be a higher life than not to gain our bread with the sweat of our brow . . .

What I want to say is this: Everybody ought to understand that the first of the defence has been terrible. My first lawyer did not stick to defend us. He had made no work to collect witnesses and evidence in our favour. The record in the Plymouth court is a pity. I am told that they are almost gone – half lost. So the defence had a tremendous work to do in order to collect some evidence, to collect some testimony to offset and to learn what the testimony of the state has done. And in this consideration it take double time of the state without delay, double time that they delay the case it would have been reasonable, whereas it took less than the state.

Well, I have already say that I am not guilty of these two crimes, but I never commit a crime in my life – I have never steal and I have never kill and I have never spilled blood, and I have fought against the crime, and I have fought and I have sacrificed myself even to eliminate the crimes that the law and the church legitimate and sanctify.

That is what I say: I would not wish to a dog or a snake, to the most low and misfortunate creature of the earth – I would not wish to any of them what I have had to suffer for things that I am not guilty of. But my conviction is that I have suffered for things that I am guilty of. I am suffering because I am a radical, and indeed I am a radical; I have suffered because I was an Italian, and indeed I am an Italian; I have suffered more for my family and for my beloved than for myself; but I am so convinced to be right that if you would execute me two times, and if I could be reborn two other times, I would live again to do what I have done already.

*Sacco and Vanzetti were electrocuted on 23 August and their execution started riots in London, Paris and Germany. Their case provoked the first serious rebellion against the conservatism of the Republican ascendancy.*

•

## HERBERT HOOVER
### New York, 22 October 1928

### *'Rugged individualism'*

*Herbert Hoover (1874–1964) accumulated a personal fortune as a mining engin-
eer before directing relief work in Europe during and after the First World War.
He was Secretary of Commerce under Presidents Harding and Coolidge from
1921, when he speeded the modernization of industry which increased the people's
prosperity. He became the Republican candidate in the 1928 presidential election,
when he was seen as the only man certain to beat the popular Democrat candidate
Al Smith, who had been chosen by the liberal, urban element in the party. Smith's
record of progressive social reform as governor of New York compelled Hoover to
express the political philosophy that was to dominate Republican thinking in the
harsh depression years of his own administration from 1929 to 1933.*

*His speech on rugged individualism delivered at the very end of the 1928
campaign ranks as a classic statement of American conservatism (even though
his philosophy was found tragically inadequate in the Wall Street crash of 1929).
He implied that government interference in economic activities must necessarily
lead to socialism and insisted that its ultimate effect would be to impair the very
basis of liberty and freedom.*

After the war, when the Republican Party assumed administration of
the country, we were faced with the problem of determination of the
very nature of our national life. During one hundred and fifty years
we have builded up a form of self-government and a social system
which is peculiarly our own. It differs essentially from all others in the
world. It is the American system. It is just as definite and positive a
political and social system as has ever been developed on earth. It is
founded upon a particular conception of self-government in which
decentralized local responsibility is the very base. Further than this, it
is founded upon the conception that only through ordered liberty,
freedom, and equal opportunity to the individual will his initiative

and enterprise spur on the march of progress. And in our insistence upon equality of opportunity has our system advanced beyond all the world . . .

When the war closed, the most vital of all issues both in our own country and throughout the world was whether Governments should continue their wartime ownership and operation of many instrumentalities of production and distribution. We were challenged with a peacetime choice between the American system of rugged individualism and a European philosophy of diametrically opposed doctrines – doctrines of paternalism and state socialism. The acceptance of these ideas would have meant the destruction of self-government through centralization of government. It would have meant the undermining of the individual initiative and enterprise through which our people have grown to unparalleled greatness . . .

There is, therefore, submitted to the American people a question of fundamental principle. That is, shall we depart from the principles of our American political and economic system, upon which we have advanced beyond all the rest of the world, in order to adopt methods based on principles destructive of its very foundations? And I wish to emphasize the seriousness of these proposals. I wish to make my position clear; for this goes to the very roots of American life and progress . . .

Bureaucracy is ever desirous of spreading its influence and its power. You cannot extend the mastery of the Government over the daily working life of a people without at the same time making it the master of the people's souls and thoughts. Every expansion of Government in business means that Government in order to protect itself from the political consequences of its errors and wrongs is driven irresistibly without peace to greater and greater control of the nation's press and platform. Free speech does not live many hours after free industry and free commerce die.

It is a false liberalism that interprets itself into the Government operation of commercial business. Every step of bureaucratizing of the business of our country poisons the very roots of liberalism – that is, political equality, free speech, free assembly, free press, and equality of opportunity. It is the road not to more liberty but to less liberty. Liberalism should be found not striving to spread bureaucracy but striving to set bounds to it. True liberalism seeks all legitimate freedom, first in the confident belief that without such freedom the pursuit of all other blessings and benefits is vain. That belief is the foundation of all American progress, political as well as economic.

Liberalism is a force truly of the spirit, a force proceeding from the deep realization that economic freedom cannot be sacrificed if political freedom is to be preserved. Even if governmental conduct of business could give us more efficiency instead of less efficiency, the fundamental objection to it would remain unaltered and unabated. It would destroy political equality. It would increase rather than decrease abuse and corruption. It would stifle initiative and invention. It would undermine the development of leadership. It would cramp and cripple the mental and spiritual energies of our people. It would extinguish equality and opportunity. It would dry up the spirit of liberty and progress. For these reasons primarily it must be resisted. For a hundred and fifty years liberalism has found its true spirit in the American system, not in the European systems . . .

Our people have the right to know whether we can continue to solve our great problems without abandonment of our American system. I know we can. We have demonstrated that our system is responsive enough to meet any new and intricate development in our economic and business life. We have demonstrated that we can meet any economic problem and still maintain our democracy as master in its own house and that we can at the same time preserve equality of opportunity and individual freedom . . .

And what have been the results of our American system? Our country has become the land of opportunity to those born without inheritance, not merely because of the wealth of its resources and industry, but because of this freedom of initiative and enterprise. Russia has natural resources equal to ours. Her people are equally industrious, but she has not had the blessing of one hundred and fifty years of our form of government and of our social system.

By adherence to the principles of decentralized self-government, ordered liberty, equal opportunity, and freedom to the individual our American experiment in human welfare has yielded a degree of well-being unparalleled in all the world. It has come nearer to the abolition of poverty, to the abolition of fear of want, than humanity has ever reached before.

*Hoover beat Smith but was reluctant to extend federal power during the Depression and was decisively beaten by Franklin Delano Roosevelt in the 1932 election.*

•

## OSWALD MOSLEY
### London, 28 May 1930

### *'The nation has to be mobilized'*

*Oswald Mosley (1896–1980) was one of the most tragic personalities of twentieth-century British politics, a charismatic Labour politician who became a figure of ridicule after he founded the British Union of Fascists, which promoted anti-Semitic and Hitlerite policies in the 1930s.*

*Sitting initially in the House of Commons as an independent MP, he joined the Labour Party in 1924 and entered Ramsay MacDonald's government in 1929. Mosley wanted to solve the Depression by stimulating foreign trade and pumping public funds into industrial projects to create jobs.*

*The proposals were rejected by the Cabinet. Mosley's resignation speech to parliament was considered as one of the most outstanding oratorical performances of the century. Its admirers included both Lloyd George and Winston Churchill.*

We have to face up to this fact, that if men are to be employed on any large scale that employment has to be paid for either by the State or by local authorities. There is a tremendous struggle, an incessant struggle, going on in every Government department to put every penny they can off the taxpayer and on to the ratepayer. What holds up these plans for months is the struggle for these pennies, these minor details. What does it matter? What is the use of shifting the burden from the taxpayer to the ratepayer? What is the use of lifting the burden from the right shoulder to the left? It is the same man who has to carry it, and the economic fact is this, as the Colwyn and every other authoritative inquiry upon the economic side has said, that the burden on the ratepayer is more onerous upon industry than the burden upon the taxpayer. If this burden has to be carried, need we struggle and waste time in deciding whether it is to be carried by the taxpayer or by the ratepayer? . . .

If you are pursuing a deflation policy, restricting the whole basis of credit, there is some force in what is known as the Treasury view, that it is difficult to raise large loans for such purposes as this.

Given, however, a financial policy of stabilization, that Treasury point of view cannot hold water. It would mean that every single new enterprise is going to put as many men out of employment as it will employ. That is a complete absurdity if you pursue that argument to its logical conclusion. If it is true it means that nothing can ever be done by the Government or by Parliament. It means that no Government has any function or any purpose; it is a policy of complete surrender. It has been said rather curiously, in view of the modesty of my programme, that it is the policy of the 'red flag'. I might reply that what is known as the Treasury view is the policy of the 'white' flag. It is a policy of surrender, of negation, by which any policy can be frustrated and blocked in this country.

Hanging all over that policy is the great conception of conversion. There are two ways of achieving conversion. One through the inherent financial strength of your position, leading to a strengthening of Government credit. The other is by the simple process of deflation to make all industrial investments unprofitable and drive your investor into Government securities because he has no other profitable outlet. But there may be another effect of that policy; that the money goes abroad, and then you get the local effect of that policy suggested by the President of the Board of Trade as the only means of solving our industrial problems, when he said on the 14th May: 'During the past fortnight alone £16,000,000 of new capital has been authorized or raised for overseas investment, and so I trust the process will continue.'

Why? Why is it so right and proper and desirable that capital should go overseas to equip factories to compete against us, to build roads and railways in the Argentine or in Timbuctoo, to provide employment for people in those countries while it is supposed to shake the whole basis of our financial strength if anyone dares to suggest the raising of money by the Government of this country to provide employment for the people of this country? If those views are passed without examination or challenge the position of this country is serious indeed. In conclusion let me say that the situation which faces us is, of course, very serious. Everybody knows that; and perhaps those who have been in office for a short time know it even better. It is not, I confidently believe, irreparable, but I feel this from the depths of my being, that the days of muddling through are over, that this time we cannot muddle through.

This nation has to be mobilized and rallied for a tremendous effort, and who can do that except the Government of the day? If that effort is not made we may soon come to crisis, to a real crisis. I do not fear that so much, for this reason, that in a crisis this nation is always at its best. This people knows how to handle a crisis, it cools their heads and steels their nerves. What I fear much more than a sudden crisis is a long, slow, crumbling through the years until we sink to the level of a Spain, a gradual paralysis beneath which all the vigour and energy of this country will succumb. That is a far more dangerous thing, and far more likely to happen unless some effort is made. If the effort is made how relatively easily can disaster be averted. You have in this country resources, skilled craftsmen among the workers, design and technique among the technicians, unknown and unequalled in any other country in the world. What a fantastic assumption it is that a nation which within the lifetime of everyone has put forth efforts of energy and vigour unequalled in the history of the world, should succumb before an economic situation such as the present. If the situation is to be overcome, if the great powers of this country are to be rallied and mobilized for a great national effort, then the Government and Parliament must give a lead. I beg the Government tonight to give the vital forces of this country the chance that they await. I beg Parliament to give that lead.

*Mosley carried his fight to the Labour Party conference that autumn but was
again defeated by MacDonald. In December he published the Mosley Manifesto, which was backed by seventeen Labour MPs, but he was expelled after
founding the progressive socialist New Party.*

*Mosley was ruined politically and his ideas were ruined with him. A. J. P.
Taylor describes the rejection of Mosley's programme as a decisive, though negative, event in British history, the moment when the British people resolved to
stand on the ancient ways.*

•

# RAMSAY MacDONALD
Llandudno, 7 October 1930

### 'We are not on trial'

*With Keir Hardie, Ramsay MacDonald (1856–1937) was one of the main
founders of the British Labour Party. He became an MP in 1906, led the parliamentary Labour Party from 1911, but opposed the First World War and lost
his seat in 1918. On re-election in 1922, he again led the party, briefly formed
a minority Labour government in 1924 and was again prime minister from
1929.*

*Confronted by prolonged unemployment and a growing budget deficit, Mac-
Donald's government was beset by economic crisis. Feelers were put out by Lloyd
George for a coalition government. The annual Labour Party conference in 1930
met not only against this worsening economic background but also on the day
after the R101 airship crash in which forty-eight people died, including Lord
Thomson, MacDonald's closest friend in politics.*

*At the start of his speech, MacDonald paid an emotional tribute to the dead.
Then he straightened himself up and launched into a passionate defence of the
government and its record.*

The Government has fulfilled the confidence that you reposed in it
at the last Election. (*Cheers.*) I have no apologies – none whatever. I
am not one of those who, standing aside, imagine that pettifogging
criticism is either helpful or illuminating. Not at all. The plough, my

friends, is in the furrow, and the place for you and me is in the furrow dragging the plough. (*Cheers.*) We have not fulfilled all our pledges – no. Did you expect us to do so? Our pledges are the pledges of men and women who are Socialists, our pledges are the pledges of men and women who know that this system of society cannot and will not work smoothly, and that the great task of statesmen of vision is to transform that system of society from the 'is' until it has become the 'is to be'; and in the course of that transformation, rightly or wrongly, my creed, and, I think, the creed of the great majority, if not all of my colleagues, has been evolution – evolution applied in precisely the same way as the scientific medical man, the scientific healer, applies his knowledge and his art to the frail and the ailing body. He does not prescribe straightaway the final food, the final exercise, the final standard of life, but being a knowing man, a man with an eye, a man not only with scientific knowledge but psychological knowledge, a man who knows how to lead gently and truly as well as to feed accurately, knowing his problem, knowing that it is not a problem of mathematics, not a problem of material things only, but a problem of mental and psychological things, works out a great policy and goes on with it from stage to stage. The men who remain out may say: 'You have not got to your journey's end,' but the men who remain in say, 'No, we have not, but we are going to get there.' (*Cheers . . .*)

It is not the Labour Government that is on trial; it is Capitalism that is being tried. We told you in those days that the time would come when finance would be more powerful than industry. That day has come. We told you in those days that people would say: 'Trade is all right, but finance is all wrong.' That day has come. We told you in those days that the time would come when the man who went into the workshop and into the factory, and his employer as well, would no longer be in the simple relationship of master and man, but that the master would become impersonal, and that powers that have nothing to do with industry would control industry – the powers of gambling with credit. That day has come . . .

So, my friends, we are not on trial; it is the system under which we live. It has broken down, not only in this little island, it has broken

down in Europe, in Asia, in America; it has broken down everywhere, as it was bound to break down. And the cure, the new path,
the new idea is organization – organization which will protect life,
not property; organization which may protect property, but protect
property in proper relation to life; organization which will see to it
that when science discovers and inventors invent, the class that will
be crushed down by reason of knowledge shall not be the working
class, but the loafing class. That is the policy that we are going to
pursue slowly, steadily, persistently, with knowledge, and with our
minds working upon a plan. And I appeal to you, my friends, today,
with all that is going on outside – I appeal to you to go back on to
your Socialist faith. Do not mix that up with pettifogging patching,
either of a Poor Law kind or of Relief Work kind. Construction,
ideas, architecture, building line upon line, stone upon stone, storey
upon storey: it will not be your happiness, it will certainly not be
mine, to see that fabric finished. It will not be your happiness, and it
will certainly not be mine, to see that every stone laid in sincerity has
been well laid. But I think it will be your happiness, as it is mine, to
go on convinced that the great foundations are being well laid, that
the ennobling plan is being conceived, and that by skilled craftsmen,
confident in each other's goodwill and sincerity, the temple will rise
and rise and rise until at last it is complete, and the genius of humanity will find within it an appropriate resting place.

*There was tumultuous applause. A later vote of censure was defeated by
1,800,000 votes to 330,000. A year later after a run on the pound, MacDonald formed a National Government with the Conservatives which the majority
of Labour MPs refused to support. MacDonald was condemned as a traitor to
socialism. Although he had towered over British politics in the 1920s, his reputation thereafter was doomed.*

# JOSEPH STALIN
## Moscow, 4 February 1931

*'Either we do it – or they crush us'*

*After assisting Lenin in Petrograd, Joseph Stalin (1879–1953) became the Bolsheviks' first Commissar for Nationalities and helped to defend Petrograd during the Civil War. At the party congress in 1923 he seized control of the party machine and manoeuvred to deny power to Trotsky. He succeeded Lenin and created one of the worst dictatorial tyrannies of the century. In 1928 he began his policy of achieving Socialism in One Country through the five-year plans.*

*About 1,500 big enterprises were built during the first five-year plan, including the largest power station in Europe; new sectors of industry were established; thousands of kilometres of roads and canals were constructed; and many new cities were built. It was a gigantic achievement, won at appalling cost in human lives.*

*Yet although there was mounting strain in the country, Stalin was still unsatisfied with the rate of progress and in this speech to industrial managers he appealed to the spirit of Russian nationalism to goad workers towards the social and economic transformation he sought to impose on the Russians.*

*His message was simple – either we do it or the West crushes us; and as his speech turned to the spirit of old Russia his words began to throb with the emotion that was mostly lacking from his lifeless oratory.*

It is sometimes asked whether it is not possible to slow down the tempo somewhat, to put a check on the movement. No, comrades, it is not possible! The tempo must not be reduced! On the contrary, we must increase it as much as is within our powers and possibilities. This is dictated to us by our obligations to the workers and peasants of the USSR. This is dictated to us by our obligations to the working class of the whole world.

To slacken the tempo would mean falling behind. And those who fall behind get beaten. But we do not want to be beaten. No, we refuse to be beaten! One feature of the history of old Russia was the continual defeats she suffered because of her backwardness. She was beaten by the Mongol khans. She was beaten by the Turkish beys. She was beaten by the Swedish feudal lords. She was beaten by the Polish and Lithuanian gentry. She was beaten by the British and French capitalists. She was beaten by the Japanese barons. All beat her – because of her backwardness, because of her military backwardness, cultural backwardness, political backwardness, industrial backwardness, agricultural backwardness. They beat her because to do so was profitable and could be done with impunity. You remember the words of the pre-revolutionary poet: 'You are poor and abundant, mighty and impotent, Mother Russia.' Those gentlemen were quite familiar with the verses of the old poet. They beat her, saying: 'You are abundant,' so one can enrich oneself at your expense. They beat her, saying: 'You are poor and impotent,' so you can be beaten and plundered with impunity. Such is the law of the exploiters – to beat the backward and the weak. It is the jungle law of capitalism. You are backward, you are weak – therefore you are wrong; hence you can be beaten and enslaved. You are mighty – therefore you are right; hence we must be wary of you.

That is why we must no longer lag behind.

In the past we had no fatherland, nor could we have had one. But now that we have overthrown capitalism and power is in our hands, in the hands of the people, we have a fatherland, and we will uphold its independence. Do you want our socialist fatherland to be beaten and to lose its independence? If you do not want this, you must put an end to its backwardness in the shortest possible time and develop a genuine Bolshevik tempo in building up its socialist economy. There is no other way. That is why Lenin said on the eve of the October Revolution: 'Either perish, or overtake and outstrip the advanced capitalist countries.'

We are fifty or a hundred years behind the advanced countries. We must make good this distance in ten years. Either we do it, or they crush us.

That is what our obligations to the workers and peasants of the USSR dictate to us.

In ten years at most we must make good the distance that separates us from the advanced capitalist countries. We have all the 'objective' possibilities for this. The only thing lacking is the ability to make proper use of these possibilities. And that depends on us. *Only* on us! It is time we learned to make use of these possibilities. It is time to put an end to the rotten line of non-interference in production. It is time to adopt a new line, one corresponding to the present period – the line of *interfering in everything*. If you are a factory manager – interfere in all the affairs of the factory, look into everything, let nothing escape you, learn and learn again. Bolsheviks must master technique. It is time Bolsheviks themselves became experts. In the period of reconstruction, technique decides everything. And a business executive who does not want to study technique, who does not want to master technique, is a joke and not an executive.

It is said that it is hard to master technique. That is not true! There are no fortresses that Bolsheviks cannot capture. We have solved a number of most difficult problems. We have overthrown capitalism. We have assumed power. We have built up a huge socialist industry. We have transferred the middle peasants on to the path of socialism. We have already accomplished what is most important from the point of view of construction. What remains to be done is not so much: to study technique, to master science. And when we have done that we shall develop a tempo of which we dare not even dream at present.

And we shall do it if we really want to.

•

PHILIP SNOWDEN
London, 17 October 1931

*'Bolshevism run mad'*

*The first National Government was formed by the Labour prime minister Ramsay MacDonald in August 1931. Most of the Labour Party went into opposition. The new government took Britain off the Gold Standard and decided to fight a general election against Labour.*

*As Labour Chancellor, Philip Snowden (1864–1937) had been forced to introduce deflationary measures to meet the British economic crisis. During the election he made this broadcast speech attacking his party and its new leader Arthur Henderson.*

*Snowden's speech was regarded as the most decisive of the election and he was held responsible for preventing Labour's return to power until 1945. He was created a viscount in 1931.*

You have been told by a spokesman of the Labour Party this week that the resources of the country are enormous and that we have money enough to go on spending to our hearts' content. This is appalling ignorance or wilful deception. It is true the resources of the country are great; but the fact is that they cannot continue to be mortgaged for current expenditure . . . The majority of the Labour Government, after agreeing to most of the economies, shirked the responsibility of placing the proposals before Parliament . . . So the National Government was formed to deal with the situation. By drastic economies, and by heavy taxation spread fairly over the whole population, the Budget has been balanced. I know the economies we have had to make are disagreeable. It has been no pleasure to impose them. They were necessary to prevent a far more serious reduction in working-class conditions. They are far less drastic than reductions which the Labour Government of Australia has been compelled to make, and far less than the economies made in Germany. After the cuts have been made the unemployed in this country are far more generously provided for than in any other country. In America they are left to private charity or to beg or starve. After the reduction in unemployment pay the benefits are now 17 per cent more in value than the Labour Government in 1924 considered adequate, and at a time when there was a Budget surplus of £30,000,000 – not a deficit of £170,000,000 . . . There is no more stern and unbending Free Trader than I am . . . The Labour Party is not a Free Trade Party . . . A month ago the Trade Union Council was preparing a tariff policy. When the General Election became imminent they dropped that in order to pose as an anti-tariff party.

Mr Henderson is quoted in the *Daily Herald* this morning as having said that if he were faced with a large cut in unemployment pay or a 20 per cent revenue tariff as an emergency expedient he was going to try the value of that expedient. Now he is denouncing tariffs as an expedient to raise prices and lower wages . . .

I hope you have read the Election programme of the Labour Party. It is the most fantastic and impracticable programme ever put before the electors. All the derelict industries are to be taken over by the State, and the taxpayer is to shoulder the losses. The banks and financial houses are to be placed under national ownership and control, which means, I suppose, that they are to be run by a joint committee of the Labour Party and the Trade Union Council. Your investments are to be ordered by some board, and your foreign investments are to be mobilized to finance this madcap policy. This is not Socialism. It is Bolshevism run mad.

•

### ADOLF HITLER
Düsseldorf, 27 January 1932

*'An indomitable aggressive spirit'*

*By 1932, Adolf Hitler (1889–1945) was within a year of becoming German chancellor. The greatest orator of the twentieth century, albeit allied to its most evil policies, Hitler had discovered his demagogic gifts in open-air tirades against Jews and the Treaty of Versailles after he joined the National Socialist German Workers' Party (the NSDAP, derisively nicknamed 'Nazi') in Munich in 1919. His failed putsch in 1923 won him national fame and imprisonment. While in prison, he wrote* Mein Kampf, *which preached a doctrine of racial-nationalist struggle for survival, advocated a German empire in Europe and the purging of the 'Jewish bacillus' from national life.*

*One of the Nazis' greatest anxieties in 1932 was the financing of the election campaign. After Hitler's speech to the Industry Club at the Park Hotel in Düsseldorf, arranged by Fritz Thyssen, the anxiety was over. It was the first time that many of the industrialists had met Hitler and his reception was cool and reserved but he spoke for two and a half hours without pause and made one of the best speeches of his life.*

In the year 1918, as I considered the position with cool and considered judgement, I was bound to confess: it is an appallingly difficult course to come before the people at such a time and to form for myself a new organization. It is naturally much easier to join one of the existing formations and thence to seek to overcome the inner division of the nation. But is that at all possible when one starts from the existing organizations? Has not every organization in the last resort the spirit, the men who can find satisfaction in its programme and in its struggle? If an organization has continually given way before Marxism and at length one day simply capitulated like a coward, has it not during sixty years been completely filled with a spirit and with men who neither understand the other way nor wish to pursue it? On the contrary, at a period of such confusion, will not the future lie with those who are prepared once more to pass through a sieve the body-politic, which has fallen into such disorder, so that from out of the people a new political leadership can crystallize, which knows how to take the mass of the nation in hand and can avoid the mistakes which led to downfall in the past?

I was naturally forced to say to myself that it would mean an appalling struggle, for I was not so fortunate as to possess an outstanding name; I was only a nameless German soldier, with a very small zinc identification number on my breast. But I came to realize that if a beginning was not made with the smallest cell, if a new body-politic was not thus formed within the nation, a body-politic which could overcome the existing 'ferments of decomposition', then the nation itself as a whole could never rise again. We have indeed in the past had a practical experience of that; it took 150 years before, from the fallen German Reich of ancient days, Prussia arose to fulfil its historic mission as the germ-cell of a new Reich. And believe me, the case is the same in the question of the internal regeneration of a people. Every idea must draw men to itself. Every idea must step out before the nation, must win from the nation the fighters whom it needs, and must tread alone the difficult way with all its necessary consequences that it may one day gain the strength to turn the course of destiny.

Events have proved that this reasoning was right in the end. For though even today there are many in Germany who believe that we National Socialists would not be capable of constructive work – they deceive themselves! If we were not, already today there would be no more bourgeoisie alive in Germany: the question Bolshevism or not Bolshevism would long ago have been decided . . .

Today that Movement cannot be destroyed: it is there: people must reckon with it, whether they like it or not. (*Loud applause.*) And I am convinced that for all those who still believe in a future for Germany it is clear what their attitude must be. For here they see before them an organization inspired to the highest degree by national sentiment, constructed on the conception of an absolute authority in the leadership in all spheres, at every stage – the solitary party which amongst its members has completely overcome not only the conception of internationalism but also the idea of democracy, which in its entire organization acknowledges only the principles of Responsibility, Command, and Obedience, and which besides all this for the first time has introduced into the political life of Germany a body numbering millions which is built up on the principle of achievement.

Here is an organization which is filled with an indomitable aggressive spirit, an organization which when a political opponent says 'your behaviour we regard as a provocation' for the first time does not see fit immediately to retire from the scene but brutally enforces its own will and hurls against the opponent the retort, 'We fight today! We fight tomorrow! And if you regard our meeting today as a provocation we shall hold yet another next week – until you have learned that it is no provocation when *German* Germany also professes its belief!' And when you say 'You must not come into the street' we go into the street in spite of you. And when you say, 'Then we shall kill you', however many sacrifices you force upon us, this young Germany will always continue its marches, and one day it will completely reconquer for the Germans the German street.

And when people cast in our teeth our intolerance, we proudly acknowledge it – yes, we have formed the inexorable decision to destroy Marxism in Germany down to its very last root. And this decision we formed not from any love of brawling: I could easily imagine a life which in itself was fairer than to be hunted through Germany, to be persecuted by countless Government regulations, to stand constantly with one foot in gaol, and to have in the State no right which one can call one's own. I could imagine for myself a fairer destiny than that of fighting a battle which at least at the outset was regarded by all as an insane chimera. Finally I believe that I have the capacity to occupy some post or other in the Social Democratic Party: and one thing is certain: if I had turned my capacity to *this* service, I should today presumably be fit even to enter the Government. But for me it was a greater decision to choose a way on which I was guided by nothing save my own faith, my indestructible confidence in the natural forces – still assuredly present – of our people, and in its importance which with good leadership would one day necessarily reappear.

And now behind us there lie twelve years of fighting. That fight has not been waged in theory only and in the Party alone turned into practice: we are also ready to wage that fight on the larger scale. I cast my mind back to the time when with six other unknown men I founded this association, when I spoke before eleven, twelve, thirteen, fourteen, twenty, thirty, and fifty persons; when I recall how after a year I had won sixty-four members for the Movement, how our small circle kept on growing, I must confess that that which has today been created, when a stream of millions of our German fellow-countrymen is flowing into our Movement, represents something which is unique in German history. The bourgeois parties have had seventy years to work in; where, I ask you, is the organization which could be compared with ours? Where is the organization which can boast, as ours can, that, at need, it can summon 400,000 men into the street, men who are schooled to blind obedience and are ready to execute any order – provided that it does not violate the law? Where is the organization that in seventy years has achieved what we have achieved in barely twelve years? – and achieved with means which were of so improvised a character that one can hardly avoid a feeling of shame when one confesses to an opponent how poverty-stricken the birth and the growth of this great Movement were in the early days.

Today we stand at the turning-point of Germany's destiny. If the present development continues, Germany will one day of necessity land in Bolshevist chaos, but if this development is broken, then our people must be taken into a school of iron discipline and gradually freed from the prejudices of both camps. A hard schooling, but one we cannot escape!

If one thinks that one can preserve for all time the conceptions of 'bourgeois' and 'proletarian' then one will either preserve the weakness of Germany – which means our downfall – or one ushers in the victory of Bolshevism. If one refuses to surrender those conceptions, then in my judgement a resurrection of the German nation is no longer possible. The chalk line which *Weltanschauungen* have drawn for peoples in the history of the world already more than once has proved to be the death-line. Either we shall succeed in working out a body-politic hard as iron from this conglomerate of parties, associations, unions, and conceptions of the world, from this pride of rank and madness of class, or else, lacking this internal consolidation, Germany will fall in final ruin.

Even if another batch of twenty emergency decrees is rained down on our people, these will not stay the great line which leads to destruction, but if one day the road be rediscovered which leads upwards, then first of all the German people must be bent straight again. That is a process which none can escape! It is no good to say that the proletarians are alone responsible. No, believe me, our whole German people of all ranks has a full measure of responsibility for our collapse – a measure pressed down and running over – some because they willed it and have consciously sought to bring it about, the others because they looked on and were too weak to stop our downfall. In history the failure to act is weighed as strictly as is the purpose or the deed. Today no one can escape the obligation to complete the regeneration of the German body-politic: every one must show his personal sympathy, must take his place in the common effort.

If I speak to you today it is not to ask for your votes or to induce you on my account to do this or that for the Party. No, I am here to expound a point of view, and I am convinced that the victory of this point of view would mean the only possible starting-point for a German recovery; it is indeed the last item standing to the credit of the German people. I hear it said so often by our opponents, 'You, too, will be unable to master the present crisis.' Supposing, gentlemen, that they are right, what would that mean? It would mean that we should be facing a ghastly period and that we should have to meet it with no other defences than a purely materialistic outlook on every side. And then the distress would, simply in its material aspect, be a thousandfold harder to bear, if one had failed to restore to the people any ideal whatsoever.

People say to me so often: 'You are only the drummer of national Germany.' And supposing that I were only the drummer? It would today be a far more statesmanlike achievement to drum once more into this German people a new faith than gradually to squander the only faith they have. Take the case of a fortress, imagine that it is reduced to extreme privations: as long as the garrison sees a possible salvation, believes in it, hopes for it, so long they can bear the reduced ration. But take from the hearts of men their last belief in the possibility of salvation, in a better future – take that completely from them, and you will see how these men suddenly regard their reduced rations as the most important thing in life. The more you bring it home to their consciousness that they are only objects for men to bargain with, that they are only prisoners of world-politics, the more will they, like all prisoners, concentrate their thoughts on purely material interests.

On the other hand, the more you bring back a people into the sphere of faith, of ideals, the more will it cease to regard material distress as the one and only thing which counts. And the weightiest evidence for the truth of that statement is our own German people. We would not ever forget that the German people waged wars of religion for 150 years with prodigious devotion, that hundreds of thousands of men once left their plot of land, their property, and their belongings simply for an ideal, simply for a conviction. We would never forget that during those 150 years there was no trace of even an ounce of material interests. Then you will understand how mighty is the force of an idea, of an ideal.

Only so can you comprehend how it is that in our Movement today hundreds of thousands of young men are prepared at the risk of their lives to withstand our opponents. I know quite well, gentlemen, that when National Socialists march through the streets and suddenly in the evening there arise a tumult and commotion, then the bourgeois draws back the window-curtain, looks out, and says: Once more my night's rest disturbed: no more sleep for me. Why must the Nazis always be so provocative and run about the place at night?

Gentlemen, if everyone thought like that, then no one's sleep at nights would be disturbed, it is true, but then the bourgeois today could not venture into the street. If everyone thought in that way, if these young folk had no ideal to move them and drive them forward, then certainly they would gladly be rid of these nocturnal fights. But remember that it means sacrifice when today many hundred thousands of SA and SS men of the National Socialist Movement every day have to mount on their lorries, protect meetings, undertake marches, sacrifice themselves night after night and then come back in the grey dawn either to workshop and factory or as unemployed to take the pittance of the dole: it means sacrifice when from the little which they possess they have further to buy their uniforms, their shirts, their badges, yes, and even pay their own fares. Believe me, there is already in all this the force of an ideal – a great ideal!

And if the whole German nation today had the same faith in its vocation as these hundred thousands, if the whole nation possessed this idealism, Germany would stand in the eyes of the world otherwise than she stands now! For our situation in the world in its fatal effects is but the result of our own underestimate of German strength. Only when we have once more changed this fatal valuation of ourselves can Germany take advantage of the political possibilities which, if we look far enough into the future, can place German life once more upon a natural and secure basis – and that means either new living-space and the development of a great internal market or protection of German economic life against the world without the utilization of all the concentrated strength of Germany. The labour resources of our people, the capacities, we have them already: no one can deny that we are industrious. But we must first refashion the political preconditions: without that, industry and capacity, diligence and economy are in the last resort of no avail, for an oppressed nation will not be able to spend on its own welfare even the fruits of its own economy but must sacrifice them on the altar of exactions and tribute.

And so in contrast to our own official Government I cannot see any hope for the resurrection of Germany if we regard the foreign politics of Germany as the primary factor: the primary necessity is the restoration of a sound national German body-politic armed to strike. In order to realize this end I founded thirteen years ago the National Socialist Movement: that Movement I have led during the last twelve years, and I hope that one day it will accomplish this task and that, as the fairest result of its struggle, it will leave behind it a German body-politic completely renewed internally, intolerant of anyone who sins against the nation and its interests, intolerant against anyone who will not acknowledge its vital interests or who opposes them, intolerant and pitiless against anyone who shall attempt once more to destroy or disintegrate this body-politic, and yet ready for friendship and peace with anyone who has a wish for peace and friendship.

*When Hitler sat down, the audience rose and cheered him wildly. Substantial contributions quickly flowed into the Nazi treasury from heavy industrial companies. Hitler had won an important victory, says his biographer Alan Bullock. German industrialists came to see in him the man who would defend their interests against the threat of Communism and the claims of the trade unions.*

•

## STANLEY BALDWIN
London, 10 November 1932

### 'The bomber will always get through'

*By 1932, the year that Hitler came to power, Baldwin had twice been prime minister and was now Lord President of the Council in Ramsay MacDonald's National Government. He had developed a horror of air warfare and bombing, especially after seeing the results of a study by the Committee of Imperial Defence, and believed that the League of Nations should ban the building of new military aircraft. The argument was pursued in Cabinet but inconclusively. Meanwhile President Hoover had also proposed that bombers should be abolished. Yet by the autumn Baldwin had decided that Britain could no longer proceed with unilateral disarmament.*

*On 10 November (moved according to his most recent biographers by a 'truly daemonic force'), he delivered a short but sensational speech to the Commons arguing that disarmament by itself would not stop war but that it would reduce the dangers and opportunities of making war – and ending with an appeal to the conscience of the young.*

What the world suffers from – and I have said this before – is a sense of fear, a want of confidence, and it is a fear held instinctively and without knowledge very often. But in my view, and I have slowly and deliberately come to this conclusion, there is no one thing more responsible for that fear – I am speaking now of what the Hon. Gentleman the Member for Limehouse (Mr Attlee) called the common people of whom I am chief – there is no greater cause of that fear than the fear of the air. Up to the time of the last war, civilians were exempt from the worst perils of war. They suffered sometimes from hunger, sometimes from the loss of sons and relatives serving in the Army, but now, in addition, they suffer from the fear, not only of being killed themselves, but, what is perhaps worse for a man, the fear of seeing his wife and children killed from the air.

These feelings exist among the ordinary people throughout the whole civilized world, and I doubt if many of those who have that fear realize one or two things with reference to its cause. One is the appalling speed which the air has brought into modern warfare. The speed of air attack, compared with the attack of an army, is as the speed of a motor car to that of a four-in-hand and in the next war you will find that any town which is within reach of an aerodrome can be bombed within the first five minutes of war from the air, to an extent which was inconceivable in the last war, and the question will be, whose morale will be shattered quickest by that preliminary bombing? I think it is well also for the man in the street to realize that there is no power on earth that can protect him from being bombed. Whatever people may tell him, the bomber will always get through, and it is very easy to understand that, if you realize the area of space.

I said that any town within reach of an aerodrome could be bombed. Take any large town you like in this island or on the Continent within such reach. For the defence of that town and its suburbs, you have to split up the air into sectors for defence. Calculate that the bombing aeroplanes will be at least 20,000 feet high in the air, and perhaps higher, and it is a matter of simple mathematical calculation – or I will omit the word 'simple' – that you will have sectors of from ten to hundreds of cubic miles to defend.

Now imagine 100 cubic miles covered with cloud and fog, and you can calculate how many aeroplanes you would have to throw into that to have much chance of catching odd aeroplanes as they fly through it. It cannot be done, and there is no expert in Europe who will say that it can. The only defence is in offence, which means that you have to kill more women and children more quickly than the enemy if you want to save yourselves.

I will not pretend that we are not taking our precautions in this country. We have done it. We have made our investigations, much more quietly and hitherto without any publicity, but, considering the years that are required to make your preparations, any Government of this country in the present circumstances of the world would have been guilty of criminal negligence had they neglected to make their preparations. The same is true of other nations. What more potent cause of fear can there be than this kind of thing that is going on on the Continent? And fear is a very dangerous thing. It is quite true that it may act as a deterrent in people's minds against war, but it is much more likely to act to make them want to increase armaments to protect them against the terrors that they know may be launched against them. We have to remember that aerial warfare is still in its infancy, and its potentialities are incalculable and inconceivable.

As far as the air is concerned, there is, as has been most truly said, no way of complete disarmament except the abolition of flying. Now that, again, is impossible. We have never known mankind go back on a new invention. It might be a good thing for this world, as I have heard some of the most distinguished men in the Air Service say, if man had never learned to fly. But he has learned to fly, and there is no more important question, not only before this House, but before every man, woman and child in Europe, than: 'What are we going to do with this power now we have got it?' I make no excuse for bringing this subject forward tonight to ventilate it in this first Assembly in the world, in the hope that perhaps what is said here may be read in other countries and may be considered and pondered, because on the solution of this question hangs not only, in my view, our civilization, but before that terrible day comes there hangs the lesser question, but a difficult one, of the possible rearmament of Germany with an air force. The two things are inextricably wrapped up together.

As long as the air exists, you cannot get rid of the fear of which I spoke, and which I believe to be the parent of many troubles. One cannot help reflecting that, after the hundreds of millions of years during which the human race has been on this earth, it is only within our generation that we have secured the mastery of the air. I certainly do not know how the youth of the world may feel, but it is not a cheerful thought to the older men that, having got that mastery of the air, we are going to defile the earth from the air as we have defiled the soil during all the years that mankind has been on it. This is a question for the younger men far more than it is for us. They are the men who fly in the air. Future generations will fly in the air more and more.

Few of my colleagues around me here, probably, will see another great war. I do not think that we have seen the last great war, but I do not think there will be one just yet; at any rate, if it does come, we shall be too old to be of use to anyone. What about the younger men? How will they investigate this matter? It is they who will have to fight, and it is they who will have to fight out this bloody issue of war. It is really for them to decide. They are the majority upon the earth, and the matter touches them far more closely. The instrument is in their hands. There are some instruments so terrible that mankind has resolved not to use them. I myself happen to know of at least three inventions, deliberately proposed for use in the last war, that were never used – potent to a degree and inhuman.

If the conscience of the young men should ever come to feel with regard to this one instrument that it is evil and should go, the thing will be done; but if they do not feel like that – well, as I say, the future is in their hands. But when the next war comes, and European civilization is wiped out, as it will be and by no force more than by that force, then do not let them lay the blame upon the old men. Let them remember that they, they principally or they alone, are responsible for the terrors that have fallen upon the earth.

*Members of parliament were shaken, even moved, by the speech, but its ambiguity left many anxious and perplexed. Where did the speech lead? Churchill asked. There was a sense of fatalism and helplessness about it. 'Tell the truth, tell the truth to the British people.' Although Baldwin had indeed told the truth, albeit in his gnomic manner, the speech did more harm than good because his striking phrase about the bomber always getting through was taken for defeatism and used to prove the futility of rearmament and disarmament alike.*

•

# FRANKLIN DELANO ROOSEVELT
## Washington, DC, 4 March 1933

### *'The only thing we have to fear is fear itself'*

*On Inauguration Day 1933 all the banks were closed, trading had ceased, and the Depression was at its worst. Widespread unemployment had created a feeling of utter helplessness.*

*America seemed beyond help – until Franklin D. Roosevelt, crippled since 1921 when he contracted polio and lost the use of both legs, won the 1932 presidential election by a majority of more than twelve million votes, winning forty-two states.*

*Now on a cold March day the crippled Roosevelt (1882–1945), a man of power and vision who knew that he could save his country, took the oath and addressed the millions of Americans listening to their radios. (He had written the first draft in four hours, adding the memorable 'freedom from fear' phrase only the day before the inauguration, perhaps prompted by Henry David Thoreau's 'Nothing is so much to be feared as fear'. He had just been given a copy of Thoreau's writings.)*

*His inaugural speech was one of the turning-points of American history, says historian Hugh Brogan. In a few minutes he achieved what had eluded Herbert Hoover for four wearying years: he gave back to his countrymen their hope and energy.*

President Hoover, Mr Chief Justice, my friends.

This is a day of national consecration, and I am certain that my fellow-Americans expect that on my induction into the Presidency I will address them with a candour and a decision which the present situation of our nation impels.

This is pre-eminently the time to speak the truth, the whole truth, frankly and boldly. Nor need we shrink from honestly facing conditions in our country today. This great nation will endure as it has endured, will revive and will prosper.

So first of all let me assert my firm belief that the only thing we have to fear is fear itself – nameless, unreasoning, unjustified terror which paralyses needed efforts to convert retreat into advance.

In every dark hour of our national life a leadership of frankness and vigour has met with that understanding and support of the people themselves which is essential to victory. I am convinced that you will again give that support to leadership in these critical days.

In such a spirit on my part and on yours we face our common difficulties. They concern, thank God, only material things. Values have shrunken to fantastic levels; taxes have risen; our ability to pay has fallen, government of all kinds is faced by serious curtailment of income; the means of exchange are frozen in the currents of trade; the withered leaves of industrial enterprise lie on every side; farmers find no markets for their produce; the savings of many years in thousands of families are gone.

More important, a host of unemployed citizens face the grim problem of existence, and an equally great number toil with little return. Only a foolish optimist can deny the dark realities of the moment.

Yet our distress comes from no failure of substance. We are stricken by no plague of locusts. Compared with the perils which our forefathers conquered because they believed and were not afraid, we have still much to be thankful for. Nature still offers her bounty and human efforts have multiplied it. Plenty is at our doorstep, but a generous use of it languishes in the very sight of the supply.

Primarily, this is because the rulers of the exchange of mankind's goods have failed through their own stubbornness and their own incompetence, have admitted that failure and abdicated. Practices of the unscrupulous money changers stand indicted in the court of public opinion, rejected by the hearts and minds of men.

True, they have tried, but their efforts have been cast in the pattern of an outworn tradition. Faced by failure of credit, they have proposed only the lending of more money.

Stripped of the lure of profit by which to induce our people to follow their false leadership, they have resorted to exhortations, pleading tearfully for restored confidence. They know only the rules of a generation of self-seekers.

They have no vision, and when there is no vision the people perish.

The money changers have fled from their high seats in the temple of our civilization. We may now restore that temple to the ancient truths.

The measure of the restoration lies in the extent to which we apply social values more noble than mere monetary profit.

Happiness lies not in the mere possession of money; it lies in the joy of achievement, in the thrill of creative effort.

The joy and moral stimulation of work no longer must be forgotten in the mad chase of evanescent profits. These dark days will be worth all they cost us if they teach us that our true destiny is not to be ministered unto but to minister to ourselves and to our fellow-men.

Recognition of the falsity of material wealth as the standard of success goes hand in hand with the abandonment of the false belief that public office and high political position are to be valued only by the standards of pride of place and personal profit; and there must be an end to a conduct in banking and in business which too often has given to a sacred trust the likeness of callous and selfish wrongdoing.

Small wonder that confidence languishes, for it thrives only on honesty, on honour, on the sacredness of obligations, on faithful protection, on unselfish performance. Without them it cannot live.

Restoration calls, however, not for changes in ethics alone. This nation asks for action, and action now.

Our greatest primary task is to put people to work. This is no unsolvable problem if we face it wisely and courageously

I favour as a practical policy the putting of first things first. I shall spare no effort to restore world trade by international economic readjustment, but the emergency at home cannot wait on that accomplishment.

The basic thought that guides these specific means of national recovery is not narrowly nationalistic.

It is the insistence, as a first consideration, upon the interdependence of the various elements in, and parts of, the United States – a recognition of the old and permanently important manifestation of the American spirit of the pioneer.

It is the way to recovery. It is the immediate way. It is the strongest assurance that the recovery will endure.

In the field of world policy I would dedicate this nation to the policy of the good neighbour – the neighbour who resolutely respects himself and, because he does so, respects the rights of others – the neighbour who respects his obligations and respects the sanctity of his agreements in and with a world of neighbours.

If I read the temper of our people correctly, we now realize as we have never before, our interdependence on each other; that we cannot merely take, but we must give as well; that if we are to go forward we must move as a trained and loyal army willing to sacrifice for the good of a common discipline, because, without such discipline, no progress is made, no leadership becomes effective.

We are, I know, ready and willing to submit our lives and property to such discipline because it makes possible a leadership which aims at a larger good.

This I propose to offer, pledging that the larger purposes will bind upon us all as a sacred obligation with a unity of duty hitherto evoked only in time of armed strife.

With this pledge taken, I assume unhesitatingly the leadership of this great army of our people, dedicated to a disciplined attack upon our common problems.

Action in this image and to this end is feasible under the forms of government which we have inherited from our ancestors.

Our Constitution is so simple and practical that it is possible always to meet extraordinary needs by changes in emphasis and arrangement without loss of essential form.

That is why our constitutional system has proved itself the most superbly enduring political mechanism the modern world has produced. It has met every stress of vast expansion of territory, of foreign wars, of bitter internal strife, of world relations . . .

I am prepared under my constitutional duty to recommend the measures that a stricken nation in the midst of a stricken world may require.

These measures, or such other measures as the Congress may

build out of its experience and wisdom, I shall seek, within my constitutional authority, to bring to speedy adoption.

But in the event that the Congress shall fail to take one of these two courses, and in the event that the national emergency is still critical, I shall not evade the clear course of duty that will then confront me.

I shall ask the Congress for the one remaining instrument to meet the crisis – broad executive power to wage a war against the emergency as great as the power that would be given me if we were in fact invaded by a foreign foe.

For the trust reposed in me I will return the courage and the devotion that befit the time. I can do no less.

We face the arduous days that lie before us in the warm courage of national unity; with the clear consciousness of seeking old and precious moral values; with the clean satisfaction that comes from the stern performance of duty by old and young alike.

We aim at the assurance of a rounded and permanent national life.

We do not distrust the future of essential democracy. The people of the United States have not failed. In their need they have registered a mandate that they want direct, vigorous action.

They have asked for discipline and direction under leadership. They have made me the present instrument of their wishes. In the spirit of the gift I take it.

In this dedication of a nation we humbly ask the blessing of God. May He protect each and every one of us! May He guide me in the days to come!

*By the end of the week half a million letters had been sent to the White House. Here for once were words that were not mere rhetoric, says Hugh Brogan. Words became deeds after 4 March and Roosevelt went on to win four successive elections.*

•

## ADOLF HITLER
Berlin, 13 July 1934

### '*The supreme justiciar of the German people*'

*Hitler was made chancellor of Germany on 30 January 1933 and four weeks later the Reichstag Fire gave him the opportunity to establish a one-party system. A little over a year later on 30 June 1934, he eliminated his rivals on the Night of the Long Knives, when he used Nazi élite units (the SS) in the private army of Himmler, the Nazi police chief, to murder the older and more radical Nazi private army, the Brown-shirts (the SA), led by Ernst Röhm. There were more than one hundred victims of the killings, which made Hitler undisputed leader of the Nazi revolution.*

*After the blood bath, Joseph Goebbels, Hitler's propagandist, forbade German newspapers to carry obituary notices of the victims, which only fed and intensified rumour, horror and fear. Hitler did not appear before the Reichstag until 13 July, when he spoke for two hours.*

*Never had Hitler made so evident his contempt for the law or humanity and his determination to preserve his power at any cost.*

At one o'clock in the night I received the last dispatches telling me of the alarm summonses; at two o'clock in the morning I flew to Munich. Meanwhile Minister-President Göring had previously received from me the commission that if I proceeded to apply a purge he was to take similar measures at once in Berlin and in Prussia. With an iron fist he beat down the attack on the National Socialist state before it could develop. The necessity for acting with lightning speed meant that in this decisive hour I had very few men with me. In the presence of the Minister Goebbels and of the new Chief of Staff the action of which you are already informed was executed and brought to a close in Munich. Although only a few days before I had been prepared to exercise clemency, at this hour there was no place for any such consideration. Mutinies are suppressed in accordance with laws of iron that are eternally the same. If anyone reproaches me and asks why I did not resort to the regular courts of justice for conviction of the offenders, then all that I can say to him is this: in this hour I was responsible for the fate of the German people, and thereby I became the supreme justiciar of the German people!

Mutinous divisions have in all periods been recalled to order by decimation. Only one state has failed to make any use of its articles of war, and this state paid for that failure by collapse – Germany. I did not wish to deliver up the young Reich to the fate of the old Reich. I gave the order to shoot those who were the ringleaders in this treason, and I further gave the order to burn out down to the raw flesh the ulcers of this poisoning of the wells in our domestic life and of the poisoning of the outside world. And I further ordered that if any of the mutineers should attempt to resist arrest, they were immediately to be struck down with armed force. The nation must know that its existence – and that is guaranteed through its internal order and security – can be threatened by no one with impunity! And everyone must know for all future time that if he raises his hand to strike the state, then certain death is his lot. And every National Socialist must know that no rank and no position can protect him from his personal responsibility and therefore from his punishment. I have prosecuted thousands of our former opponents on account of their corruption. I should in my own mind reproach myself if I were now to tolerate similar offences in our own ranks. No people and no government can help it if creatures arise such as we once knew in Germany, a Kutisker, for example, such as France came to know in a Stavisky, or such as we today have once more experienced – men whose aim is to sin against a nation's interests. But every people is itself guilty if it does not find the strength to destroy such noxious creatures.

If people bring against me the objection that only a judicial procedure could precisely weigh the measure of the guilt and of its expiation, then against this view I lodge my most solemn protest. He who rises against Germany is a traitor to his country: and the traitor to his country is not to be punished according to the range and the extent of his act, but according to the purpose that that act has revealed. He who in his heart purposes to raise a mutiny and thereby breaks loyalty, breaks faith, breaks sacred pledges, he can expect nothing else than that he himself will be the first sacrifice. I have no intention to have the little culprits shot and to spare the great criminals. It is not my duty to inquire whether it was too hard a lot that was inflicted on these conspirators, these agitators and destroyers, these poisoners of the wellsprings of German public opinion and in a wider sense of world opinion: it is not mine to consider which of them suffered too severely: I have only to see to it that Germany's lot should not be intolerable . . .

In these days, which have been days of severe trial both for me and for its members, the SA [storm troopers] has preserved the spirit of loyalty. Thus for the third time the SA has proved that it is mine, just as I will prove at any time that I belong to my SA men. In a few weeks' time the Brown Shirt will once more dominate the streets of Germany and will give to one and all clear evidence that because it has overcome its grievous distress the life of National Socialist Germany is only the more vigorous.

When in March of last year our young revolution stormed through Germany, my highest endeavour was to shed as little blood as possible. To millions of my former opponents, on behalf of the new state and in the name of the National Socialist party, I offered a general amnesty; millions of them have since joined us and are loyally cooperating in the rebuilding of the Reich.

I hoped that it might not be necessary any longer to be forced to defend this state yet again with arms in our hands. But since fate has now none the less put us to this test, all of us wish to pledge ourselves with only the greater fanaticism to hold fast to that which was formerly won at the price of the blood of so many of our best men and which today had to be maintained once more through the blood of German fellow countrymen. Just as one and a half years ago I offered reconciliation to our former opponents, so would I from henceforth also promise forgetfulness to all those who shared in the guilt of this act of madness. Let them bethink themselves, and remembering this melancholy calamity in our new German history let them devote themselves to the task of reparation. May they now recognize with surer insight than before the great task that fate sets us, which civil war and chaos cannot perform. May we all feel responsible for the most precious treasure that there can be for the German people: internal order, internal and external peace, just as I am ready to undertake responsibility at the bar of history for the twenty-four hours in which the bitterest decisions of my life were made, in which fate once again taught me in the midst of anxious care with every thought to hold fast to the dearest thing that has been given us in this world – the German people and the German Reich!

*After President von Hindenburg died on 2 August, an announcement was made within an hour that the office of president was being merged with that of the chancellor and that Hitler would become head of the state as well as Supreme Commander of the Armed Forces of the Reich. The same day the officers and men of the German army took their oath of allegiance not to the constitution or to the fatherland but to Hitler himself.*

•

## OSWALD MOSLEY
### London, 24 March 1935

#### *'England again dares to be great'*

*Oswald Mosley announced the establishment of the British Union of Fascists in October 1932, three months after Hitler's Nazis had won power in the German elections. 'My duty was to awaken the will to live and to live greatly, to dedicate myself to a national renaissance,' he wrote later. A year later the movement became anti-Semitic and Hitlerite rather than fascist. Dressed in black shirts, riding breeches and jackboots the British fascists staged marches through the streets, particularly in the East End of London, distributing propaganda against democracy and socialism and making vicious attacks on the Jews. Their rallies were attended by thousands and often marked by ugly scenes of violence.*

*An audience of 8,000 heard this speech at the Albert Hall in which Mosley set out the vision he saw emanating from the 'first instinct of patriotism'.*

We count it a privilege to live in an age when England demands that great things shall be done, a privilege to be of the generation which learns to say what can we give instead of what can we take. For thus our generation learns there are greater things than slothful ease; greater things than safety; more terrible things than death.

This shall be the epic generation which scales again the heights of time and history to see once more the immortal lights – the lights of sacrifice and high endeavour summoning through ordeal the soul of humanity to the sublime and the eternal. The alternatives of our age are heroism or oblivion. There are no lesser paths in the history of great nations. Can we, therefore, doubt which path to choose?

Let us tonight at this great meeting give the answer. Hold high the head of England; lift strong the voice of Empire. Let us to Europe and to the world proclaim that the heart of this great people is undaunted and invincible. This flag still challenges the winds of destiny. This flame still burns. This glory shall not die. The soul of Empire is alive, and England again dares to be great.

*Mosley's fascist movement was a failure. After riots in London in October 1936 the Public Order Act was passed, banning political uniforms and private armies and limiting the right to march in the streets. Mosley was interned during the war and unsuccessfully fought general elections in 1959 and 1966. He lived in Paris and died in 1980.*

•

## LA PASIONARIA (DOLORES IBARRURI)
### Madrid, 19 July 1936

#### 'They shall not pass'

*Dolores Ibárruri (1895–1989), the daughter of a Basque miner, joined the Spanish Socialist Party in 1917 and worked as a journalist for the workers' press, using the pseudonym La Pasionaria (the passion flower). She helped to found the Spanish Communist Party in 1920.*

*For millions of people, as her biographer Robert Low records, La Pasionaria was the personification of the Spanish Civil War, which polarized world opinion between 1936 and 1939 as the republicans fought Franco's fascists. A tall, dark woman, dressed in mourner's black, she was the republic's principal mouthpiece to the world. Her speeches were reproduced in a million leaflets.*

*At the urging of José Díaz, general secretary of the Communist Party, La Pasionaria delivered this speech, broadcast on Radio Union from the Ministry of the Interior, on behalf of the Communists to boost the morale of the people.*

Workers, anti-fascists, working people: everyone stands ready to defend the republic, popular liberties and the democratic conquests of the people. The seriousness of the situation is known by all through the bulletins of the government and the Popular Front. In Morocco and the Canaries the fight goes on with enthusiasm and courage, the workers united with forces loyal to the republic. To the cry of 'Fascism will not pass, the hangmen of October [i.e. Asturias] will not pass!' communists, socialists, anarchists and republicans, soldiers and all those forces loyal to the will of the people are destroying the insurrectionary traitors who have dragged through dirt and treason the military pride of which they have so often boasted. The whole country is shaking with indignation faced with these heartless men who, with fire and terror, want to plunge popular and democratic Spain into an inferno of terror. But they shall not pass [*no pasarán*]! The whole of Spain is on a war footing. In Madrid the people are on the streets, warning the government with their decisiveness and spirit of combat so that the crushing of the reactionaries and fascists who have rebelled will be achieved. Women, heroic women of the people, remember the heroism of the Asturian women! Fight alongside the men to defend the bread and security of your threatened children. Soldiers, sons of the people! Stand firm, as one man, beside the government, beside the workers, beside the Popular Front, your parents, your brothers and comrades. Fight for the Spain of the sixteenth of February; take it to triumph. Workers of all persuasions: the government has placed in your hands the necessary means of defence so that we know how to honour our obligation to prevent in Spain the shame which a triumph of the bloody hangmen of the October revolution would imply. Let nobody hesitate: let us be able to celebrate victory tomorrow. Everyone be ready for action. Every worker, every anti-fascist, should consider himself a soldier at arms. People of Catalonia, Vasconia, Galicia, all Spaniards: defend the democratic republic; consolidate the victory won by the people on the sixteenth of February! The Communist Party calls you all to the struggle. It calls on all workers to take a place in the combat to crush once and for all the enemies of the republic and of popular liberties. Long live the Popular Front! Long live the union of anti-fascists! Long live the republic and the people!

*The phrase No pasarán spread swiftly through Spain and entered revolutionary folklore around the world. (It had been made famous twenty years earlier by the French general Pétain during the siege of Verdun in 1916.) La Pasionaria sought refuge in the Soviet Union after Franco took power in 1939, returned to Spain in 1977 after his death and reentered the National Assembly when she was eighty-one.*

•

## FRANKLIN DELANO ROOSEVELT
### New York, 31 October 1936

### *'The forces of selfishness and of lust for power met their match'*

*The New Deal had created six million jobs. Roosevelt had given America ideas, leadership and help. The Depression had been mitigated. The spectre of unemployment no longer haunted the land. As Hitler instituted his German dictatorship and Mussolini conquered Abyssinia, Roosevelt had vindicated American democracy and rescued the profit system.*

*So wherever he spoke during the 1936 presidential campaign, he was greeted as a saviour. His last major speech was in Madison Square Garden in New York City and was considered his best of the campaign. His four speechwriters as well as the president spent more time on it than on any other as he ordered them to take off all gloves. The speech summed up the campaign as well as the record of the previous four years and showed Roosevelt as supremely confident in the creativity of the New Deal and determined to combat and defeat the forces that still opposed him, mainly the business leaders who thought that it was now their turn to rule America again.*

*The mounting cheers during each shouted sentence of his peroration rose to tumultuous applause as he reached his conclusion.*

I submit to you a record of peace; and on that record a well-founded expectation for future peace – peace for the individual, peace for the community, peace for the Nation, and peace with the world.

Tonight I call the roll – the roll of honour of those who stood with us in 1932 and still stand with us today.

Written on it are the names of millions who never had a chance – men at starvation wages, women in sweatshops, children at looms.

Written on it are the names of those who despaired, young men and young women for whom opportunity had become a will-o'-the-wisp.

Written on it are the names of farmers whose acres yielded only bitterness, business men whose books were portents of disaster, home owners who were faced with eviction, frugal citizens whose savings were insecure.

Written there in large letters are the names of countless other Americans of all parties and all faiths, Americans who had eyes to see and hearts to understand, whose consciences were burdened because too many of their fellows were burdened, who looked on these things four years ago and said, 'This can be changed. We will change it.'

We still lead that army in 1936. They stood with us then because in 1932 they believed. They stand with us today because in 1936 they know. And with them stand millions of new recruits who have come to know.

Their hopes have become our record.

We have not come this far without a struggle and I assure you we cannot go further without a struggle.

For twelve years this Nation was afflicted with hear-nothing, see-nothing, do-nothing Government. The Nation looked to Government but the Government looked away. Nine mocking years with the golden calf and three long years of the scourge! Nine crazy years at the ticker and three long years in the breadlines! Nine mad years of mirage and three long years of despair! Powerful influences strive today to restore that kind of Government with its doctrine that that Government is best which is most indifferent.

For nearly four years you have had an Administration which instead of twirling its thumbs has rolled up its sleeves. We will keep our sleeves rolled up.

We had to struggle with the old enemies of peace – business and financial monopoly, speculation, reckless banking, class antagonism, sectionalism, war profiteering.

They had begun to consider the Government of the United States as a mere appendage to their own affairs. We know now that Government by organized money is just as dangerous as Government by organized mob.

Never before in all our history have these forces been so united against one candidate as they stand today. They are unanimous in their hate for me – and I welcome their hatred.

I should like to have it said of my first Administration that in it the forces of selfishness and of lust for power met their match. I should like to have it said of my second Administration that in it these forces met their master.

*Republican leaders seized on Roosevelt's attack on the forces of reaction that had sought to block his programme and said he was trying to make himself 'master' of the American people, but Roosevelt won every state except Maine and Vermont and polled more than twenty-seven million votes against his opponent Governor Alfred Landon of Kansas, who got more than sixteen million votes.*

•

## WINSTON CHURCHILL
London, 12 November 1936

### *'The locust years'*

*By 1936 Winston Churchill, abandoned by his party, betrayed by his friends and stripped of office, was convinced that Germany was stronger in air power than Britain and France combined. He urged Stanley Baldwin to allow a House of Commons debate on defence, during which he delivered this speech, one of the greatest of his career. It was the day that Churchill spoke for all who knew that sooner or later Britain must confront Hitler and he worked on the speech through the night, dictating and revising passages to hone one of his finest philippics — aimed directly at Baldwin.*

*'He drives his points home with a sledgehammer,' Harold Nicolson recorded as he watched Churchill deliver the speech, which ended with a remarkable peroration in which he damned the House of Commons.*

The First Lord of the Admiralty in his speech the other night went even farther. He said, 'We are always reviewing the position.' Everything, he assured us, is entirely fluid. I am sure that that is true. Anyone can see what the position is. The Government simply cannot make up their minds, or they cannot get the Prime Minister to make up his mind. So they go on in strange paradox, decided only to be undecided, resolved to be irresolute, adamant for drift, solid for fluidity, all-powerful to be impotent. So we go on preparing more months and years – precious, perhaps vital to the greatness of Britain – for the locusts to eat. They will say to me, 'A Minister of Supply is not necessary, for all is going well.' I deny it. 'The position is satisfactory.' It is not true. 'All is proceeding according to plan.' We know what that means . . .

Owing to past neglect, in the face of the plainest warnings, we have now entered upon a period of danger greater than has befallen Britain since the U-boat campaign was crushed; perhaps, indeed, it is a more grievous period than that, because at that time at least we were possessed of the means of securing ourselves and of defeating that campaign. Now we have no such assurance. The era of procrastination, of half-measures, of soothing and baffling expedients, of delays, is coming to its close. In its place we are entering a period of consequences. We have entered a period in which for more than a year, or a year and a half, the considerable preparations which are now on foot in Britain will not, as the Minister clearly showed, yield results which can be effective in actual fighting strength; while during this very period Germany may well reach the culminating point of her gigantic military preparations, and be forced by financial and economic stringency to contemplate a sharp decline, or perhaps some other exit from her difficulties. It is this lamentable conjunction of events which seems to present the danger of Europe in its most disquieting form. We cannot avoid this period; we are in it now. Surely, if we can abridge it by even a few months, if we can shorten this period when the German Army will begin to be so much larger than the French Army, and before the British Air Force has come to play its complementary part, we may be the architects who build the peace of the world on sure foundations.

Two things, I confess, have staggered me, after a long Parliamentary experience, in these Debates. The first has been the dangers that have so swiftly come upon us in a few years, and have been transforming our position and the whole outlook of the world. Secondly, I have been staggered by the failure of the House of Commons to react effectively against those dangers. That, I am bound to say, I never expected. I never would have believed that we should have been allowed to go on getting into this plight, month by month and year by year, and that even the Government's own confessions of error would have produced no concentration of Parliamentary opinion and force capable of lifting our efforts to the level of emergency. I say that unless the House resolves to find out the truth for itself it will have committed an act of abdication of duty without parallel in its long history.

•

## STANLEY BALDWIN
London, 12 November 1936

*'I shall always trust the instincts of our democratic people'*

*Baldwin reacted immediately to Churchill's jibe about the years that the locusts had eaten. He conceded that Britain had cut down the services during 1924–9 because it hoped for disarmament and believed there was no danger of a major war. Nor, he argued, was British public opinion ready for rearmament until 1934–5. Addressing much of his speech to the member for Epping, Churchill, and declaring that he would speak with the 'utmost frankness', he then set out his defence.*

Supposing I had gone to the country and said that Germany was rearming and that we must rearm, does anybody think that this pacific democracy would have rallied to that cry at that moment? I cannot think of anything that would have made the loss of the election from my point of view more certain. I think the country itself learned by certain events that took place during the winter of 1934–5 what the perils might be to it. All I did was to take a moment perhaps less unfortunate than another might have been, and we won the election with a large majority; but frankly I could conceive that we should at that time, by advocating certain courses, have been a great deal less successful. We got from the country – with a large majority – a mandate for doing a thing that no one, twelve months before, would have believed possible. It is my firm conviction that had the Government, with this great majority, used that majority to do anything that might be described as arming without a mandate – and they did not do anything, except the slightly increased air programme for which they gave their reasons – had I taken such action as my Right Hon. Friend desired me to take, it would have defeated entirely the end I had in view. I may be wrong, but I put that to the House as an explanation of my action in that respect.

I shall always trust the instincts of our democratic people. They may come a little late, but my word, they come with a certainty when they do come; they come with a unity not imposed from the top, not imposed by force, but a unity that nothing can break. I believe today that, whatever differences there may be among us in the country on various questions – as there must be – the conviction is biting deep into our country, with all its love of peace, that there must be no going back on our resolution for such rearmament as we deem necessary to meet any possible peril from whatever quarter it may come. That feeling is coupled with the feeling which we all have that we are as anxious as ever to see all the countries of Europe considering disarmament, especially in the air. But until that day comes, nothing will shake the resolution either of the Government or of this House or of our people.

It is very easy to be led into supposing that dictatorial methods are necessarily more effective than the coordination of free effort, but we must not imagine that other countries whose governments do not submit their plans for defence to Parliament and do not require the approval of the legislature for the power which they exercise, whose Ministers are never criticized and have not to explain themselves, therefore escape all trouble. The last war showed one thing plainly and it was that at times when we might have suspected that the enemy was prepared to the last button, that all was going happily with him and that he had no difficulties, he was, even then, struggling with handicaps and confusions of which we knew nothing. It is a mistake to suppose that our methods are necessarily inferior to other methods which are largely concealed from the public gaze. My Right Hon. Friend the Member for Epping seldom speaks nowadays without a quotation from the Latin tongue and I rejoice that it should be so. He gave us one today, and I, at this point, would like to give another: 'Omne ignotum pro terribili', which I might translate thus: 'Things you know nothing about are always bogies.'

Experience in the House of Commons has taught me the lesson that more is to be gained in this country by relying on willing cooperation than by adopting dictatorial methods, until they are forced upon you and become essential. The House of Commons and the British people are very alike. The exercise of compulsory powers inevitably involves, at any rate at first, a most serious dislocation of industry, a dislocation which may be out of all proportion to the benefits obtained. It may well be that, instead of being hastened, production for some time may be retarded. But it is certain – and I must repeat this – that it would so dislocate the ordinary free working of industry as to reduce our effective financial strength; and that financial strength, so carefully nursed and looked after through all these years, is one of the strongest weapons we have if war ever comes upon us.

The whole of our efforts in the field of diplomacy and foreign policy will be aimed at bringing agreement and peace to all foreign Powers. At the same time all our efforts will be devoted to this great question of defence – the protection of our own people – and we will not relax our efforts for one moment, because we know that while we shall work for the blessings of peace, there can be no peace, in Europe certainly, unless every country knows that we are prepared for war.

*Baldwin's speech, a limp and lame reply, delivered haltingly, haunted his reputation to the grave and increased the sense of unease created by Churchill's speech – but he was to win a triumph the following month when the abdication crisis erupted. He stood accused of acting complacently as Hitler built up German military power.- Yet the archives for the era suggest that Baldwin was certainly more aware of the need to build up Britain's defences than his successor Neville Chamberlain.*

•

## CHAIM WEIZMANN
### Jerusalem, 25 November 1936

### 'The Jews carry Palestine in their hearts'

*David Ben-Gurion, the great prime minister of Israel, described Chaim Weizmann (1874–1952) as the most gifted envoy the Jewish people ever produced. 'There was no other Jew in whom the non-Jewish world perceived the embodiment of the Jewish people, with their ability, their will, and their longings,' Ben-Gurion wrote. 'He was perhaps the only truly great ambassador produced by the Jewish people throughout the generations.'*

*At no moment in his life was Weizmann a greater ambassador for the establishment of a state of Israel than when he addressed the royal commission under Lord Peel, set up by Stanley Baldwin in 1936 to consider the working of the mandate after a series of Arab attacks on Jews. Weizmann was convinced that the Peel Commission offered the hope that a new and possibly decisive phase in the Zionist movement might now be beginning.*

*As he arrived to meet the commission, there were audible whispers from the spectators on either side of him: 'Ha-shem yatzliach darkecho' (God prosper you on your mission). 'I felt that I would be speaking for generations long since dead, for those who lay buried on Mount Scopus and those whose last resting places were scattered all over the world,' Weizmann wrote in his autobiography. 'I knew that any misstep of mine, any error, however involuntary, would be not mine alone but would redound to the discredit of my people. I was aware of a crushing sense of responsibility.'*

*Speaking without a prepared text, he began his address in slow measured sentences and sought to put before the commission the permanent principles of the Zionist movement and the immediate urgency of the Jewish problem. He spoke for two and a half hours.*

I should like to put before you the Jewish problem as it presents itself today. It is a twofold problem; but its nature can perhaps be expressed in one word: it is the problem of the homelessness of a people. Speaking of homelessness, I should like to state that individual Jews, and individual groups of Jews, may have homes and sometimes very comfortable homes. Indeed, if one thinks of the small communities in the west of Europe beginning with England and continuing further down to the South – France, Switzerland, Italy, Belgium, and Holland – these Jewish communities are, as compared to the Jews in Central, Eastern and South-eastern Europe, in a fairly comfortable position. Then again, the position of the great Jewish community further west in America is, economically, and to a certain extent politically and morally, such that Jews there are free to work and labour without let or hindrance. But if one draws a line and takes the Rhine as the geographical boundary, almost everything to the east of the Rhine is today in a position, politically and economically, which may be described – and I am not given, I think, to exaggeration – as something that is neither life nor death; and one may add that if Europe today were in the same state as it was in 1914 before the War, with the highways and byways of Europe and the world in general open, then we should have witnessed an emigration of Jews that would probably have dwarfed the pre-war emigration – and the pre-war emigration was not by any means small. I think that in the year 1914 alone there emigrated out of Russia, which then included Poland as well, something in the neighbourhood of 120,000 Jews.

They went in the majority of cases to America, where they could readily be absorbed in a highly developed industrial country. The emigrant found his livelihood almost immediately on arrival. This, as

Your Lordship and the members of the Commission are well aware,
cannot happen today. The world is closed; and we have recently
heard it said in authoritative quarters in Geneva, in Poland, and in
England, that there are one million Jews too many in Poland. This is
not the place to enter into a discussion as to why exactly one million
*Jews*? They are citizens of Poland; their fate and their destinies have
been bound up with the fate and destinies of Poland for wellnigh
a thousand years. They passed through all the vicissitudes of the
Polish nation. They desire to make their contribution, good, bad or
indifferent – like everybody else – to Polish development. Why
should they be singled out as being a million too many?

What does it mean? Where can they go? Is there any place in the
world which can rapidly absorb one million people, whoever they
may be, Jews or non-Jews? The poor Polish peasant, perhaps ignorant and not very subtle, when he hears people in authority making a
pronouncement like that, may possibly interpret it as meaning: here
is a superfluous people standing in my way, which must be got rid of
somehow.

I do not want to press the point any further. I shall not waste the
time of the Commission by describing in any way what is happening
in Germany. It is too well known to need elaboration. This accounts
for the position of something like 3,600,000 Jews. Poland has slightly
over three million; Germany had in 1932 or 1933 something like
600,000, but that number has since diminished. If one goes further
afield, and takes the Jewries of Rumania, Latvia, Austria, one sees
practically the same picture, and it is no exaggeration on my part to
say that today almost six million Jews – I am not speaking of the
Jews in Persia and Morocco and such places, who are very inarticu-
late, and of whom one hears very little – there are in this part of the
world six million people pent up in places where they are not wanted,
and for whom the world is divided into places where they cannot
live, and places into which they may not enter.

Now we think this is not merely a problem which concerns the
Jewish community. It is in our view a world problem of considerable
importance. Naturally, it is one which affects primarily the Jewish
community, and secondarily the state of affairs in that particular part

of the world, a part of the world which since the War has moved towards new forms of political and social life, and which is not yet very strong or very mature either politically or economically. These six million people to whom I have referred are condemned to live from hand to mouth, they do not know today what is going to happen tomorrow. I am not speaking now of organized anti-Semitism; even assuming the host-nations were quite friendly, there would still be purely objective reasons in those parts of the world which would tend to grind down the Jewish community and make it into the flotsam and jetsam of the world – grind it into economic dust, so to speak.

Since my early youth, My Lord, I have fought destructive tendencies in Jewry, but it is almost impossible to avoid destructive tendencies amongst a younger generation which lives in the state I have described, unless some hope is given to the young people that one day, some day in some distant future, one in five, one in ten, one in twenty, will find a refuge somewhere where he can work, where he can live, and where he can straighten himself up and look with open eyes at the world and at his fellow men and women. It is no wonder that a certificate for Palestine is considered the highest boon in this part of the world. One in twenty, one in thirty, may get it, and for them it is redemption; it is tantamount to freedom, the opportunity to live and work, and that is why they watch with such intensity all that is going on here, and whether or not the doors of Palestine will remain open or will remain closed.

I could go on dwelling on the tense position in Jewry today, aggravated, as it naturally has been, by the effects of the Great War. This is the moral side of the problem. In all countries we try to do our best, but somehow in many countries we are not entirely accepted as an integral part of the communities to which we belong. This feeling is one of the causes which have prompted Jews throughout the ages, and particularly in the last hundred years, to try to make a contribution towards the solution of the problem and to normalize – to some extent to normalize – the position of the Jews in the world. We are sufficiently strong, My Lord, to have preserved our identity, but an identity which is *sui generis* and not like the identity of other nations.

When one speaks of the English or the French or the German nation, one refers to a definite State, a definite organization, a language, a literature, a history, a common destiny; but it is clear that when one speaks of the Jewish people, one speaks of a people which is a minority everywhere, a majority nowhere, which is to some extent identified with the races among which it lives, but still not quite identical. It is, if I may say so, a disembodied ghost of a race, without a body, and it therefore inspires suspicion, and suspicion breeds hatred. There should be one place in the world, in God's wide world, where we could live and express ourselves in accordance with our character, and make our contribution towards the civilized world, in our own way and through our own channels. Perhaps if we had, we would be better understood in ourselves, and our relation to other races and nations would become more normal. We would not have to be always on the defensive or, on the contrary, become too aggressive, as always happened with a minority forced to be constantly on the defensive.

What has produced this particular mentality of the Jews which makes me describe the Jewish race as a sort of disembodied ghost – an entity and yet not an entity in accordance with the usual standards which are applied to define an entity? I believe the main cause which has produced the particular state of Jewry in the world is its attachment to Palestine. We are a stiff-necked people and a people of long memory. We never forget. Whether it is our misfortune or whether it is our good fortune, we have never forgotten Palestine, and this steadfastness, which has preserved the Jew throughout the ages and throughout a career that is almost one long chain of inhuman suffering, is primarily due to some physiological or psychological attachment to Palestine. We have never forgotten it nor given it up. We have survived our Babylonian and Roman conquerors. The Jews put up a fairly severe fight, and the Roman Empire, which digested half of the civilized world, did not digest small Judaea. Whenever they once got a chance, the slightest chance, there the Jews returned, there they created their literature, their villages, towns, and communities. If the Commission would take the trouble to study the post-Roman period of the Jews and the life of the Jews in Palestine, they would find that during the nineteen centuries which have passed since the destruction of Palestine as a Jewish political entity, there was not a single century in which the Jews did not attempt to come back.

It is, I believe, a fallacy to regard those 1,900 years as, so to say, a desert of time; they were not. When the material props of the Jewish commonwealth were destroyed, the Jews carried Palestine in their hearts and in their heads wherever they went. That idea continued to express itself in their ritual and in their prayers. In the East End of London the Jew still prays for dew in the summer and for rain in the winter, and his seasons and festivals are all Palestinian seasons and Palestinian festivals. When Rome destroyed their country, the intellectual leader of the Jewish community came to the Roman commander and said, 'You have destroyed all our material possessions; give us, I pray, some refuge for our houses of learning.' A refuge was found; the place still exists; it was then a big place, and is now a tiny railway station by the name of Yebna – in Hebrew, *Yabneh*. There were schools there, and there the Jews continued their intellectual output, so that those schools became, so to speak, the spiritual homes, not only of Palestinian Jewry, but of Jewry at large, which was gradually filtering out of Palestine and dispersing all over the world. They replaced the material Palestine, the political Palestine, by a moral Palestine which was indestructible, which remained indestructible; and this yearning found its expression in a mass of literature, sacred and non-sacred, secular and religious.

The Balfour Declaration was issued by His Majesty's Government on 2 November 1917.

It has sometimes glibly been said, 'Here is a document, somewhat vague in its nature, issued in time of war. It was a wartime expedient.' I have a much higher opinion of British statesmen than to attribute to them an act of that kind. It was a solemn act, a promise given to a people, an ancient people, which finds itself in the position which I have described.

What did the Balfour Declaration mean? It meant something quite simple at that time, and I am saying so advisedly. It meant that Judaea was restored to the Jews or the Jews were restored to Judaea. I could submit to the Commission a series of utterances of responsible statesmen and men in every walk of life in England to show that this Declaration was at the time regarded as the Magna Carta of the Jewish people; it was in a sense comparable with another Declaration made thousands of years before, when Cyrus allowed a remnant of the Jews to return from Babylon and to rebuild the Temple. To the ordinary man at that time reading the Declaration, what it meant is broadly indicated by the various speeches at a solemn meeting at the Opera House in London, where (among others) Lord Cecil spoke and said: 'Arabia for the Arabs, Judaea for the Jews, Armenia for the Armenians.' Much water and much blood have flowed under the various bridges of the world since that time, and not all of his predictions have been realized; but we read into the Declaration what the statesmen of Great Britain told us it meant. It meant a National Home, 'national' meaning that we should be able to live like a nation in Palestine, and 'Home' a place where we might live as free men in contradistinction to living on sufferance everywhere else. To English people I need not explain what the word 'home' means, or what it does *not* mean, to us everywhere else.

The meaning is clear, and the Jewry of the world, in the trenches of Europe, in the pogrom-swept area of Russia, saw it like that. Tens of thousands of Jews marched before the house of the British Consul at Odessa at the time. Behind them were half-organized bands of marauders and murderers sweeping the countryside and destroying everything in their wake. But those Jews poured out their hearts in gratitude to the one accessible representative of the British Government, whom they had never seen, of whom they had never heard, whose language they could not speak, whose mentality they could not understand. They felt that here something had been done for us which, after two thousand years of hope and yearning, would at last give us a resting-place in this terrible world.

*The Peel Report recommended partition into separate Arab and Jewish states, a drastic solution that was rejected by the Arabs and most Zionists (but accepted by Weizmann). It was never implemented by the British government. The six million Jews for whom Weizmann spoke were exterminated by the Nazis, Israel was established as a Jewish state in Palestine in 1946 and Weizmann was elected president.*

•

EDWARD VIII
London, 10 December 1936

*'I have determined to renounce the Throne'*

*Edward VIII (1894–1972) succeeded George V as king on 20 January. Within a year and without being crowned, he abdicated rather than give up the woman he loved, Mrs Wallis Simpson, whose divorce had gone through three weeks earlier. A morganatic marriage, denying Mrs Simpson the title of queen but allowing the king to remain on the throne, was considered but rejected by Stanley Baldwin and his government. Given the choice between his throne and Mrs Simpson, the king abdicated, renouncing the throne for himself and his descendants in a personally signed message to Parliament.*

After long and anxious consideration, I have determined to renounce the Throne to which I succeeded on the death of My father, and I am now communicating this, My final and irrevocable decision. Realizing as I do the gravity of this step, I can only hope that I shall have the understanding of My peoples in the decision I have taken and the reasons which have led Me to take it. I will not enter now into My private feelings, but I would beg that it should be remembered that the burden which constantly rests upon the shoulders of a Sovereign is so heavy that it can only be borne in circumstances different from those in which I now find Myself. I conceive that I am not overlooking the duty that rests on Me to place in the forefront the public interest, when I declare that I am conscious that I can no longer discharge this heavy task with efficiency or with satisfaction to Myself.

I have accordingly this morning executed an Instrument of Abdication in the terms following:

'I, Edward VIII, of Great Britain, Ireland and the British Dominions beyond the Seas, King, Emperor of India, do hereby declare My irrevocable determination to renounce the Throne for Myself and for My descendants, and My desire that effect should be given to this Instrument of Abdication immediately.

'In token whereof I have hereunto set My hand this tenth day of December, nineteen hundred and thirty-six, in the presence of the witnesses whose signatures are subscribed.

(Signed) EDWARD RI'

My execution of this Instrument has been witnessed by My three brothers, Their Royal Highnesses the Duke of York, the Duke of Gloucester and the Duke of Kent.

I deeply appreciate the spirit which has actuated the appeals which have been made to Me to take a different decision, and I have, before reaching My final determination, most fully pondered over them. But My mind is made up. Moreover, further delay cannot but be most injurious to the peoples whom I have tried to serve as Prince of Wales and as King and whose future happiness and prosperity are the constant wish of My heart.

I take My leave of them in the confident hope that the course which I have thought it right to follow is that which is best for the stability of the Throne and Empire and the happiness of My peoples. I am deeply sensible of the consideration which they have always extended to Me both before and after My accession to the Throne and which I knew they will extend in full measure to My successor.

I am most anxious that there should be no delay of any kind in giving effect to the Instrument which I have executed and that all necessary steps should be taken immediately to secure that My lawful successor, My brother, His Royal Highness the Duke of York, should ascend the Throne.

EDWARD RI

## STANLEY BALDWIN
### London, 10 December 1936

*'The House today is a theatre which is being watched by the whole world'*

*King Edward VIII signed his instrument of abdication on the morning of 10 December. Afterwards Baldwin went to see Queen Mary, the king's mother, and then lunched at 10 Downing Street with his wife. He wrote his speech for the Commons himself, sitting alone, on small scraps of paper. Then he left them behind and they had to be fetched for him. After all that he began by dropping them and spoke extempore from notes that appeared to be in alarming disarray.*

*'To a quiet attentive House of Commons he made one of his greatest speeches, lasting just under an hour,' say his biographers Keith Middlemas and John Barnes, 'a triumph of art that concealed art, that gave the King the most favourable interpretation . . . and which lifted the crisis at last from rumour and scandal on to the high dramatic plane where it has since largely remained.'*

The House must remember – it is difficult to realize – that His Majesty is not a boy, although he looks so young. We have all thought of him as our Prince, but he is a mature man, with wide and great experience of life and the world, and he always had before him three, nay, four, things, which in these conversations at all hours, he repeated again and again – That if he went he would go with dignity. He would not allow a situation to arise in which he could not do that. He wanted to go with as little disturbance of his Ministers and his people as possible. He wished to go in circumstances that would make the succession of his brother as little difficult for his brother as possible; and I may say that any idea to him of what might be called a King's party, was abhorrent. He stayed down at Fort Belvedere because he said that he was not coming to London while these things were in dispute, because of the cheering crowds. I honour and respect him for the way in which he behaved at that time.

I have something here which, I think, will touch the House. It is a pencilled note, sent to me by His Majesty this morning, and I have his authority for reading it. It is just scribbled in pencil:

> Duke of York. He and the King have always been on the best of terms as brothers and the King is confident that the Duke deserves and will receive the support of the whole Empire.

I would say a word or two on the King's position. The King cannot speak for himself. The King has told us that he cannot carry, and does not see his way to carry, these almost intolerable burdens of Kingship without a woman at his side, and we know that. This crisis, if I may use the word, has arisen now rather than later from that very frankness of His Majesty's character which is one of his many attractions. It would have been perfectly possible for His Majesty not to have told me of this at the date when he did, and not to have told me for some months to come. But he realized the damage that might be done in the interval by gossip, rumours and talk, and he made that declaration to me when he did, on purpose to avoid what he felt might be dangerous, not only here but throughout the Empire, to the moral force of the Crown which we are all determined to sustain.

He told me his intentions, and he has never wavered from them. I want the House to understand that. He felt it his duty to take into his anxious consideration all the representations that his advisers might give him and not until he had fully considered them did he make public his decision. There has been no kind of conflict in this matter. My efforts during these last days have been directed, as have the efforts of those most closely round him, in trying to help him to make the choice which he has not made; and we have failed. The King has made his decision to take this moment to send this Gracious Message because of his confident hope that by that he will preserve the unity of this country and of the whole Empire, and avoid those factious differences which might so easily have arisen.

It is impossible, unfortunately, to avoid talking to some extent today about oneself. These last days have been days of great strain, but it was a great comfort to me, and I hope it will be to the House, when I was assured before I left him on Tuesday night, by that intimate circle that was with him at the Fort that evening, that I had left nothing undone that I could have done to move him from the decision at which he had arrived, and which he has communicated to us. While there is not a soul among us who will not regret this from the bottom of his heart, there is not a soul here today that wants to judge. We are not judges. He has announced his decision. He has told us what he wants us to do, and I think we must close our ranks, and do it . . .

This House today is a theatre which is being watched by the whole world. Let us conduct ourselves with that dignity which His Majesty is showing in this hour of his trial. Whatever our regret at the contents of the Message, let us fulfil his wish, do what he asks, and do it with speed. Let no word be spoken today that the utterer of that word may regret in days to come, let no word be spoken that causes pain to any soul, and let us not forget today the revered and beloved figure of Queen Mary, what all this time has meant to her, and think of her when we have to speak, if speak we must, during this Debate. We have, after all, as the guardians of democracy in this little island to see that we do our work to maintain the integrity of that democracy and of the monarchy, which, as I said at the beginning of my speech, is now the sole link of our whole Empire and the guardian of our freedom. Let us look forward and remember our country and the trust reposed by our country in this, the House of Commons, and let us rally behind the new King – (*Hon. Members: 'Hear, hear'*) – stand behind him, and help him; and let us hope that, whatever the country may have suffered by what we are passing through, it may soon be repaired and that we may take what steps we can in trying to make this country a better country for all the people in it.

*Baldwin retired six months later and played no further part in public life – but his speech on the abdication crowned his political career with adulation.*

•

## EDWARD VIII
### Windsor, 11 December 1936

#### 'God Save the King'

*Seated alone in Windsor Castle, a few miles outside London, after Baldwin's speech to the Commons, the former king broadcast to the nation. It was a poignant moment for both the nation and the king, embroiled in one of the great love stories of the century.*

*A few brushstrokes were added to the speech by Winston Churchill, who had been one of the king's few supporters in the Commons. The sentence which speaks of the 'matchless blessing' of a happy home shows the Churchill touch.*

At long last I am able to say a few words of my own. I have never wanted to withhold anything, but until now it has not been constitutionally possible for me to speak.

A few hours ago I discharged my last duty as King and Emperor, and now that I have been succeeded by my brother, the Duke of York, my first words must be to declare my allegiance to him. This I do with all my heart.

You all know the reasons which have impelled me to renounce the Throne. But I want you to understand that in making up my mind I did not forget the country or the Empire which as Prince of Wales, and lately as King, I have for twenty-five years tried to serve. But you must believe me when I tell you that I have found it impossible to carry the heavy burden of responsibility and to discharge my duties as King as I would wish to do without the help and support of the woman I love.

And I want you to know that the decision I have made has been mine and mine alone. This was a thing I had to judge entirely for myself. The other person most nearly concerned has tried up to the last to persuade me to take a different course. I have made this, the most serious decision of my life, only upon the single thought of what would in the end be best for all.

This decision has been made less difficult to me by the sure knowledge that my Brother, with his long training in the public affairs of this country and with his fine qualities, will be able to take my place forthwith, without interruption or injury to the life and progress of the Empire. And he has one matchless blessing, enjoyed by so many of you and not bestowed on me – a happy home with his wife and children.

During these hard days I have been comforted by Her Majesty my Mother and by my Family. The Ministers of the Crown, and in particular Mr Baldwin, the Prime Minister, have always treated me with full consideration. There has never been any constitutional difference between me and them and between me and Parliament. Bred in the constitutional tradition by my Father, I should never have allowed any such issue to arise.

Ever since I was Prince of Wales, and later on when I occupied the Throne, I have been treated with the greatest kindness by all classes of the people, wherever I have lived or journeyed throughout the Empire. For that I am very grateful.

I now quit altogether public affairs, and I lay down my burden. It may be some time before I return to my native land, but I shall always follow the fortunes of the British race and Empire with profound interest, and if at any time in the future I can be found of service to His Majesty in a private station I shall not fail.

And now we all have a new King. I wish him, and you, his people, happiness and prosperity with all my heart. God bless you all. God Save the King.

*After his abdication, Edward VIII was created Duke of Windsor by his successor George VI, his brother. He married Mrs Simpson on 3 June 1937, was governor of the Bahamas during the Second World War, and lived in exile for the rest of his life, mostly in Paris.*

•

## LEON TROTSKY
### New York, 9 February 1937

*'I stake my life'*

*Ousted from power and then exiled by Stalin, Trotsky by 1937 had been living in Mexico for a year. The Moscow show trials initiated by Stalin after the assassination of Kirov, the party boss in Leningrad, had started in 1936 with Trotsky chosen to play the part of chief defendant* in absentia.

*Stalin's aim was to link Trotsky and alleged Trotskyite conspirators such as Bukharin, Rykov, Zinoviev, Kamenev, Radek and Piatakov (all of them old Bolsheviks) to the different types of opposition, terror, counter-revolution, wrecking, espionage and treason in the Soviet Union and to destroy any potential opposition. The state prosecutor was Andrei Vyshinsky.*

*More than six thousand people had gathered in the New York Hippodrome, on 9 February 1937, at a mass meeting called by the American Committee for the Defence of Leon Trotsky to hear him speak in his own cause. Arrangements had been made for the speech to be transmitted from Mexico direct to the hall. The meeting was to have been Trotsky's first opportunity of speaking directly to a large audience in defence of the accused in the Moscow trials.*

*For reasons which are still unknown the speech could not be heard – but it was a passionate, eloquent and prophetic denunciation of Stalin.*

Dear Listeners, Comrades, and Friends: Why does Moscow so fear the voice of a single man? Only because I know the truth, the whole truth. Only because I have nothing to hide. Only because I am ready to appear before a public and impartial commission of inquiry with documents, facts, and testimonies in my hands, and to disclose the truth to the very end. I declare: if this commission decides that I am guilty in the slightest degree of the crimes which Stalin imputes to me, I pledge in advance to place myself voluntarily in the hands of the executioners of the GPU. That, I hope, is clear. Have you all heard? I make this declaration before the entire world. I ask the Press to publish my words in the farthest corners of our planet. But if the commission establishes – do you hear me? – that the Moscow trials are a conscious and premeditated frame-up, constructed with the bones and nerves of human beings, I will not ask my accusers to place themselves voluntarily before a firing-squad. No, the eternal disgrace in the memory of human generations will be sufficient for them! Do the accusers of the Kremlin hear me? I throw my defiance in their faces. And I await their reply!

At the heart of the Moscow trials is an absurdity. According to the official version, the Trotskyists had been organizing the most monstrous plot since 1931. However, all of them, as if by command, spoke and wrote in one way but acted in another. In spite of the hundreds of persons implicated in the plot, over a period of five years, not a trace of it was revealed: no splits, no denunciations, no confiscated letters, until the hour of the general confessions arrived! Then a new miracle came to pass. People who had organized assassinations, prepared war, divided the Soviet Union, these hardened criminals suddenly confessed in August 1936 not under the pressure of proofs – no, because there were no proofs – but for certain mysterious reasons, which hypocritical psychologists declare are peculiar attributes of the 'Russian soul'. Just think: yesterday they carried out railroad wrecking and poisoning of workers – by unseen order of Trotsky. Today they are Trotsky's accusers and heap upon him their pseudo-crimes. Yesterday they dreamed only of killing Stalin. Today they all sing hymns of praise to him. What is it: a madhouse? No, they tell us, it is not a madhouse, but the 'Russian soul'. You lie, gentlemen, about the Russian soul. You lie about the human soul in general.

The miracle consists not only in the simultaneity and the universality of the confessions. The miracle, above all, is that, according to the general confessions, the conspirators did something which was fatal precisely to their own political interests, but extremely useful to the leading clique. Once more the conspirators before the tribunal said just what the most servile agents of Stalin would have said. Normal people, following the dictates of their own will, would never have been able to conduct themselves as Zinoviev, Kamenev, Radek, Piatakov, and the others did. Devotion to their ideas, political dignity, the simple instinct of self-preservation would force them to struggle for themselves, for their personalities, for their interests, for their lives. The only reasonable and fitting question is this: Who led these people into a state in which all human reflexes are destroyed, and how did he do it? There is a very simple principle in jurisprudence, which holds the key to many secrets: *is fecit cui prodest*; he who benefits by it, he is the guilty one. The entire conduct of the accused has been dictated from beginning to end, not by their own ideas and interests, but by the interests of the ruling clique. And the pseudo-plot, and the confessions, the theatrical judgement and the entirely real executions, all were arranged by one and the same hand. Whose? *Cui prodest?* Who benefits? The hand of Stalin! The rest is deceit, falsehood, the idle babbling about the 'Russian soul'! In the trials there did not figure fighters, nor conspirators, but puppets in the hands of the GPU. They played assigned roles. The aim of the disgraceful performance: to eliminate the whole opposition, to poison the very source of critical thought, to definitely ensconce the totalitarian regime of Stalin.

We repeat: the accusation is a premeditated frame-up. This frame-up must inevitably appear in each of the defendants' confessions, if they are examined alongside the facts. The prosecutor Vyshinsky knows this very well. That is why he did not address a single concrete question to the accused, which would have embarrassed them considerably. The names, documents, dates, places, means of transportation, circumstances of the meetings – around these decisive facts Vyshinsky has placed a cloak of shame, or to be more exact, a shameless cloak. Vyshinsky dealt with the accused, not in the language of the jurist, but in the conventional language of the past-master of frame-up, in the jargon of the thief. The insinuating character of Vyshinsky's questions – along with the complete absence of material proofs – this represents the second crushing evidence against Stalin.

Among you, dear listeners, there must be not a few people who freely say: 'The confessions of the accused are false, that is clear; but how was Stalin able to obtain such confessions; therein lies the secret!' In reality the secret is not so profound. The Inquisition, with a much more simple technique, extorted all sorts of confessions from its victims. That is why the democratic penal law renounced the methods of the Middle Ages, because they led not to the establishment of the truth, but to a simple confirmation of the accusations dictated by the inquiring judge. The GPU trials have a thoroughly inquisitorial character: that is the simple secret of the confessions! . . .

Let him who has a particle of imagination picture to himself an unfortunate Soviet citizen, an oppositionist, isolated and persecuted, a pariah, who is constrained to write, not telegrams of salutation to Stalin, but dozens and scores of confessions of his crimes. Perhaps in this world there are many heroes who are capable of bearing all kinds of tortures, physical or moral, which are inflicted on themselves, their wives, their children. I do not know . . . My personal observations inform me that the capacities of the human nervous system are limited. Through the GPU Stalin can trap his victim in an abyss of black despair, humiliation, infamy, in such a manner that he takes upon himself the most monstrous crimes with the prospect of imminent death or a feeble ray of hope for the future as the sole outcome. If, indeed, he does not contemplate suicide.

Suicide or moral prostration: there is no other choice! But do not forget that in the prisons of the GPU even suicide is often an inaccessible luxury!

The Moscow trials do not dishonour the revolution, because they are the progeny of reaction. The Moscow trials do not dishonour the old generation of Bolsheviks; they only demonstrate that even Bolsheviks are made of flesh and blood, and that they do not resist endlessly when over their heads swings the pendulum of death. The Moscow trials dishonour the political regime which has conceived them: the regime of Bonapartism, without honour and without conscience! All of the executed died with curses on their lips for this regime.

The Moscow trials are a signal. Woe to them who do not heed! The Reichstag trial surely had a great importance. But it concerned only vile Fascism, this embodiment of all the vices of darkness and barbarism. The Moscow trials are perpetrated under the banner of socialism. We will not concede this banner to the masters of falsehood! If our generation happens to be too weak to establish socialism over the earth, we will hand the spotless banner down to our children. The struggle which is in the offing transcends by far the importance of individuals, factions, and parties. It is a struggle for the future of all mankind. It will be severe. It will be lengthy. Whoever seeks physical comfort and spiritual calm, let him step aside. In time of reaction it is more convenient to lean on the bureaucracy than on the truth. But all those for whom the word socialism is not a hollow sound but the content of their moral life – forward! Neither threats nor persecutions nor violations can stop us! Be it even over our bleaching bones, the truth will triumph! We will blaze the trail for it. It will conquer! Under all the severe blows of fate, I shall be happy, as in the best days of my youth, if together with you I can contribute to its victory! Because, my friends, the highest human happiness is not the exploitation of the present but the cooperation of the future.

*The show trials went on, culminating in the trial of Bukharin and Rykov in 1938. On a single day in December 1938 Stalin sanctioned the execution of 3,167 prisoners. On 20 August 1940, Trotsky was battered to death in his Mexican home by one of Stalin's agents.*

•

## MARTIN NIEMÖLLER
### Berlin-Dahlem, 27 June 1937

### 'The oppression is growing'

*As Martin Niemöller (1892–1984) celebrated Holy Communion on Friday, 25 June 1937, he was incensed to discover that three members of the Gestapo were present. He had also heard that Hans Asmussen, theological adviser to the council of the German church, had gone into hiding from the Nazis.*

*On the following Sunday, the subject of Niemöller's sermon was Rabbi Gamaliel who, according to Acts 5, had persuaded the Jewish Sanhedrin to show tolerance to the teaching of St Peter and his fellow Christians. The result was that the apostles were released from custody. Neutrality was impossible, Niemöller preached. Persecution had begun.*

(The Lord shall yet comfort Zion) Acts 5: 33–42:
Jesus Christ says: 'Blessed are ye when men shall revile you and persecute you for My sake.' And faith hears that, and faith clings to that promise, and faith is happy and comforted, as Jesus bade it: 'Rejoice and be exceeding glad!'

But, brothers and sisters, can this *really* be so? Can we be happy and comforted in our faith? We see today that this matter of a happy and comforted faith is no child's play, that it is not enough to be able to quote passages from the Bible; that we do not go far with a little inspired protestation and our usual normal measure of inextinguishable optimism, and that we have reached the point where we cannot resist alone, without help.

The oppression is growing, and anyone who has had to submit to the Tempter's machine-gun fire during this last week thinks differently from what he did even three weeks ago. I have in mind how on Wednesday the Secret Police forced their way into the locked church at Friedrichwerder and in the vestry arrested eight members of the Reich Council of Brethren who were holding a meeting there, and took them away. I have in mind how yesterday at Saarbrücken six women and a male member of the congregation were taken into custody because they were distributing an election leaflet of the Confessional Church, at the request of the Council of Brethren. I say to you: anyone who knows these things and who has actually had to suffer these things, is not far from uttering the Prophet's words – indeed such a one would fain say with the Prophet: 'It is enough – no, it is too much! – now, O Lord, take away my life!'

And anyone who has the experience I had the night before last at an evening Communion service and sees beside him nothing less than three young members of the Secret Police who have come in their official capacity to spy upon the community of Jesus Christ in their praying, singing and preaching – three young men who were also assuredly baptized once upon a time in the name of the Lord Jesus Christ and who also assuredly vowed loyalty to their Saviour at the confirmation altar, and whose office and duty it now is to set traps for the community of Jesus Christ – anyone who sees that cannot escape so easily from the shame of the Church; he cannot pass the matter off with a pious phrase and an inspired protest: such a sight may cost him a sleepless and most certainly a restless night, and he may even cry from the depths of his despair: 'Lord, have mercy upon me!'

*Niemöller never again preached in Dahlem church until after the death of Adolf Hitler. On 1 July, he was arrested by the secret police. A year later he was taken to Sachsenhausen Concentration Camp, and then to Dachau. He spent four years in solitary confinement before being liberated by the Allies in 1945.*

•

## ADOLF HITLER
### Berlin, 26 September 1938

*'My patience is now at an end'*

*Among all the millions of words of twentieth-century oratory, none are more chilling than the seven that Hitler uttered at the Berlin Sportspalast in September 1938: 'My patience is now at an end.'*

*The British prime minister Neville Chamberlain had visited Hitler twice in the previous ten days but had been snubbed, even after offering a plan agreed by Britain and France and accepted by the Czechs – but later repudiated by the British Cabinet – for the Sudeten districts of Czechoslovakia to be transferred to Germany without a plebiscite.*

*Chamberlain refused to give up hope and dispatched Sir Horace Wilson to Germany with a personal appeal to Hitler suggesting direct negotiations between the German and Czech governments, with the British present as a third party, in the hope of persuading him to moderate the tone of the speech he was due to make in the Sportspalast.*

*When Wilson arrived three hours before the speech was due, Hitler was in his most intransigent mood, working his resentment, hatred and opposition up to the pitch where they would provide the necessary stimulus for his speech.*

*Three hours later, Chamberlain and Beneš, the Czech president, got their answer.*

And now before us stands the last problem that must be solved and will be solved. It is the last territorial claim which I have to make in Europe, but it is the claim from which I will not recede and which, God willing, I will make good.

The history of the problem is as follows: in 1918 under the watchword 'The Right of the Peoples to Self-determination' Central Europe was torn in pieces and was newly formed by certain crazy so-called 'statesmen'. Without regard for the origin of the peoples, without regard for either their wish as nations or for economic necessities Central Europe at that time was broken up into atoms and new so-called States were arbitrarily formed. To this procedure Czechoslovakia owes its existence. This Czech State began with a single lie and the father of this lie was named Beneš. This Mr Beneš at that time appeared in Versailles and he first of all gave the assurance that there was a Czechoslovak nation. He was forced to invent this lie in order to give to the slender number of his own fellow-countrymen a somewhat greater range and thus a fuller justification. And the Anglo-Saxon statesmen, who were, as always, not very adequately versed in respect of questions of geography or nationality, did not at that time find it necessary to test these assertions of Mr Beneš. Had they done so, they could have established the fact that there is no such thing as a Czechoslovak nation but only Czechs and Slovaks and that the Slovaks did not wish to have anything to do with the Czechs but . . . *(the rest of the sentence was drowned in a tumultuous outburst of applause)*.

So in the end through Mr Beneš these Czechs annexed Slovakia. Since this State did not seem fitted to live, out of hand three and a half million Germans were taken in violation of their right to self-determination and their wish for self-determination. Since even that did not suffice, over a million Magyars had to be added, then some Carpathian Russians, and at last several hundred thousand Poles.

That is this State which then later proceeded to call itself Czechoslovakia—in violation of the right of the peoples to self-determination, in violation of the clear wish and will of the nations to which this violence had been done . . .

Now the shameless part of this story begins. This State whose Government is in the hands of a minority compels the other nationalities to cooperate in a policy which will oblige them one of these days to shoot at their own brothers. Mr Beneš demands of the German: 'If I wage war against Germany, then you have to shoot against the Germans. And if you refuse to do this, you are a traitor against the State and I will have you yourself shot.' And he makes the same demand of Hungary and Poland. He demands of the Slovaks that they should support aims to which the Slovak people are completely indifferent. For the Slovak people wishes to have peace – and not adventures. Mr Beneš thus actually turns these folk either into traitors to their country or traitors to their people. Either they betray their people, are ready to fire on their fellow-countrymen, or Mr Beneš says: 'You are traitors to your country and you will be shot for that by me.' Can there be anything more shameless than to compel folk of another people, in certain circumstances, to fire on their own fellow-countrymen only because a ruinous, evil, and criminal Government so demands it? I can here assert: when we had occupied Austria, my first order was: no Czech needs to serve, rather he must not serve, in the German Army. I have not driven him to a conflict with his conscience . . .

Mr Beneš now places his hopes on the world! And he and his diplomats make no secret of the fact. They state: it is our hope that Chamberlain will be overthrown, that Daladier will be removed, that on every hand revolutions are on the way. They place their hope on Soviet Russia. He still thinks then that he will be able to evade the fulfilment of his obligations.

And then I can say only one thing: now two men stand arrayed one against the other: there is Mr Beneš and here stand I. We are two men of a different make-up. In the great struggle of the peoples while Mr Beneš was sneaking about through the world, I as a decent German soldier did my duty. And now today I stand over against this man as the soldier of my people!

I have only a few statements still to make: I am grateful to Mr Chamberlain for all his efforts. I have assured him that the German people desires nothing else than peace, but I have also told him that I cannot go back behind the limits set to our patience. I have further assured him, and I repeat it here, that when this problem is solved there is for Germany no further territorial problem in Europe. And I have further assured him that at the moment when Czechoslovakia solves her problems, that means when the Czechs have come to terms with their other minorities, and that peaceably and not through oppression, then I have no further interest in the Czech State. And that is guaranteed to him! We want no Czechs!

But in the same way I desire to state before the German people that with regard to the problem of the Sudeten Germans my patience is now at an end! I have made Mr Beneš an offer which is nothing but the carrying into effect of what he himself has promised. The decision now lies in his hands: Peace or War! He will either accept this offer and now at last give to the Germans their freedom or we will go and fetch this freedom for ourselves. The world must take note that in four and a half years of war and through the long years of my political life there is one thing which no one could ever cast in my teeth: I have never been a coward!

Now I go before my people as its first soldier and behind me – that the world should know – there marches a people and a different people from that of 1918!

If at that time a wandering scholar was able to inject into our people the poison of democratic catchwords – the people of today is no longer the people that it was then. Such catchwords are for us like wasp-stings: they cannot hurt us: we are now immune.

In this hour the whole German people will unite with me! It will feel my will to be its will. Just as in my eyes it is its future and its fate which give me the commission for my action.

And we wish now to make our will as strong as it was in the time of our fight, the time when I, as a simple unknown soldier, went forth to conquer a Reich and never doubted of success and final victory.

Then there gathered close about me a band of brave men and brave women, and they went with me. And so I ask you my German people to take your stand behind me, man by man, and woman by woman.

In this hour we all wish to form a common will and that will must be stronger than every hardship and every danger.

And if this will is stronger than hardship and danger then one day it will break down hardship and danger.

We are determined!

Now let Mr Beneš make his choice!

*Alan Bullock, the distinguished Hitler biographer, describes this speech as a masterpiece of invective which even Hitler never surpassed. Rarely, he said, had the issue of war or peace been so nakedly reduced to the personal resentment and vanity of one man.*

*Chamberlain tried yet again. Three days later a settlement of the crisis was reached in Munich by the heads of government of Germany, Britain, France and Italy (Hitler, Chamberlain, Daladier and Mussolini) and the Sudetenland was annexed to Germany.*

*On 1 October German troops marched into the Sudetenland. The Second World War started on 3 September the following year.*

•

## NEVILLE CHAMBERLAIN
### London, 30 September 1938

#### *'Peace for our time'*

*If Hitler's declaration that his patience was at an end was the most ominous sentence of the century, Neville Chamberlain's belief that he had won peace from Hitler was the most complacent. After conferring with Hitler, Mussolini and Daladier, Chamberlain (1869–1940), British prime minister since May 1937, had signed the Munich Pact and returned to London a hero.*

*He addressed the cheering crowd from a first-floor window at 10 Downing Street.*

My good friends, this is the second time in our history that there has come back from Germany to Downing Street peace with honour. (*After the cheering stopped, Chamberlain continued.*) I believe it is peace for our time. We thank you from the bottom of our hearts. (*To this the crowd responded: 'We thank you. God bless you.' Then a pause until Chamberlain said:*) And now I recommend you to go home and sleep quietly in your beds.

·

DUFF COOPER
London, 3 October 1938

'My head erect'

*Duff Cooper (1890–1954) entered parliament as a Conservative in 1924 and was Secretary for War from 1935 to 1937, when he became First Lord of the Admiralty. When the House of Commons met after the Munich agreement Conservatives rose and cheered when Chamberlain entered the chamber. He also had the tacit support of the Labour benches.*

*In his memoir* Old Men Forget, *Cooper recalled that members were anxious to hear Chamberlain: 'As I had to speak first, I had an unsympathetic and impatient audience.'*

*As he explained the reasons for his dramatic resignation – Sir Anthony Eden, Chamberlain's Foreign Secretary, had resigned earlier over the Italian invasion of Abyssinia – he said Britain should have been fighting to prevent one great power from dominating the continent of Europe by 'brute force', in defiance of treaty obligations, of the laws of nations and the decrees of morality.*

When Herr Hitler broke the Treaty of Versailles he undertook to keep the Treaty of Locarno, and when he broke the Treaty of Locarno, he undertook not to interfere further or to have any territorial aims in Europe. When he entered Austria by force he authorized his henchmen to give an authoritative assurance that he would not interfere with Czechoslovakia. That was less than six months ago. Still the Prime Minister believes that he can rely upon 'the good faith of Hitler' . . .

The Prime Minister may be right. I can assure you, Mr Speaker, with the deepest sincerity, that I hope and pray that he is right, but I cannot believe what he believes. I wish I could. Therefore, I can be of no assistance to him in his Government. I should only be a hindrance, and it is much better that I should go. I remember when we were discussing the Godesberg ultimatum that I said that if I were a party to persuading, or even to suggesting to, the Czechoslovak Government that they should accept that ultimatum, I should never be able to hold up my head again. I have forfeited a great deal. I have given up an office that I loved, work in which I was deeply interested and a staff of which any man might be proud. I have given up association in that work with my colleagues with whom I have maintained for many years the most harmonious relations, not only as colleagues but as friends. I have given up the privilege of serving as lieutenant to a leader whom I still regard with the deepest admiration and affection. I have ruined, perhaps, my political career. But that is a little matter; I have retained something which is to me of greater value – I can still walk about the world with my head erect.

*Chamberlain made no attempt to answer Cooper, who had immediate notes of congratulation from Winston Churchill and Harold Macmillan. 'Your speech . . . was admirable in form, massive in argument and shone with courage and public spirit,' said Churchill. Cooper, who became the first Viscount Norwich, was Churchill's Minister of Information (1940–42) and ambassador to France (1944–7).*

•

## WINSTON CHURCHILL
### London, 5 October 1938

### 'A total and unmitigated defeat'

*The Munich debate went on for four days, though Chamberlain's majority was never in doubt. After Cooper, several powerful speeches lamenting British humiliation and weakness were made by prominent Conservatives, including Anthony Eden.*

*Speaking on the third day, Churchill pronounced the most damning indictment of Chamberlain's policies.*

When I think of the fair hopes of a long peace which still lay before Europe at the beginning of 1933 when Herr Hitler first obtained power, and of all the opportunities of arresting the growth of the Nazi power which have been thrown away, when I think of the immense combinations and resources which have been neglected or squandered, I cannot believe that a parallel exists in the whole course of history. So far as this country is concerned the responsibility must rest with those who have had the undisputed control of our political affairs. They neither prevented Germany from rearming, nor did they rearm ourselves in time. They quarrelled with Italy without saving Ethiopia. They exploited and discredited the vast institution of the League of Nations and they neglected to make alliances and combinations which might have repaired previous errors, and thus they left us in the hour of trial without adequate national defence or effective international security . . .

Many people, no doubt, honestly believe that they are only giving away the interests of Czechoslovakia, whereas I fear we shall find that we have deeply compromised, and perhaps fatally endangered, the safety and even the independence of Great Britain and France. This is not merely a question of giving up the German colonies, as I am sure we shall be asked to do. Nor is it a question only of losing influence in Europe. It goes far deeper than that. You have to consider the character of the Nazi movement and the rule which it implies. The Prime Minister desires to see cordial relations between this country and Germany. There is no difficulty at all in having cordial relations between the peoples. Our hearts go out to them. But they have no power. But never will you have friendship with the present German government. You must have diplomatic and correct relations, but there can never be friendship between the British democracy and the Nazi power, that power which spurns Christian ethics, which cheers its onward course by a barbarous paganism, which vaunts the spirit of aggression and conquest, which derives strength and perverted pleasure from persecution, and uses, as we have seen, with pitiless brutality the threat of murderous force. That power cannot ever be the trusted friend of the British democracy.

What I find unendurable is the sense of our country falling into the power, into the orbit and influence of Nazi Germany, and of our existence becoming dependent upon their good will or pleasure. It is to prevent that that I have tried my best to urge the maintenance of every bulwark of defence – first, the timely creation of an Air Force superior to anything within striking distance of our shores; secondly, the gathering together of the collective strength of many nations; and thirdly, the making of alliances and military conventions, all within the Covenant, in order to gather together forces at any rate to restrain the onward movement of this power. It has all been in vain. Every position has been successfully undermined and abandoned on specious and plausible excuses.

We do not want to be led upon the high road to becoming a satellite of the German Nazi system of European domination. In a very few years, perhaps in a very few months, we shall be confronted with demands with which we shall no doubt be invited to comply. Those demands may affect the surrender of territory or the surrender of liberty. I foresee and foretell that the policy of submission will carry with it restrictions upon the freedom of speech and debate in Parliament, on public platforms, and discussions in the Press, for it will be said – indeed, I hear it said sometimes now – that we cannot allow the Nazi system of dictatorship to be criticized by ordinary, common English politicians. Then, with a Press under control, in part direct but more potently indirect, with every organ of public opinion doped and chloroformed into acquiescence, we shall be conducted along further stages of our journey . . .

I have been casting about to see how measures can be taken to protect us from this advance of the Nazi power, and to secure those forms of life which are so dear to us. What is the sole method that is open? The sole method that is open for us is to regain our old island independence by acquiring that supremacy in the air which we were promised, that security in our air defences which we were assured we had, and thus to make ourselves an island once again. That, in all this grim outlook, shines out as the overwhelming fact. An effort at rearmament the like of which has not been seen ought to be made forthwith, and all the resources of this country and all its united strength should be bent to that task . . .

I do not begrudge our loyal, brave people, who were ready to do their duty no matter what the cost, who never flinched under the strain of last week – I do not grudge them the natural, spontaneous outburst of joy and relief when they learned that the hard ordeal would no longer be required of them at the moment; but they should know the truth. They should know that there has been gross neglect and deficiency in our defences; they should know that we have sustained a defeat without a war, the consequences of which will travel far with us along our road; they should know that we have passed an awful milestone in our history, when the whole equilibrium of Europe has been deranged, and that the terrible words have for the time being been pronounced against the Western democracies: 'Thou art weighed in the balance and found wanting.' And do not suppose that this is the end. This is only the beginning of the reckoning. This is only the first sip, the first foretaste of a bitter cup which will be proffered to us year by year unless by a supreme recovery of moral health and martial vigour, we arise again and take our stand for freedom as in the olden time.

*Chamberlain won the vote but the abstention of thirty Conservative MPs was the most convincing demonstration yet of the opposition to his policies among his own supporters. Churchill was condemned by* The Times *as treating the Commons to prophecies that made Jeremiah appear an optimist.*

•

## NEVILLE CHAMBERLAIN
### Birmingham, 17 March 1939

*'Is this an attempt to dominate the world by force?'*

*Already diminished by Munich, Czechoslovakia fell to Hitler on 15 March 1939. Two days later, Neville Chamberlain addressed his own people, the Birmingham Conservative Association. His prepared speech was an elaborate defence of Munich – but at the last moment he threw in a reference to what had happened two days before. The audience applauded his protest and with each roar Chamberlain's improvisations grew stronger.*

*With this speech, appeasement and Munich were eclipsed. Chamberlain turned British foreign policy upside down.*

Surely as a joint signatory of the Munich Agreement I was entitled, if Herr Hitler thought it ought to be undone, to that consultation which is provided for in the Munich declaration. Instead of that he has taken the law into his own hands. Before even the Czech President was received, and confronted with demands which he had no power to resist, the German troops were on the move, and within a few hours they were in the Czech capital.

According to the proclamation which was read out in Prague yesterday Bohemia and Moravia have been annexed to the German Reich. Non-German inhabitants, who of course include the Czechs, are placed under the German Protector in the German Protectorate. They are to be subject to the political, military, and economic needs of the Reich. They are called self-governing States, but the Reich is to take charge of their foreign policy, their Customs and their Excise, their bank reserves, and the equipment of the disarmed Czech forces. Perhaps most sinister of all, we hear again of the appearance of the Gestapo, the secret police, followed by the usual tale of wholesale arrests of prominent individuals, with consequences with which we are all familiar.

Every man and woman in this country who remembers the fate of the Jews and the political prisoners in Austria must be filled today with distress and foreboding. Who can fail to feel his heart go out in sympathy to the proud and brave people who have so suddenly been subjected to this invasion, whose liberties are curtailed, whose national independence has gone? What has become of this declaration of, 'No further territorial ambition'? What has become of the assurance, 'We don't want Czechs in the Reich'? What regard had been paid here to that principle of self-determination on which Herr Hitler argued so vehemently with me at Berchtesgaden when he was asking for the severance of Sudetenland from Czecho-Slovakia and its inclusion in the German Reich?

Now we are told that this seizure of territory has been necessitated by disturbances in Czecho-Slovakia. We are told that the proclamation of this new German Protectorate against the will of its inhabitants has been rendered inevitable by disorders which threatened the peace and security of her mighty neighbour. If there were disorders, were they not fomented from without? (*Cheers.*) And can anybody outside Germany take seriously the idea that they could be a danger to that great country, that they could provide any justification for what has happened?

Does not the question inevitably arise in our minds, if it is so easy to discover good reasons for ignoring assurances so solemnly and so repeatedly given, what reliance can be placed upon any other assurances that come from the same source?

There is another set of questions which almost inevitably must occur in our minds and to the minds of others, perhaps even in Germany herself. Germany, under her present regime, has sprung a series of unpleasant surprises upon the world. The Rhineland, the Austrian *Anschluss*, the severance of Sudetenland – all these things shocked and affronted public opinion throughout the world. Yet, however much we might take exception to the methods which were adopted in each of those cases, there was something to be said, whether on account of racial affinity or of just claims too long resisted – there was something to be said for the necessity of a change in the existing situation.

But the events which have taken place this week in complete disregard of the principles laid down by the German Government itself, seem to fall into a different category, and they must cause us all to be asking ourselves, 'Is this the end of an old adventure, or is it the beginning of a new? Is this the last attack upon a small State, or is it to be followed by others? Is this, in fact, a step in the direction of an attempt to dominate the world by force?'

Those are grave and serious questions. I am not going to answer them tonight. But I am sure they will require the grave and serious consideration, not only of Germany's neighbours but of others, perhaps even beyond the confines of Europe. Already there are indications that the process has begun, and it is obvious that it is likely now to be speeded up.

We ourselves will naturally turn first to our partners in the British Commonwealth of Nations – (*cheers*) – and to France – (*cheers*) – to whom we are so closely bound, and I have no doubt that others, too, knowing that we are not disinterested in what goes on in South-Eastern Europe, will wish to have our counsel and advice.

In our own country we must all review the position with that sense of responsibility which its gravity demands. Nothing must be excluded from that review which bears upon the national safety. Every aspect of our national life must be looked at again from that angle. The Government, as always, must bear the main responsibility, but I know that all individuals will wish to review their own position, too, and to consider again if they have done all they can to offer their service to the State.

I do not believe there is anyone who will question my sincerity when I say there is hardly anything I would not sacrifice for peace. (*Cheers.*) But there is one thing that I must except, and that is the liberty that we have enjoyed for hundreds of years, and which we will never surrender. (*Loud cheers.*) That I, of all men, should feel called upon to make such a declaration – that is the measure of the extent to which these events have shattered the confidence which was just beginning to show its head and which, if it had been allowed to grow, might have made this year memorable for the return of all Europe to sanity and stability.

It is only six weeks ago that I was speaking in this city, and that I alluded to rumours and suspicions which I said ought to be swept away. I pointed out that any demand to dominate the world by force was one which the democracies must resist, and I added that I could not believe that such a challenge was intended, because no Government with the interests of its own people at heart could expose them for such a claim to the horrors of world war.

And indeed, with the lessons of history for all to read, it seems incredible that we should see such a challenge. I feel bound to repeat that, while I am not prepared to engage this country by new unspecified commitments operating under conditions which cannot now be foreseen, yet no greater mistake could be made than to suppose that, because it believes war to be a senseless and cruel thing, this nation has so lost its fibre that it will not take part to the utmost of its power, resisting such a challenge if it ever were made. For that declaration

I am convinced that I have not merely the support, the sympathy, the confidence of my fellow-countrymen and countrywomen, but I shall have also the approval of the whole British Empire and of all other nations who value peace indeed, but who value freedom even more.

*The speech was described in the London* Times *as 'momentous'. It was broadcast and heard throughout the British Empire and the United States and also broadcast fully in German. Chamberlain declared war on Germany on 3 September (see next speech).*

•

## NEVILLE CHAMBERLAIN
London, 3 September 1939

*'This country is at war with Germany'*

I am speaking to you from the Cabinet Room at 10 Downing Street.

This morning the British Ambassador in Berlin handed the German Government a final Note stating that, unless we heard from them by 11 o'clock that they were prepared at once to withdraw their troops from Poland, a state of war would exist between us.

I have to tell you now that no such undertaking has been received, and that consequently this country is at war with Germany.

You can imagine what a bitter blow it is to me that all my long struggle to win peace has failed. Yet I cannot believe that there is anything more or anything different that I could have done and that would have been more successful.

Up to the very last it would have been quite possible to have arranged a peaceful and honourable settlement between Germany and Poland, but Hitler would not have it. He had evidently made up his mind to attack Poland whatever happened, and although he now says he put forward reasonable proposals which were rejected by the Poles, that is not a true statement.

The proposals were never shown to the Poles, nor to us, and, though they were announced in a German broadcast on Thursday night, Hitler did not wait to hear comments on them, but ordered his troops to cross the Polish frontier. His action shows convincingly that there is no chance of expecting that this man will ever give up his practice of using force to gain his will. He can only be stopped by force.

We and France are today, in fulfilment of our obligations, going to the aid of Poland, who is so bravely resisting this wicked and unprovoked attack on her people. We have a clear conscience. We have done all that any country could do to establish peace. The situation in which no word given by Germany's ruler could be trusted and no people or country could feel themselves safe has become intolerable. And now that we have resolved to finish it, I know that you will all play your part with calmness and courage.

At such a moment as this the assurances of support that we have received from the Empire are a source of profound encouragement to us.

When I have finished speaking certain detailed announcements will be made on behalf of the Government. Give these your closest attention. The Government have made plans under which it will be possible to carry on the work of the nation in the days of stress and strain that may be ahead. But these plans need your help.

You may be taking your part in the fighting services or as a volunteer in one of the branches of Civil Defence. If so you will report for duty in accordance with the instructions you have received. You may be engaged in work essential to the prosecution of war for the maintenance of the life of the people – in factories, in transport, in public utility concerns, or in the supply of other necessaries of life. If so, it is of vital importance that you should carry on with your jobs.

Now may God bless you all. May He defend the right. It is the evil things that we shall be fighting against – brute force, bad faith, injustice, oppression and persecution – and against them I am certain that the right will prevail.

•

## LEO AMERY
### London, 7 May 1940

*'In the name of God, go'*

*By 1940, Leo Amery (1873–1955) was almost at the end of his political career, during which he had been First Lord of the Admiralty, Colonial Secretary and Dominions Secretary in the 1920s. Now a distinguished elder statesman, he was a fierce critic of Chamberlain's vacillation and weak leadership. On the day before war was declared, it was Amery who had shouted to Arthur Greenwood, the former Labour leader, to 'Speak for England' when he rose to speak after Chamberlain.*

*On 7 May 1940, Chamberlain opened a debate on the disastrous Norwegian campaign. Among the younger Conservative MPs, there were many territorial officers who spoke for the units which had suffered in Norway. Among them, wearing the uniform of Admiral of the Fleet, was Sir Roger Keyes, who denounced the government.*

*Then Amery, a friend and colleague of Chamberlain's for many years and a fellow Birmingham MP, stood up to speak. He was called during the dinner hour but the House quickly filled up as he moved the target of Chamberlain's critics from the navy towards the prime minister and his conduct of the war. Sensing the mood of the Commons, and with devastating effect, he ended his speech with the angry words used by Oliver Cromwell to the Long Parliament in the seventeenth century. As he uttered them, he pointed at the prime minister and delivered his pitiless attack. It was one of the most dramatic moments in the tumultuous two-day debate.*

Believe me, as long as the present methods prevail, all our valour and all our resources are not going to see us through. Above all, so long as they prevail, time is not going to be on our side, because they are methods which, inevitably and inherently, waste time and weaken decisions. What we must have, and have soon, is a supreme war directorate of a handful of men free from administrative routine, free to frame policy among themselves, and with the task of supervising, inspiring, and impelling a group of departments clearly allocated to each one of them. That is the only way. We learned that in the last war. My Right Hon. Friend the Member for Caernarfon Boroughs (Mr Lloyd George) earned the undying gratitude of the nation for the courage he showed in adopting what was then a new experiment. The experiment worked, and it helped to win the war. After the war years, the Committee of Imperial Defence laid it down as axiomatic that, while in a minor war you might go on with an ordinary Cabinet, helped perhaps by a War Committee, in a major war you must have a War Cabinet – meaning precisely the type of Cabinet that my Right Hon. Friend introduced then. The overwhelming opinion of this House and of the public outside has been demanding that for a long while. We are told that there would be no particular advantage in it at the present time. I ask, Is this or is this not a major war?

We must have, first of all, a right organization of government. What is no less important today is that the Government shall be able to draw upon the whole abilities of the nation. It must represent all the elements of real political power in this country, whether in this House or not. The time has come when Hon. and Right Hon. Members opposite must definitely take their share of the responsibility. The time has come when the organization, the power and influence of the Trades Union Congress cannot be left outside. It must, through one of its recognized leaders, reinforce the strength of the national effort from inside. The time has come, in other words, for a real National Government . . .

Just as our peacetime system is unsuitable for war conditions, so does it tend to breed peacetime statesmen who are not too well fitted for the conduct of war. Facility in debate, ability to state a case, caution in advancing an unpopular view, compromise and procrastination are the natural qualities – I might almost say, virtues – of a political leader in time of peace. They are fatal qualities in war. Vision, daring, swiftness and consistency of decision are the very essence of victory. In our normal politics, it is true, the conflict of party did encourage a certain combative spirit. In the last war we Tories found that the most perniciously aggressive of our opponents, the Right Hon. Member for Caernarfon Boroughs, was not only aggressive in words, but was a man of action. In recent years the normal weakness of our political life has been accentuated by a coalition based upon no clear political principles. It was in fact begotten of a false alarm as to the disastrous results of going off the Gold Standard. It is a coalition which has been living ever since in a twilight atmosphere between Protection and Free Trade and between unprepared collective security and unprepared isolation. Surely, for the Government of the last ten years to have bred a band of warrior statesmen would have been little short of a miracle. We have waited for eight months, and the miracle has not come to pass. Can we afford to wait any longer?

Somehow or other we must get into the Government men who can match our enemies in fighting spirit, in daring, in resolution and in thirst for victory. Some three hundred years ago, when this House found that its troops were being beaten again and again by the dash and daring of the Cavaliers, by Prince Rupert's Cavalry, Oliver Cromwell spoke to John Hampden. In one of his speeches he recounted what he said. It was this:

'I said to him, "Your troops are most of them old, decayed serving men and tapsters and such kind of fellows ... You must get men of a spirit that are likely to go as far as they will go, or you will be beaten still."'

It may not be easy to find these men. They can be found only by trial and by ruthlessly discarding all who fail and have their failings discovered. We are fighting today for our life, for our liberty, for our all; we cannot go on being led as we are. I have quoted certain words of Oliver Cromwell. I will quote certain other words. I do it with great reluctance, because I am speaking of those who are old friends and associates of mine, but they are words which, I think, are applicable to the present situation. This is what Cromwell said to the Long Parliament when he thought it was no longer fit to conduct the affairs of the nation:

'You have sat too long here for any good you have been doing. Depart, I say, and let us have done with you. In the name of God, go.'

•

# DAVID LLOYD GEORGE
London, 7 May 1940

### *'Sacrifice the seals of office'*

*Leo Amery had pointed his finger at Neville Chamberlain and used Cromwell's words: 'In the name of God, go.' Then, as one of the most memorable debates in British history went into its second day, the Labour Party decided to call for a vote of censure.*

*Chamberlain was startled, angry, and taken unawares. He jumped up and declared: 'I do not seek to evade criticism but I say to my friends in the House, and I have friends in the House, no government can prosecute a war efficiently unless it has public and parliamentary support. I accept this challenge. I welcome it indeed. At least I shall see who is with us and who is against us and I call on my friends to support us in the lobby tonight.'*

*Chamberlain's intervention was a major miscalculation and provoked an unforgettable speech – the last decisive intervention in the House of Commons by Lloyd George. Aroused by Chamberlain's appeal to his 'friends' and the prime minister's cheapening of the office he had held with such distinction during the last world war, he now had his revenge for years of exclusion from power.*

The situation is a grave one – I agree with what was said about that by the Prime Minister – and it would be a fatal error on our part not to acknowledge it. In such experience as I have had of war direction I have never tried to minimize the extent of a disaster. I try to get the facts, because unless you really face the facts you cannot overcome the difficulties and restore the position. There is no case, in my judgement, for panic. I say that deliberately, after a good deal of reflection, but there is a grave case for pulling ourselves together. We cannot do that unless we tell the country the facts. They must realize the magnitude of our jeopardy. We have two immense Empires federated in the struggle for liberty, the two greatest Empires in the world, the British Empire and the French Empire, with almost inexhaustible resources but not easily mobilized, not easily roused, especially ours.

You are not going to rouse the British Empire – because you will have to do it not merely in Britain but throughout the world – to put forth the whole of its strength unless and until you tell it the facts and realities of the peril that confronts it. At the cost of unpleasantness, I am going to do that, not with a view to terrifying them or spreading dismay and consternation, but with a view to rousing real action and not sham action such as we have had. It is no use saying that the balance of advantage is in our favour, or adding up the numbers of ships sunk on either side. That kind of petty-cash balance-sheet is not the thing to look at. There are more serious realities than that.

We promised Poland; we promised Czecho-Slovakia. We said: 'We will defend your frontiers if you will revise them.' There was a promise to Poland, to Norway, and to Finland. Our promissory notes are now rubbish on the market. (*Hon. Members: 'Shame.'*) Tell me one country at the present moment, one neutral country, that would be prepared to stand up and finance us on a mere promise from us? What is the use of not facing facts? . . .

The Hon. Member for Stockton-on-Tees (Mr Harold Macmillan) gave the whole of the facts, and they have never been answered yet. That is the situation with regard to our strategical position. What is the use of denying it? It is one of the facts that we have to face. We have to restore that prestige in the world if we are to win this war. There is also the fact that the state of our preparations is known to the world. We started these preparations five years ago, in 1935. In 1935 a promise of rearmament was made; in 1936 active proposals were submitted to this House and were passed without a Division. The Government said they would commit us to £1,500 million. If they had asked for more and had said that it was necessary, there was no party in this House which would have challenged it. (*Interruption.*) If any party had challenged it, you had your majority. What has been done? Is there anyone in this House who will say that he is satisfied with the speed and efficiency of the preparations in any respect for air, for Army, yea, for Navy? Everybody is disappointed. Everybody knows that whatever was done was done half-heartedly, ineffectively, without drive and unintelligently. For three or four years I thought to myself that the facts with regard to

Germany were exaggerated by the First Lord, because the then Prime Minister – not this Prime Minister – said that they were not true. The First Lord was right about it. Then came the war. The tempo was hardly speeded up. There was the same leisureliness and inefficiency. Will anybody tell me that he is satisfied with what we have done about aeroplanes, tanks, guns, especially anti-aircraft guns? Is anyone here satisfied with the steps we took to train an Army to use them? Nobody is satisfied. The whole world knows that. And here we are in the worst strategic position in which this country has ever been placed.

*Sir Patrick Hannon (Birmingham, Moseley):* We have our sea power.

*Mr J. J. Davidson (Glasgow, Maryhill):* And your dividends.

*Mr Lloyd George:* I wish we had used it in some parts of Norway. I do not think that the First Lord was entirely responsible for all the things that happened there.

*Mr Churchill:* I take complete responsibility for everything that has been done by the Admiralty, and I take my full share of the burden.

*Mr Lloyd George:* The Right Hon. Gentleman must not allow himself to be converted into an air-raid shelter to keep the splinters from hitting his colleagues. But that is the position, and we must face it. I agree with the Prime Minister that we must face it as a people and not as a party, nor as a personal issue. The Prime Minister is not in a position to make his personality in this respect inseparable from the interests of the country.

*The Prime Minister:* What is the meaning of that observation? I have never represented that my personality – (*Hon. Members:* 'You did') On the contrary, I took pains to say that personalities ought to have no place in these matters.

*Mr Lloyd George:* I was not here when the Right Hon. Gentleman made the observation, but he definitely appealed on a question which is a great national, Imperial and world issue. He said, 'I have got my friends.' It is not a question of who are the Prime Minister's friends. It is a far bigger issue. The Prime Minister must remember that he has met this formidable foe of ours in peace and in war. He has always been worsted. He is not in a position to appeal on the grounds of friendship. He has appealed for sacrifice. The nation is prepared for every sacrifice so long as it has leadership, so long as the

Government show clearly what they are aiming at and so long as the nation is confident that those who are leading it are doing their best. I say solemnly that the Prime Minister should give an example of sacrifice, because there is nothing which can contribute more to victory in this war than that he should sacrifice the seals of office.

*When the Commons voted, the government's majority was reduced to 81 from its usual figure of 200. Forty-one Tories voted with the opposition and some sixty abstained. As Chamberlain left the House, a few Tory rebels, among them Harold Macmillan (who was later to be prime minister) sang 'Rule Britannia!' and shouted 'Go, Go, Go!' Winston Churchill became prime minister of a coalition government on 10 May.*

•

## WINSTON CHURCHILL
London, 13 May 1940

*'I have nothing to offer but blood, toil, tears and sweat'*

*On becoming prime minister, Churchill mobilized the language and made it fight. The first occasion occurred only three days after he had formed his coalition Cabinet. It was Whit Monday and Churchill made a short speech to the House of Commons. Yet on entering the chamber it was Chamberlain who got more cheers than Churchill, whose support was mostly on the Labour benches.*

*The speech was unforgettable, imposing Churchill's character and resolve on the Commons whether they liked it or not. The effect was electrifying, says Robert Rhodes James, one of his biographers. As he walked out of the chamber, he said to one of his aides: 'That got the SODS, didn't it!'*

*Churchill's war speeches, with their bulldog spirit, their refusal to acknowledge the prospect of defeat, rallied the British at the most critical period of the war when Hitler was advancing to Dunkirk and threatening to invade England.*

It must be remembered that we are in the preliminary stage of one of the greatest battles in history, that we are in action at many points in Norway and in Holland, that we have to be prepared in the Mediterranean, that the air battle is continuous and that many preparations have to be made here at home. In this crisis I hope I may be pardoned if I do not address the House at any length today. I hope that any of my friends and colleagues, or former colleagues, who are affected by the political reconstruction, will make all allowance for any lack of ceremony with which it has been necessary to act. I would say to the House, as I said to those who have joined the Government: 'I have nothing to offer but blood, toil, tears and sweat.'

We have before us an ordeal of the most grievous kind. We have before us many, many long months of struggle and of suffering. You ask, what is our policy? I will say: It is to wage war, by sea, land and air, with all our might and with all the strength that God can give us: to wage war against a monstrous tyranny, never surpassed in the dark, lamentable catalogue of human crime. That is our policy. You ask, What is our aim? I can answer in one word: Victory – victory at all costs, victory in spite of all terror, victory, however long and hard the road may be; for without victory, there is no survival. Let that be realized; no survival for the British Empire; no survival for all that the British Empire has stood for, no survival for the urge and impulse of the ages, that mankind will move forward towards its goal. But I take up my task with buoyancy and hope. I feel sure that our cause will not be suffered to fail among men. At this time I feel entitled to claim the aid of all, and I say, 'Come, then, let us go forward together with our united strength.'

•

## WINSTON CHURCHILL
### BBC Radio, 19 May 1940

*'Be ye men of valour'*

*Churchill's war of words began in earnest when he made his first broadcast to the nation as prime minister on 19 May. The Germans had invaded Holland and Belgium and broken through the French defences at Sedan. It was clear that French resistance could not long continue and that the position of British troops on the continent was perilous.*

*After only three hours to compose the speech, Churchill broadcast live and warned that a German attack on Britain might be imminent. It was a call to arms that caught the imagination of the nation.*

Our task is not only to win the battle – but to win the War. After this battle in France abates its force, there will come the battle for our island – for all that Britain is, and all that Britain means. That will be the struggle. In that supreme emergency we shall not hesitate to take every step, even the most drastic, to call forth from our people the last ounce and the last inch of effort of which they are capable. The interests of property, the hours of labour, are nothing compared with the struggle for life and honour, for right and freedom, to which we have vowed ourselves.

I have received from the Chiefs of the French Republic, and in particular from its indomitable Prime Minister, M. Reynaud, the most sacred pledges that whatever happens they will fight to the end, be it bitter or be it glorious. Nay, if we fight to the end, it can only be glorious.

Having received His Majesty's commission, I have found an administration of men and women of every party and of almost every point of view. We have differed and quarrelled in the past; but now one bond unites us all – to wage war until victory is won, and never to surrender ourselves to servitude and shame, whatever the cost and the agony may be. This is one of the most awe-striking periods in the long history of France and Britain. It is also beyond doubt the most sublime. Side by side, unaided except by their kith and kin in the great Dominions and by the wide Empires which rest beneath their shield – side by side, the British and French peoples have advanced to rescue not only Europe but mankind from the foulest and most soul-destroying tyranny which has ever darkened and stained the pages of history. Behind them – behind us – behind the armies and fleets of Britain and France – gather a group of shattered States and bludgeoned races: the Czechs, the Poles, the Norwegians, the Danes, the Dutch, the Belgians – upon all of whom the long night of barbarism will descend, unbroken even by a star of hope, unless we conquer, as conquer we must; as conquer we shall.

Today is Trinity Sunday. Centuries ago words were written to be a call and a spur to the faithful servants of Truth and Justice: 'Arm yourselves, and be ye men of valour, and be in readiness for the conflict; for it is better for us to perish in battle than to look upon the outrage of our nation and our altar. As the Will of God is in Heaven, even so let it be.'

•

# WINSTON CHURCHILL
## London, 18 June 1940

### 'This was their finest hour'

*The crumbling French resistance to Hitler could not be maintained much longer. On 10 June the government left Paris; on 16 June Marshal Pétain formed a new government. The next day France sued for peace. As Churchill predicted in this House of Commons speech, the Battle of France was over and the Battle of Britain had begun. Britain, he declared, was now resolved to fight on alone.*

*The defiant words were heard by millions when it was broadcast four hours later and it is probably the best remembered Churchill speech of the war, particularly for the magnificent peroration. Even so, as Churchill wrote later, rhetoric was no guarantee of survival.*

We do not yet know what will happen in France or whether the French resistance will be prolonged, both in France and in the French Empire overseas. The French Government will be throwing away great opportunities and casting adrift their future if they do not continue the war in accordance with their Treaty obligations, from which we have not felt able to release them. The House will have read the historic declaration in which, at the desire of many Frenchmen – and of our own hearts – we have proclaimed our willingness at the darkest hour in French history to conclude a union of common citizenship in this struggle. However matters may go in France or with the French Government, or other French Governments, we in this island and in the British Empire will never lose our sense of comradeship with the French people. If we are now called upon to endure what they have been suffering, we shall emulate their courage, and if final victory rewards our toils they shall share the gains, aye, and freedom shall be restored to all. We abate nothing of our just demands: not one jot or tittle do we recede. Czechs, Poles, Norwegians, Dutch, Belgians have joined their causes to our own. All these shall be restored.

What General Weygand called the Battle of France is over. I expect that the Battle of Britain is about to begin. Upon this battle depends the survival of Christian civilization. Upon it depends our own British life, and the long continuity of our institutions and our Empire. The whole fury and might of the enemy must very soon be turned on us. Hitler knows that he will have to break us in this island or lose the war. If we can stand up to him, all Europe may be free and the life of the world may move forward into broad, sunlit uplands. But if we fail, then the whole world, including the United States, including all that we have known and cared for, will sink into the abyss of a new Dark Age made more sinister, and perhaps more protracted, by the lights of perverted science. Let us therefore brace ourselves to our duties and so bear ourselves that, if the British Empire and its Commonwealth last for a thousand years, men will still say, 'This was their finest hour.'

•

## CHARLES DE GAULLE
London, 18–19 June 1940

*'The flame of French resistance'*

*A veteran of the First World War, when he served under Colonel Pétain, General de Gaulle (1890–1970) successfully commanded an armoured division in May 1940 and briefly held the junior post of under-secretary for war under Paul Reynaud, the French prime minister. When the French armies collapsed, Reynaud sent for Pétain, who soon became premier himself and made arrangements for surrender and an armistice. De Gaulle escaped to England to organize the Free French movement and was sentenced to death* in absentia *by a French court.*

*The Battle of France was over, the Battle of Britain about to begin and the fortunes of the allies against Hitler stood at their lowest ebb as the tall French officer stood before the microphone to rally Frenchmen throughout the world.*

## I

The leaders who, for many years past, have been at the head of the French armed forces have set up a government.

Alleging the defeat of our armies, this government has entered into negotiations with the enemy with a view to bringing about a cessation of hostilities. It is quite true that we were, and still are, overwhelmed by enemy mechanized forces, both on the ground and in the air. It was the tanks, the planes, and the tactics of the Germans, far more than the fact that we were outnumbered, that forced our armies to retreat. It was the German tanks, planes, and tactics that provided the element of surprise which brought our leaders to their present plight.

But has the last word been said? Must we abandon all hope? Is our defeat final and irremediable? To those questions I answer – No!

Speaking in full knowledge of the facts, I ask you to believe me when I say that the cause of France is not lost. The very factors that brought about our defeat may one day lead us to victory.

For, remember this, France does not stand alone. She is not isolated. Behind her is a vast empire, and she can make common cause with the British Empire, which commands the seas and is continuing the struggle. Like England, she can draw unreservedly on the immense industrial resources of the United States.

This war is not limited to our unfortunate country. The outcome of the struggle has not been decided by the Battle of France. This is a world war. Mistakes have been made, there have been delays and untold suffering, but the fact remains that there still exists in the world everything we need to crush our enemies some day. Today we are crushed by the sheer weight of mechanized force hurled against us, but we can still look to a future in which even greater mechanized force will bring us victory. The destiny of the world is at stake.

I, General de Gaulle, now in London, call on all French officers and men who are at present on British soil, or may be in the future, with or without their arms; I call on all engineers and skilled work-men from the armaments factories who are at present on British soil, or may be in the future, to get in touch with me.

Whatever happens, the flame of French resistance must not and shall not die.

Tomorrow I shall broadcast again from London.

## II

Frenchmen must now be fully aware that all ordinary forms of authority have disappeared.

Faced by the bewilderment of my countrymen, by the disintegration of a government in thrall to the enemy, by the fact that the institutions of my country are incapable, at the moment, of functioning, I, General de Gaulle, a French soldier and military leader, realize that I now speak for France.

In the name of France, I make the following solemn declaration:

It is the bounden duty of all Frenchmen who still bear arms to continue the struggle. For them to lay down their arms, to evacuate any position of military importance, or agree to hand over any part of French territory, however small, to enemy control, would be a crime against our country. For the moment I refer particularly to French North Africa – to the *integrity* of French North Africa.

The Italian armistice is nothing but a clumsy trap. In the Africa of Clauzel, Bugeaud, Lyautey, and Noguès, honour and duty strictly enjoin that the French should refuse to carry out the conditions imposed by the enemy.

The thought that the panic of Bordeaux could make itself felt across the sea is not to be borne.

Soldiers of France, wherever you may be, arise!

*De Gaulle acted as an inspiration to the French resistance. In June 1943 he became head of the French Committee of National Liberation in Algiers. He landed in Normandy a week after D-Day and marched into Paris on 25 August 1944, while German sharpshooters were still on the roofs.*

•

## J. B. PRIESTLEY
London, 1940

### 'This little steamer'

*Churchill did not speak alone after Dunkirk. J. B. Priestley, the British novel-ist, commanded almost as big an audience for his Postscript broadcasts on BBC Radio with their cheerful, chatty understatements.*

*Priestley, the author of* Good Companions *and* English Journey, *cap-tured not only the mood of defiance of the British but also their deeply held inner conviction that they would triumph over 'little old Hitler' as well as the quintes-sential English spirit (echoing Stanley Baldwin's speech on England, page 94) that eventually conquered Hitler — as these two short Postscripts demonstrate.*

Here at Dunkirk is another English epic. And to my mind what was most characteristically English about it — so typical of us, so absurd and yet so grand and gallant that you hardly know whether to laugh or to cry when you read about them — was the part played in the difficult and dan-gerous embarkation — not by the warships, magnificent though they were — but by the little pleasure-steamers. We've known them and laughed at them, these fussy little steamers, all our lives. We have called them 'the shilling sicks'. We have watched them load and unload their crowds of holiday passengers — the gents full of high spirits and bottled beer, the ladies eating pork pies, the children sticky with peppermint rock. Sometimes they only went as far as the next seaside resort. But the boldest of them might manage a Channel crossing, to let everybody have a glimpse of Boulogne. They were usually paddle steamers, mak-ing a great deal more fuss with all their churning than they made speed; and they weren't proud, for they let you see their works going round. They liked to call themselves *Queens* and *Belles*, and even if they were new, there was always something old-fashioned, a Dickens touch, a mid-Victorian air, about them. They seemed to belong to the same ridiculous holiday world as pierrots and piers, sand castles, ham-and-egg teas, palmists, automatic machines, and crowded sweating promenades. But they were called out of that world – and, let it be noted – they were called out in good time and good order. Yes, those 'Brighton Belles' and 'Brighton Queens' left that innocent foolish world of theirs – to sail into the inferno, to defy bombs, shells, magnetic mines, torpedoes, machine-gun fire – to rescue our soldiers. Some of them – alas – will never return. Among those paddle steamers that will never return was one that I knew well, for it was the pride of our ferry service to the Isle of Wight – none other than the good ship *Gracie Fields*. I tell you, we were proud of the *Gracie Fields*, for she was the glittering queen of our local line, and instead of taking an hour over her voyage, used to do it, churning like mad, in forty-five minutes. And now never again will we board her at Cowes and go down into her dining saloon for a fine breakfast of bacon and eggs. She has paddled and churned away – for ever. But now – look – this little steamer, like all her brave and battered sisters, is immortal. She'll go sailing proudly down the years in the epic of Dunkirk. And our great-grandchildren, when they learn how we began this War by snatching glory out of defeat, and then swept on to victory, may also learn how the little holiday steamers made an excursion to hell and came back glorious.

I think the countryman knows, without being told, that we hold our lives here, as we hold our farms, upon certain terms. One of those terms is that while wars still continue, while one nation is ready to hurl its armed men at another, you must if necessary stand up and fight for your own. And this decision comes from the natural piety of simple but sane men. Such men, you will notice, are happier now than the men who have lost that natural piety.

Well, as we talked on our post on the hilltop, we watched the dusk deepen in the valleys below, where our women-folk listened to the news as they knitted by the hearth, and we remembered that these were our homes and that now at any time they might be blazing ruins, and that half-crazy German youths, in whose empty eyes the idea of honour and glory seems to include every form of beastliness, might soon be let loose down there. The sentries took their posts. There was a mist coming over the down. Nothing much happened for a time. A green light that seemed to defy all black-out regulations turned out to be merely an extra large and luminous glow-worm; the glow-worms, poor ignorant little creatures, don't know there's a war on and so continue lighting themselves up. A few searchlights went stabbing through the dusk and then faded. The mist thickened, and below in all the valleys, there wasn't the faintest glimmer of light. You heard the ceaseless high melancholy singing of the telegraph wires in the wind.

So we talked about what happened to us in the last war, and about the hay and the barley, about beef and milk and cheese and tobacco. Then a belt of fog over to the left became almost silvery, because somewhere along there all the searchlights were sweeping the sky. Then somewhere behind that vague silveriness, there was a sound as if gigantic doors were being slammed to. There was the rapid stabbing noise of anti-aircraft batteries, and far away some rapping of machine-guns. Then the sirens went, in our two nearest towns, as if all that part of the darkened countryside, like a vast trapped animal, were screaming at us.

*J. B. Priestley was included among the 2,820 people who were to be rounded up by the Nazis as dangerous adversaries after they had conquered Britain. They also included Noël Coward, Virginia Woolf, Aldous Huxley, E. M. Forster, H. G. Wells and Bertrand Russell.*

•

## FRANKLIN DELANO ROOSEVELT
### Washington, DC, 29 December 1940

### *'The arsenal of democracy'*

*Although the Battle of Britain had been won, the Battle of the Atlantic was intensifying. Vessels were being sunk faster than British shipyards could replace them. Money was running out and soon Britain would not be able to pay for the supplies she needed.*

*Apart from responding to Britain's plight by increasing American naval activity in the Atlantic, Roosevelt aired the idea of Lend-Lease. 'If your neighbour's house is on fire and he wants to borrow your garden hose, you don't ask to*

*be paid, you just want your hose back.' Roosevelt also educated the American*
*public about what was at stake in the war in some of his most dramatic speeches.*
*One of them was this fireside chat.*

The experience of the past two years has proven beyond doubt that
no nation can appease the Nazis. No man can tame a tiger into a kit-
ten by stroking it. There can be no appeasement with ruthlessness.
There can be no reasoning with an incendiary bomb. We know now
that a nation can have peace with the Nazis only at the price of total
surrender . . .

The people of Europe who are defending themselves do not ask
us to do their fighting. They ask us for the implements of war, the
planes, the tanks, the guns, the freighters which will enable them to
fight for their liberty and for our security. Emphatically we must get
these weapons to them in sufficient volume and quickly enough, so
that we and our children will be saved the agony and suffering of war
which others have had to endure.

Let not the defeatists tell us that it is too late. It will never be earlier. Tomorrow will be later than today.

Certain facts are self-evident.

In a military sense Great Britain and the British Empire are today
the spearhead of resistance to world conquest. They are putting up
a fight which will live for ever in the story of human gallantry.

There is no demand for sending an American Expeditionary
Force outside our own borders. There is no intention by any member of your Government to send such a force. You can, therefore,
nail any talk about sending armies to Europe as deliberate untruth.

Our national policy is not directed toward war. Its sole purpose is
to keep war away from our country and our people . . .

Democracy's fight against world conquest is being greatly aided,
and must be more greatly aided, by the rearmament of the United
States and by sending every ounce and every ton of munitions and
supplies that we can possibly spare to help the defenders who are in
the front lines. It is no more unneutral for us to do that than it is for
Sweden, Russia and other nations near Germany, to send steel and ore
and oil and other war materials into Germany every day of the week.

We are planning our own defence with the utmost urgency; and in its vast scale we must integrate the war needs of Britain and the other free nations which are resisting aggression . . .

No pessimistic policy about the future of America shall delay the immediate expansion of those industries essential to defence. We need them. It is the purpose of the nation to build now with all possible speed every machine, every arsenal, every factory that we need to manufacture our defence material. We have the men – the skill – the wealth – and above all, the will.

I am confident that if and when production of consumer or luxury goods in certain industries requires the use of machines and raw materials that are essential for defence purposes, then such production must yield, and will gladly yield, to our primary and compelling purpose.

I appeal to the owners of plants – to the managers – to the workers – to our own Government employees – to put every ounce of effort into producing these munitions swiftly and without stint. With this appeal I give you the pledge that all of us who are officers of your Government will devote ourselves to the same whole-hearted extent to the great task that lies ahead.

As planes and ships and guns and shells are produced, your Government, with its defence experts, can then determine how best to use them to defend this hemisphere. The decision as to how much shall be sent abroad and how much shall remain at home must be made on the basis of our over-all military necessities.

We must be the great arsenal of democracy. For us this is an emergency as serious as war itself. We must apply ourselves to our task with the same resolution, the same sense of urgency, the same spirit of patriotism and sacrifice as we would show were we at war.

*This fireside chat was the most successful that Roosevelt had ever given. According to opinion polls, more than sixty per cent of Americans agreed with what he said.*

•

FRANKLIN DELANO ROOSEVELT
Washington, DC, 6 January 1941

*'The four freedoms'*

*Only eight days after promising to make America the arsenal of democracy,
Roosevelt addressed Congress and made perhaps the most famous speech of his
career, in which he declared that America would support all nations that struggled on behalf of four essential freedoms: freedom of speech and religion and
freedom from want and fear (an echo of his inaugural address).*

*Roosevelt was again offering implicit support to Britain and coaxing Americans
towards a war that he was convinced they would sooner or later be forced to enter.*

Every realist knows that the democratic way of life is at this moment
being directly assailed in every part of the world – assailed either by
arms, or by secret spreading of poisonous propaganda by those who
seek to destroy unity and promote discord in nations that are still at
peace.

During sixteen long months this assault has blotted out the whole
pattern of democratic life in an appalling number of independent
nations, great and small. The assailants are still on the march, threatening other nations, great and small.

Therefore, as your President, performing my constitutional duty
to 'give to the Congress information of the state of the Union', I
find it, unhappily, necessary to report that the future and the safety
of our country and of our democracy are overwhelmingly involved
in events far beyond our borders.

Armed defence of democratic existence is now being gallantly
waged in four continents. If that defence fails, all the population and
all the resources of Europe, Asia, Africa and Australasia will be
dominated by the conquerors. Let us remember that the total of
those populations and their resources in those four continents
greatly exceeds the sum total of the population and the resources of
the whole of the Western Hemisphere many times over.

In times like these it is immature – and incidentally, untrue – for anybody to brag that an unprepared America, single-handed, and with one hand tied behind its back, can hold off the whole world.

No realistic American can expect from a dictator's peace international generosity, or return of true independence, or world disarmament, or freedom of expression, or freedom of religion, or even good business.

Such a peace would bring no security for us or for our neighbours. 'Those, who would give up essential liberty to purchase a little temporary safety, deserve neither liberty nor safety.'

As a nation, we may take pride in the fact that we are soft-hearted; but we cannot afford to be soft-headed.

We must always be wary of those who with sounding brass and a tinkling cymbal preach the 'ism' of appeasement.

We must especially beware of that small group of selfish men who would clip the wings of the American eagle in order to feather their own nests.

I have recently pointed out how quickly the tempo of modern warfare could bring into our very midst the physical attack which we must eventually expect if the dictator nations win this war.

There is much loose talk of our immunity from immediate and direct invasion from across the seas. Obviously, as long as the British Navy retains its power, no such danger exists. Even if there were no British Navy, it is not probable that any enemy would be stupid enough to attack us by landing troops in the United States from across thousands of miles of ocean, until it had acquired strategic bases from which to operate.

But we learn much from the lessons of the past years in Europe – particularly the lesson of Norway, whose essential seaports were captured by treachery and surprise built up over a series of years.

As long as the aggressor nations maintain the offensive, they – not we – will choose the time and the place and the method of their attack.

That is why the future of all the American Republics is today in serious danger.

That is why this Annual Message to the Congress is unique in our history.

That is why every member of the Executive Branch of the Government and every member of the Congress faces great responsibility and great accountability.

The need of the moment is that our actions and our policy should be devoted primarily – almost exclusively – to meeting this foreign peril. For all our domestic problems are now a part of the great emergency.

Just as our national policy in internal affairs has been based upon a decent respect for the rights and the dignity of all our fellow men within our gates, so our national policy in foreign affairs has been based on a decent respect for the rights and dignity of all nations, large and small. And the justice of morality must and will win in the end.

Our national policy is this:

First, by an impressive expression of the public will and without regard to partisanship, we are committed to all-inclusive national defence.

Second, by an impressive expression of the public will and without regard to partisanship, we are committed to full support of all those resolute peoples, everywhere, who are resisting aggression and are thereby keeping war away from our Hemisphere. By this support, we express our determination that the democratic cause shall prevail; and we strengthen the defence and the security of our own nation.

Third, by an impressive expression of the public will and without regard to partisanship, we are committed to the proposition that principles of morality and considerations for our own security will never permit us to acquiesce in a peace dictated by aggressors and sponsored by appeasers. We know that enduring peace cannot be bought at the cost of other people's freedom.

In the future days, which we seek to make secure, we look forward to a world founded upon four essential human freedoms.

The first is freedom of speech and expression – everywhere in the world.

The second is freedom of every person to worship God in his own way – everywhere in the world.

The third is freedom from want – which, translated into world terms, means economic understandings which will secure to every nation a healthy peacetime life for its inhabitants – everywhere in the world.

The fourth is freedom from fear – which, translated into world terms, means a world-wide reduction of armaments to such a point and in such a thorough fashion that no nation will be in a position to commit an act of physical aggression against any neighbour – anywhere in the world.

That is no vision of a distant millennium. It is a definite basis for a kind of world attainable in our own time and generation. That kind of world is the very antithesis of the so-called new order of tyranny which the dictators seek to create with the crash of a bomb.

To that new order we oppose the greater conception – the moral order. A good society is able to face schemes of world domination and foreign revolutions alike without fear.

Since the beginning of our American history, we have been engaged in change – in a perpetual peaceful revolution – a revolution which goes on steadily, quietly adjusting itself to changing conditions – without the concentration camp or the quick-lime in the ditch. The world order which we seek is the cooperation of free countries, working together in a friendly, civilized society.

This nation has placed its destiny in the hands and heads and hearts of its millions of free men and women; and its faith in freedom under the guidance of God. Freedom means the supremacy of human rights everywhere. Our support goes to those who struggle to gain those rights or keep them. Our strength in our unity of purpose.

To that high concept there can be no end save victory.

·

## JOSEPH STALIN
### Moscow, 3 July 1941

### 'A grave danger hangs over our country'

*Stalin was taken by surprise in 1941 when Hitler tore up the Nazi–Soviet Pact, launched Operation Barbarossa and invaded Russia. For the first week, he suffered some kind of mental breakdown, especially when he realized the speed with which the Germans were advancing. When members of the Politburo arrived to meet him at Kuntsevo on 30 June, he seems to have thought they had come to arrest him. Only after being urged to establish a state defence committee under his chairmanship did Stalin begin to recover his self-confidence and to reappear in the Kremlin.*

*Once he had overcome his own fears, he emerged once again as the indispensable leader – and on 3 July spoke to the people over the radio. Appealing to Russian patriotism, he made an awe-inspiring call to the people to destroy everything if forced to retreat – to scorch the earth. It was as if the Russia of 1812 had been resurrected and spoken through Stalin's mouth, said one commentator.*

Comrades! Citizens! Brothers and Sisters! Men of our Army and Navy!

I am addressing you, my friends!

The perfidious military attack on our fatherland, begun on 22 June by Hitler's Germany, is continuing.

In spite of heroic resistance of the Red Army, and although the enemy's finest divisions and finest air-force units have already been smashed and have met their doom on the field of battle, the enemy continues to push forward, hurling fresh forces into the attack.

Hitler's troops have succeeded in capturing Lithuania, a considerable part of Latvia, the western part of White Russia, and a part of the western Ukraine.

The Fascist air force is extending the range of operations of its bombers and is bombing Murmansk, Orsha, Mogilev, Smolensk, Kiev, Odessa, and Sevastopol.

A grave danger hangs over our country.

How could it have happened that our glorious Red Army surrendered a number of our cities and districts to the Fascist armies?

Is it really true that German Fascist troops are invincible, as is ceaselessly trumpeted by boastful Fascist propagandists? Of course not!

History shows that there are no invincible armies, and never have been. Napoleon's army was considered invincible, but it was beaten successively by Russian, English, and German armies. Kaiser Wilhelm's German army in the period of the first imperialist war was also considered invincible, but it was beaten several times by Russian and Anglo-French forces, and was finally smashed by Anglo-French forces.

The same must be said of Hitler's German Fascist army today. This army has not yet met with serious resistance on the Continent of Europe. Only on our territory has it met serious resistance, and if as a result of this resistance the finest divisions of Hitler's German Fascist army have been defeated by our Red Army, it means that this army, too, can be smashed and will be smashed as were the armies of Napoleon and Wilhelm.

There can be no doubt that this short-lived military gain for Germany is only an episode, while the tremendous political gain of the USSR is a serious and lasting factor that is bound to form the basis for development of decisive military successes of the Red Army in the war with Fascist Germany . . .

In case of a forced retreat of Red Army units, all rolling stock must be evacuated; to the enemy must not be left a single engine, a single railway car, not a single pound of grain or a gallon of fuel.

Collective farmers must drive off all their cattle and turn over their grain to the safekeeping of state authorities for transportation to the rear. All valuable property including nonferrous metals, grain, and fuel which cannot be withdrawn must without fail be destroyed.

In areas occupied by the enemy, guerrilla units, mounted and foot, must be formed, diversionist groups must be organized to combat enemy troops, to foment guerrilla warfare everywhere, to blow up bridges, roads, damage telephone and telegraph lines, and to set fire to forests, stores, and transports.

In occupied regions conditions must be made unbearable for the enemy and all his accomplices. They must be hounded and annihilated at every step and all their measures frustrated.

This war with Fascist Germany cannot be considered an ordinary war. It is not only a war between two armies, it is also a great war of the entire Soviet people against the German Fascist forces.

The aim of this national war in defence of our country against the Fascist oppressors is not only elimination of the danger hanging over our country, but also aid to all European peoples groaning under the yoke of German Fascism.

In this war of liberation we shall not be alone.

In this great war we shall have loyal allies in the peoples of Europe and America, including German people who are enslaved by Hitlerite despots.

Our war for the freedom of our country will merge with the struggle of the peoples of Europe and America for their independence, for democratic liberties. It will be a united front of peoples standing for freedom and against enslavement and threats of enslavement by Hitler's Fascist armies.

In this connection the historic utterance of British Prime Minister Churchill regarding aid to the Soviet Union and the declaration of the USA government signifying readiness to render aid to our country, which can only evoke a feeling of gratitude in the hearts of the peoples of the Soviet Union, are fully comprehensible and symptomatic.

Comrades, our forces are numberless. The overweening enemy will soon learn this to his cost. Side by side with the Red Army and Navy thousands of workers, collective farmers, and intellectuals are rising to fight the enemy aggressor. The masses of our people will rise up in their millions. The working people of Moscow and Leningrad already have commenced to form vast popular levies in support of the Red Army.

Such popular levies must be raised in every city that is in danger of an enemy invasion; all working people must be roused to defend our freedom, our honour, our country – in our patriotic war against German Fascism.

In order to insure a rapid mobilization of all forces of the peoples of the USSR, and to repulse the enemy who treacherously attacked our country, a State Committee of Defence has been formed in whose hands the entire power of the state has been vested.

The State Committee of Defence has entered into its functions and calls upon all our people to rally around the party of Lenin–Stalin and around the Soviet government so as self-denyingly to support the Red Army and Navy, demolish the enemy, and secure victory.

All our forces for the support of our heroic Red Army and our glorious Red Navy!

All the forces of the people – for the demolition of the enemy! Forward, to our victory!

•

# FRANKLIN DELANO ROOSEVELT
## Washington, DC, 8 December 1941

### *'A date which will live in infamy'*

*From the fall of France in 1940, Britain had conducted war with Germany and Italy on her own, and by the autumn of 1941 the Japanese were in Indo-China, on Singapore's doorstep. Only strong support from the United States might make the Japanese hesitate but the Americans were hard to draw.*

*Then on 7 December, the Japanese attacked Pearl Harbor with 360 planes, sinking three battleships, destroying 120 planes and killing 2,403 Americans (mostly sailors).*

*In this brief speech, Roosevelt asked Congress to declare war on Japan. The opening line of Roosevelt's first draft read: 'a date which will live in world history'. He crossed out 'world history' and substituted 'infamy'.*

*As A. J. P. Taylor wrote, the doubts of Roosevelt were resolved. A true world war began. Churchill said: 'So we had won after all!'*

Mr Vice-President, Mr Speaker, members of the Senate and the House of Representatives:

Yesterday, December 7, 1941 – a date which will live in infamy – the

United States of America was suddenly and deliberately attacked by naval and air forces of the empire of Japan.

The United States was at peace with that nation and, at the solicitation of Japan, was still in conversation with its government and its emperor looking toward the maintenance of peace in the Pacific.

Indeed, one hour after Japanese air squadrons had commenced bombing in the American island of Oahu the Japanese ambassador to the United States and his colleague delivered to our secretary of state a formal reply to a recent American message. And, while this reply stated that it seemed useless to continue the existing diplomatic negotiations, it contained no threat or hint of war or of armed attack.

It will be recorded that the distance of Hawaii from Japan makes it obvious that the attack was deliberately planned many days or even weeks ago. During the intervening time the Japanese government has deliberately sought to deceive the United States by false statements and expressions of hope for continued peace.

The attack yesterday on the Hawaiian Islands has caused severe damage to American naval and military forces. I regret to tell you that very many American lives have been lost. In addition, American ships have been reported torpedoed on the high seas between San Francisco and Honolulu.

Yesterday the Japanese government also launched an attack against Malaya.

Last night Japanese forces attacked Hong Kong.

Last night Japanese forces attacked Guam.

Last night Japanese forces attacked the Philippine Islands.

Last night the Japanese attacked Wake Island.

And this morning the Japanese attacked Midway Island.

Japan has therefore undertaken a surprise offensive extending throughout the Pacific area. The facts of yesterday and today speak for themselves. The people of the United States have already formed their opinions and well understand the implications to the very life and safety of our nation.

As commander in chief of the army and navy I have directed that all measures be taken for our defence. Always will we remember the character of the onslaught against us.

No matter how long it may take us to overcome this premeditated invasion, the American people, in their righteous might, will win through to absolute victory.

I believe that I interpret the will of the Congress and of the people when I assert that we will not only defend ourselves to the uttermost but will make it very certain that this form of treachery shall never again endanger us.

Hostilities exist. There is no blinking at the fact that our people, our territory, and our interests are in grave danger.

With confidence in our armed forces, with the unbounding determination of our people, we will gain the inevitable triumph. So help us God.

I ask that the Congress declare that since the unprovoked and dastardly attack by Japan on Sunday, December 7, 1941, a state of war has existed between the United States and the Japanese Empire.

•

# REINHARD HEYDRICH
## Wannsee, 20 January 1942

### 'The final solution'

*One of the most important events in the history of the twentieth century occurred at a villa on the banks of the Wannsee, a lake near Berlin, on 20 January 1942. It was a conference under the chairmanship of Reinhard Heydrich, head of the SS Intelligence Service, at which Hitler's Nazis planned the final solution, the extermination of about eleven million Jews in Europe. Heydrich had been appointed 'Plenipotentiary for the Preparation of the Final Solution of the European Jewish Question'.*

*This was his address to the senior civil servants.*

We have the means, the methods, the organization, experience and people. And we have the will. This is a historic moment in the struggle against Jewry. The Führer has declared his determination . . . to destroy European Jewry. The Führer sees himself . . . as exterminating fatal bacteria to save the organism. It is them or us. What has happened so far? Step by step we have forced the Jews out of all levels of German life . . .

We have forced them out of the *Lebensraum* of the people partly by transfers to concentration camps, and partly due to Obersturmbannführer Eichmann's organization by permitting 537,000 Jews to emigrate before the war; and finally . . .

We have seen since the beginning of the war the liquidation of hundreds of thousands of Polish, Baltic and Russian Jews. You gentlemen from the Party Chancellery, the Reich Chancellery, the Foreign Office, General Government and Ministry for the East have been kept informed by Gestapo reports of the Action groups' activities . . .

The Reichsführer SS has forbidden any further emigration of Jews. The Jews remaining in the Reich and all European Jews in our present and future spheres of influence will be evacuated to the East for the final solution . . .

We shall work effectively but silently. Total cooperation will be required in this matter of life or death for the Reich. So that we can all envisage what the Jewish question in the Reich involves (*pointing to a map of Europe*) the red area shows the Reich on the eve of war. This is the Eastern front. Behind in white conquered Eastern territories under Germany's civilian rule. In pink territories subject to the Reich – in vertical red stripes occupied territories in the rest of Europe. Horizontal red stripes, our Allies or countries under our influence. The dots on the map like fly spots represent the density of the Jewish population. That is our problem the further we advance between Riga and Odessa.

We must deal with the settlements of our Jewish opponents. They've made themselves comfortable there for centuries. In my own home town of Odessa there are more than 70,000 Jewish inhabitants. There were, used to be (*laughter*). To sum up, gentlemen, our Action groups following hard on the heels of our troops have virtually eliminated the Jewish concentrations. We have influenced the old anti-Semitism by certain procedural measures.

Now the rough work has been done we begin the period of finer work. We need to work in harmony with the civil administration. We count on you gentlemen as far as the final solution is concerned. What is to be resolved will be resolved here (*pointing to the East*), at the world's arse, as my men say. War and gunsmoke have made immense achievements possible. It is the Reichsführer SS's will that the Jewish question is settled there in one clean sweep. The total Jews concerned – 11,000,000.

This breaks down as follows:

In the old Reich – 130,000
In Austria – 43,000
In the Protectorate – 75,000
In the General Government – 2,500,000
In the Balkans – 1,600,000
In Occupied France – 165,000
In Unoccupied France – 740,000 (Quite a task!)
In the New Europe for which we shall be responsible, in
    foreign unoccupied countries, like England – 330,000
In neutral countries like Switzerland – 18,000 of the Chosen
    People.

In the final solution we will use the Jews as labour in the East. They will be marched, both sexes segregated, in columns, building roads on the way, breaking rocks, draining marshes. We'll give them every opportunity to find out what work means, on the extensive industrial plants now being constructed by Comrade Pohl of the SS's Economic Office . . .

Of course, most of these Jews will succumb to natural wastage; the remainder, the toughest, will have to be processed accordingly. Why? Because it is the survival of the fittest. Otherwise they'd seed a new Jewish resurrection. Look at history!

*Heydrich was wounded in Prague on 27 May 1942 by two Czechs parachuted in from Britain. He died eight days later. His death was revenged by the massacre at Lidice. Wherever Heydrich went, a trail of blood was always left behind. He was correctly described as a butcher and a hangman.*

## GENERAL BERNARD MONTGOMERY
Cairo, 13 August 1942

*'We will stand and fight* here'

*The fame of Bernard Montgomery (1887–1976) as a field commander was established with the British Eighth Army from July 1942 to January 1944 as the Desert Rats fought Erwin Rommel, the brilliant German general, from Alamein across north Africa and then into Sicily and southern Italy.*

*Monty, as he was universally known, was an inspiring leader who cared for his soldiers' morale. He could play with an audience of British troops like a fanatical ecclesiastic launching a crusade, said one contemporary observer. Monty arrived in Cairo on 12 August 1942, and assumed command of the Eighth Army the next day, when he made this address to his demoralized officers.*

I want first of all to introduce myself to you. You do not know me. I do not know you. But we have got to work together; therefore we must understand each other, and we must have confidence each in the other. I have only been here a few hours. But from what I have seen and heard since I arrived I am prepared to say, here and now, that I have confidence in you. We will then work together as a team; and together we will gain the confidence of this great Army and go forward to final victory in Africa.

I believe that one of the first duties of a commander is to create what I call 'atmosphere', and in that atmosphere his staff, subordinate commanders, and troops will live and work and fight.

I do not like the general atmosphere I find here. It is an atmosphere of doubt, of looking back to select the next place to which to withdraw, of loss of confidence in our ability to defeat Rommel, of desperate defence measures by reserves in preparing positions in Cairo and the Delta.

All that must cease.

Let us have a new atmosphere.

The defence of Egypt lies here at Alamein and on the Ruweisat

Ridge. What is the use of digging trenches in the Delta? It is quite useless; if we lose this position we lose Egypt; all the fighting troops now in the Delta must come here at once, and will. *Here* we will stand and fight; there will be no further withdrawal. I have ordered that all plans and instructions dealing with further withdrawal are to be burnt, and at once. We will stand and fight *here*.

If we can't stay here alive, then let us stay here dead.

I want to impress on everyone that the bad times are over. Fresh Divisions from the UK are now arriving in Egypt, together with ample reinforcements for our present Divisions. We have 300 to 400 Sherman new tanks coming and these are actually being unloaded at Suez *now*. Our mandate from the Prime Minister is to destroy the Axis forces in North Africa; I have seen it, written on half a sheet of notepaper. And it will be done. If anyone here thinks it can't be done, let him go at once; I don't want any doubters in this party. It can be done, and it will be done: beyond any possibility of doubt.

Now I understand that Rommel is expected to attack at any moment. Excellent. Let him attack.

I would sooner it didn't come for a week, just give me time to sort things out. If we have two weeks to prepare we will be sitting pretty; Rommel can attack as soon as he likes, after that, and I hope he does.

Meanwhile, we ourselves will start to plan a great offensive; it will be the beginning of a campaign which will hit Rommel and his Army for six right out of Africa.

But first we must create a reserve Corps, mobile and strong in armour, which we will train *out of the line*. Rommel has always had such a force in his Africa Corps, which is never used to hold the line but which is always in reserve, available for striking blows. Therein has been his great strength. We will create such a Corps ourselves, a British Panzer Corps; it will consist of two armoured Divisions and one motorized Division; I gave orders yesterday for it to begin to form, back in the Delta.

I have no intention of launching our great attack until we are completely ready; there will be pressure from many quarters to attack soon; *I will not attack until we are ready*, and you can rest assured on that point.

Meanwhile, if Rommel attacks while we are preparing, let him do so with pleasure; we will merely continue with our own preparations and *we* will attack when *we* are ready, and not before.

I want to tell you that I always work on the Chief of Staff system. I have nominated Brigadier de Guingand as Chief of Staff Eighth Army. I will issue orders through him. Whatever he says will be taken as coming from me and will be acted on *at once*. I understand there has been a great deal of 'bellyaching' out here. By bellyaching I mean inventing poor reasons for *not* doing what one has been told to do.

All this is to stop at once.

I will tolerate no bellyaching.

If anyone objects to doing what he is told, then he can get out of it: and at once. I want that made very clear right down through the Eighth Army.

I have little more to say just at present. And some of you may think it is quite enough and may wonder if I am mad.

I assure you I am quite sane.

I understand there are people who often think I am slightly mad; so often that I now regard it as rather a compliment.

All I have to say to that is that if I am slightly mad, there are a large number of people I could name who are raving lunatics!!

What I have done is to get over to you the 'atmosphere' in which we will now work and fight; you must see that that atmosphere permeates right through the Eighth Army to the most junior private soldier. All the soldiers must know what is wanted; when they see it coming to pass there will be a surge of confidence throughout the Army.

I ask you to give me your confidence and to have faith that what I have said will come to pass.

There is much work to be done.

The orders I have given about no further withdrawal will mean a complete change in the layout of our dispositions; also, we must begin to prepare for our great offensive.

The first thing to do is to move our HQ to a decent place where we can live in reasonable comfort and where the Army Staff can all be together and side by side with the HQ of the Desert Air Force. This is a frightful place here, depressing, unhealthy and a rendezvous for every fly in Africa; we shall do no good work here. Let us get over there by the sea where it is fresh and healthy. If officers are to do good work they must have decent messes, and be comfortable. So off we go on the new line.

The Chief of Staff will be issuing orders on many points very shortly, and I am always available to be consulted by the senior officers of the staff. The great point to remember is that we are going to finish with this chap Rommel once and for all. It will be quite easy. There is no doubt about it.

He is definitely a nuisance. Therefore we will hit him a crack and finish with him.

*Montgomery's speech to his officers marked one of the turning points of the war. Rommel's offensive at Alam Halfa began on the night of 30–31 August. The attack was held. Monty had gained the initiative and at El Alamein in October he won a decisive victory. He went on to command Allied ground troops in the Normandy landings and he played a decisive role in checking the German counter-offensive in the Ardennes in 1944. On 4 May 1945 he formally accepted the surrender of all German forces in north-western Europe at Lüneburg Heath.*

•

## CHAIM RUMKOWSKI
### Łódź ghetto, 4 September 1942

### *'Give me your children'*

*At the Łódź ghetto in Poland, which the Germans used to incarcerate the old and sick and other unwanted Jews from the cities of western Europe, Chaim Rumkowski, aged sixty, a widower without children and Elder of the ghetto, believed he was ruling a Jewish state. He loved the ghetto, where more than 160,000 Jews were contained. It was his dominion and he tried to point out the value of ghettoization, a partial fulfilment of the Zionist goals he embraced. He repeatedly told Jews at Łódź that when the war was over he would be chosen to run a protectorate that the Nazis would establish to contain all the Jews of Europe.*

*Although Rumkowski bargained with the Germans to minimize deportations from the ghetto, his Faustian pact with the Nazis obliged him to fulfil an unending series of deportation orders imposed on him by the Nazis: ten thousand, fifteen thousand, twenty thousand – and then ten thousand more. Finally the entire ghetto was gone.*

*The most chilling of all his exhortations to the inhabitants of Łódź ghetto (perhaps indeed the most horrifying speech in this anthology) was this address in which he urged the Jews to give up their children to the Nazis – and the gas ovens.*

*In* The Drowned and the Saved, *Primo Levi describes Rumkowski's oratorical style as unmistakable. He adopted the technique of Mussolini and Hitler, the style of inspired recitation, pseudo-colloquy with the crowd, the creation of consent through subjugation and plaudit. 'The man who has throne and sceptre, who is not afraid of being contradicted or derided, speaks like this.'*

A grievous blow has struck the ghetto. They are asking us to give up the best we possess – the children and the elderly. I was unworthy of having a child of my own, so I gave the best years of my life to children. I've lived and breathed with children. I never imagined that I would be forced to deliver this sacrifice to the altar with my own hands. In my old age I must stretch out my hands and beg: Brothers and sisters, hand them over to me! Fathers and mothers, give me your children! (*Horrible, terrifying wailing among the assembled crowd.*)

I had a suspicion something was about to befall us. I anticipated 'something' and was always like a watchman on guard to prevent it. But I was unsuccessful because I did not know what was threatening us. I did not know the nature of the danger. The taking of the sick from the hospitals caught me completely by surprise. And I give you the best proof there is of this: I had my own nearest and dearest among them, and I could do nothing for them.

I thought that that would be the end of it, that after that they'd leave us in peace, the peace for which I long so much, for which I've always worked, which has been my goal. But something else, it turned out, was destined for us. Such is the fate of the Jews: always more suffering and always worse suffering, especially in times of war.

Yesterday afternoon, they gave me the order to send more than 20,000 Jews out of the ghetto, and if not – 'We will do it!' So, the question became: 'Should we take it upon ourselves, do it ourselves, or leave it for others to do?' Well, we – that is, I and my closest associates – thought first not about 'How many will perish?' but 'How many is it possible to save?' And we reached the conclusion that, however hard it would be for us, we should take the implementation of this order into our own hands.

I must perform this difficult and bloody operation – I must cut off limbs in order to save the body itself! – I must take children because, if not, others may be taken as well, God forbid.

(*Horrible wailing.*)

I have no thought of consoling you today. Nor do I wish to calm you. I must lay bare your full anguish and pain. I come to you like a bandit, to take from you what you treasure most in your hearts! I have tried, using every possible means, to get the order revoked. I tried – when that proved to be impossible – to soften the order. Just yesterday I ordered a list of children aged nine – I wanted, at least, to save this one age group, the nine- to ten-year-olds. But I was not granted this concession. On only one point did I succeed, in saving the ten-year-olds and up. Let this be a consolation in our profound grief.

There are, in the ghetto, many patients who can expect to live only a few days more, maybe a few weeks. I don't know if the idea is diabolical or not, but I must say it: 'Give me the sick. In their place, we can save the healthy.' I know how dear the sick are to any family, and particularly to Jews. However, when cruel demands are made, one has to weigh and measure: who shall, can and may be saved? And common sense dictates that the saved must be those who can be saved and those who have a chance of being rescued, not those who cannot be saved in any case.

We live in the ghetto, mind you. We live with so much restriction that we do not have enough even for the healthy, let alone for the sick. Each of us feeds the sick at the expense of our own health: we give our bread to the sick. We give them our meagre ration of sugar, our little piece of meat. And what's the result? Not enough to cure the sick, and we ourselves become ill. Of course, such sacrifices are the most beautiful and noble. But there are times when one has to choose: sacrifice the sick, who haven't the slightest chance of recovery and who also may make others ill, or rescue the healthy.

I could not deliberate over this problem for long; I had to resolve it in favour of the healthy. In this spirit, I gave the appropriate instructions to the doctors, and they will be expected to deliver all incurable patients, so that the healthy, who want and are able to live, will be saved in their place.

(*Horrible weeping.*)

I understand you, mothers; I see your tears, all right. I also feel what you feel in your hearts, you fathers who will have to go to work the morning after your children have been taken from you, when just yesterday you were playing with your dear little ones. I know and feel all this. Since four o'clock yesterday, when I first found out about the order, I have been utterly broken. I share your pain. I suffer because of your anguish, and I don't know how I'll survive this – where I'll find the strength.

I must tell you a secret: they requested 24,000 victims, 3,000 a day for eight days. I succeeded in reducing the number to 20,000, but only on the condition that these would be children below the age of ten. Children ten and older are safe. Since the children and the aged together equal only some 13,000 souls, the gap will have to be filled with the sick.

I can barely speak. I am exhausted; I only want to tell you what I am asking of you: Help me carry out this action! I am trembling. I am afraid that others, God forbid, will do it themselves . . .

A broken Jew stands before you. Do not envy me. This is the most difficult of all the orders I've ever had to carry out at any time. I reach out to you with my broken, trembling hands and I beg: Give into my hands the victims, so that we can avoid having further victims, and a population of a hundred thousand Jews can be preserved. So they promised me: if we deliver our victims by ourselves, there will be peace . . .

(*Shouts: 'We all will go!' 'Mr Chairman, an only child should not be taken; children should be taken from families with several children!'*)

These are empty phrases! I don't have the strength to argue with you! If the authorities were to arrive, none of you would shout.

I understand what it means to tear off a part of the body. Yesterday I begged on my knees, but it didn't work. From small villages with Jewish populations of seven to eight thousand, barely a thousand arrived here. So which is better? What do you want: that eighty to ninety thousand Jews remain, or, God forbid, that the whole population be annihilated?

You may judge as you please; my duty is to preserve the Jews who remain. I do not speak to hotheads. I speak to your reason and conscience. I have done and will continue doing everything possible to keep arms from appearing in the streets and blood from being shed. The order could not be undone; it could only be reduced.

One needs the heart of a bandit to ask from you what I am asking. But put yourself in my place, think logically, and you'll reach the conclusion that I cannot proceed any other way. The part that can be saved is much larger than the part that must be given away.

*By 1 September 1944, nearly all the Jews of Łódź had been murdered. Rumkowski was told he could remain in the ghetto. He declined the offer and joined the last transport for Auschwitz where he too was murdered. Soviet troops liberated the ghetto on 19 January 1945. Of the 160,000 original inhabitants, there remained 870 starving human beings.*

•

## ÉAMON DE VALERA
### Dublin, 17 March 1943

*'The vision of such an Ireland'*

*Guerrilla commander, political prisoner, successful revolutionary, a partisan in civil war, Éamon de Valera (1882–1975) was prime minister of Ireland for more than twenty years and president for fourteen years until he retired in 1973 at the age of ninety. He was elected president of Sinn Féin, the Irish republican party, in 1917, but subsequently founded Fianna Fáil and formed a government in 1932. As prime minister he gradually cut the links binding Dublin to British rule. A new constitution in 1937 created the sovereign democratic state of Eire.*

*As Roy Foster, the historian of Ireland, says, Fianna Fáil Ireland was a nation set apart by Catholicism and nationality: the interlocking relationships of Church and politics helped to define a unique, God-given way of life. There was also revealed a fierce suspicion of cosmopolitanism and what it stood for, as shown in de Valera's St Patrick's Day broadcasts on the new national radio station.*

*The most celebrated of those broadcasts was made in 1943 when he called up a vision of an Ireland characterized by cosy homesteads, athletic youths and comely maidens.*

Before the present war began I was accustomed on St Patrick's Day to speak to our kinsfolk in foreign lands, particularly those in the United States, and to tell them year by year of the progress being made towards building up the Ireland of their dreams and ours – the Ireland that we believe is destined to play, by its example and its inspiration, a great part as a nation among the nations.

Acutely conscious though we all are of the misery and desolation in which the greater part of the world is plunged, let us turn aside for a moment to that ideal Ireland that we would have. That Ireland which we dreamed of would be the home of a people who valued material wealth only as the basis of right living, of a people who were satisfied with frugal comfort and devoted their leisure to the things of the spirit – a land whose countryside would be bright with cosy homesteads, whose fields and villages would be joyous with the sounds of industry, with the romping of sturdy children, the contests of athletic youths and the laughter of comely maidens, whose firesides would be forums for the wisdom of serene old age. It would, in a word, be the home of a people living the life that God desires that man should live.

With the tidings that make such an Ireland possible, St Patrick came to our ancestors 1,500 years ago, promising happiness here as well as happiness hereafter. It was the pursuit of such an Ireland that later made our country worthy to be called the Island of Saints and

Scholars. It was the idea of such an Ireland, happy, vigorous, spiritual, that fired the imagination of our poets, that made successive generations of patriotic men give their lives to win religious and political liberty, and that will urge men in our own and future generations to die, if need be, so that these liberties may be preserved.

One hundred years ago the Young Irelanders, by holding up the vision of such an Ireland before the people, inspired our nation and moved it spiritually as it had hardly been moved since the golden age of Irish civilization. Fifty years after the Young Irelanders, the founders of the Gaelic League similarly inspired and moved the people of their day, as did later the leaders of the Volunteers. We of this time, if we have the will and the active enthusiasm, have the opportunity to inspire and move our generation in like manner. We can do so by keeping this thought of a noble future for our country constantly before our minds, ever seeking in action to bring that future into being, and ever remembering that it is to our nation as a whole that future must apply.

For many the pursuit of the material is a necessity. Man, to express himself fully and to make the best use of the talents God has given him, needs a certain minimum of comfort and leisure. A section of our people have not yet this minimum. They rightly strive to secure it, and it must be our aim and the aim of all who are just and wise to assist in the effort. But many have got more than is required and are free, if they choose, to devote themselves more completely to cultivating the things of the mind, and in particular those which mark us out as a distinct nation.

The first of these latter is the national language. It is for us what no other language can be. It is our very own. It is more than a symbol; it is an essential part of our nationhood. It has been moulded by the thought of a hundred generations of our forebears. In it is stored the accumulated experience of a people, our people, who even before Christianity was brought to them were already cultured and living in a well-ordered society. The Irish language spoken in Ireland today is the direct descendant without break of the language our ancestors spoke in those far-off days.

As a vehicle of three thousand years of our history, the language is for us precious beyond measure. As the bearer to us of a philosophy, of an outlook on life deeply Christian and rich in practical wisdom, the language today is worth far too much to dream of letting it go. To part with it would be to abandon a great part of ourselves, to lose the key of our past, to cut away the roots from the tree. With the language gone we could never aspire again to being more than half a nation.

For my part, I believe that this outstanding mark of our nationhood can be preserved and made forever safe by this generation. I am indeed certain of it, but I know that it cannot be saved without understanding and cooperation and effort and sacrifice. It would be wrong to minimize the difficulties. They are not slight. The task of restoring the language as the everyday speech of our people is a task as great as any nation ever undertook. But it is a noble task. Other nations have succeeded in it, though in their case, when the effort was begun, their national language was probably more widely spoken among their people than is ours with us. As long as the language lives, however, on the lips of the people as their natural speech in any substantial part of this land we are assured of success if – *if* we are in earnest.

•

## GENERAL GEORGE PATTON
### England and France, 1943–4

*'That son of a bitch Patton again'*

*'Old Blood and Guts' was the nickname given to General George Patton (1885–1945) by his troops during the Second World War as a testimony to his reputation for recklessness and hot-headed daring.*

*That daring was shown at its most flamboyant in 1944 when his Third Army advanced across France in a sweep through Brittany, round Paris, up the Marne and the Moselle, across the Rhine and eventually into Czechoslovakia in April 1945.*

*As they went into battle, Patton, puffing his cigar, was given to making short, sharp, morale-boosting addresses at his staff conferences and to his men.*

*The three published here were given to his troops in England and Normandy. The third was his welcome to the 761st 'Black Panther' Tank Battalion. They show that you don't need to be long-winded to be eloquent or to allow your audience to get the message, and raised profanity to a fine art.*

I am not supposed to be commanding this Army – I am not even supposed to be in England. Let the first bastards to find out be the goddam Germans. Some day I want them to rise on their hind legs and howl: 'Jesus Christ, it's that goddam Third Army and that son of a bitch Patton again' . . . There's one great thing that you men can say when it's all over and you're home once more. You can thank God that twenty years from now when you're sitting by the fireside with your grandson on your knee, and he asks you what you did in the war, you won't have to shift him to the other knee, cough and say, 'I shovelled crap in Louisiana.'

Now, gentlemen, doubtless from time to time there will be some complaints that we are pushing people too hard. I don't give a good goddam about such complaints. I believe in the old and sound rule that an ounce of sweat is worth a gallon of blood. The harder we push, the more Germans we'll kill, and gentlemen, the more Germans we kill, the fewer of our men will be killed. Pushing means fewer casualties. I want you to remember that.

There's another thing I want you to remember. Forget this goddam business of worrying about our flanks. We must guard our flanks, but not to the extent that we don't do anything else. Some goddammed fool once said that flanks must be secured and since then sons of bitches all over the world have been going crazy guarding their flanks. We don't want any of that in the Third Army. Flanks are something for the enemy to worry about, not us.

Also, I don't want to get any messages saying, 'I'm holding my position.' We're not holding anything! Let the Hun do that. We are advancing constantly and are not interested in holding anything, except the enemy. We're going to hold on to him and kick the hell out of him all the time.

Our basic plan of operation is to advance and to keep on advancing regardless of whether we have to go over, under, or through the enemy. We have one motto, 'L'audace, l'audace, toujours l'audace!' Remember that, gentlemen. From here on out, until we win or die in the attempt, we will always be audacious.

Men, you are the first Negro tankers ever to fight in the American army. I would never have asked for you if you were not good. I have nothing but the best in my army. I don't care what colour you are as long as you go up there and kill those Kraut sons of bitches. Everyone has their eyes on you and are expecting great things from you. Most of all, your race is looking forward to your success. Don't let them down, and, damn you, don't let me down!

    If you want me you can always find me in the lead tank.

*Patton was killed in a road accident while commanding the US Fifth Army in occupied Germany in December 1945.*

•

## BISHOP GEORGE BELL
London, 9 February 1944

*'Obliteration is not a justifiable act of war'*

*The Anglican churchman George Bell (1893–1958) was Dean of Canterbury and then Bishop of Chichester from 1929 to 1958. Bell was a bishop with an international outlook and moral courage. That courage was demonstrated when he exposed the anti-Christian trend of Hitlerism at its beginnings, for which he was sharply criticized. It was shown again during the Second World War when he attacked the Allied policy of bombing cities and civilian homes in Germany, as in this House of Lords speech. His criticism made him deeply unpopular but he did not flinch from his moral position.*

I turn to the situation in February 1944, and the terrific devastation by Bomber Command of German towns. I do not forget the Luftwaffe, or its tremendous bombing of Belgrade, Warsaw, Rotterdam, London,

Portsmouth, Coventry, Canterbury and many other places of military, industrial and cultural importance. Hitler is a barbarian. There is no decent person on the Allied side who is likely to suggest that we should make him our pattern or attempt to be competitors in that market. It is clear enough that large-scale bombing of enemy towns was begun by the Nazis. I am not arguing that point at all. The question with which I am concerned is this. Do the Government understand the full force of what area bombardment is doing and is destroying now? Are they alive not only to the vastness of the material damage, much of which is irreparable, but also to the harvest they are laying up for the future relationships of the peoples of Europe as well as to its moral implications? The aim of Allied bombing from the air, said the Secretary of State for Air at Plymouth on 22 January, is to paralyse German war industry and transport. I recognize the legitimacy of concentrated attack on industrial and military objectives, on airfields and air bases, in view especially of the coming of the Second Front. I fully realize that in attacks on centres of war industry and transport the killing of civilians when it is the result of bona-fide military activity is inevitable. But there must be a fair balance between the means employed and the purpose achieved. To obliterate a whole town because certain portions contain military and industrial establishments is to reject the balance.

Let me take two crucial instances, Hamburg and Berlin. Hamburg has a population of between one and two million people. It contains targets of immense military and industrial importance. It also happens to be the most democratic town in Germany where the anti-Nazi opposition was strongest. Injuries to civilians resulting from bona-fide attacks on particular objectives are legitimate according to International Law. But owing to the methods used the whole town is now a ruin. Unutterable destruction and devastation were wrought last autumn. On a very conservative estimate, according to the early German statistics, 28,000 persons were killed. Never before in the history of air warfare was an attack of such weight and persistence carried out against a single industrial concentration. Practically all the buildings, cultural, military, residential, industrial, religious – including the famous University Library with its 800,000 volumes, of which three-quarters have perished – were razed to the ground.

Berlin, the capital of the Reich, is four times the size of Hamburg. The offices of the Government, the military, industrial, war-making establishments in Berlin are a fair target. Injuries to civilians are inevitable. But up to date half Berlin has been destroyed, area by area, the residential and the industrial portions alike. Through the dropping of thousands of tons of bombs, including fire-phosphorus bombs, of extraordinary power, men and women have been lost, overwhelmed in the colossal tornado of smoke, blast and flame. It is said that 74,000 persons have been killed and that three million are already homeless. The policy is obliteration, openly acknowledged. That is not a justifiable act of war. Again, Berlin is one of the greatest centres of art collections in the world. It has a large collection of Oriental and classical sculpture. It has one of the best picture galleries in Europe, comparable to the National Gallery. It has a gallery of modern art better than the Tate, a museum of ethnology without parallel in this country, one of the biggest and best organized libraries – State and university, containing two and a half million books – in the world. Almost all these non-industrial, non-military buildings are grouped together near the old Palace and in the Street of the Linden. The whole of that street, which has been constantly mentioned in the accounts of the raids, has been demolished. It is possible to replace flat houses by mass production. It is not possible so quickly to rebuild libraries or galleries or churches or museums. It is not very easy to rehouse those works of art which have been spared. Those works of art and those libraries will be wanted for the re-education of the Germans after the war. I wonder whether your Lordships realize the loss involved in that.

How is it, then, that this wholesale destruction has come about? The answer is that it is the method used, the method of area bombing. The first outstanding raid of area bombing was, I believe, in the spring of 1942, directed against Lübeck, then against Rostock, followed by the thousand-bomber raid against Cologne at the end of May 1942. The point I want to bring home, because I doubt whether it is sufficiently realized, is that it is no longer definite military and industrial objectives which are the aim of the bombers, but the whole town, area by area, is plotted carefully out. This area is singled out and plastered on one night; that area is singled out and plastered on another night; a third, a fourth, a fifth area is similarly singled out and plastered night after night, till, to use the language of the Chief of Bomber Command with regard to Berlin, the heart of Nazi Germany ceases to beat. How can there be discrimination in such matters when civilians, monuments, military objectives and industrial objectives all together form the target? How can the bombers aim at anything more than a great space when they see nothing and the bombing is blind?

Is it a matter for wonder that anti-Nazis who long for help to over-throw Hitler are driven to despair? I have here a telegram, which I have communicated to the Foreign Office, sent to me on 27 December last by a well-known anti-Nazi Christian leader who had to flee from Germany for his life long before the war. It was sent from Zürich, and puts what millions inside Germany must feel. He says:

'Is it understood that present situation gives us no sincere opportunity for appeal to people because one cannot but suspect effect of promising words on practically powerless population convinced by bombs and phosphor that their annihilation is resolved?'

If we wish to shorten the war, as we must, then let the Government speak a word of hope and encouragement both to the tortured millions of Europe and to those enemies of Hitler to whom in 1939 Mr Churchill referred as 'millions who stand aloof from the seething mass of criminality and corruption constituted by the Nazi Party machine'.

Why is there this blindness to the psychological side? Why is there this inability to reckon with the moral and spiritual facts? Why is there this forgetfulness of the ideals by which our cause is inspired? How can the War Cabinet fail to see that this progressive devastation of cities is threatening the roots of civilization? How can they be blind to the harvest of even fiercer warring and desolation, even in this country, to which the present destruction will inevitably lead when the members of the War Cabinet have long passed to their rest? How can they fail to realize that this is not the way to curb military aggression and end war? This is an extraordinarily solemn moment. What we do in war – which, after all, lasts a comparatively short time – affects the whole character of peace, which covers a much longer period. The sufferings of Europe, brought about by the demoniac cruelty of Hitler and his Nazis, and hardly imaginable to those in this country who for the last five years have not been out of this island or had intimate association with Hitler's victims, are not to be healed by the use of power only, power exclusive and unlimited. The Allies stand for something greater than power. The chief name inscribed on our banner is 'Law'. It is of supreme importance that we who, with our Allies, are the liberators of Europe should so use power that it is always under the control of law. It is because the bombing of enemy towns – this area bombing – raises this issue of power unlimited and exclusive that such immense importance is bound to attach to the policy and action of His Majesty's Government. I beg to move.

*Bell was the natural choice to become Archbishop of Canterbury, but was ignored by Winston Churchill, who had disliked his attacks on British war policy.*

•

## J. ROBERT OPPENHEIMER
### Los Alamos, New Mexico, 2 November 1945

### 'Our deep moral dependence'

*Ever since the discovery of nuclear fission, Julius Robert Oppenheimer (1904–67), one of the world's greatest nuclear scientists, carried in his mind the possibility of powerful explosives based on it. He realized how much it might do for the Allies in the Second World War and how much it might change the course of history – and also how ominous the developments could be for the future of the human race.*

*He became the first director of the Los Alamos atomic-bomb project in 1943 and led the scientists who produced the atomic bombs that fell on Hiroshima and Nagasaki.*

*He resigned in 1945 and made this speech, as a fellow scientist and 'fellow worrier', to the Association of Los Alamos Scientists – a defence of the atomic bomb that was permeated with uneasiness about how it might now be used.*

The reason that we did this job is because it was an organic necessity. If you are a scientist you cannot stop such a thing. If you are a scientist you believe that it is good to find out how the world works; that it is good to find out what the realities are; that it is good to turn over to mankind at large the greatest possible power to control the world and to deal with it according to its lights and its values.

There has been a lot of talk about the evil of secrecy, of concealment, of control, of security. Some of that talk has been on a rather low plane, limited really to saying that it is difficult or inconvenient to work in a world where you are not free to do what you want. I think that the talk has been justified, and that the almost unanimous resistance of scientists to the imposition of control and secrecy is a justified position, but I think that the reason for it may lie a little deeper. I think that it comes from the fact that secrecy strikes at the very root of what science is, and what it is for. It is not possible to be a scientist unless you believe that it is good to learn. It is not good to be a scientist, and it is not possible, unless you think that it is of the highest value to share your knowledge, to share it with anyone who is interested. It is not possible to be a scientist unless you believe that the knowledge of the world, and the power which this gives, is a thing which is of intrinsic value to humanity, and that you are using it to help in the spread of knowledge, and are willing to take the consequences. And, therefore, I think that this resistance which we feel and see all around us to anything which is an attempt to treat science of the future as though it were rather a dangerous thing, a thing that must be watched and managed, is resisted not because of its inconvenience – I think that we are in a position where we must be willing to take any inconveniences – but resisted because it is based on a philosophy incompatible with that by which we live, and learned to live in the past.

There are many people who try to wriggle out of this. They say the real importance of atomic energy does not lie in the weapons that have been made; the real importance lies in all the great benefits which atomic energy, which the various radiations, will bring to mankind. There may be some truth in this. I am sure that there is truth in it, because there has never in the past been a new field opening up where the real fruits of it have not been invisible at the beginning. I have a very high confidence that the fruits – the so-called peacetime applications – of atomic energy will have in them all we think, and more. There are others who try to escape the immediacy of this situation by saying that, after all, war has always been very terrible; after all, weapons have always got worse and worse; that this is just another weapon and it doesn't create a great change; that they are not so bad; bombings have been bad in this war and this is not a change in that – it just adds a little to the effectiveness of bombing; that some sort of protection will be found. I think that these efforts to diffuse and weaken the nature of the crisis make it only more dangerous. I think it is for us to accept it as a very grave crisis, to realize that these atomic weapons which we have started to make are very terrible, that they involve a change, that they are not just a slight modification: to accept this, and to accept with it the necessity for those transformations in the world that will make it possible to integrate these developments into human life.

As scientists I think we have perhaps a little greater ability to accept change, and accept radical change, because of our experiences in the pursuit of science. And that may help us – that, and the fact that we have lived with it – to be of some use in understanding these problems . . .

The control of atomic weapons cannot be in itself the unique end of such operation [of international collaboration]. The only unique end can be a world that is united, and a world in which war will not occur. But those things don't happen overnight, and in this field it would seem that one could get started, and get started without meeting those insuperable obstacles which history has so often placed in the way of any effort of cooperation. Now this is not an easy thing, and the point I want to make, the one point I want to hammer home, is what an enormous change in spirit is involved. There are things which we hold very dear, and I think rightly hold very dear; I would say that the word democracy perhaps stood for some of them as well as any other word. There are many parts of the world in which there is no democracy. There are other things which we hold dear, and which we rightly should. And when I speak of a new spirit in international affairs I mean that even to these deepest of things which we cherish, and for which Americans have been willing to die – and certainly most of us would be willing to die – even in these deepest things, we realize that there is something more profound than that; namely, the common bond with other men everywhere. It is only if you do that that this makes sense; because if you approach the problem and say, 'We know what is right and we would like to use the atomic bomb to persuade you to agree with us,' then you are in a very weak position and you will not succeed, because under those conditions you will not succeed in delegating responsibility for the survival of men. It is a purely unilateral statement; you will find yourselves attempting by force of arms to prevent a disaster.

I want to express the utmost sympathy with the people who have to grapple with this problem and in the strongest terms to urge you not to underestimate its difficulty. I can think of an analogy, and I hope it is not a completely good analogy: in the days in the first half of the nineteenth century there were many people, mostly in the North, but some in the South, who thought that there was no evil on earth more degrading than human slavery, and nothing that they would more willingly devote their lives to than its eradication. Always when I was young I wondered why it was that when Lincoln was President he did not declare that the war against the South, when it broke out, was a war that slavery should be abolished, that this was the central point, the rallying point, of that war. Lincoln was severely criticized by many of the Abolitionists as you know, by many then called radicals, because he seemed to be waging a war which did not hit the thing that was most important. But Lincoln realized, and I have only in the last months come to appreciate the depth and wisdom of it, that beyond the issue of slavery was the issue of the community of the people of the country, and the issue of the Union. I hope that today this will not be an issue calling for war; but I wanted to remind you that in order to preserve the Union Lincoln had to subordinate the immediate problem of the eradication of slavery, and trust – and I think that if he had had his way it would have gone so – to the conflict of these ideas in a united people to eradicate it . . .

It is everywhere felt that the fraternity between us and scientists in other countries may be one of the most helpful things for the future; yet it is apparent that even in this country not all of us who are scientists are in agreement. There is no harm in that; such disagreement is healthy. But we must not lose the sense of fraternity because of it; we must not lose our fundamental confidence in our fellow scientists.

I think that we have no hope at all if we yield in our belief in the value of science, in the good that it can be to the world to know about reality, about nature, to attain a gradually greater and greater control of nature, to learn, to teach, to understand. I think that if we lose our faith in this we stop being scientists, we sell out our heritage, we lose what we have most of value for this time of crisis.

But there is another thing: we are not only scientists; we are men, too. We cannot forget our dependence on our fellow men. I mean not only our material dependence, without which no science would be possible, and without which we could not work; I mean also our deep moral dependence, in that the value of science must lie in the world of men, that all our roots lie there. These are the strongest bonds in the world, stronger than those even that bind us to one another, these are the deepest bonds – that bind us to our fellow men.

*Oppenheimer became chairman of the Atomic Energy Commission but opposed the hydrogen bomb. His career ended after he was brought before Joseph Mc-Carthy's UnAmerican Affairs Committee, labelled as a poor security risk and kept from seeing classified information.*

# WINSTON CHURCHILL
Fulton, Missouri, 5 March 1946

## The 'iron curtain'

*Winston Churchill had lost the British general election in 1945 and was now leader of the Opposition. In 1946 he decided to absent himself from parliament for a few months and accepted an invitation to deliver an address at Westminster College in Fulton, Missouri, the home state of President Truman. Truman and Churchill travelled together in the president's special train.*

*At Fulton, Churchill made the most important and influential of his post-war speeches, in which he advocated a United Nations peace-keeping force and the strengthening of the 'special relationship' between Britain and the United States. The speech is remembered most, however, for Churchill's description of the 'iron curtain' that had descended across Europe.*

A shadow has fallen upon the scenes so lately lighted by the Allied victory. Nobody knows what Soviet Russia and its Communist international organization intends to do in the immediate future, or what are the limits, if any, to their expansive and proselytizing tendencies. I have a strong admiration and regard for the valiant Russian people and for my wartime comrade, Marshal Stalin. There is deep sympathy and goodwill in Britain – and I doubt not here also – towards the peoples of all the Russias and a resolve to persevere through many differences and rebuffs in establishing lasting friendships. We understand the Russian need to be secure on her western frontiers by the removal of all possibility of German aggression. We welcome Russia to her rightful place among the leading nations of the world. We welcome her flag upon the seas. Above all, we welcome constant, frequent and growing contacts between the Russian people and our own people on both sides of the Atlantic. It is my duty, however, for I am sure you would wish me to state the facts as I see them to you, to place before you certain facts about the present position in Europe.

From Stettin in the Baltic to Trieste in the Adriatic, an iron curtain has descended across the Continent. Behind that line lie all the capitals of the ancient states of Central and Eastern Europe. Warsaw, Berlin, Prague, Vienna, Budapest, Belgrade, Bucharest and Sofia, all these famous cities and the populations around them lie in what I must call the Soviet sphere, and all are subject in one form or another, not only to Soviet influence but to a very high and, in many cases, increasing measure of control from Moscow. Athens alone – Greece with its immortal glories – is free to decide its future at an election under British, American and French observation. The Russian-dominated Polish Government has been encouraged to make enormous and wrongful inroads upon Germany, and mass expulsions of millions of Germans on a scale grievous and undreamed-of are now taking place. The Communist parties, which were very small in all these Eastern states of Europe, have been raised to pre-eminence and power far beyond their numbers and are seeking everywhere to obtain totalitarian control. Police governments are prevailing in nearly every case, and so far, except in Czechoslovakia, there is no true democracy.

Turkey and Persia [Iran] are both profoundly alarmed and disturbed at the claims which are being made upon them and at the pressure being exerted by the Moscow Government. An attempt is being made by the Russians in Berlin to build up a quasi-Communist party in their zone of Occupied Germany by showing special favours to groups of left-wing German leaders. At the end of the fighting last June, the American and British Armies withdrew westwards, in accordance with an earlier agreement, to a depth at some points of one hundred and fifty miles upon a front of nearly four hundred miles, in order to allow our Russian allies to occupy this vast expanse of territory which the Western Democracies had conquered.

If now the Soviet Government tries, by separate action, to build up a pro-Communist Germany in their areas, this will cause new serious difficulties in the British and American zones, and will give the defeated Germans the power of putting themselves up to auction between the Soviets and the Western Democracies. Whatever conclusions may be drawn from these facts – and facts they are – this is certainly not the Liberated Europe we fought to build up. Nor is it one which contains the essentials of permanent peace.

The safety of the world requires a new unity in Europe, from which no nation should be permanently outcast. It is from the quarrels of the strong parent races in Europe that the world wars we have witnessed, or which occurred in former times, have sprung. Twice in our own lifetime we have seen the United States, against their wishes and their traditions, against arguments, the force of which it is impossible not to comprehend, drawn by irresistible forces, into these wars in time to secure the victory of the good cause, but only after frightful slaughter and devastation had occurred. Twice the United States has had to send several millions of its young men across the Atlantic to find the war; but now war can find any nation, wherever it may dwell between dusk and dawn. Surely we should work with conscious purpose for a grand pacification of Europe, within the structure of the United Nations and in accordance with its Charter. That I feel is an open cause of policy of very great importance.

*Churchill became prime minister in 1951 and resigned office in 1955. He was made an honorary citizen of the United States in 1963 – a unique distinction – and won the Nobel Prize for Literature in 1953. He died in 1965 and was given a state funeral.*

•

# BERNARD BARUCH
New York, 14 June 1946

### *'A choice between the quick and the dead'*

*Bernard Baruch (1870–1965) began life as an office boy and made his fortune as a speculator and Wall Street financier. He was chosen by Woodrow Wilson to head the War Industries Board in the First World War and helped to draft the Versailles Treaty in 1919. He became a valued adviser to presidents – he also advised Churchill during the Second World War.*

    *As an elder statesman he was the United States representative to the United*

*Nations Atomic Energy Commission in 1946 and 1947. There was a note of apocalyptic foreboding at the start of his address to the commission at its opening session. The American plan for the control of atomic weapons became known as the Baruch Plan.*

We are here to make a choice between the quick and the dead.

That is our business.

Behind the black portent of the new atomic age lies a hope which, seized upon with faith, can work our salvation. If we fail, then we have damned every man to be the slave of fear. Let us not deceive ourselves: we must seek world peace or world destruction.

Science has torn from nature a secret so vast in its potentialities that our minds cower from the terror it creates. Yet terror is not enough to inhibit the use of the atomic bomb. The terror created by weapons has never stopped man from employing them. For each new weapon a defence has been produced, in time. But now we face a condition in which adequate defence does not exist.

Science, which gave us this dread power, shows that it can be made a giant help to humanity, but science does not show us how to prevent its baleful use. So we have been appointed to obviate that peril by finding a meeting of the minds and the hearts of our peoples. Only in the will of mankind lies the answer.

In this crisis we represent not only our governments but, in a larger way, we represent the peoples of the world. We must remember that the peoples do not belong to the governments, but that the governments belong to the peoples. We must answer their demands; we must answer the world's longing for peace and security.

In that desire the United States shares ardently and hopefully. The search of science for the absolute weapon has reached fruition in this country. But she stands ready to proscribe and destroy this instrument – to lift its use from death to life – if the world will join in a pact to that end.

In our success lies the promise of a new life, freed from the heart-stopping fears that now beset the world. The beginning of victory for the great ideals for which millions have bled and died lies in building a workable plan. Now we approach the fulfilment of the aspirations of mankind. At the end of the road lies the fairer, better, surer life we crave and mean to have.

Only by a lasting peace are liberties and democracies strengthened and deepened. War is their enemy. And it will not do to believe that any of us can escape war's devastation. Victor, vanquished and neutrals alike are affected physically, economically and morally.

Against the degradation of war we can erect a safeguard. That is the guerdon for which we reach. Within the scope of the formula we outline here, there will be found, to those who seek it, the essential elements of our purpose. Others will see only emptiness. Each of us carries his own mirror in which is reflected hope – or determined desperation – courage or cowardice.

There is famine throughout the world today. It starves men's bodies. But there is a greater famine – the hunger of men's spirit. That starvation can be cured by the conquest of fear, and the substitution of hope, from which springs faith – faith in each other; faith that we want to work together toward salvation; and determination that those who threaten the peace and safety shall be punished.

The peoples of these democracies gathered here have a particular concern with our answer, for their peoples hate war. They will have a heavy exaction to make of those who fail to provide an escape. They are not afraid of an internationalism that protects; they are unwilling to be fobbed off by mouthings about narrow sovereignty, which is today's phrase for yesterday's isolationism.

The basis of a sound foreign policy, in this new age, for all the nations here gathered, is that: anything that happens, no matter where or how, which menaces the peace of the world, or the economic stability, concerns each and all of us.

That, roughly, may be said to be the central theme of the United Nations. It is with that thought we gain consideration of the most important subject that can engage mankind – life itself.

Now, if ever, is the time to act for the common good. Public opinion supports a world movement toward security. If I read the signs aright, the peoples want a programme, not composed merely of pious thoughts, but of enforceable sanctions – an international law with teeth in it.

We of this nation, desirous of helping to bring peace to the world and realizing the heavy obligations upon us, arising from our possession of the means for producing the bomb and from the fact that it is part of our armament, are prepared to make our full contribution toward effective control of atomic energy.

But before a country is ready to relinquish any winning weapons, it must have more than words to reassure it. It must have a guarantee of safety, not only against the offenders in the atomic area, but against the illegal users of other weapons – bacteriological, biological, gas – perhaps – why not? – against war itself.

In the elimination of war lies our solution, for only then will nations cease to compete with one another in the production and use of dread 'secret' weapons which are evaluated solely by their capacity to kill. This devilish programme takes us back not merely to the Dark Ages, but from cosmos to chaos. If we succeed in finding a suitable way to control atomic weapons, it is reasonable to hope that we may also preclude the use of other weapons adaptable to mass destruction. When a man learns to say 'A' he can, if he chooses, learn the rest of the alphabet, too.

Let this be anchored in our minds:

Peace is never long preserved by weight of metal or by an armament race. Peace can be made tranquil and secure only by understanding and agreement fortified by sanctions. We must embrace international cooperation or international disintegration.

Science has taught us how to put the atom to work. But to make it work for good instead of for evil lies in the domain dealing with the principles of human duty. We are now facing a problem more of ethics than of physics.

The solution will require apparent sacrifice in pride and in position, but better pain as the price of peace than death as the price of war.

•

# JAWAHARLAL NEHRU
Delhi, 14 August 1947

### *'The noble mansion of free India'*

*Jawaharlal Nehru (1889–1964) became active in the Indian Congress move-
ment in 1919 and spent the next twenty-eight years at the forefront of the
struggle for Indian independence, spending nine years in gaol and long periods
under partial restraint. He became president of the Congress movement in 1929
with the support of Gandhi and was subsequently re-elected four times.*

*Now in August 1947 he had helped to negotiate India's freedom from the
British government of Clement Attlee and it was the eve of independence. At
this moment of triumph, Nehru made two great speeches, the first to the Indian
parliament, the second to the nation over the radio.*

## I

Long years ago we made a tryst with destiny, and now the time comes
when we shall redeem our pledge, not wholly or in full measure, but
very substantially. At the stroke of the midnight hour, when the
world sleeps, India will awake to life and freedom. A moment comes,
which comes but rarely in history, when we step out from the old to
the new, when an age ends, and when the soul of a nation, long suppressed, finds utterance. It is fitting that at this solemn moment we
take the pledge of dedication to the service of India and her people
and to the still larger cause of humanity.

At the dawn of history India started on her unending quest, and
trackless centuries are filled with her striving and the grandeur of her
success and her failures. Through good and ill fortune alike she has
never lost sight of that quest or forgotten the ideals which gave her
strength. We end today a period of ill fortune and India discovers
herself again. The achievement we celebrate today is but a step, an
opening of opportunity, to the greater triumphs and achievements
that await us. Are we brave enough and wise enough to grasp this
opportunity and accept the challenge of the future?

Freedom and power bring responsibility. The responsibility rests upon this Assembly, a sovereign body representing the sovereign people of India. Before the birth of freedom we have endured all the pains of labour and our hearts are heavy with the memory of this sorrow. Some of those pains continue even now. Nevertheless, the past is over and it is the future that beckons to us now.

That future is not one of ease or resting but of incessant striving so that we may fulfil the pledges we have so often taken and the one we shall take today. The service of India means the service of the millions who suffer. It means the ending of poverty and ignorance and disease and inequality of opportunity. The ambition of the greatest man of our generation has been to wipe every tear from every eye. That may be beyond us, but as long as there are tears and suffering, so long our work will not be over.

And so we have to labour and to work, and work hard, to give reality to our dreams. Those dreams are for India, but they are also for the world, for all the nations and peoples are too closely knit together today for any one of them to imagine that it can live apart. Peace has been said to be indivisible; so is freedom, so is prosperity now, and so also is disaster in this One World that can no longer be split into isolated fragments.

To the people of India, whose representatives we are, we make an appeal to join us with faith and confidence in this great adventure. This is no time for petty and destructive criticism, no time for ill-will or blaming others. We have to build the noble mansion of free India where all her children may dwell.

II

The appointed day has come – the day appointed by destiny – and India stands forth again, after long slumber and struggle, awake, vital, free and independent. The past clings on to us still in some measure and we have to do much before we redeem the pledges we have so often taken. Yet the turning-point is past, and history begins anew for us, the history which we shall live and act and others will write about.

It is a fateful moment for us in India, for all Asia and for the world. A new star rises, the star of freedom in the East, a new hope comes into being, a vision long cherished materializes. May the star never set and that hope never be betrayed!

We rejoice in that freedom, even though clouds surround us, and many of our people are sorrow-stricken and difficult problems encompass us. But freedom brings responsibilities and burdens and we have to face them in the spirit of a free and disciplined people.

On this day our first thoughts go to the architect of this freedom, the Father of our Nation [Gandhi], who, embodying the old spirit of India, held aloft the torch of freedom and lighted up the darkness that surrounded us. We have often been unworthy followers of his and have strayed from his message, but not only we but succeeding generations will remember this message and bear the imprint in their hearts of this great son of India, magnificent in his faith and strength and courage and humility. We shall never allow that torch of freedom to be blown out, however high the wind or stormy the tempest.

Our next thoughts must be of the unknown volunteers and soldiers of freedom who, without praise or reward, have served India even unto death.

We think also of our brothers and sisters who have been cut off from us by political boundaries and who unhappily cannot share at present in the freedom that has come. They are of us and will remain of us whatever may happen, and we shall be sharers in their good [or] ill fortune alike.

The future beckons to us. Whither do we go and what shall be our endeavour? To bring freedom and opportunity to the common man, to the peasants and workers of India; to fight and end poverty and ignorance and disease; to build up a prosperous, democratic and progressive nation, and to create social, economic and political institutions which will ensure justice and fullness of life to every man and woman.

We have hard work ahead. There is no resting for any one of us till we redeem our pledge in full, till we make all the people of India what destiny intended them to be. We are citizens of a great country, on the verge of bold advance, and we have to live up to that high standard. All of us, to whatever religion we may belong, are equally the children of India with equal rights, privileges and obligations. We cannot encourage communalism or narrow-mindedness, for no nation can be great whose people are narrow in thought or in action.

To the nations and peoples of the world we send greetings and pledge ourselves to cooperate with them in furthering peace, freedom and democracy.

And to India, our much-loved motherland, the ancient, the eternal and the ever-new, we pay our reverent homage and we bind ourselves afresh to her service. JAI HIND.

*Nehru became an international statesman, mediating in Korea (1951) and Vietnam (1954) as well as sending Indian troops on United Nations peacekeeping missions in Palestine, the Congo and Cyprus. He rationalized Hindu laws and won acceptance of plans for a mixed economy. His death in 1964 deprived India of moral leadership of the developing Third World, but Nehru founded a dynasty. He was succeeded by his daughter, Indira Gandhi (1917–84), who was, in turn, succeeded by her son, Rajiv Gandhi, in 1984.*

•

## JAWAHARLAL NEHRU
### Delhi, 30 January 1948

*'The light has gone out of our lives'*

*When Gandhi was assassinated by a Hindu nationalist, the world mourned one of the greatest figures of the twentieth century. The Indian government received more than 3,400 unsolicited messages of sympathy from foreign governments. The United Nations lowered its flag to half-mast.*

*'Mahatma Gandhi was the spokesman for the conscience of all mankind,' said General George Marshall, United States Secretary of State. 'Gandhi had demonstrated that a powerful human following can be assembled . . . through the cogent example of a morally superior conduct of life,' asserted Professor Albert Einstein.*

*There were expressions of sympathy from the Pope, the Dalai Lama, the*

*Archbishop of Canterbury, the Chief Rabbi of London, King George VI, President Truman, Chiang Kai-shek and the president of France.*

*No tribute, however, was more simply or movingly expressed than this radio speech by Gandhi's disciple, the prime minister of the independent India that Gandhi worked to achieve throughout his life.*

Friends and comrades, the light has gone out of our lives and there is darkness everywhere. I do not know what to tell you and how to say it. Our beloved leader, Bapu as we called him, the father of the nation, is no more. Perhaps I am wrong to say that. Nevertheless, we will not see him again as we have seen him for these many years. We will not run to him for advice and seek solace from him, and that is a terrible blow, not to me only, but to millions and millions in this country, and it is a little difficult to soften the blow by any other advice that I or anyone else can give you.

The light has gone out, I said, and yet I was wrong. For the light that shone in this country was no ordinary light. The light that has illumined this country for these many years will illumine this country for many more years, and a thousand years later that light will still be seen in this country and the world will see it and it will give solace to innumerable hearts. For that light represented the living truth . . . the eternal truths, reminding us of the right path, drawing us from error, taking this ancient country to freedom.

All this has happened when there was so much more for him to do. We could never think that he was unnecessary or that he had done his task. But now, particularly, when we are faced with so many difficulties, his not being with us is a blow most terrible to bear.

A madman has put an end to his life, for I can only call him mad who did it, and yet there has been enough of poison spread in this country during the past years and months, and this poison has had effect on people's minds. We must face this poison, we must root out this poison, and we must face all the perils that encompass us and face them not madly or badly but rather in the way that our beloved teacher taught us to face them. The first thing to remember now is that no one of us dare misbehave because we are angry. We have to behave like strong and determined people, determined to face all the perils that surround us, determined to carry out the mandate that our great teacher and our great leader has given us, remembering always that if, as I believe, his spirit looks upon us and sees us, nothing would displease his soul so much as to see that we have indulged in any small behaviour or any violence.

So we must not do that. But that does not mean that we should be weak, but rather that we should in strength and in unity face all the troubles that are in front of us. We must hold together, and all our petty troubles and difficulties and conflicts must be ended in the face of this great disaster. A great disaster is a symbol to us to remember all the big things of life and forget the small things, of which we have thought too much.

•

## JOSEPH McCARTHY
### Wheeling, West Virginia, 20 February 1950

*'I have in my hand . . .'*

*Joseph McCarthy (1908–57), the junior Republican senator from Wisconsin, began his career as America's leading Red hunter on 9 February 1950, when he made this speech at the McLure Hotel in Wheeling.*

*McCarthy's accusation that fifty-seven members of the State Department were card-carrying members of the Communist Party instantly became national news and provoked denials from the president and the State Department.*

*Controversy about what McCarthy really said raged for years. This version of his infamous speech is taken from the statement he made on the Senate floor on 20 February, when he put into the Congressional record a copy of what he really said at Wheeling.*

Today we are engaged in a final, all-out battle between communistic atheism and Christianity. The modern champions of communism have selected this as the time. And, ladies and gentlemen, the chips are down – they are truly down . . .

Can there be anyone here tonight who is so blind as to say that the war is not on? Can there be anyone who fails to realize that the Communist world has said, 'The time is now' – that this is the time for the showdown between the democratic Christian world and the Communist atheistic world?

Unless we face this fact, we shall pay the price that must be paid by those who wait too long.

Six years ago, at the time of the first conference to map out the peace – Dumbarton Oaks – there was within the Soviet orbit 180 million people. Lined up on the antitotalitarian side there were in the world at that time roughly 1,625 million people. Today, only six years later, there are 800 million people under the absolute domination of Soviet Russia – an increase of over 400 per cent. On our side, the figure has shrunk to around 500 million. In other words, in less than six years the odds have changed from 9 to 1 in our favour to 8 to 5 against us. This indicates the swiftness of the tempo of Communist victories and American defeats in the Cold War. As one of our outstanding historical figures once said, 'When a great democracy is destroyed, it will not be because of enemies from without, but rather because of enemies from within.'

The truth of this statement is becoming terrifyingly clear as we see this country each day losing on every front.

At war's end we were physically the strongest nation on earth and, at least potentially, the most powerful intellectually and morally. Ours could have been the honour of being a beacon in the desert of destruction, a shining living proof that civilization was not ready to destroy itself. Unfortunately, we have failed miserably and tragically to arise to the opportunity.

The reason why we find ourselves in a position of impotency is not because our only powerful potential enemy has sent men to invade our shores, but rather because of the traitorous actions of those who have been treated so well by this Nation. It has not been the less fortunate or members of minority groups who have been selling this Nation out, but rather those who have had all the benefits that the wealthiest nation on earth has had to offer – the finest homes, the finest college education, and the finest jobs in Government we can give.

This is glaringly true in the State Department. There the bright young men who are born with silver spoons in their mouths are the ones who have been worst . . .

I have in my hand fifty-seven cases of individuals who would appear to be either card-carrying members or certainly loyal to the Communist Party, but who nevertheless are still helping to shape our foreign policy . . .

One of the important reasons for the graft, the corruption, the dishonesty, the disloyalty, the treason in high Government positions – one of the most important reasons why this continues is a lack of moral uprising on the part of the 140 million American people. In the light of history, however, this is not hard to explain.

It is the result of an emotional hangover and a temporary moral lapse which follows every war. It is the apathy to evil which people who have been subjected to the tremendous evils of war feel. As the people of the world see mass murder, the destruction of defenceless and innocent people, and all of the crime and lack of morals which go with war, they become numb and apathetic. It has always been thus after war.

However, the morals of our people have not been destroyed. They still exist. This cloak of numbness and apathy has only needed a spark to rekindle them. Happily, this spark has finally been supplied.

As you know, very recently the Secretary of State [Dean Acheson] proclaimed his loyalty to a man guilty of what has always been considered as the most abominable of all crimes – of being a traitor to the people who gave him a position of great trust [Alger Hiss]. The Secretary of State in attempting to justify his continued devotion to the man who sold out the Christian world to the atheistic world, referred to Christ's Sermon on the Mount as a justification and reason therefor, and the reaction of the American people to this would have made the heart of Abraham Lincoln happy.

When this pompous diplomat in striped pants, with a phony British accent, proclaimed to the American people that Christ on the Mount endorsed communism, high treason, and betrayal of a sacred trust, the blasphemy was so great that it awakened the dormant indignation of the American people.

He has lighted the spark which is resulting in a moral uprising and will end only when the whole sorry mess of twisted, warped thinkers are swept from the national scene so that we may have a new birth of national honesty and decency in Government.

*The smear tactics of McCarthy and his philistine contempt for intellectuals did untold damage to the American tradition of freedom of thought. He even denounced General George Marshall as a front man for Communism.*

*McCarthyism, the practice of accusing individuals of belonging to Communist front organizations with little evidence for the accusation, destroyed the careers of many men and women and created a sense of Red menace which won the 1952 election for the Republicans.*

*Then McCarthy sought to discredit the army. The army demonstrated that McCarthy had sought preferential treatment for one of his aides. A Senate motion of censure condemned McCarthy's conduct in 1954 and he discredited his cause a few days later by attacking President Eisenhower by name.*

•

## WILLIAM FAULKNER
### Stockholm, 10 December 1950

#### 'The agony and the sweat'

*When William Faulkner (1897–1962), the creator of Yoknapatawpha County and author of* As I Lay Dying *and* The Sound and the Fury, *won the Nobel Prize, he bought his first dress suit for the occasion and decided to go to Stockholm for the prize-giving.*

*At the state banquet, the quiet farmer from Oxford, Mississippi, appeared before a microphone and television camera for the first time and said that he declined to accept the end of man.*

I feel that this award was not made to me as a man, but to my work – a life's work in the agony and sweat of the human spirit, not for glory and least of all for profit, but to create out of the materials of the human spirit something which did not exist before. So this award is only mine in trust. It will not be difficult to find a dedication for the money part of it commensurate with the purpose and significance of its origin. But I would like to do the same with the acclaim too, by using this moment as a pinnacle from which I might be listened to by the young men and women already dedicated to the same anguish and travail, among whom is already that one who will someday stand here where I am standing.

Our tragedy today is a general and universal physical fear so long sustained by now that we can even bear it. There are no longer problems of the spirit. There is only the question: when will I be blown up? Because of this, the young man or woman writing today has forgotten the problems of the human heart in conflict with itself which alone can make good writing because only that is worth writing about, worth the agony and the sweat.

He must learn them again. He must teach himself that the basest of all things is to be afraid; and, teaching himself that, forget it for ever, leaving no room in his workshop for anything but the old verities and truths of the heart, the old universal truths lacking which any story is ephemeral and doomed – love and honour and pity and pride and compassion and sacrifice. Until he does so, he labours under a curse. He writes not of love but of lust, of defeats in which nobody loses anything of value, of victories without hope, and, worst of all, without pity or compassion. His griefs grieve on no universal bones, leaving no scars. He writes not of the heart but of the glands.

Until he relearns these things, he will write as though he stood among and watched the end of man. I decline to accept the end of man. It is easy enough to say that man is immortal simply because he will endure; that when the last ding-dong of doom has clanged and faded from the last worthless rock hanging tideless in the last red and dying evening, that even then there will still be one more sound: that of his puny inexhaustible voice, still talking. I refuse to accept this. I believe that man will not merely endure: he will prevail. He is immortal, not because he alone among creatures has an inexhaustible voice, but because he has a soul, a spirit capable of compassion and sacrifice and endurance. The poet's, the writer's, duty is to write about these things. It is his privilege to help man endure by lifting his heart, by reminding him of the courage and honour and hope and pride

and compassion and pity and sacrifice which have been the glory of
his past. The poet's voice need not merely be the record of man; it
can be one of the props, the pillars, to help him endure and prevail.

•

## ANEURIN BEVAN
London, 23 April 1951

### 'There is only one hope for mankind'

*Aneurin Bevan (1897–1960) was the son of a miner who left school at thirteen
to work on the coal-face and rose to become the spokesman for the South Wales
miners during the General Strike of 1926. He became an MP in 1929, was the
most constructive of Churchill's critics during the Second World War and was
one of the greatest Labour orators.*

*As minister of health from 1945 to 1951, he was the founder of the British
National Health Service – but he resigned from the government on 21 April
1951 in protest at the imposition of health-service charges to meet defence costs.
He told Clement Attlee, the prime minister, that he could not carry out policies
which were 'repugnant' to his conscience.*

*Two days later he made his resignation speech to the Commons. He stood
almost alone. There was no sympathy on the Conservative benches and Labour
MPs feared he would destroy the government.*

The western world has embarked upon a campaign of arms production upon a scale, so quickly, and of such an extent that the
foundations of political liberty and Parliamentary democracy will
not be able to sustain the shock. This is a very grave matter indeed.
I have always said that the defence programme must always be consistent with the maintenance of the standard of life of the British
people and the maintenance of the social services, and that as soon
as it became clear we had engaged upon an arms programme inconsistent with those considerations, I could no longer remain a Member
of the Government.

I therefore beg the House and the country, and the world, to think before it is too late. It may be that on such an occasion as this the dramatic nature of a resignation might cause even some of our American friends to think before it is too late. It has always been clear that the weapons of the totalitarian States are, first, social and economic, and only next military; and if in attempting to meet the military effect of those totalitarian machines, the economies of the western world are disrupted and the standard of living is lowered or industrial disturbances are created, then Soviet Communism establishes a whole series of Trojan horses in every nation of the western economy . . .

This great nation has a message for the world which is distinct from that of America or that of the Soviet Union. Ever since 1945 we have been engaged in this country in the most remarkable piece of social reconstruction the world has ever seen. By the end of 1950 we had assumed the moral leadership of the world. (*Interruption.*) It is no use Hon. Members opposite sneering, because when they come to the end of the road it will not be a sneer which will be upon their faces. There is only one hope for mankind, and that hope still remains in this little island. It is from here that we tell the world where to go and how to go there, but we must not follow behind the anarchy of American competitive capitalism which is unable to restrain itself at all, as is seen in the stockpiling that is now going on, and which denies to the economy of Great Britain even the means of carrying on our civil production . . .

The Chancellor of the Exchequer in this year's Budget proposes to reduce the Health expenditure by £13 million – only £13 million out of £4,000 million.

If he finds it necessary to mutilate, or begin to mutilate, the Health Services for £13 million out of £4,000 million, what will he do next year? Or are you next year going to take your stand on the upper denture? The lower half apparently does not matter, but the top half is sacrosanct. Is that right? If my Hon. Friends are asked questions at meetings about what they will do next year, what will they say?

The Chancellor of the Exchequer is putting a financial ceiling on the Health Service. With rising prices the Health Service is squeezed between that artificial figure and rising prices. What is to be squeezed out next year? Is it the upper half? When that has been squeezed out and the same principle holds good, what do you squeeze out the year after? Prescriptions? Hospital charges? Where do you stop? I have been accused of having agreed to a charge on prescriptions. That shows the danger of compromise. Because if it is pleaded against me that I agreed to the modification of the Health Service, then what will be pleaded against my Right Hon. Friends next year, and indeed what answer will they have if the vandals opposite come in? What answer? The Health Service will be like Lavinia – all the limbs cut off and eventually her tongue cut out, too.

I should like to ask my Right Hon. and Hon. Friends, where are they going? (*Hon. Members:* '*Where are you going?*') Where am I going? I am where I always was. Those who live their lives in mountainous and rugged countries are always afraid of avalanches, and they know that avalanches start with the movement of a very small stone. First, the stone starts on a ridge between two valleys – one valley desolate and the other valley populous. The pebble starts, but nobody bothers about the pebble until it gains way, and soon the whole valley is overwhelmed. That is how the avalanche starts, that is the logic of the present situation, and that is the logic my Right Hon. and Hon. Friends cannot escape. Why, therefore, has it been done in this way?

After all, the National Health Service was something of which we were all very proud, and even the Opposition were beginning to be proud of it. It only had to last a few more years to become a part of our traditions, and then the traditionalists would have claimed the credit for all of it. Why should we throw it away? In the Chancellor's Speech there was not one word of commendation for the Health Service – not one word. What is responsible for that?

Why has the cut been made? He cannot say, with an overall surplus of over £220 million and a conventional surplus of £39 million, that he had to have the £13 million. That is the arithmetic of Bedlam. He cannot say that his arithmetic is so precise that he must have the £13 million, when last year the Treasury were £247 million out. Why?

What is the cause of it? Why has it been done? . . .

I say this, in conclusion. There is only one hope for mankind – and that is democratic Socialism. There is only one party in Great Britain which can do it – and that is the Labour Party. But I ask them carefully to consider how far they are polluting the stream. We have gone a long way – a very long way – against great difficulties. Do not let us change direction now. Let us make it clear, quite clear, to the rest of the world that we stand where we stood, that we are not going to allow ourselves to be diverted from our path by the exigencies of the immediate situation. We shall do what is necessary to defend ourselves – defend ourselves by arms, and not only with arms but with the spiritual resources of our people.

*The speech stunned the House of Commons. Newspapers jeered and even the miners of Durham were critical. Bevan was defeated by Hugh Gaitskell (the chancellor who imposed the health charges) in the contest for the Labour leadership of 1955 but then became official spokesman on foreign affairs.*

•

## ADLAI STEVENSON
### Illinois, 26 July 1952

*'Let's talk sense to the American people'*

*When the Republicans selected General Eisenhower as their presidential candidate in 1952, the Democrats responded by nominating their best man, Governor Adlai Stevenson (1900–1965) of Illinois, who had proved himself an effective reforming governor.*

*Until then, few Americans had heard of Stevenson, although he had served in government, been a delegate to the UN General Assembly and was elected governor of Illinois by a record-breaking half million votes in 1948.*

*As Stevenson accepted the Democratic nomination, the nation heard for the first time the eloquence that made him so memorable a speaker.*

The ordeal of the twentieth century – the bloodiest, most turbulent era of the Christian age – is far from over. Sacrifice, patience, understanding, and implacable purpose may be our lot for years to come.

Let's face it. Let's talk sense to the American people. Let's tell them the truth, that there are no gains without pains, that we are now on the eve of great decisions, not easy decisions, like resistance when you're attacked, but a long, patient, costly struggle which alone can assure triumph over the great enemies of man – war, poverty, and tyranny – and the assaults upon human dignity which are the most grievous consequences of each.

Let's tell them that the victory to be won in the twentieth century, this portal to the golden age, mocks the pretensions of individual acumen and ingenuity. For it is a citadel guarded by thick walls of ignorance and mistrust which do not fall before the trumpets' blast or the politicians' imprecations or even a general's baton. They are, my friends, walls that must be directly stormed by the hosts of courage, morality, and of vision, standing shoulder to shoulder, unafraid of ugly truth, contemptuous of lies, half-truths, circuses, and demagoguery.

The people are wise – wiser than the Republicans think. And the Democratic party is the people's party, not the labour party, not the farmers' party, not the employers' party – it is the party of no one because it is the party of everyone.

That, I think, is our ancient mission. Where we have deserted it we have failed. With your help there will be no desertion now. Better we lose the election than mislead the people; and better we lose than misgovern the people.

Help me do the job in this autumn of conflict and of campaign; help me to do the job in these years of darkness, of doubt, and of crisis which stretch beyond the horizon of tonight's happy vision, and we will justify our glorious past and the loyalty of silent millions who look to us for compassion, for understanding, and for honest purpose. Thus we will serve our great tradition greatly.

I ask of you all you have; I will give to you all I have, even as he who came here tonight and honoured me, as he has honoured you – the Democratic party – by a lifetime of service and bravery that will find him an imperishable page in the history of the Republic and of the Democratic party – President Harry S. Truman.

And finally, my friends, in the staggering task that you have assigned me, I shall always try 'to do justly, to love mercy, and walk humbly with my God'.

*Eisenhower won the election by a landslide and Stevenson lost again in 1956 – but his liberalism captured a generation of Democrats, saved the Republicans from falling back into the clutches of the Southern conservatives, and prepared the way for the reformers of the Kennedy and Johnson administrations.*

•

## KWAME NKRUMAH
### Accra, 10 July 1953

### 'The motion of destiny'

*After graduating from Achimoto College at Lincoln University in Pennsylvania and the London School of Economics, Kwame Nkrumah (1909–72) returned to his homeland and founded the Convention People's Party in 1949. He sought immediate self-government for the Gold Coast, which he renamed Ghana. During his ten years in America he had acquired a strong sense of black solidarity and a burning vision of an independent United States of Africa.*

*His party won an overwhelming election victory in 1951 and Nkrumah, who had been imprisoned by the British for sedition, was released to head the government. He cooperated with the British governor in a peaceful transfer of power. A white paper on constitutional reform was published in July 1953 – and on 10 July Nkrumah moved his independence motion, known popularly as 'The motion of destiny'.*

I am asking you to give my Government the power to bring to fruition the longing hopes, the ardent dreams, the fervent aspirations of the chiefs and people of our country. Throughout a century of alien rule our people have, with ever increasing tendency, looked forward to that bright and glorious day when they shall regain their ancient heritage, and once more take their place rightly as free men in the world.

Mr Speaker, we have frequent examples to show that there comes a time in the history of all colonial peoples when they must, because of their will to throw off the hampering shackles of colonialism, boldly assert their God-given right to be free of a foreign ruler. Today we are here to claim this right to our independence . . .

The right of a people to decide their own destiny, to make their way in freedom, is not to be measured by the yardstick of colour or degree of social development. It is an inalienable right of peoples which they are powerless to exercise when forces, stronger than they themselves, by whatever means, for whatever reasons, take this right away from them. If there is to be a criterion of a people's preparedness for self-government, then I say it is their readiness to assume the responsibilities of ruling themselves. For who but a people themselves can say when they are prepared? How can others judge when that moment has arrived in the destiny of a subject people? What other gauge can there be?

Mr Speaker, never in the history of the world has an alien ruler granted self-rule to a people on a silver platter. Therefore, Mr Speaker, I say that a people's readiness and willingness to assume the responsibilities of self-rule is the single criterion of their preparedness to undertake those responsibilities . . .

In the very early days of the Christian era, long before England had assumed any importance, long even before her people had united into a nation, our ancestors had attained a great empire, which lasted until the eleventh century, when it fell before the attacks of the Moors of the North. At its height that empire stretched from Timbuktu to Bamako, and even as far as to the Atlantic. It is said that lawyers and scholars were much respected in that empire and that the inhabitants of Ghana wore garments of wool, cotton, silk and velvet. There was trade in copper, gold and textile fabrics, and jewels and weapons of gold and silver were carried.

Thus may we take pride in the name of Ghana, not out of romanticism, but as an inspiration for the future. It is right and proper that we should know about our past. For just as the future moves from the present so the present has emerged from the past. Nor need we be ashamed of our past. There was much in it of glory. What our ancestors achieved in the context of their contemporary society gives us confidence that we can create, out of that past, a glorious future, not in terms of war and military pomp, but in terms of social progress and of peace. For we repudiate war and violence. Our battles shall be against the old ideas that keep men trammelled in their own greed; against the crass stupidities that breed hatred, fear and inhumanity. The heroes of our future will be those who can lead our people out of the stifling fog of disintegration through serfdom, into the valley of light where purpose, endeavour and determination will create that brotherhood which Christ proclaimed two thousand years ago, and about which so much is said, but so little done . . .

Honourable Members, you are called, here and now, as a result of the relentless tide of history, by Nemesis as it were, to a sacred charge, for you hold the destiny of our country in your hands. The eyes and ears of the world are upon you; yea, our oppressed brothers throughout this vast continent of Africa and the New World are looking to you with desperate hope, as an inspiration to continue their grim fight against cruelties which we in this corner of Africa have never known – cruelties which are a disgrace to humanity, and to the civilization which the white man has set himself to teach us. At this time, history is being made; a colonial people in Africa has put forward the first definite claim for independence. An African colonial people proclaim that they are ready to assume the stature of free men and to prove to the world that they are worthy of the trust.

I know that you will not fail those who are listening for the mandate that you will give to your Representative Ministers. For we are ripe for freedom, and our people will not be denied. They are conscious that the right is theirs, and they know that freedom is not something that one people can bestow on another as a gift. They claim it as their own and none can keep it from them.

As long as we remain subject to an alien power, too much of our energy is diverted from constructive enterprise. Oppressive forces breed frustration. Imperialism and colonialism are a twofold evil. This theme is expressed in the truism that 'no nation which oppresses another can itself be free'. Thus we see that this evil not only wounds the people which is subject, but the dominant nation pays the price in a warping of their finer sensibilities through arrogance and greed. Imperialism and colonialism are a barrier to true friendship . . .

In our daily lives, we may lack those material comforts regarded as essential by the standards of the modern world, because so much of our wealth is still locked up in our land; but we have the gifts of laughter and joy, a love of music, a lack of malice, an absence of the desire for vengeance for our wrongs, all things of intrinsic worth in a world sick of injustice, revenge, fear and want.

We feel that there is much the world can learn from those of us who belong to what we might term the pre-technological societies. These are values which we must not sacrifice unheedingly in pursuit of material progress. That is why we say that self-government is not an end in itself.

We have to work hard to evolve new patterns, new social customs, new attitudes to life, so that while we seek the material, cultural and economic advancement of our country, while we raise their standards of life, we shall not sacrifice their fundamental happiness. That, I should say, Mr Speaker, has been the greatest tragedy of Western society since the industrial revolution.

In harnessing the forces of nature, man has become the slave of the machine, and of his own greed. If we repeat these mistakes and suffer the consequences which have overtaken those that made them, we shall have no excuse. This is a field of exploration for the young men and women now in our schools and colleges, for our sociologists and economists, for our doctors and our social welfare workers, for our engineers and town planners, for our scientists and our philosophers.

Mr Speaker, when we politicians have long passed away and been forgotten, it is upon their shoulders that will fall the responsibility of evolving new forms of social institutions, new economic instruments to help build in our rich and fertile country a society where men and women may live in peace, where hate, strife, envy and greed, shall have no place.

Mr Speaker, we can only meet the challenge of our age as a free people. Hence our demand for our freedom, for only free men can shape the destinies of their future.

Mr Speaker, Honourable Members, we have great tasks before us. I say, with all seriousness, that it is rarely that human beings have such an opportunity for service to their fellows.

Mr Speaker, for my part, I can only re-echo the words of a great man: 'Man's dearest possession is life, and since it is given him to live but once, he must so live as not to be besmeared with the shame of a cowardly existence and trivial past, so live that dying he might say: all my life and all my strength were given to the finest cause in the world – the liberation of mankind.'

Mr Speaker, 'Now God be thank'd, Who has match'd us with His hour!' I beg to move.

*'The acclamation that burst forth was such that one expected the roof and walls to collapse,' Nkrumah wrote later. Nkrumah became president when Ghana became a republic on 1 July 1960. He was respected as a Pan-African leader but once in power became increasingly dictatorial at home and was overthrown in a military coup in 1966. A statue was erected and a park opened in his memory in Accra in 1992. His body was reinterred in a mausoleum.*

•

### FIDEL CASTRO
Santiago, Cuba, 16 October 1953

*'History will absolve me'*

*On 26 July 1953 Fidel Castro, a Cuban lawyer and defender of the poor in Havana, led an unsuccessful armed revolt against the Moncada Barracks. A mass trial of Castro and 122 other defendants started in the Santiago Palace of Justice on 21 September. Castro was eventually confined to prison and his trial was held in virtual secrecy in a small nurses' lodge at the Saturnino Lora hospital – a decision made to perpetuate the official fiction that he was too ill to attend the Palace of Justice.*

*Castro's speech from the dock, inspired by his hero José Martí, the Cuban philosopher, remains the fundamental document of the subsequent Cuban revolution and the most venerated scripture of the rebel movement. The speech built up history's case to justify taking up arms against tyrants, summoning up the spirit of Luther and Calvin, Montesquieu and Rousseau, Milton, Locke, Paine and Balzac.*

*Castro practised the delivery of his speech in his cell until dawn. Then he went before the judges and declared: 'When men carry the same ideals in their hearts, nothing can isolate them — neither prison walls nor the sod of cemeteries. For a single memory, a single spirit, a single conscience, a single dignity will sustain them all.'*

Honourable Judges: If there is in your hearts a vestige of love for your country, love for humanity, love for justice, listen carefully. I know that I will be silenced for many years; I know that the regime will try to suppress the truth by all possible means; I know that there will be a conspiracy to bury me in oblivion. But my voice will not be stilled — it will rise from my breast even when I feel most alone, and my heart will give it all the fire that callous cowards deny it . . .

From a shack in the mountains on Monday, July the 27th, I listened to the dictator's voice on the air while there were still eighteen of our men in arms against the government. Those who have never experienced similar moments will never know that kind of bitterness and indignation. While the long cherished hopes of freeing our people lay in ruins about us we heard those crushed hopes gloated over by a tyrant more vicious, more arrogant than ever. The endless stream of lies and slanders, poured forth in his crude, odious, repulsive language, may only be compared to the endless stream of clean young blood which had flowed since the previous night — with his knowledge, consent, complicity and approval — being spilled by the most inhuman gang of assassins it is possible to imagine.

To have believed him for a single moment would have sufficed to fill a man of conscience with remorse and shame for the rest of his life. At that time I could not even hope to brand his miserable forehead with the mark of truth which condemns him for the rest of his days and for all time to come. Already a circle of more than a thousand men, armed with weapons more powerful than ours and with peremptory orders to bring in our bodies, was closing in around us. Now that the truth is coming out, now that speaking before you I am carrying out the mission I set for myself, I may die peacefully and content. So I shall not mince any words about those savage murderers . . .

Moncada Barracks were turned into a workshop of torture and death. Some shameful individuals turned their uniforms into butchers' aprons. The walls were splattered with blood. The bullets imbedded in the walls were encrusted with singed bits of skin, brains and human hair, the grisly reminders of rifle shots fired full in the face. The grass around the barracks was dark and sticky with human blood. The criminal hands that are guiding the destiny of Cuba had written for the prisoners at the entrance of that den of death the very inscription of Hell: 'Forsake all hope.'

They did not even attempt to cover appearances. They did not bother in the least to conceal what they were doing. They thought they had deceived the people with their lies and they ended up deceiving themselves. They felt themselves lords and masters of the universe, with power over life and death. So the fear they had experienced upon our attack at daybreak was dissipated in a feast of corpses, in a drunken orgy of blood . . .

Dante divided his *Inferno* into nine circles. He put the criminals in the seventh, the thieves in the eighth and the traitors in the ninth. Difficult dilemma the devils will be faced with, when they try to find an adequate spot for this man's soul – if this man has a soul. The man who instigated the atrocious acts in Santiago de Cuba doesn't even have a heart.

In every society there are men of base instincts. The sadists, brutes, conveyors of all the ancestral atavisms go about in the guise of human beings, but they are monsters, only more or less restrained by discipline and social habit. If they are offered a drink from a river of blood, they will not be satisfied until they drink the river dry. All these men needed was the order. At their hands the best and noblest Cubans perished: the most valiant, the most honest, the most idealistic. The tyrant called them mercenaries. There they were dying as heroes at the hands of men who collect a salary from the Republic and who, with the arms the Republic gave them to defend her, serve the interests of a clique and murder her best citizens.

Throughout their torturing of our comrades, the Army offered them the chance to save their lives by betraying their ideology and falsely declaring that Prío had given them money. When they indignantly rejected that proposition, the Army continued with its horrible tortures. They crushed their testicles and they tore out their eyes. But no one yielded. No complaint was heard nor a favour asked. Even when they had been deprived of their virile organs, our men were still a thousand times more men than all their tormentors together. Photographs, which do not lie, show the bodies torn to pieces. Other methods were used. Frustrated by the valour of the men, they tried to break the spirit of our women. With a bleeding human eye in their hands, a sergeant and several other men went to the cell where our comrades Melba Hernández and Haydée Santamaría were held. Addressing the latter, and showing her the eye, they said: 'This eye belonged to your brother. If you will not tell us what he refused to say, we will tear out the other.' She, who loved her valiant brother above all things, replied full of dignity: 'If you tore out an eye and he did not speak, much less will I.' Later they came back and burned their arms with lit cigarettes until at last, filled with spite, they told the young Haydée Santamaría: 'You no longer have a fiancé because we have killed him too.' But, still imperturbable, she answered: 'He is not dead, because to die for one's country is to live forever.' Never had the heroism and the dignity of Cuban womanhood reached such heights . . .

We are Cubans and to be Cuban implies a duty; not to fulfil that duty is a crime, is treason. We are proud of the history of our country; we learned it in school and have grown up hearing of freedom, justice and human rights. We were taught to venerate the glorious example of our heroes and martyrs. Céspedes, Agramonte, Maceo, Gómez, and Martí were the first names engraved in our minds. We were taught that the Titan once said that liberty is not begged for but won with the blade of a machete. We were taught that for the guidance of Cuba's free citizens, the Apostle wrote in his book *The Golden Age*: 'The man who abides by unjust laws and permits any man to trample and mistreat the country in which he was born, is not an honourable man . . . In the world there must be a certain degree of honour just as there must be a certain amount of light. When there are many men without honour, there are always others who bear in themselves the honour of many men. These are the men who rebel with great force against those who steal the people's freedom, that is to say, against those who steal human honour itself. In those men thousands more are contained, an entire people is contained, human dignity is contained . . .' We were taught that the 10th of October and the 24th of February are glorious anniversaries of national rejoicing because they mark days on which Cubans rebelled against the yoke of infamous tyranny. We were taught to cherish and defend the beloved flag of the lone star, and to sing every afternoon the verses of our National Anthem: 'To live in chains is to live in disgrace and in opprobrium' and 'To die for one's homeland is to live forever!' All this we learned and will never forget, even though today in our land there is murder and prison for the men who practise the ideas taught to them since the cradle. We were born in a free country that our parents bequeathed to us and the Island will sink into the sea before we consent to be slaves of anyone.

It seemed that the Apostle would die during his Centennial. It seemed that his memory would be extinguished forever. So great was the affront! But he is alive; he has not died. His people are rebellious. His people are worthy. His people are faithful to his memory. There are Cubans who have fallen defending his doctrines. There are young men who in magnificent selflessness came to die beside his tomb, giving their blood and their lives so that he could keep on living in the heart of his nation. Cuba, what would have become of you had you let your Apostle die?

I come to the close of my defence plea but I will not end it as lawyers usually do, asking that the accused be freed. I cannot ask freedom for myself while my comrades are already suffering in the ignominious prison of the Isle of Pines. Send me there to join them and to share their fate. It is understandable that honest men should be dead or in prison in a Republic where the President is a criminal and a thief . . .

I know that imprisonment will be harder for me than it has ever been for anyone, filled with cowardly threats and hideous cruelty. But I do not fear prison, as I do not fear the fury of the miserable tyrant who took the lives of seventy of my comrades. Condemn me. It does not matter. History will absolve me.

*Castro was sentenced to fifteen years but was freed two years later and went into exile. He returned to Cuba with his brother Raúl and Che Guevara in December*

*1956 and conducted guerrilla operations from the Sierra Maestra. On 8 January 1959, he entered Havana in triumph and became prime minister a year later. Castro and Guevara became worldwide symbols of rebellion during the student revolts of the 1960s in the United States and Europe.*

•

## BERTRAND RUSSELL
### BBC Radio, London, 30 December 1954

*'Shall we choose death?'*

*Bertrand Russell's claim to be remembered by history rests on his work in mathematical and symbolic logic and his profound influence on philosophy. Yet he was also constantly involved in political affairs. Russell (1872–1970) was deprived of his fellowship at Trinity College, Cambridge, during the First World War because of his pacifism. He was imprisoned in 1918. During the Second World War, however, he abandoned his pacifism because of his hatred of fascism. When the atom bomb was followed by the hydrogen bomb, he became a campaigner for nuclear disarmament – and this speech on BBC Radio was a characteristic example of the powerful rhetoric he used against the arms race that built up between the United States and the Soviet Union, the two great superpowers, and which, he argued, was endangering the human race.*

*The broadcast was made after the explosion of the first H-bomb, his thin singsong voice charged with the detached intensity of a prophet.*

I am speaking not as a Briton, not as a European, not as a member of a western democracy, but as a human being, a member of the species Man, whose continued existence is in doubt. The world is full of conflicts: Jews and Arabs; Indians and Pakistanis; white men and Negroes in Africa; and, overshadowing all minor conflicts, the titanic struggle between communism and anti-communism.

Almost everybody who is politically conscious has strong feelings about one or more of these issues; but I want you, if you can, to set aside such feelings for the moment and consider yourself only as a member of a biological species which has had a remarkable history and whose disappearance none of us can desire. I shall try to say no single word which should appeal to one group rather than to another. All, equally, are in peril, and, if the peril is understood, there is hope that they may collectively avert it. We have to learn to think in a new way. We have to learn to ask ourselves not what steps can be taken to give military victory to whatever group we prefer, for there no longer are such steps. The question we have to ask ourselves is: What steps can be taken to prevent a military contest of which the issue must be disastrous to all sides?

The general public, and even many men in positions of authority, have not realized what would be involved in a war with hydrogen bombs. The general public still thinks in terms of the obliteration of cities. It is understood that the new bombs are more powerful than the old and that, while one atomic bomb could obliterate Hiroshima, one hydrogen bomb could obliterate the largest cities such as London, New York, and Moscow. No doubt in a hydrogen-bomb war great cities would be obliterated. But this is one of the minor disasters that would have to be faced. If everybody in London, New York, and Moscow were exterminated, the world might, in the course of a few centuries, recover from the blow. But we now know, especially since the Bikini test, that hydrogen bombs can gradually spread destruction over a much wider area than had been supposed. It is stated on very good authority that a bomb can now be manufactured which will be 25,000 times as powerful as that which destroyed Hiroshima. Such a bomb, if exploded near the ground or under water, sends radioactive particles into the upper air. They sink gradually and reach the surface of the earth in the form of a deadly dust or rain. It was this dust which infected the Japanese fishermen and their catch of fish although they were outside what American experts believed to be the danger zone. No one knows how widely such lethal radioactive particles might be diffused, but the best authorities are unanimous in saying that a war with hydrogen bombs is quite likely to put an end to the human race. It is feared that if many hydrogen bombs are used there will be universal death – sudden only for a fortunate minority, but for the majority a slow torture of disease and disintegration . . .

Here, then, is the problem which I present to you, stark and dreadful and inescapable: Shall we put an end to the human race; or shall mankind renounce war? People will not face this alternative because it is so difficult to abolish war. The abolition of war will demand distasteful limitations of national sovereignty. But what perhaps impedes understanding of the situation more than anything else is that the term 'mankind' feels vague and abstract. People scarcely realize in imagination that the danger is to themselves and their children and their grandchildren, and not only to a dimly apprehended humanity. And so they hope that perhaps war may be allowed to continue provided modern weapons are prohibited. I am afraid this hope is illusory. Whatever agreements not to use hydrogen bombs had been reached in time of peace, they would no longer be considered binding in time of war, and both sides would set to work to manufacture hydrogen bombs as soon as war broke out, for if one side manufactured the bombs and the other did not, the side that manufactured them would inevitably be victorious . . .

As geological time is reckoned, Man has so far existed only for a very short period – one million years at the most. What he has achieved, especially during the last 6,000 years, is something utterly new in the history of the Cosmos, so far at least as we are acquainted with it. For countless ages the sun rose and set, the moon waxed and waned, the stars shone in the night, but it was only with the coming of Man that these things were understood. In the great world of astronomy and in the little world of the atom, Man has unveiled secrets which might have been thought undiscoverable. In art and literature and religion, some men have shown a sublimity of feeling which makes the species worth preserving. Is all this to end in trivial horror because so few are able to think of Man rather than of this or that group of men? Is our race so destitute of wisdom, so incapable of impartial love, so blind even to the simplest dictates of self-preservation, that the last proof of its silly cleverness is to be the extermination of all life on our planet? – for it will be not only men who will perish, but also the animals, whom no one can accuse of communism or anti-communism.

I cannot believe that this is to be the end. I would have men forget their quarrels for a moment and reflect that, if they will allow themselves to survive, there is every reason to expect the triumphs of the future to exceed immeasurably the triumphs of the past. There lies before us, if we choose, continual progress in happiness, knowledge, and wisdom. Shall we, instead, choose death, because we cannot forget our quarrels? I appeal, as a human being to human beings: remember your humanity, and forget the rest. If you can do so, the way lies open to a new Paradise; if you cannot, nothing lies before you but universal death.

*Russell reiterated his prophetic message for the rest of his life. He helped to found the Campaign for Nuclear Disarmament in 1958 and became its president. He was imprisoned in 1961 for inciting the public to commit a breach of the peace as part of the protest movement against nuclear weapons. During the Cuban missile crisis of 1962 he corresponded directly with President Kennedy and President Khrushchev.*

•

# MARTIN LUTHER KING
## Montgomery, Alabama, 5 December 1955

### *'There comes a time when people get tired'*

*Martin Luther King (1929–68), a black American Baptist pastor, was the right man in the right place at a moment when history demanded a man of stature to become the leader of his people. That moment occurred in 1954, when King led the victorious campaign against segregated seating in Montgomery's buses. Never before in American history had any black leader succeeded in carrying out a prolonged and victorious attack upon oppression by white people. King subsequently led the civil-rights movement, insisting, like Gandhi, on non-violence.*

*About a thousand black Americans packed Holt Street Baptist Church on the night of 5 December 1955, the day when the first campaign started. Outside, another five thousand, mainly labourers and servants, listened to the speeches over loudspeakers. With only twenty minutes to prepare his speech, King wrote later that he decided that he would seek to arouse his followers to action by insisting their self-respect was at stake and that if they accepted such injustices without protesting they*

*would betray their own sense of dignity and the eternal edicts of God himself. 'But*
*I would balance this with a strong affirmation of the Christian doctrine of love.'*
   *As King and Ralph Abernathy entered the church together, all heads turned.*
*King led the congregation in singing 'Onward Christian Soldiers' and 'Leaning*
*on the Everlasting Arms'. After prayers and a reading from the Scriptures, he*
*advanced to the lectern. As the audience applauded and television cameras began*
*to shoot from all sides, the crowd grew quiet. Then King, speaking without notes*
*or a manuscript, delivered the speech that first drew him to national attention.*

We're here this evening for serious business. We're here in a general
sense because first and foremost, we are American citizens, and we are
determined to acquire our citizenship to the fullness of its meaning.
We are here also because of our deep-seated belief that democracy
transformed from thin paper to thick action is the greatest form of
government on earth.

There comes a time that people get tired. We are here this evening
to say to those who have mistreated us so long that we are tired –
tired of being segregated and humiliated; tired of being kicked about
by the brutal feet of oppression.

There comes a time my friends when people get tired of being
plunged across the abyss of humiliation, when they experience the
bleakness of nagging despair. There comes a time when people get
tired of being pushed out of the glimmering sunlight of last July and
left standing amid the piercing chill of an Alpine November.

We had no alternative but to protest. For many years, we have
shown amazing patience. We have sometimes given our white
brothers the feeling that we liked the way we were being treated. But
we come here tonight to be saved from that patience that makes us
patient with anything less than freedom and justice.

One of the great glories of democracy is the right to protest for
right.

These organizations [White Citizens' Councils and the Ku Klux
Klan] are protesting for the perpetuation of injustice in the community, we are protesting for the birth of justice in the community.
Their methods lead to violence and lawlessness. But in our protest
there will be no cross burnings. No white person will be taken from

his home by a hooded Negro mob and brutally murdered. There will be no threats and intimidation. We will be guided by the highest principles of law and order.

Our method will be that of persuasion, not coercion. We will only say to the people, 'Let your conscience be your guide.' Our actions must be guided by the deepest principles of our Christian faith. Love must be our regulating ideal. Once again we must hear the words of Jesus echoing across the centuries ('Love your enemies, bless them that curse you, and pray for them that despitefully use you'). If we fail to do this our protest will end up as a meaningless drama on the stage of history, and its memory will be shrouded with the ugly garments of shame. In spite of the mistreatment that we have confronted we must not become bitter, and end up by hating our white brothers. As Booker T. Washington said, 'Let no man pull you so low as to make you hate him.'

We are not wrong in what we are doing. If we are wrong, the Supreme Court of this nation is wrong. If we are wrong, the Constitution of the United States is wrong. If we are wrong, God Almighty is wrong. If we are wrong, Jesus of Nazareth was merely a Utopian dreamer who never came down to earth.

If you will protest courageously, and yet with dignity and Christian love, when the history books are written in future generations, the historians will have to pause and say, 'There lived a great people – a black people – who injected new meaning and dignity into the veins of civilization.' This is our challenge and our overwhelming responsibility.

•

## NIKITA KHRUSHCHEV
Moscow, 25 February 1956

*'We must abolish the cult of the individual'*

*Six months after the death of Stalin, Nikita Khrushchev (1894–1971) became first secretary of the Communist Party and started to build his power at the top of the Soviet Union. He secured the succession of his nominee, Bulganin, to the premiership in 1955.*

*The twentieth congress of the party, in 1956, held at the Kremlin with 1,355 voting delegates, was the first since Stalin's death. At the first meeting, the delegates noticed that there was no photograph of Stalin in the conference hall. Khrushchev gave his seven-hour report with hardly any allusion to Stalin. After the regular session on 24 February, the delegates were summoned to a closely guarded night meeting. At this secret meeting, Khrushchev made one of the most sensational speeches of the century in which he attacked the cult of personality during Stalin's reign of terror and introduced an era of liberalization in which many of Stalin's victims were rehabilitated.*

Comrades! In the report of the Central Committee of the party at the twentieth Congress, in a number of speeches by delegates to the Congress, and also formerly during the plenary CC-CPSU sessions, quite a lot has been said about the cult of the individual and about its harmful consequences.

After Stalin's death the Central Committee of the party began to implement a policy of explaining concisely and consistently that it is impermissible and foreign to the spirit of Marxism–Leninism to elevate one person, to transform him into a superman possessing supernatural characteristics akin to those of a god. Such a man supposedly knows everything, sees everything, thinks for everyone, can do anything, is infallible in his behaviour.

Such a belief about a man, and specifically about Stalin, was cultivated among us for many years . . .

In December 1922, in a letter to the Party Congress, Vladimir Ilyich wrote.

After taking over the position of Secretary-General Comrade Stalin accumulated in his hands immeasurable power and I am not certain whether he will be always able to use this power with the required care.

This letter – a political document of tremendous importance, known in the party history as Lenin's 'testament' – was distributed among the delegates to the twentieth Party Congress. You have read it, and will undoubtedly read it again more than once. You might reflect on Lenin's plain words, in which expression is given to Vladimir Ilyich's anxiety concerning the party, the people, the State, and the future direction of party policy.

Vladimir Ilyich said:

> Stalin is excessively rude, and this defect, which can be freely tolerated in our midst and in contacts among us Communists, becomes a defect which cannot be tolerated in one holding the position of the Secretary-General. Because of this I propose that the comrades consider the method by which Stalin would be removed from this position and by which another man would be selected for it, a man who, above all, would differ from Stalin in only one quality, namely, greater tolerance, greater loyalty, greater kindness and more considerate attitude towards the comrades, a less capricious temper, &c.

This document of Lenin's was made known to the delegates at the thirteenth Party Congress, who discussed the question of transferring Stalin from the position of Secretary-General. The delegates declared themselves in favour of retaining Stalin in this post, hoping that he would heed the critical remarks of Vladimir Ilyich and would be able to overcome the defects which caused Lenin serious anxiety . . .

As later events have proven, Lenin's anxiety was justified: in the first period after Lenin's death Stalin still paid attention to his advice, but later he began to disregard the serious admonitions of Vladimir Ilyich.

When we analyse the practice of Stalin in regard to the direction of the party and of the country, when we pause to consider everything which Stalin perpetrated, we must be convinced that Lenin's fears were justified. The negative characteristics of Stalin, which, in Lenin's time, were only incipient, transformed themselves during the last years into a grave abuse of power by Stalin, which caused untold harm to our party.

We have to consider seriously and analyse correctly this matter in order that we may preclude any possibility of a repetition in any form whatever of what took place during the life of Stalin, who absolutely did not tolerate collegiality in leadership and in work, and who practised brutal violence, not only towards everything which opposed him but also towards that which seemed to his capricious and despotic character contrary to his concepts.

Stalin acted not through persuasion, explanation, and patient cooperation with people, but by imposing his concepts and demanding absolute submission to his opinion. Whoever opposed this concept or tried to prove his viewpoint, and the correctness of his position, was doomed to removal from the leading collective and to subsequent moral and physical annihilation. This was especially true during the period following the seventeenth Party Congress, when many prominent party leaders and rank-and-file party workers, honest and dedicated to the cause of Communism, fell victim to Stalin's despotism . . .

Stalin originated the concept 'enemy of the people'. This term automatically rendered it unnecessary that the ideological errors of a man or men engaged in a controversy be proven: this term made possible the usage of the most cruel repression, violating all norms of revolutionary legality, against anyone who in any way disagreed with Stalin, against those who were only suspected of hostile intent, against those who had bad reputations. This concept, 'enemy of the people', actually eliminated the possibility of any kind of ideological fight or the making of one's views known on this or that issue, even those of a practical character. In the main, and in actuality, the only proof of guilt used, against all norms of current legal science, was the 'confession' of the accused himself: and, as subsequent probing proved, 'confessions' were acquired through physical pressures against the accused.

This led to glaring violations of revolutionary legality, and to the fact that many entirely innocent persons, who in the past had defended the party line, became victims. We must assert that in regard to those persons who in their time had opposed the party line, there were often no sufficiently serious reasons for their physical annihilation. The formula 'enemy of the people' was specifically introduced for the purpose of physically annihilating such individuals.

Everyone knows how irreconcilable Lenin was with the ideological enemies of Marxism, with those who deviated from the correct party line. At the same time, however, Lenin, as is evident from the given document, in his practice of directing the party demanded the most intimate party contact with people who had shown indecision or temporary nonconformity with the party line, but whom it was possible to return to the party path. Lenin advised that such people should be patiently educated without the application of extreme methods. Lenin's wisdom in dealing with people was evident in his work with cadres.

An entirely different relationship with people characterized Stalin. Lenin's traits – patient work with people; stubborn and painstaking education of them; the ability to induce people to follow him without using compulsion, but rather through the ideological influence on them of the whole collective – were entirely foreign to Stalin. He discarded the Leninist method of convincing and educating: he abandoned the method of ideological struggle for that of administrative violence, mass repressions, and terror. He acted on an increasingly larger scale and more stubbornly through punitive organs, at the same time often violating all existing norms of morality and of Soviet laws.

Arbitrary behaviour by one person encouraged and permitted arbitrariness in others. Mass arrests and deportations of many thousands of people, execution without trial and without normal investigation . . .

Lenin used severe methods only in the most necessary cases, when the exploiting classes were still in existence and were vigorously opposing the Revolution, when the struggle for survival was decidedly assuming the sharpest forms, even including a Civil War.

Stalin, on the other hand, used extreme methods and mass repressions at a time when the Revolution was already victorious, when the Soviet State was strengthened, when the exploiting classes were already liquidated and Socialist relations were rooted solidly in all phases of national economy, when our party was politically consolidated and had strengthened itself both numerically and ideologically. It is clear that here Stalin showed in a whole series of cases his intolerance, his brutality, and his abuse of power. Instead of proving his political correctness and mobilizing the masses, he often chose the path of repression and physical annihilation, not only against actual enemies but also against individuals who had not committed any crimes against the party and the Soviet Government. Here we see no wisdom but only a demonstration of the brutal force which had once so alarmed V. I. Lenin . . .

I recall the first days when the conflict between the Soviet Union and Yugoslavia began artificially to be blown up. Once, when I came from Kiev to Moscow, I was invited to visit Stalin who, pointing to the copy of a letter lately sent to Tito, asked me: 'Have you read this?'

Not waiting for my reply, he answered: 'I will shake my little finger – and there will be no more Tito. He will fall.'

We have dearly paid for this 'shaking of the little finger'. This statement reflected Stalin's mania for greatness, but he acted just that way: 'I will shake my little finger – and there will be no Kossior'; 'I will shake my little finger once more and Postyshev and Chubar will be no more'; 'I will shake my little finger again – Voznesensky, Kuznetsov and many others will disappear.'

But this did not happen to Tito. No matter how much or how little Stalin shook, not only his little finger but everything else that he could shake, Tito did not fall. Why? The reason was that, in this case of disagreement with the Yugoslav comrades, Tito had behind him a State and a people who had gone through a severe school of fighting for liberty and independence, a people which gave support to its leaders.

You see to what Stalin's mania for greatness led. He had completely lost consciousness of reality; he demonstrated his suspicion and haughtiness not only in relation to individuals in the USSR but in relation to whole parties and nations.

Stalin's reluctance to consider life's realities and the fact that he was not aware of the real state of affairs in the provinces can be illustrated by his direction of agriculture. All those who interested themselves even a little in the national situation saw the difficult situation in agriculture, but Stalin never even noted it. Did we tell Stalin about this? Yes, we told him, but he did not support us. Why? Because Stalin never travelled anywhere, did not meet city and kolkhoz workers; he did not know the actual situation in the provinces. He knew the country and agriculture only from films. And these films had dressed up and beautified the existing situation in agriculture.

Many films so pictured kolkhoz life that the tables were bending from the weight of turkeys and geese. Evidently Stalin thought that it was actually so.

Vladimir Ilyich Lenin looked at life differently; he was always close to the people; he used to receive peasant delegates, and often spoke at factory gatherings; he used to visit villages and talk with the peasants.

Stalin separated himself from the people and never went anywhere. This went on for dozens of years. The last time he visited a village was in January 1928, when he went to Siberia in connection with grain deliveries. How then could he have known the situation in the provinces?

We should in all seriousness consider the question of the cult of the individual. We cannot let this matter get out of the party, especially not to the press. It is for this reason that we are considering it here at a closed congress session. We should know the limits: we should not give ammunition to the enemy: we should not wash our dirty linen before their eyes. I think that the delegates to the congress will understand and assess properly all these proposals. (*Tumultuous applause.*)

Comrades! We must abolish the cult of the individual decisively, once and for all; we must draw the proper conclusions concerning both ideological-theoretical and practical work.

It is necessary for this purpose:

First, in a Bolshevik manner, to condemn and to eradicate the cult of the individual as alien to Marxism–Leninism and not consonant with the principles of party leadership and the norms of party life, and to fight inexorably all attempts at bringing back this practice in one form or another.

To return to and actually practise in all our ideological work the most important theses of Marxist–Leninist science about the people as the creator of history and as the creator of all material and spiritual good of humanity, about the decisive role of the Marxist party in the revolutionary fight for the transformation of society, about the victory of communism.

Comrades: The twentieth Congress of the Communist Party of the Soviet Union has manifested with a new strength the unshakable unity of our party, its cohesiveness around the Central Committee, its resolute will to accomplish the great task of building communism. (*Tumultuous applause.*) And the fact that we present in all their ramifications the basic problems of overcoming the cult of the individual which is alien to Marxism–Leninism, as well as the problem of liquidating its burdensome consequences, is evidence of the great moral and political strength of our party. (*Prolonged applause.*)

We are absolutely certain that our party, armed with the historical resolutions of the twentieth congress, will lead the Soviet people along the Leninist path to new successes, to new victories. (*Tumultuous, prolonged applause.*)

Long live the victorious banner of our party – Leninism! (*Tumultuous, prolonged applause ending in standing ovation.*)

*Although delivered in secret, the speech reached other Communist countries and eventually leaked out in the West. It encouraged restlessness in Poland, revolt in Hungary and hastened the rift with Chairman Mao and Peking, the main reasons for Khrushchev's downfall in 1964, two years after the United States and the Soviet Union nearly came to war over the Cuban missile crisis.*

•

## ANEURIN BEVAN
London, 5 December 1956

### 'We have to act up to different standards'

*The Suez Crisis of 1956, initiated after President Nasser of Egypt nationalized the Suez Canal Company, divided British public opinion more bitterly than any other post-war dispute – and also diverted British and American attention from Soviet intervention to suppress the Hungarian national uprising. An Anglo-French invasion of Egypt started on 5 November but was halted two days later after being condemned by the United Nations, as well as the United States.*

*Aneurin Bevan, now the official Labour spokesman on foreign affairs, was the fiercest British critic of Suez. The first inquest on the disaster was held in the Commons on 5 December, when Bevan, according to his biographer Michael Foot, made what many considered the greatest speech of his life: 'Bevan welded the scattered indictment into a single, glittering synthesis; the wit merged with the wisdom and the wisdom with the wit, like two edges of the same sword.' This was the peroration.*

The social furniture of modern society is so complicated and fragile that it cannot support the jackboot. We cannot run the processes of modern society by attempting to impose our will upon nations by armed force. If we have not learned that we have learned nothing. Whatever may have been the morality of the Government's action – and about that there is no doubt – there is no doubt about its imbecility. There is not the slightest shadow of doubt that we have attempted to use methods which were bound to destroy the objectives we had, and, of course, this is what we have discovered.

It has been proved over and over again now in the modern world that men and women are often prepared to put up with material losses for things that they really think worthwhile. It has been shown in Budapest, and it could be shown in the Middle East. That is why I beg Hon. Members to turn their backs on this most ugly chapter and realize that if we are to live in the world and are to be regarded as a decent nation, decent citizens in the world, we have to act up to different standards than the one that we have been following in the last few weeks.

I resent most bitterly this unconcern for the lives of innocent men and women. It may be that the dead in Port Said are 100, 200 or 300. If it is only one, we had no business to take it. Do Hon. Members begin to realize how this is going to revolt the world when it passes into the imagination of men and women everywhere, and in this country, that we, with eight million here in London, the biggest single civilian target in the world, with our crowded island exposed, as no nation in the world is exposed, to the barbarism of modern weapons, we ourselves set the example.

We ourselves conscript our boys and put guns and aeroplanes in their hands and say, 'Bomb there.' Really, this is so appalling that human language can hardly describe it. And for what? The Government resorted to epic weapons for squalid and trivial ends, and that is why all through this unhappy period Ministers – all of them – have spoken and argued and debated well below their proper form – because they have been synthetic villains. They are not really villains. They have only set off on a villainous course, and they cannot even use the language of villainy.

It is no use Hon. Members consoling themselves that they have more support in the country than many of them feared they might have. Of course they have support in the country. They have support among many of the unthinking and unreflective who still react to traditional values, who still think that we can solve all these problems in the old ways. Of course they have. Not all the human race has grown to adult state yet. But do not let them take comfort in that thought. The Right Hon. Member for Woodford (Sir Winston Churchill) has warned them before. In the first volume of his *Second World War*, he writes about the situation before the war and he says this:

> Thus an Administration more disastrous than any in our history saw all its errors and shortcomings acclaimed by the nation. There was however a bill to be paid, and it took the new House of Commons nearly ten years to pay it.

*The speech was acclaimed both inside and outside the House of Commons and made even Bevan's former critics believe that he should be the next Foreign Secretary.*

•

## ANEURIN BEVAN
### Brighton, 3 October 1957

*'Naked into the conference chamber'*

*Why has he done it? Why, why, why? was the angry, bemused reaction of the Bevanites, Aneurin Bevan's allies on the left of the Labour Party, after the speech to the party conference in which he opposed resolution 24 calling for unilateral British disarmament.*

*His speech in the 1957 H-bomb debate was the bravest of Bevan's career: he*

*was siding with his old enemy, Hugh Gaitskell, and denouncing the views of his*
*closest political friends. 'I have thought about this very anxiously,' he said. 'I*
*knew that I was going to make a speech that would offend and even hurt many*
*of my friends.' He was interrupted by cries of protest. 'But do you think I am*
*afraid?' There was no answer. 'I shall say what I believe.' This is what Bevan*
*then said.*

If you carry this resolution and follow out all its implications and do
not run away from it you will send a British Foreign Secretary, whoever
he may be, naked into the conference chamber. Able to preach sermons, of course; he could make good sermons. But action of that sort
is not necessarily the way in which you take the menace of this bomb
from the world. It might be that action of that sort will still be there
available to us if our other actions fail. It is something you can always
do. You can always, if the influence you have upon your allies and
upon your opponents is not yielding any fruits, take unilateral action
of that sort. (*A cry of 'Do it now.'*) 'Do it now,' you say. This is the
answer I give from the platform. Do it now as a Labour Party Conference? You cannot do it now. It is not in your hands to do it. All you can
do is pass a resolution. What you are saying is that a British Foreign
Secretary gets up in the United Nations, without consultation – mark
this; this is a responsible attitude! – without telling any members of the
Commonwealth, without concerting with them, that the British
Labour movement decides unilaterally that this country contracts out
of all its commitments and obligations entered into with other countries and members of the Commonwealth – without consultation at
all. And you call that statesmanship? I call it an emotional spasm . . .

If any Socialist Foreign Secretary is to have a chance he must be
permitted to substitute good policies for bad policies. Do not disarm
him diplomatically, intellectually, and in every other way before he
has a chance to turn round.

This country could be destroyed merely as an incident of a war
between Russia and the USA. It is not necessary for any bombs to
drop on us. If war broke out between the USA and the Soviet Union,
this country would be poisoned with the rest of mankind. What we
have, therefore, to consider is how far the policies we are considering

can exert an influence and a leverage over the policies of the USA and of the Soviet Union . . .

I do seriously believe in the rejection of the bomb. But that is not the issue. That is what I am telling you. If resolution 24 only meant that we would have very little difficulty with it. But if resolution 24 is read with its implications it means that as decent folk you must immediately repudiate all the protection and all the alliances and all the entanglements you have with anybody who uses or possesses or manufactures hydrogen bombs. That is our dilemma. I find it a very, very serious dilemma. This problem is without precedent in the history of the world. I consider that it is not only a question of practical statesmanship . . .

No nation is entitled to try to exterminate an evil by invoking a greater evil than the one it is trying to get rid of. The hydrogen bomb is, of course, a greater evil than any evil it is intended to meet. But, unfortunately, the USSR and the USA are in possession of this weapon, and we are in danger of being exterminated as a consequence of their rivalries and their antagonisms. What I would like to have is the opportunity of exerting influence upon the policies of those countries, but this is not the way to do it. You do not give us a chance. It was said to me during the week, 'What is the use of getting up on the platform and saying you are going to stop or suspend the tests?' We have said that already. Are we thinking merely in terms of stronger and stronger resolutions accompanied by no action at all?

I am begging and praying our comrades here to reconsider the demands they have made, because I agree that those who support resolution No. 24 do it with complete sincerity. They do it because they believe that the resolution embodies their detestation of the bomb. But I am sure that in your secret hearts you will admit that you have not fully thought out the implications of that. You have not realized that the consequence of passing that resolution would be to drive Great Britain into a diplomatic purdah.

*Bevan became deputy leader of the Labour Party in 1959.*

.

# ENOCH POWELL
House of Commons, 27 July 1959

### '*Hola Camp*'

*Enoch Powell (1912–98) was one of the most gifted, principled and controversial Conservative politicians of his era. Once a professor of Greek (and a future Minister of Health), Powell was still a backbencher when an official inquiry confirmed allegations of brutality at the Kenyan detention camp at Hola, where batons and rifle butts had been used on Mau Mau detainees and ten men had died (allegedly after drinking dirty water). His coruscating speech, insisting on ministerial responsibility, was remembered by many MPs on both sides of the House as the best they ever heard. As Powell ended, he sat down and cried. He said later: 'One of the exhilarations of being a member of the House of Commons, if you experience it, are the moments when you actually have it in your hand, in which you play upon it like an instrument.'*

*The speech remained the most powerful memory of his long career.*

I am as certain of this as I am of anything, that my Right Hon. Friend the Secretary of State from the beginning to the end of this affair is without any jot or tittle of blame for what happened in Kenya, that he could not be expected to know, that it could not be within the administrative conventions that these matters should be brought to his attention before or during the execution. When I say my Right Hon. Friend was in this matter utterly and completely blameless, that is of a piece with his administration of his high office generally, which has been the greatest exercise of the office of Colonial Secretary in modern times. It is in the name of that record, it is in the name of his personal blamelessness, that I beg of him to ensure that the responsibility is recognized and carried where it properly belongs, and is seen to belong.

I have heard it suggested that there were circumstances surrounding this affair at Hola Camp which, it is argued, might justify the passing over of this responsibility – which might justify one in saying,

'Well, of course, strictly speaking, that is quite correct: but then here there were special circumstances.'

It has been said – and it is a fact – that these eleven men were the lowest of the low; sub-human was the word which one of my Hon. Friends used. So be it. But that cannot be relevant to the acceptance of responsibility for their death. I know that it does not enter into my Right Hon. Friend's mind that it could be relevant, because it would be completely inconsistent with his whole policy of rehabilitation, which is based upon the assumption that whatever the present state of these men, they can be reclaimed. No one who supports the policy of rehabilitation can argue from the character and condition of these men that responsibility for their death should be different from the responsibility for anyone else's death. In general, I would say that it is a fearful doctrine, which must recoil upon the heads of those who pronounce it, to stand in judgement on a fellow human being and to say, 'Because he was such-and-such, therefore the consequences which would otherwise flow from his death shall not flow.'

It is then said that the morale of the Prison Service, the morale of the whole Colonial Service, is above all important and that whatever we do, whatever we urge, whatever we say, should have regard to that morale. 'Amen' say I. But is it for the morale of the Prison Service that those who executed a policy should suffer – whether inadequately or not is another question – and those who authorized it, those to whom they appealed, should be passed over? I cannot believe that that supports the morale of a service.

Going on beyond that, my Hon. Friend the Member for Leicester, South-East (Mr Peel) reminded the House how proud the Colonial Service is of the integrity of its administration and its record. Nothing could be more damaging to the morale of such a service than that there should be a breath of a blemish left upon it. No, sir; that argument from the morale of the Prison Service and the Colonial Service stands on its head if what we mean is that therefore the consequences of responsibility should not follow in this case as they would in any other similar case.

Finally it is argued that this is Africa, that things are different there. Of course they are. The question is whether the difference between things there and here is such that the taking of responsibility there and here should be upon different principles. We claim that it is our object – and this is something which unites both sides of the House – to leave representative institutions behind us wherever we give up our rule. I cannot imagine that it is a way to plant representative institutions to be seen to shirk the acceptance and the assignment of responsibility, which is the very essence of responsible government.

Nor can we ourselves pick and choose where and in what parts of the world we shall use this or that kind of standard. We cannot say, 'We will have African standards in Africa, Asian standards in Asia and perhaps British standards here at home.' We have not that choice to make. We must be consistent with ourselves everywhere. All government, all influence of man upon man, rests upon opinion. What we can do in Africa, where we still govern and where we no longer govern, depends upon the opinion which is entertained of the way in which this country acts and the way in which Englishmen act. We cannot, we dare not, in Africa of all places, fall below our own highest standards in the acceptance of responsibility.

•

## ANEURIN BEVAN
### Blackpool, 29 November 1959

*'An ugly society, a vulgar society, a meretricious society'*

*The Labour Party, led by Hugh Gaitskell, had lost the 1959 general election to the Conservatives, led by Harold Macmillan. As it met for a special inquest on its defeat, Labour was once again divided over its commitment to nationalization, with the revisionist Gaitskell urging that the constitution should be brought 'up to date' and arguing that public ownership was no longer the be-all and end-all of party policy.*

*The next day, overcoming his sickness of the previous months, Aneurin Bevan, now deputy leader, reopened the socialist argument, yet preserved the unity of the party. 'It was the classic Bevan speech,' says Michael Foot, his biographer, 'shaped to secure an immediate end and yet elevating the party debate to the realm of political philosophy ... Samson's locks had grown again but he used his strength not to destroy but to sustain.'*

If it is said that we lost the election because of our belief in public ownership, then 12,250,000 people voted for us because they believed in public ownership. It is not a bad start-off, is it? Now you may say: 'Ah, but they did not vote for you because they believed in public ownership.' Well, you cannot have it both ways, can you? Or even suppose you were allowed to have it both ways, then you must conclude that 12,250,000 people did vote for us despite their distaste for public ownership. That is the biggest single vote ever given for public ownership in any country in the whole world. Then why the hell this defeatism? Why all this talk that we have actually gone back? Of course it is true that in the present-day affluent society a very large number of people are not as discontented as they were, and because we are a Party that stands for the redress of discontent and the wrongs caused by discontent, the absence of so much discontent therefore has reduced our popularity. But you know, comrades, I have been in this movement now for many years. I was in this movement in between the war years when there were two million unemployed, and still the Tories got a majority. You would have thought that there was some spontaneous generation of Socialist conviction; but we lost before the war years. Even the unemployed voted against us. Even in the areas where there was as much as 20 per cent and 30 per cent of unemployment we lost seats. Should we not therefore have voted in favour of unemployment?

The fact is – and that is accepted, and derive your lessons from it – that a very considerable number of young men and women in the course of the last five or ten years have had their material conditions improved and their status has been raised in consequence and their discontents have been reduced, so that temporarily their personalities are satisfied with the framework in which they live. They are not conscious of constriction; they are not conscious of frustration or of limitation as formerly they were, in exactly the same way as even before the war large numbers of workers were not sufficiently conscious of frustration and of limitation, even on unemployment benefit, to vote against the Tories.

What is the lesson for us? It is that we must enlarge and expand those personalities, so that they can become again conscious of limitation and constriction. The problem is one of education, not of surrender! This so-called affluent society is an ugly society still. It is a vulgar society. It is a meretricious society. It is a society in which priorities have gone all wrong. I once said – and I do not want to quote myself too frequently – that the language of priorities was the religion of Socialism, and there is nothing wrong with that statement either, but you can only get your priorities right if you have the power to put them right, and the argument, comrades, is about power in society. If we managed to get a majority in Great Britain by the clever exploitation of contemporary psychology, and we did not get the commanding heights of the economy in our power, then we did not get the priorities right. The argument is about power and only about power, because only by the possession of power can you get the priorities correct . . .

Frank Pakenham made a speech here yesterday in which he said that his beliefs were derived from his religion. I do not claim to be a very religious man; I never have. But I must remind Frank Pakenham that Christ drove the money-changers from the Temple. He did not open the doors wide for them to enter. He drove them away. If we go on to apply the principles of Christianity to contemporary British society, they have been done elsewhere rather better than they have been done here. I think there is something evil, something abominable, something disgraceful in a country that can turn its back on Hola, that can turn its back on the old-age pensioners, that can starve the Health Service, and reap £1,500 million from the Stock Exchange boom immediately after the election is over.

What are we going to say, comrades? Are we going to accept the defeat? Are we going to say to India, where Socialism has been adopted as the official policy despite all the difficulties facing the Indian community, that the British Labour movement has dropped Socialism here? What are we going to say to the rest of the world?

Are we going to send a message from this great Labour movement, which is the father and mother of modern democracy and modern Socialism, that we in Blackpool in 1959 have turned our backs on our principles because of a temporary unpopularity in a temporarily affluent society?

Let me give you a personal confession of faith. I have found in my life that the burdens of public life are too great to be borne for trivial ends. The sacrifices are too much, unless we have something really serious in mind; and therefore, I hope we are going to send from this Conference a message of hope, a message of encouragement, to the youth and to the rest of the world that is listening very carefully to what we are saying.

I was rather depressed by what Denis Healey [a fellow Labour MP] said. I have a lot of respect for him: but you know, Denis, you are not going to be able to help the Africans if the levers of power are left in the hands of their enemies in Britain. You cannot do it! Nor can you inject the principles of ethical Socialism into an economy based upon private greed. You cannot do it! You cannot mix them, and therefore I beg and pray that we should wind this Conference up this time on a message of hope, and we should say to India and we should say to Africa and Indonesia, and not only to them, but we should say to China and we should say to Russia, that the principles of democratic Socialism have not been extinguished by a temporary defeat at the hands of the Tories a few weeks ago!

You know, comrades, parliamentary institutions have not been destroyed because the Left was too vigorous; they have been destroyed because the Left was too inert. You cannot give me a single illustration in the Western world where Fascism conquered because Socialism was too violent. You cannot give me a single illustration where representative government has been undermined because the representatives of the people asked for too much. But I can give you instance after instance we are faced with today where representative government has been rendered helpless because the representatives of the people did not ask enough. We have never suffered from too much vitality; we have suffered from too little.

That is why I say that we are going to go from this Conference a united Party. We are going to go back to the House of Commons, and we are going to fight the Tories. But we are not only going to fight them there; we are going to fight them in the constituencies and inside the trade unions. And we are going to get the youth! Let them start. Do not let them wait for the Executive, for God's sake! Start getting your youth clubs, go in and start now! Go back home and start them, and we will give all the help and encouragement that we can.

I have enough faith in my fellow creatures in Great Britain to believe that when they have got over the delirium of the television, when they realize that their new homes that they have been put into are mortgaged to the hilt, when they realize that the moneylender has been elevated to the highest position in the land, when they realize that the refinements for which they should look are not there, that it is a vulgar society of which no decent person could be proud, when they realize all those things, when the years go by and they see the challenge of modern society not being met by the Tories who can consolidate their political powers only on the basis of national mediocrity, who are unable to exploit the resources of their scientists because they are prevented by the greed of their capitalism from doing so, when they realize that the flower of our youth goes abroad today because they are not being given opportunities of using their skill and their knowledge properly at home, when they realize that all the tides of history are flowing in our direction, that we are not beaten, that we represent the future: then, when we say it and mean it, then we shall lead our people to where they deserve to be led!

*This characteristically emotional affirmation of British democratic socialism was almost Bevan's last speech and he won a tumultuous reception. He died the following summer.*

•

# HAROLD MACMILLAN
Cape Town, 3 February 1960

*'The wind of change'*

*Harold Macmillan (1894–1986) had been British prime minister for three years when in January 1960 he left for a tour of Africa that took him through Ghana, Nigeria, Rhodesia, and Nyasaland and then to the apartheid state of South Africa, where he made the most famous speech of his life.*

*The speech to both houses of parliament was the most important event of the tour. 'I approached this ordeal with much trepidation,' Macmillan wrote in his memoirs. 'I knew that much of what I would be constrained to say would be disagreeable to many of my hearers.' Dr Hendrik Verwoerd, the South African prime minister [and also one of the prime movers of apartheid], had seen the outlines of the text and what Macmillan was to say had come as a shock.*

*Standing in the chamber of the Old Cape Colony parliament, Macmillan, who had encouraged independence in Britain's former colonies, delivered a fifty-minute speech in which he made plain Britain's deep distaste for the racial policies of his hosts, who were still then members of the British Commonwealth.*

Ever since the break-up of the Roman Empire one of the constant facts of political life in Europe has been the emergence of independent nations. They have come into existence over the centuries in different forms, with different kinds of Government, but all have been inspired by a deep, keen feeling of nationalism, which has grown as the nations have grown.

In the twentieth century, and especially since the end of the war, the processes which gave birth to the nation states of Europe have been repeated all over the world. We have seen the awakening of national consciousness in peoples who have for centuries lived in dependence upon some other power. Fifteen years ago this movement spread through Asia. Many countries there of different races and civilizations pressed their claim to an independent national life. Today the same thing is happening in Africa, and the most striking of all the impressions I have formed is of the strength of this African national consciousness. In different places it takes different forms, but it is happening everywhere. The wind of change is blowing through this continent, and, whether we like it or not, this growth of national consciousness is a political fact. We must all accept it as a fact, and our national policies must take account of it.

Of course, you understand this better than anyone. You are sprung from Europe, the home of nationalism, and here in Africa you have yourselves created a new nation. Indeed, in the history of our times yours will be recorded as the first of the African nationalisms, and this tide of national consciousness which is now rising in Africa is a fact for which you and we and the other nations of the Western World are ultimately responsible. For its causes are to be found in the achievements of Western civilization, in the pushing forward of the frontiers of knowledge, in the applying of science in the service of human needs, in the expanding of food production, in the speeding and multiplying of the means of communication, and perhaps, above all, the spread of education . . .

As I see it the great issue in this second half of the twentieth century is whether the uncommitted peoples of Asia and Africa will swing to the East or to the West. Will they be drawn into the Communist camp? Or will the great experiments in self-government that are now being made in Asia and Africa, especially within the Commonwealth, prove so successful, and by their example so compelling, that the balance will come down in favour of freedom and order and justice?

The struggle is joined, and it is a struggle for the minds of men. What is now on trial is much more than our military strength or our diplomatic and administrative skill. It is our way of life. The uncommitted nations want to see before they choose.

What can we show them to help them choose right? Each of the independent members of the Commonwealth must answer that question for itself. It is a basic principle of our modern Commonwealth that we respect each other's sovereignty in matters of internal policy. At the same time we must recognize that in this shrinking world in which we live today the internal policies of one nation may have effects outside it. We may sometimes be tempted to say to each other, 'Mind your own business,' but in these days I would myself expand the old saying so that it runs: 'Mind your own business, but mind how it affects my business, too.'

Let me be very frank with you, my friends. What Governments and Parliaments in the United Kingdom have done since the war in according independence to India, Pakistan, Ceylon, Malaya and Ghana, and what they will do for Nigeria and other countries now nearing independence, all this, though we take full and sole responsibility for it, we do in the belief that it is the only way to establish the future of the Commonwealth and of the Free World on sound foundations. All this of course is also of deep and close concern to you for nothing we do in this small world can be done in a corner or remain hidden. What we do today in West, Central and East Africa becomes known tomorrow to everyone in the Union, whatever his language, colour or traditions. Let me assure you, in all friendliness, that we are well aware of this and that we have acted and will act with full knowledge of the responsibility we have to all our friends.

Nevertheless I am sure you will agree that in our own areas of responsibility we must each do what we think right. What we think right derives from a long experience both of failure and success in the management of our own affairs. We have tried to learn and apply the lessons of our judgement of right and wrong. Our justice is rooted in the same soil as yours – in Christianity and in the rule of law as the basis of a free society. This experience of our own explains why it has been our aim in the countries for which we have borne responsibility, not only to raise the material standards of living, but also to create a society which respects the rights of individuals, a society in which men are given the opportunity to grow to their full stature – and that must in our view include the opportunity to have an increasing share in political power and responsibility, a society in which individual merit and individual merit alone is the criterion for a man's advancement, whether political or economic . . .

The attitude of the United Kingdom towards this problem was clearly expressed by the Foreign Secretary, Mr Selwyn Lloyd, speaking at the United Nations General Assembly on 17 September 1959. These were his words:

In those territories where different races or tribes live side by side the task is to ensure that all the people may enjoy security and freedom and the chance to contribute as individuals to the progress and well being of these countries. We reject the idea of any inherent superiority of one race over another. Our policy therefore is non-racial. It offers a future in which Africans, Europeans, Asians, the peoples of the Pacific and others with whom we are concerned, will all play their full part as citizens in the countries where they live, and in which feelings of race will be submerged in loyalty to new nations.

I have thought you would wish me to state plainly and with full candour the policy for which we in Britain stand. It may well be that in trying to do our duty as we see it we shall sometimes make difficulties for you. If this proves to be so we shall regret it. But I know that even so you would not ask us to flinch from doing our duty.

As a fellow member of the Commonwealth it is our earnest desire to give South Africa our support and encouragement, but I hope you won't mind my saying frankly that there are some aspects of your policies which make it impossible for us to do this without being false to our own deep convictions about the political destinies of free men to which in our own territories we are trying to give effect. I think we ought, as friends, to face together, without seeking to apportion credit or blame, the fact that in the world of today this difference of outlook lies between us . . .

The fact is that in this modern world no country, not even the greatest, can live for itself alone. Nearly two thousand years ago, when the whole of the civilized world was comprised within the confines of the Roman Empire, St Paul proclaimed one of the great truths of history – we are all members one of another. During this twentieth century that eternal truth has taken on a new and exciting significance. It has always been impossible for the individual man to live in isolation from his fellows, in the home, the tribe, the village, or the city. Today it is impossible for nations to live in isolation from one another. What Dr John Donne said of individual men three hundred years ago is true today of my country, your country, and all the countries of the world:

Any man's death diminishes me, because I am involved in Mankind. And therefore never send to know for whom the bell tolls; it tolls for thee.

All nations now are interdependent one upon another, and this is generally realized throughout the Western World . . . Those of us who by grace of the electorate are temporarily in charge of affairs in your country and in mine, we fleeting transient phantoms on the great stage of history, we have no right to sweep aside on this account the friendship that exists between our countries, for that is the legacy of history. It is not ours alone to deal with as we wish. To adapt a famous phrase, it belongs to those who are living, but it also belongs to those who are dead and to those who are yet unborn. We must face the differences, but let us try to see beyond them down the long vista of the future.

I hope – indeed, I am confident – that in another fifty years we shall look back on the differences that exist between us now as matters of historical interest, for as time passes and one generation yields to another, human problems change and fade. Let us remember these truths. Let us resolve to build, not to destroy, and let us remember always that weakness comes from division, strength from unity.

*Verwoerd made an impromptu defence of 'justice for the white man' within his official vote of thanks. White South Africans voted eight months later to leave the British Commonwealth and the Independent Republic of South Africa was formed on 31 May 1961.*

•

## EUGENE McCARTHY
Los Angeles, 13 July 1960

*'Do not reject this man'*

*There were five strong candidates for the Democratic nomination for the presidential election in 1960: Adlai Stevenson, Stuart Symington, Hubert Humphrey, Lyndon Baines Johnson and John F. Kennedy.*

*Stevenson had lost the two previous elections to Eisenhower but was still keen for the nomination that was to be denied to him when the convention opted for Kennedy. Among those who were thinking uneasily of deserting Stevenson for Kennedy, there were many who nevertheless thought Stevenson alone had the intellectual stature and integrity required by the next American president – and this address by Senator Eugene McCarthy of Minnesota, an eloquent and moving tribute to Stevenson's distinguished career in American politics, stood out from the other nomination speeches for its dramatic boldness.*

These times, men say, are out of joint. They say these are the worst of times without being the best of times – this may be true. But I say to you these external signs, these practical problems which face us, are nothing compared to the problems of the mind and of the spirit which face the United States and the free world today.

If the mind is clouded and if the will is confused and uncertain, there can be no sound decision and no sound action.

There's demagoguery abroad in the land at all times, and demagoguery, I say to you, takes many forms. There's that which says 'here is wealth, and here is material comfort'. We suffer a little from that in the United States.

There's demagoguery which promises people power, which is used for improper purposes and ends. And we have seen in this century and in this generation what happens when power is abused.

I say to you there's a subtle kind of demagoguery which erodes the spirit. And this is the demagoguery which has affected this United States in the last eight years.

What are we told? What have we been told? We've been told that we can be strong without sacrifice. This is what we've been told. We've been told that we can be good without any kind of discipline if we just say we're humble and sincere – this is the nature of goodness. We've been told that we can be wise without reflection. We can be wise without study, we've been told. I say this is the erosion of the spirit which has taken place in this United States in the last eight years. And I say to you that the time has come to raise again the cry of the ancient prophet. What did he say? He said the prophets prophesy falsely and the high priests, he said, ruled by their word, and my people love to have it so. But what will be the end?

I say to you the political prophets have prophesied falsely in these eight years. And the high priests of government have ruled by that false prophecy. And the people seemed to have loved it so.

But there was one man – there was one man who did not prophesy falsely, let me remind you. There was one man who said: Let's talk sense to the American people.

What did the scoffers say? The scoffers said: Nonsense. They said: Catastrophic nonsense. But we know it was the essential and the basic and the fundamental truth that he spoke to us.

There was a man who talked sense to the American people. There was one man who said: This is a time for self-examination. This is a time for us to take stock, he said. This is a time to decide where we are and where we're going.

This, he said, is a time for virtue. But what virtues did he say we needed? Oh yes, he said we need the heroic virtues – we always do. We need fortitude; we need courage; we need justice. Everyone cheers when you speak out for those virtues.

But what did he say in addition to that? He said we need the unheroic virtues in America. We need the virtue, he said, of patience. There were those who said we've had too much of patience.

We need, he said, the virtue of tolerance. We need the virtue of forbearance. We need the virtues of patience and understanding.

This was what the prophet said. This is what he said to the American people. I ask you, did he prophesy falsely? Did he prophesy falsely?

He said this is a time for greatness. This is a time for greatness for America. He did not say he possessed it. He did not even say he was destined for it. He did say that the heritage of America is one of greatness.

And he described the heritage to us. And he said the promise of America is a promise of greatness. And he said, this promise we must fulfill.

This was his call to greatness. This was the call to greatness that was issued in 1952.

He did not seek power for himself in 1952. He did not seek power in 1956.

He does not seek it for himself today.

This man knows – this man knows, as all of us do from history, that power often comes to those who seek it. But history does not prove that power is always well used by those who seek it.

On the contrary, the whole history of democratic politics is to this end, that power is best exercised by those who are sought out by the people, by those to whom power is given by a free people.

And so I say to you Democrats here assembled: Do not turn away from this man. Do not reject this man. He has fought gallantly. He has fought courageously. He has fought honourably. In 1952 in the great battle. In 1956 he fought bravely. And between those years and since, he has stood off the guerrilla attacks of his enemies and the sniping attacks of those who should have been his friends. Do not reject this man who has made us all proud to be called Democrats. Do not reject this man who, his enemies said, spoke above the heads of the people, but they said it only because they didn't want the people to listen. He spoke to the people. He moved their minds and stirred their hearts, and this was what was objected to. Do not leave this prophet without honour in his own party. Do not reject this man.

I submit to you a man who is not the favourite son of any one state. I submit to you the man who is the favourite son of fifty states.

And not only of fifty states but the favourite son of every country in the world in which he is known – the favourite son in every country in which he is unknown but in which some spark even though unexpressed of desire for liberty and freedom still lives.

This favourite son I submit to you: Adlai E. Stevenson of Illinois.

*Stevenson became ambassador to the United Nations in the Kennedy administration. McCarthy challenged President Johnson in 1968 and got forty per cent of the vote in the New Hampshire primary – which caused Robert Kennedy to declare and persuaded Johnson to stand down. After the assassination of Kennedy, Hubert Humphrey won the nomination.*

•

## JOHN F. KENNEDY
Los Angeles, 15 July 1960

### 'A new frontier'

*After the stolid, dull Eisenhower years, Senator John Fitzgerald Kennedy (1917–63) offered new horizons and new hope to Americans, summoning them to join him on the new frontier.*

*At the Democratic Convention in Los Angeles he had defeated Hubert Humphrey, Stuart Symington, Lyndon Johnson and Adlai Stevenson to win the nomination for the presidential election. As he spoke at the ceremony of acceptance, he was flanked by his mother and sister, and by his defeated rivals. As the sun set he spoke, facing west, to 80,000 Democrats in the Los Angeles Coliseum – and to thirty-five million Americans watching him on television.*

*His face was tired and haggard after a year of strain and a week of sleeplessness. His voice was high and sad.*

The American people expect more from us than cries of indignation and attack. The times are too grave, the challenge too urgent, and the stakes too high – to permit the customary passions of political debate. We are not here to curse the darkness, but to light the candle that can guide us through that darkness to a safe and sane future. As Winston Churchill said on taking office some twenty years ago:

'If we open a quarrel between the present and the past, we shall be in danger of losing the future.'

Today our concern must be with that future. For the world is changing. The old era is ending. The old ways will not do.

All over the world, particularly in the newer nations, young men are coming to power – men who are not bound by the traditions of the past – men who are not blinded by the old fears and hates and rivalries – young men who can cast off the old slogans and delusions and suspicions.

The Republican nominee-to-be,* of course, is also a young man.

*Richard Nixon.

But his approach is as old as McKinley. His party is the party of the past. His speeches are generalities from Poor Richard's Almanac. Their platform, made up of left-over Democratic planks, has the courage of our old convictions. Their pledge is a pledge to the status quo – and today there can be no status quo.

For I stand tonight facing west on what was once the last frontier. From the lands that stretch 3,000 miles behind me, the pioneers of old gave up their safety, their comfort and sometimes their lives to build a new world here in the West.

They were not the captives of their own doubts, the prisoners of their own price tags. Their motto was not 'every man for himself' – but 'all for the common cause'. They were determined to make that new world strong and free, to overcome its hazards and its hardships, to conquer the enemies that threatened from without and within.

Today some would say that those struggles are all over – that all the horizons have been explored – that all the battles have been won – that there is no longer an American frontier.

But I trust that no one in this assemblage will agree with those sentiments. For the problems are not all solved and the battles are not all won – and we stand today on the edge of a new frontier – the frontier of the 1960s – a frontier of unknown opportunities and perils – a frontier of unfulfilled hopes and threats.

Woodrow Wilson's New Freedom promised our nation a new political and economic framework. Franklin Roosevelt's New Deal promised security and succour to those in need. But the New Frontier of which I speak is not a set of promises – it is a set of challenges. It sums up not what I intend to offer the American people, but what I intend to ask of them. It appeals to their pride, not their pocketbook – it holds out the promise of more sacrifice instead of more security.

But I tell you the New Frontier is here, whether we seek it or not. Beyond that frontier are uncharted areas of science and space, unsolved problems of peace and war, unconquered pockets of ignorance and prejudice, unanswered questions of poverty and surplus.

It would be easier to shrink back from that frontier, to look to the safe mediocrity of the past, to be lulled by good intentions and high rhetoric – and those who prefer that course should not cast their votes for me, regardless of party.

But I believe the times demand invention, innovation, imagination, decision. I am asking each of you to be new pioneers on that New Frontier. My call is to the young in heart, regardless of age – to the stout in spirit, regardless of party – to all who respond to the scriptural call:

'Be strong and of good courage; be not afraid, neither be thou dismayed.'

For courage – not complacency – is our need today – leadership – not salesmanship. And the only valid test of leadership is the ability to lead, and lead vigorously. A tired nation, said David Lloyd George, is a tory nation – and the United States today cannot afford to be either tired or tory.

There may be those who wish to hear more – more promises to this group or that – more harsh rhetoric about the men in the Kremlin – more assurances of a golden future, where taxes are always low and subsidies ever high. But my promises are in the platform you have adopted. Our ends will not be won by rhetoric and we can have faith in the future only if we have faith in ourselves.

For the harsh facts of the matter are that we stand on this frontier at a turning-point in history. We must prove all over again whether this nation – or any nation so conceived – can long endure – whether our society – with its freedom of choice, its breadth of opportunity, its range of alternatives – can compete with the single-minded advance of the Communist system.

Can a nation organized and governed such as ours endure? That is the real question. Have we the nerve and the will? Can we carry through in an age where we will witness not only new breakthroughs in weapons of destruction – but also a race for mastery of the sky and the rain, the ocean and the tides, the far side of space and the inside of men's minds?

Are we up to the task? Are we equal to the challenge? Are we willing to match the Russian sacrifice of the present for the future? Or must we sacrifice our future in order to enjoy the present?

That is the question of the New Frontier. That is the choice our nation must make – a choice that lies not merely between two men or two parties, but between the public interest and private comfort – between national greatness and national decline – between the fresh air of progress and the stale, dank atmosphere of 'normalcy' – between determined dedication and creeping mediocrity.

All mankind waits upon our decision. A whole world looks to see what we will do. We cannot fail their trust; we cannot fail to try.

*John Kennedy won the election by a narrow margin over Richard Nixon and became in January the following year the youngest – and first Roman Catholic – president in US history.*

•

## JOHN F. KENNEDY
### Washington, DC, 20 January 1961

*'The torch has been passed to a new generation of Americans'*

*For men and women born during or after the Second World War, John Kennedy's inaugural address, signalling the arrival in power of a new generation and a forty-four-year-old president, still burns in the memory. The new president instructed his speechwriter, Theodore Sorensen, to find the secret of Abraham Lincoln's Gettysburg Address. Kennedy (1917–63) adopted the cadences of Lincoln. Most Lincolnesque of all was his use of the oratorical 'Let', a device used to start eight sentences. Many phrases were made memorable by his use of contrapuntalism, as in 'Let us never negotiate out of fear. But let us never fear to negotiate.'*

*Critics have since ranked Kennedy's inaugural with Jefferson (the first), Lincoln (the second), Wilson (the first) and Franklin D. Roosevelt (first and second). According to the American student of oratory William Safire, Kennedy set the standard by which modern presidential inaugurals are judged.*

We observe today not a victory of party, but a celebration of freedom – symbolizing an end, as well as a beginning – signifying renewal, as well as change. For I have sworn before you and Almighty God the same solemn oath our forebears prescribed nearly a century and three-quarters ago.

The world is very different now. For man holds in his mortal hands the power to abolish all forms of human poverty and all forms of human life. And yet the same revolutionary beliefs for which our forebears fought are still at issue around the globe – the belief that the rights of man come not from the generosity of the state, but from the hand of God.

We dare not forget today that we are the heirs of that first revolution. Let the word go forth from this time and place, to friend and foe alike, that the torch has been passed to a new generation of Americans – born in this century, tempered by war, disciplined by a hard and bitter peace, proud of our ancient heritage – and unwilling to witness or permit the slow undoing of those human rights to which this nation has always been committed, and to which we are committed today at home and around the world.

Let every nation know, whether it wishes us well or ill, that we shall pay any price, bear any burden, meet any hardship, support any friend, oppose any foe, in order to assure the survival and the success of liberty.

This much we pledge – and more.

To those old allies whose cultural and spiritual origins we share, we pledge the loyalty of faithful friends. United, there is little we cannot do in a host of cooperative ventures. Divided, there is little we can do – for we dare not meet a powerful challenge at odds and split asunder.

To those new states whom we welcome to the ranks of the free, we pledge our word that one form of colonial control shall not have passed away merely to be replaced by a far more iron tyranny. We shall not always expect to find them supporting our view. But we shall always hope to find them strongly supporting their own freedom – and to remember that, in the past, those who foolishly sought power by riding the back of the tiger ended up inside.

To those peoples in the huts and villages across the globe struggling to break the bonds of mass misery, we pledge our best efforts to help them help themselves, for whatever period is required – not because the Communists may be doing it, not because we seek their votes, but because it is right. If a free society cannot help the many who are poor, it cannot save the few who are rich.

To our sister republics south of our border, we offer a special pledge – to convert our good words into good deeds – in a new alliance for progress – to assist free men and free governments in casting off the chains of poverty. But this peaceful revolution of hope cannot become the prey of hostile powers. Let all our neighbours know that we shall join with them to oppose aggression or subversion anywhere in the Americas. And let every other power know that this hemisphere intends to remain the master of its own house.

To that world assembly of sovereign states, the United Nations, our last best hope in an age where the instruments of war have far outpaced the instruments of peace, we renew our pledge of support – to prevent it from becoming merely a forum for invective – to strengthen its shield of the new and the weak – and to enlarge the area in which its writ may run.

Finally, to those nations who would make themselves our adversary, we offer not a pledge but a request: that both sides begin anew the quest for peace, before the dark powers of destruction unleashed by science engulf all humanity in planned or accidental self-destruction.

We dare not tempt them with weakness. For only when our arms are sufficient beyond doubt can we be certain beyond doubt that they will never be employed.

But neither can two great and powerful groups of nations take comfort from our present course – both sides overburdened by the cost of modern weapons, both rightly alarmed by the steady spread of the deadly atom, yet both racing to alter that uncertain balance of terror that stays the hand of mankind's final war.

So let us begin anew – remembering on both sides that civility is not a sign of weakness, and sincerity is always subject to proof. Let us never negotiate out of fear. But let us never fear to negotiate.

Let both sides explore what problems unite us instead of belabouring those problems which divide us.

Let both sides, for the first time, formulate serious and precise proposals for the inspection and control of arms – and bring the absolute power to destroy other nations under the absolute control of all nations.

Let both sides seek to invoke the wonders of science instead of its terrors. Together let us explore the stars, conquer the deserts, eradicate disease, tap the ocean depths, and encourage the arts and commerce.

Let both sides unite to heed in all corners of the earth the command of Isaiah – to 'undo the heavy burdens ... and to let the oppressed go free'.

And if a beachhead of cooperation may push back the jungle of suspicion, let both sides join in creating a new endeavour, not a new balance of power, but a new world of law, where the strong are just and the weak secure and the peace preserved.

All this will not be finished in the first 100 days. Nor will it be finished in the first 1,000 days, nor in the life of this Administration, nor even perhaps in our lifetime on this planet. But let us begin.

In your hands, my fellow citizens, more than in mine, will rest the final success or failure of our course. Since this country was founded, each generation of Americans has been summoned to give testimony to its national loyalty. The graves of young Americans who answered the call to service surround the globe.

Now the trumpet summons us again – not as a call to bear arms, though arms we need; not as a call to battle, though embattled we are – but a call to bear the burden of a long twilight struggle, year in and year out, 'rejoicing in hope, patient in tribulation' – a struggle against the common enemies of man: tyranny, poverty, disease, and war itself.

Can we forge against these enemies a grand and global alliance, North and South, East and West, that can assure a more fruitful life for all mankind? Will you join in that historic effort?

In the long history of the world, only a few generations have been granted the role of defending freedom in its hour of maximum danger. I do not shrink from this responsibility – I welcome it. I do not believe that any of us would exchange places with any other people or any other generation. The energy, the faith, the devotion which we bring to this endeavour will light our country and all who serve it – and the glow from that fire can truly light the world.

And so, my fellow Americans, ask not what your country can do for you – ask what you can do for your country.

My fellow citizens of the world, ask not what America will do for you, but what together we can do for the freedom of man.

Finally, whether you are citizens of America or citizens of the world, ask of us the same high standards of strength and sacrifice which we ask of you. With a good conscience our only sure reward, with history the final judge of our deeds, let us go forth to lead the land we love, asking His blessing and His help, but knowing that here on earth God's work must truly be our own.

•

## GIDEON HAUSNER
### Jerusalem, 17–18 April 1961

*'That man was Eichmann'*

*As a young Nazi SS officer, Adolf Eichmann (1906–62) was appointed head of the Central Office for Jewish Emigration in Vienna in 1938 and from 1942 assumed responsibility for the extinction of unwanted Jewish internees.*

*He supervised the deportation of slave labourers from among them. After the war he fled to South America. He was kidnapped in Argentina by Israeli agents in 1960 and charged with crimes against the Jewish people at his trial in Jerusalem in 1961.*

*As Attorney-General of the State of Israel, Gideon Hausner, at the age of forty-six, led the prosecution of Eichmann – the spokesman for six million Jews. He spoke for ten hours.*

*The following extracts are from his speeches at the opening and conclusion of the trial.*

When I stand before you, O Judges of Israel, to lead the prosecution of Adolf Eichmann, I do not stand alone. With me here are six million accusers. But they cannot rise to their feet and point their finger at the man in the dock with the cry 'J'accuse' on their lips. For they are now only ashes – ashes piled high on the hills of Auschwitz and the fields of Treblinka and strewn in the forests of Poland. Their graves are scattered throughout Europe. Their blood cries out, but their voice is stilled. Therefore will I be their spokesman. In their name will I unfold this terrible indictment . . .

. . . never, down the long, bloodstained road travelled by this people, never since the first days of its nationhood, has any man arisen who succeeded in dealing so grievous a blow as did Hitler and his regime, and Adolf Eichmann, as its executive arm for the destruction of Jewry. Human history knows no other example of a man against whom could be drawn up such a bill of indictment. The deeds of those classic figures of barbarism, Nero, Attila, Genghis Khan, pale into insignificance when set against the abominations, the murderous horrors, which will be presented to you in this trial . . . only in our generation has an organized state set upon an entire defenceless and peaceful population, men, women, and children, greybeards and babies, incarcerated them behind electrified fences, imprisoned them in concentration camps, and resolved to destroy them utterly . . .

In this trial, we shall encounter a new kind of killer, the kind that exercises his bloody craft behind a desk, and only occasionally does the deed with his own hands . . . But it was his word that put gas chambers into action; he lifted the telephone, and railway trains left for the extermination centres; his signature it was that sealed the doom of tens of thousands. He had but to give the order, and troopers took off to rout Jews out of their homes, to beat and torture them and drive them into ghettos, to steal their property and, after brutality and pillage, after all had been wrung from them, when even their hair had been taken, to transport them en masse to their slaughter. Even their dead bodies were not immune. Gold teeth were extracted and wedding rings torn from fingers . . .

Eichmann was the one who *planned, initiated and organized,* who instructed others to spill this ocean of blood, and to use all the means of murder, theft and torture. He is responsible, therefore, as though he with his own hands had knotted the hangman's noose, lashed the victims into the gas chambers, shot and thrust into the open pits every single one of the millions who were murdered. Such is his responsibility in the eyes of the law. And such is his responsibility by every standard of conscience and morality. His accomplices in the crime were . . . the leaders of a nation – including professors and scholars, robed dignitaries with academic degrees, educated persons, the 'intelligentsia'. We shall encounter them – the doctors and lawyers, scholars, bankers and economists – in those councils which resolved to exterminate the Jews, and among them officers and directors of the work of murder in all its terrible phases . . .

. . . words exist to express what man's reason can conceive and his heart contain, and here we are dealing with actions which transcend our human grasp. Yet this is what did happen: millions were condemned to death, not for any crime, not for anything they had done, but only because they belonged to the Jewish people. The development of technology placed at the disposal of the destroyers efficient equipment for the execution of their appalling designs . . .

. . . there was only one man who had been concerned almost entirely with the Jews, whose business had been their destruction, whose role in the establishment of the iniquitous regime had been limited to them. That man was Adolf Eichmann. If we charge him also with crimes against people who were not Jews, committed, as it were, 'by the way', this is because we make no ethnic distinctions. But we should remember that the mission of the accused, in which for years he saw his destiny and calling, and to which he devoted himself with enthusiasm and endless zeal, was the destruction of the Jews . . .

Eichmann will tell you that he carried out the orders of his superiors. But the conscience of the world, speaking with the voice of the International Military Tribunal, has declared that orders contrary to the principles of conscience and morality, orders that violate the essential imperatives on which human society is based and negate the basic rules without which men cannot live together – such orders constitute no defence, legal or moral. Therefore, in the light of the ruling, our own law in Israel has denied the accused the legal right to submit such a defence. But that is by no means all. We shall prove to the court that he went far beyond his actual orders, that he took the initiative in extermination operations for which he had been given no orders whatsoever, and carried them out only because of his devotion to the task in which he saw his life's mission . . .

. . . the first and principal means of repression used by the SS was the concentration camp, in which were developed and perfected systems of terror employing all the resources available to modern technology. The Nazi, the romantic mystic, the family man, who on the surface seemed to be a loving husband to his wife and a merciful father to his children, the lover of nature, was revealed in the concentration camps as a monster of insane brutality, who did not hesitate to trample on human beings, without blinking an eye, as if they were insects. One of the shocking chapters in *Commandant of Auschwitz* the story of Rudolf Hoess, is the part where Hoess describes his own peaceful family life at home: the education he gave his sons, his affectionate regard for his wife – and all this going on just on the other side of the high-tension barbed-wire fence of the terrible extermination camp in which between five and ten thousand people were being put to death *each day* – and sometimes even more.

The Gestapo knew well how to exploit all the human frailties of their victims. They knew that starvation and torture, given time, can break even strong men; that by brutality and humiliation it is possible to efface the divine image, leaving a man insensitive, inert, an obedient robot doing as he is told, even when he is ordered to dig his own grave . . . Every means of humiliation was deliberately employed to destroy the Jew's faith in himself. When a man is whipped across the face and he is unable to react; when he is deprived of food until he aches with hunger; when men and women, boys and girls, are given orders to perform their excretory functions in full sight of one another, like beasts; when women are made to run naked before the guards; when, morning and night, executions by shooting and hanging prove that the lives of Jews are absolutely worthless; when senseless butchery takes place before your eyes for the sport of capricious guards; when twenty times a day you are made aware that you are abandoned and defenceless, your life dependent on the mood of any one of the SS men on that particular day – under such circumstances it was not difficult to create a condition in which most of these unfortunates were stripped of all faith and feeling, bereft for the most part of any will to go on living, their supreme desire being a speedy and painless death . . .

The Nazis . . . were skilled in lies and chicanery. They knew how to use every expedient to deceive their victims. After every manhunt, in which thousands and tens of thousands of Jews would be sent to their deaths and others would manage to hide or escape, a rumour would be deliberately spread by the Nazis that this was the last operation of its kind, and that the survivors would no longer be touched, that there would be no more transports. Many individuals of the type that cling to hope, those who could not or would not believe that the fate of all the Jews had indeed been sealed, or who were exhausted by hunger, misery and suffering, would venture out of their hiding places or return from the forests, only to be captured by their persecutors in a new manhunt. The tiger played with his victims at his own sweet will. We shall find some Jews among those carrying out Nazi orders, in the Jewish police in the ghettos and in the Councils of Elders. Even at the entrance to the gas chambers there were often Jews whose task it was to calm the victims and persuade them that they were merely going to showers. This was one of the most satanic aspects of the entire programme: to deaden men's senses, to deprive them of all emotional and intellectual vigour, to leave no more than a terrified and lifeless robot, so that it was possible to use the prisoners in the camps themselves as part of the murder machine against their own people . . .

You will hear evidence of deeds which the mind of man does not want to believe. You will hear about little ones thrown out of windows of hospitals when they failed to respond to orders that they report for parade.

We shall present to you the instructions issued by Eichmann and his office about the transport of children. One of these said that the children were to be divided among the transports intended for Auschwitz. Children of fourteen were considered 'independent' for purposes of transport to the extermination camps. Nor can we say who suffered the more terrible fate: those who died, or those who concealed themselves in every conceivable hiding-place and crevice, who lived in perpetual terror of expulsion, who survived through the kindness of Christian neighbours who agreed to hide them. Children would come home from the schools and centres organized by the community to find their parents' home was empty, for they had been sent by some 'aktion' or 'operation' to their deaths; and the apartment had in the meantime been occupied by others.

You will hear evidence of tender infants pressed by their mothers to their bodies in the gas chambers so that they should not inhale the poisonous gas, until the executioners came and threw them alive into the furnaces or the waiting graves.

Those unhappy children who lived for years in fear of the beating of a rifle butt on their door; who had been sent by their parents to the woods in an attempt to save them, who had been taught to choke their tears and sighs because a weeping child would be shot on the spot; who had been ordered to deny their origins and pretend to be Christians; who saw their fathers being lashed with whips before their eyes; in front of whom 'discussions' would be carried on by the German executioners as to who should be killed first – the father or the son; who went to the open grave with 'Hear, O Israel!' on their lips – these children and youths . . . are the very soul and hard core of the indictment. Those Anne Franks and Justine Drangers and a million others.

We shall present the pictures of some of those children swollen with hunger, frightened and crushed, with eyes frozen with terror. We shall show you the photographs of their starved bodies thrown into manure wagons, of the helpless little ones on the threshold of the extermination chambers.

At Auschwitz the killings were carried out by every method, shooting, hanging, and beating, but mainly in the massive gas chambers. In each such chamber 2,000 people were herded together for a 'shower' – a flow of poison gas. The death factory operated unceasingly. The extermination of 2,000 people lasted 25 minutes, after which the bodies were taken to one of the five giant furnaces. Medical experiments were made on human beings as if they were guinea pigs. Parts of female sex organs were cut out, or limbs were subjected to X-rays until the unfortunate creatures writhed in pain prior to their

death. Men were castrated. Experiments were made on the influence
of paraffin and petrol injections on human skin and the effects of
chemical substances on mental resistance. The methods of punishment would not have shamed the most cruel barbarians in history.
Beating on the naked body was a comparatively light punishment.
Water was poured into people's ears, fingernails were extracted, prisoners starved until they went out of their minds. In the bunker of
those sentenced for punishment by starvation a dead prisoner was
found, bent over whom was a second prisoner, also dead, grasping
the liver from the corpse of the first. He had died while tearing at the
liver of a fellow human being. The Nazi contribution to European
culture was the reintroduction of cannibalism . . .

We shall prove that the accused performed all these deeds with the
set purpose of destroying the Jewish people, wholly or in part. Adolf
Eichmann will enjoy a privilege which he did not accord to a single
one of his victims. He will be able to defend himself before the court.
His fate will be decided according to law and according to the evidence, with the burden of proof resting upon the prosecution. And
the judges of Israel will pronounce true and righteous judgement.

It is no wonder that the German Foreign Ministry passed on for
Eichmann's information the warning, broadcast by London Radio,
that those responsible for the murders in Auschwitz would be
brought to judgement. Even on the verge of the German collapse in
April 1945, in that atmosphere of the twilight of the gods, when the
Allies from the East, West and South were closing in – Eichmann
still told a German Red Cross representative that he could not agree
to the more humanitarian methods of dealing with Jews then being
considered by Himmler.

Many millions of non-Jews also perished in the Great War. We
shall not attempt to decide here, at this trial, which of the acts of
hostility were contrary to the laws and customs of war as laid down
by international law. But we shall say, with all the emphasis at our
command, that the extermination of the Jewish people was not connected with any military action. It cannot be compared with the
bombing of cities or with submarine warfare. These were acts of
war, and whether they were legitimate or not they were carried out in

connection with and in the process of waging war. The extermination of the Jews had no connection with the war effort of Germany and her allies. The extermination was carried out *at the time* of the war, when the battle-smoke to some extent covered and concealed the atrocities; but it was not done in pursuit of war, nor was it impelled by the needs or necessities of war.

*Eichmann was hanged on 31 May 1962.*

•

# HUGH GAITSKELL
## Scarborough, 5 October 1961

### 'We will fight, fight and fight again'

*As leader of the Labour Party since 1955, Hugh Gaitskell (1906–63) had led opposition to the Suez invasion of 1956 but clashed with his left wing over nationalization and unilateral nuclear disarmament.*

*At the 1961 party conference, he faced a challenge to his leadership from Harold Wilson (which he defeated) as well as a resolution seeking to commit Labour to unilateral disarmament.*

*His speech was therefore the most important of his political life. He had not slept the previous night and wrote the peroration at 4 a.m. Gaitskell thought he would lose and be forced to resign the leadership. As he rose to speak he looked overtired and white with tension and he was continually interrupted by boos and howls of protest, particularly when he referred to 'fellow travellers'.*

I would not wish for one day to remain a Leader who had lost the confidence of his colleagues in Parliament. It is perfectly reasonable to try to get rid of somebody, to try to get rid of a man you do not agree with, who you think perhaps is not a good Leader. But there are ways of doing this. What would be wrong, in my opinion, and would not be forgiven, is if, in order to get rid of a man, you supported a policy in which you did not wholeheartedly believe, a policy which, as far as the resolution is concerned, is not clear.

Before you take the vote on this momentous occasion, allow me a last word. Frank Cousins [leader of the unilateralist Transport and General Workers' Union] has said this is not the end of the problem. I agree with him. It is not the end of the problem because Labour Members of Parliament will have to consider what they do in the House of Commons. What do you expect of them? You know how they voted in June overwhelmingly for the policy statement. It is not in dispute that the vast majority of Labour Members of Parliament are utterly opposed to unilateralism and neutralism. So what do you expect them to do? Change their minds overnight? To go back on the pledges they gave to the people who elected them from their constituencies? And supposing they did do that. Supposing all of us, like well-behaved sheep, were to follow the policies of unilateralism and neutralism, what kind of an impression would that make upon the British people? You do not seem to be clear in your minds about it, but I will tell you this. I do not believe that the Labour Members of Parliament are prepared to act as time servers. I do not believe they will do this, and I will tell you why: because they are men of conscience and honour. People of the so-called Right and so-called Centre have every justification for having a conscience, as well as people of the so-called Left. I do not think they will do this because they are honest men, loyal men, steadfast men, experienced men, with a lifetime of service to the Labour Movement.

There are other people too, not in Parliament, in the Party who share our convictions. What sort of people do you think they are? What sort of people do you think we are? Do you think we can simply accept a decision of this kind? Do you think that we can become overnight the pacifists, unilateralists and fellow travellers that other people are? How wrong can you be? As wrong as you are about the attitude of the British people.

In a few minutes the Conference will make its decision. Most of the votes, I know, are predetermined and we have been told what is likely to happen. We know how it comes about. I sometimes think, frankly, that the system we have, by which great unions decide their policy before even their conferences can consider the Executive recommendation, is not really a very wise one or a good one. Perhaps in a calmer moment this situation could be looked at.

I say this to you: we may lose the vote today and the result may deal this Party a grave blow. It may not be possible to prevent it, but I think there are many of us who will not accept that this blow need be mortal, who will not believe that such an end is inevitable. There are some of us, Mr Chairman, who will fight and fight and fight again to save the Party we love. We will fight and fight and fight again to bring back sanity and honesty and dignity, so that our Party with its great past may retain its glory and its greatness.

It is in that spirit that I ask delegates who are still free to decide how they vote, to support what I believe to be a realistic policy on defence, which yet could so easily have united the great Party of ours, and to reject what I regard as the suicidal path of unilateral disarmament which will leave our country defenceless and alone.

*Gaitskell was greeted by the biggest ovation of his life and one journalist wrote that this was his finest hour. Although the Left won the vote, the margin was only 300,000 instead of the expected million or more. Gaitskell's political courage and integrity and his appeal to those 'still free to decide' switched votes and turned a triumph into a hollow victory.*

•

## IAIN MACLEOD
### Brighton, 11 October 1961

*'The brotherhood of man'*

*As British Colonial Secretary from 1959 to 1961, Iain Macleod (1913–70) pursued a historic policy of granting independence to the British colonies in Africa more quickly than many Conservatives wished and defying some of the most powerful sectors of the Tory Party. Although he was woundingly described as 'too clever by half' (by the Marquess of Salisbury), he achieved his purpose in ensuring that Britain's withdrawal from most parts of Africa was accomplished with more speed and goodwill than it otherwise would have been.*

*Speaking to the Conservative conference on the day before Harold Macmillan made him chairman of the party and leader of the House of Commons, Macleod defined the British imperial mission and the moral principles on which it was based. Its most memorable phrase was based on Robert Burns:*

> *That man to man the whole world o'er*
> *Shall brothers be for a' that.*

*Many contemporaries considered Macleod, with his rasping voice, with scorn or passion controlled, the best parliamentary debater of his generation – and this speech to an audience in which many disagreed violently with his policy was one of his finest.*

At the end of the last war, something like 630 million people lived in the dependent territories of the Crown. Now, that figure is about 40 million. Indeed, when this week started, the figure was 30 million. Think, then, of that change from 630 million and reflect that at the same time, over the same period, Russian imperialism has shackled 100 million men and women who once were free. And when you compare those two records, I hope you will share my indignation that in international forums, in the United Nations itself, most of all in the countries where tyranny itself reigns, our British colonial record should be attacked . . .

It has fallen to me to be Colonial Secretary during two of the most tremendous years of advance that the world has ever seen. You must be in no doubt that you are watching one of the great dramas of history, as so many countries thrust forwards through nationalism towards their independence . . .

The tightrope of timing which the Colonial Secretary has to walk in every territory every week, sometimes almost every day, is the most difficult of all his tasks – how you try to reconcile the emerging nationalism of these countries with the need for the surest possible protection for the minority. As you walk this tightrope, you must realize that if you fall from it it will bring disaster and perhaps bloodshed to so many people to whom you stand in a position of trustee.

How, then, do you go forward? On what moral principles should you base your policy, for be very sure that in this field, as in every other field, if your policies are not based on principle they will fail? I can only give you my own personal belief. First, I believe in the rights and duties of men, and that means of all men. But do not ever fall into the error of assuming that, because you give a man better housing, because you give a man better education, because you improve the health services, somehow that will satisfy his craving for basic political rights. It cannot do. Indeed, it is bound to sharpen it.

Remember also that however great your services may have been to a country, however noble the contribution we have made in the five continents of the world to the developing countries has been – and it has been noble – that will never always be accepted as a reason why automatically you should govern. We would never have accepted – we did not accept – this from the Romans. The Irish never accepted it from us. Be quite sure that the inheritors of the British Empire equally would not accept it from our people. But yet there is a way. Let me remind you of something that I said at last year's Conference when I quoted the Prime Minister of Nigeria. He was referring to the British Colonial record in Nigeria. He said that we had been, first, masters, then leaders, and finally partners, but always friends. This is the answer – in partnership and in friendship. This can be done.

Secondly, I believe in what our grandfathers would have called the British Imperial mission. It is not yet completed. Since the world began, empires have grown and flourished and decayed, some into a sort of genteel obscurity, some leaving little heritage and culture behind them, some even no more than stones covered by the sand. They are one with Nineveh and Tyre, but we are the only empire leaving behind us a coherent political scheme of development. We are the only people who, with all the hesitations and failures that there have been, are genuinely resolved on turning, to use Harold Macmillan's phrase, an empire into a commonwealth and a commonwealth into a family. This is what we are doing.

. . . The third principle is that I believe quite simply in the brotherhood of man – men of all races, of all colours, of all creeds. I think it is this that must be in the centre of our thinking.

And now what lies ahead in this event? It is perhaps strange to an English and to a Welsh audience to quote the greatest of our Scottish native poets, but nobody has put this in simpler or finer words than Burns:

> It is coming yet for a' that,
> That man to man the whole world o'er,
> Shall brothers be for a' that.

And this is coming. There are foolish men who will deny it, but they will be swept away; but if we are wise then indeed the task of bringing these countries towards their destiny of free and equal partners and friends with us in the Commonwealth of Nations can be a task as exciting, as inspiring and as noble as the creation of empire itself.

*Macleod became Chancellor of the Exchequer when Edward Heath was elected prime minister in 1970 but died within a month of taking office.*

•

# DOUGLAS MacARTHUR
## West Point, New York, 12 May 1962

### *'Duty – Honour – Country'*

*As Supreme Allied Commander in the south-west Pacific during the Second World War, General Douglas MacArthur (1880–1964) halted the advance of the Japanese and then, as commander of the occupation forces in Japan from 1945 to 1957, was virtually a pro-consul, organizing the rehabilitation of the defeated nation.*

*After becoming commander-in-chief of US forces in the Korean War, he was relieved of command by President Truman in 1951 after advocating carrying the war into China.*

*On his return to America he was given a hero's welcome and made a moving speech to Congress which he concluded by saying:*

*'When I joined the Army even before the turn of the century, it was the fulfilment of all my boyish hopes and dreams. The world has turned over many times since I took the oath on the Plain at West Point, and the hopes and dreams have*

*long since vanished. But I still remember the refrain of one of the most popular barrack ballads of that day which proclaimed most proudly that –*

*'Old soldiers never die, they just fade away.*

*'And like the old soldier of that ballad, I now close my military career and just fade away – an old soldier who tried to do his duty as God gave him the light to see that duty.*
   *'Goodbye.'*

*Three weeks later MacArthur was awarded the Sylvanus Thayer Medal, the highest honour of the United States Military Academy. He reviewed the Corps of Cadets on the Plain at West Point and then, speaking without preparation, responded to the presentation. This speech was the real soldier's farewell. After this speech, MacArthur really did fade away.*

Duty – Honour – Country. Those three hallowed words reverently dictate what you ought to be, what you can be, what you will be. They are your rallying points; to build courage when courage seems to fail; to regain faith when there seems to be little cause for faith; to create hope when hope becomes forlorn. Unhappily, I possess neither that eloquence of diction, that poetry of imagination, nor that brilliance of metaphor to tell you all that they mean. The unbelievers will say they are but words, but a slogan, but a flamboyant phrase. Every pedant, every demagogue, every cynic, every hypocrite, every troublemaker, and, I am sorry to say, some others of an entirely different character, will try to downgrade them even to the extent of mockery and ridicule.

But these are some of the things they do. They build your basic character; they mould you for your future roles as custodians of the nation's defence; they make you strong enough to know when you are weak, and brave enough to face yourself when you are afraid. They teach you to be proud and unbending in honest failure, but humble and gentle in success, not to substitute words for actions, not to seek the path of comfort, but to face the stress and spur of difficulty and challenge; to learn to stand up in the storm but to have compassion on those who fail; to master yourself before you seek to master others; to have a heart that is clean, a goal that is high; to learn to laugh yet never forget how to weep; to reach into the future yet never neglect the past; to be serious yet never to take yourself too seriously; to be modest so that you will remember the simplicity of true greatness, the open mind of true wisdom, the meekness of true strength. They give you a temper of the will, a quality of the imagination, a vigour of the emotions, a freshness of the deep springs of life, a temperamental predominance of courage over timidity, an appetite for adventure over love of ease. They create in your heart the sense of wonder, the unfailing hope of what next, and the joy and inspiration of life. They teach you in this way to be an officer and a gentleman.

And what sort of soldiers are those you are to lead? Are they reliable, are they brave, are they capable of victory? Their story is known to all of you; it is the story of the American man-at-arms. My estimate of him was formed on the battlefield many years ago, and has never changed. I regarded him then as I regard him now – as one of the world's noblest figures, not only as one of the finest military characters, but also as one of the most stainless. His name and fame are the birthright of every American citizen. In his youth and strength, his love and loyalty, he gave all that mortality can give. He needs no eulogy from me or from any other man. He has written his own history and written it in red on his enemy's breast. But when I think of his patience under adversity, of his courage under fire, and of his modesty in victory, I am filled with an emotion of admiration I cannot put into words. He belongs to history as furnishing one of the greatest examples of successful patriotism; he belongs to posterity as the instructor of future generations in the principles of liberty and freedom; he belongs to the present, to us, by his virtues and by his achievements. In twenty campaigns, on a hundred battlefields, around a thousand campfires, I have witnessed that enduring fortitude, that patriotic self-abnegation, and that invincible determination which have carved his status in the hearts of his people. From one end of the world to the other he has drained deep the chalice of courage.

As I listened to those songs of the glee club, in memory's eye I could see those staggering columns of the First World War, bending under soggy packs, on many a weary march from dripping dusk to drizzling dawn, slogging ankle deep through the mire of shell-shocked roads, to form grimly for the attack, blue-lipped, covered with sludge and mud, chilled by the wind and rain, driving home to their objective, and, for many, to the judgement seat of God. I do not know the dignity of their birth but I do know the glory of their death. They died unquestioning, uncomplaining, with faith in their hearts, and on their lips the hope that we would go on to victory. Always for them – Duty – Honour – Country; always their blood and sweat and tears as we sought the way and the light and the truth.

And twenty years after, on the other side of the globe, again the filth of murky foxholes, the stench of ghostly trenches, the slime of dripping dugouts; those broiling suns of relentless heat, those torrential rains of devastating storm, the loneliness and utter desolation of jungle trails, the bitterness of long separation from those they loved and cherished, the deadly pestilence of tropical disease, the horror of stricken areas of war; their resolute and determined defence, their swift and sure attack, their indomitable purpose, their complete and decisive victory – always victory – always through the bloody haze of their last reverberating shot, the vision of gaunt, ghastly men reverently following your password of Duty – Honour – Country.

The code which those words perpetrate embraces the highest moral laws and will stand the test of any ethics or philosophies ever promulgated for the uplift of mankind. Its requirements are for the things that are right, and its restraints are from the things that are wrong. The soldier, above all other men, is required to practise the greatest act of religious training – sacrifice. In battle and in the face of danger and death, he discloses those divine attributes which his Maker gave when He created man in His own image. No physical courage and no brute instinct can take the place of the Divine help which alone can sustain him. However horrible the incidents of war may be, the soldier who is called upon to offer and to give his life for his country is the noblest development of mankind.

You now face a new world – a world of change. The thrust into outer space of the satellites, spheres and missiles marked the beginning of another epoch in the long story of mankind – the chapter of the space age. In the five or more billions of years the scientists tell us it has taken to form the earth, in the three or more billion years of development of the human race, there has never been a greater, a more abrupt or staggering evolution. We deal now not with things of this world alone, but with the illimitable distances and as yet unfathomed mysteries of the universe. We are reaching out for a new and boundless frontier. We speak in strange terms: of harnessing the cosmic energy; of making winds and tides work for us; of creating unheard-of synthetic materials to supplement or even replace our old standard basics; of purifying sea water for our drink; of mining ocean floors for new fields of wealth and food; of disease preventatives to expand life into the hundreds of years; of controlling the weather for a more equitable distribution of heat and cold, of rain and shine; of space ships to the moon; of the primary target in war, no longer limited to the armed forces of an enemy, but instead to include his civil populations; of ultimate conflict between a united human race and the sinister forces of some other planetary galaxy; of such dreams and fantasies as to make life the most exciting of all time.

And through all this welter of change and development, your mission remains fixed, determined, inviolable – it is to win our wars. Everything else in your professional career is but a corollary to this vital dedication. All other public purposes, all other public projects, all other public needs, great or small, will find others for their accomplishment; but you are the ones who are trained to fight; yours is the profession of arms – the will to win, the sure knowledge that in war there is no substitute for victory; that if you lose, the nation will be destroyed; that the very obsession of your public service must be Duty – Honour – Country. Others will debate the controversial issues, national and international, which divide men's minds; but serene, calm, aloof, you stand as the nation's war guardian, as its lifeguard from the raging tides of international conflict; as its gladiator in the arena of battle. For a century and a half, you have defended, guarded, and protected its hallowed traditions of liberty and freedom, of right and justice. Let civilian voices argue the merits or demerits of our processes of government; whether our strength is being sapped by deficit financing, indulged in too long; by federal paternalism grown too mighty; by power groups grown too arrogant; by politics grown too corrupt; by crime grown too rampant; by morals grown too low; by taxes grown too high; by extremists grown too violent; whether our personal liberties are as thorough and complete as they should be. These great national problems are not for your professional participation or military solution. Your guidepost stands out like a tenfold beacon in the night – Duty – Honour – Country.

You are the leaven which binds together the entire fabric of our national system of defence. From your ranks come the great captains who hold the nation's destiny in their hands the moment the war tocsin sounds. The Long Grey Line has never failed us. Were you to do so, a million ghosts in olive drab, in brown khaki, in blue and grey, would rise from their white crosses thundering those magic words – Duty – Honour – Country.

This does not mean that you are war mongers. On the contrary, the soldier, above all other people, prays for peace, for he must suffer and bear the deepest wounds and scars of war. But always in our ears ring the ominous words of Plato, that wisest of all philosophers, 'Only the dead have seen the end of war.'

The shadows are lengthening for me. The twilight is here. My days of old have vanished tone and tint; they have gone glimmering through the dreams of things that were. Their memory is one of wondrous beauty, watered by tears, and coaxed and caressed by the smiles of yesterday. I listen vainly, but with thirsty ear, for the witching melody of faint bugles blowing reveille, of far drums beating the long roll. In my dreams I hear again the crash of guns, the rattle of musketry, the strange mournful mutter of the battlefield. But in the evening of my memory, always I come back to West Point. Always there echoes and re-echoes in my ears – Duty – Honour – Country.

## HUGH GAITSKELL
### Brighton, 3 October 1962

*'The end of a thousand years of history'*

*Hugh Gaitskell was a fighter, a politician with a stubborn faith in the power of reasoned argument. A year earlier he had defeated a challenge to his leadership and won acceptance for his opposition to unilateral disarmament. Now he was determining the policy of the Labour Party on joining the European Common Market, the issue that has dominated and divided British politics ever since. To the anguish of his right-wing supporters, most of whom backed entry into Europe, Gaitskell swung the party into a position of hostility towards the Common Market.*

*No other living British politician could have so dominated a mass conference by the sheer force of intellect and personality, said Anthony Crosland, one of Gaitskell's friends. Yet Dora, Gaitskell's wife, observed during the standing ovation: 'All the wrong people are cheering.'*

I understand and deeply sympathize with the people of France and of Germany in their desire to get rid of the conflicts which have so often broken out between them and which indeed are all too fresh in our minds. But I sometimes wonder whether the great problems of the world today are to be found in the unity or disunity of Western Europe. I would have said there were two problems outstanding above all others: the problem of peace and the problems of poverty; the problem of East–West relations that plagues us and the problem of the division of the world into the 'haves' and the 'have nots'.

I know some will say with great sincerity: 'But we recognize that and we believe that by Britain going into Europe a great contribution can be made to these problems.' Maybe so, but it is for them to submit the proof. So far it is hard to be convinced. For although, of course, Europe has had a great and glorious civilization, although Europe can claim Goethe and Leonardo, Voltaire and Picasso, there have been evil features in European history too – Hitler and Mussolini and today the attitude of some Europeans to the Congo problem, the attitude of at least one European government to the United Nations. You cannot say what this Europe will be: it has its two faces and we do not know as yet which is the one which will dominate.

But here is another question we have to ask; what exactly is involved in the concept of political union? We hear a lot about it; we are told that the Economic Community is not just a customs union, that all who framed it saw it as a stepping stone towards political integration. We ought to be told what is meant by that, for if this be true our entry into the Common Market carries with it some very serious political obligations. But when you ask it is not easy to get a clear answer . . .

I can see only three possibilities outside the obligations that we accept specifically in the Treaty of Rome. It may mean that there is no obligation upon the Government of Britain to do more than talk, consult more frequently with the President of France and the Chancellor of Germany. I see no harm in these talks, but I am not terribly optimistic about what they will produce . . .

But what else? If it is not just talking, what is it? The second possibility is majority decisions on political issues, just as we are to have majority decisions on economic issues. Do we want that? Well, I suppose you might say we would be able somehow or other to outvote those we disagree with. I would like to be very sure of that before I committed myself.

Then, of course, there is the idea and the ideal of Federal Europe. Now I know it will be said by some, 'Why bring up federation? It is not immediate, it is not imposed upon us, it may not happen.' But we would be foolish to deny, not to recognize and indeed sympathize with the desire of those who created the Economic Community for political federation. That is what they mean, that is what they are after when they admit freely that under the present constitution of EEC the Assembly has no powers except the very far-reaching, overriding one, which they are most unlikely to use, of dismissing the Commission by a two-thirds majority. When it is pointed out that the Commission is a body which has powers but is not responsible or under anybody's control, what is the answer? The answer they give us: 'That is why we should set up a Federal Assembly with powers over them.' This is what they are arguing.

What does federation mean? It means that powers are taken from national governments and handed over to federal governments and to federal parliaments. It means – I repeat it – that if we go into this we are no more than a state (as it were) in the United States of Europe, such as Texas and California. They are remarkably friendly examples, you do not find every state as rich or having such good weather as those two! But I could take others: it would be the same as in Australia, where you have Western Australia, for example, and New South Wales. We should be like them. This is what it means; it does mean the end of Britain as an independent nation state. It may be a good thing or a bad thing but we must recognize that this is so . . .

We must be clear about this: it does mean, if this is the idea, the end of Britain as an independent European state. I make no apology for repeating it. It means the end of a thousand years of history. You may say, 'Let it end,' but, my goodness, it is a decision that needs a little care and thought. And it does mean the end of the Commonwealth. How can one really seriously suppose that if the mother country, the centre of the Commonwealth, is a province of Europe (which is what federation means) it could continue to exist as the mother country of a series of independent nations? It is sheer nonsense.

*Although nobody knew it at the time, Gaitskell was making his last speech to a Labour Party conference. He died unexpectedly early the following year and his epitaph from his political allies was that he was the greatest prime minister who never was.*

•

## JOHN F. KENNEDY
### Berlin, 11 June 1963

### *'Ich bin ein Berliner'*

*When President Kennedy went to West Berlin for an eight-hour visit in 1963, his motorcade was cheered every foot of the way. He got his first sight of the Berlin Wall as he approached the Brandenburg Gate. He had been scheduled to gaze over the wall through the gate on to the Unter den Linden, once the main avenue of the German capital, but the five arches of the gate were covered by red banners blocking his view of East Berlin.*

*Kennedy's speech that day, from the city where the Iron Curtain showed the great divide between Communist East and capitalist West at its most cruel in the symbolism of the Berlin Wall, struck a chord that reverberated around the world.*

Two thousand years ago the proudest boast was 'civis Romanus sum'. Today in the world of freedom the proudest boast is 'Ich bin ein Berliner.'

There are many people in the world who really don't understand – or say they don't – what is the great issue between the free world and the Communist world. Let them come to Berlin.

There are some who say that Communism is the wave of the future, Let them come to Berlin.

And there are some who say in Europe and elsewhere 'We can work with the Communists.' Let them come to Berlin.

And there are even a few who say that it's true that Communism is an evil system but it permits us to make economic progress. Let them come to Berlin.

Freedom has many difficulties and democracy is not perfect. But we have never had to put a wall up to keep our people in, to prevent them from leaving us.

I want to say on behalf of my countrymen who live many miles away on the other side of the Atlantic, who are far distant from you, that they take the greatest pride that they have been able to share with you, even from a distance, the story of the last eighteen years.

I know of no town, no city that has been besieged for eighteen years that still lives with the vitality and the force and the hope and the determination of the city of West Berlin.

While the wall is the most obvious and vivid demonstration of the failures of the Communist system, all the world can see we take no satisfaction in it, for it is, as your Mayor has said, an offence not only against history, but an offence against humanity, separating families, dividing husbands and wives and brothers and sisters and dividing a people who wish to be joined together.

What is true of this city is true of Germany. Real lasting peace in Europe can never be assured as long as one German out of four is denied the elementary right of free men, and that is to make a free choice.

In eighteen years of peace and good faith this generation of Germans has earned the right to be free, including the right to unite their families and their nation in lasting peace with goodwill to all people.

You live in a defended island of freedom, but your life is part of the main. So let me ask you as I close, to lift your eyes beyond the dangers of today to the hopes of tomorrow, beyond the freedom merely of this city of Berlin and all your country of Germany to the advance of freedom everywhere, beyond the wall to the day of peace with justice, beyond yourselves and ourselves to all mankind.

Freedom is indivisible and when one man is enslaved who are free? When all are free, then we can look forward to that day when this city will be joined as one and this country and this great continent of Europe in a peaceful and hopeful globe.

When that day finally comes, as it will, the people of West Berlin can take sober satisfaction in the fact that they were in the front lines for almost two decades.

All free men, wherever they may live, are citizens of Berlin. And therefore, as a free man, I take pride in the words 'Ich bin ein Berliner.'

•

# NIGEL BIRCH
London, 17 June 1963

### 'Never glad confident morning again'

*The Profumo scandal of 1963 arose after John Profumo, Secretary of State for War, was forced to resign after admitting to an affair with Christine Keeler, a call-girl who was simultaneously involved with a Russian naval attaché, about which he had lied to the House of Commons.*

*In a statement to the Commons, Harold Macmillan, the prime minister, emphasized that Profumo was dismissed from the government for lying – but the general effect of his speech and his conduct throughout the scandal was to show Macmillan as naïve and out of touch.*

*Nigel Birch, who had resigned from Macmillan's government in 1958 in protest at increases in government spending, was one of the most accomplished speakers in the Commons. He was pithy, with a coruscating wit, and his interventions often turned a parliamentary debate into an occasion.*

*The most notable was when he attacked Macmillan in the Profumo debate and ended his speech with a quotation from Robert Browning, as deadly a use of quotation as Leo Amery's dismissal of Neville Chamberlain.*

We know a deal more now about Profumo than we did at the time of the statement, but we have all known him pretty well for a number of years in this House. I must say that he never struck me as a man at all like a cloistered monk; and Miss Keeler was a professional prostitute . . . Here one had an active, busy man and a professional prostitute. On his own admission, Profumo had a number of meetings with her, and, if we are to judge by the published statements, she is not a woman who would be intellectually stimulating. Is it really credible that the association had no sexual content? There seems to me to be a certain basic improbability about the proposition that their relationship was purely platonic. What are whores about? Yet Profumo's word was accepted. It was accepted from a colleague. Would that word have been accepted if Profumo had not been a colleague or even if he had been a political opponent? Everyone must, I think, make his own judgement about that.

We were told that special consideration ought to have been given to Profumo because he was a colleague. It is certainly true that a Prime Minister owes to his subordinates all the help, comfort and protection that he can give them. But surely that help, that comfort and that protection must stop short of condoning a lie in a personal statement to this House.

Then we are told that special weight ought to have been given to Profumo's words because he was a Privy Councillor and a Secretary of State. I am a Privy Councillor and I have been a Secretary of State, but when I sustained the burden of both offices I did not feel that any sea change had taken place in my personality. I remained what I was, what I had always been and what I am today; and I do not believe it reasonable to suppose that any sea change took place in Mr Profumo's personality.

He was not a man who was ever likely to tell the absolute truth in a tight corner, and at the time the statement was made he was in a very tight corner indeed. There are people – and it is to the credit of our poor, suffering humanity that it is so – who will tell the whole truth about themselves whatever the consequences may be. Of such are saints and martyrs, but most of us are not like that. Most people in a tight corner either prevaricate – or, as in this case, they lie.

This lie was accepted. I have meditated very deeply on this, and though I have given some rather tough reasons for not accepting that Profumo's statement was credible, I have after deep consideration come to the conclusion that my Right Hon. Friend did absolutely genuinely believe it. I will give my reasons now for taking that view, and these reasons concern the competence and the good sense with which the affair was handled.

Profumo on his own admission had been guilty of a very considerable indiscretion, for a Minister at any rate. He was not a particularly successful Minister. He had no great place in this House or in the country. I cannot really see that the Prime Minister was under any obligation whatever to retain his services, nor do I think that getting rid of Mr Profumo would, in fact, have made the political situation any worse than it then was. On the other hand, to retain him entailed a colossal risk and a colossal gamble. The difficulties and dangers were obvious enough. The Press were in full cry. They were in possession of letters. They were hardly likely to have bought letters unless they had something of interest in them. Miss Keeler was pretty certain to turn up again, and if she did, editors were sure to make use of her literary talent. The dangers were enormous, and yet this colossal gamble was taken, and in this gamble, as it seems to me, the possible gain was negligible and the possible loss devastating.

The conclusion that I draw from that is that the course adopted by my Right Hon. Friend the Prime Minister could have been adopted only by someone who genuinely and completely believed the statements of Profumo, and therefore, I absolutely acquit my Right Hon. Friend of any sort of dishonour. On the other hand, on the question of competence and good sense I cannot think that the verdict can be favourable.

What is to happen now? I cannot myself see at all that we can go on acting as if nothing had happened. We cannot just have business as usual. I myself feel that the time will come very soon when my Right Hon. Friend ought to make way for a much younger colleague. I feel that that ought to happen. I certainly will not quote at him the savage words of Cromwell, but perhaps some of the words of Browning might be appropriate in his poem on 'The Lost Leader', in which he wrote:

> . . . let him never come back to us!
> There would be doubt, hesitation and pain.
> Forced praise on our part – the glimmer of twilight,
> Never glad confident morning again!

'Never glad confident morning again!' – so I hope that the change will not be too long delayed.

Ahead of us we have a Division. We have the statement of my Right Hon. and noble Friend Lord Hailsham, in a personal assurance on television, that a Whip is not a summons to vote but a summons to attend. I call the Whips to witness that I at any rate have attended.

*The speech electrified the Commons. The publicity it received and its effect on Birch's fellow Tories weakened Macmillan's hold over the Tory Party. Macmillan retired four months later. Birch was created a life peer and became Lord Rhyl in 1970.*

·

## MARTIN LUTHER KING
### Washington, DC, 28 August 1963

*'I have a dream'*

*As the centenary of Abraham Lincoln's emancipation proclamation was cele-brated in 1963, the National Association for the Advancement of Colored People, using the slogan 'Free by '63', launched a massive campaign for justice for America's blacks. The most important demonstrations were in Birmingham, Alabama (where Martin Luther King, 1929–68, led a march on the city hall, was twice thrown into gaol but won substantial measures of desegregation) and in Selma where a grand march of protest to Montgomery was addressed by King and Ralph Bunche, until then the only black American winner of the Nobel Peace Prize.*

*Then Philip Randolph, dean of the black American leaders, proposed a march on Washington for jobs and freedom. 'There was no precedent for a convo-cation of national scope and gargantuan size,' King wrote later. 'Complicating the situation were innumerable prophets of doom who feared that the slightest incident of violence would alienate Congress and destroy all hope of legislation.'*

*Yet 210,000 gathered at the Washington Monument in August and marched to the Lincoln Memorial, where the high point of the day was the speech by Mar-tin Luther King, the voice of black Americans. He had written it in longhand the night before and did not finish it until 4 a.m. Now, standing before the marchers, King rose to the drama of the occasion, and delivered one of the most memorable speeches of the century. No public figure of his generation could match the skill with which he made a mastery of the spoken word the servant of his cause.*

Five score years ago, a great American, in whose symbolic shadow we stand, signed the Emancipation Proclamation. This momentous decree came as a great beacon light of hope to millions of Negro slaves who had been seared in the flames of withering injustice. It came as a joyous daybreak to end the long night of captivity.

But one hundred years later, we must face the tragic fact that the Negro is still not free. One hundred years later, the life of the Negro is still sadly crippled by the manacles of segregation and the chains of discrimination. One hundred years later, the Negro lives on a lonely island of poverty in the midst of a vast ocean of material prosperity. One hundred years later, the Negro is still languished in the corners of American society and finds himself an exile in his own land. So we have come here today to dramatize an appalling condition.

In a sense we have come to our nation's Capital to cash a cheque. When the architects of our republic wrote the magnificent words of the Constitution and the Declaration of Independence, they were signing a promissory note to which every American was to fall heir. This note was a promise that all men would be guaranteed the un-alienable rights of life, liberty, and the pursuit of happiness.

It is obvious today that America has defaulted on this promissory note insofar as her citizens of colour are concerned. Instead of hon-ouring this sacred obligation, America has given the Negro people a bad cheque; a cheque which has come back marked 'insufficient funds'. But we refuse to believe that the bank of justice is bankrupt. We refuse to believe that there are insufficient funds in the great vaults of opportunity of this nation. So we have come to cash this cheque – a cheque that will give us upon demand the riches of free-dom and the security of justice. We have also come to this hallowed spot to remind America of the fierce urgency of *now*. This is no time to engage in the luxury of cooling off or to take the tranquillizing drug of gradualism.

*Now* is the time to make real the promises of Democracy.

*Now* is the time to rise from the dark and desolate valley of segrega-tion to the sunlit path of racial justice.

*Now* is the time to open the doors of opportunity to all of God's children.

*Now* is the time to lift our nation from the quicksands of racial injustice to the solid rock of brotherhood.

It would be fatal for the nation to overlook the urgency of the moment and to underestimate the determination of the Negro. This sweltering summer of the Negro's legitimate discontent will not pass until there is an invigorating autumn of freedom and equality. Nineteen sixty-three is not an end, but a beginning. Those who hope that the Negro needed to blow off steam and will now be content will have a rude awakening if the nation returns to business as usual. There will be neither rest nor tranquillity in America until the Negro is granted his citizenship rights. The whirlwinds of revolt will continue to shake the foundations of our nation until the bright day of justice emerges.

But there is something that I must say to my people who stand on the warm threshold which leads into the palace of justice. In the process of gaining our rightful place we must not be guilty of wrongful deeds. Let us not seek to satisfy our thirst for freedom by drinking from the cup of bitterness and hatred. We must forever conduct our struggle on the high plane of dignity and discipline. We must not allow our creative protest to degenerate into physical violence. Again and again we must rise to the majestic heights of meeting physical force with soul force. The marvellous new militancy which has engulfed the Negro community must not lead us to a distrust of all white people, for many of our white brothers, as evidenced by their presence here today, have come to realize that their destiny is tied up with our destiny and their freedom is inextricably bound to our freedom. We cannot walk alone.

And as we walk, we must make the pledge that we shall march ahead. We cannot turn back. There are those who are asking the devotees of civil rights, 'When will you be satisfied?' We can never be satisfied as long as the Negro is the victim of the unspeakable horrors of police brutality. We can never be satisfied as long as our bodies, heavy with the fatigue of travel, cannot gain lodging in the motels of the highways and the hotels of the cities. We cannot be satisfied as long as the Negro's basic mobility is from a smaller ghetto to a larger one. We can never be satisfied as long as a Negro in Mississippi cannot vote and a Negro in New York believes he has nothing for which to vote. No, no, we are not satisfied, and we will not be satisfied until justice rolls down like waters and righteousness like a mighty stream.

I am not unmindful that some of you have come here out of great trials and tribulations. Some of you have come fresh from narrow jail cells. Some of you have come from areas where your quest for freedom left you battered by the storms of persecution and staggered by the winds of police brutality. You have been the veterans of creative suffering. Continue to work with the faith that unearned suffering is redemptive.

Go back to Mississippi, go back to Alabama, go back to South Carolina, go back to Georgia, go back to Louisiana, go back to the slums and ghettos of our northern cities, knowing that somehow this situation can and will be changed. Let us not wallow in the valley of despair.

I say to you today, my friends, that in spite of the difficulties and frustrations of the moment I still have a dream. It is a dream deeply rooted in the American dream.

I have a dream that one day this nation will rise up and live out the true meaning of its creed: 'We hold these truths to be self-evident; that all men are created equal.'

I have a dream that one day on the red hills of Georgia the sons of former slaves and the sons of former slaveowners will be able to sit down together at the table of brotherhood.

I have a dream that one day even the state of Mississippi, a desert state sweltering with the heat of injustice and oppression, will be transformed into an oasis of freedom and justice.

I have a dream that my four little children will one day live in a nation where they will not be judged by the colour of their skin but by the content of their character.

I have a dream today.

I have a dream that one day the state of Alabama, whose governor's lips are presently dripping with the words of interposition and nullification, will be transformed into a situation where little black boys and black girls will be able to join hands with little white boys and white girls and walk together as sisters and brothers.

I have a dream today.

I have a dream that one day every valley shall be exalted, every hill and mountain shall be made low, the rough places will be made plains, and the crooked places will be made straight, and the glory of the Lord shall be revealed, and all flesh shall see it together.

This is our hope. This is the faith with which I return to the South. With this faith we will be able to hew out of the mountain of despair a stone of hope. With this faith we will be able to transform the jangling discords of our nation into a beautiful symphony of brotherhood. With this faith we will be able to work together, to pray together, to struggle together, to go to jail together, to stand up for freedom together, knowing that we will be free one day.

This will be the day when all of God's children will be able to sing with new meaning

> My country, 'tis of thee,
> Sweet land of liberty,
> Of thee I sing:
> Land where my fathers died,
> Land of the pilgrims' pride,
> From every mountainside
> Let freedom ring.

And if America is to be a great nation this must become true. So let freedom ring from the prodigious hilltops of New Hampshire. Let freedom ring from the mighty mountains of New York. Let freedom ring from the heightening Alleghenies of Pennsylvania!

Let freedom ring from the snowcapped Rockies of Colorado!

Let freedom ring from the curvacious peaks of California!

But not only that; let freedom ring from Stone Mountain of Georgia!

Let freedom ring from Lookout Mountain of Tennessee!

Let freedom ring from every hill and molehill of Mississippi. From every mountainside, let freedom ring.

When we let freedom ring, when we let it ring from every village and every hamlet, from every state and every city, we will be able to speed up that day when all of God's children, black men and white men, Jews and Gentiles, Protestants and Catholics, will be able to join hands and sing in the words of the old Negro spiritual, 'Free at last! free at last! thank God almighty, we are free at last!'

*James Reston, one of America's most distinguished journalists, described the speech as 'an anguished echo from all the old American reformers' – from Roger Williams calling for religious liberty, Sam Adams for political liberty and Thoreau denouncing coercion to William Lloyd Garrison demanding emancipation and Eugene V. Debs crying for economic equality. King echoed them all.*

*Martin Luther King was* Time's *Man of the Year in 1963 and was awarded the Nobel Peace Prize in 1964. Civil-rights Acts, initiated by President Kennedy, were put on the statute book by President Johnson in 1964 and 1965. King was assassinated on a civil-rights mission to Memphis, Tennessee, on 4 April 1968.*

•

# HAROLD WILSON
## Scarborough, 1 October 1963

### 'The white heat of technology'

*Harold Wilson (1916–95) became leader of the Labour Party in 1963 after the death of Hugh Gaitskell. His challenge to the Tories, now led after the retirement of Harold Macmillan by the aristocratic Sir Alec Douglas-Home, was mounted with dramatic effect at the Labour Party conference, an annual platform for a major speech by the party leader.*

*In a speech that was rewritten during the small hours of the morning, Wilson summoned Labour to embrace the cult of the new and to harness the white heat of the technological revolution, and identified himself with the technicians and white-coat workers. There should be more scientists in government, he urged, more investment in scientific research and a new minister of technology. There was no room in the Labour movement for Luddites or antique working practices.*

*The contrast between Wilson and Douglas-Home, who confessed to doing his sums with matchsticks, was dramatic. 'We are living in the jet age,' Wilson said in other speeches, 'but we are governed by an Edwardian establishment mentality.' Wilson's message swept the political board. After twelve years of Tory rule, it chimed with the public mood and was compared to President Kennedy's 'new frontier'.*

We are redefining and we are restating our Socialism in terms of the scientific revolution. But that revolution cannot become a reality unless we are prepared to make far-reaching changes in economic and social attitudes which permeate our whole system of society.

The Britain that is going to be forged in the white heat of this revolution will be no place for restrictive practices or for outdated methods on either side of industry. We shall need a totally new attitude to the problems of apprenticeship, of training and retraining for skill. If there is one thing where the traditional philosophy of capitalism breaks down it is in training for apprenticeship, because quite frankly it does not pay any individual firm, unless it is very altruistic or quixotic or farsighted, to train apprentices if it knows at the end of the period of training they will be snapped up by some unscrupulous firm that makes no contribution to apprenticeship training. That is what economists mean when they talk about the difference between marginal private cost and net social cost.

So we are going to need a new attitude. In some industries we shall have to get right away from the idea of apprenticeship to a single firm. There will have to be apprenticeship with the industry as a whole, and the industry will have to take responsibility for it. Indeed, if we are going to end demarcation and snobbery in our training for skill and for science why should not these apprenticeship contracts be signed with the State itself? Then again, in the Cabinet room and the board room alike those charged with the control of our affairs must be ready to think and to speak in the language of our scientific age.

For the commanding heights of British industry to be controlled today by men whose only claim is their aristocratic connections or the power of inherited wealth or speculative finance is as irrelevant to the twentieth century as would be the continued purchase of commissions in the armed forces by lordly amateurs. At the very time that even the MCC has abolished the distinction between amateurs and professionals, in science and industry we are content to remain a nation of Gentlemen in a world of Players.

For those of us who have studied the formidable Soviet challenge in the education of scientists and technologists, and above all, in the ruthless application of scientific techniques in Soviet industry, know that our future lies not in military strength alone but in the efforts, the sacrifices, and above all the energies which a free people can mobilize for the future greatness of our country. Because we are democrats, we reject the methods which Communist countries are deploying in applying the results of scientific research to industrial life, but because we care deeply about the future of Britain, we must use all the resources of democratic planning, all the latent and under-developed energies and skills of our people, to ensure Britain's standing in the world. That is the message which I believe will go out from this Conference to the people of Britain and to the people of the world.

*The speech was greeted with a long standing ovation. Almost every correspondent was instantly seduced by Wilson's pseudo-scientific jargon, a disenchanted critic wrote later. Yet it had a big impact on floating middle-class voters and Wilson became prime minister in 1964. He won two subsequent elections in 1966 and 1974 and retired in 1976.*

•

# LYNDON B. JOHNSON
## Washington, DC, 27 November 1963

### 'Let us continue'

*According to the historian Theodore White, there was no word less than superb to describe the performance of Lyndon Johnson (1908–73) as he became presi-dent of the United States after the assassination of John Kennedy. All accounts of his behaviour through that week of tragedy endowed him with 'superlative grace'. At his inauguration, Kennedy had declared: 'Let us begin.' Now Johnson used the healing words: 'Let us continue' and proceeded to make continuity the watchword of Washington.*

*On the Sunday after the assassination, Johnson detailed some of the best brains of Kennedy's staff – Theodore Sorensen, McGeorge Bundy and J. K. Galbraith – to draft his first speech to Congress, adding to the team his old friend Abe Fortas, a Washington lawyer, and Bill Moyers and Horace Busby from his personal staff to add ideas.*

*He laboured on the speech throughout the next two days, changing words and phrases as he sought the right tone. When Bundy and Moyers brought him the finished speech, he pencilled in freshly the words that came from his own heart – 'For thirty-two years Capitol Hill has been my home' – and was ready to deliver the address that made his personal policy into national policy.*

Mr Speaker, Mr President, Members of the House, Members of the Senate, my fellow Americans:

All I have I would have given gladly not to be standing here today.

The greatest leader of our time has been struck down by the foulest deed of our time. Today John Fitzgerald Kennedy lives on in the immortal words and works that he left behind. He lives on in the mind and memories of mankind. He lives on in the hearts of his countrymen.

No words are sad enough to express our sense of loss. No words are strong enough to express our determination to continue the forward thrust of America that he began.

The dream of conquering the vastness of space – the dream of partnership across the Atlantic – and across the Pacific as well – the dream of a Peace Corps in less developed nations – the dream of education for all of our children – the dream of jobs for all who seek them and need them – the dream of care for our elderly – the dream of an all-out attack on mental illness – and above all, the dream of equal rights for all Americans, whatever their race or colour – these and other American dreams have been vitalized by his drive and by his dedication.

And now the ideas and the ideals which he so nobly represented must and will be translated into effective action.

Under John Kennedy's leadership, this Nation has demonstrated that it has the courage to seek peace, and it has the fortitude to risk war. We have proved that we are a good and reliable friend to those who seek peace and freedom. We have shown that we can also be a formidable foe to those who reject the path of peace and those who seek to impose upon us or our allies the yoke of tyranny.

This Nation will keep its commitments from South Viet-Nam to West Berlin. We will be unceasing in the search for peace; resourceful in our pursuit of areas of agreement even with those with whom we differ; and generous and loyal to those who join with us in common cause.

In this age when there can be no losers in peace and no victors in war, we must recognize the obligation to match national strength with national restraint. We must be prepared at one and the same time for both the confrontation of power and the limitation of power. We must be ready to defend the national interest and to negotiate the common interest. This is the path that we shall continue to pursue. Those who test our courage will find it strong, and those who seek our friendship will find it honourable. We will demonstrate anew that the strong can be just in the use of strength; and the just can be strong in the defence of justice.

And let all know we will extend no special privilege and impose no persecution. We will carry on the fight against poverty and misery, and disease and ignorance, in other lands and in our own.

We will serve all the Nation, not one section or one sector, or one group, but all Americans. These are the United States – a united people with a united purpose.

Our American unity does not depend upon unanimity. We have differences; but now, as in the past, we can derive from those differences strength, not weakness, wisdom, not despair. Both as a people and a government, we can unite upon a programme, a programme which is wise and just, enlightened and constructive.

For thirty-two years Capitol Hill has been my home. I have shared many moments of pride with you, pride in the ability of the Congress of the United States to act, to meet any crisis, to distil from our differences strong programmes of national action.

An assassin's bullet has thrust upon me the awesome burden of the Presidency. I am here today to say I need your help; I cannot bear this burden alone. I need the help of all Americans, and all America. This Nation has experienced a profound shock, and in this critical moment, it is our duty, yours and mine, as the Government of the United States, to do away with uncertainty and doubt and delay, and to show that we are capable of decisive action; that from the brutal loss of our leader we will derive not weakness, but strength; that we can and will act and act now.

From this chamber of representative government, let all the world know and none misunderstand that I rededicate this Government to the unswerving support of the United Nations, to the honourable and determined execution of our commitments to our allies, to the maintenance of military strength second to none, to the defence of the strength and the stability of the dollar, to the expansion of our foreign trade, to the reinforcement of our programmes of mutual assistance and cooperation in Asia and Africa, and to our Alliance for Progress in this hemisphere.

On the 20th day of January, in 1961, John F. Kennedy told his countrymen that our national work would not be finished 'in the first thousand days, nor in the life of this administration, nor even perhaps in our lifetime on this planet. But,' he said, 'let us begin.'

Today, in this moment of new resolve, I would say to all my fellow Americans, let us continue.

This is our challenge – not to hesitate, not to pause, not to turn about and linger over this evil moment, but to continue on our course so that we may fulfil the destiny that history has set for us.

•

## NELSON MANDELA
### Johannesburg, 20 April 1964

*'An ideal for which I am prepared to die'*

*After being sentenced to life imprisonment in 1964, Nelson Mandela (1918–) became a worldwide symbol of heroic black resistance to the apartheid regime of South Africa. He was described as the Black Pimpernel.*

*He joined the African National Congress in 1952 and became a member of a small action group whose main task was to launch Umkhonto we Sizwe (Spear of the Nation) or MK. From a safe house in Rivonia, MK planned sabotage of strategic targets — after its first terrorist attacks in 1961 bombs exploded in Johannesburg, Port Elizabeth and Durban.*

*When the ANC was banned in 1961, Mandela evaded arrest for a year but was gaoled for five years in 1962 and sent to Robben Island. His prison term was interrupted by the Rivonia trial, brought after a police raid on ANC headquarters in 1963. Mandela and his colleagues were charged under the Suppression of Communism Act.*

*The trial opened on 9 October 1963, with Mandela named as Accused Number One and facing the death penalty. As he entered the court, wearing prison clothes of khaki shorts and flimsy sandals, Mandela and the other accused made a clenched fist ANC salute. The defence case opened the following April.*

*Mandela decided to make a statement of ANC ideals and politics from the dock. It meant that he could not be cross-examined. The speech lasted four hours. He denied he was a Communist and described himself as an African patriot who admired the Magna Carta and the Bill of Rights. This extract covers his opening words and the peroration — which inspired support throughout the world.*

I am the First Accused. I hold a Bachelor's Degree in Arts and practised as an attorney in Johannesburg for a number of years in partnership with Oliver Tambo. I am a convicted prisoner serving five years for leaving the country without a permit and for inciting people to go on strike at the end of May 1961.

At the outset, I want to say that the suggestion made by the State in its opening that the struggle in South Africa is under the influence of foreigners or Communists is wholly incorrect. I have done whatever I did, both as an individual and as a leader of my people, because of my experience in South Africa and my own African background, not because of what any outsider might have said.

I admit immediately that I was one of the persons who helped to form Umkhonto we Sizwe, and that I played a prominent role in its affairs until I was arrested in August 1962. I, and the others who started the organization, did so for two reasons. Firstly, we believed that as a result of government policy, violence by the African people had become inevitable, and that unless responsible leadership was given to channel and control the feelings of our people, there would be outbreaks of terrorism which would produce an intensity of bitterness and hostility between the various races of this country which is not produced even by war. Secondly, we felt that without violence there would be no way open to the African people to succeed in their struggle against the principle of white supremacy. All lawful methods of expressing opposition to this principle had been closed by legislation, and we were placed in a position in which we had either to accept a permanent state of inferiority, or to defy the government. We chose to defy the law. We first broke the law in a way which avoided any recourse to violence; when this form was legislated against, and the government resorted to a show of force to crush opposition to its policies, only then did we decide to answer violence with violence.

But the violence which we chose to adopt was not terrorism. We who formed Umkhonto were all members of the African National Congress, and had behind us the ANC tradition of nonviolence and negotiation as a means of solving political disputes. We believed that South Africa belonged to all the people who lived in it, and not to one group, be it black or white. We did not want an interracial war, and tried to avoid it to the last. But the hard facts were that fifty years of nonviolence had brought the African people nothing but more and more repressive legislation, and fewer and fewer rights. Four forms of violence were considered – sabotage, guerrilla warfare, terrorism, and open revolution. We chose to adopt the first method and to exhaust it before making any other decision.

The initial plan was based on a careful analysis of the political and economic situation of our country. We believed that South Africa depended to a large extent on foreign capital and foreign trade. We felt that planned destruction of power plants, and interference with rail and telephone communications, would tend to scare away capital from the country, make it more difficult for goods from the industrial areas to reach the seaports on schedule, and would in the long run be a heavy drain on the economic life of the country, thus compelling the voters of the country to reconsider their position.

Attacks on the economic lifelines of the country were to be linked with sabotage on government buildings and other symbols of apartheid. These attacks would serve as a source of inspiration to our people. In addition, they would provide an outlet for those people who were urging the adoption of violent methods and would enable us to give concrete proof to our followers that we had adopted a stronger line and were fighting back against government violence. In addition, if mass action was successfully organized, and mass reprisals taken, we felt that sympathy for our cause would be roused in other countries, and that greater pressure would be brought to bear on the South African government.

This then was the plan. Umkhonto was to perform sabotage, and strict instructions were given to its members that on no account were they to injure or kill people in planning or carrying out operations.

Experience convinced us that rebellion would offer the government limitless opportunities for the indiscriminate slaughter of our people, but it was precisely because the soil of South Africa was already drenched with the blood of innocent Africans that we felt it our duty to make preparations as a long-term undertaking to use force in order to defend ourselves against force. If war was inevitable, we wanted the fight to be conducted on terms most favourable to our people. The fight which held out prospects best for us and the least risk of life to both sides was guerrilla warfare. We decided, therefore, in our preparations for the future, to make provision for the possibility of guerrilla warfare. All whites undergo compulsory military training, but no such training was given to Africans. It was in our view essential to build up a nucleus of trained men who would be able to provide the leadership which would be required if guerrilla warfare started . . .

I turn now to my own position. I have denied that I am a Communist, and I think that in the circumstances I am obliged to state exactly what my political beliefs are. I have always regarded myself, in the first place, as an African patriot. I am attracted by the idea of a classless society, an attraction which springs partly from Marxist reading and partly from my admiration of the structure and organization of early African societies in this country. The land, then the main means of production, belonged to the tribe. There were no rich or poor and there was no exploitation.

Yes, I have been influenced by Marxist thought, but so have other leaders such as Gandhi, Nehru, Nkrumah, and Nasser. We all accept the need for some form of socialism to enable our people to catch up with the advanced countries of this world and to overcome their legacy of extreme poverty. But this does not mean we are Communists, or even Marxists. Indeed, for my own part, I believe that it is open to debate whether the Communist Party has any specific role to play at this particular stage of our political struggle. The basic task at the present moment is the removal of race discrimination and the attainment of democratic rights on the basis of the Freedom Charter. Insofar as that party furthers this task, I welcome its assistance. I realize that it is one of the means by which people of all races can be drawn into our struggle . . .

Our fight is against real, and not imaginary hardships, or, to use the language of the State Prosecutor, 'so-called hardships'. We fight against two features which are the hallmarks of African life in South Africa, and which are entrenched by legislation which we seek to have repealed. These features are poverty and lack of human dignity, and we do not need Communists, or so-called 'agitators', to teach us about these things.

The whites enjoy what may well be the highest standard of living in the world, whilst Africans live in poverty and misery. Forty per cent of the Africans live in hopelessly overcrowded and, in some cases, drought-stricken reserves, where soil erosion and the over-working of the soil make it impossible for them to live properly off the land. Thirty per cent are labourers, labour tenants, and squatters on white farms and work and live under conditions similar to those of the serfs of the Middle Ages. The other thirty per cent live in towns where they have developed economic and social habits which bring them closer, in many respects, to white standards. Yet forty-six per cent of all African families in Johannesburg do not earn enough to keep them going.

The complaint of Africans, however, is not only that they are poor and whites are rich, but that the laws which are made by the whites are designed to preserve this situation. There are two ways to break out of poverty. The first is by formal education, and the second is by the worker acquiring a greater skill at his work and thus higher wages. As far as Africans are concerned, both these avenues of advancement are deliberately curtailed by legislation.

The present Government has always sought to hamper Africans in their search for education. There is compulsory education for all white children at virtually no cost to their parents, be they rich or poor. Similar facilities are not provided for African children. In 1960–61, the per capita government spending on African students at state-funded schools was estimated at R12.46. In the same year, the per capita spending on white children in the Cape Province (which are the only figures available to me) was R144.57. The present Prime Minister said during the debate on the Bantu Education Bill in 1953: 'When I have control of Native education, I will reform it so that Natives will be taught from childhood to realize that equality with Europeans is not for them . . . People who believe in equality are not desirable teachers for Natives. When my Department controls Native education, it will know for what class of higher education a Native is fitted, and whether he will have a chance in life to use his knowledge.'

The other main obstacle to the economic advancement of the Africans is the industrial colour bar by which all the better jobs of industry are reserved for whites only. Moreover, Africans are not allowed to form trade unions, which have recognition under the Industrial Conciliation Act. The Government often answers its critics by saying that Africans in South Africa are economically better off than the inhabitants of the other countries in Africa. Our complaint is not that we are poor by comparison with people in other countries, but that we are poor by comparison with white people in our own country, and that we are prevented by legislation from altering this imbalance.

Hundreds and thousands of Africans are thrown into gaol each year under pass laws. Even worse than this is the fact that pass laws keep husband and wife apart and lead to the breakdown of family life.

Poverty and the breakdown of family life have secondary effects. Children wander about the streets of the townships because they have no schools to go to, or no money to enable them to go to school, or no parents at home to see that they go to school because both parents, if there be two, have to work to keep the family alive. This leads to a breakdown in moral standards, to an alarming rise in illegitimacy and to growing violence which erupts not only politically but everywhere. Life in the townships is dangerous; there is not a day that goes by without somebody being stabbed or assaulted. And violence is carried out of the townships into the white living areas. People are afraid to walk alone in the streets after dark. House-breakings and robberies are increasing despite the fact that the death sentence can now be imposed for such offences. Death sentences cannot cure the festering sore. The only cure is to alter the conditions under which the Africans are forced to live, and to meet their legitimate grievances.

We want to be part of the general population, and not confined to living in our ghettos. African men want to have their wives and children to live with them where they work, and not to be forced into an unnatural existence in men's hostels. Our women want to be left with their men folk, and not to be left permanently widowed in the Reserves. We want to be allowed out after 11 p.m. and not to be confined to our rooms like little children. We want to be allowed to travel in our own country, and seek work where we want to, and not where the Labour Bureau tells us to. We want a just share in the whole of South Africa; we want security and a stake in society.

Above all, my lord, we want equal political rights, because without them our disabilities will be permanent. I know this sounds revolutionary to the whites in this country, because the majority of voters will be Africans. This makes the white man fear democracy. But this fear cannot be allowed to stand in the way of the only solution which will guarantee racial harmony and freedom for all. It is not true that the enfranchisement of all will result in racial domination. Political division, based on colour, is entirely artificial, and when it disappears, so will the domination of one colour group by another. The ANC has spent half a century fighting against racialism. When it triumphs, as it certainly must, it will not change that policy.

This then is what the ANC is fighting. Our struggle is a truly national one. It is a struggle of the African people, inspired by our own suffering and our own experience. It is a struggle for the right to live.

During my lifetime I have dedicated my life to this struggle of the

African people. I have fought against white domination, and I have fought against black domination. I have cherished the ideal of a democratic and free society in which all persons live together in harmony with equal opportunities. It is an ideal which I hope to live for, and to see realized. But my lord, if needs be, it is an ideal for which I am prepared to die.

*On 11 June, Mandela and the seven other defendants were sentenced to life imprisonment. Mandela returned to Robben Island, where he was put in a stone cell measuring two metres by two metres, lit by a forty-watt bulb and set to hard labour in a quarry. He spent twenty-seven years in prison.*

•

## LYNDON B. JOHNSON
### Ann Arbor, Michigan, 22 May 1964

#### 'The Great Society'

*At first, as he sought a slogan to encapsulate the mission of his presidency and to follow the idealism of the New Deal, Lyndon Johnson thought of A Better Deal.*

*It was one of his speechwriters, Richard Goodwin, who had earlier worked with President Kennedy, who dreamt up the phrase The Great Society. When Johnson failed to arouse any strong enthusiasm for A Better Deal, he began to weave the theme of The Great Society into his speeches – and used the phrase on nineteen occasions in March and April, but it was not recognized as his slogan until Goodwin wrote Johnson's speech for the University of Michigan.*

For a century we laboured to settle and to subdue a continent. For half a century we called upon unbounded invention and untiring industry to create an order of plenty for all of our people.

The challenge of the next half century is whether we have the wisdom to use that wealth to enrich and elevate our national life, and to advance the quality of our American civilization.

Your imagination, your initiative, and your indignation will determine whether we build a society where progress is the servant of our needs, or a society where old values and new visions are buried under unbridled growth. For in your time we have the opportunity to move not only towards the rich society and the powerful society, but upward to the Great Society.

The Great Society rests on abundance and liberty for all. It demands an end to poverty and racial injustice, to which we are totally committed in our time. But that is just the beginning.

The Great Society is a place where every child can find knowledge to enrich his mind and to enlarge his talents. It is a place where leisure is a welcome chance to build and reflect, not a feared cause of boredom and restlessness. It is a place where the city of man serves not only the needs of the body and the demands of commerce but the desire for beauty and the hunger for community.

It is a place where man can renew contact with nature. It is a place which honours creation for its own sake and for what it adds to the understanding of the race. It is a place where men are more concerned with the quality of their goals than the quantity of their goods.

But most of all, the Great Society is not a safe harbour, a resting place, a final objective, a finished work. It is a challenge constantly renewed, beckoning us towards a destiny where the meaning of our lives matches the marvellous products of our labour . . .

Our society will never be great until our cities are great. Today the frontier of imagination and innovation is inside those cities and not beyond their borders.

New experiments are already going on. It will be the task of your generation to make the American city a place where future generations will come, not only to live but to live the good life . . .

A second place where we begin to build the Great Society is in our countryside. We have always prided ourselves on being not only America the strong and America the free, but America the beautiful. Today that beauty is in danger. The water we drink, the food we eat, the very air that we breathe, are threatened with pollution. Our parks are overcrowded, our seashores overburdened. Green fields and dense forests are disappearing.

A few years ago we were greatly concerned about the 'Ugly American'. Today we must act to prevent an ugly America.

For once the battle is lost, once our natural splendour is destroyed, it can never be recaptured. And once man can no longer walk with beauty or wonder at nature his spirit will wither and his sustenance be wasted.

A third place to build the Great Society is in the classrooms of America. There your children's lives will be shaped. Our society will not be great until every young mind is set free to scan the farthest reaches of thought and imagination. We are still far from that goal.

Today, eight million adult Americans, more than the entire population of Michigan, have not finished five years of school. Nearly twenty million have not finished eight years of school. Nearly fifty-four million – more than one-quarter of all America – have not even finished high school . . .

In many places, classrooms are overcrowded and curricula are outdated. Most of our qualified teachers are underpaid, and many of our paid teachers are unqualified. So we must give every child a place to sit and a teacher to learn from. Poverty must not be a bar to learning, and learning must offer an escape from poverty . . .

There are those timid souls who say this battle cannot be won; that we are condemned to a soulless wealth. I do not agree. We have the power to shape the civilization that we want. But we need your will, your labour, your hearts, if we are to build that kind of society.

Those who came to this land sought to build more than just a new country. They sought a new world. So I have come here today to your campus to say that you can make their vision our reality. So let us from this moment begin our work so that in the future men will look back and say: It was then, after a long and weary way, that man turned the exploits of his genius to the full enrichment of his life.

*The Civil Rights bill, which was part of the Kennedy legislative programme, was hurried on to the statute book by Johnson and became law on 2 July 1964. It was the most important measure passed in the aftermath of President Kennedy's assassination and tackled almost all the problems about which Southern blacks had been protesting so strongly.*

•

# BARRY GOLDWATER
San Francisco, 16 July 1964

*'Extremism in defence of liberty is no vice'*

*By the summer of 1964, Barry Goldwater (1909–98), the leading Conservative political spokesman in the United States during the Kennedy administration, had arrived centre stage in American history at a time when intellectual vitality seemed to have run out of the generations-old liberal orthodoxy that had dominated American politics since Roosevelt.*

*At the Cow Palace, Richard Nixon was about to nominate him as Republican candidate against Lyndon Johnson in the presidential election. His speechwriters had worked on his speech for more than two weeks. Goldwater had gone through it five times. No word was unmeasured. The speech was to proclaim a new morality, an uncompromising challenge to the course American politics had followed for the past thirty years within his own party as well as the Democrats.*

*After being portrayed as crazy, stupid and bloodthirsty, Goldwater was an embittered man who decided to go it alone and offer no compromise. The speech signalled the tenor of his campaign which became notorious for his advocacy of increased opposition to world Communism and hostility to the power of federal government. The last two lines were underlined in his text.*

The Good Lord raised this mighty Republican Republic to be a home for the brave and to flourish as the land of the free – not to stagnate in the swampland of collectivism, not to cringe before the bully of Communism.

Now my fellow Americans, the tide has been running against freedom. Our people have followed false prophets. We must, and we shall, return to proven ways – not because they are old, but because they are true.

We must, and we shall, set the tide running again in the cause of freedom. And this party, with its every action, every word, every breath and every heartbeat, has but a single resolve, and that is freedom.

Freedom made orderly for this nation by our constitutional

government. Freedom under a government limited by laws of nature and of nature's God. Freedom balanced so that order lacking liberty will not become the slavery of the prison cell; balanced so that liberty lacking order will not become the licence of the mob and of the jungle.

Now, we Americans understand freedom. We have earned it: we have lived for it, and we have died for it. This nation and its people are freedom's models in a searching world. We can be freedom's missionaries in a doubting world . . .

Those who seek to live your lives for you, to take your liberty in return for relieving you of yours; those who elevate the state and downgrade the citizen, must see ultimately a world in which earthly power can be substituted for Divine Will. And this nation was founded upon the rejection of that notion and upon the acceptance of God as the author of freedom.

Now those who seek absolute power, even though they seek it to do what they regard as good, are simply demanding the right to enforce their own version of heaven on earth, and let me remind you they are the very ones who always create the most hellish tyranny.

Absolute power does corrupt, and those who seek it must be suspect and must be opposed. Their mistaken course stems from false notions, ladies and gentlemen, of equality. Equality, rightly understood as our founding fathers understood it, leads to liberty and to the emancipation of creative differences; wrongly understood, as it has been so tragically in our time, it leads first to conformity and then to despotism.

Fellow Republicans, it is the cause of Republicanism to resist concentrations of power, private or public, which enforce such conformity and inflict such despotism.

It is the cause of Republicanism to insure that power remains in the hands of the people – and, so help us God, that is exactly what a Republican President will do with the help of a Republican Congress.

It is further the cause of Republicanism to restore a clear understanding of the tyranny of man over man in the world at large. It is our cause to dispel the foggy thinking which avoids hard decisions in the delusion that a world of conflict will somehow resolve itself into a world of harmony, if we just don't rock the boat or irritate the forces of aggression – and this is hogwash.

It is, further, the cause of Republicanism to remind ourselves, and the world, that only the strong can remain free: that only the strong can keep the peace.

Today – today in our beloved country – we have an Administration which seems eager to deal with Communism in every coin known – from gold to wheat; from consulates to confidence, and even human freedom itself.

Now the Republican cause demands that we brand Communism as the principal disturber of peace in the world. Indeed, we should brand it as the only significant disturber of the peace . . .

And I want to make this abundantly clear – I don't intend to let peace or freedom be torn from our grasp, because of lack of strength, or lack of will – and that I promise you Americans.

I can see a day when all the Americas – North and South – will be linked in a mighty system – a system in which the errors and misunderstandings of the past will be submerged one by one in a rising tide of prosperity and interdependence . . .

Balance, diversity, creative difference – these are the elements of the Republican equation. Republicans agree, Republicans agree heartily, to disagree on many, many of their applications. But we have never disagreed on the basic fundamental issues of why you and I are Republicans.

This is a party – this Republican party is a party – for free men. Not for blunt followers and not for conformists.

Back in 1858 Abraham Lincoln said this of the Republican party, and I quote him because he probably could have said it during the last week or so: it was so composed of strained, discordant, and even hostile elements . . .

Yet all of these elements agreed on one paramount objective: to arrest the programme of slavery, and place it in the course of its ultimate extinction.

Anyone who joins us in all sincerity we welcome. Those, those who do not care for our cause, we don't expect to enter our ranks in any case. And let our Republicanism so focused and so dedicated not be made fuzzy and futile by unthinking and stupid labels.

I would remind you that extremism in the defence of liberty is no vice!

And let me remind you also that moderation in the pursuit of justice is no virtue!

*Goldwater's speech ended not only the Eisenhower era in American politics but also the reign of pragmatism in the Republican party. He won only five states in the election which Johnson won with sixty-one per cent of the popular vote, the biggest majority ever achieved by an American president at that time. Goldwater returned to the Senate in 1969 and was later influential in persuading Richard Nixon to step down from the presidency after the Watergate scandal in 1974.*

•

## RONALD REAGAN
### Nationwide television address, 27 October 1964

#### 'A time for choosing'

*A lifelong Democrat, Ronald Reagan (1911–2004) switched sides and became co-chairman of Californians for Barry Goldwater in 1964. Reagan got his first real exposure to the airwaves as a salesman for General Electric, travelling the country to host GE Theater. As he campaigned for Goldwater, his campaign speeches were similar in their tone and message to those he had been giving in his GE presentations.*

*'One night a few weeks before the election,' Reagan recalled later, 'I addressed a fundraiser at the Coconut Grove in Los Angeles. When the evening was over, a delegation of high-powered Republicans waited for me. They asked whether I would deliver that same speech on nationwide TV if they raised the money to buy the time.'*

*Goldwater at one stage wanted to cancel the address, since he had been attacked for his views on social security, but relented after he heard a copy of the soundtrack. Reagan's election address, which became known as The Speech, was broadcast on NBC.*

Those who would trade our freedom for the soup kitchen of the welfare state have told us that they have a utopian solution of peace without victory. They call their policy 'accommodation'. And they say if we only avoid any direct confrontation with the enemy, he will forget his evil ways and learn to love us. All who oppose them are indicted as warmongers. They say we offer simple answers to complex problems. Well, perhaps there is a simple answer . . . not an easy one . . . but a simple one, if you and I have the courage to tell our elected officials that we want our *national* policy based upon what we know in our hearts is morally right.

We cannot buy our security, our freedom from the threat of the bomb by committing an immorality so great as saying to a billion human beings now in slavery behind the Iron Curtain, 'Give up your dreams of freedom because to save our own skin, we are willing to make a deal with your slave-masters.' Alexander Hamilton said, 'A nation which can prefer disgrace to danger is prepared for a master, and deserves one!' Let's set the record straight. There is no argument over the choice between peace and war, but there is only one guaranteed way you can have peace . . . and you can have it in the next second . . . surrender!

Admittedly there is a risk in any course we follow other than this, but every lesson in history tells us that the greater risk lies in appeasement, and this is the spectre our well-meaning liberal friends refuse to face . . . that their policy of accommodation is appeasement, and it gives no choice between peace and war, only between fight or surrender. If we continue to accommodate, continue to back and retreat, eventually we have to face the final demand – the ultimatum. And what then? When Nikita Khrushchev has told his people he knows what our answer will be? He has told them that we are retreating under the pressure of the Cold War, and someday when the time comes to deliver the ultimatum, our surrender will be voluntary because by that time we will have been weakened from within spiritually, morally, and economically. He believes this because from our side he has heard voices pleading for 'peace at any price' or 'better Red than dead', or as one commentator put it, he would rather 'live on his knees than die on his feet'. And therein lies the road to war, because those voices don't speak for the rest of us. You and I know and do not believe that life is so dear and peace so sweet as to be purchased at the price of chains and slavery. If nothing in life is worth dying for, when did this begin – just in the face of this enemy? – or should Moses have told the children of Israel to live in slavery under the pharaohs? Should Christ have refused the cross? Should the patriots at Concord Bridge have thrown down their guns and refused to fire the shot heard round the world? The martyrs of history were not fools, and our honoured dead who gave their lives to stop the advance of the Nazis didn't die in vain! Where, then, is the road to peace? Well, it's a simple answer after all.

You and I have the courage to say to our enemies, 'There is a price we will not pay.' There is a point beyond which they must not advance! This is the meaning in the phrase of Barry Goldwater's 'peace through strength!' Winston Churchill said that 'the destiny of man is not measured by material computation. When great forces are on the move in the world, we learn we are spirits – not animals.' And he said, 'There is something going on in time and space, and beyond time and space, which, whether we like it or not, spells duty.' You and I have a rendezvous with destiny. We will preserve for our children this, the last best hope of man on earth, or we will sentence them to take the last step into a thousand years of darkness.

We will keep in mind and remember that Barry Goldwater has faith in us. He has faith that you and I have the ability and the dignity and the right to make our own decisions and determine our own destiny.

Thank you.

*Reagan's speech raised $8 million. Whatever its effect on Goldwater's defeat, it soon changed Reagan's entire life and contributed significantly to his emergence as the spokesman of the Republican right.*

•

## MALCOLM X
### Detroit, 14 February 1965

*'More African than American'*

*Malcolm X (1925–65) was born in Nebraska, the son of a radical Baptist minister who was murdered by the Ku Klux Klan, and raised in Michigan and Boston. His name, he said, symbolized his life — ex-smoker, ex-drinker, ex-Christian, ex-slave. He became a pimp and hustler and was jailed for drug pushing and burglary in 1946. In 1952 he discovered the Nation of Islam and became a Black Muslim minister preaching vengeance against the 'white devil' and advocating violence and black separation. He was suspended from the Black Muslims in 1963 after a conflict with their leader Elijah Muhammad and travelled to Mecca. He realized that orthodox Muslims preached racial equality, abandoned his attacks on the white devils and founded the Organization of Afro-American Unity.*

*He was the most articulate Black Muslim of the early 1960s. He delivered this speech to the Afro-American Broadcasting Company on the evening after his house had been bombed by Black Muslims enraged by his change of heart. What effect did the struggle over Africa have on black Americans, he asked?*

*A week later, as he began another speech in New York, he was assassinated.*

Why should the black man in America concern himself since he's been away from the African continent for three or four hundred years? Why should we concern ourselves? What impact does what happens to them have upon us? Number one, you have to realize that up until 1959 Africa was dominated by the colonial powers. Having complete control over Africa, the colonial powers of Europe projected the image of Africa negatively. They always project Africa in a negative light: jungle savages, cannibals, nothing civilized. Why then, naturally it was so negative that it was negative to you and me, and you and I began to hate it. We didn't want anybody telling us anything about Africa, much less calling us Africans. In hating Africa and in hating the Africans, we ended up hating ourselves, without even realizing it. Because you can't hate the roots of a tree, and not hate the tree. You can't hate your origin and not end up hating yourself. You can't hate Africa and not hate yourself.

You show me one of these people over here who has been thoroughly brainwashed and has a negative attitude toward Africa, and I'll show you one who has a negative attitude toward himself. You can't have a positive attitude toward yourself and a negative attitude toward Africa at the same time. To the same degree that your understanding of and attitude toward Africa becomes positive, you'll find that your understanding of and your attitude toward yourself will also become positive. And this is what the white man knows. So they very skilfully make you and me hate our African identity, our African characteristics.

You know yourself that we have been a people who hated our African characteristics. We hated our heads, we hated the shape of our nose, we wanted one of those long doglike noses, you know; we hated the colour of our skin, hated the blood of Africa that was in our veins. And in hating our features and our skin and our blood, why, we had to end up hating ourselves. And we hated ourselves. Our colour became to us a chain – we felt that it was holding us back; our colour became to us like a prison which we felt was keeping us confined, not letting us go this way or that way. We felt that all of these restrictions were based solely upon our colour, and the psychological reaction to that would have to be that as long as we felt imprisoned or chained or trapped by black skin, black features, and black blood, that skin and those features and that blood holding us back automatically had to become hateful to us. And it became hateful to us.

It made us feel inferior; it made us feel inadequate, made us feel helpless. And when we fell victims to this feeling of inadequacy or inferiority or helplessness, we turned to somebody else to show us the way. We didn't have confidence in another black man to show us the way, or black people to show us the way. In those days we didn't. We didn't think a black man could do anything except play some horns – you know, make some sound and make you happy with some songs and in that way. But in serious things, where our food, clothing, shelter, and education were concerned, we turned to the man. We never thought in terms of bringing these things into existence for ourselves, we never thought in terms of doing things for ourselves. Because we felt helpless. What made us feel helpless was our hatred for ourselves. And our hatred for ourselves stemmed from our hatred for things African . . .

One of the things that made the Black Muslim movement grow was its emphasis upon things African. This was the secret to the growth of the Black Muslim movement. African blood, African origin, African culture, African ties. And you'd be surprised – we discovered that deep within the subconscious of the black man in this country, he is still more African than he is American. He *thinks* that he's more American than African, because the man is jiving him, the man is brainwashing him every day. He's telling him, 'You're an American, you're an American.' Man, how could you think you're an American when you haven't ever had any kind of an American treat over here? You have never, never. Ten men can be sitting at a table eating, you know, dining, and I can come and sit down where they're dining. They're dining; I've got a plate in front of me, but nothing is on it. Because all of us are sitting at the same table, are all of us diners? I'm not a diner until you let me dine. Just being at the table with others who are dining doesn't make me a diner, and this is what you've got to get in your head here in this country.

Just because you're in this country doesn't make you an American. No, you've got to go farther than that before you can become an American. You've got to enjoy the fruits of Americanism. You haven't enjoyed those fruits. You've enjoyed the thorns. You've enjoyed the thistles. But you have not enjoyed the fruits, no sir. You have fought harder for the fruits than the white man has, but you've enjoyed less. When the man put the uniform on you and sent you abroad, you fought harder than they did. Yes, I know you – when you're fighting for them, you can fight . . .

Brothers and sisters, let me tell you, I spend my time out there in the streets with people, all kinds of people, listening to what they have to say. And they're dissatisfied, they're disillusioned, they're fed up, they're getting to the point of frustration where they begin to feel, 'What do we have to lose?' When you get to that point, you're the type of person who can create a very dangerously explosive atmosphere. This is what's happening in our neighbourhoods, to our people.

I read a poll taken by *Newsweek* magazine this week saying that Negroes are satisfied. Oh, yes, *Newsweek*, you know, supposed to be a top magazine with a top pollster, talking about how satisfied Negroes are. Maybe I haven't met the Negroes he met. Because I know he hasn't met the ones that I've met. And this is dangerous. This is where the white man does himself the most harm. He invents statistics to create an image, thinking that that image is going to hold things in check. You know why they always say Negroes are lazy? Because they want Negroes to be lazy. They always say Negroes can't unite, because they don't want Negroes to unite. And once they put this thing in the Negro's mind, they feel that he tries to fulfil their image. If they say you can't unite black people, and then you come to them to unite them, they won't unite, because it's been said that they're not supposed to unite. It's a psycho that they work, and it's the same way with these statistics.

When they think that an explosive era is coming up, then they grab their press again and begin to shower the Negro public, to make it appear that all Negroes are satisfied. Because if you know you're dissatisfied all by yourself and ten others aren't, you play it cool; but if you know that all ten of you are dissatisfied, you get with it. This is what the man knows. The man knows that if these Negroes find out how dissatisfied they really are — even Uncle Tom is dissatisfied, he's just playing his part for now — this is what makes the man frightened. It frightens them in France and frightens them in England, and it frightens them in the United States.

And it is for this reason that it is so important for you and me to start organizing among ourselves, intelligently, and try to find out: 'What are we going to do if this happens, that happens or the next thing happens?' Don't think that you're going to run to the man and say, 'Look, boss, this is me.' Why, when the deal goes down, you'll look just like me in his eyesight; I'll make it tough for you. Yes, when the deal goes down, he doesn't look at you in any better light than he looks at me . . .

I say again that I'm not a racist, I don't believe in any form of seg-regation or anything like that. I'm for brotherhood for everybody, but I don't believe in forcing brotherhood upon people who don't want it. Let us practise brotherhood among ourselves, and then if others want to practise brotherhood with us, we're for practising it with them also. But I don't think that we should run around trying to love somebody who doesn't love us.

•

# LYNDON B. JOHNSON
## Washington, DC, 15 March 1965

### '*We shall overcome*'

*Although his achievements were to be overshadowed by Vietnam, Lyndon John-son's five years in the White House saw the completion of civil-rights legislation, the Federal Education Act of 1965 and the establishment of Medicare in pur-suit of his ideal of The Great Society.*

*As he contemplated the Voting Rights Act of 1965, Johnson was worried about the reaction of Congress but was persuaded that a speech to the House would not be interpreted as a sign of panic and would also show that he was being bipartisan.*

*At 8 p.m. and due to deliver his speech at 9 p.m., he was still writing. The speech never made the teleprompter and was read from a rough copy. As he came to the most famous section, Johnson paused for breath. 'In that fleeting moment,' he wrote in his memoirs, 'my thoughts turned to the picket lines in Birmingham, the sit-ins in North Carolina, the marches in Selma. A picture rose before my eyes – a picture of blacks and whites marching together, side by side, chanting and singing the anthem of the civil rights movement. I raised my arms.'*

Mr Speaker, Mr President, members of the Congress, I speak tonight for the dignity of man and the destiny of democracy.

I urge every member of both parties, Americans of all religions and of all colours, from every section of this country, to join me in that cause.

At times, history and fate meet at a single time in a single place to shape a turning-point in man's unending search for freedom.

So it was at Lexington and Concord. So it was a century ago at Appomattox. So it was last week in Selma, Alabama.

There, long suffering men and women peacefully protested the denial of their rights as Americans. Many were brutally assaulted. One good man – a man of God – was killed.

There is no cause for pride in what has happened in Selma. There is no cause for self-satisfaction in the long denial of equal rights of millions of Americans. But there is cause for hope and for faith in our democracy in what is happening here tonight.

For the cries of pain and the hymns of oppressed people have summoned into convocation all the majesty of great Government – the Government of the greatest nation on earth.

Our mission is at once the oldest and the most basic of this country – to right wrong, to do justice, to serve man.

In our time we have come to live with the moments of great crisis. Our lives have been marked with debate about great issues, issues of war and peace, issues of prosperity and depression.

But rarely in any time does an issue bare the secret heart of America itself. Rarely are we met with a challenge, not to our growth or abundance, or our welfare or our security, but rather to the values and the purposes and the meaning of our beloved nation.

The issue of equal rights for American Negroes is such an issue.

And should we defeat every enemy, and should we double our wealth and conquer the stars, and still be unequal to this issue, then we will have failed as a people and as a nation.

For, with a country as with a person, 'What is a man profited if he shall gain the whole world, and lose his own soul?'

There is no Negro problem. There is no Southern problem. There is no Northern problem. There is only an American problem.

And we are met here tonight as Americans – not as Democrats or Republicans; we're met here as Americans to solve that problem.

This was the first nation in the history of the world to be founded with a purpose. The great phrases of that purpose still sound in every American heart, North and South:

'All men are created equal.' 'Government by consent of the governed.' 'Give me liberty or give me death.'

And those are not just clever words, and those are not just empty theories.

In their name Americans have fought and died for two centuries and tonight around the world they stand there as guardians of our liberty risking their lives.

Those words are promised to every citizen that he shall share in the dignity of man. This dignity cannot be found in a man's possessions. It cannot be found in his power or in his position: it really rests on his right to be treated as a man equal in opportunity to all others.

It says that he shall share in freedom. He shall choose his leaders, educate his children, provide for his family according to his ability and his merits as a human being.

To apply any other test, to deny a man his hopes because of his colour or race or his religion or the place of his birth is not only to do injustice, it is to deny America and to dishonour the dead who gave their lives for American freedom.

Our fathers believed that if this noble view of the rights of man was to flourish it must be rooted in democracy. The most basic right of all was the right to choose your own leaders.

The history of this country in large measure is the history of expansion of that right to all of our people. Many of the issues of civil rights are very complex and most difficult. But about this there can and should be no argument: every American citizen must have an equal right to vote.

There is no reason which can excuse the denial of that right. There is no duty which weighs more heavily on us than the duty we have to insure that right. Yet the harsh fact is that in many places in this country men and women are kept from voting simply because they are Negroes.

Every device of which human ingenuity is capable has been used to deny this right. The Negro citizen may go to register only to be told that the day is wrong, or the hour is late, or the official in charge is absent.

And if he persists and if he manages to present himself to the registrar, he may be disqualified because he did not spell out his middle name, or because he abbreviated a word on the application. And if he manages to fill out an application, he is given a test.

The registrar is the sole judge of whether he passes this test. He may be asked to recite the entire Constitution, or explain the most complex provisions of state law.

And even a college degree cannot be used to prove that he can read and write. For the fact is that the only way to pass these barriers is to show a white skin.

Experience has clearly shown that the existing process of law cannot overcome systematic and ingenious discrimination. No law that we now have on the books, and I have helped to put three of them there, can insure the right to vote when local officials are determined to deny it. In such a case, our duty must be clear to all of us.

The Constitution says that no person shall be kept from voting because of his race or his colour. We have all sworn an oath before God to support and to defend that Constitution. We must now act in obedience to that oath.

On Wednesday, I will send to Congress a law designed to eliminate illegal barriers to the right to vote . . .

Outside this chamber is the outraged conscience of a nation, the grave concern of many nations and the harsh judgement of history on our acts.

But even if we pass this bill the battle will not be over.

What happened in Selma is part of a far larger movement which reaches into every section and state of America. It is the effort of American Negroes to secure for themselves the full blessings of American life.

Their cause must be our cause too. Because it's not just Negroes but really it's all of us who must overcome the crippling legacy of bigotry and injustice. And we shall overcome.

As a man whose roots go deeply into Southern soil, I know how agonizing racial feelings are. I know how difficult it is to reshape the attitudes and the structure of our society. But a century has passed – more than one hundred years – since the Negro was freed.

And he is not fully free tonight.

It was more than one hundred years ago that Abraham Lincoln – a great President of another party – signed the Emancipation Proclamation. But emancipation is a proclamation and not a fact.

A century has passed – more than one hundred years – since equality was promised, and yet the Negro is not equal.

A century has passed since the day of promise, and the promise is unkept. The time of justice has now come, and I tell you that I believe sincerely that no force can hold it back. It is right in the eyes of man and God that it should come, and when it does, I think that day will brighten the lives of every American.

For Negroes are not the only victims. How many white children have gone uneducated? How many white families have lived in stark poverty? How many white lives have been scarred by fear, because we wasted energy and our substance to maintain the barriers of hatred and terror?

And so I say to all of you here and to all in the nation tonight that those who appeal to you to hold on to the past do so at the cost of denying you your future. This great rich, restless country can offer opportunity and education and hope to all – all, black and white, all, North and South, sharecropper and city dweller.

These are the enemies: poverty, ignorance, disease. They are our enemies, not our fellow man, not our neighbour. And these enemies too – poverty, disease and ignorance – we shall overcome.

*The speech was seen as the zenith of the first three years of Johnson's presidency. Johnson signed the Voting Rights Bill four months later on 6 August.*

•

ROY JENKINS
London, 23 May 1966

*'This is the goal'*

*Roy Jenkins (1920–2003) was one of the great reforming Labour home secretaries of twentieth-century British politics as well as one of the best chancellors. He quickly determined to strike a more upbeat note on race relations and wanted to provide a 'favourable splash' for the launching of Mark Bonham Carter as the first chairman of the new Race Relations Board. The speech was memorable in its definition of racial integration, which became one of the most provocative issues in British politics in the 1960s.*

*The weekend before the speech Jenkins stayed in the Provost's Lodge at King's College, Cambridge. 'On the Saturday evening,' he wrote in his memoirs, 'we went to the Founder's Obit Service in the chapel, during which, in the obscurity of the provostial stalls, I continued to scribble away . . .' That was when he wrote the passage about the universities and culture, of which he was subsequently 'rather proud'.*

Integration is perhaps rather a loose word. I do not regard it as meaning the loss, by immigrants, of their own national characteristics and culture. I do not think that we need in this country a 'melting-pot', which will turn everybody out in a common mould, as one of a series of carbon copies of someone's misplaced vision of the stereotyped Englishman.

It would be bad enough if that were to occur to the relatively few in this country who happen to have pure Anglo-Saxon blood in their veins. If it were to happen to the rest of us, to the Welsh (like myself), to the Scots, to the Irish, to the Jews, to the mid-European, and to still more recent arrivals, it would be little short of a national disaster. It would deprive us of most of the positive advantages of immigration, which, as I shall develop in a moment, I believe to be very great indeed.

I define integration, therefore, not as a flattening process of assimilation but as equal opportunity, accompanied by cultural diversity, in an atmosphere of mutual tolerance. This is the goal. We may fall a little short of its full attainment, as have other communities both in the past and in the present. But if we are to maintain any sort of world reputation for civilized living and social cohesion, we must get far nearer to its achievement than is the case today. In so far as this is something which can be brought about by Government action, this is now a Home Office responsibility. I welcome this. We have traditionally had the responsibility for the control of admission – of aliens for many years past, and more recently of Commonwealth citizens. I regard this as a distasteful but necessary duty. My instincts are all against the restriction of free movement, whether for work or education or pleasure, from one country to another. Distasteful though it may be, however, it remains a duty.

In present circumstances we are bound, as almost everyone now recognizes, to contain the flow of immigrants within the economic and social capacity of the country to absorb them – the social factor being for the moment, I believe, more restrictive than the economic. There are of course differing views about that absorptive capacity, but the Government has a clear responsibility to see that it is not put so high as to create a widespread resistance to effective integration policies. Equally it must not be so unreasonably low as to create an embittered sense of apartness in the immigrant community itself. But this will depend, in my view, not only on the numerical decisions but on the way these decisions are administered; and it is my firm intention to do so as sympathetically as I possibly can, especially when dealing with hard borderline cases.

There are some people, many of them by no means illiberal, who believe that if everybody would only stay at home in their own countries, the world would be a much easier and better place. From this view I firmly dissent. Easier it might conceivably be, but certainly not better or more civilized or innovating.

For centuries past this and every other country which has played a part in the mainstream of world events has benefited immensely from its immigrants. Some of them came in much more aggressive ways than those we are discussing today, but at least from the Norman Conquest, to the wave of German and Austrian and Czechoslovak refugees in the thirties, we have been constantly stimulated and jolted out of our natural island lethargy by a whole series of immigrations. Those who came were always made unwelcome by some people, but they have rarely failed to make a contribution out of proportion to their numbers. If anyone doubts this let them look at British business today, and at the phenomenal extent to which the more successful companies have been founded – or rejuvenated – by men whose origin was outside these islands.

But this is not merely a matter of business. Where in the world is there a university which could preserve its fame, or a cultural centre which would keep its eminence, or a metropolis which could hold its drawing power if it were to turn inwards and serve only its own hinterland and its own racial group? To live apart, for a person, a city, a country, is to lead a life of declining intellectual stimulation.

Nor should we underestimate the special contribution which has been made by the recent immigrants from the West Indies, from India and Pakistan, and from other Commonwealth countries. Some are highly gifted with outstanding talents in a wide variety of human activities. They and many others are making a major contribution to our national welfare and prosperity. They work in our hospitals as doctors and nurses, they build houses and run transport services in our cities. They help to fill the many labour shortages, particularly in urban areas, particularly in vital but undermanned public services which go with a full employment society.

Let there be no suggestion therefore that immigration, in reasonable numbers, is a cross we have to bear, and no pretence that if only those who have come could find jobs back at home, our problems could be at an end. So far from this being the case, our doctor shortage would become still more chronic; many of our hospitals and institutions, particularly those performing tasks (like the care of the aged) which are medically unglamorous but socially essential, would have to close down; and our urban public transport systems would be reduced to skeleton services with mounting public inconvenience and a disastrous effect upon private car road congestion.

There is therefore no overall rational basis for resentment of the coloured immigrant population in our midst. Far from hindering our successful national development, they positively help it. But resentment does not always spring from rational causes, particularly when, as is the case with coloured immigrants, their skin and their cultural differences make them natural targets for those who are looking for scapegoats.

A few people, whether out of political opportunism or personal inadequacy, have deliberately whipped up prejudice, playing on fear and ignorance, and blaming the immigrants for problems which were none of their making – but which stemmed from previous parsimony in housing, schools and welfare services. Of course there are some who have legitimate individual grievances against an immigrant, just as white men can have against white men, or black men against black men. But this is not the root of the problem. The root is community prejudice, and it is that with which, whether it springs from fear or inadequacy or less reputable motives, we have to deal.

I say *have to deal* because I am perfectly sure, first, that American experience, although it can sometimes be misleading in this field, shows clearly that this is not a problem which solves itself without positive action; and, secondly, because, unless we can solve it this will be a major blot on our record for the rest of this century, a constant source of weakness abroad, a handicap to full economic development . . .

The task which confronts us all is a crucial but not a daunting one. We have a population which is only two per cent coloured, although the proportion is of course appreciably higher in some areas. More important perhaps is the fact that we have as yet no established habit of hostility or bitterness on either side of the colour frontier. Such a habit could grow and grow quickly but it is hardly there yet. The problem is too new for that. We therefore start not indeed with a clean slate – there are already a few ugly marks upon it, but they are still relatively few.

But what we do have in this country is a great absorptive and adaptative tradition. For three centuries we have softened civil conflicts and adjusted our political system to the demands of a constantly changing economic and class structure. The problem we are discussing today makes less demands upon our capacity for tolerance and change than many which we have successfully surmounted in the past. But the way in which we face it, particularly in the next few years, can have a great effect upon our future. If we overcome we shall have a new message to offer the world. If we fail we shall be building up, both inside and outside the country, vast difficulties for future generations of English people.

·

# ROBERT KENNEDY
## Cape Town, 7 June 1966

### 'A tiny ripple of hope'

*The address by Robert Kennedy (1925–68) to the National Union of South African Students' Day of Affirmation, an annual protest affirming the students' commitment to human liberty and academic freedom in the face of government oppression, was his finest speech.*

*As Attorney-General in his brother's administration, Robert Kennedy had championed civil rights for black Americans. After his election as senator for New York in 1965, he began campaigning for the Democratic nomination for the presidency in 1968 and won wide support from the blacks and underprivileged.*

*His visit to South Africa was ignored by the Verwoerd Government but there was pandemonium when Kennedy arrived at the University of Cape Town where he was greeted by a crowd of 18,000. An unlit Grecian torch, carried at the head of the procession, symbolized the fate of academic freedom in South Africa.*

*In a speech that skilfully placed the South African struggle for freedom in the context of the worldwide campaign to break down the barriers of nationality, race and class, Kennedy expressed his fundamental political philosophy. He spoke not only to the students of South Africa but to the youth of the world.*

We stand here in the name of freedom.

At the heart of that Western freedom and democracy is the belief that the individual man, the child of God, is the touchstone of value and all society, groups, the state, exist for his benefit. Therefore the enlargement of liberty for individual human beings must be the supreme goal and the abiding practice of any Western society.

The first element of this individual liberty is the freedom of speech.

The right to express and communicate ideas, to set oneself apart from the dumb beasts of field and forest; to recall governments to their duties and obligations; above all, the right to affirm one's membership and allegiance to the body politic – to society – to the men with whom we share our land, our heritage and our children's future.

Hand in hand with freedom of speech goes the power to be heard – to share in the decisions of government which shape men's lives. Everything that makes life worthwhile – family, work, education, a place to rear one's children and a place to rest one's head – all this rests on decisions of government; all can be swept away by a government which does not heed the demands of its people. Therefore, the essential humanity of men can be protected and preserved only where government must answer – not just to those of a particular religion, or a particular race; but to all its people.

And even government by the consent of the governed, as in our own Constitution, must be limited in its power to act against its people: so that there may be no interference with the right to worship, or with the security of the home; no arbitrary imposition of pains or penalties by officials high or low; no restriction on the freedom of men to seek education or work or opportunity of any kind, so that each man may become all he is capable of becoming.

These are the sacred rights of Western society. These are the essential differences between us and Nazi Germany as they were between Athens and Persia.

They are the essence of our difference with Communism today. I am inalterably opposed to Communism because it exalts the state over the individual and the family, and because of the lack of freedom of speech, of protest, of religion and of the press, which is characteristic of totalitarian states.

The way of opposition to Communism is not to imitate its dictatorship, but to enlarge individual human freedom – in our own countries and all over the globe. There are those in every land who would label as 'Communist' every threat to their privilege. But as I have seen on my travels in all sections of the world, reform is not Communism. And the denial of freedom, in whatever name, only strengthens the very Communism it claims to oppose.

For two centuries, my own country has struggled to overcome the self-imposed handicap of prejudice and discrimination based on nationality, social class or race – discrimination profoundly repugnant to the theory and command of our Constitution. Even as my father grew up in Boston, signs told him that 'No Irish need apply.'

Two generations later President Kennedy became the first Catholic to head the nation; but how many men of ability had, before 1961, been denied the opportunity to contribute to the nation's progress because they were Catholic, or of Irish extraction.

In the last five years, the winds of change have blown as fiercely in the United States as anywhere in the world. But they will not – they cannot – abate.

For there are millions of Negroes untrained for the simplest of jobs, and thousands every day denied their full equal rights under the law; and the violence of the disinherited, the insulted and injured, looms over the streets of Harlem and Watts and Southside Chicago.

But a Negro American trains as an astronaut, one of mankind's first explorers into outer space; another is the chief barrister of the United States Government, and dozens sit on the benches of court; and another, Dr Martin Luther King, is the second man of African descent to win the Nobel Peace Prize for his nonviolent efforts for social justice between the races.

We must recognize the full human equality of all our people – before God, before the law, and in the councils of government. We must do this not because it is economically advantageous – although it is; not because the laws of God and man command it – although they do command it; not because people in other lands wish it so. We must do it for the single and fundamental reason that it is the right thing to do.

And this must be our commitment outside our borders as it is within.

It is your job, the task of the young people of this world, to strip the last remnants of that ancient, cruel belief from the civilization of man.

Each nation has different obstacles and different goals, shaped by the vagaries of history and experience. Yet as I talk to young people around the world I am impressed not by diversity but by the closeness of their goals, their desires and concerns and hope for the future. There is discrimination in New York, apartheid in South

Africa and serfdom in the mountains of Peru. People starve in the streets in India; intellectuals go to jail in Russia; thousands are slaughtered in Indonesia; wealth is lavished on armaments everywhere. These are differing evils. But they are the common works of man.

And therefore they call upon common qualities of conscience and of indignation, a shared determination to wipe away the unnecessary sufferings of our fellow human beings at home and particularly around the world.

It is these qualities which make of youth today the only true international community. More than this I think that we could agree on what kind of a world we want to build. It would be a world of independent nations, moving towards international community, each of which protected and respected basic human freedoms. It would be a world which demanded of each government that it accept its responsibility to insure social justice.

Just to the north here are lands of challenge and opportunity – rich in natural resources, land and minerals and people. Yet they are also lands confronted by the greatest odds – overwhelming ignorance, internal tensions and strife, and an often destructive and hostile nature. Many of these nations, as colonies, were oppressed and exploited. Yet they have not estranged themselves from the broad traditions of the West; they are hoping and gambling their progress and stability on the chance that we will meet our responsibilities to help them overcome their poverty.

In another world, cleansed of hate and fear and artificial barriers, South Africa could play an outstanding role in that effort. This is without question a pre-eminent repository of the wealth and knowledge and skill of the continent. Here are the greater part of Africa's research scientists and steel production, most of its reservoirs of coal and electric power. In your faculties and councils, here in this very audience, are hundreds and thousands of men who could transform the lives of millions for all time to come.

But that help cannot be accepted if we – within our own countries or in our relations with others – deny individual integrity and the common humanity of man.

Our answer is the world's hope; it is to rely on youth. The cruelties and obstacles of this swiftly changing planet will not yield to obsolete dogmas and outworn slogans. It cannot be moved by those who cling to a present which is already dying, who prefer the illusion of security to the excitement of danger.

It demands the qualities of youth: not a time of life but a state of mind, a temper of the will, a quality of the imagination, a predominance of courage over timidity, of the appetite for adventure over the love of ease.

As I have seen, and as I have said – in Europe, in Asia, in Latin America, and now in South Africa – it is a revolutionary world we live in; and thus, I have said in Latin America, in Asia, in Europe and in the United States, it is young people who must take the lead.

'There is,' said an Italian philosopher, 'nothing more difficult to take in hand, more perilous to conduct, or more uncertain in its success than to take the lead in the introduction of a new order of things.' Yet this is the measure of the task of your generation and the road is strewn with many dangers.

First, is the danger of futility; the belief there is nothing one man or one woman can do against the enormous array of the world's ills – against misery and ignorance, injustice and violence. Yet many of the world's great movements of thought and action have flowed from the world of a single man. A young monk began the Protestant Reformation, a young general extended an empire from Macedonia to the borders of the earth and a young woman reclaimed the territory of France.

Each time a man stands up for an ideal, or acts to improve the lot of others, or strikes out against injustice, he sends forth a tiny ripple of hope, and crossing each other from a million different centres of energy and daring, those ripples build a current that can sweep down the mightiest walls of oppression and resistance.

The second danger is that of practicality; of those who say that hopes and beliefs must bend before immediate necessities. Of course if we would act effectively we must deal with the world as it is. We must get things done.

But if there was one thing President Kennedy stood for that touched the most profound feeling of young people across the world, it was the belief that idealism, high aspirations and deep convictions are not incompatible with the most practical and efficient of programmes – that there is no basic inconsistency between ideals and realistic possibilities – no separation between the deepest desires of heart and mind and the rational application of human effort to human problems.

A third danger is timidity. For every ten men who are willing to face the guns of an enemy there is only one willing to brave the disapproval of his fellow, the censure of his colleagues, the wrath of his society. Moral courage is a rarer commodity than bravery in battle or great intelligence. Yet it is the one essential, vital quality for those who seek to change a world which yields most painfully to change.

For the fortunate among us is comfort; the temptation to follow the easy and familiar paths of personal ambition and financial success so grandly spread before those who have the privilege of education. But that is not the road history has marked out for us.

There is a Chinese curse which says, 'May he live in interesting times.' Like it or not, we live in interesting times. They are times of danger and uncertainty; but they are also more open to the creative energy of men than any other time in history. And everyone here will ultimately be judged – will ultimately judge himself – on the effort he has contributed to building a new world society and the extent to which his ideals and goals have shaped that effort.

So we part, I to my country and you to remain. We are – if a man of forty can claim that privilege – fellow members of the world's largest younger generation. Each of us have our own work to do. I know at times you must feel very alone with your problems and difficulties. But I want to say how impressed I am with what you stand for and the effort you are making.

Like the young people of my own country and of every country I have visited, you are in many ways more closely united to these brothers of your time than to the older generations in your nation; determined to build a better future; that you know, as President Kennedy said to the youth of my country, that 'the energy, the faith, the devotion which we bring to this endeavour will light our country and all who serve it – and the glow from that fire can truly light the world.'

*Robert Kennedy won a thundering ovation. Two years later, after winning the California primary election, he was shot and died on 6 June. On the stark white wall over his grave is carved a sentence from his South African speech: 'Each time a man stands up for an ideal, or acts to improve the lot of others, or strikes out against injustice, he sends forth a tiny ripple of hope.'*

•

## EUGENE McCARTHY
Chicago, 2 December 1967

### *'The decent opinion of mankind'*

*After waiting in vain for Senator Robert Kennedy ( John F. Kennedy's brother) to move against President Johnson, the Minnesota Democrat Senator Eugene McCarthy (1916–91) announced his candidacy for the presidential nomination in 1968 and won forty per cent of the vote in the New Hampshire primary. His move prompted Johnson to stand down and Kennedy to enter the race. He was in sight of winning the nomination when he was assassinated. Hubert Humphrey became the candidate.*

*As the Vietnam dissenters awaited the politician who would speak for them, McCarthy lit the candle in this December speech to the Conference of Concerned Democrats. The critical word in America's new vocabulary, he declared, was war – war on poverty, ignorance, crime, pollution, none of which could be solved by war.*

But we do have one war which is properly called a war – the war in Vietnam, which is central to all of the problems of America.

A war of questionable legality and questionable constitutionality.

A war which is diplomatically indefensible; the first war in this century in which the United States, which at its founding made an appeal to the decent opinion of mankind in the Declaration of Independence, finds itself without the support of the decent opinion of mankind.

A war which cannot be defended in the context of the judgement of history. It is being presented in the context of an historical judgement of an era which is past. Munich appears to be the starting point of history for the secretary of state and for those who attempt to support his policies. What is necessary is a realization that the United States is a part of the movement of history itself; that it cannot stand apart, attempting to control the world by imposing covenants and treaties and by violent military intervention; that our role is not to police the planet but to use military strength with restraint and within limits, while at the same time we make available to the world the great power of our economy, of our knowledge, and of our goodwill.

A war which is not defensible even in military terms, which runs contrary to the advice of our greatest generals – Eisenhower, Ridgway, Bradley, and MacArthur – all of whom admonished us against becoming involved in a land war in Asia. Events have proved them right, as estimate after estimate as to the time of success and the military commitment necessary to success has had to be revised – always upward: more troops, more extensive bombing, a widening and intensification of the war. Extension and intensification have been the rule, and projection after projection of success have been proved wrong.

With the escalation of our military commitment has come a parallel of overleaping of objectives: from protecting South Vietnam, to nation building in South Vietnam, to protecting all of Southeast Asia, and ultimately to suggesting that the safety and security of the United States itself is at stake.

Finally, it is a war which is morally wrong. The most recent statement of objectives cannot be accepted as an honest judgement as to why we are in Vietnam. It has become increasingly difficult to justify the methods we are using and the instruments of war which we are using as we have moved from limited targets and somewhat restricted weapons to greater variety and more destructive instruments of war, and also have extended the area of operations almost to the heart of North Vietnam.

Even assuming that both objectives and methods can be defended, the war cannot stand the test of proportion and of prudent judgement. It is no longer possible to prove that the good that may come with what is called victory, or projected as victory, is proportionate to the loss of life and property and to other disorders that follow from this war . . .

Beyond all of these considerations, two further judgements must be passed: a judgement of individual conscience, and another in the broader context of the movement of history itself.

The problem of individual conscience is, I think, set most clearly before us in the words of Charles Péguy in writing about the Dreyfus case: 'a single injustice, a single crime, a single illegality, if it is officially recorded, . . . will bring about the loss of one's honour, the dishonour of a whole people.'

And the broader historical judgement as suggested by Arnold Toynbee in his comments on Rome's war with Carthage: 'Nemesis is a potent goddess . . . War posthumously avenges the dead on the survivors, and the vanquished on the victors. The nemesis of war is intrinsic. It did not need the invention of the atomic weapon to make this apparent. It was illustrated more than two thousand years before our time, by Hannibal's legacy to Rome. Hannibal gained a posthumous victory over Rome. Although he failed to defeat the great nation militarily because of the magnitude of her military manpower and solidity of the structure of the Roman Commonwealth, he did succeed in inflicting grievous wounds on the Commonwealth's body social and economic. They were so grievous that they festered into the revolution that was precipitated by Tiberius Gracchus and that did not cease till it was arrested by Augustus a hundred years later . . . This revolution,' Toynbee said, 'was the nemesis of Rome's superficially triumphant career of military conquest,' and ended, of course, the Republic and substituted for it the spirit of the dictators and of the Caesars.

Those of us who are gathered here tonight are not advocating peace at any price. We are willing to pay a high price for peace – for an honourable, rational, and political solution to this war, a solution which will enhance our world position, which will permit us to give the necessary attention to our other commitments abroad, both military and nonmilitary, and leave us with both human and physical resources and with moral energy to deal effectively with the pressing domestic problems of the United States itself.

I see little evidence that the administration has set any limits on the price which it will pay for a military victory which becomes less and less sure and more hollow and empty in promise.

The scriptural promise of the good life is one in which the old men see visions and the young men dream dreams. In the context of this war and all of its implications, the young men of America do not dream dreams, but many live in the nightmare of moral anxiety, of concern and great apprehension; and the old men, instead of visions which they can offer to the young, are projecting, in the language of the secretary of state, a spectre of one billion Chinese threatening the peace and safety of the world . . . a frightening and intimidating future.

The message from the administration today is a message of apprehension, a message of fear, yes – even a message of fear of fear.

This is not the real spirit of America. I do not believe that it is. This is a time to test the mood and spirit:

To offer in place of doubt – trust.

In place of expediency – right judgement.

In place of ghettos, let us have neighbourhoods and communities.

In place of incredibility – integrity.

In place of murmuring, let us have clear speech; let us again hear America singing.

In place of disunity, let us have dedication of purpose.

In place of near despair, let us have hope.

This is the promise of greatness which was stated for us by Adlai Stevenson and which was brought to form and positive action in the words and actions of John Kennedy.

Let us pick up again these lost strands and weave them again into the fabric of America.

Let us sort out the music from the sounds and again respond to the trumpet and the steady drum.

•

# MELINA MERCOURI
## Washington, 23 January 1968

### *'We will be free'*

*The Greek film actress and politician Melina Mercouri (1923–94) was born into a political family. Her grandfather was mayor of Athens and her father was deputy mayor and Minister of State. Against her parents' wishes, she became an actress and is still remembered for her dazzling performance in the film* Never on Sunday. *After 1967, however, she devoted all her energy to campaigning against the military junta – the Greek colonels – who seized power and imposed a dictatorship in 1967. She was declared an enemy of the state and lived in exile in Paris and the United States.*

*She made this powerful speech to the Women's Democratic Club. This is the first half. She went on to plead with the United States to help Greece instead of aiding the colonels and asked: 'Is America the moral leader of the world – or is it not?'*

I have been asked to speak on the subject 'The Artist and Politics'. I'll try to do so. But I must immediately tell you that I consider the artist no less a citizen than anyone else. And I believe that those who say the artist has no place in politics not only would strip him of his citizenship but would also deny all of history. I know that some artists have accepted the address of the ivory tower. Perhaps they are comfortable, but they collaborate with those who want them excluded from the movement of the world.

I am an artist by vocation and profession. I am a citizen by obligation and responsibility. And as an actress I am happiest when I work in a play or a film that makes both artistic and social contribution.

There is a beautiful story about Picasso. It was during the Nazi occupation in France. The great painter was summoned to Gestapo headquarters. He found a Nazi officer studying one of Picasso's most famous paintings. The canvas depicted the brutal destruction of the town of Guernica by the Nazis during the Spanish Civil War. The Gestapo man looked with menace at Picasso and pointed to the painting.

'Did you do this?' he asked. Picasso looked at the Nazi and said, 'No, you did.'

That was a fine moment. A moment when the artist and the citizen were one. I am a Greek artist, a Greek citizen. Technically, perhaps there might be some question of this. When the military junta seized power in Greece and destroyed the constitution and the freedom of my people, I spoke out against them. The colonels then declared me *anti-Greek*. They announced that my citizenship was taken away and my property confiscated. Perhaps they have the means to take my property. That is physical and tangible. But my citizenship is within me. I drank it with my mother's milk. It is my identity. It is my love for Greece, for my friends, for Greek music and art.

It is my soul. And as the Russian girl says in the story, 'My soul they cannot touch.'

Like everything else, dictatorship has its textbooks and manuals. One of the first things to do is to silence the artist. The artist by his very nature, must have the most immediate, the most intimate contact with people. His life is communication. And dictatorship would keep the people incommunicado. So beware of the artist who *informs*, who exposes, who inspires, who enflames. Silence the composer Mikis Theodorakis. He might write another 'La Marseillaise'. Beware even of the dead. Sophocles, Euripides, Aeschylus, those giant artists, those giant citizens, are censored in Greece. They are dangerous because they wrote of freedom and the excellence of man. This junta stands for slavery and the degradation of man.

The artist is never attacked as such. Ibsen, Shelley, Byron, Keats, Picasso, Leger, Rivera, Joyce, Sinyavsky, Pasternak, Miller, Charlie Chaplin and countless more all through history, were attacked not because they were artists, but because they used their art to uplift, to expose, to protest, to make man better, to make man free.

So, I think I have made myself clear. I am here to talk politically. *Politically*, not *politics*. I am not a politician. Politicians are more dangerous than artists and often funnier.

In 1964 the people of Greece having fought for free elections proceeded to choose the Centre-Union Party to govern Greece. They elected George Papandreou to be prime minister. And this by a majority without precedent in Greece. I will immediately confess to you that I am not an admirer of George Papandreou but, of course, that is beside the point. The people of Greece voted for him. I was not quite sure of his liberalism but to the conservatives and the extreme right wing he was considered a dangerous radical. He *did* talk of reform, a more fair distribution of wealth and free education. This obviously made him a Bolshevik. He took every opportunity to denounce the Communists in Greece, but that did not stop his enemies from calling him a 'sympathizer', a 'fellow traveller' or a 'bedfellow'. We know these clichés in Greece just as well as you do. But it didn't work. His popular support remained strong.

Yet on 15 July 1965, Greece was stunned to learn that he had been dismissed from office by King Constantine and his government was dissolved. The country was shocked. The eyebrows of constitutional experts were raised in horror.

Why was he so rudely and illegally dismissed? He and his son Andreas, the Minister of Economic Co-ordination, insisted that the army needed some reorganization. They naively believed that the army's loyalty should be to the constitution and the government and not to the extreme right or to the palace.

And in 1967 the world learned how right they were.

On 21st April of that year the army tanks crashed through the streets of Athens and democracy was destroyed.

But let me talk a little of those two years between 1965 and 1967. Nothing makes me angrier than to read those so-called 'authorities' who say that prior to the coming of the junta, Greece was in political chaos. I have seen this statement repeated a thousand times and it makes my blood boil. Who created this chaos?

For two years after the dismissal of the freely elected government the palace made repeated attempts to create a government of its own. But always with unpopular, right-wing elements and not one of them could stand up. It drives me crazy to hear this chaos attributed to the forces of democracy. You all remember the definition of the

Hebrew word 'chutzpah'. 'Chutzpah' is when a man kills his mother and father and then asks for clemency on the grounds that he is an orphan.

I shall not dwell upon the role of King Constantine except to make a short review. He created the crisis. Then when the junta came, and all of Greece would have supported him if he opposed them, he made no move. He himself swore in the junta. He himself collaborated in the elimination from the army of all democratic elements. He said that he behaved this way to spare Greece from shedding its blood. But eight months later when he saw his own position threatened, he asked the Greek people to shed its blood to save his crown. His counter-coup was a pitiful operetta, a masterpiece of ineptitude, a tragic farce. Now he is in Rome working out a deal for an ignominious return. He is a king without a people, a king of shreds and patches. And I charge that those individuals and those governments who are working for his return do so with the knowledge that he will never have the support of the people. So here we are. Greece that made the gift of democracy to the world is in chains. The constitution destroyed, parliament dissolved, trade unions illegal. The civil services, the schools, the church have been purged. The press, the artist, totally censored and muzzled. The court martials make a mockery of justice. The junta rules by terror, by imprisonment and by torture. And when I say torture, it is not a phrase. The authenticated stories and checked reports of inhuman tortures are at the same time revolting and heartbreaking. I shall spare you the details but if you really want to know them ask me and I will tell you. And then there is the most horrible crime of all, the plot to corrupt the youth of Greece. The school system is being completely revised, the textbooks are being rewritten, teachers who believe in democracy are thrown out of the schools. The young people are being taught ideals that are Nazi. The junta's intention is to create a generation of fascists. And so there is the most terrible of fears, the father afraid of his son. The son afraid of his father, the teacher afraid of his student.

How then are the Greek people to understand the apologists for this medieval, this barbarous regime? I could understand approval from the dead Hitler, from the dead Mussolini, from the dead Stalin, but how can I understand the *live* Dean Acheson?

In a letter to the *Washington Post*, Mr Acheson expressed an opinion that authoritarian rule is what the Greeks need. Now we all know that Mr Acheson is an honourable man, yet he comes to bury democracy in Greece. He is an honourable man and he adds his spadeful of earth into democracy's grave. Evil tongues say that Mr Acheson has a pique against the former Greek government because they rejected his solution to the Cyprus issue. I must doubt this because Mr Acheson is an honourable man. It is his honourable judgement that the people of Greece are ignorant and backward and not ready for democracy. I am only an unlearned actress and the honourable Mr Acheson is a former secretary of state, yet I will stand up to my full height and say, 'Mr Secretary, you are wrong. You are tragically wrong. We know the meaning of democracy. We invented it. We will refuse your counsel, Mr Secretary. We will be free.'

*The speech was read into the Congressional record by Don Edwards of California. Mercouri returned to Greece in 1974 after the fall of the colonels and became Minister of Culture from 1981 to 1990. She led the campaign, so far unsuccessful, to persuade the British government to return the Elgin Marbles.*

•

## LYNDON B. JOHNSON
Washington, DC, 31 March 1968

*'I shall not seek nor will I accept nomination as your president'*

*As America sank deeper into the quagmire of the Vietnam War in 1968, President Johnson was spiritually and physically exhausted. Television screens were filled with images of horror showing the devastation of Vietnam, the sufferings of its people and the sufferings of American soldiers.*

*On 20 January, the Vietcong launched the Tet offensive, which involved American troops in desperate battles for control of their bases at Da Nang and*

*Khe Sanh and even the grounds of the US embassy in Saigon. Robert Kennedy and Eugene McCarthy were openly campaigning for the Democratic nomination for the presidential election. Johnson, who said in his memoirs that he had always intended to retire at the end of his first full term, read the signals.*

*He hoped that by suspending the bombing of North Vietnam he would open the way to peace negotiations and accepted that his candidacy would both split the Democrats further and weaken the United States' negotiating position.*

*Johnson prepared two perorations for his speech, given from the White House at the end of March. At 9.35 p.m. and well into his speech, his mind was made up. Watched by eighty-five million Americans, his face registering powerful emotions, he glanced at his wife and raised his right arm – the prearranged signal that he was going, after all, to speak the extra words that had been prepared.*

*Then the president looked into the camera. 'Fifty-two months and ten days ago . . .' he began, and gave up his burden.*

Of those to whom much is given, much is asked. I cannot say and no man could say that no more will be asked of us.

Yet, I believe that now, no less than when the decade began, this generation of Americans is willing to 'pay any price, bear any burden, meet any hardship, support any friend, oppose any foe to assure the survival and the success of liberty'.

Since those words were spoken by John F. Kennedy, the people of America have kept that compact with mankind's noblest cause.

And we shall continue to keep it.

Yet, I believe we must always be mindful of this one thing, whatever the trials and the tests ahead. The ultimate strength of our country and our cause will lie not in powerful weapons or infinite resources or boundless wealth, but will lie in the unity of our people.

This I believe very deeply.

Throughout my entire public career I have followed the personal philosophy that I am a free man, an American, a public servant, and a member of my party, in that order always and only.

For thirty-seven years in the service of our Nation, first as a Congressman, as a Senator, and as Vice-President, and now as your President, I have put the unity of the people first. I have put it ahead of any divisive partisanship.

And in these times as in times before, it is true that a house divided against itself by the spirit of faction, of party, of region, of religion, of race, is a house that cannot stand.

There is division in the American house now. There is divisiveness among us all tonight. And holding the trust that is mine, as President of all the people, I cannot disregard the peril to the progress of the American people and the hope and the prospect of peace for all peoples.

So, I would ask all Americans, whatever their personal interests or concern, to guard against divisiveness and all its ugly consequences.

Fifty-two months and ten days ago, in a moment of tragedy and trauma, the duties of this office fell upon me. I asked then for your help and God's, that we might continue America on its course, binding up our wounds, healing our history, moving forward in new unity, to clear the American agenda and to keep the American commitment for all of our people.

United we have kept that commitment. United we have enlarged that commitment.

Through all time to come, I think America will be a stronger nation, a more just society, and a land of greater opportunity and fulfilment because of what we have all done together in these years of unparalleled achievement.

Our reward will come in the life of freedom, peace, and hope that our children will enjoy through ages ahead.

What we won when all of our people united just must not now be lost in suspicion, distrust, selfishness, and politics among any of our people.

Believing this as I do, I have concluded that I should not permit the Presidency to become involved in the partisan divisions that are developing in this political year.

With America's sons in the fields far away, with America's future under challenge right here at home, with our hopes and the world's hopes for peace in the balance every day, I do not believe that I should devote an hour or a day of my time to any personal partisan causes or to any duties other than the awesome duties of this office – the Presidency of your country.

Accordingly, I shall not seek, and I will not accept, the nomination of my party for another term as your President.

But let men everywhere know, however, that a strong, a confident, and a vigilant America stands ready tonight to seek an honourable peace – and stands ready tonight to defend an honoured cause – whatever the price, whatever the burden, whatever the sacrifice that duty may require.

*Hubert Humphrey, Johnson's chosen successor, was narrowly defeated in the election by Richard Nixon.*

•

## ENOCH POWELL
### Birmingham, 20 April 1968

*'I seem to see "the River Tiber foaming with much blood"'*

*No speech in Britain in the past fifty years had so violent and powerful an impact on public opinion or was more notorious and memorable than the address Enoch Powell gave in Birmingham in 1968. It was one of a series of inflammatory speeches, initially attacking Kenyan Asian immigrants, which Powell's critics considered a particularly potent stimulus to racial antagonism but which nevertheless articulated the fears and prejudices of many Britons, particularly in working-class inner cities.*

*Powell had become a right-wing nationalist who had quarrelled violently with the Tory leader Edward Heath. He believed that the British Nationality Act had enabled the arrival of a big immigrant population with consequences so long ignored that when it was no longer possible for the government and parliament to remain blind to them they had become all but irremediable.*

*In this speech in April, Powell openly raised the spectre of racial conflict and called for the repatriation of black and other Commonwealth immigrants.*

The supreme function of statesmanship is to provide against preventable evils. In seeking to do so, it encounters obstacles which are deeply rooted in human nature. One is that by the very order of things such evils are not demonstrable until they have occurred: at each stage in their onset there is room for doubt and for dispute whether they be real or imaginary. By the same token, they attract little attention in comparison with current troubles, which are both indisputable and pressing. Hence the besetting temptation of all politics to concern itself with the immediate present at the expense of the future. Above all, people are disposed to mistake predicting troubles for causing troubles and even for desiring troubles: 'if only', they love to think, 'if only people wouldn't talk about it, it probably wouldn't happen'. Perhaps this habit goes back to the primitive belief that the word and the thing, the name and the object, are identical. At all events, the discussion of future grave but, with effort now, avoidable evils is the most unpopular and at the same time the most necessary occupation for the politician. Those who knowingly shirk it, deserve, and not infrequently receive, the curses of those who come after.

A week or two ago I fell into conversation with a constituent, a middle-aged, quite ordinary working man employed in one of our nationalized industries. After a sentence or two about the weather, he suddenly said: 'If I had the money to go, I wouldn't stay in this country.' I made some deprecatory reply, to the effect that even this government wouldn't last for ever; but he took no notice, and continued: 'I have three children, all of them been through grammar school and two of them married now, with family. I shan't be satisfied till I have seen them all settled overseas. In this country in fifteen or twenty years' time the black man will have the whip hand over the white man.'

I can already hear the chorus of execration. How dare I say such a horrible thing? How dare I stir up trouble and inflame feelings by repeating such a conversation? The answer is that I do not have the right not to do so. Here is a decent, ordinary fellow-Englishman, who in broad daylight in my own town says to me, his Member of Parliament, that this country will not be worth living in for his children. I simply do not have the right to shrug my shoulders and think about something else. What he is saying, thousands and hundreds of thousands are saying and thinking – not throughout Great Britain, perhaps, but in the areas that are already undergoing the total transformation to which there is no parallel in a thousand years of English history.

In fifteen or twenty years, on present trends, there will be in this country three and a half million Commonwealth immigrants and their descendants. That is not my figure. That is the official figure given to Parliament by the spokesman of the Registrar-General's office. There is no comparable official figure for the year 2000; but it must be in the region of five to seven million, approximately one-tenth of the whole population, and approaching that of Greater London. Of course, it will not be evenly distributed from Margate to Aberystwyth and from Penzance to Aberdeen. Whole areas, towns and parts of towns across England will be occupied by different sections of the immigrant and immigrant-descended population.

As time goes on, the proportion of this total who are immigrant descendants, those born in England, who arrived here by exactly the same route as the rest of us, will rapidly increase. Already by 1985 those born here would constitute the majority. It is this fact above all which creates the extreme urgency of action now, of just that kind of action which is hardest for politicians to take, action where the difficulties lie in the present but evils to be prevented or minimized lie several parliaments ahead.

The natural and rational first question for a nation confronted by such a prospect is to ask: 'How can its dimensions be reduced?' Granted it be not wholly preventable, can it be limited, bearing in mind that numbers are of the essence. The significance and consequences of an alien element introduced into a country or population are profoundly different according to whether that element is one per cent or ten per cent. The answers to the simple and rational question are equally simple and rational: by stopping, or virtually stopping, further inflow, and by promoting the maximum outflow. Both answers are part of the official policy of the Conservative Party.

It almost passes belief that at this moment twenty or thirty additional immigrant children are arriving from overseas in Wolverhampton alone every week – and that means fifteen or twenty additional families a decade or two hence. Those whom the gods wish to destroy, they first make mad. We must be mad, literally mad, as a nation to be permitting the annual inflow of some fifty thousand dependants, who are for the most part the material of the future growth of the immigrant-descended population. It is like watching a nation busily engaged in heaping up its own funeral pyre. So insane are we that we actually permit unmarried persons to immigrate for the purpose of founding a family with spouses and fiancés whom they have never seen. Let no one suppose that the flow of dependants will automatically tail off. On the contrary, even at the present admission rate of only five thousand a year by voucher, there is sufficient for a further twenty-five thousand dependants per annum *ad infinitum*, without taking into account the huge reservoir of existing relations in this country – and I am making no allowance at all for fraudulent entry. In these circumstances nothing will suffice but that the total inflow for settlement be reduced at once to negligible proportions, and that the necessary legislative and administrative measures be taken without delay. I stress the words 'for settlement'. This has nothing to do with the entry of Commonwealth citizens, any more than of aliens, into this country, for the purposes of study or of improving their qualifications, like (for instance) the Commonwealth doctors who, to the advantage of their own countries, have enabled our hospital service to be expanded faster than would otherwise have been possible. These are not, and never have been, immigrants.

I turn to re-emigration. If all immigration ended tomorrow, the rate of growth of the immigrant-descended population would be substantially reduced, but the prospective size of this element in the population would still leave the basic character of the national danger unaffected. This can only be tackled while a considerable proportion of the total still comprises persons who entered this country during the last ten years or so. Hence the urgency of implementing now the second element of the Conservative Party's policy: the encouragement of re-emigration. Nobody can make an estimate of the numbers which, with generous grants and assistance would choose either to return to their countries of origin or go to other countries anxious to receive the manpower and the skills they represent. Nobody knows, because no such policy has yet been attempted. I can only say that, even at present, immigrants in my own constituency from time to time come to me, asking if I can find them assistance to return home. If such a policy were adopted and pursued, with the determination which the gravity of the alternative justifies, the resultant outflow could appreciably alter the prospects for the future.

It can be no part of any policy that existing families should be kept divided; but there are two directions in which families can be reunited, and if our former and present immigration laws have brought about the division of families, albeit voluntary or semi-voluntary, we ought to be prepared to arrange for them to be reunited in their countries of origin. In short, suspension of immigration and encouragement of re-emigration belong together, logically and humanly, as two aspects of the same approach.

The third element of the Conservative Party's policy is that all who are in this country as citizens should be equal before the law and that there shall be no discrimination or difference made between them by public authority. As Mr Heath has put it, we will have no 'first-class citizens' and 'second-class citizens'. This does not mean that the immigrant and his descendants should be elevated into a privileged or special class or that the citizen should be denied his right to discriminate in the management of his own affairs between one fellow-citizen and another or that he should be subjected to inquisition as to his reasons and motives for behaving in one lawful manner rather than another.

There could be no grosser misconception of the realities than is entertained by those who vociferously demand legislation as they call it 'against discrimination', whether they be leaderwriters of the same kidney and sometimes on the same newspapers which year after year in the 1930s tried to blind this country to the rising peril which confronted it, or archbishops who live in palaces, faring delicately, with the bedclothes pulled right over their heads. They have got it exactly and diametrically wrong. The discrimination and the deprivation, the sense of alarm and of resentment, lies not with the immigrant population but with those among whom they have come and are still coming. This is why to enact legislation of the kind before Parliament at this moment is to risk throwing a match on to gunpowder. The kindest thing that can be said about those who propose and support it is that they know not what they do.

Nothing is more misleading than comparison between the

Commonwealth immigrant in Britain and the American Negro. The Negro population of the United States, which was already in existence before the United States became a nation, started literally as slaves and were later given the franchise and other rights of citizenship, to the exercise of which they have only gradually and still incompletely come. The Commonwealth immigrant came to Britain as a full citizen, to a country which knew no discrimination between one citizen and another, and he entered instantly into the possession of the rights of every citizen, from the vote to free treatment under the National Health Service. Whatever drawbacks attended the immigrants – and they were drawbacks which did not, and do not, make admission into Britain by hook or by crook appear less than desirable – arose not from the law or from public policy or from administration but from those personal circumstances and accidents which cause, and always will cause, the fortunes and experience of one man to be different from another's.

But while to the immigrant entry to this country was admission to privileges and opportunities eagerly sought, the impact upon the existing population was very different. For reasons which they could not comprehend, and in pursuance of a decision by default, on which they were never consulted, they found themselves made strangers in their own country. They found their wives unable to obtain hospital beds in childbirth, their children unable to obtain school places, their homes and neighbourhoods changed beyond recognition, their plans and prospects for the future defeated; at work they found that employers hesitated to apply to the immigrant worker the standards of discipline and competence required of the native-born worker; they began to hear, as time went by, more and more voices which told them that they were now the unwanted. On top of this, they now learn that a one-way privilege is to be established by Act of Parliament: a law, which cannot, and is not intended, to operate to protect them or redress their grievances, is to be enacted to give the stranger, the disgruntled and the *agent provocateur* the power to pillory them for their private actions.

In the hundreds upon hundreds of letters I received when I last spoke on this subject two or three months ago, there was one striking feature which was largely new and which I find ominous. All Members of Parliament are used to the typical anonymous correspondent; but what surprised and alarmed me was the high proportion of ordinary, decent, sensible people, writing a rational and often well-educated letter, who believed that they had to omit their address because it was dangerous to have committed themselves to paper to a Member of Parliament agreeing with the views I had expressed, and that they would risk either penalties or reprisals if they were known to have done so. The sense of being a persecuted minority which is growing among ordinary English people in the areas of the country which are affected is something that those without direct experience can hardly imagine. I am going to allow just one of those hundreds of people to speak for me. She did give her name and address, which I have detached from the letter which I am about to read. She was writing from Northumberland about something which is happening at this moment in my own constituency:

Eight years ago in a respectable street in Wolverhampton a house was sold to a Negro. Now only one white (a woman old-age pensioner) lives there. This is her story. She lost her husband and both her sons in the war. So she turned her seven-roomed house, her only asset, into a boarding house. She worked hard and did well, paid off her mortgage and began to put something by for her old age. Then the immigrants moved in. With growing fear, she saw one house after another taken over. The quiet street became a place of noise and confusion. Regretfully, her white tenants moved out.

The day after the last one left, she was awakened at 7 a.m. by two Negroes who wanted to use her phone to contact their employer. When she refused, as she would have refused any stranger at such an hour, she was abused and feared she would have been attacked but for the chain on her door. Immigrant families have tried to rent rooms in her house, but she always refused. Her little store of money went, and after paying her rates, she has less than £2 per week. She went to apply for a rate reduction and was seen by a young girl, who on hearing she had a seven-roomed house, suggested she should let part of it. When she said the only people she could get were Negroes, the girl said 'racial prejudice won't get you anywhere in this country'. So she went home.

The telephone is her lifeline. Her family pay the bill, and help her out as best they can. Immigrants have offcred to buy her house – at a price which the prospective landlord would be able to recover from his tenants in weeks, or at most a few months. She is becoming afraid to go out. Windows are broken. She finds excreta pushed through her letterbox. When she goes to the shops, she is followed by children, charming, wide-grinning piccaninnies. They cannot speak English, but one word they know. 'Racialist', they chant. When the new Race Relations Bill is passed, this woman is convinced she will go to prison. And is she so wrong? I begin to wonder.

The other dangerous delusion from which those who are wilfully or otherwise blind to realities suffer, is summed up in the word 'integration'. To be integrated into a population means to become for all practical purposes indistinguishable from its other members. Now, at all times, where there are marked physical differences, especially of colour, integration is difficult, though over a period, not impossible. There are among the Commonwealth immigrants who have come to live here in the last fifteen years or so, many thousands whose wish and purpose is to be integrated and whose every thought and endeavour is bent in that direction. But to imagine that such a thing enters the heads of a great and growing majority of immigrants and their descendants is a ludicrous misconception, and a dangerous one to boot.

We are on the verge of a change. Hitherto it has been force of circumstance and of background which has rendered the very idea of integration inaccessible to the greater part of the immigrant population – that they never conceived or intended such a thing, and that their numbers and physical concentration meant the pressures towards integration which normally bear upon any small minority did not operate. Now we are seeing the growth of positive forces acting against integration, of vested interests in the preservation and sharpening of racial and religious differences, with a view to the exercise of actual domination, first over fellow-immigrants and then over the rest of the population. The cloud no bigger than a man's hand, that can so rapidly overcast the sky, has been visible recently in Wolverhampton and has shown signs of spreading quickly. The words I am about to use, verbatim as they appeared in the local press of 17 February [1968], are not mine, but those of a Labour Member of Parliament who is a Minister in the Government. 'The Sikh community's campaign to maintain customs inappropriate in Britain is much to be regretted. Working in Britain, particularly in the public services, they should be prepared to accept the terms and conditions of their employment. To claim special communal rights (or should one say rites?) leads to a dangerous fragmentation within society. This communalism is a canker; whether practised by one colour or another it is to be strongly condemned.' All credit to John Stonehouse for having had the insight to perceive that, and the courage to say it.

For these dangerous and divisive elements the legislation proposed in the Race Relations Bill is the very pabulum they need to flourish. Here is the means of showing that the immigrant communities can organize to consolidate their members, to agitate and campaign against their fellow-citizens, and to overawe and dominate the rest with legal weapons which the ignorant and the ill-informed have provided. As I look ahead, I am filled with foreboding. Like the Roman, I seem to see 'the River Tiber foaming with much blood'. The tragic and intractable phenomenon which we watch with horror on the other side of the Atlantic but which there is interwoven with the history and existence of the States itself, is coming upon us here by our own volition and our own neglect. Indeed, it has all but come. In numerical terms, it will be of American proportions long before the end of the century. Only resolute and urgent action will avert it even now. Whether there will be the public will to demand and obtain that action, I do not know. All I know is that to see, and not to speak, would be the great betrayal.

*After the uproar provoked by the speech, Powell was disowned by Tory leader Edward Heath – but in the East End of London dockers and immigration officers from Heathrow airport marched on behalf of Powell's views. The Race Relations Act, introducing measures against discrimination on grounds of race, colour or ethnic or national origin, became law the following November.*

•

# RICHARD NIXON
## Miami, 8 August 1968

*'The time has come for an honest government'*

*Richard Nixon (1913–94) was General Eisenhower's vice-president but lost the presidential battle narrowly to John F. Kennedy in 1960. Two years later he failed to become governor of California, ascribing his defeat to the hostility of the media. His political career seemed over. Yet the Republican disaster of 1964, when Goldwater lost to Lyndon Johnson, encouraged Nixon's supporters to run him for the presidency in 1968 and he gained the nomination.*

*Nixon declared that his nomination address was designed to let his audience see the whole man. After his years in the political wilderness, the speech was the most important of Nixon's political life and was made even as news of the violence in the Miami ghetto was starting to filter out. Nixon cribbed an oratorical device from Martin Luther King. I have a dream, said King. I see a day, declared Nixon.*

As we look at America, we see cities enveloped in smoke and flame. We hear sirens in the night. We see Americans dying on distant battlefields abroad. We see Americans hating each other, fighting each other, killing each other at home.

And as we see and hear these things, millions of Americans cry out in anguish: Did we come all this way for this? Did American boys die in Normandy and Korea and in Valley Forge for this?

Listen to the answers to those questions.

It is another voice, it is a quiet voice in the tumult of the shouting. It is the voice of the great majority of Americans, the forgotten Americans, the nonshouters, the nondemonstrators. They're not racists or sick; they're not guilty of the crime that plagues the land;

they are black, they are white; they're native born and foreign born; they're young and they're old.

They work in American factories, they run American businesses. They serve in government; they provide most of the soldiers who die to keep it free. They give drive to the spirit of America. They give lift to the American dream. They give steel to the backbone of America.

They're good people. They're decent people; they work and they save and they pay their taxes and they care.

Like Theodore Roosevelt, they know that this country will not be a good place for any of us to live in unless it's a good place for all of us to live in . . .

America's in trouble today not because her people have failed, but because her leaders have failed. And what America needs are leaders to match the greatness of her people.

And this great group of Americans – the forgotten Americans and others – know that the great question Americans must answer by their votes in November is this: whether we shall continue for four more years the policies of the last five years.

And this is their answer, and this is my answer to that question. When the strongest nation in the world can be tied down for four years in a war in Vietnam with no end in sight, when the richest nation in the world can't manage its own economy, when the nation with the greatest tradition of the rule of law is plagued by unprecedented lawlessness, when a nation that has been known for a century for equality of opportunity is torn by unprecedented racial violence, and when the President of the United States cannot travel abroad or to any major city at home without fear of a hostile demonstration – then it's time for new leadership for the United States of America.

My fellow Americans, tonight I accept the challenge and the commitment to provide that new leadership for America and I ask you to accept it with me.

And let us accept this challenge not as a grim duty but as an exciting adventure in which we are privileged to help a great nation realize its destiny and let us begin by committing ourselves to the truth, to see it like it is and tell it like it is, to find the truth, to speak the truth and to live the truth. That's what we will do.

We've had enough of big promises and little action. The time has come for an honest government in the United States of America.

My fellow Americans, I believe that historians will recall that 1968 marked the beginning of the American generation in world history. Just to be alive in America, just to be alive at this time is an experience unparalleled in history. Here's where the action is.

Think: thirty-two years from now most of Americans living today will celebrate a New Year that comes once in a thousand years.

Eight years from now, in the second term of the next President, we will celebrate the 200th anniversary of the American Revolution.

And by our decision in this we – all of us here, all of you listening on television and radio – we will determine what kind of nation America will be on its 200th birthday. We will determine what kind of a world America will live in in the year 2000.

This is the kind of day I see for America on that glorious Fourth eight years from now: I see a day when Americans are once again proud of their flag; when once again at home and abroad it is honoured as the world's greatest symbol of liberty and justice.

I see a day when the President of the United States is respected and his office is honoured because it is worthy of respect and worthy of honour. I see a day when every child in this land, regardless of his background, has a chance for the best education that our wisdom and schools can provide, and an equal chance to go just as high as his talents will take him . . .

Government can provide opportunity, but opportunity means nothing unless people are prepared to seize it.

A President can ask for reconciliation in the racial conflict that divides Americans, but reconciliation comes only from the hearts of people.

And tonight, therefore, as we make this commitment, let us look into our hearts, and let us look down into the faces of our children.

Is there anything in the world that should stand in their way? None of the old hatreds mean anything when you look down into the faces of our children. In their faces is our hope, our love and our courage.

Tonight, I see the face of a child. He lives in a great city, he's black or he's white, he's Mexican, Italian, Polish, none of that matters. What matters: he's an American child.

That child in that great city is more important than any politician's promise. He is America, he is a poet, he is a scientist, he's a great teacher, he's a proud craftsman, he's everything we've ever hoped to be in everything we dare to dream about.

He sleeps the sleep of a child, and he dreams the dreams of a child. And yet when he awakens, he awakens to a living nightmare of poverty, neglect and despair.

He fails in school, he ends up on welfare. For him the American system is one that feeds his stomach and starves his soul. It breaks his heart. And in the end it may take his life on some distant battlefield.

To millions of children in this rich land this is their prospect, but this is only part of what I see in America.

I see another child tonight. He hears a train go by. At night he dreams of faraway places where he'd like to go. It seems like an impossible dream. But he is helped on his journey through life. A father who had to go to work before he finished the sixth grade sacrificed everything he had so that his sons could go to college.

A gentle Quaker mother with a passionate concern for peace quietly wept when he went to war but she understood why he had to go.

A great teacher, a remarkable football coach, an inspirational minister encouraged him on his way. A courageous wife and loyal children stood by him in victory and also in defeat.

And in his chosen profession of politics, first there were scores, then hundreds, then thousands, and finally millions who worked for his success.

And tonight he stands before you, nominated for President of the United States of America.

You can see why I believe so deeply in the American dream.

For most of us the American revolution has been won, the American dream has come true. What I ask of you tonight is to help me make that dream come true for millions to whom it's an impossible dream today.

# BETTY FRIEDAN
Chicago, 1969

## 'A woman's civil right'

*A forty-two-year-old housewife and mother of three shocked American social
structures to the core in 1963 when she published* The Feminine Mystique,
*the bestseller that launched the modern women's movement. Betty Friedan
(1921–2006) contended that deeply entrenched attitudes and social barriers
imprisoned women in a 'housewife trap'. She called for expanded career opportunities and equality with men, and set out to destroy the myth of the happy
housewife. Some women burned their bras; others cast off their aprons – or their
husbands.*

*'I did not set out consciously to start a revolution when I wrote* The Feminine Mystique,*' Friedan wrote later, 'but it changed my life, as a woman and as
a writer, and other women tell me it changed theirs.' She went on to become the
first president of the National Organization of Women and Founder of the
National Women's Political Caucus.*

*At the first national conference for repeal of abortion laws, Betty Friedan
gave this powerful speech proclaiming abortion as a woman's civil right.*

Women, even though they're almost too visible as sex objects in this
country, are invisible people. As the Negro was the invisible man, so
women are the invisible people in America today: women who have a
share in the decisions of the mainstream of government, of politics,
of the church – who don't just cook the church supper, but preach
the sermon; who don't just look up the ZIP codes and address the
envelopes, but make the political decisions; who don't just do the
housework of industry, but make some of the executive decisions.
Women, above all, who say what their own lives and personalities are
going to be, and no longer listen to or even permit male experts to
define what 'feminine' is or isn't.

The essence of the denigration of women is our definition as sex
object. To confront our inequality, therefore, we must confront both

society's denigration of us in these terms and our own self-denigration as people.

Am I saying that women must be liberated from sex? No. I am saying that sex will only be liberated to be a human dialogue, sex will only cease to be a sniggering, dirty joke and an obsession in this society, when women become active self-determining people, liberated to a creativity beyond motherhood, to a full human creativity.

Am I saying that women must be liberated from motherhood? No. I am saying that motherhood will only be a joyous and responsible human act when women are free to make, with full conscious choice and full human responsibility, the decisions to become mothers. Then, and only then, will they be able to embrace motherhood without conflict, when they will be able to define themselves not just as somebody's mother, not just as servants of children, not just as breeding receptacles, but as people for whom motherhood is a freely chosen part of life, freely celebrated while it lasts, but for whom creativity has many more dimensions, as it has for men.

Then, and only then, will motherhood cease to be a curse and a chain for men and for children. For despite all the lip service paid to motherhood today, all the roses sent on Mother's Day, all the commercials and the hypocritical ladies' magazines' celebration of women in their roles as housewives and mothers, the fact is that all television or night-club comics have to do is go before a microphone and say the words 'my wife', and the whole audience erupts into gales of guilty, vicious and obscene laughter.

The hostility between the sexes has never been worse. The image of women in avant-garde plays, novels and movies, and behind the family situation comedies on television is that mothers are man-devouring, cannibalistic monsters, or else Lolitas, sex objects – and objects not even of heterosexual impulse, but of sadomasochism. That impulse – the punishment of women – is much more of a factor in the abortion question than anybody ever admits.

Motherhood is a bane almost by definition, or at least partly so, as long as women are forced to be mothers – and only mothers – against their will. Like a cancer cell living its life through another cell, women today are forced to live too much through their children and husbands (they are too dependent on them, and therefore are forced to take too much varied resentment, vindictiveness, inexpressible resentment and rage out on their husbands and children).

Perhaps it is the least understood fact of American political life: the enormous buried violence of women in this country today. Like all oppressed people, women have been taking their violence out on their own bodies, in all the maladies with which they plague the MDs and the psychoanalysts. Inadvertently, and in subtle and insidious ways, they have been taking their violence out, too, on their children and on their husbands, and sometimes they're not so subtle.

The battered-child syndrome that we are hearing more and more about from our hospitals is almost always to be found in the instance of unwanted children, and women are doing the battering, as much or more than men. In the case histories of psychologically and physically maimed children, the woman is always the villain, and the reason is our definition of her not only as passive sex object, but as mother, servant, someone else's mother, someone else's wife.

Am I saying that women have to be liberated from men? That men are the enemy? No. I am saying the *men* will only be truly liberated to love women and to be fully themselves when women are liberated to have a full say in the decisions of their lives and their society.

Until that happens, men are going to bear the guilty burden of the passive destiny they have forced upon women, the suppressed resentment, the sterility of love when it is not between two fully active, joyous people, but has in it the element of exploitation. And men will not be free to be all they can be as long as they must live up to an image of masculinity that disallows all the tenderness and sensitivity in a man, all that might be considered feminine. Men have enormous capacities in them that they have to repress and fear in order to live up to the obsolete, brutal, bear-killing, Ernest Hemingway, crew-cut Prussian, napalm-all-the-children-in-Vietnam, bang-bang-you're-dead image of masculinity. Men are not allowed to admit that they sometimes are afraid. They are not allowed to express their own sensitivity, their own need to be passive sometimes and not always active. Men are not allowed to cry. So they are only half-human, as women are only half-human, until we can go this next step forward. All the burdens and responsibilities that men are supposed to shoulder alone makes them, I think, resent women's pedestal, much as that pedestal may be a burden for women.

This is the real sexual revolution. Not the cheap headlines in the papers about at what age boys and girls go to bed with each other and whether they do it with or without the benefit of marriage. That's the least of it. The real sexual revolution is the emergence of women from passivity, from the point where they are the easiest victims for all the seductions, the waste, the worshipping of false gods in our affluent society, to full self-determination and full dignity. And it is the emergence of men from the stage where they are inadvertent brutes and masters to sensitive, complete humanity.

This revolution cannot happen without radical changes in the family as we know it today; in our concepts of marriage and love, in our architecture, our cities, our theology, our politics, our art. Not that women are special. Not that women are superior. But these expressions of human creativity are bound to be infinitely more various and enriching when women and men are allowed to relate to each other beyond the strict confines of the *Ladies' Home Journal*'s definition of the Mamma and Papa marriage.

If we are finally allowed to become full people, not only will children be born and brought up with more love and responsibility than today, but we will break out of the confines of that sterile little suburban family to relate to each other in terms of all of the possible dimensions of our personalities – male and female, as comrades, as colleagues, as friends, as lovers. And without so much hate and jealousy and buried resentment and hypocrisies, there will be a whole new sense of love that will make what we call love on Valentine's Day look very pallid.

It's crucial, therefore, that we see this question of abortion as more than a quantitative move, more than a politically expedient move. Abortion repeal is not a question of political expediency. It is part of something greater. It is historic that we are addressing ourselves this weekend to perhaps the first national confrontation of women and men. Women's voices are finally being heard aloud, saying it the way it is about the question of abortion both in its most basic sense of morality and in its new political sense as part of the unfinished revolution of sexual equality.

In this confrontation, we are making an important milestone in this marvellous revolution that began long before any of us here were born and which still has a long way to go. As the pioneers from Mary Wollstonecraft to Margaret Sanger gave us the consciousness that brought us from our several directions here, so we here, in changing the very terms of the debate on abortion to assert woman's right to choose, and to define the terms of our lives ourselves, move women further to full human dignity. Today, we moved history forward . . .

•

## EDWARD HEATH
### London, 28 October 1971

### *'Millions will rejoice'*

*Edward Heath (1916–2005), who became British prime minister in 1970, had always been a strong supporter of British entry into the European Common Market. The Schuman plan for a European Iron and Steel Commission was the subject of his maiden speech in 1950. He had been Britain's chief negotiator when Harold Macmillan tried to join the Common Market in 1961 but was foiled by Charles de Gaulle, the French president.*

*Negotiations to join the Common Market began again as soon as Heath became prime minister. There were crucial talks with de Gaulle's successor, Georges Pompidou, in May 1971 which removed many of the obstacles to British membership.*

*When the House of Commons debated the decision of principle of whether to apply for membership in October 1971, both the Labour and Tory parties were split. Heath made the concluding speech of the great debate which marked a decisive turning-point in British history.*

I have sometimes felt that among those who have been in this debate seeking to balance up the advantages and disadvantages there was a desire for a degree of certainty which is never obtainable in human affairs. Hon. Members will not ask for it in their lives, in their own businesses. As a nation we have never hitherto asked for it in a trading agreement or in international affairs, either economic or political. Anyone who studies the length of our trading agreements outside will accept that that is the case . . .

It is understandable after ten years of negotiation and frustration that many in debate and many in the country outside have fought and talked in terms of 'we' and 'they'. Some, I think, have been overwhelmed by a fear that this country in an organization such as the Community must always be dominated by 'they'. That is certainly not how the rest of the Community sees it. But we are approaching the point where, if this House so decides tonight, it will become just as much our Community as their Community. We shall be partners, or shall be cooperating, and we shall be trying to find common solutions to common problems of all the members of an enlarged Community.

We have confidence that we can benefit as well as contribute, that we can further our own interests and the interests of the Community at one and the same time. After all, the leaders of all three parties in this House accept the principle of entry into the European Community, as the Right Hon. Gentleman reaffirmed this afternoon. The Community is not governed by any particular party ideology. How can it be, with a Socialist Government in the Federal Republic, with a Right-wing Government in France, with a coalition in Italy containing Socialists? Of course not. What is more, all the opposition parties in the member countries of the Community support membership of the Community just as much as the governing parties . . .

Surely we must consider the consequences of staying out. We cannot delude ourselves that an early chance would be given us to take the decision again. We should be denying ourselves and succeeding generations the opportunities which are available to us in so many spheres; opportunities which we ourselves in this country have to seize. We should be leaving so many aspects of matters affecting our daily lives to be settled outside our own influence. That surely cannot be acceptable to us. We should be denying to Europe, also – let us look outside these shores for a moment – its full potential, its opportunities of developing economically and politically, maintaining its security, and securing for all its people a higher standard of prosperity.

All the consequences of that for many millions of people in Europe must be recognized tonight in the decision the House is taking. In addition, many projects for the future of Europe have been long delayed. There has been great uncertainty, and tonight all that can be removed – (*Hon. Members: 'No.'*)

Throughout my political career it is well known that I have had the vision of a Britain in a united Europe; a Britain which would be united economically to Europe and which would be able to influence decisions affecting our own future, and which would enjoy a better standard of life and a fuller life. I have worked for a Europe which will play an increasing part in meeting the needs of those parts of the world which still lie in the shadow of want . . . I want Britain as a member of a Europe which is united politically, and which will enjoy lasting peace and the greater security which would ensue.

Nor do I believe that the vision of Europe – and the Right Hon. Gentleman raised this specific point – is an unworthy vision, or an ignoble vision or an unworthy cause for which to have worked – (*Interruption.*) I have always made it absolutely plain to the British people that consent to this course would be given by Parliament – (*Hon. Members: 'Resign.'*) Parliament is the Parliament of all the people.

When we came to the end of the negotiations in 1963, after the veto had been imposed, the negotiator on behalf of India said:

> When you left India some people wept. And when you leave Europe tonight some will weep. And there is no other people in the world of whom these things could be said.

That was a tribute from the Indian to the British. But tonight when this House endorses this Motion many millions of people right across the world will rejoice that we have taken our rightful place in a truly united Europe.

*Sixty-seven Labour MPs defied the party whip and voted with the Tories.*
*Another twenty abstained. Acceptance of applying for entry to Europe was*
*passed by a majority of 112. The European Community Bill passed through the*
*Commons in 1972 by seventeen votes. Britain became a member of the Euro-*
*pean Economic Community on 1 January 1973.*

•

## RICHARD NIXON
### Washington, DC, 9 August 1974

### 'Au revoir'

*The Watergate scandal arose after employees of a Republican Party organization*
*were caught seeking to remove bugging devices from the Democratic Party cam-*
*paign headquarters in the Watergate apartment block in 1972. As the scandal*
*grew, mainly because of the reporting of the* Washington Post, *it became clear*
*that Richard Nixon had secretly taped all conversations in his White House*
*office. Many also became convinced that he was either implicated in illegal activ-*
*ities or so abnormally suspicious that he was not fit to be president.*

*Steps were taken to secure his removal by impeachment – but Nixon became*
*the first United States president to resign from office. Gerald Ford, his successor,*
*gave him a comprehensive pardon.*

*As he left the White House, Nixon made this speech to the staff.*

You are here to say goodbye to us, and we don't have a good word
for it in English – the best is *au revoir*. We will see you again . . .

Sure, we have done some things wrong in this Administration,
and the top man always takes the responsibility, and I have never
ducked it. But I want to say one thing: We can be proud of it – five
and a half years. No man or no woman came into this Administration and left it with more of this world's goods than when he came
in. No man or no woman ever profited at the public expense or the
public till. That tells something about you.

Mistakes, yes. But for personal gain, never. You did what you
believed in. Sometimes right, sometimes wrong. And I only wish that

I were a wealthy man – at the present time, I have got to find a way to pay my taxes – (*laughter*) – and if I were, I would like to recompense you for the sacrifices that all of you have made to serve in government.

But you are getting something in government – and I want you to tell this to your children, and I hope the Nation's children will hear it, too – something in government service that is far more important than money. It is a cause bigger than yourself. It is the cause of making this the greatest nation in the world, the leader of the world, because without our leadership, the world will know nothing but war, possibly starvation or worse, in the years ahead. With our leadership it will know peace, it will know plenty . . .

We think sometimes when things happen that don't go the right way; we think that when you don't pass the bar exam the first time – I happened to, but I was just lucky; I mean, my writing was so poor the bar examiner said, 'We have just got to let the guy through.' We think that when someone dear to us dies, we think that when we lose an election, we think that when we suffer a defeat that all is ended.

Not true. It is only a beginning, always. The young must know it; the old must know it. It must always sustain us, because the greatness comes not when things go always good for you, but the greatness comes and you are really tested, when you take some knocks, some disappointments, when sadness comes, because only if you have been in the deepest valley can you ever know how magnificent it is to be on the highest mountain.

•

### SIR KEITH JOSEPH
Birmingham, 19 October 1974

*'Our human stock is threatened'*

*Sir Keith Joseph (1918–94) was Secretary of State for Social Services in Edward Heath's Conservative government from 1970 to 1974. He was an intellectual, a fellow of All Souls, Oxford, and a One-Nation Tory who became disillusioned by Heath's policies which led to defeat in 1974. He founded the Centre for Policy Studies with Margaret Thatcher and challenged Conservative economic and social philosophy from the right.*

*Joseph was a serious candidate to lead the party in the event of a challenge to Heath but the uproar created by this speech, mostly on the moral or spiritual state of the nation, in which he advocated restraint on the breeding capacities of the poorest social classes, effectively ended any ambition he may have held to lead his party. 'Our human stock is threatened,' he declared. (Joseph protested that he had been referring to children born to unmarried or single parent, teenage households NOT NOT NOT – as he wrote in capital letters in The Times – because they were in solo-economic classes 4 and 5, but the damage was done and he had failed to check his statistics.)*

*Joseph became the main supporter of Margaret Thatcher who beat Heath in the 1975 Tory leadership election. He was her first Industry Secretary from 1979 to 1981 and was Secretary of State for Education from 1981 to 1986.*

The facile rhetoric of absolute liberty has become a cover for irresponsibility; instant social protest an excuse for anti-social behaviour.

The old virtues of patriotism and national pride have been denigrated in the name of internationalism, love of all our fellow men. But no one can love mankind if he does not love his own countrymen.

It was the radical socialist writer and patriot, the late George Orwell, who described the left-wing intellectuals as men motivated primarily by hatred of their own country. Socialists who spoke most about brotherhood of man could not bear their fellow Englishmen, he complained. Their well-orchestrated sneers from their strongpoint in the educational system and media have weakened the national will to transmit to future generations those values, standards and aspirations which made England admired the world over.

It is just because their message is that self-discipline is out of date and that the poor cannot be expected to help themselves, that they want the state to do more. That is why they believe in state ownership and control of economic life, education, health. Their wish to end parental choice in where and how their children shall be educated, in spending their money on better education and health for their children instead of on a new car, leisure, pleasure, is all part of the attempt to diminish self and self-discipline and real freedoms in favour of the state, ruled by socialists — the new class, as one disillusioned Communist leader called them.

Of course I shall be misrepresented, but let me ward off what misunderstanding I can. I am not saying that we should not help the poor, far from it. But the only real lasting help we can give to the poor is helping them to help themselves; to do the opposite, to create more dependence, is to destroy them morally while throwing an unfair burden on society. The populist rulers of Rome thought they had hit on a foolproof method of achieving a permanent curb on their patrician rivals when they created a dependent proletariat relying on them for bread and circuses: but in the end it destroyed the political stability of Rome, and so Rome itself fell, destroyed from inside.

Are we to be destroyed from inside too, a country which successfully repelled and destroyed Philip of Spain, Napoleon, the Kaiser, Hitler, are we to be destroyed by ideas, mischievous, wrongheaded, debilitating, yet seductive because they are fashionable and promise so much on the cheap?

It is up to us. History is not made by abstract forces, or classes; it is made by people. If we have the moral courage to say what we believe to be true, right and good, the people will be with us.

Let us take inspiration from that admirable woman Mary Whitehouse. I do not accept all her ideas, she will not accept all mine. Yet we can see in her a shining example of what one person can do single-handedly when inspired by faith and compassion. An unknown middle-aged woman, a schoolteacher in the Midlands, set out to protect adolescents against the permissiveness of our time.

Look at the scale of the opposing forces. On the one side, the whole of the new establishment with their sharp words and sneers poised; against them stood this one middle-aged woman. Today her name is a household word, made famous by the very assaults of her by her enemies. She has mobilized and given fresh heart to many who see where this current fashion is leading. Her book, *Who Does She Think She Is?*, took its title from the outraged cry of an acolyte of the new hierarchy, who asked how an unknown woman dare speak up against the BBC, the educators and false shepherds.

We too can take courage from her, and dedicate ourselves to fighting back on issues which will decide the nation's future far more than economics, however important it remains. And I welcome the opportunity to express my admiration for another brave woman with us tonight, Mrs Jill Knight, who speaks up when others prefer discretion in public and speak their minds only in private.

What are we to do? Are we to place it all in the lap of the government, the police, the courts? No, not all.

Gladstone, who entered politics as a field for moral endeavour, and never forgot the supremacy of the moral over the expedient, put the matter cogently: he argued that his colleagues were right in thinking that 'there are great evils in the state of society, but wrong when they think them so superficial that they can be cured by legislation'. How well he understood matters too serious to be left to government!

We must do more as Tories to make our voices heard and our influence felt, as a party, as people in public life, high or lowly, in religious life, on councils, voluntary bodies, educational institutions. The arguments are on our side and we have good friends among the teachers, the sociologists, the psychologists, if only we will call on them, give the lead for them to follow.

We must fight the battle of ideas in every school, university, publication, committee, TV studio even if we have to struggle for our toehold there. We have the truth – if we fail to make it shine clear, we shall be to blame no less than the exploiters, the casuists, the commercializers.

There is much for government to do as well. But we shall need intellectual as well as moral courage to grapple with the dilemmas inherent in the remoralization of public life. I shall confine myself to one example here, because I have been talking longer than you may have bargained for already.

The balance of our population, our human stock is threatened. A recent article in *Poverty*, published by the Child Poverty Action Group, showed that a high and rising proportion of children are being born to mothers least fitted to bring children into the world and bring them up. They are born to mothers who were first pregnant in adolescence in social classes four and five. Many of these girls are unmarried, many are deserted or divorced or soon will be. Some are of low intelligence, most of low educational attainment.

They are unlikely to be able to give children the stable emotional background, the consistent combination of love and firmness which are more important than riches. They are producing problem children, the future unmarried mothers, delinquents, denizens of our borstals, subnormal educational establishments, prisons, hostels for drifters. Yet, these mothers, the under-twenties in many cases, single parents, from classes four and five, are now producing a third of all births. A high proportion of these births are a tragedy for the mother, the child and for us.

Yet what shall we do? If we do nothing, the nation moves towards degeneration, however much resources we pour into preventative work and the over-burdened educational system. It is all the more serious when we think of the loss of people with talent and initiative through emigration as our semi-socialism deprives them of adequate opportunities, rewards and satisfaction.

Yet proposals to extend birth control facilities to these classes of people, particularly the young unmarried girls, the potential young unmarried mothers, evokes entirely understandable moral opposition. Is it not condoning immorality? I suppose it is. But which is the lesser evil, until we are able to remoralize whole groups of classes of people, undoing the harm done when already weak restraints on strong instincts are further weakened by permissiveness in television, in films, on bookstalls? ...

[According to the Press Association, Sir Keith, at this point in his speech, added a passage to the prepared text 'in view of misunderstandings'.]

The worship of instinct, of spontaneity, the rejection of self-discipline, is not progress: it is degeneration.

It was Freud who argued that repression of instincts is the price we pay for civilization. He considered the price well paid. So can we, now. But we must see the dilemmas, we must argue it out among ourselves to find a way through these moral dilemmas, while we fight for our ideals in wider form through words and deeds. But you may ask what can fallible politicians in short-lived governments do in the face of all these tidal forces? Most of what needs to be done, I have stressed, is for individuals as themselves, and as members of all manner of bodies. But some tasks are for government, and to these I will return on a future occasion.

This could be a watershed in our national existence. Are we to move towards moral decline, reflected and intensified by economic decline, by the corrosive effects of inflation? Or can we remoralize our national life in which the economy is an integral part? It is up to us, to people like you and me.

•

## MARGARET THATCHER
Brighton, 10 October 1975

*'Let me give you my vision'*

*Margaret Thatcher (1925–) became the first woman leader of the Conservative Party when she beat Edward Heath in the leadership ballot of February 1975. Her election marked a significant shift within the party towards a more radical version of Toryism and away from the consensual centrism of the Keynesian mixed-economy policies of the previous thirty years. Monetarism, denationalization, tax cuts and control of the money supply were the policies that were soon to be espoused.*

*She set out the new Thatcherite political stall in her first speech as leader to the Conservative Party conference and was greeted by rolling breakers of cheers, shouts and foot-stamping. The speech had a difficult birth. Sir Ronald Millar, her principal speechwriter, has described how it was not finished until ten past five on the morning it was to be delivered as Mrs Thatcher sought a peroration that satisfied her. 'Oh no! No, that won't do at all,' she said at one stage. 'Sorry, what's wrong with it?' 'It's just not me, dear.'*

Whenever I visit Communist countries their politicians never hesitate to boast about their achievements. They know them all by heart; they reel off the facts and figures, claiming this is the rich harvest of the Communist system. Yet they are not prosperous as we in the West are prosperous, and they are not free as we in the West are free.

Our capitalist system produces a far higher standard of prosperity and happiness because it believes in incentive and opportunity, and because it is founded on human dignity and freedom. Even the Russians have to go to a capitalist country – America – to buy enough wheat to feed their people – and that after more than fifty years of a State-controlled economy. Yet they boast incessantly, while we, who have so much more to boast about, for ever criticize and decry. Is it not time we spoke up for our way of life? After all, no Western nation has to build a wall round itself to keep its people in.

So let us have no truck with those who say the free-enterprise system has failed. What we face today is not a crisis of capitalism but of Socialism. No country can flourish if its economic and social life is dominated by nationalization and State control.

The cause of our shortcomings does not, therefore, lie in private enterprise. Our problem is not that we have too little Socialism. It is that we have too much. If only the Labour Party in this country would act like Social Democrats in West Germany. If only they would stop trying to prove their Socialist virility by relentlessly nationalizing one industry after another.

Of course, a halt to further State control will not on its own restore our belief in ourselves, because something else is happening to this country. We are witnessing a deliberate attack on our values, a deliberate attack on those who wish to promote merit and excellence, a deliberate attack on our heritage and our great past, and there are those who gnaw away at our national self-respect, rewriting British history as centuries of unrelieved gloom, oppression and failure – as days of hopelessness, not days of hope. And others, under the shelter of our education system, are ruthlessly attacking the minds of the young . . . blatant tactics of intimidation designed to undermine the fundamental beliefs and values of every student, tactics pursued by people who are the first to insist on their own civil rights while seeking to deny them to the rest of us.

We must not be bullied or brainwashed out of our beliefs. No wonder so many of our people, some of the best and the brightest, are depressed and talking of emigrating. Even so, I think they are wrong. They are giving up too soon. Many of the things we hold dear are threatened as never before, but none has yet been lost, so stay here, stay and help us defeat Socialism so that the Britain you have known may be the Britain your children will know.

These are the two great challenges of our time – the moral and political challenge, and the economic challenge. They have to be faced together and we have to master them both.

What are our chances of success? It depends on what kind of people we are. What kind of people are we? We are the people that in the past made Great Britain the workshop of the world, the people who persuaded others to buy British, not by begging them to do so but because it was best.

We are a people who have received more Nobel Prizes than any other nation except America, and head for head we have done better than America, twice as well in fact.

We are the people who, among other things, invented the computer, the refrigerator, the electric motor, the stethoscope, rayon, the steam turbine, stainless steel, the tank, television, penicillin, radar, the jet engine, hovercraft, float glass and carbon fibres, et cetera – and the best half of Concorde.

We export more of what we produce than either West Germany, France, Japan or the United States, and well over ninety per cent of these exports come from private enterprise. It is a triumph for the private sector and all who work in it, and let us say so loud and clear.

With achievements like that who can doubt that Britain can have a great future, and what our friends abroad want to know is whether that future is going to happen.

Well, how can we Conservatives make it happen?

Let me give you my vision: a man's right to work as he will, to spend what he earns, to own property, to have the State as servant and not as master – these are the British inheritance. They are the essence of a free country and on that freedom all our other freedoms depend.

But we want a free economy, not only because it guarantees our liberties, but also because it is the best way of creating wealth and prosperity for the whole country, and it is this prosperity alone which can give us the resources for better services for the community, better services for those in need.

By their attack on private enterprise, this Labour Government has made certain that there will be next to nothing available for improvements in our social services over the next few years. We must get private enterprise back on the road to recovery, not merely to give people more of their own money to spend as they choose, but to have more money to help the old and the sick and the handicapped. And the way to recovery is through profits, good profits today leading to high investment, leading to well-paid jobs, leading to a better standard of living tomorrow. No profits mean no investment and that means a dying industry geared to yesterday's world, and that means fewer jobs tomorrow.

Some Socialists seem to believe that people should be numbers in a State computer. We believe they should be individuals. We are all unequal. No one, thank heavens, is quite like anyone else, however much the Socialists may pretend otherwise. We believe that everyone has the right to be unequal. But to us, every human being is equally important. Engineers, miners, manual workers, shop assistants, farmworkers, postmen, housewives – these are the essential foundations of our society, and without them there would be no nation. But there are others with special gifts who should also have their chance, because if the adventurers who strike out in new directions in science, technology, medicine, commerce and industry are hobbled, there can be no advance. The spirit of envy can destroy, it can never build. Everyone must be allowed to develop the abilities he knows he has within him, and she knows she has within her, in the way they choose.

Freedom to choose is something we take for granted until it is in danger of being taken away. Socialist Governments set out perpetually to restrict the area of choice, and Conservative Governments to increase it. We believe that you become a responsible citizen by making decisions for yourself, not by having them made for you. But they are made for you by Labour all right!

•

CHAIM HERZOG
New York, 10 November 1975

*'Hate, ignorance and evil'*

*The United Nations offered the state of Israel almost immediate recognition in 1948.*

*By the 1970s, however, the twenty Arab states, the Soviet Union and a majority of Third World countries under dictatorships, controlled most of the votes in the UN General Assembly, and on 10 November 1975, Resolution 3379, calling on all nations to combat Zionism as a form of racism, was passed by 72 votes to 35, with 32 abstentions. All Jews became vulnerable to the charge of racism.*

*One of the most dramatic moments in the UN's history occurred when Chaim Herzog (1918–97), Israel's ambassador to the UN, after making this speech opposing the resolution, tore it in half and left the podium.*

I do not come to this rostrum to defend the moral and historical values of the Jewish people. They do not need to be defended. They speak for themselves. They have given to mankind much of what is great and eternal. They have done for the spirit of man more than can readily be appreciated in a forum such as this one.

I come here to denounce the two great evils which menace society in general and a society of nations in particular. These two evils are hatred and ignorance. These two evils are the motivating force behind the proponents of this draft resolution and their supporters. These two evils characterize those who would drag this world organization, the idea of which was first conceived by the prophets of Israel, to the depths to which it has been dragged today.

The key to understanding Zionism lies in its name. In the Bible, the easternmost of the two hills of ancient Jerusalem was called Zion. The period was the tenth century BC. In fact, the name 'Zion' appears 152 times in the Old Testament, referring to Jerusalem. The name is overwhelmingly a poetic and prophetic designation. The religious and emotional qualities of the name arise from the importance of Jerusalem as the Royal City and the City of the Temple. 'Mount Zion' is the place where God dwells according to the Bible. Jerusalem or Zion is a place where the Lord is King according to Isaiah and where he has installed his King, David, as quoted in the Psalms.

King David made Jerusalem the capital of Israel almost 3,000 years ago, and Jerusalem has remained the capital ever since. During the centuries the term 'Zion' grew and expanded to mean the whole of Israel. The Israelites in exile could not forget Zion.

The Hebrew psalmist sat by the waters of Babylon and swore 'If I forget thee, O Jerusalem, let my right hand forget her cunning.' This oath has been repeated for thousands of years by Jews throughout the world. It is an oath which was made over 700 years before the advent of Christianity and over 1,200 years before the advent of Islam.

In view of all these connotations, Zion came to mean the Jewish homeland, symbolic of Judaism, of Jewish national aspirations.

Every Jew, while praying to his God, wherever he is in the world, faces towards Jerusalem. These prayers have expressed for over 2,000 years of exile the yearning of the Jewish people to return to its ancient homeland, Israel. In fact, a continuous Jewish presence, in larger or smaller numbers, has been maintained in the country over the centuries.

Zionism is the name of the national movement of the Jewish people and is the modern expression of the ancient Jewish heritage. The Zionist ideal, as set out in the Bible, has been, and is, an integral part of the Jewish religion.

Zionism is to the Jewish people what the liberation movements of Africa and Asia have been to their peoples. Zionism is one of the most stirring and constructive national movements in human history. Historically, it is based on a unique and unbroken connection, extending some 4,000 years, between the People of the Book and the Land of the Bible.

In modern times, in the late nineteenth century, spurred by the twin forces of anti-Semitic persecution and of nationalism, the Jewish people organized the Zionist movement in order to transform its dream into reality. Zionism as a political movement was the revolt of an oppressed nation against the depredations and wicked discrimination and oppression of the countries in which anti-Semitism flourished. It is indeed no coincidence at all and not surprising that the sponsors and supporters of this draft resolution include countries which are guilty of the horrible crime of anti-Semitism and discrimination to this very day.

Support for the aim of Zionism was written into the League of Nations Mandate for Palestine, and was again endorsed by the United Nations in 1947 when the General Assembly voted by an overwhelming majority for the restoration of Jewish independence in our ancient land.

The re-establishment of Jewish independence in Israel after centuries of struggle to overcome foreign conquest and exile is a vindication of the fundamental concepts of the equality of nations and self-determination. To question the Jewish people's right to national existence and freedom is not only to deny to the Jewish people the right accorded to every other people on this globe but is also to deny the central precepts of the United Nations.

For Zionism is nothing more – and nothing less – than the Jewish people's sense of origin and destination in the land linked eternally with its name. It is also the instrument whereby the Jewish nation seeks an authentic fulfilment of itself. And the drama is enacted in the region in which the Arab nation has realized its sovereignty in twenty states comprising a hundred million people in four and a half million square miles, with vast resources. The issue therefore is not whether the world will come to terms with Arab nationalism. The question is at what point Arab nationalism, with its prodigious glut of advantage, wealth, and opportunity, will come to terms with the modest but equal rights of another Middle Eastern nation to pursue its life in security and peace . . .

Over the centuries it has fallen to the lot of my people to be the testing agent of human decency, the touchstone of civilization, the crucible in which enduring human values are to be tested. A nation's level of humanity could invariably be judged by its behaviour towards its Jewish population. It always began with the Jews but never ended with them.

The anti-Jewish pogroms in Czarist Russia were but the tip of the iceberg which revealed the inherent rottenness of the regime which was soon to disappear in the storm of revolution. The anti-Semitic excesses of the Nazis merely foreshadowed the catastrophe which was to befall mankind in Europe.

This wicked resolution must sound the alarm for all decent people in the world. The Jewish people as a testing agent has unfortunately never erred. The implications inherent in this shameful move are terrifying indeed.

On this issue, the world as represented in this hall has divided itself into good and bad, decent and evil, human and debased. We, the Jewish people, will recall in history our gratitude to those nations who stood up and were counted and who refused to support this wicked proposition. I know that this episode will have strengthened the forces of freedom and decency in the world and will have fortified them in their resolve to strengthen the ideals they so value. I know that this episode will have strengthened Zionism, as it has weakened the United Nations.

As I stand on this rostrum, the long and proud history of my people unravels itself before my inward eye. I see the oppressors of our people over the ages as they pass one after another in evil procession into oblivion. I stand here before you as the representative of a strong and flourishing people which has survived them all and which will survive this shameful exhibition and the proponents of this resolution. I stand here as the representative of a people one of whose prophets gave to this world the sublime prophecy which animated the founders of this world organization and which graces the entrance to this building: '. . . nation shall not lift up sword against nation, neither shall they learn war any more' (Isaiah 2:4). In the verses before that, the prophet Isaiah proclaimed: 'And it shall come to pass in the last days . . . for out of Zion shall go forth the law, and the word of the Lord from Jerusalem' (Isaiah 2:2–3).

As I stand on this rostrum, the great moments of Jewish history come to mind as I face you, once again outnumbered and the would-be victim of hate, ignorance and evil. I look back on those great moments. I recall the greatness of a nation which I have the honour to represent in this forum. I am mindful at this moment of the Jewish people throughout the world wherever they may be, be it in freedom or in slavery, whose prayers and thoughts are with me at this moment.

I stand not here as a supplicant. Vote as your moral conscience dictates to you. For the issue is not Israel or Zionism. The issue is the continued existence of the organization, which has been dragged to its lowest point of discredit by a coalition of despotisms and racists.

The vote of each delegation will record in history its country's stand on anti-Semitic racism and anti-Judaism. You yourselves bear the responsibility for your stand before history, for as such will you be viewed in history. But we, the Jewish people, will not forget.

For us, the Jewish people, this is but a passing episode in a rich and an event-filled history. We put our trust in our Providence, in our faith and beliefs, in our time-hallowed tradition, in our striving for social advance and human values and in our people, wherever they may be. For us, the Jewish people, this resolution, based on hatred, falsehood, and arrogance, is devoid of any moral or legal value. For us, the Jewish people, this is no more than a piece of paper, and we shall treat it as such.

*The resolution was rescinded in 1992.*

•

## MICHAEL FOOT
### Blackpool, 29 September 1976

*'The red flame of Socialist courage'*

*Michael Foot (1913–2010) was one of the great dissenters and romantics of British politics, a man whose heroes were Swift, Hazlitt and Byron. He identified with the Levellers as well as Cromwell and Whigs as well as Nonconformists. According to the British historian Kenneth O. Morgan, he embodied a powerful creative thrust of popular radicalism that has been constant in British public life for two centuries.*

*Foot was also a magnificent orator, at his best when defying and denouncing*

*Tories and defending his beloved Labour Party against the slurs and sneers of its opponents. After years as a rebel on the left wing of the Party, he became Secretary of State for Employment in Harold Wilson's third government in 1974.*

*Trade unionists were angry with the Labour government in 1976. It was dealing with an inflation rate of twenty per cent and the unions were opposing government intervention in collective wage bargaining and wanted utterly to reject statutory incomes control.*

*On the first day of the Labour Party conference, Foot, for many years the idol of the conference as the bitterest critic of official policies but now a Cabinet minister, made a dramatic appeal to the conference to endorse the Wilson government's anti-inflation policy. If they failed to support the government's policy, he said in a passionate speech, they could bring about the end of the Labour government.*

No one is less surprised than myself that this Conference has been dominated, and will continue to be dominated in my judgement, by the rising anxieties and fears and anger of our people about unemployment up and down this country ... Unemployment on this level is totally unacceptable to the Labour Movement. Of course, our unemployment is part of an affliction affecting the whole Western world; the Western world is gripped by the most complex and perilous recession which we have seen since 1945. It is indeed, in my judgement, a crisis of Capitalism of a most formidable character, and we have to muster all our energies, all our skill, to deal with it.

Let me start therefore by telling you what is my deepest instinct about the whole of this situation; it is of first importance for our country, and no less for our Labour Movement, that this crisis should be faced and surmounted by a Labour Government acting in the closest alliance and good faith with the trade-union movement of this country. (*Applause.*) If we were to fall apart, I shudder to think what would be the consequences for our people, for our young people and old alike, in unemployment and in all the other associated consequences. I shudder to think also what would be the consequence for our democratic institutions themselves. It is only three or four years ago that a Conservative Government used the opportunity which we gave them after 1970 to introduce the most insidious attack on trade unionism in this country which we have seen in this century.

If we were ever fools enough to allow them to get the levers of power again, the whips would be changed to scorpions for our chastisement. Let us not make any mistake about that . . .

People sometimes say: we will agree to some arrangement between the Government and the trade unions about wages, but only when you have the full panoply of Socialist measures actually put into full operation. I understand the argument, but I say it is unworkable. There is not a single Government in the world aspiring to change society that could work upon that system of transition, whether it is Communist, Maoist, Yugoslav, anything. Of course you could not work on that basis, and so I say, for anyone to argue that there shall be no concession to a Labour Government on these measures until all the other measures are in operation, that is not merely a recipe for the destruction of this Labour Government, it is a recipe for the destruction of any Labour Government. That has to be faced, too.

I am very glad that this Conference is going to be dominated also by the demand for new systems of investment, in the National Enterprise Board and the planning agreements and all the other matters that we have discussed and which we have had in our Party programmes. Of course, that is of paramount importance. But do not let anybody imagine that investment is a soft option. Investment is not a soft option. You can learn it from *Das Kapital* as well as from anywhere else, and I hope I will not be convicted for that. You can read it all there. Investment means very often, almost always, forgoing present claims in order to have future benefits. And you can do it by not so many methods. You can do it by the brutal capitalist methods of the nineteenth century, or you can do it by the equally brutal, or maybe even more outrageous, methods of twentieth-century Stalinism, or you can do it by the politics of persuasion, by the Social Contract. You can do it that way. You can do it the democratic way, which is the heart and soul of our Labour Movement, and always has been. And it is that method by which we are going to seek for our success.

We must face the crisis, beat the inflation, start the regeneration of British industry, lift this scourge of unemployment from our people. This is what we must do. It is the greatest summons that has come to our Labour Party in the seventy-five years of its existence.

We face an economic typhoon of unparalleled ferocity, the worst the world has seen since the 1930s. Joseph Conrad wrote a book called *Typhoon*, and at the end he told people how to deal with it. He said, 'Always facing it, Captain McWhirr: that's the way to get through.' Always facing it, that is the way we have got to solve this problem. We do not want a Labour Movement that tries to dodge it; we do not want people in a Labour Cabinet to try to dodge it. We want people who are prepared to show how they are going to face it, and we need the united support of the Labour Movement to achieve it.

I believe that we can make this Conference one of the greatest in our history, not by stifling dissent or criticism or debate, however ferociously the criticisms may be put: of course not. Indeed, there would not be any life left in this Party if it had not been for those prepared to come along and advocate sometimes unpopular opinions and stand up for them, and discover that those unpopular opinions sometimes became accepted. So I am not asking for any dull uniformity or anything of the sort. I am asking this Movement to exert itself as it has never done before, to show the qualities which we have, the Socialist imagination that exists in our Movement, the readiness to re-forge the alliance, stronger than ever, between the Government and the trade unions, and above all to show the supreme quality in politics, the red flame of Socialist courage. That is what we have got to do to save our country, and that is what can come from this Conference. (*Applause. A standing ovation.*)

*When Harold Wilson resigned in 1976, James Callaghan defeated Michael Foot for the leadership of the Labour Party and became prime minister. Foot became leader of the House of Commons and succeeded Callaghan in 1980 as leader of the party which had been defeated in the 1979 general election by Margaret Thatcher. Foot was beaten by Margaret Thatcher in the election of 1983. He retired from the House of Commons in 1992.*

## ALEXANDER SOLZHENITSYN
### Cambridge, Massachusetts, 8 June 1978

*'What is the joy about?'*

*After serving in the Red Army and being decorated for bravery during the Second World War, Alexander Solzhenitsyn (1918–2008) was sent to a labour camp from 1945 to 1953 after making critical remarks about Stalin in letters to a friend. He was then sent into exile in Siberia until 1956.*

One Day in the Life of Ivan Denisovich, *his novel exposing the misery of Stalin's 'gulags', was published in 1962 and approved by Khrushchev. His experience of the gulags also inspired* Cancer Ward, The First Circle *and* The Gulag Archipelago, *all of which were banned.*

*Although Solzhenitsyn was awarded the Nobel Prize for Literature in 1970, he was harangued in the Soviet press, charged with treason and sent into exile in 1974 after* The Gulag Archipelago *was published in the West.*

*As this speech at Harvard University's annual commencement ceremony demonstrated, Solzhenitsyn did not trumpet his gratitude to the West. Instead he denounced a Western way of life that he saw as spoilt, silly and empty of spiritual values.*

A decline in courage may be the most striking feature which an outside observer notices in the West today. The Western world has lost its civic courage, both as a whole and separately, in each country, in each government, in each political party and, of course, in the United Nations. Such a decline in courage is particularly noticeable among the ruling and intellectual élites, causing an impression of a loss of courage by the entire society. There remain many courageous individuals, but they have no determining influence on public life. Political and intellectual functionaries exhibit this depression, passivity and perplexity in their actions and in their statements, and even more so in their self-serving rationales as to how realistic, reasonable and intellectually and even morally justified it is to base state policies on weakness and cowardice . . .

Must one point out that from ancient times a decline in courage has been considered the beginning of the end? . . .

When the modern Western states were being formed, it was proclaimed as a principle that governments are meant to serve man and that man lives in order to be free and pursue happiness. (See, for example, the American Declaration of Independence.) Now at last during past decades technical and social progress has permitted the realization of such aspirations: the welfare state. Every citizen has been granted the desired freedom and material goods in such quantity and of such quality as to guarantee in theory the achievement of happiness, in the debased sense of the word which has come into being during those same decades. (In the process, however, one psychological detail has been overlooked: the constant desire to have still more things and a still better life, and the struggle to this end imprints many Western faces with worry and even depression, though it is customary to carefully conceal such feelings. This active and tense competition comes to dominate all human thought and does not in the least open a way to free spiritual development.) The individual's independence from many types of state pressure has been guaranteed; the majority of the people have been granted well-being to an extent their fathers and grandfathers could not even dream about; it has become possible to raise young people according to these ideals, preparing them for and summoning them towards physical bloom, happiness, possession of material goods, money and leisure, towards an almost unlimited freedom in the choice of pleasures. So who should now renounce all this, why and for the sake of what should one risk one's precious life in defence of the common good, and particularly in the nebulous case when the security of one's nation must be defended in an as yet distant land?

Even biology tells us that a high degree of habitual well-being is not advantageous to a living organism. Today, well-being in the life of Western society has begun to reveal its pernicious mask . . .

Should I be asked whether I would propose the West, such as it is today, as a model to my country, I would frankly have to answer negatively. No, I could not recommend your society as an ideal for the transformation of ours. Through deep suffering, people in our country have now achieved a spiritual development of such intensity that the Western system in its present state of spiritual exhaustion does not look attractive. Even those characteristics of your life which I have just enumerated are extremely saddening.

A fact which cannot be disputed is the weakening of human personality in the West, while in the East it has become firmer and stronger. Six decades for our people and three decades for the people of Eastern Europe; during that time we have been through a spiritual training far in advance of Western experience. The complex and deadly crush of life has produced stronger, deeper and more interesting personalities than those generated by standardized Western wellbeing. Therefore, if our society were to be transformed into yours, it would mean an improvement in certain aspects, but also a change for the worse on some particularly significant points. Of course, a society cannot remain in an abyss of lawlessness as is the case in our country. But it is also demeaning for it to stay on such a soulless and smooth plane of legalism as is the case in yours. After the suffering of decades of violence and oppression, the human soul longs for things higher, warmer and purer than those offered by today's mass living habits, introduced as by a calling card by the revolting invasion of commercial advertising, by TV stupor and by intolerable music.

All this is visible to numerous observers from all the worlds of our planet. The Western way of life is less and less likely to become the leading model.

There are telltale symptoms by which history gives warning to a threatened or perishing society. Such are, for instance, a decline of the arts or a lack of great statesmen. Indeed, sometimes the warnings are quite explicit and concrete. The centre of your democracy and of your culture is left without electric power for a few hours only, and all of a sudden crowds of American citizens start looting and creating havoc. The smooth surface film must be very thin, then, the social system quite unstable and unhealthy.

But the fight for our planet, physical and spiritual, a fight of cosmic proportions, is not a vague matter of the future; it has already started. The forces of Evil have begun their decisive offensive; you can feel their pressure, yet your screens and publications are full of prescribed smiles and raised glasses. What is the joy about?

*Solzhenitsyn was pardoned in 1991, after the collapse of the Soviet Union.*

•

## ROY JENKINS
London, 22 November 1979

*'Home Thoughts from Abroad'*

*The 1979 Dimbleby Lecture, broadcast annually by the BBC in memory of the great broadcaster Richard Dimbleby, helped to change the course of British politics.*

*Roy Jenkins had resigned as the Labour government's Home Secretary in 1976 to prepare for his appointment as president of the European Economic Community commission and had left the Labour Party. He used the opportunity of the Dimbleby Lecture to voice his disenchantment with the warring ideologies of the two main British political parties and offered the hope of a new party of the centre based on European models.*

*Jenkins offers in his memoirs a fascinating insight into the hard work of writing such a speech. His first attempt at composition occurred on 14 August and by 15 October he had a text, nearly sufficient to fill the forty-eight minutes required. But it was not right. 'It was far too long and leisurely on historical analysis and not nearly strong enough on prescription.' On 1 November he wrote from 9.15 a.m. to 1.00 and then from 3.15 to 8.15 p.m. and had a comprehensive text, about fifteen hundred words too long.*

*Six days later he read a tautened and typed version through during a train journey and did a run-through of the full text at a BBC studio on 12 November. He then continued to titivate the lecture in Brussels until he had to seal it up for the release of copies to the press.*

*On the day of the lecture, he also made three speeches in Brussels before departing for London.*

A few decades ago there were quite a lot of people who believed that a single election victory could be the beginning of the millennium. It was a view perhaps more prevalent, because of greater optimism or utopianism, on the Left than on the Right. It was certainly held by many Labour supporters in 1945. More recently, however, I have the impression that it applies equally or more strongly on the Right.

A governing party must have the self-confidence to want power and to believe that its exercise of it can tilt the country in the right direction. But it should also have the humility to recognize on any likely projection of the past, its power will come to an end, probably in about six years, maybe less, only exceptionally more. The test of its statesmanship in the context of history will not therefore be how many trees it pulls up by the roots but how it fits into a continuous process of adaptation in which leadership is combined with sensitivity to national mood . . .

This is not a recipe for inaction or for the avoidance of controversy. Some of the most bitterly contested measures of the past 150 years – the electoral reform bills, the repeal of the Corn Laws, the curbing of the powers of the House of Lords, the initiation of social security, or, to take an example from the Right, the setting up of independent television – have been inviolate once they were on the statute book because they quickly became part of the social fabric and could only have been undone at the cost of unacceptable electoral damage to the opposing party.

All this implies a certain respect by politicians for the opinions of their opponents. But that is surely both possible and desirable. In their memoirs, written with the benignity of old age, it generally comes through. Indeed, where bitterness remains, it is more often directed against previous colleagues than against previous opponents.

Yet when they are seeking or exercising power there is only too often a shrill and unconvincing attempt to portray almost everyone on the other side as either a fool or a knave. Each successive Tory government is the most reactionary since that of Lord Liverpool, or some other hobgoblin figure shrouded in the past. Each successive Labour government has been the most rapacious, doctrinaire and unpatriotic conspiracy to be seen this side of the Iron Curtain. Either might, I suppose, be true in the future, but it cannot all have been true in the past, and I do not believe that it either convinces or pleases the electorate.

One major disadvantage of excessive political partisanship is that it fosters precisely the sort of industrial mood which is rapidly turning Britain into a manufacturing desert. If, on the House of Commons floor, it is always the fault of the other side, how can politicians preach convincingly against the prevalence of such a mood on the shop-floor?

This, some people will say with horror, is an unashamed plea for the strengthening of the political centre. Why not? The vocation of politicians ought to be to represent, to channel, to lead the aspirations of the electorate. These aspirations, not on every issue, but in essential direction, pull far more towards the centre than towards the extremes. The general mood is not that of reaction or of putting the clock back. But nor is it one of support for class selfishness or for revolution, whether it be utopian or malevolent.

Our great failure, now for decades past, has been lack of adaptability. Sometimes this rigidity is a source of strength. It was very good not to be too adaptable in 1940. But overall it is a source of weakness. Some societies – France in the second half of the Third Republic, pre-revolutionary Russia, the Austro-Hungarian Empire – have been still less adaptable than our own. But they hardly provide grounds for comfort. Compared with post-war Germany, post-war Japan, Fifth Republican France (industrially at least), the United States for virtually the whole of its history, compared for that matter with early Victorian Britain – modern Britain has been sluggish, unimaginative and resistant to voluntary change, not merely economically but socially and politically as well. We cannot successfully survive unless we can make our society more adaptable; and an unadaptable political system works heavily against this. Politicians cannot cling defensively to their present somewhat ossified party and political system while convincingly advocating the acceptance of change everywhere else in industry and society. 'Everybody change but us' is never a good slogan.

The paradox is that we need more change accompanied by more stability of direction. It is a paradox but not a contradiction. Too often we have superficial and quickly reversed political change without much purpose or underlying effect. This is not the only paradox. We need the innovating stimulus of the free-market economy without either the unacceptable brutality of its untrammelled distribution of rewards or its indifference to unemployment. This is by no means an impossible combination. It works well in a number of countries. It means that you accept the broad line of division between the public and the private sectors and do not constantly threaten those in the private sector with nationalization or expropriation.

You encourage them without too much interference to create as much wealth as possible, but use the wealth so created both to give a return for enterprise and to spread the benefits throughout society in a way that avoids the disfigurement of poverty, gives a full priority to public education and health services, and encourages cooperation and not conflict in industry and throughout society. You use taxation for this purpose, but not just to lop off rewards. The state must know its place, which should be an important but far from an omnipotent one. You recognize that there are certain major economic objectives, well beyond merely regulatory ones like the control of the money supply, which can only be achieved by public action, often on an international scale. Two clear contemporary examples are first the breaking of the link, now fairly long-standing, but by no means inevitable, between economic growth and the consumption of oil; and second, by coordinated government purchasing policy, ensuring that this country and Europe as a whole is a major producer and not merely a passive purchaser of the products of the electronic/telecommunications revolution. Success or failure on these two points will largely determine whether we with our partners are a leading or second-rate industrial group in the world of the 1990s. You use market forces to help achieve such objectives but do not for a moment pretend that they, unguided and unaided, can do the whole job.

You also make sure that the state knows its place, not only in relation to the economy, but in relation to the citizen. You are in favour of the right of dissent and the liberty of private conduct. You are against unnecessary centralization and bureaucracy. You want to devolve decision-making wherever you sensibly can. You want parents in the school system, patients in the health service, residents in the neighbourhood, customers in both nationalized and private industry, to have as much say as possible. You want the nation to be self-confident and outward-looking, rather than insular, xenophobic and suspicious. You want the class system to fade without being replaced either by an aggressive and intolerant proletarianism or by the dominance of the brash and selfish values of a 'get rich quick' society. You want the nation, without eschewing necessary controversy, to achieve a renewed sense of cohesion and common purpose.

These are some of the objectives which I believe could be assisted by a strengthening of the radical centre. I believe that such a development could bring into political commitment the energies of many people of talent and goodwill who, although perhaps active in many other voluntary ways, are at present alienated from the business of government, whether national or local, by the sterility and formalism of much of the political game. I am sure this would improve our politics. I think the results might also help to improve our national performance. But of that I cannot be certain. I am against too much dogmatism here. We have had more than enough of it. But at least we could escape from the pessimism of Yeats's 'Second Coming', where

> The best lack all conviction, while the worst
> Are full of passionate intensity

and

> Things fall apart; the centre cannot hold.

*Two Saturdays later both Shirley Williams and Bill Rodgers, who with Jenkins were to be three of the Gang of Four who founded the Social Democratic Party in 1981, visited Jenkins. Neither had been frightened off by the lecture and both were prepared in certain circumstances to break with the Labour Party.*

*Jenkins's lecture proved to be the single most important event in placing on the agenda for serious discussion the idea of a new party in the middle ground of British politics; it was a seminal text of what a new party could stand for.*

*After the SDP was formed, initially with Jenkins as leader, it subsequently entered an alliance with the Liberal Party – and the alliance briefly threatened to overtake the Labour Party and become the dominant party of opposition to the Tories. After the 1987 general election, the SDP faded away and many members joined a new Liberal Democrat Party. But the threat from the alliance trans-formed the Labour Party, whose policies became similar to those that Jenkins espoused in his Dimbleby Lecture.*

•

## EDWARD KENNEDY
### New York, 12 August 1980

### *'The dream shall never die'*

*Senator Edward Kennedy's campaign for president in 1980 ended when he was decisively beaten by President Jimmy Carter at the Democratic Convention. Yet although Carter won the nomination, it was Kennedy (1932–2009) who made the best speech and who got the loudest cheers when he and Carter appeared together on the platform.*

*On the day after his defeat, Kennedy brought the convention alive with a bril-liant defence of the Democrats' traditional policies, a scathing attack on Ronald Reagan, and a moving and defiant statement of the Kennedys' faith.*

There were hard hours on our journey, and often we sailed against the wind. But always we kept our rudder true, and there were so many of you who stayed the course and shared our hope. You gave your help; but even more, you gave your hearts.

Because of you, this has been a happy campaign. You welcomed Joan, me and our family into your homes and neighbourhoods, your churches, your campuses, your union halls. When I think back of all the miles and all the months and all the memories, I think of you. I recall the poet's words, and I say: What golden friends I have.

Among you, my golden friends across this land, I have listened and learned.

I have listened to Kenny Dubois, a glassblower in Charleston, West Virginia, who has ten children to support but has lost his job after thirty-five years, just three years short of qualifying for his pension ...

I have listened to the grandmother in East Oakland who no longer has a phone to call her grandchildren because she gave it up to pay the rent on her small apartment.

I have listened to young workers out of work, to students without the tuition for college, and to families without the chance to own a home. I have seen the closed factories and the stalled assembly lines of Anderson, Indiana and South Gate, California, and I have seen too many, far too many idle men and women desperate to work. I have seen too many, far too many working families desperate to protect the value of their wages from the ravages of inflation.

Yet I have also sensed a yearning for new hope among the people in every state where I have been. And I have felt it in their handshakes, I saw it in their faces, and I shall never forget the mothers who carried children to our rallies. I shall always remember the elderly who have lived in an America of high purpose and who believe that it can all happen again.

Tonight, in their name, I have come here to speak for them. And for their sake, I ask you to stand with them. On their behalf I ask you to restate and reaffirm the timeless truth of our party.

I congratulate President Carter on his victory here. (*Applause.*)

I am confident that the Democratic Party will reunite on the basis of Democratic principles, and that together we will march towards a Democratic victory in 1980. (*Applause.*)

And someday, long after this convention, long after the signs come down, and the crowds stop cheering, and the bands stop playing, may it be said of our campaign that we kept the faith. May it be said of our party in 1980 that we found our faith again.

And may it be said of us, both in dark passages and in bright days, in the words of Tennyson that my brothers quoted and loved, and that have special meaning for me now: 'I am a part of all that I have met/Tho' much is taken, much abides/That which we are, we are /One equal temper of heroic hearts/strong in will/To strive, to seek, to find, and not to yield.'

For me, a few hours ago, this campaign came to an end. For all those whose cares have been our concern, the work goes on, the cause endures, the hope still lives, and the dream shall never die.

•

## MICHAEL HESELTINE
### Blackpool, 15 October 1981

*'We are reaping the whirlwind of all our yesterdays'*

*As Secretary of State for the Environment in Margaret Thatcher's first government, Michael Heseltine (1933–), one of the outstanding orators of the contemporary British Tory Party, was charged with studying the problems of Merseyside, the region around the declining seaport of Liverpool, after the summer riots of 1980. Heseltine always sat uncomfortably in Thatcher governments: he still believed in what had become the unfashionable view that state intervention could help to reverse decades of decline in Britain's inner cities.*

*Speaking to the Conservative conference a year later, he made an impassioned call that Conservative politics must deny rioters and wreckers any fertile ground to sow the seeds of discontent. He appealed to the one-nation doctrines of Disraeli and Iain Macleod that had kept the Tory Party in the forefront of British politics. Self-help (the Thatcherite creed) had a limited meaning in an inner-city community where forty per cent of young kids were without work, he declared.*

*Then he moved into the main thrust of his speech.*

I come from South Wales. This nation is still suffering from the legacies, from the folklore and from the memories of those bitter inter-war years. They have fuelled a venom in the Labour Party and in the trade unions that has set back our industrial society almost beyond redemption.

This is the great challenge for our party, for we alone believe in politics as a process of healing, of drawing together and of building together on common strengths. There is not a person here who has not cheered to the echo the great names, the great phrases that secured for our party a well-nigh incredible record of governing Britain over so long a period.

It required great courage when Disraeli first talked of one nation. It did not represent a conventional view of the time. It flew in the teeth of much that was contemporary experience. But he led the Tory Party through the great traumas of his day because he, in advance of his time, had the vision to lead in his time. Today we cheer the memory of that man. When I joined this party Iain Macleod was a deeply controversial politician, fighting against bitter criticism to keep us close to those same traditions of compassion and tolerance. Those traditions are not ours to squander or abuse. For a brief time they are entrusted to us to make relevant in today's world. They are the traditions that have kept our party in the forefront of British politics in the centre of power.

In our generation we must show the same courage and vision as the leaders whose memories we so frequently applaud. What talk of equality of opportunity? What do those words actually mean in the inner cities today? What do they mean to the black communities? We now have large immigrant communities in British cities. Let this party's position be absolutely clear. They are British. They live here. They vote here. However tight the immigration legislation – and in everyone's interests it should be tight – there will be a large black community in this country tomorrow, just as there is today. There are no schemes of significant repatriation that have any moral, social or political credibility.

I will and I do condemn the handful of blacks who rioted. But I condemn just as strongly the whites who rioted alongside them. I totally support the police in their brave and unenviable task of restoring stability in our society.

But the rioters were a tiny section of the black and white populations, the overwhelming majority of whom deplore the riots as vehemently as we do. But the fact remains that of those black communities, who stand for the same values that I have described, far too many – our people – know that the education they obtain, the jobs they are offered and the careers that are opened to them do not match up to the finest traditions upon which we pride ourselves.

There is a challenge here in the conditions that we took on from the Labour Party – because it totally failed to match the scale of the challenge to be found in the inner cities . . .

Few of us can remember such testing times for this nation . . . we are reaping the whirlwind of all our yesterdays. Decade after decade we have denied our industry the climate for sufficient innovation and investment. Too often we have slaughtered the capital programmes to pay for the over-burgeoning consumption of the public sector. We have extracted as wages today what we should have left as investment for tomorrow. We have, too often, squandered our inheritance, and our inner cities are just a signpost of a journey of despair.

There will be no recovery without more resources. Preferably those resources will be in the form of investment from the private sector or from the better use of existing public programmes. But if the case can be made it may also be from extra public expenditure. From wherever it comes it will require an effort of will by a community of people for a common purpose.

You will say to me, 'What of the wreckers? What of those who will not work, those who strike without cause, those who thump the elderly, smash in the windows and thrive on a life of crime?' Every generation has its wreckers. There have been riots in other times, but our faith has always told us that one cannot sow the seeds of discontent on a stable society. They can flourish only if they find fertile ground. Our politics and policies must deny that fertile ground. Yes, of course, our political opponents will fight us – as soon as they stop fighting each other. But we have the mettle for that fight.

*Heseltine won a standing ovation. He resigned from Margaret Thatcher's government in 1986 and challenged her for the leadership of the Tory Party in 1990. On the first ballot he won more votes than Mrs Thatcher and precipitated her downfall, but lost to John Major, whose Cabinet he subsequently joined.*

•

# MARGARET THATCHER
Cheltenham, 3 July 1982

### 'The Falklands Factor'

*When Margaret Thatcher decided to send a task force of 10,000 men to recapture the Falkland Islands after they had been invaded by Argentina, she played for the highest stakes and won triumphantly. The British success was attributed to Mrs Thatcher's nerve and determination. The 'Iron Lady' of Soviet propaganda proved iron indeed. From being the least popular British prime minister of modern times, Mrs Thatcher became the new Boadicea, the embodiment of toughness and resolve.*

*The 'Falklands Factor', noted in this nationalistic speech to a rally of Conservative women, ensured that she won the general election of 1983, her second election victory.*

Today we meet in the aftermath of the Falklands Battle. Our country has won a great victory and we are entitled to be proud. This nation had the resolution to do what it knew had to be done — to do what it knew was right.

We fought to show that aggression does not pay, and that the robber cannot be allowed to get away with his swag. We fought with the support of so many throughout the world: the Security Council, the Commonwealth, the European Community, and the United States. Yet we also fought alone — for we fought for our own people and for our own sovereign territory.

Now that it is all over, things cannot be the same again, for we have learnt something about ourselves — a lesson which we desperately needed to learn. When we started out, there were the waverers and the faint-hearts: the people who thought that Britain could no longer seize the initiative for herself; the people who thought we could no longer do the great things which we once did; and those who believed that our decline was irreversible — that we could never again be what we were. There were those who would not admit it — even perhaps some here today – people who would have strenuously denied the suggestion but – in their heart of hearts – they too had their secret fears that it was true: that Britain was no longer the nation that had built an Empire and ruled a quarter of the world.

Well, they were wrong. The lesson of the Falklands is that Britain has not changed and that this nation still has those sterling qualities which shine through our history. This generation can match their fathers and grandfathers in ability, in courage, and in resolution. We have not changed. When the demands of war and the dangers to our own people call us to arms – then we British are as we have always been – competent, courageous and resolute.

When called to arms – ah, that's the problem. It took the battle in the South Atlantic for the shipyards to adapt ships way ahead of time; for dockyards to refit merchantmen and cruise liners, to fix helicopter platforms, to convert hospital ships – all faster than was thought possible; it took the demands of war for every stop to be pulled out and every man and woman to do their best.

British people had to be threatened by foreign soldiers and British territory invaded and then – why then – the response was incomparable. Yet why does it need a war to bring out our qualities and reassert our pride? Why do we have to be invaded before we throw aside our selfish aims and begin to work together as only we can work, and achieve as only we can achieve?

That really is the challenge we as a nation face today. We have to see that the spirit of the South Atlantic – the real spirit of Britain – is kindled not only by war but can now be fired by peace.

We have the first prerequisite. We know we can do it – we haven't lost the ability. That is the Falklands Factor. We have proved ourselves to ourselves. It is a lesson we must not now forget. Indeed, it is a lesson which we must apply to peace just as we have learnt it in war. The faltering and the self-doubt has given way to achievement and pride. We have the confidence and we must use it.

Just look at the Task Force as an object lesson. Every man had his own task to do and did it superbly. Officers and men, senior NCO and newest recruit – every one realized that his contribution was essential for the success of the whole. All were equally valuable – each was differently qualified. By working together, each was able to do more than his best. As a team they raised the average to the level of the best and by each doing his utmost together they achieved the impossible. That's an accurate picture of Britain at war – not yet of Britain at peace. But the spirit has stirred and the nation has begun to assert itself. Things are not going to be the same again.

•

## ROBERT RUNCIE
London, 26 July 1982

*'Our neighbours are indeed like us'*

*Although it continued to lose members during the 1970s and 1980s, the Church of England remained a powerful source of social criticism and often upset Conservative ministers.*

*Dr Robert Runcie (1921–2000), who won the Military Cross during the Second World War, was appointed Archbishop of Canterbury by Margaret Thatcher but their relationship was uneasy. After her own triumphalism over victory in the Falklands war, she was said to be particularly upset by this muted and moderate sermon from Dr Runcie at a service of thanksgiving in St Paul's Cathedral, although she never commented publicly on her views of the sermon. Runcie dared to suggest that people were mourning Argentina as well as Britain – and that they should also be remembered in the nation's prayers.*

Our hope as Christians is not fundamentally in man's naked goodwill and rationality. We believe that he can overcome the deadly selfishness of class or sect or race by discovering himself as a child of the universal God of love. When a man realizes that he is a beloved child of the Creator of all, then he is ready to see his neighbours in the world as brothers and sisters. That is one reason why those who dare to interpret God's will must never claim him as an asset for one nation or group rather than another. War springs from the love and loyalty which should be offered to God being applied to some God-substitute, one of the most dangerous being nationalism.

This is a dangerous world where evil is at work nourishing the mindless brutality which killed and maimed so many in this city last week. Sometimes, with the greatest reluctance, force is necessary to hold back the chaos which injustice and the irrational element in man threaten to make of the world. But having said that, all is not lost and there is hope. Even in the failure of war there are springs of hope. In that great war play by Shakespeare, Henry V says: 'There is some soul of goodness in things evil, would men observingly distill it out.' People are mourning on both sides of this conflict. In our prayers we shall quite rightly remember those who are bereaved in our own country and the relations of the young Argentinian soldiers who were killed. Common sorrow could do something to reunite those who were engaged in this struggle. A shared anguish can be a bridge of reconciliation. Our neighbours are indeed like us.

I have had an avalanche of letters and advice about this service. Some correspondents have asked 'why drag God in?' as if the intention was to wheel up God to endorse some particular policy or attitude rather than another. The purpose of prayer and of services like this is very different and there is hope for the world in the difference. In our prayers we come into the presence of the living God. We come with our very human emotions, pride in achievement and courage, grief at loss and waste. We come as we are and not just mouthing opinions and thanksgiving which the fashion of the moment judges acceptable. As we pour into our prayer our mourning, our pride, our shame and our convictions, which will inevitably differ from person to person, if we are really present and really reaching out to God and not just demanding his endorsement, then God is able to work upon us. He is able to deepen and enlarge our compassion and to purify our thanksgiving. The parent who comes mourning the loss of a son may find here consolation, but also a spirit which enlarges our compassion to include all those Argentinian parents who have lost sons.

Man without God finds it difficult to achieve this revolution inside himself. But talk of peace and reconciliation is just fanciful and theoretical unless we are prepared to undergo such a revolution. Many of the reports I have heard about the troops engaged in this war refer to moments when soldiers have been brought face to face with what is fundamental in life and have found new sources of strength and compassion even in the midst of conflict. Ironically, it has sometimes been those spectators who remained at home, whether supporters or opponents of the conflict, who continue to be most violent in their attitudes and untouched in their deepest selves.

Man without God is less than man. In meeting God, a man is shown his failures and his lack of integrity, but he is also given strength to turn more and more of his life and actions into love and compassion for other men like himself. It is necessary to the continuance of life on this planet that more and more people make this discovery. We have been given the choice. Man possesses the power to obliterate himself, sacrificing the whole race on the altar of some God-substitute. Or he can choose life in partnership with God the Father of all. I believe that there is evidence that more and more people are waking up to the realization that this crucial decision peers us in the face here and now.

Cathedrals and churches are always places into which we bring human experiences – birth, marriage, death, our flickering communion with God, our fragile relationships with each other, so that they may be deepened and directed by the spirit of Christ. Today we bring our mixture of thanksgiving, sorrows and aspirations for a better ordering of this world. Pray God that he may purify, enlarge and redirect these in the ways of his kingdom of love and peace. Amen.

*Dr Runcie retired in 1991.*

•

## NEIL KINNOCK
### Bridgend, 7 June 1983

*'I warn you'*

*The Labour Party, led by Michael Foot, was in deep disarray during the British general election of 1983 and its manifesto was described as the longest suicide note in history. One of Foot's most devoted lieutenants was Neil Kinnock (1942–), a Welsh Labour MP on the left wing of the party and a rising star.*

*Kinnock showed in this speech, delivered on the eve of the election, that he is a natural orator. It was clear, he declared, that a new Thatcher government would cut spending on health, education, and pensions and increase unemployment, taxes and interest rates. 'I warn you,' he went on . . .*

If Margaret Thatcher is re-elected as Prime Minister, *I warn you*

I warn you that you will have pain –
When healing and relief depend upon payment.

I warn you that you will have ignorance –
When talents are untended and wits are wasted, when learning is a privilege and not a right.

I warn you that you will have poverty –
When pensions slip and benefits are whittled away by a Government that won't pay in an economy that can't pay.

I warn you that you will be cold –
When fuel charges are used as a tax system that the rich don't notice and the poor can't afford.

I warn you that you must not expect work –
When many cannot spend, more will not be able to earn. When they don't earn, they don't spend. When they don't spend, work dies.

I warn you not to go into the streets alone after dark or into the streets in large crowds of protest in the light.

I warn you that you will be quiet –
When the curfew of fear and the gibbet of unemployment make you obedient.

I warn you that you will have defence of a sort –
With a risk and at a price that passes all understanding.

I warn you that you will be home-bound –
When fares and transport bills kill leisure and lock you up.

I warn you that you will borrow less –
When credit, loans, mortgages and easy payments are refused to people on your melting income.

If Margaret Thatcher wins, she will be more a Leader than a Prime Minister. That power produces arrogance and when it is toughened by Tebbitry and flattered and fawned upon by spineless sycophants, the boot-licking tabloid Knights of Fleet Street and placemen in the Quangos, the arrogance corrupts absolutely.

If Margaret Thatcher wins –

I warn you not to be ordinary.

I warn you not to be young.

I warn you not to fall ill.

I warn you not to get old.

*The successful resolution of the Falklands conflict was still vivid in the British memory and Margaret Thatcher won an easy election victory.*
*Four months later Neil Kinnock was elected leader of the Labour Party.*

•

## POPE JOHN PAUL II
Częstochowa, Poland, 18 June 1983

*'We do not want a Poland which costs us nothing'*

*John Paul II, the Polish Pope, made three visits to his native land. The third of these, in 1983, when Solidarity, the Polish workers' union, had been banned, was the most significant. On this visit, John Paul II said he had come to cry out before Europe and the world for the forgotten people of Eastern Europe.*

*On Saturday, 18 June, the Pope's helicopter took him to Częstochowa where he spoke, often in code, to what the London* Times *described as 'a ragamuffin army of a million young pilgrims' from the weather-worn battlement of the Jasna Góra monastery.*

*Dozens of Solidarity banners sprouted in the crowd as the Pope uttered certain trigger words − 'workers', or 'solidarity' (with a small 's') − or made any reference to truth or oppression or human rights.*

*He was greeted by huge applause, applause that was almost frightening, according to* The Times, *when voiced by so many people in such a confined space.*

Our Lady of Jasna Góra is the teacher of true love for all. And this is particularly important for you, dear young people. In you, in fact, is decided that form of love which all of your life will have and, through you, human life on Polish soil: the matrimonial, family, social and national form − but also the priestly, religious and missionary one. Every life is determined and evaluated by the interior form of love. Tell me what you love, and I will tell you who you are.

I watch! How beautiful it is that this word is found in the call of Jasna Góra. It possesses a profound evangelical ancestry: Christ says many times: 'Watch' (Matt. 26: 41). Perhaps also from the Gospel it passed into the tradition of scouting. In the call of Jasna Góra it is the essential element of the reply that we wish to give to the love by which we are surrounded in the sign of the Sacred Icon.

The response to this love must be precisely the fact that I watch! What does it mean, 'I watch'?

It means that I make an effort to be a person with a conscience. I do not stifle this conscience and I do not deform it; I call good and evil by name, and I do not blur them; I develop in myself what is good, and I seek to correct what is evil, by overcoming it in myself. This is a fundamental problem which can never be minimized or put on a secondary level. No! It is everywhere and always a matter of the first importance. Its importance is all the greater in proportion to the increase of circumstances which seem to favour our tolerance of evil and the fact that we easily excuse ourselves from this, especially if adults do so.

My dear friends! It is up to you to put up a firm barrier against immorality, a barrier – I say – to those social vices which I will not here call by name but which you yourselves are perfectly aware of. You must demand this of yourselves, even if others do not demand it of you. Historical experiences tell us how much the immorality of certain periods cost the whole nation. Today when we are fighting for the future form of our social life, remember that this form depends on what people will be like. Therefore: watch!

Christ said to the apostles, during his prayer in Gethsemane: 'Watch and pray that you may not enter into temptation' (Matt. 26: 41).

'I watch' also means: I see another. I do not close in on myself, in a narrow search for my own interests, my own judgements. 'I watch' means: love of neighbour; it means: fundamental interhuman solidarity.

Before the Mother of Jasna Góra I wish to give thanks for all the proofs of this solidarity which have been given by my compatriots, including Polish youth, in the difficult period of not many months ago. It would be difficult for me to enumerate here all the forms of this solicitude which surrounded those who were interned, imprisoned, dismissed from work, and also their families. You know this better than I. I received only sporadic news about it.

May this good thing, which appeared in so many places and so many ways, never cease on Polish soil. May there be a constant confirmation of that 'I watch' of the call of Jasna Góra, which is a response to the presence of the Mother of Christ in the great family of the Poles.

'I watch' also means: I feel responsible for this great common inheritance whose name is Poland. This name defines us all. This name obliges us all. This name costs us all.

Perhaps at times we envy the French, the Germans or the Americans because their name is not tied to such a historical price and because they are so easily free: while our Polish freedom costs so much.

My dear ones, I will not make a comparative analysis. I will only say that it is what costs that constitutes value. It is not, in fact, possible to be truly free without an honest and profound relationship with values. We do not want a Poland which costs us nothing. We watch, instead, beside all that makes up the authentic inheritance of the generations, seeking to enrich it. A nation, then, is first of all rich in its people. Rich in man. Rich in youth. Rich in every individual who watches in the name of truth: it is truth, in fact, that gives form to love.

My dear young friends! Before our common Mother and the Queen of our hearts, I desire finally to say to you that she knows your sufferings, your difficult youth, your sense of injustice and humiliation, the lack of prospects for the future that is so often felt, perhaps the temptations to flee to some other world.

Even if I am not among you every day, as was the case for many years in the past, nevertheless I carry in my heart a great solicitude. A great, enormous solicitude. A solicitude for you. Precisely because 'on you depends tomorrow'.

I pray for you every day.

It is good that we are here together at the hour of the call of Jasna Góra. In the midst of the trials of the present time, in the midst of the trial through which your generation is passing, this call of the millennium continues to be a programme.

In it is contained a fundamental way out. Because the way out in whatever dimension – economic, social, political – must happen first in man. Man cannot remain with no way out.

Mother of Jasna Góra, you who have been given to us by Providence for the defence of the Polish nation, accept this evening this call of the Polish youth together with the Polish Pope, and help us to persevere in hope! Amen.

*When freedom came to Eastern Europe in 1989, the Pope's speeches in Poland in 1983 were considered as one of the main contributions in bolstering the defiant human spirit that brought the walls of oppression tumbling down.*

·

## DENIS HEALEY
London, 27 February 1984

*'The great she-elephant, she who must be obeyed'*

*One of the earliest and most memorable attacks on the prime ministerial style of Margaret Thatcher was made by Denis Healey (1917–), one of the most combative and bruising speakers in the House of Commons. Healey, a former Labour Defence Secretary and Chancellor of the Exchequer, was speaking during a debate on a proposal by the Thatcher government to abolish the right of workers at GCHQ, the British intelligence eavesdropping station at Cheltenham, to belong to a union.*

Every trade unionist in Britain feels threatened by what the Government have done. The anger felt by trade unionists was felt deeply by everyone, not least Mr Murray [Lionel 'Len' Murray, leader of the Trades Union Congress], who attended the meeting with the Prime Minister last week, because she was felt to be accusing trade unions of lack of patriotism, of being prepared to risk people's lives and to break their promises. The Foreign Secretary made it crystal clear in his speech that that, in his view, is what trade union membership at GCHQ must imply. I ask the Government to recognize that they really cannot talk in those terms to people such as Terry Duffy and Kate Losinska, who are now leading the campaign against the Government. What a miracle the Government have achieved in the trade union movement.

I have not wasted time on the Foreign Secretary this afternoon, although I am bound to say that I feel that some of his colleagues must be a bit tired by now of his hobbling around from one of the doorsteps to another, with a bleeding hole in his foot and a smoking gun in his hand, telling them that he did not know it was loaded.

The Foreign Secretary, however, is not the real villain in this case; he is the fall guy. Those of us with long memories will feel that he is rather like poor van der Lubbe in the Reichstag fire trial. We are asking ourselves the question that was asked at the trial: who is the Mephistopheles behind this shabby Faust? The answer to that is clear. The handling of this decision by – I quote her own Back Benchers – the great she-elephant, she who must be obeyed, the Catherine the Great of Finchley, the Prime Minister herself, has drawn sympathetic trade unionists, such as Len Murray, into open revolt. Her pig-headed bigotry has prevented her closest colleagues and Sir Robert Armstrong from offering and accepting a compromise.

The Right Hon. Lady, for whom I have a great personal affection, has formidable qualities, a powerful intelligence and immense courage, but those qualities can turn into horrendous vices, unless they are moderated by colleagues who have more experience, understanding and sensitivity. As she has got rid of all those colleagues, no one is left in the Cabinet with both the courage and the ability to argue with her.

I put it to all Conservative Members, but mainly to the Government Front Bench, that to allow the Right Hon. Lady to commit Britain to another four years of capricious autocracy would be to do fearful damage not just to the Conservative Party but to the state. She has faced them with the most damaging of all conflicts of loyalty. They must choose between the interests of their country, our nation's security and our cohesion as a people and the obstinacy of an individual. I hope that they resolve this conflict in the interests of the nation. If not, they will carry a heavy responsibility for the tragedies that are bound to follow.

•

PRINCE CHARLES
London, 30 May 1984

*'A monstrous carbuncle'*

*It was the 150th anniversary of the Royal Institute of British Architects and the anniversary dinner was being held in the historic setting of Hampton Court, a few miles from central London. The hall was lit by candles, the evening was graced by the first masque commissioned since the eighteenth century – and the annual gold medal was being presented by Britain's future king, Charles, Prince of Wales.*

*The 700 architects were in for a shock if they were expecting princely platitudes from their honoured guest. Instead the prince launched into a forthright attack on architects who designed houses for the approval of fellow architects instead of the tenants. Ever since, however, the speech has been remembered for his damning indictment of a proposed extension to the National Gallery in London's Trafalgar Square as a 'monstrous carbuncle'.*

At last people are beginning to see that it is possible, and important in human terms, to respect old buildings, street plans and traditional scales and at the same time not to feel guilty about a preference for façades, ornaments and soft materials. At last, after witnessing the wholesale destruction of Georgian and Victorian housing in most of our cities, people have begun to realize that it *is* possible to restore old buildings and, what is more, that there are architects willing to undertake such projects.

For far too long, it seems to me, some planners and architects have consistently ignored the feelings and wishes of the mass of ordinary people in this country. Perhaps, when you think about it, it is hardly surprising as architects tend to have been trained to design buildings from scratch – to tear down and rebuild . . . A large number of us have developed a feeling that architects tend to design houses for the approval of fellow architects and critics, not for the tenants.

To be concerned about the way people live, about the environment they inhabit and the kind of community that is created by that environment should surely be one of the prime requirements of a really good architect. It has been most encouraging to see the development of community architecture as a natural reaction to the policy of decanting people to new towns and overspill estates where the extended family patterns of support were destroyed and the community life was lost. Now, moreover, we are seeing the gradual expansion of housing cooperatives, particularly in the inner-city areas of Liverpool, where the tenants are able to work with an architect of their own who listens to their comments and their ideas and tries to design the kind of environment they want, rather than the kind which tends to be imposed upon them without any degree of choice . . .

What I believe is important about community architecture is that it has shown ordinary people that their views are worth having; that architects and planners do not necessarily have the monopoly of knowing best about taste, style and planning; that they need not be made to feel guilty or ignorant if their natural preference is for the more traditional designs – for a small garden, for courtyards, arches and porches – and that there is a growing number of architects prepared to listen and to offer imaginative ideas . . .

It would be a tragedy if the character and skyline of our capital city were to be further ruined and St Paul's dwarfed by yet another giant glass stump, better suited to downtown Chicago than the City of London. It is hard to imagine that London before the last war must have had one of the most beautiful skylines of any great city, if those who recall it are to be believed. Those who do, say that the affinity between buildings and the earth, in spite of the city's immense size, was so close and organic that the houses looked almost as though they had grown out of the earth and had not been imposed upon it – grown, moreover, in such a way that as few trees as possible were thrust out of the way. Those who knew it then and loved it, as so many British love Venice without concrete stumps and glass towers, and those who can imagine what it was like, must associate with the sentiments in one of Aldous Huxley's earliest and most successful novels, *Antic Hay*, where the main character, an unsuccessful architect, reveals a model of London as Christopher Wren wanted to rebuild it after the Great Fire and describes how Wren was so obsessed with the opportunity the fire gave the city to rebuild itself into a greater and more glorious vision. What, then, are we doing to our capital city now? What have we done to it since the bombing during the war? What are we shortly going to do to one of its most famous areas – Trafalgar Square? Instead of designing an extension to the elegant façade of the National Gallery which complements it and continues the concept of columns and domes, it looks as if we may be presented with a kind of vast municipal fire station, complete with the sort of tower that contains the siren.

I would understand better this type of High Tech approach if you demolished the whole of Trafalgar Square and started again with a single architect responsible for the entire layout, but what is proposed is like a monstrous carbuncle on the face of a much loved and elegant friend. Apart from anything else, it defeats me why anyone wishing to display the early Renaissance pictures belonging to the gallery should do so in a new gallery so manifestly at odds with the whole spirit of that age of astonishing proportion. Why can't we have those curves and arches that express feeling in design? What is wrong with them? Why has everything got to be vertical, straight, unbending, only at right angles – and functional?

*The 'monstrous carbuncle' was never built. The plan by Peter Abrends was scrapped and Robert Venturi, an American architect, won a competition to design the gallery's new Sainsbury wing. In 1988 Prince Charles wrote and produced* A Vision of Britain, *a television documentary about his views on architecture which was later published as a book.*

•

## RONALD REAGAN
### Pointe du Hoc, Normandy, 6 June 1984

*'Let us make a vow to the dead'*

*According to his speechwriter Peggy Noonan, Ronald Reagan would and did read out anything she put in front of him. Even so, there was a quality to Reagan's speeches, whatever their cosy folksiness or the showbiz schmaltz that so infuriated his detractors, that touched hearts and made people weep genuine tears – as they did on this occasion commemorating the Normandy invasion of the Second World War.*

*It was an emotional day which became a celebration of heroism and sacrifice, Reagan wrote in his retirement. 'I stood there on that windswept point with the ocean behind me. Before me were the boys who forty years before had fought their way up from the ocean. Some rested under the white crosses and Stars of David that stretched out across the landscape. Others sat right in front of me. They looked like elderly businessmen, yet these were the kids who climbed the cliffs.'*

We're here to mark that day in history when the Allied peoples joined in battle to reclaim this continent to liberty. For four long years, much of Europe had been under a terrible shadow. Free nations had fallen, Jews cried out in the camps, millions cried out for liberation. Europe was enslaved, and the world prayed for its rescue. Here in Normandy the rescue began. Here the Allies stood and fought against tyranny in a giant undertaking unparalleled in human history.

We stand on a lonely, windswept point on the northern shore of France. The air is soft, but forty years ago at this moment, the air was dense with smoke and the cries of men, and the air was filled with the crack of rifle fire and the roar of cannon. At dawn, on the morning of the 6th of June 1944, 225 Rangers jumped off the British landing craft and ran to the bottom of these cliffs. Their mission was one of the most difficult and daring of the invasion: to climb these sheer and desolate cliffs and take out the enemy guns. The Allies had been told that some of the mightiest of these guns were here and they would be trained on the beaches to stop the Allied advance.

The Rangers looked up and saw the enemy soldiers – at the edge of the cliffs shooting down at them with machine-guns and throwing grenades. And the American Rangers began to climb. They shot rope ladders over the face of these cliffs and began to pull themselves up. When one Ranger fell, another would take his place. When one rope was cut, a Ranger would grab another and begin his climb again. They climbed, shot back, and held their footing. Soon, one by one, the Rangers pulled themselves over the top, and in seizing the firm land at the top of these cliffs, they began to seize back the continent of Europe. Two hundred and twenty-five came here. After two days of fighting only ninety could still bear arms.

Behind me is a memorial that symbolizes the Ranger daggers that were thrust into the top of these cliffs. And before me are the men who put them there.

These are the boys of Pointe du Hoc. These are the men who took the cliffs. These are the champions who helped free a continent. These are the heroes who helped end a war.

Gentlemen, I look at you and I think of the words of Stephen

Spender's poem. You are men who in your 'lives fought for life . . . and left the vivid air signed with your honour' . . .

Forty summers have passed since the battle that you fought here. You were young the day you took these cliffs; some of you were hardly more than boys, with the deepest joys of life before you. Yet you risked everything here. Why? Why did you do it? What impelled you to put aside the instinct for self-preservation and risk your lives to take these cliffs? What inspired all the men of the armies that met here? We look at you, and somehow we know the answer. It was faith, and belief; it was loyalty and love.

The men of Normandy had faith that what they were doing was right, faith that they fought for all humanity, faith that a just God would grant them mercy on this beachhead or on the next. It was the deep knowledge – and pray God we have not lost it – that there is a profound moral difference between the use of force for liberation and the use of force for conquest. You were here to liberate, not to conquer, and so you and those others did not doubt your cause. And you were right not to doubt.

You all knew that some things are worth dying for. One's country is worth dying for, and democracy is worth dying for, because it's the most deeply honourable form of government ever devised by man. All of you loved liberty. All of you were willing to fight tyranny, and you knew the people of your countries were behind you.

•

## NEIL KINNOCK
### Bournemouth, 1 October 1985

*'You can't play politics with people's jobs'*

*As Labour leader from 1983, Neil Kinnock, by insisting on the modernization of the party, prepared the ground which led to New Labour's historic election victory under Tony Blair in 1997. Kinnock made his reputation as leader in this scornful denunciation of the militants of Merseyside in his address to the party conference.*

*Forty-eight hours before the conference the Militant Tendency, which effectively controlled Liverpool City Council, hired a fleet of taxis to send redundancy notices to all council employees. For Militant, led by Derek Hatton, the tactic was a consciousness-raising element of its strategy of confronting the Thatcher government, but Kinnock saw it as cynical extremism that would give Labour a bad name.*

*When the conference met, with Hatton sitting only twenty feet away, Kinnock made a searing denunciation of Militant tactics. Hatton rose to his feet, shouting 'Liar, liar', which only heightened the drama of the leader's declaration of war on the Trotskyists.*

If socialism is to be successful in this country, it must relate to the practical needs and the mental and moral traditions of the men and women of this country. We must emphasize what we have in common with those people who are our neighbours, workmates and fellow countrymen and women – and we have everything in common with them – in a way we could not do if we were remote, if, like the Tories, we were in orbit around the realities of our society, if, like the Social Democrats and the Liberals, we stood off from those realities, retreated from them, deserted them. But we are of, from, for the people. That is our identity, that is our commitment, that is how much we have in common with the people. Let us emphasize that, let us demonstrate it, let us not hide it away as if it was something extraordinary or evidence of reaction. Let us emphasize what we have in common with the people of this country.

We must not dogmatize or browbeat. We have got to reason with people; we have got to persuade people. That is their due. We have voluntarily, every one of us, joined a political party. We wish a lot more people would come and join us, help us, give us their counsel, their energies, their advice, broaden our participation. But in making the choice to join a political party we took a decision, and it was that, by persuasion, we hoped that we could bring more people with us. So that is the basis on which we have got to act, want to act . . .

[There is] something else you know. There is anger in this country at the devastation brought about by these last six years of Tory government, but strangely that anger is mixed with despair, a feeling that the problems are just too great, too complex, to be dealt with by any government or any policy. That feeling is abroad. We disagree with it, we contend it, we try to give people the rational alternatives, but it exists. If our response to that despair, anger and confusion amounts to little more than slogans, if we give the impression to the British people that we believe that we can just make a loud noise and the Tory walls of Jericho will fall down, they are not going to treat us very seriously at all – and we won't deserve to be treated very seriously . . .

I shall tell you again what you know. Because you are from the people, because you are of the people, because you live with the same realities as everybody else lives with, implausible promises don't win victories. I'll tell you what happens with impossible promises. You start with far-fetched resolutions. They are then pickled into a rigid dogma, a code, and you go through the years sticking to that, out-dated, misplaced, irrelevant to the real needs, and you end in the grotesque chaos of a Labour council – a *Labour council* – hiring taxis to scuttle round a city handing out redundancy notices to its own workers. I am telling you, no matter how entertaining, how fulfilling to short-term egos – I'm telling you, and you'll listen – you can't play politics with people's jobs and with people's services or with their homes. Comrades, the voice of the people – not the people here; the voice of the real people with real needs – is louder than all the boos that can be assembled. Understand that, please, comrades. In your socialism, in your commitment to those people, understand it. The people will not, cannot, abide posturing. They cannot respect the gesture-generals or the tendency-tacticians

Comrades, it seems to me lately that some of our number have become like latter-day public school boys. It seems it matters not whether you won or lost, but how you played the game. We cannot take that inspiration from Rudyard Kipling. Those game players get isolated, hammered, blocked off. They might try to blame others – workers, trade unions, some other leadership, the people of the city – for not showing sufficient revolutionary consciousness, always somebody else, and then they claim a rampant victory. Whose victory? Not victory for the people, not victory for them. I see the casualties; we all see the casualties. They are not to be found amongst the leaders and some of the enthusiasts; they are to be found amongst the people whose jobs are destroyed, whose services are crushed, whose living standards are pushed down to deeper depths of insecurity and misery. Comrades, these are vile times under this Tory government for local democracy, and we have got to secure power to restore real local democracy.

But I look around this country and I see Labour councils, I see socialists, as good as any other socialists, who fought the good fight and who, at the point when they thought they might jeopardize people's jobs and people's services, had the intelligence, yes, and the courage to adopt a different course. They truly put jobs and services first before other considerations. They had to make hellish choices. I understand it. You must agonize with them in the choices they had to make – very unpalatable, totally undesirable, but they did it. They found ways. They used all their creativity to find ways that would best protect those whom they employed and those whom they were elected to defend. Those people are leaders prepared to take decisions, to meet obligations, to give service. They know life is real, life is earnest – too real, too earnest to mistake a Conference Resolution for an accomplished fact; too real, too earnest to mistake a slogan for a strategy; too real, too earnest to allow them to mistake their own individual enthusiasms for mass movement; too real, too earnest to mistake barking for biting. I hope that becomes universal too.

Comrades, I offer you this counsel. The victory of socialism, said a great socialist, does not have to be complete to be convincing. I have no time, he went on, for those who appear to threaten the whole of private property but who in practice would threaten nothing; they are purists and therefore barren. Not the words of some hypnotized moderate, not some petrified pragmatist, but Aneurin Bevan in 1950 at the height of his socialist vision and his radical power and conviction. There are some who will say that power and principle are somehow in conflict. Those people who think that power and principle are in conflict only demonstrate the superficiality, the shallowness, of their own socialist convictions; for whilst they are bold enough to preach those convictions in little coteries, they do not have the depth of conviction to subject those convictions, those beliefs, that analysis, to the real test of putting them into operation in power.

*Most delegates were delighted by the speech. Kinnock's rating in a Harris poll two days later climbed fourteen points and he overtook Thatcher.*

•

## RONALD REAGAN
### Oval Office of the White House, 28 January 1986

*'The future doesn't belong to the fainthearted'*

*A few hours after the spectacular* Challenger *space shuttle disaster, President Reagan delivered this address to the nation. It was a characteristic example of the Reagan style – homely, almost conversational but achieving exactly the right emotion. The speech was memorable for its closing lines, which were from the poem 'High Flight', a sonnet written by John Gillespie Magee, a Canadian pilot who flew Spitfires from Britain during the Second World War and who was killed at the age of nineteen in December 1941.*

*This was a classic case of a speechwriter – Peggy Noonan, who learned the poem at school – remembering the appropriate quotation at the right moment. Reagan was present when the actor Tyrone Power returned from the war and recited 'High Flight' from memory at a homecoming party. The poem was used for years as the close-down reading of a Washington television station.*

Nineteen years ago, almost to the day, we lost three astronauts in a terrible accident on the ground. But we've never lost an astronaut in flight; we've never had a tragedy like this. And perhaps we've forgotten the courage it took for the crew of the shuttle; but they, the *Challenger* Seven, were aware of the dangers, but overcame them and did their jobs brilliantly. We mourn seven heroes: Michael Smith, Dick Scobee, Judith Resnik, Ronald McNair, Ellison Onizuka, Gregory Jarvis, and Christa McAuliffe. We mourn their loss as a nation together.

For the families of the seven, we cannot bear, as you do, the full impact of this tragedy. But we feel the loss, and we're thinking about you so very much. Your loved ones were daring and brave, and they had that special grace, that special spirit that says, 'Give me a challenge and I'll meet it with joy.' They had a hunger to explore the universe and discover its truths. They wished to serve, and they did. They served all of us.

We've grown used to wonders in this century. It's hard to dazzle us. But for twenty-five years the United States space programme has been doing just that. We've grown used to the idea of space, and perhaps we forget that we've only just begun. We're still pioneers. They, the members of the *Challenger* crew, were pioneers.

And I want to say something to the schoolchildren of America who were watching the live coverage of the shuttle's takeoff. I know it is hard to understand, but sometimes painful things like this happen. It's all part of the process of exploration and discovery. It's all part of taking a chance and expanding man's horizons. The future doesn't belong to the fainthearted; it belongs to the brave. The *Challenger* crew was pulling us into the future, and we'll continue to follow them . . .

There's a coincidence today. On this day 390 years ago, the great explorer Sir Francis Drake died aboard ship off the coast of Panama. In his lifetime the great frontiers were the oceans, and a historian later said, 'He lived by the sea, died on it, and was buried in it.' Well, today we can say of the *Challenger* crew: their dedication was, like Drake's, complete.

The crew of the space shuttle *Challenger* honoured us by the manner in which they lived their lives. We will never forget them, nor the last time we saw them, this morning, as they prepared for the journey and waved goodbye and 'slipped the surly bonds of earth' to 'touch the face of God.'

•

## NEIL KINNOCK
Llandudno, 15 May 1987

*'Why am I the first Kinnock in a thousand generations to be able
to get to university?'*

*Even his rivals acknowledged that Neil Kinnock, in his first election as leader of
the Labour Party in 1987, fought an energetic and effective campaign. That was
particularly true on television where his party political broadcasts were made by
Hugh Hudson, the celebrated director of the Oscar-winning* Chariots of Fire.

*The most memorable of the television broadcasts showed Kinnock and
Glenys, his wife, strolling in the hills above Llandudno on the North Wales
coast, and included extracts from this speech to the Welsh Labour Party.*

*The rousing passion of his speech and the emotional atmosphere in the packed
conference hall became a hallmark of Kinnock's election rallies and demonstrated
that, when he spoke from the soul rather than a sanitized script prepared so as
not to frighten away potential voters with the bogy of a socialist government, he
was the greatest British orator of his generation.*

We are democratic socialists. We care all the time. We don't think it's
a soft sentiment, we don't think it's 'wet'.

We think that care is the essence of strength.

And we believe that because we know that strength without care
is savage and brutal and selfish.

Strength with care is compassion – the practical action that is
needed to help people lift themselves to their full stature.

That's real care – it is not soft or weak. It is tough and strong.

But where do we get that strength to provide that care?

Do we wait for some stroke of good fortune, some benign giant,
some socially conscious Samson to come along and pick up the
wretched of the earth?

Of course we don't.

We cooperate, we collect together, we coordinate so that everyone
can contribute and everyone can benefit, everyone has responsibilities,

everyone has rights. That is how we put care into action. That is how we make the weak strong, that is how we lift the needy, that is how we make the sick whole, that is how we give talent the chance to flourish, that is how we turn the unemployed claimant into the working contributor.

We do it together. It is called collective strength, collective care. And its whole purpose is individual freedom.

When we speak of collective strength and collective freedom, collectively achieved, we are not fulfilling that nightmare that Mrs Thatcher tries to paint, and all her predecessors have tried to saddle us with.

We're not talking about uniformity; we're not talking about regimentation; we're not talking about *conformity* – that's their creed. The uniformity of the dole queue; the regimentation of the unemployed young and their compulsory work schemes. The *conformity* of people who will work in conditions, and take orders, and accept pay *because of* mass unemployment that they would laugh at in a free society with full employment.

That kind of freedom for the individual, that kind of liberty can't be secured by most of the people for most of the time if they're just left to themselves, isolated, stranded, with their whole life chances dependent upon luck!

Why am I the first Kinnock in a thousand generations to be able to get to university? Why is Glenys the first woman in her family in a thousand generations to be able to get to university?

Was it because *all* our predecessors were 'thick'? Did they lack talent – those people who could sing, and play, and recite and write poetry; those people who could make wonderful, beautiful things with their hands; those people who could dream dreams, see visions; those people who had such a sense of perception as to know in times so brutal, so oppressive, that they could win their way out of that by coming together?

Were those people not university material? Couldn't they have knocked off all their A-levels in an afternoon?

But why didn't they get it?

Was it because they were weak? – those people who could work eight hours underground and then come up and play football?

Weak? Those women who could survive eleven childbearings, were they weak? Those people who could stand with their backs and their legs straight and face the people who had control over their lives, the ones who owned their workplaces and tried to own them, and tell them, 'No. I won't take your orders.' Were they weak?

Does anybody really think that they didn't gct what we had because they didn't have the talent, or the strength, or the endurance, or the commitment?

Of course not. It was because there was no platform upon which they could stand; no arrangement for their neighbours to subscribe to their welfare; no method by which the communities could translate their desires for those individuals into provision for those individuals.

And now, Mrs Thatcher, by dint of privatization, and means test, and deprivation, and division, wants to nudge us back into the situation where everybody can either stand on their own feet, or live on their knees.

*The 1987 British general election marked the high noon of Margaret Thatcher's three governments and she won her third victory – but Kinnock destroyed the Alliance of the Liberals and the Social Democrats as the main alternative to the Tories. The American politician Joe Biden was later to pinch a theme from Kinnock's speech and ask 'Why am I the fourteenth Joe Biden . . .?' Kinnock lost his second general election in 1992 and subsequently resigned as leader of the Labour Party.*

•

# EDWARD KENNEDY
Atlanta, 19 July 1988

*'Now is the time'*

*At the Democrat Convention in Atlanta in 1988, Senator Edward Kennedy introduced by his nephew John Fitzgerald Kennedy Jr, spoke in support of Michael Dukakis, who had been chosen to fight George Bush.*

*As his speech ended, he pledged 'every resource' of his mind and spirit to the Democrat cause – and then movingly recalled the dream, and the dreamers, who had inspired Democrats since the 1960s.*

You and I have stood together many times, but no time has been more important than this.

The campaign that stretches before us now is a struggle for the souls and the future of America. For we are more than a political coalition, more than a collection of programmes, more than the sum of our prospects and our strategy. Most of all, we are the trustees of a dream.

Twenty years ago, in 1968, we lost two of the most powerful voices of that dream. But they left us their vision, their values, and the hopes they awakened.

In the countless millions of people whose hearts they touched, we remember them now to remind ourselves that the American journey is unfinished, that we stand for change in order to march again towards enduring ideals, that we do not have to settle for things as they are.

Martin Luther King Jr told us something we need to hear anew. He said, 'We are now faced with the fact that tomorrow is today. We are confronted with the fierce urgency of now, in the unfolding life and history. There is such a thing as being too late.' (*Applause.*)

And Dr King also said, 'We must work unceasingly to lift this Nation to a higher destiny, to a new plateau of compassion.'

And in that time there was another voice, only briefly heard, but whose words too have outlasted all the loss in years. Robert Kennedy said, 'Each time a man stands up for an ideal, or acts to improve the lot of others, or strikes out against injustice, he sends forth a tiny ripple of hope. And crossing each other from a million different centres of energy and daring, those ripples build a current that can sweep down the mightiest walls of oppression and resistance.' (*Applause.*)

He was my brother. But he and Dr King were also in the deepest sense brothers to us all. These two, these valiant two, lived for the same dream and were gone only months apart.

And if they were here with us, two decades later, I think I know what they would say: 'Now is the time. Some men see things as they are and say, why? We dream things that never were and say, why not? Now is the time.' (*Spontaneous demonstration.*)

•

## JESSE JACKSON
Atlanta, 19 July 1988

### *'Keep hope alive'*

*As a charismatic preacher and black activist, Jesse Jackson (1941–) worked with Martin Luther King and was ordained a Baptist minister in 1968, the year King was assassinated. He subsequently assumed King's mantle as America's most articulate spokesman for black rights and established PUSH (People United to Save Humanity) in 1971 to promote the economic advancement of black people.*

*He was the first black American to mount a serious campaign for the presidency when in 1984 he constructed a 'rainbow coalition' of minority groups. He lost to Walter Mondale.*

*Four years later he came second to Michael Dukakis. He made this memorable speech, of which this is the peroration, as he accepted the nomination as vice-president.*

I'm often asked, 'Jesse, why do you take on these tough issues? They're not very political. We can't win that way.'

If an issue is morally right, it will eventually be political. It may be political and never be right. Fannie Lou Hamer didn't have the most votes in Atlantic City, but her principles have outlasted every delegate who voted to lock her out. Rosa Parks did not have the most votes, but she was morally right. Dr King didn't have the most votes about the Vietnam war, but he was morally right. If we're principled first, our politics will fall in place.

'Jesse, why did you take these big bold initiatives?' A poem by an unknown author went something like this: We mastered the air, we've conquered the sea, and annihilated distance and prolonged life, we were not wise enough to live on this earth without war and without hate.

As for Jesse Jackson, I'm tired of sailing my little boat, far inside the harbour bar. I want to go out where the big ships float, out on the deep where the great ones are. And should my frail craft prove too slight, the waves that sweep those billows o'er, I'd rather go down in a stirring fight than drown to death in the sheltered shore.

We've got to go out, my friends, where the big boats are.

And then, for our children, young America, hold your head high now. We can win. We must not lose you to drugs and violence, premature pregnancy, suicide, cynicism, pessimism and despair. We can win.

Wherever you are tonight, I challenge you to hope and to dream. Don't submerge your dreams. Exercise above all else, even on drugs, dream of the day you're drug-free. Even in the gutter, dream of the day that you'll be upon your feet again. You must never stop dreaming. Face reality, yes. But don't stop with the way things are; dream of things as they ought to be. Dream. Face pain, but love, hope, faith, and dreams will help you rise above the pain.

Use hope and imagination as weapons of survival and progress, but you keep on dreaming, young America. Dream of peace. Peace is rational and reasonable. War is irrational in this age and unwinnable.

Dream of teachers who teach for life and not for living. Dream of doctors who are concerned more about public health than private wealth. Dream of lawyers more concerned about justice than a judgeship. Dream of preachers who are concerned more about prophecy than profiteering. Dream on the high road of sound values.

And in America, as we go forth to September, October and November and then beyond, America must never surrender to a high moral challenge.

Do not surrender to drugs. The best drug policy is a no first use. Don't surrender with needles and cynicism. Let's have no first use on the one hand, or clinics on the other. Never surrender, young America.

Go forward. America must never surrender to malnutrition. We can feed the hungry and clothe the naked. We must never surrender. We must go forward. We must never surrender to illiteracy. Invest in our children. Never surrender; and go forward.

We must never surrender to inequality. Women cannot compromise ERA [Equal Rights Amendment] or comparable worth. Women are making 60 cents on the dollar to what a man makes. Women cannot buy milk cheaper. Women deserve to get paid for the work that you do. It's right and it's fair.

Don't surrender, my friends. Those who have AIDS tonight, you deserve our compassion. Even with AIDS you must not surrender in your wheelchairs. I see you sitting here tonight in those wheelchairs. I've stayed with you. I've reached out to you across our nation. Don't you give up. I know it's tough sometimes. People look down on you. It took you a little more effort to get here tonight.

And no one should look down on you, but sometimes mean people do. The only justification we have for looking down on someone is that we're going to stop and pick them up. But even in your wheelchairs, don't you give up. We cannot forget fifty years ago when our backs were against the wall, [Franklin D.] Roosevelt was in a wheelchair. I would rather have Roosevelt in a wheelchair than Reagan and [George] Bush on a horse. Don't you surrender and don't give up.

Don't surrender and don't give up. Why can I challenge you this way? 'Jesse Jackson, you don't understand my situation. You be on television. You don't understand. I see you with the big people. You don't understand my situation.' I understand. You're seeing me on TV but you don't know the me that makes me, me. They wonder why does Jesse run, because they see me running for the White House. They don't see the house I'm running from.

I have a story. I wasn't always on television. Writers were not always outside my door. When I was born late one afternoon, October 8th, in Greenville, SC, no writers asked my mother her name. Nobody chose to write down her address. My mama was not supposed to make it. And I was not supposed to make it. You see, I was born to a teenage mother who was born to a teenage mother.

I understand. I know abandonment and people being mean to you, and saying you're nothing and nobody, and can never be anything. I understand. Jesse Jackson is my third name. I'm adopted. When I had no name, my grandmother gave me her name. My name was Jesse Burns until I was twelve. So I wouldn't have a blank space, she gave me a name to hold me over. I understand when nobody knows your name. I understand when you have no name. I understand.

I wasn't born in the hospital. Mama didn't have insurance. I was born in the bed at the house. I really do understand. Born in a three-room house, bathroom in the backyard, slop jar by the bed, no hot and cold running water. I understand. Wallpaper used for decoration? No. For a windbreaker. I understand. I'm a working person's person, that's why I understand you whether you're black or white.

I understand work. I was not born with a silver spoon in my mouth. I had a shovel programmed for my hand. My mother, a working woman. So many days she went to work with runs in her stockings. She knew better, but she wore runs in her stockings so that my brother and I could have matching socks and not be laughed at at school.

I understand. At three o'clock on Thanksgiving Day we couldn't eat turkey because mama was preparing someone else's turkey at three o'clock. We had to play football to entertain ourselves and then around six o'clock she would get off the Alta Vista bus when we would bring up the leftovers and eat our turkey – leftovers, the carcass, the cranberries around eight o'clock at night. I really do understand.

Every one of these funny labels they put on you, those of you who are watching this broadcast tonight in the projects, on the corners, I understand. Call you outcast, low down, you can't make it, you're nothing, you're from nobody, subclass, underclass – when you see Jesse Jackson, when my name goes in nomination, your name goes in nomination.

I was born in the slum, but the slum was not born in me. And it wasn't born in you, and you can make it. Wherever you are tonight you can make it. Hold your head high, stick your chest out. You can make it. It gets dark sometimes, but the morning comes. Don't you surrender. Suffering breeds character. Character breeds faith. In the end faith will not disappoint.

You must not surrender. You may or may not get there, but just know that you're qualified and you hold on and hold out. We must never surrender. America will get better and better. Keep hope alive. Keep hope alive. Keep hope alive. On tomorrow night and beyond, keep hope alive.

I love you very much. I love you very much.

*The presidential election was won by George Bush, the Republican candidate.*

•

# MARGARET THATCHER
## Bruges, 20 September 1988

### 'The frontiers of the State'

*Margaret Thatcher's attitude to the European Community, which constantly made Britain appear the odd nation out, split her Cabinet, led to the resignation of both Nigel Lawson, Chancellor of the Exchequer, and Sir Geoffrey Howe, Foreign Secretary, and was one of the main reasons for her downfall in 1990. Thatcher was suspicious that the European Community was a recipe for the creeping state socialism and trade-union power that she had seen off in Britain.*

*No speech by Mrs Thatcher provoked more controversy during her eleven years as prime minister of Britain than her address – drafted by Sir Charles Powell, her adviser on foreign affairs – to the College of Europe in Bruges. The Bruges speech set out in the sharpest focus her opposition to any form of European federalism that would undermine the sovereignty of the nation state – the F word issue that has since been a dominant theme of principle in British politics.*

Europe is not the creation of the Treaty of Rome. Nor is the European idea the property of any group or institution. We British are as much heirs to the legacy of European culture as any other nation. Our links to the rest of Europe, the continent of Europe, have been the *dominant* factor in our history. For 300 years we were part of the Roman Empire and our maps still trace the straight lines of the roads the Romans built. Our ancestors – Celts, Saxons and Danes – came from the continent.

Our nation was – in that favourite Community word – 'restructured' under Norman and Angevin rule in the eleventh and twelfth centuries.

This year we celebrate the three-hundredth anniversary of the Glorious Revolution in which the British crown passed to Prince William of Orange and Queen Mary.

Visit the great churches and cathedrals of Britain, read our literature and listen to our language: all bear witness to the cultural riches which we have drawn from Europe – and other Europeans from us.

We in Britain are rightly proud of the way in which, since Magna Carta in 1215, we have pioneered and developed representative institutions to stand as bastions of freedom. And proud too of the way in which for centuries Britain was a home for people from the rest of Europe who sought sanctuary from tyranny.

But we know that without the European legacy of political ideas we could not have achieved as much as we did. From classical and medieval thought we have borrowed that concept of the rule of law which marks out a civilized society from barbarism. And on that idea of Christendom – for long synonymous with Europe – with its recognition of the unique and spiritual nature of the individual, we still base our belief in personal liberty and other human rights.

Too often the history of Europe is described as a series of interminable wars and quarrels. Yet from our perspective today surely what strikes us most is our common experience. For instance, the story of how Europeans explored and colonized and – yes, without apology – civilized much of the world is an extraordinary tale of talent, skill and courage.

We British have in a special way contributed to Europe. Over the centuries we have fought to prevent Europe from falling under the dominance of a single power. We have fought and we have died for her freedom. Only miles from here in Belgium lie the bodies of 120,000 British soldiers who died in the First World War. Had it not been for that willingness to fight and to die, Europe *would* have been united long before now – but not in liberty, not in justice. It was British support to resistance movements throughout the last war that helped to keep alive the flame of liberty in so many countries until the day of liberation.

All these things alone are proof of our commitment to Europe's future.

The European Community is *one* manifestation of that European identity. But it is not the only one. We must never forget that east of the Iron Curtain peoples who once enjoyed a full share of European culture, freedom and identity have been cut off from their roots. We shall always look on Warsaw, Prague and Budapest as great European cities.

Nor should we forget that European values have helped to make the United States of America into the valiant defender of freedom which she has become.

This is no arid chronicle of obscure facts from the dust-filled libraries of history. It is the record of nearly two thousand years of British involvement *in* Europe, cooperation *with* Europe and contribution *to* Europe, a contribution which today is as valid and as strong as ever. Yes, we have looked also to wider horizons – as have others – and thank goodness for that, because Europe never would have prospered and never will prosper as a narrow-minded, inward-looking club.

The European Community belongs to *all* its members. It must reflect the traditions and aspirations of *all* its members.

And let me be quite clear. Britain does not dream of some cosy, isolated existence on the fringes of the European Community. Our destiny is in Europe, as part of the Community. That is not to say that our future lies *only* in Europe. But nor does that of France or Spain, or indeed any other member.

The Community is not an end in itself. Nor is it an institutional device to be constantly modified according to the dictates of some abstract intellectual concept. Nor must it be ossified by endless regulation.

The European Community is the practical means by which Europe can ensure the future prosperity and security of its people in a world in which there are many other powerful nations and groups of nations . . .

To try to suppress nationhood and concentrate power at the centre of a European conglomerate would be highly damaging and would jeopardize the objectives we seek to achieve.

Europe will be stronger precisely because it has France as France, Spain as Spain, Britain as Britain, each with its own customs, traditions and identity. It would be folly to try to fit them into some sort of identikit European personality.

Some of the founding fathers of the Community thought that the United States of America might be its model.

But the whole history of America is quite different from Europe. People went there to get away from the intolerance and constraints of life in Europe. They sought liberty and opportunity; and their strong sense of purpose has, over two centuries, helped create a new unity and pride in being American – just as our pride lies in being British or Belgian or Dutch or German.

I am the first to say that on many great issues the countries of Europe should try to speak with a single voice. I want to see us work more closely on the things we can do better together than alone. Europe is stronger when we do so, whether it be in trade, in defence, or in our relations with the rest of the world.

But working more closely together does *not* require power to be centralized in Brussels or decisions to be taken by an appointed bureaucracy.

Indeed, it is ironic that just when those countries such as the Soviet Union, which have tried to run everything from the centre, are learning that success depends on dispersing power and decisions away from the centre, some in the Community seem to want to move in the opposite direction.

We have not successfully rolled back the frontiers of the State in Britain only to see them reimposed at a European level, with a European super-State exercising a new dominance from Brussels.

Certainly we want to see Europe more united and with a greater sense of common purpose. But it must be in a way which preserves the different traditions, parliamentary powers and sense of national pride in one's own country; for these have been the source of Europe's vitality through the centuries.

•

## VÁCLAV HAVEL
Prague, 1 January 1990

*'A contaminated moral environment'*

*Communism in Eastern Europe died in 1989 as one by one the Communist regimes in Poland, Czechoslovakia, Hungary, Romania and Bulgaria collapsed. The year ended with the crumbling of the Berlin Wall. It was the springtime of nations, the most exciting year in European history since 1848.*

*The motto of the year was 'Truth shall prevail' and it was a year of truth for Communism. As Timothy Garton Ash, an eyewitness to the events, puts it: 'There is a real sense in which these regimes lived by the word and perished by the word. For what, after all, happened? A few thousands, then tens of thousands, then hundreds of thousands went on to the streets. They spoke a few words. "Resign," they said. "No more shall we be slaves!" "Free elections." "Freedom!" And the walls of Jericho fell. And with the walls, the communist parties simply crumbled.'*

*That sense that truth will prevail is what made the first speech by Václav Havel, the playwright who was elected Czech president on 29 December 1989, so moving and uplifting in its expression of the defiant human spirit that conquered Communism during that memorable year.*

*One theme of Havel's work was that under Communism almost everybody lived a double life, saying one thing in public and another in private. It was a theme to which he returned in this speech on New Year's Day, broadcast on radio and television, with his comments on the 'contaminated moral environment' under the Communist regime.*

My dear fellow citizens, for forty years you heard from my predecessors on this day different variations of the same theme: how our country flourished, how many million tons of steel we produced, how happy we all were, how we trusted our government, and what bright perspectives were unfolding in front of us.

I assume you did not propose me for this office so that I, too, would lie to you.

Our country is not flourishing. The enormous creative and spiritual potential of our nation is not being used sensibly. Entire branches of industry are producing goods which are of no interest to anyone, while we are lacking the things we need. A state which calls itself a workers' state humiliates and exploits workers. Our obsolete economy is wasting the little energy we have available. A country that once could be proud of the educational level of its citizens spends so little on education that it ranks today as seventy-second in the world. We have polluted our soil, our rivers and forests, bequeathed to us by our ancestors, and we have today the most contaminated environment in Europe. Adult people in our country die earlier than in most other European countries . . .

But all this is still not the main problem. The worst thing is that we live in a contaminated moral environment. We fell morally ill because we became used to saying something different from what we thought. We learned not to believe in anything, to ignore each other, to care only about ourselves. Concepts such as love, friendship, compassion, humility, or forgiveness lost their depth and dimensions, and for many of us they represented only psychological peculiarities, or they resembled gone-astray greetings from ancient times, a little ridiculous in the era of computers and spaceships. Only a few of us were able to cry out loud that the powers that be should not be all-powerful, and that special farms, which produce ecologically pure and top-quality food just for them, should send their produce to schools, children's homes, and hospitals if our agriculture was unable to offer them to all. The previous regime – armed with its arrogant and intolerant ideology – reduced man to a force of production and nature to a tool of production. In this it attacked both their very substance and their mutual relationship. It reduced gifted and autonomous people, skilfully working in their own country, to nuts and bolts of some monstrously huge, noisy, and stinking machine, whose real meaning is not clear to anyone. It cannot do more than slowly but inexorably wear down itself and all its nuts and bolts.

When I talk about contaminated moral atmosphere, I am not talking just about the gentlemen who eat organic vegetables and do not look out of the plane windows. I am talking about all of us. We had all become used to the totalitarian system and accepted it as an unchangeable fact and thus helped to perpetuate it. In other words, we are all – though naturally to differing extents – responsible for the operation of the totalitarian machinery, none of us is just its victim: we are all also its co-creators.

Why do I say this? It would be very unreasonable to understand the sad legacy of the last forty years as something alien, which some distant relative bequeathed us. On the contrary, we have to accept this legacy as a sin we committed against ourselves. If we accept it as such, we will understand that it is up to us all, and up to us only, to do something about it. We cannot blame the previous rulers for everything, not only because it would be untrue but also because it could blunt the duty that each of us faces today, namely, the obligation to act independently, freely, reasonably, and quickly. Let us not be mistaken: the best government in the world, the best parliament and the best president, cannot achieve much on their own. And it would also be wrong to expect a general remedy from them only. Freedom and democracy include participation and therefore responsibility from us all.

If we realize this, then all the horrors that the new Czechoslovak democracy inherited will cease to appear so terrible. If we realize this, hope will return to our hearts.

In the effort to rectify matters of common concern, we have something to lean on. The recent period – and in particular, the last six weeks of our peaceful revolution – has shown the enormous human, moral, and spiritual potential and civic culture that slumbered in our society under the enforced mask of apathy. Whenever someone categorically claimed that we were this or that, I always objected that society is a very mysterious creature and that it is not wise to trust only the face it presents to you. I am happy that I was not mistaken. Everywhere in the world people wonder where those meek, humiliated, sceptical, and seemingly cynical citizens of Czechoslovakia found the marvellous strength to shake from their shoulders in several weeks and in a decent and peaceful way the totalitarian yoke. And let us ask: from where did the young people who never knew another system take their desire for truth, their love of free thought, their political ideas, their civic courage and civic

prudence? How did it happen that their parents – the very generation that had been considered as lost – joined them? How is it
possible that so many people immediately knew what to do and
none of them needed any advice or instruction? . . .

Masaryk* based his politics on morality. Let us try in a new time
and in a new way to restore this concept of politics. Let us teach ourselves and others that politics should be an expression of a desire to
contribute to the happiness of the community rather than of a need
to cheat or rape the community. Let us teach ourselves and others
that politics can be not only the art of the possible, especially if this
means the art of speculation, calculation, intrigue, secret deals, and
pragmatic manoeuvring, but that it can even be the art of the impossible, namely, the art of improving ourselves and the world . . .

There are free elections and an election campaign ahead of us. Let
us not allow this struggle to dirty the so far clean face of our gentle
revolution. Let us not allow the sympathies of the world which we
have won so fast to be equally rapidly lost through our becoming
entangled in the jungle of skirmishes for power. Let us not allow the
desire to serve oneself to bloom once again under the fair mask of
the desire to serve the common good. It is not really important now
which party, club, or group will prevail in the elections. The important thing is that the winners will be the best of us, in the moral, civic,
political, and professional sense, regardless of their political affilia-
tions. The future policies and prestige of our state will depend on the
personalities we select and later elect to our representative bodies . . .

In conclusion, I would like to say that I want to be a president
who will speak less and work more. To be a president who will not
only look out of the windows of his aeroplane but who, first and
foremost, will always be present among his fellow citizens and listen
to them well.

You may ask what kind of republic I dream of. Let me reply: I
dream of a republic independent, free, and democratic, of a republic

---

*Thomas Masaryk (1850–1937) was the first president of Czechoslovakia
after it won independence in 1918. The name was anathema to the Communist regime.

economically prosperous and yet socially just, in short, of a humane republic which serves the individual and which therefore holds the hope that the individual will serve it in turn. Of a republic of well-rounded people, because without such it is impossible to solve any of our problems, human, economic, ecological, social, or political.

The most distinguished of my predecessors opened his first speech with a quotation from the great Czech educator Comenius. Allow me to round off my first speech with my own paraphrase of the same statement:

People, your government has returned to you!

•

## NELSON MANDELA
Cape Town, 11 February 1990

*'Our march to freedom is irreversible'*

*Twenty-seven years after he was first imprisoned, Nelson Mandela, a worldwide symbol of resistance to apartheid, then seventy-one and white-haired, walked out of prison with a smile on his face, raised his hand in the clenched-fist salute of the African National Congress, and made his first speech since he stood in the dock accused of treason. Speaking to a crowd of 50,000 under the majestic shadow of Table Mountain, and watched by a global audience of millions on television, he placed the remaining years of his life in the hands of his people and ended his speech with the words he had uttered from the dock in 1964.*

Friends, Comrades and fellow South Africans. I greet you all in the name of peace, democracy and freedom for all. I stand here before you not as a prophet but as a humble servant of you, the people. Your tireless and heroic sacrifices have made it possible for me to be here today. I therefore place the remaining years of my life in your hands . . .

Today the majority of South Africans, black and white, recognize that apartheid has no future. It has to be ended by our own decisive mass action in order to build peace and security. The mass campaign of defiance and other actions of our organization and people can only culminate in the establishment of democracy.

The apartheid destruction on our subcontinent is incalculable. The fabric of family life of millions of my people has been shattered. Millions are homeless and unemployed. Our economy lies in ruins and our people are embroiled in political strife.

Our resort to the armed struggle in 1960 with the formation of the military wing of the ANC, Umkhonto we Sizwe (Spear of the Nation), was a purely defensive action against the violence of apartheid. The factor which necessitated the armed struggle still exists today. We have no option but to continue . . .

Negotiations on the dismantling of apartheid will have to address the overwhelming demand of our people for a democratic, non-racial and unitary South Africa.

There must be an end to white monopoly on political power, and a fundamental restructuring of our political and economic systems to ensure that the inequalities of apartheid are addressed and our society thoroughly democratized.

It must be added that Mr de Klerk himself is a man of integrity, who is acutely aware of the dangers of a public figure not honouring his undertakings. But as an organization, we base our policy and strategy on the harsh reality we are faced with. And this reality is that we are still suffering under the policies of the Nationalist government.

Our struggle has reached a decisive moment. We call on our people to seize this moment, so that the process towards democracy is rapid and uninterrupted.

We have waited too long for our freedom! We can no longer wait. Now is the time to intensify the struggle on all fronts. To relax our efforts now would be a mistake which generations to come will not be able to forgive. The sight of freedom looming on the horizon should encourage us to redouble our efforts. It is only through disciplined mass action that our victory can be assured.

We call on our white compatriots to join us in the shaping of a new South Africa. The freedom movement is a political home for you, too. We call on the international community to continue the campaign to isolate the apartheid regime. To lift sanctions now would be to run the risk of aborting the process towards the complete eradication of apartheid.

Our march to freedom is irreversible. We must not allow fear to stand in our way. Universal suffrage on a common voters' roll in a united, democratic and non-racial South Africa is the only way to peace and racial harmony.

In conclusion I wish to go to my own words during my trial in 1964. They are as true today as they were then. I quote:

'I have fought against white domination and I have fought against black domination. I have cherished the ideal of a democratic and free society in which all persons live together in harmony and with equal opportunity. It is an ideal which I hope to live for and to achieve. But if needs be, it is an ideal for which I am prepared to die. *Amandla* (power)!'

*A year later President de Klerk of South Africa announced proposals to disman- tle the structure of apartheid. Mandela and de Klerk were awarded the Nobel Peace Prize in 1993, and Nelson Mandela became South Africa's first black president in May 1994. He retired in 1999.*

•

# SIR GEOFFREY HOWE
## London, 13 November 1990

### 'A conflict of loyalty'

*Sir Geoffrey Howe (1926–) served throughout the eleven years of Margaret Thatcher's three administrations, first as Chancellor of the Exchequer, then as Foreign Secretary and finally as leader of the Commons. By 1990 he was the sole survivor from her first Cabinet. Yet their relationship, which had never been founded on mutual admiration, had sharply deteriorated, mainly because of Mrs Thatcher's distrust of the instincts of the Foreign Office, and her frequent humil- iations of Howe, who was also her deputy. The apparently faithful and imperturbable Howe finally snapped and he resigned on 1 November, saying he could no longer serve her with honour.*

*Howe's pedestrian style was once memorably summed up. Being attacked by him was like being savaged by a dead sheep, said his opponent Denis Healey. Yet in his resignation speech the dead sheep became a lion, drawing audible gasps of surprise from fellow Conservatives (who included Mrs Thatcher). It was 'an act of brilliantly executed matricide', says Sir Ronald Millar, Mrs Thatcher's principal speechwriter, 'each word honed with Aesculapian skill for maximum effect'.*

It has been suggested – even, indeed, by some of my Right Hon. and Hon. Friends – that I decided to resign solely because of questions of style and not on matters of substance at all. Indeed, if some of my former colleagues are to be believed, I must be the first minister in history who has resigned because he was in full agreement with government policy. The truth is that, in many aspects of politics, style and substance complement each other. Very often, they are two sides of the same coin . . .

It was a great honour to serve for six years as Foreign and Commonwealth Secretary and to share with my Right Hon. Friend [Margaret Thatcher] in some notable achievements in the European Community. But it was as we moved on to consider the crucial monetary issues in the European context that I came to feel increasing concern. Some of the reasons for that anxiety were made very clear by my Right Hon. Friend the Member for Blaby [Nigel Lawson] in his resignation speech just over twelve months ago. Like him, I concluded at least five years ago that the conduct of our policy against inflation could no longer rest solely on attempts to measure and control the domestic money supply. We had no doubt that we should be helped in that battle, and, indeed, in other respects, by joining the exchange rate mechanism of the European monetary system.

There was, or should have been, nothing novel about joining the ERM; it has been a long-standing commitment. For a quarter of a century after the Second World War, we found that the very similar Bretton Woods regime did serve as a useful discipline. Now, as my Right Hon. Friend the Prime Minister acknowledged two weeks ago, our entry into the ERM can be seen as an 'extra discipline for keeping down inflation'. However, it must be said that the practical conclusion has been achieved only at the cost of substantial damage to her Administration and, more serious still, to its inflation achievements.

It was the late Lord Stockton, formerly Harold Macmillan, who first put the central point clearly. As long ago as 1962, he argued that we had to place and keep ourselves within the Community. He saw it as essential then as it is today not to cut ourselves off from the realities of power, not to retreat into a ghetto of sentimentality about our past and so diminish our control over our own destiny in the future.

The pity is that the Macmillan view had not been perceived more clearly a decade before in the fifties. It would have spared so many of the struggles of the past twenty years had we been in the Community from the outset, had we been ready, in the much too simple phrase, to 'surrender some sovereignty' at a much earlier stage.

Had we been in from the start we should have had more not less influence over the Europe in which we live today. We should never forget the lesson of that isolation, of being on the outside looking in, for the conduct of today's affairs.

We have done best when we have seen the Community not as a static entity to be resisted and contained, but as an active process which we can shape often decisively provided we allow ourselves to be fully engaged in it with confidence and enthusiasm and in good faith.

We must at all costs avoid presenting ourselves yet again with an over-simplified choice, a false antithesis, a bogus dilemma, between one alternative clearly labelled 'cooperation between independent sovereign states' and a second equally crudely labelled alternative 'a centralized federal super-state' as if there were no middle way in between.

We commit a serious error if we think always in terms of 'surrendering' sovereignty and seek to stand pat for all time on a given deal by proclaiming, as the prime minister did two weeks ago, that we have 'surrendered enough'. The European enterprise is not and should not be seen like that, as some kind of zero sum gain.

Sir Winston Churchill put it much more positively forty years ago when he said: 'It is also possible and not less agreeable to regard [this sacrifice or merger of national sovereignty] as the gradual assumption by all the nations concerned of that larger sovereignty which can alone protect their diverse and distinctive customs and characteristics and their national traditions.'

I find Winston Churchill's perception a good deal more convincing and encouraging for the interests of our nation than the nightmare image sometimes conjured up by the Prime Minister who sometimes seems to look out on a Continent that is positively teeming with ill-intentioned people scheming, in her words, to 'extinguish democracy', to 'dissolve our national identities', to lead us 'through the back door into a federal Europe'.

What kind of vision is that for our business people who trade there each day, for our financiers who seek to make London the money capital of Europe, or for all the young people of today? These concerns are especially important as we approach the crucially important topic of EMU. We must be positively and centrally involved in this debate and not fearfully and negatively detached. The cost of disengagement here could be very serious indeed . . .

The tragedy is – and it is for me personally, for my party, for our whole people, for the Prime Minister herself a very real tragedy – that the Prime Minister's perceived attitude towards Europe is running increasingly serious risks for the future of our nation. It risks minimizing our influence and maximizing our chances of being once again shut out.

We have paid heavily in the past for late starts and squandered opportunities in Europe. We dare not let that happen again. If we detach ourselves completely as a party or as a nation from the middle ground of Europe, the effects will be incalculable and very hard ever to correct.

In my letter of resignation, which I tendered with the utmost sadness and dismay, I said: 'Cabinet government is about trying to persuade one another from within.' That was my commitment to government by persuasion, persuading colleagues and the nation.

I have tried to do that as Foreign Secretary and since, but I realize now that the task has become futile, of trying to stretch the meaning of words beyond what was credible, and trying to pretend there was a common policy when every step forward risked being subverted by some casual comment or impulsive answer.

The conflict of loyalty, of loyalty to my Right Hon. Friend the Prime Minister – and, after all, in two decades together that instinct of loyalty is still very real – and of loyalty to what I perceive to be the true interests of the nation, has become all too great. I no longer believe it possible to resolve that conflict from within this government. That is why I have resigned. In doing so, I have done what I believe to be right for my party and my country. The time has come for others to consider their own response to the tragic conflict of loyalties with which I have myself wrestled for perhaps too long.

*Howe's speech led to the downfall of Margaret Thatcher. Shortly afterwards, Michael Heseltine announced that he would stand against her in the annual leadership election. Mrs Thatcher failed to muster enough votes to win on the first round, subsequently withdrew, and John Major won on the second ballot.*

•

## AUNG SAN SUU KYI
### Burma, 1990

#### 'Freedom from fear'

*Aung San Suu Kyi has been described as the most famous woman in the world never to have held office and, along with the Dalai Lama, as one of the most fêted exponents of non-violent political protest since Mahatma Gandhi. She was put under house arrest by Burma's military government after her National League for Democracy Party won an overwhelming victory in the 1990 general election when she made this speech – and spent fifteen of the next twenty-one years without her freedom. She sacrificed life with her husband and two sons rather than yield to the junta and refused to return to England when her husband was dying of cancer because she feared she would not be allowed to return to Burma. She was awarded the Nobel Peace Prize in 1991.*

It is not power that corrupts but fear. Fear of losing power corrupts those who wield it and fear of the scourge of power corrupts those who are subject to it. Most Burmese are familiar with the four *a-gati*, the four kinds of corruption. *Chanda-gati*, corruption induced by desire, is deviation from the right path in pursuit of bribes or for the sake of those one loves. *Dosa-gati* is taking the wrong path to spite those against whom one bears ill will, and *moga-gati* is aberration due to ignorance. But perhaps the worst of the four is *bhaya-gati*, for not only does *bhaya*, fear, stifle and slowly destroy all sense of right and wrong, it so often lies at the root of the other three kinds of corruption. Just as *chanda-gati*, when not the result of sheer avarice, can be caused by fear of want or fear of losing the goodwill of those one loves, so fear of being surpassed, humiliated or injured in some way can provide the impetus for ill will. And it would be difficult to dispel ignorance unless there is freedom to pursue the truth unfettered by fear. With so close a relationship between fear and corruption it is little wonder that in any society where fear is rife corruption in all forms becomes deeply entrenched.

Public dissatisfaction with economic hardships has been seen as the chief cause of the movement for democracy in Burma, sparked off by the student demonstrations in 1988. It is true that years of incoherent policies, inept official measures, burgeoning inflation and falling real income had turned the country into an economic shambles. But it was more than the difficulties of eking out a barely acceptable standard of living that had eroded the patience of a traditionally good-natured, quiescent people – it was also the humiliation of a way of life disfigured by corruption and fear.

The students were protesting not just against the death of their comrades but against the denial of their right to life by a totalitarian regime which deprived the present of meaningfulness and held out no hope for the future. And because the students' protests articulated the frustrations of the people at large, the demonstrations quickly grew into a nationwide movement. Some of its keenest supporters were businessmen who had developed the skills and the contacts necessary not only to survive but to prosper within the system. But their affluence offered them no genuine sense of security or fulfilment, and they could not but see that if they and their fellow citizens, regardless of economic status, were to achieve a worthwhile existence, an accountable administration was at least a necessary if not a sufficient condition. The people of Burma had wearied of a precarious state of passive apprehension . . .

The effort necessary to remain uncorrupted in an environment where fear is an integral part of everyday existence is not immediately apparent to those fortunate enough to live in states governed by the rule of law. Just laws do not merely prevent corruption by meting out impartial punishment to offenders. They also help to create a society in which people can fulfil the basic requirements necessary for the preservation of human dignity without recourse to corrupt practices. Where there are no such laws, the burden of upholding the principles of justice and common decency falls on the ordinary people. It is the cumulative effect on their sustained effort and steady endurance which will change a nation where reason and conscience are warped by fear into one where legal rules exist to promote man's desire for harmony and justice while restraining the less desirable destructive traits in his nature.

In an age when immense technological advances have created lethal weapons which could be, and are, used by the powerful and the unprincipled to dominate the weak and the helpless, there is a compelling need for a closer relationship between politics and ethics at both the national and international levels. The Universal Declaration of Human Rights of the United Nations proclaims that 'every individual and every organ of society' should strive to promote the basic rights and freedoms to which all human beings regardless of race, nationality or religion are entitled. But as long as there are governments whose authority is founded on coercion rather than on the mandate of the people, and interest groups which place short-term profits above long-term peace and prosperity, concerted international action to protect and promote human rights will remain at best a partially realized struggle. There will continue to be arenas of struggle where victims of oppression have to draw on their own inner resources to defend their inalienable rights as members of the human family . . .

Within a system which denies the existence of basic human rights, fear tends to be the order of the day. Fear of imprisonment, fear of torture, fear of death, fear of losing friends, family, property or means of livelihood, fear of poverty, fear of isolation, fear of failure. A most insidious form of fear is that which masquerades as common sense or even wisdom, condemning as foolish, reckless, insignificant or futile the small daily acts of courage which help to preserve man's self-respect and inherent human dignity. It is not easy for a people conditioned by fear under the iron rule of the principle that might is right to free themselves from the enervating miasma of fear. Yet even under the most crushing state machinery courage rises up again and again, for fear is not the natural state of civilized man.

The wellspring of courage and endurance in the face of unbridled power is generally a firm belief in the sanctity of ethical principles combined with a historical sense that despite all setbacks the condition of man is set on an ultimate course for both spiritual and material advancement. It is his capacity for self-improvement and self-redemption which most distinguishes man from the mere brute. At the root of human responsibility is the concept of perfection, the urge to achieve it, the intelligence to find a path towards it, and the will to follow that path if not to the end at least the distance needed to rise above individual limitations and environmental impediments. It is man's vision of a world fit for rational, civilized humanity which leads him to dare and to suffer to build societies free from want and fear. Concepts such as truth, justice and compassion cannot be dismissed as trite when these are often the only bulwarks which stand against ruthless power.

•

### TONY BENN
London, 20 November 1991

*'I cannot hand away powers lent to me'*

*Although he is one of the most controversial politicians in Britain, described by one historian as a populist guru of the left, a dissident, an individualist, almost an anarchist, even his most dedicated political opponents acknowledge the power and persuasiveness of Tony Benn's oratory.*

*That is particularly true of his speeches on Europe. Benn (1925–) campaigned against joining the European Community from the outset of the British debate and has consistently warned against what he sees as the perils of federalism.*

*As the debate in Britain over a federal Europe intensified towards the end of 1991, with the signing of the Maastricht treaty imminent, Benn, Labour MP for Chesterfield, made this speech to the House of Commons. It was admired by many Conservatives, some his fiercest critics, who believed that on this occasion he spoke for England. Norman Tebbit, a staunch ally of Margaret Thatcher, said it was the best speech he had ever heard in the House.*

Some people genuinely believe that we shall never get social justice from the British Government, but we shall get it from Jacques Delors. They believe that a good king is better than a bad Parliament. I have never taken that view. Others believe that the change is inevitable, and that the common currency will protect us from inflation and will provide a wage policy. They believe that it will control speculation and that Britain cannot survive alone. None of those arguments persuade me because the argument has never been about sovereignty.

I do not know what a sovereign is, apart from the one that used to be in gold and the Pope who is a sovereign in the Vatican. We are talking about democracy. No nation – not even the great United States which could, for all I know, be destroyed by a nuclear weapon from a third-world country – has the power to impose its will on other countries. We are discussing whether the British people are to be allowed to elect those who make the laws under which they are governed. The argument is nothing to do with whether we should get more maternity leave from Madame Papandreou than from Madame Thatcher. That is not the issue.

I recognize that when the members of the three Front Benches agree, I am in a minority. My next job therefore is to explain to the people of Chesterfield what we have decided. I will say first, 'My dear constituents, in future you will be governed by people whom you do not elect and cannot remove. I am sorry about it. They may give you better crèches and shorter working hours but you cannot remove them.'

I know that it sounds negative but I have always thought it positive to say that the important thing about democracy is that we can remove without bloodshed the people who govern us. We can get rid of a Callaghan, a Wilson or even a Right Hon. Lady by internal processes. We can get rid of the Right Hon. Member for Huntingdon [Mr Major]. But that cannot be done in the structure that is proposed. Even if one likes the policies of the people in Europe one cannot get rid of them.

Secondly, we say to my favourite friends, the Chartists and suffragettes, 'All your struggles to get control of the ballot box were a waste of time. We shall be run in future by a few white persons, as in 1832.' The instrument, I might add, is the Royal Prerogative of treaty making. For the first time since 1649 the Crown makes the laws – advised, I admit, by the Prime Minister.

We must ask what will happen when people realize what we have done. We have had a marvellous debate about Europe, but none of us has discussed our relationship with the people who sent us here . . .

If people lose the power to sack their Government one of several things happens. First, people may just slope off. Apathy could destroy democracy. When the turnout drops below 50 per cent, we are in danger . . .

The second thing that people can do is to riot. Riot is an old-fashioned method for drawing the attention of the Government to what is wrong. It is difficult for an elected person to admit it, but the riot at Strangeways produced some prison reforms. Riot has historically played a much larger part in British politics than we are ever allowed to know.

Thirdly, nationalism can arise. Instead of blaming the Treaty of Rome, people say, 'It is those Germans' or 'It is the French'. Nationalism is built out of frustration that people feel when they cannot get their way through the ballot box. With nationalism comes repression. I hope that it is not pessimistic – in my view it is not – to say that democracy hangs by a thread in every country of the world. Unless we can offer people a peaceful route to the resolution of injustices through the ballot box they will not listen to a House that has blocked off that route.

There are many alternatives open to us. One Hon. Member said that he was young and had not fought in the war. He looked at a new Europe. But there have been five Europes this century. There was one run by the King, the Kaiser and the Tsar – they were all cousins so that was very comfortable. They were all Queen Victoria's grandsons. And there was no nonsense about human rights when Queen Victoria's grandsons repressed people. Then there was the Russian revolution. Then there was the inter-war period. Then there was the Anglo-Soviet alliance. Then there was the cold war. Now we have a Boris Yeltsin who has joined the Monday Club. There have been many Europes. This is not the only Europe on offer . . .

Another way would be to have a looser, wider Europe. I have an idea for a Commonwealth of Europe. I am introducing a bill on the subject. Europe would be rather like the British Commonwealth. We would work by consent with people. Or we could accept this ghastly proposal, which is clumsy, secretive, centralized, bureaucratic and divisive. That is how I regard the Treaty of Rome. I was born a European and I will die one. But I have never put my alliance behind the Treaty of Rome. I object to it. I hate being called an anti-European. How can one be anti-European when one is born in Europe? It is like saying that one is anti-British if one does not agree with the Chancellor of the Exchequer. What a lot of nonsense it is.

I ask myself why the House is ready to contemplate abandoning its duties, as I fear that it is. I was elected forty-nine years ago this month. This Chamber has lost confidence in democracy. It believes that it must be governed by someone else. It is afraid to use the powers entrusted to it by its constituents. It has traded power for status. One gets asked to go on the telly if one is a Member of Parliament. The Chamber does not want to use its power. It has accepted the role of a spectator and joined what Bagehot called the dignified part of the constitution, leaving the Crown, under the control of the Prime Minister, to be the Executive part.

If democracy is destroyed in Britain it will be not the communists, Trotskyists or subversives but this House which threw it away.

The rights that are entrusted to us are not for us to give away. Even if I agree with everything that is proposed, I cannot hand away powers lent to me for five years by the people of Chesterfield. I just could not do it. It would be theft of public rights.

Therefore, there is only one answer. If people are determined to submit themselves to Jacques Delors, Madame Papandreou and the Council of Ministers, we must tell the people what is planned. If people vote for that, they will all have capitulated. Julius Caesar said, 'We are just merging our sovereignty.' So did William the Conqueror.

It is not possible to support the Government's motion. I have told the Chief Whip that I cannot support the Labour motion. I invite the House to vote against the Government's motion and not to support a motion which purports to take us faster into a Community which cannot reflect the aspirations of those who put us here. That is not a nationalist argument nor is it about sovereignty. It is a democratic argument and it should be decisive in a democratic Chamber.

•

## SALMAN RUSHDIE
### New York, December 1991

#### *'What is my single life worth?'*

*After publication of his novel* The Satanic Verses *Salman Rushdie became the first Western writer to become the subject of a* fatwa, *a death sentence issued by Ayatollah Khomeini of Iran, who decreed that his book was a blasphemy on the Muslim faith. For several years after 1989 he lived in hiding under 24-hour-a-day protection by British Special Branch bodyguards.*

*Rushdie spent the day of this speech, honouring the 200th anniversary of the First Amendment, in a fourteenth-floor suite with twenty armed bodyguards. The windows were blocked by bullet-proof mattresses. At the Columbia Graduate School of Journalism the audience were frisked before entry and the bomb squad was outside the hall. At the end three plain-clothed policemen escorted Rushdie back into hiding.*

A hot-air balloon drifts slowly over a bottomless chasm, carrying several passengers. A leak develops; the balloon starts losing height. The pit, a dark yawn, comes closer. Good grief! The wounded balloon can bear just one passenger to safety; the many must be sacrificed to save the one! But who should live, who should die? And who could make such a choice?

In point of fact, debating societies everywhere regularly make such choices without qualms, for of course what I've described is the given situation of that evergreen favourite, the Balloon Debate, in which, as the speakers argue over the relative merits and demerits of the well-known figures they have placed in disaster's mouth, the assembled company blithely accepts the faintly unpleasant idea that a human being's right to life is increased or diminished by his or her virtues or vices – that we may be born equal but thereafter our lives weigh differently in the scales.

It's only make-believe, after all. And while it may not be very nice, it does reflect how people actually think.

I have now spent over a thousand days in just such a balloon; but, alas, this isn't a game. For most of these thousand days, my fellow-travellers included the Western hostages in the Lebanon, and the British businessmen imprisoned in Iran and Iraq, Roger Cooper and Ian Richter. And I had to accept, and did accept, that for most of my countrymen and countrywomen, my plight counted for less than the others'. In any choice between us, I'd have been the first to be pitched out of the basket and into the abyss. 'Our lives teach us who we are,' I wrote at the end of my essay 'In Good Faith'. Some of the lessons have been harsh, and difficult to learn.

Trapped inside a metaphor, I've often felt the need to redescribe it, to change the terms. This isn't so much a balloon, I've wanted to say, as a bubble, within which I'm simultaneously exposed and sealed off. The bubble floats above and through the world, depriving me of reality, reducing me to an abstraction. For many people, I've ceased to be a human being. I've become an issue, a bother, an 'affair'. Bullet-proofed bubbles, like this one, are reality-proof, too. Those who travel in them, like those who wear Tolkien's rings of invisibility, become wraith-like if they're not careful. They get lost. In this phantom space a man may become the bubble that encases him, and then one day – pop! – he's gone forever.

It's ridiculous – isn't it? – to have to say, but I *am* a human being, unjustly accused, unjustly embubbled. Or is it I who am being ridiculous, as I call out from my bubble, *I'm still trapped in here, folks; somebody, please, get me out?*

Out there where you are, in the rich and powerful and lucky West, has it really been so long since religions persecuted people, burning them as heretics, drowning them as witches, that you can't recognize religious persecution when you see it? . . . The original metaphor has reasserted itself. I'm back in the balloon, asking for the right to live.

What is my single life worth? Despair whispers in my ear: 'Not a lot.' But I refuse to give in to despair.

I refuse to give in to despair because I've been shown love as well as hatred. I know that many people do care, and are appalled by the crazy, upside-down logic of the post-*fatwa* world, in which a single novelist can be accused of having savaged or 'mugged' a whole community, becoming its tormentor (instead of its tarred and feathered victim) and the scapegoat for all its discontents. Many people do ask, for example: When a white pop-star-turned-Islamic-fanatic speaks approvingly about killing an Indian immigrant, how does the Indian immigrant end up being called the racist?

Or, again: What minority is smaller and weaker than a minority of one?

I refuse to give in to despair even though, for a thousand days and more, I've been put through a degree course in worthlessness, my own personal and specific worthlessness. My first teachers were the mobs marching down distant boulevards, baying for my blood, and finding, soon enough, their echoes on English streets. I could not understand the force that makes parents hang murderous slogans around their children's necks. I have learned to understand it. It burns books and effigies and thinks itself holy. But at first, as I watched the marchers, I felt them trampling on my heart.

Once again, however, I have been saved by instances of fair-mindedness, of goodness. Every time I learn that a reader somewhere has been touched by *The Satanic Verses*, moved and entertained and stimulated by it, it arouses deep feelings in me. And there are more and more such readers nowadays, my postbag tells me, readers (including Muslims) who are willing to give my burned, spurned child a fair hearing at long last.

Sometimes I think that, one day, Muslims will be ashamed of what Muslims did in these times, will find the 'Rushdie affair' as improbable as the West now finds martyr-burning. One day they may agree that – as the European Enlightenment demonstrated – freedom of thought is precisely freedom from religious control, freedom from accusations of blasphemy.

Maybe they'll agree, too, that the row over *The Satanic Verses* was at bottom an argument about who should have power over the grand narrative, the Story of Islam, and that that power must belong equally to everyone. That even if my novel were incompetent, its attempt to retell the story would still be important. That if I've failed, others must succeed, because those who do not have power over the story that dominates their lives, power to retell it, rethink it, deconstruct it, joke about it, and change it as times change, truly are powerless, because they cannot think new thoughts.

One day. Maybe. But not today.

Today, my education in worthlessness continues, and what Saul Bellow would call my 'reality instructors' include: the media pundit who suggests that a manly death would be better for me than hiding like a rat; the letter-writer who points out that of course the trouble is that I *look* like the Devil, and wonders if I have hairy shanks and cloven hooves; the 'moderate' Muslim who writes to say that Muslims find it 'revolting' when I speak about the Iranian death threats (it's not the *fatwa* that's revolting, you understand, but my mention of it); the rather more immoderate Muslim who tells me to 'shut up', explaining that if a fly is caught in a spider's web, it should not attract the attention of the spider. I ask the reader to imagine how it might feel to be intellectually and emotionally bludgeoned, from a thousand different directions, every day for a thousand days and more.

Back in the balloon, something longed-for and heartening has happened. On this occasion, *mirabile dictu*, the many have not been sacrificed, but saved. That is to say, my companions, the Western hostages and the gaoled businessmen, have by good fortune and the efforts of others managed to descend safely to earth, and have been reunited with their families and friends, with their own, free lives. I rejoice for them, and admire their courage, their resilience. And now I'm alone in the balloon.

Surely I'll be safe now? Surely, now, the balloon will drop safely towards some nearby haven, and I, too, will be reunited with my life? Surely it's my turn now?

But the balloon is over the chasm again; and it's still sinking. I realize that it's carrying a great deal of valuable freight. Trading relations, armaments deals, the balance of power in the Gulf – these and other matters of great moment are weighing down the balloon. I hear voices suggesting that if I stay aboard, this precious cargo will be endangered. The national interest is being redefined; am I being redefined out of it? Am I to be jettisoned, after all?

When Britain renewed relations with Iran at the United Nations in 1990, the senior British official in charge of the negotiations assured me in unambiguous language that something very substantial had been achieved on my behalf. The Iranians, laughing merrily, had secretly agreed to forget the *fatwa*. (The diplomat put great stress on this cheery Iranian laughter.) They would 'neither encourage nor allow' their citizens, surrogates or proxies to act against me.

Oh, how I wanted to believe that. But in the year-and-a-bit that followed, we saw the *fatwa* restated in Iran, the bounty money doubled, the book's Italian translator severely wounded, its Japanese translator stabbed to death; there was news of an attempt to find and kill me by contract killers working directly for the Iranian government through its European embassies. Another such contract was successfully carried out in Paris, the victim being the harmless and aged ex-Prime Minister of Iran, Shapour Bakhtiar.

It seems reasonable to deduce that the secret deal made at the United Nations hasn't worked. Dismayingly, however, the talk as I write is all of improving relations with Iran still further, while the 'Rushdie case' is described as a side-issue.

Is this a balloon I'm in, or the dustbin of history?

At the end of 1990, dispirited and demoralized, feeling abandoned, even then, in consequence of the British government's decision to patch things up with Iran, and with my marriage at an end, I faced my deepest grief, my unquenchable sorrow at having been torn away from, cast out of, the cultures and societies from which I'd always drawn my strength and inspiration – that is, the broad community of British Asians, and the broader community of Indian Muslims. I determined to make my peace with Islam, even at the cost of my pride. Those who were surprised and displeased by what I did perhaps failed to see that I was not some deracinated Uncle Tom Wog.

To these people it was apparently incomprehensible that I should seek to make peace between the warring halves of the world, which were also the warring halves of my soul – and that I should seek to do so in a spirit of humility, instead of the arrogance so often attributed to me.

In 'In Good Faith' I wrote: 'Perhaps a way forward might be found through the mutual recognition of [our] mutual pain', but even moderate Muslims had trouble with this notion: what pain, they asked, could I possibly have suffered? *What was I talking about?* As a result, the really important conversations I had in this period were with myself.

I said: Salman, you must send a message loud enough to be heard all over the world. You must make ordinary Muslims see that you aren't their enemy, and make the West understand a little more of the complexity of Muslim culture. It was my hope that Westerners might say, well, if he's the one in danger, and yet he's willing to acknowledge the importance of his Muslim roots, then perhaps we ought to start thinking a little less stereotypically ourselves. (No such luck, though. The message you send isn't always the one that's received.)

I reminded myself that I had always argued that it was necessary to develop the nascent concept of the 'secular Muslim', who, like the secular Jews, affirmed his membership of the culture while being separate from the theology. I had recently read the contemporary Muslim philosopher Fouad Zakariya's *Laïcité ou Islamisme*, and been encouraged by Zakariya's attempt to modernize Islamic thought. But, Salman, I told myself, you can't argue from outside the debating chamber. You've got to cross the threshold, go inside the room, and *then* fight for your humanized, historicized, secularized way of being a Muslim.

I recalled my near-namesake, the twelfth-century philosopher Ibn Rushd (Averroës), who argued that (to quote the great Arab historian Albert Hourani), 'not all the words of the Qu'ran should be taken literally. When the literal meaning of Qu'ranic verses appeared to contradict the truths to which philosophers arrived by the exercise of reason, those verses needed to be interpreted metaphorically.'

But Ibn Rushd was a snob. Having propounded an idea far in advance of its time, he qualified it by saying that such sophistication was only suitable for the élite; literalism would do for the masses. Salman, I asked myself, is it time to pick up Ibn Rushd's banner and carry it forward; to say, nowadays such ideas are fit for everybody, for the beggar as well as the prince?

It was with such things in mind – and with my thoughts in a state of some confusion and torment – that I spoke the Muslim creed before witnesses. But my fantasy of joining the fight for the modernization of Muslim thought, for freedom from the shackles of the Thought Police, was stillborn. It never really had a chance. Too many people had spent too long demonizing or totemizing me to listen seriously to what I had to say. In the West, some 'friends' turned against me, called me by yet another set of insulting names. Now I was spineless, pathetic, debased; I had betrayed myself, my Cause; above all, I had betrayed *them*.

I also found myself up against the granite, heartless certainties of Actually Existing Islam, by which I mean the political and priestly power structure that presently dominates and stifles Muslim societies. Actually Existing Islam has failed to create a free society anywhere on earth, and it wasn't about to let me, of all people, argue in favour of one.

Suddenly I was (metaphorically) among people whose social attitudes I'd fought all my life – for example, their attitudes about women (one Islamicist boasted to me that his wife would cut his toenails while he made telephone calls, and suggested I found such a spouse) or about gays (one of the Imams I met in December 1990 was on TV soon afterwards, denouncing Muslim gays as sick creatures who brought shame on their families and who ought to seek medical and psychiatric help). Had I truly fallen in among such people? *That was not what I meant at all.*

Facing the intransigence, the philistine scorn of so much of Actually Existing Islam, I reluctantly concluded that there was no way for me to help bring into the Muslim culture I'd dreamed of, the progressive, irreverent, sceptical, argumentative, playful and *unafraid* culture which is what I've always understood as *freedom.* Not me, not in this lifetime, no chance. Actually Existing Islam, which has all but deified its Prophet, a man who always fought passionately against such deification; which has supplanted a priest-free religion by a priest-ridden one; which makes literalism a weapon and redescriptions a crime, will never let the likes of me in.

Ibn Rushd's ideas were silenced in their time. And throughout the Muslim world today, progressive ideas are in retreat. Actually Existing Islam reigns supreme, and just as the recently destroyed 'Actually Existing Socialism' of the Soviet terror-state was horrifically unlike the utopia of peace and equality of which democratic socialists have dreamed, so also is Actually Existing Islam a force to which I have never given in, to which I cannot submit.

There is a point beyond which conciliation looks like capitulation. I do not believe I passed the point, but others have thought otherwise.

I have never disowned my book, nor regretted writing it. I said I was sorry to have offended people, because I had not set out to do so, and so I am. I explained that writers do not agree with every word spoken by every character they create – a truism in the world of books, but a continuing mystery to *The Satanic Verses'* opponents. I have always said that this novel has been traduced.

It has now been more than three years since *The Satanic Verses* was published; that's a long, long 'space for reconciliation'. Long enough. I accept that I was wrong to have given way on this point. *The Satanic Verses* must be freely available and easily affordable, if only because if it is not read and studied, then these years will have no meaning. Those who forget the past are condemned to repeat it.

'Our lives teach us who we are.' I have learned the hard way that when you permit anyone else's description of reality to supplant your own – and such descriptions have been raining down on me, from security advisers, governments, journalists, archbishops, friends, enemies, mullahs – then you might as well be dead. Obviously, a rigid, blinkered, absolutist world-view is the easiest to keep hold of; whereas the fluid, uncertain, metamorphic picture I've always carried about is rather more vulnerable.

Yet I must cling with all my might to that chameleon, that chimera, that shape-shifter, my own soul; must hold on to its mischievous, iconoclastic, out-of-step clown-instincts, no matter how great the storm. And if that plunges me into contradiction and paradox, so be it; I've lived in that messy ocean all my life. I've fished in it for my art. This turbulent sea was the sea outside my bedroom window in Bombay. It is the sea by which I was born, and which I carry within me wherever I go.

'Free speech is a non-starter,' says one of my Islamic extremist opponents. No, sir, it is not. Free speech is the whole thing, the whole ball game. Free speech is life itself.

That's the end of my speech from this ailing balloon. Now it's time to answer the question. What is my single life worth?

Is it worth more or less than the fat contracts and political treaties that are in here with me? Is it worth more or less than good relations with a country which, in April 1991, gave 800 women seventy-four lashes each for not wearing a veil; in which the eighty-year-old writer Mariam Pirouz is still in gaol, and has been tortured; and whose Foreign Minister says, in response to criticism of his country's lamentable human-rights record, 'International monitoring of the human rights situation in Iran should not continue indefinitely . . . Iran could not tolerate such monitoring for long'?

You must decide what you think a friend is worth to his friends, what you think a son is worth to his mother, or a father to his son.

You must decide what a man's conscience and heart and soul are worth. You must decide what you think a writer is worth, what value you place on a maker of stories, and an arguer with the world.

Ladies and gentlemen, the balloon is sinking into the abyss.

•

## QUEEN ELIZABETH II
London, 24 November 1992

### 'Annus horribilis'

*As Queen Elizabeth II celebrated her fortieth year on the throne in 1992, the British monarchy was in unprecedented disarray and under unprecedented attack. The Princess Royal had divorced, the Duke and Duchess of York had separated, and the marriage of the Prince and Princess of Wales had been exposed as a sham. Meanwhile, critics of the monarchy accused the Queen of being aloof and out of touch. The bill for the monarchy was too high, they said. The Queen should pay tax.*

*On 20 November Windsor Castle, one of the Queen's main homes, caught fire. Photographs of the blazing castle had a ring of the apocalypse. Sympathy for the Queen was dissipated, however, when the government said that she would not have to foot any of the bill to restore the castle.*

*Four days later the Lord Mayor of London, clad in brilliant ermine, was the Queen's host at a City of London lunch to celebrate the Queen's anniversary. The Queen was dressed in darkest navy, as if in mourning, and was suffering from a cold. She was almost croaking as she delivered the first unforgettable speech of her reign in which she accepted criticism but urged that it should be tempered with gentleness, good humour and understanding.*

Nineteen ninety-two is not a year I shall look back on with undiluted pleasure. In the words of one of my more sympathetic correspondents, it has turned out to be an 'Annus Horribilis'.

I suspect that I am not alone in thinking it so. Indeed, I suspect that there are very few people or institutions unaffected by these last months of worldwide turmoil and uncertainty. This generosity and wholehearted kindness of the Corporation of the City to Prince Philip and me would be welcome at any time, but at this particular moment, in the aftermath of Friday's tragic fire at Windsor, it is especially so. And, after this last weekend, we appreciate all the more what has been set before us today. Years of experience, however, have made us a bit more canny than the lady, less well versed than us in the splendours of City hospitality, who, when she was offered a balloon glass for her brandy, asked for 'only half a glass, please'. It is possible to have too much of a good thing. A well-meaning Bishop was obviously doing his best when he told Queen Victoria, 'Ma'am, we cannot pray too often, nor too fervently, for the Royal Family.' The Queen's reply was, 'Too fervently, no; too often, yes.'

I, like Queen Victoria, have always been a believer in that old maxim 'moderation in all things'. I sometimes wonder how future generations will judge the events of this tumultuous year. I dare say that history will take a slightly more moderate view than that of some contemporary commentators. Distance is well known to lend enchantment, even to the less attractive views. After all, it has the inestimable advantage of hindsight. But it can also lend an extra dimension to judgement, giving it a leavening of moderation and compassion – even of wisdom – that is sometimes lacking in the reactions of those whose task it is in life to offer instant opinions on all things great and small.

No section of the community has all the virtues, neither does any have all the vices. I am quite sure that most people try to do their jobs as best they can, even if the result is not always entirely successful. He who has never failed to reach perfection has a right to be the harshest critic. There can be no doubt, of course, that criticism is good for people and institutions that are part of public life. No institution – City, Monarchy, whatever – should expect to be free from the scrutiny of those who give it their loyalty and support, not to mention those who don't. But we are all part of the same fabric of our national society and that scrutiny, by one part of another, can be just as effective if it is made with a touch of gentleness, good humour and understanding. This sort of questioning can also act, and it should do so, as an effective engine for change. The City is a good example of the way the process of change can be incorporated into the stability and continuity of a great institution. I particularly admire, my Lord Mayor, the way in which the City has adapted so nimbly to what the Prayer Book calls 'the changes and chances of this mortal life'. You have set an example of how it is possible to remain effective and dynamic without losing those indefinable qualities, style and character. We only have to look around this great hall to see the truth of that.

Forty years is quite a long time. I am glad to have had the chance to witness, and to take part in, many dramatic changes in life in this country. But I am glad to say that the magnificent standard of hospitality given on so many occasions to the Sovereign by the Lord Mayor of London has not changed at all. It is an outward symbol of one other unchanging factor which I value above all – the loyalty given to me and my family by so many people in this country, and the Commonwealth, throughout my reign. You, my Lord Mayor, and all those whose prayers – fervent, I hope, but not too frequent – have sustained me through all these years, are friends indeed. Prince Philip and I give you all, wherever you may be, our most humble thanks.

*It was as if the Queen was begging for sympathy and baring her soul in public about the most horrible year of her reign, said the commentators. Annus horribilis, a phrase probably suggested by Sir Robert Fellowes, her private secretary, entered the language and was a gift to headline writers, even though the sceptical headline writers of the Sun, Britain's biggest-selling daily newspaper, rendered her message as 'One's Bum Year'. Within weeks it was announced that the Queen would pay tax and that the Prince of Wales, heir to the throne, and the Princess of Wales were to separate.*

•

## BILL CLINTON
### Memphis, 13 November 1993

### 'If Martin Luther King were to reappear'

*William Jefferson (Bill) Clinton (1946–) was born in Hope, Arkansas, educated at Georgetown, Yale and Oxford and became the youngest ever governor of Arkansas in 1978. He served five terms as governor before he defeated George Bush on a platform of hope and change in the presidential election of 1992.*

*Clinton was reared in a religious home. He made this speech to 5,000 ministers ten months after his inauguration at the Church of God in Christ in*

*Memphis from the pulpit where Martin Luther King preached his last sermon before his assassination. Clinton started the speech by describing some of the achievements of his presidency. Then he turned to what he really wanted to say, speaking impromptu.*

*William Safire, the distinguished American columnist, himself a former White House speechwriter, describes it as quintessential Clinton: 'personal, impassioned, anecdotal, self-questioning, colloquial and, with Bible-quoting Southern Baptist cadences, uplifting'.*

What I really want to say to you today, my fellow Americans, is that we can do all of this and still fail unless we meet the great crisis of the spirit that is gripping America today . . .

I tell you, unless we do something about crime and violence and drugs that is ravaging the community, we will not be able to repair this country.

If Martin Luther King, who said, 'Like Moses, I am on the mountaintop, and I can see the promised land, but I'm not going to be able to get there with you, but we will get there' – if he were to reappear by my side today and give us a report card on the last twenty-five years, what would he say? You did a good job, he would say, voting and electing people who formerly were not electable because of the colour of their skin. You have more political power, and that is good. You did a good job, he would say, letting people who have the ability to do so live wherever they want to live, go wherever they want to go in this great country. You did a good job, he would say, elevating people of colour into the ranks of the United States Armed Forces to the very top or into the very top of our Government. You did a very good job, he would say. He would say, you did a good job creating a black middle class of people who really are doing well, and the middle class is growing more among African-Americans than among non-African-Americans. You did a good job: you did a good job in opening opportunity.

But he would say: I did not live and die to see the American family destroyed. I did not live and die to see thirteen-year-old boys get automatic weapons and gun down nine-year-olds just for the kick of it. I did not live and die to see young people destroy their own lives with drugs and then build fortunes destroying the lives of others. That is not what I came here to do. I fought for freedom, he would say, but not for the freedom of people to kill each other with reckless abandon, not for the freedom of children to have children and the fathers of the children walk away from them and abandon them as if they don't amount to anything. I fought for people to have the right to work but not to have whole communities and people abandoned. This is not what I lived and died for.

My fellow Americans, he would say, I fought to stop white people from being so filled with hate that they would wreak violence on black people. I did not fight for the right of black people to murder other black people with reckless abandon.

The other day the Mayor of Baltimore, a dear friend of mine, told me a story of visiting the family of a young man who had been killed – eighteen years old – on Halloween. He always went out with little bitty kids so they could trick-or-treat safely. And across the street from where they were walking on Halloween, a fourteen-year-old boy gave a thirteen-year-old boy a gun and dared him to shoot the eighteen-year-old boy, and he shot him dead. And the Mayor had to visit the family.

In Washington, DC, where I live, your nation's Capital, the symbol of freedom throughout the world, look how that freedom is being exercised. The other night a man came along the street and grabbed a one-year-old child and put the child in his car. The child may have been the child of the man. And two people were after him, and they chased him in the car, and they just kept shooting with reckless abandon, knowing that baby was in the car. And they shot the man dead, and a bullet went through his body into the baby's body, and blew the little bootie off the child's foot.

The other day on the front page of our paper, the nation's Capital, are we talking about world peace or world conflict? No, big article on the front page of the *Washington Post* about an eleven-year-old child planning her funeral: 'These are the hymns I want sung. This is the dress I want to wear. I know I'm not going to live very long.' That is not the freedom, the freedom to die before you're a teenager is not what Martin Luther King lived and died for.

More than 37,000 people die from gunshot wounds in this country every year. Gunfire is the leading cause of death in young men. And now that we've all got so cool that everybody can get a semiautomatic weapon, a person shot now is three times more likely to die than fifteen years ago, because they're likely to have three bullets in them. A hundred and sixty thousand children stay home from school every day because they are scared they will be hurt in their schools.

The other day I was in California at a town meeting, and a handsome young man stood up and said: 'Mr President, my brother and I, we don't belong to gangs. We don't have guns. We don't do drugs. We want to go to school. We want to be professionals. We want to work hard. We want to do well. We want to have families. And we changed our school because the school we were in was so dangerous. So when we stowed up to the new school to register, my brother and I were standing in line and somebody ran into the school and started shooting a gun. My brother was shot down standing right in front of me at the safer school.' The freedom to do that kind of thing is not what Martin Luther King lived and died for, not what people gathered in this hallowed church for the night before he was assassinated in April of 1968. If you had told anybody who was here in that church on that night that we would abuse our freedom in that way, they would have found it hard to believe. And I tell you, it is our moral duty to turn it around . . .

I read a wonderful speech the other day given at Howard University in a lecture series funded by Bill and Camille Cosby, in which the speaker said, 'I grew up in Anacostia years ago. Even then it was all black, and it was a very poor neighbourhood. But you know, when I was a child in Anacostia, a 100 per cent African-American neighbourhood, a very poor neighbourhood, we had a crime rate that was lower than the average of the crime rate of our city. Why? Because we had coherent families. We had coherent communities. The people who filled the church on Sunday lived in the same place they went to church. The guy that owned the drugstore lived down the street. The person that owned the grocery store lived in our community. We were whole.' And I say to you, we have to make our people whole again.

This church has stood for that. Why do you think you have 5 million members in this country? Because people know you are filled with the spirit of God to do the right thing in this life by them. So I say to you, we have to make a partnership, all the Government agencies, all the business folks; but where there are no families, where there is no order, where there is no hope, where we are reducing the size of our armed services because we have won the cold war, who will be there to give structure, discipline, and love to these children? You must do that. And we must help you. Scripture says, you are the salt of the Earth and the light of the world, that if your light shines before men they will give glory to the Father in heaven. That is what we must do.

That is what we must do. How would we explain it to Martin Luther King if he showed up today and said, yes, we won the cold war. Yes, the biggest threat that all of us grew up under, Communism and nuclear war, Communism gone, nuclear war receding. Yes, we developed all these miraculous technologies. Yes, we all have got a VCR in our home; it's interesting. Yes, we get fifty channels on the cable. Yes, without regard to race, if you work hard and play by the rules, you can get into a service academy or a good college, you'll do just great. How would we explain to him all these kids getting killed and killing each other? How would we justify the things that we permit that no other country in the world would permit? How could we explain that we gave people the freedom to succeed, and we created conditions in which millions abuse that freedom to destroy the things that make life worth living and life itself? We cannot.

And so I say to you today, my fellow Americans, you gave me this job, and we're making progress on the things you hired me to do. But unless we deal with the ravages of crime and drugs and violence and unless we recognize that it's due to the breakdown of the family, the community, and the disappearance of jobs, and unless we say some of this cannot be done by Government, because we have to reach deep inside to the values, the spirit, the soul, and the truth of human nature, none of the other things we seek to do will ever take us where we need to go.

So in this pulpit, on this day, let me ask all of you in your heart to say: We will honour the life and the work of Martin Luther King. We will honour the meaning of our church. We will, somehow, by God's grace, we will turn this around. We will give these children a future. We will take away their guns and give them books. We will take away their despair and give them hope. We will rebuild the families and the neighbourhoods and the communities. We won't make all the work that has gone on here benefit just a few. We will do it together by the grace of God.

•

## NELSON MANDELA
### Johannesburg, 10 May 1994

#### *'Let freedom reign'*

*Nelson Mandela was released twenty-seven years after he was imprisoned, in February 1990. Four years later, after President William de Klerk initiated a historic peace accord with the black majority of South Africans, led by Mandela, he was elected president in South Africa's first democratic elections. This was his inaugural address.*

Today all of us do, by our presence here, and by our celebrations in other parts of our country and the world, confer glory and hope to newborn liberty.

Out of the experience of an extraordinary human disaster that lasted too long must be born a society of which all humanity will be proud.

Our daily deeds as ordinary South Africans must produce an actual South African reality that will reinforce humanity's belief in justice, strengthen its confidence in the nobility of the human soul and sustain all our hopes for a glorious life for all.

All this we owe both to ourselves and to the peoples of the world who are so well represented here today.

To my compatriots, I have no hesitation in saying that each one of us is as intimately attached to the soil of this beautiful country as are the famous jacaranda trees of Pretoria and the mimosa trees of the bushveld.

Each time one of us touches the soil of this land, we feel a sense of personal renewal. The national mood changes as the seasons change.

We are moved by a sense of joy and exhilaration when the grass turns green and the flowers bloom.

That spiritual and physical oneness we all share with this common homeland explains the depth of the pain we all carried in our hearts as we saw our country tear itself apart in a terrible conflict, and as we saw it spurned, outlawed and isolated by the peoples of the world, precisely because it has become the universal base of the pernicious ideology and practice of racism and racial oppression.

We, the people of South Africa, feel fulfilled that humanity has taken us back into its bosom; that we, who were outlaws not so long ago, have today been given the rare privilege to be host to the nations of the world on our own soil. We thank all our distinguished international guests for having come to take possession with the people of our country of what is, after all, a common victory for justice, for peace, for human dignity.

We trust that you will continue to stand by us as we tackle the challenges of building peace, prosperity, non-sexism, non-racialism and democracy.

We deeply appreciate the role that the masses of our people and their political mass democratic, religious, women, youth, business, traditional and other leaders have played to bring about this conclusion. Not least among them is my second deputy president, the honourable F. W. de Klerk.

We would also like to pay tribute to our security forces, in all their ranks, for the distinguished role they have played in securing our first democratic elections and the transition to democracy, from blood-thirsty forces which still refuse to see the light.

The time for the healing of the wounds has come. The moment to bridge the chasms that divide us has come. The time to build is upon us. We have, at last, achieved our political emancipation. We pledge ourselves to liberate all our people from the continuing bondage of poverty, deprivation, suffering, gender and other discrimination.

We succeeded to take our last steps to freedom in conditions of relative peace. We commit ourselves to the construction of a complete, just and lasting peace.

We have triumphed in the effort to implant hope in the breasts of the millions of our people. We enter into a covenant that we shall build the society in which all South Africans, both black and white, will be able to walk tall, without any fear in their hearts, assured of their inalienable right to human dignity – a rainbow nation at peace with itself and the world.

As a token of its commitment to the renewal of our country, the new interim Government of National Unity will, as a matter of urgency, address the issue of amnesty for various categories of our people who are currently serving terms of imprisonment.

We dedicate this day to all the heroes and heroines in this country and the rest of the world who sacrificed in many ways and surrendered their lives so that we could be free. Their dreams have become reality. Freedom is their reward.

We are both humbled and elevated by the honour and privilege that you, the people of South Africa, have bestowed on us, as the first president of a united, democratic, non-racial and non-sexist South Africa, to lead our country out of the valley of darkness.

We understand it still that there is no easy road to freedom. We know it well that none of us acting alone can achieve success. We must therefore act together as a united people, for national reconciliation, for nation building, for the birth of a new world. Let there be justice for all. Let there be peace for all. Let there be work, bread, water and salt for all.

Let each know that for each the body, the mind and the soul have been freed to fulfil themselves.

Never, never and never again shall it be that this beautiful land will again experience the oppression of one by another and suffer the indignity of being the skunk of the world.

Let freedom reign. The sun shall never set on so glorious a human achievement. God bless Africa. Thank you.

•

## ELIE WIESEL
Auschwitz, 27 January 1995

### 'Listen to the silent screams'

*As a teenager Elie Wiesel (1928–) was imprisoned in Auschwitz and Buchen-*
*wald where his parents and sister died. He became a journalist after the war and a*
*United States citizen in 1963. All his novels and plays have recalled the horror of*
*the Nazi concentration camps. He was awarded the Nobel Peace Prize in 1986.*

*The fiftieth anniversary of the liberation of Auschwitz was marked by a*
*special ceremony attended by thirteen presidents, three kings and many Nobel*
*laureates to pray for its 1.5 million victims. The Polish president, Lech Walesa,*
*was flanked by two survivors. One was Simone Veil, the French health and social*
*affairs minister. The other was Wiesel, who delivered this haunting address.*

I speak to you as a man who fifty years and nine days ago had
no name, no hope, no future and was known only by his number,
A 70713.

I speak as a Jew who has seen what humanity has done to itself
by trying to exterminate an entire people and inflict suffering and
humiliation and death on so many others.

In this place of darkness and malediction we can but stand in awe
and remember its stateless, faceless and nameless victims. Close your
eyes and look: endless nocturnal processions are converging here,
and here it is always night. Here heaven and earth are on fire.

Close your eyes and listen. Listen to the silent screams of terrified
mothers, the prayers of anguished old men and women. Listen to
the tears of children, Jewish children, a beautiful little girl among
them, with golden hair, whose vulnerable tenderness has never left
me. Look and listen as they quietly walk towards dark flames so
gigantic that the planet itself seemed in danger.

All these men and women and children came from everywhere, a
gathering of exiles drawn by death.

*Yitgadal veyitkadash, Shmay Rabba.*

In this kingdom of darkness there were many people. People who came from all the occupied lands of Europe. And then there were the Gypsies and the Poles and the Czechs . . . It is true that not all the victims were Jews. But all the Jews were victims.

Now, as then, we ask the question of all questions: what was the meaning of what was so routinely going on in this kingdom of eternal night. What kind of demented mind could have invented this system?

And it worked. The killers killed, the victims died and the world was the world and everything else was going on, life as usual. In the towns nearby, what happened? In the lands nearby, what happened? Life was going on where God's creation was condemned to blasphemy by the killers and their accomplices.

*Yitgadal veyitkadash, Shmay Rabba.*

Turning point or watershed, Birkenau produced a mutation on a cosmic scale, affecting man's dreams and endeavours. After Auschwitz, the human condition is no longer the same. After Auschwitz, nothing will ever be the same.

*Yitgadal veyitkadash, Shmay Rabba.*

As we remember the solitude and the pain of its victims, let us declare this day marks our commitment to commemorate their death, not to celebrate our own victory over death.

As we reflect upon the past, we must address ourselves to the present, and the future. In the name of all that is sacred in memory, let us stop the bloodshed in Bosnia, Rwanda and Chechenia; the vicious and ruthless terror attacks against Jews in the Holy Land. Let us reject and oppose more effectively religious fanaticism and racial hate.

Where else can we say to the world 'Remember the morality of the human condition,' if not here?

For the sake of our children, we must remember Birkenau, so that it does not become their future.

*Yitgadal veyitkadash, Shmay Rabba:* Weep for Thy children whose death was not mourned then; weep for them, our Father in heaven, for they were deprived of their right to be buried, for heaven itself became their cemetery.

•

# EARL SPENCER
## Westminster Abbey, 6 September 1997

### *'The most hunted person of the modern age'*

*People don't clap at funerals but they did – and inside Westminster Abbey – at the funeral of Diana, Princess of Wales, the divorced wife of Prince Charles, who had been killed with Dodi Fayed in a Paris car crash. The occasion was the tribute to his sister by Princess Diana's brother Earl Spencer over her catafalque. The funeral was broadcast live across the world and almost certainly reached the largest audience in history.*

*Spencer delivered a deeply felt attack on the press and then flung down a challenge to the royal family over the upbringing of the Princess's two sons, William and Harry. As he finished his oration, his voice broke. The masses outside, most of whom had been critical of the Queen's response to the Princess's death, started applauding. The sound of the applause penetrated the Abbey and the congregation joined in. It was utterly unprecedented and the Queen sat immobile as her subjects made their brief revolt.*

I stand before you today the representative of a family in grief, in a country in mourning before a world in shock.

We are all united not only in our desire to pay our respects to Diana, but rather in our need to do so.

For such was her extraordinary appeal that the tens of millions of people taking part in this service all over the world, via television and radio, who never actually met her, feel that they, too, lost someone close to them in the early hours of Sunday morning. It is a more remarkable tribute to Diana than I can ever hope to offer her today.

Diana was the very essence of compassion, of duty, of style, of beauty. All over the world she was a symbol of selfless humanity. All over the world, a standard-bearer for the rights of the truly downtrodden, a very British girl who transcended nationality. Someone with a natural nobility who was classless and who proved in the last year that she needed no royal title to continue to generate her particular brand of magic.

Today is our chance to say thank you for the way you brightened our lives, even though God granted you but half a life. We will all feel cheated always that you were taken from us so young, and yet we must learn to be grateful that you came along at all. Only now that you are gone do we truly appreciate what we are now without and we want you to know that life without you is very, very difficult.

We have all despaired at our loss over the past week, and only the strength of the message you gave us through your years of giving has afforded us the strength to move forward.

There is a temptation to rush to canonize your memory. There is no need to do so. You stand tall enough as a human being of unique qualities not to need to be seen as a saint. Indeed, to sanctify your memory would be to miss out on the very core of your being, your wonderfully mischievous sense of humour with a laugh that bent you double.

Your joy for life transmitted wherever you took your smile and the sparkle in those unforgettable eyes. Your boundless energy, which you could barely contain.

But your greatest gift was your intuition, and it was a gift you used wisely. This is what underpinned all your other wonderful attributes, and if we look to analyse what it was about you that had such a wide appeal, we find it in your instinctive feel for what was really important in all our lives. Without your God-given sensitivity we would be immersed in greater ignorance at the anguish of AIDS and HIV sufferers, the plight of the homeless, the isolation of lepers, the random destruction of landmines.

Diana explained to me once that it was her innermost feelings of suffering that made it possible for her to connect with her constituency of the rejected.

And here we come to another truth about her. For all the status, the glamour, the applause, Diana remained throughout a very insecure person at heart, almost childlike in her desire to do good for others so she could release herself from deep feelings of unworthiness, of which her eating disorders were merely a symptom.

The world sensed this part of her character and cherished her for her vulnerability while admiring her for her honesty.

The last time I saw Diana was on 1 July, her birthday, in London, when typically she was not taking time to celebrate her special day with friends but was guest of honour at a special charity fund-raising evening.

She sparkled of course, but I would rather cherish the days I spent with her in March when she came to visit me and my children in our home in South Africa.

I am proud of the fact that, apart from when she was on display meeting President Mandela, we managed to contrive to stop the ever-present paparazzi from getting a single picture of her – that meant a lot to her.

These were days I will always treasure. It was as if we had been transported back to our childhood when we spent such an enormous amount of time together – the two youngest in the family.

Fundamentally, she had not changed at all from the big sister who mothered me as a baby, fought with me at school and endured those long train journeys between our parents' homes with me at weekends. It is a tribute to her level-headedness and strength that despite the most bizarre-like life imaginable after her childhood, she remained intact, true to herself.

There is no doubt that she was looking for a new direction in her life at this time. She talked endlessly of getting away from England, mainly because of the treatment she received at the hands of the newspapers. I don't think she ever understood why her genuinely good intentions were sneered at by the media, why there appeared to be a permanent quest on their behalf to bring her down. It is baffling.

My own and only explanation is that genuine goodness is threatening to those at the opposite end of the moral spectrum. It is a point to remember that of all the ironies about Diana, perhaps the greatest was this – a girl given the name of the ancient goddess of hunting was, in the end, the most hunted person of the modern age.

She would want us today to pledge ourselves to protecting her beloved boys William and Harry from a similar fate and I do this here, Diana, on your behalf. We will not allow them to suffer the anguish that used regularly to drive you to tearful despair.

And beyond that, on behalf of your mother and sisters, I pledge that we, your blood family, will do all we can to continue the imaginative way in which you were steering these two exceptional young men so that their souls are not simply immersed by duty and tradition but can sing openly as you planned.

We fully respect the heritage into which they have both been born, and will always respect and encourage them in their Royal role.

But we, like you, recognize the need for them to experience as many different aspects of life as possible to arm them spiritually and emotionally for the years ahead. I know you would have expected nothing less from us.

William and Harry, we all care desperately for you today. We are all chewed up with sadness at the loss of a woman who was not even our mother. How great your suffering is we cannot even imagine.

I would like to end by thanking God for the small mercies he has shown us at this dreadful time; for taking Diana at her most beautiful and radiant and when she had joy in her private life.

Above all, we give thanks for the life of a woman I am so proud to be able to call my sister: the unique, the complex, the extraordinary and irreplaceable Diana, whose beauty, both internal and external, will never be extinguished from our minds.

•

## TONY BLAIR
### Brighton, 30 September 1997

### 'A beacon to the world'

*Tony Blair became the third youngest prime minister in British history (after Pitt the Younger and Lord Liverpool) when New Labour won a landslide victory over John Major's Conservatives in the 1997 general election. He was the most popular prime minister since opinion polls began.*

*There was an element of triumphalism in his speech to the first party confer-*

*ence held under a Labour government since 1979 but it also demonstrated how far the Labour Party had travelled in the previous eighteen years. There was no mention of socialism or equality or nationalization. Instead Blair emphasized duty over rights, the importance of family life, zero tolerance on crime and a more positive approach to European unity as he appealed for Britain to become a beacon to the world. Even right-wing commentators hailed the speech as a historic statement of intent.*

It has been a very long time waiting for this moment and all I can tell you is that after eighteen long years of Opposition, I am deeply proud – privileged – to stand before you as the new Labour Prime Minister of our country.

I believe in Britain. I believe in the British people. One cross on the ballot paper. One nation was reborn.

Today, I want to set an ambitious course for this country: to be nothing less than the model twenty-first-century nation, a beacon to the world. It means drawing deep into the richness of the British character. Creative. Compassionate. Outward-looking. Old British values, but a new British confidence.

We can never be the biggest. We may never again be the mightiest. But we can be the best. The best place to live. The best place to bring up children, the best place to lead a fulfilled life, the best place to grow old.

Fourteen years ago, our party was written off as history. This year we made history. And let our first thanks be to the British people. You kept faith with us. And we will keep faith with you. Thank you to the party organization, the volunteers, the professionals who fashioned the finest political fighting machine our country has ever known.

Ours was not a victory of politicians but of people. The people took their trust, and gave it to us. I want them to say, this week as they watch us here in Brighton, 'We did the right thing.' I want the British people to be as proud of having elected us as we are to serve them. We won because we are new Labour, because we had the courage to change ourselves, and the discipline to take hard decisions, whilst remaining united.

But I want to do more than keep our promises. I sense the British people demand more of us, too. People ask me the highlight of the election. Mine was driving from home to Buckingham Palace, along streets we had driven hundreds of times, past soulless buildings and sullen faces on their way to work. This drive was so different. As we turned into Gower Street, people watching our journey on TV came pouring out of the doorways, waving and shouting and clapping, with an energy and excitement that went beyond anything I imagined would happen.

They were liberated. Theirs were the smiles of tolerant, broad-minded, outward-looking, compassionate people and suddenly they learnt that they were in the majority after all. As one woman put it to me: 'We've got our Government back.' And with them I could sense confidence returning to the British people, compassion to the British soul, unity to the British nation, and that all three would give us new-found strength.

You see, the people were yearning for change in their country, at a time when they could see we had had the guts to modernize our party. The two came together.

The result is a quiet revolution now taking place. Led by the real modernizer: not me, the British people. They were the ones who had the guts to do it. And I say the size of our victory puts a special responsibility on us. To be a Government of high ideals and hard choices. Not popular for one time, but remembered for all time. Not just a better Government than the Tories but one of the great, radical, reforming governments of our history.

The British don't fear change. We are one of the great innovative peoples. From the Magna Carta to the first Parliament to the Industrial Revolution to an Empire that covered the world. Most of the great inventions of modern times with Britain stamped on them: the telephone; the television; the computer; penicillin; the hovercraft; radar.

Change is in the blood and bones of the British. We are by our nature and tradition innovators, adventurers, pioneers. As our great poet of renewal and recovery, John Milton, put it, we are 'a nation not slow or dull, but of quick, ingenious and piercing spirit, acute to invent, subtle and sinewy to discourse, not beneath the reach of any point that human capacity can soar to'.

Even today in Britain we lead the world, in design, pharmaceuticals, financial services, telecommunications. We have the world's first language, English. Britain today is an exciting, inspiring place to be. And it can be much more, if we face the challenge of a world around us today that has its finger on the fast-forward button; where every part of the picture of our life is changing, changing constantly.

So today I say to the British people the chains of mediocrity have broken, the tired days are behind us, we are free to excel once more. We are free to build that model twenty-first-century nation, to become that beacon to the world.

Creative. Compassionate. Confident of our place in the world. And you know, when people say, 'Sorry, that's too ambitious. Sorry, it can't be done,' I say: this is not a sorry country, we are not a sorry people. It can be done: if you have the will, the courage and determination to do it . . .

It's pretty simple, the type of country I want. It's a country where our children are proud and happy to grow up, feeling good not just about themselves, but about the community around them.

I don't want them living in a country where some of them go to school hungry, unable to learn because their parents can't afford to feed them; where they can see drugs being traded at school gates; where gangs of teenagers hang around street corners, doing nothing but spitting and swearing and abusing passers-by.

I don't want them brought up in a country where the only way pensioners can get long-term care is by selling their home, where people who fought to keep that country free are now faced every winter with the struggle for survival, skimping and saving, cold and alone, waiting for death to take them.

And I will not rest until that country is gone, until all our children live in a Britain where no child goes hungry, the young are employed, and the old are cherished and valued to the end of their days.

But let me spell out some facts. After eighteen years of Tory Government, of cuts and closures, of declining public services, the country was taxed more than under the last Labour Government.

This country, any country today, will not just carry on paying out more in taxes and getting less. Our new society that we want to create will have the same values as it ever did. Fighting poverty and unemployment. Securing justice and opportunity. It should be a compassionate society. It *must* be a compassionate society.

But it is compassion with a hard edge, because a strong society cannot be built in the real world on soft choices. It means fundamental reform of our welfare state, of the deal between citizen and society. It means getting money out of social breakdown and into schools and hospitals where we want to see it.

The new welfare state must encourage work, not dependency . . . We want single mothers with school-age children at least to visit a job centre, not just stay at home waiting for the benefit cheque, every week until the children are sixteen.

We cannot be that beacon to the world in the year 2005 with a welfare state built for the very different world of 1945. Our tax system should reward hard work. In the eighties, the Tories took down high marginal tax rates for high earners. It is time we did the same for Britain's working poor.

And we need to bring a change to the way we treat each other as citizens of our society. I tell you: a decent society is not based on rights. It is based on duty. Our duty to each other. To all should be given opportunity, from all responsibility demanded. The duty to show respect and tolerance to others.

I make no apology. I back zero tolerance on crime. I back powers to tackle antisocial neighbours; to make parents responsible for their children; to overhaul the youth justice system so that youngsters stop thinking they can commit a crime, get a caution and carry on being a criminal. At every level of the fight against crime – today acting on serious organized crime – this new Labour Government is taking it on. But to those who say it's all a threat to our civil liberties, I say the threat to civil liberties is of women afraid to go out, and pensioners afraid to stay in their own homes because of crime. And when we give opportunities to people, we can demand responsibility.

And we cannot say we want a strong and secure society when we ignore its very foundation: family life. This is not about preaching to individuals about their private lives. It is addressing a huge social problem. Attitudes have changed. The world has changed. But I am a modern man leading a modern country and this is a modern crisis. Nearly 100,000 teenage pregnancies every year. Elderly parents with whom families cannot cope. Children growing up without role models they can respect and learn from. More and deeper poverty. More crime. More truancy. More neglect of educational opportunities. And above all, more unhappiness. That unhappiness we must change . . .

My vision for post-Empire Britain is clear. It is to make this country pivotal, a leader in the world. With the US our friend and ally. Within the Commonwealth. In the United Nations. In Nato. To use the superb reputation of our Armed Forces, not just for defence, but as an instrument of influence in a world of collective security and co-operation.

And for Britain to lead in Europe again. Not so that we 'don't get left behind'. That is a weak reason. It is because for four centuries or more we have been a leading power in Europe. And we have at times been absolutely critical to the survival of, not just Europe, but of the whole world. It is our destiny to lead in Europe.

And Europe needs us. For we have a vision of Europe. We want a people's Europe: free trade, industrial strength, high levels of employment and social justice, a democratic Europe. And against that vision is the bureaucrat's Europe: the Europe of thwarting open trade, unnecessary rules and regulations, the Europe of the CAP and the endless committees leading nowhere. But we cannot shape Europe unless we matter in Europe.

I know there will be a hard choice to come over a single currency. And our policy, based as it is on the British national interest, remains unchanged. But in or out, we will be affected by it and must remain able to influence the way that it works . . .

So much to do. So much to change. So hard to do it. But the vision is as old as humanity. Modernization is not an end in itself. It is for a purpose. Modernization is not the enemy of justice, but its ally.

Progress and justice are the two rocks upon which the new Britain is raised to the heights. Lose either one and we come crashing down until we are just another average nation, scrabbling around for salvation in the ebbing tide of the twentieth century.

That is why we changed the Labour Party. To make new Britain. It is why we will carry on changing. It is why it was right yesterday to take another historic step on the road to reform of our party so that never again will a Labour Government be torn about by divisions between leadership in Parliament and the party in the country.

And let me tell you this directly. Yes, we are new Labour. Yes, our policies and attitudes have changed. But there are no old Labour or new Labour values. There are Labour values. They are what make us the party of compassion; of social justice; of the struggle against poverty and inequality; of liberty; of basic human solidarity; and the day we cease to be those things is the day we keep the name of the Labour Party but lose the reason for its existence. And ours, you know, is a simple enough vision. But it will require a supreme national effort. It is a task for a whole people, not just a government. Great challenges. But great rewards for all of us if we can rise to them as we can.

And rise as one nation. Held together by our values and by the strength of our character. We are a giving people. In the face of crisis or challenge, we pull together, strengthened by unity. It says nothing about our politics. It speaks volumes about our character.

You remember how your parents, like mine, used to say to you: 'Just do your best.' Well, let us do our best. On May 1, the people entrusted me with the task of leading their country into a new century. That was your challenge to me. And proudly, humbly, I accepted it.

Today, I issue a challenge to you. Help us make Britain that beacon shining throughout the world. Unite behind our mission to modernize our country for all our people. For there is a place for all the people in new Britain, and there is a role for all the people in its creation. Believe in us as much as we believe in you.

Give just as much to our country as all of us intend to give. Give your all. Make this the giving age.

'By the strength of our common endeavour, we achieve more together than we can alone.' On May 1 1997, it wasn't just the Tories who were defeated. Cynicism was defeated. Fear of change was defeated. Fear itself was defeated. Did I not say it would be a battle of hope against fear? On May 1 1997, fear lost. Hope won. The Giving Age began.

Now make the good that is in the heart of each of us serve the good of all of us. Give to our country the gift of our energy, our ideas, our hopes, our talents. Use them to build a country each of whose people will say that 'I care about Britain because I know that Britain cares about me.'

Britain, head and heart, will be unbeatable. That is the Britain I offer you. That is the Britain that together can be ours.

•

## MICHAEL PORTILLO
### Blackpool, 9 October 1997

#### 'The causes of defeat'

*Few defeats provoked more joy among Labour supporters in the 1997 general election than the humiliation of Michael Portillo (1953–) at Enfield Southgate. Yet his dignity in defeat earned new respect for Portillo who was the standard-bearer of the Euro-sceptic Tory right wing and who would otherwise have been a serious candidate to win the leadership of the Conservative Party after John Major stepped down.*

*William Hague became leader but many Tories saw Portillo as the leader in exile. That was why this speech to the Centre for Policy Studies at a fringe meeting during the party conference was important.*

*Much of the speech was devoted to Portillo's analysis of the continuing attractiveness of the Conservative message. But it was the opening, explaining why the party had lost, his section on compassion (of which he had seemed the antithesis), and his denunciation of Tony Blair's New Labour that attracted most attention.*

Let us begin by recognizing the scale of our defeat and of our problem. Perhaps as one who went in an instant from being in the Cabinet to being a member of the general public, I am qualified to offer an opinion. I do not accept the view that the Conservatives lost the election of 1997 because we abandoned one-nation Toryism or split the nation. We did not. I will return to that point in a moment. The causes of our defeat were different. I would like to identify what I believe to have been the four principal factors.

First, the party became associated increasingly with the most disagreeable messages and thoughts. Much of that linkage was unjustified, but since it is what people thought – what people still think – it must be appreciated as a deeply felt distaste, rather than momentary irritation. We cannot dismiss it as mere false perception. Tories were linked to harshness: thought to be uncaring about unemployment, poverty, poor housing, disability and single parent-hood; and considered indifferent to the moral arguments over landmines and arms sales. We were thought to favour greed and the unqualified pursuit of the free market, with a 'devil take the hindmost' attitude.

Second, we abandoned almost completely the qualities of loyalty and the bonds of party without which party effectively ceases to exist. Some of this was ideological. Passions about the future of our country rightly fired people up, but wrongly led them to attack and despise their colleagues. Part of it was egotistical. There were MPs anxious to oblige whenever the media came looking for dissent, seizing the opportunity to be famous for fifteen minutes. But now we are out of government, their views are sought more rarely, and their once-famous faces are fading in the public memory.

We must rediscover the old instincts that led Tories to support one another and to rally round. Loyalty was never a secret weapon: it was because it was so visible in *public*, and reinforced in private, that it was so effective. The impact of disunity upon us is clear to see. The party must in the very near future learn again to display the camaraderie and common purpose that are fundamental to a party's prospects. Our new leader, William Hague, has every right to expect our loyalty publicly and privately. If he does not get it, we stand no chance of being re-elected. He has shown that he will lead. Now the party must show that it can be led.

Third, we were thought to be arrogant and out of touch. Much of it may have been no more than personal mannerisms that grated on the public after years in office. Some of it was insensitivity – using the language of economics and high finance when people's jobs and self-esteem were at stake. And when people looked at the composition of our party, they thought it too elderly, or too vulgar, or too out of touch in vocabulary and perceptions, or in some other way, unfamiliar and unrepresentative.

Fourth, there was sleaze. I did not believe all that Conservatives were accused of. Even today, I do not think that wrongdoing was any more prevalent in our party than in others, and I expect the rotten boroughs of the Labour Party to prove as much in coming months. But it was certainly bad enough. Sleaze disgraced us in the eyes of the public. Their perception was of corruption and unfitness for public service. Such distasteful perceptions can endure and do us damage for a long time.

We should face these issues head on and deal with them. The last years profoundly disappointed our supporters, and disgusted many others. Those of us who were in the parliamentary party, and those of us who were in the government, bear a particular responsibility . . .

Compassion is an essential ingredient in Conservatism. We have never lost it, but the world does not believe that. Our reputation has suffered because Conservatives don't wear their hearts on their sleeves. They don't like humbug or display. Their compassion is largely of a practical sort: what can we actually do about the problems that we see around us? That is why Conservatives are to be found in such large numbers working for voluntary organizations. Conservatives have a scepticism about panaceas and about the possibility of government solving problems with a flourish of a pen. But that common sense approach must not mask the fact that concern for others and magnanimity are important qualities of Conservatism, and the instinct for social cohesion transcends the nation . . .

Now, a word about tactics. There are two things that the Conservative Party needs very badly. One, I mentioned, is loyalty. If we cannot reinvent it we cannot govern. The other is patience. I read somewhere that there was frustration with William Hague for not yet coming up with the next big idea. I accord that remark the prize for the silliest thing said since the election.

The public is not yet ready for such an innovation from us, even if a big idea were a thing to be conjured up at will. People need a rest from us, and we need time to reflect and listen and come to understand one another better than we have of late. We certainly need to do a lot about ourselves. We need better and different organization. We need a broad and stable financial base. We need to spread our appeal and attract different sorts of people: different ages, social types, ethnic groups and cultures.

As for policies, we should be in no great hurry. Get straight what are our core beliefs. Sort out the confusions and false signals that arose while we were in government. Take a fresh look in the new circumstances.

Our party will renew itself. The new intake of MPs is of extremely high quality. Just as happened with Labour, those new people will be the engine of our revival. Ministerial office will be theirs, but they must bide their time patiently too.

On the night of the election I wished our new government well, and I do so again. Conservatives are patriots and we wish to see our country succeed. You will not see us gloat over national reverses, nor talk down their successes, as Labour did when we were the government. We wish to see Britain behaving honourably, being an influence for good in Europe and the world. We wish to see the economy remain strong. We do not look to defeat Labour on the back of national failure. There will be sufficient grounds without that to argue for their removal.

I do not underestimate Mr Blair or his achievements. In the years before the election he skilfully laid bare the areas of life and policy where the public felt dissatisfied and angry with the Conservatives. He did not win merely by default, but because of his talent for capturing the public mood. We will learn from that.

Today the Labour Government looks very strong and confident. But problems lie ahead. They don't know where they are headed, and that is dangerous. Mr Blair's great achievement is directionless leadership: he appears to be in control, but no one knows to where he is leading. I have made many mistakes in my career. I suppose we all have. But few people have been consistently wrong on all the great issues that faced our nation over the last fifteen years, as Mr Blair was. Last week, in a speech which was much acclaimed, Mr Blair failed to define the purpose of his government. I perceive no ideological roots. I can detect no sense of direction. Labour has a strong sense that it cannot undo what we did. But they do not understand why it was right to do it. They do not accept the politics of freedom and choice that lay behind our agenda. Labour grasped that it had to adopt our rhetoric. But they will in the end be judged not on what they say but on what they do.

Labour has been guided by the wish to destroy us; and by the determination to be re-elected. That is not a recipe for governing well. You cannot run an administration forever on the principle that you are unwilling to do anything that offends. You cannot substitute focus-group government for Cabinet government. Labour is a coalition brought about to win power. That will to win power is the one idea that the members of the government hold in common. But with the passage of time, that will prove an insubstantial glue. The signs of division may today be no bigger than a small crab in a jar, but they will grow.

This government is too bossy, too contemptuous of parliament, too self-satisfied and too little criticized in the media for its own good or for ours. The wheel of fortune turns and that which once appeared fresh, with the passing of time goes to seed . . .

What the Tories need is patience. Principles we already have. Opportunities there will be. Our time will come again.

•

## BORIS YELTSIN
St Petersburg, 17 July 1998

### 'May they rest in peace'

*Tsar Nicholas II, the last emperor of Russia, and his entire family were shot at Yekaterinburg by the Red Guards in 1918, nearly a year after Lenin and the Bolsheviks seized power in the Russian Revolution.*

*Eighty years later to the day, Boris Yeltsin (1931–2007), who became president of Russia in 1990 after the break-up of the Soviet Union, led his nation in official apology for the murder of the Tsar at a moving ceremony in the cathedral of the Peter and Paul Fortress where his Romanov ancestors were buried.*

*Watched by millions of Russians, Yeltsin, a sick man, stood in sombre silence before the vault, while his wife, Naina, crossed herself. Yeltsin said he had no option but to be present to tell the truth.*

It's an historic day for Russia. Eighty years have passed since the slaying of the last Russian emperor and his family. We have long been silent about this monstrous crime. We must say the truth: the Yekaterinburg massacre has become one of the most shameful pages of our history.

By burying the remains of innocent victims we want to expiate the sins of our ancestors. Guilty are those who committed this heinous crime and those who have been justifying it for decades – all of us.

We must not lie to ourselves, explaining this senseless cruelty with political goals. The execution of the Romanov family was the result of an irreconcilable split in Russian society. Its results are felt to this day. The burial of the victims' remains is an act of human justice, an expiation of common guilt.

We all bear responsibility for the historical memory of the nation; and that's why I could not fail to come here. I must be here as both an individual and the president.

I bow my head before the victims of the merciless slaying. While building a new Russia we must rely on its historical experience. Many glorious pages of our history are linked with the Romanovs. But also connected with their name is one of the most bitter lessons – that attempts to change life by violence are doomed.

We must finish this century, which has become the century of blood and lawlessness for Russia, with repentance and reconciliation irrespective of political and religious views and ethnic origin. This is our historic chance. On the eve of the third millennium, we must do it for the sake of our generation, and those to come. Let's remember those innocent victims who have fallen to hatred and violence. May they rest in peace.

•

# BILL CLINTON
## Washington, DC, 17 August 1998

### 'This has hurt too many innocent people'

*One year after he started his second term as president in January 1997, President Clinton learned that Kenneth Starr was investigating accusations that he had conducted a sexual relationship with Monica Lewinsky, a White House intern, in 1995 and then tried to cover it up. After months of investigation, rumours and Clinton's denial that he had had sexual relations with 'that woman', Clinton was forced to admit to a relationship that was 'not appropriate' with the twenty-five-year-old Miss Lewinsky. The confession was made in a four-minute speech seen by nearly two-thirds of Americans. No president had ever been forced to address such personal issues in a nationally televised speech. Clinton was as defiant as he was contrite.*

This afternoon in this room, from this chair, I testified before the Office of Independent Counsel and the grand jury. I answered their questions truthfully, including questions about my private life, questions no American citizen would ever want to answer.

Still, I must take complete responsibility for all my actions, both public and private. And that is why I am speaking to you tonight.

As you know, in a deposition in January, I was asked questions about my relationship with Monica Lewinsky. While my answers were legally accurate, I did not volunteer information.

Indeed, I did have a relationship with Ms Lewinsky that was not appropriate. In fact, it was wrong. It constituted a critical lapse in judgement and a personal failure on my part for which I am solely and completely responsible.

But I told the grand jury today and I say to you now that at no time did I ask anyone to lie, to hide or destroy evidence or to take any other unlawful action.

I know that my public comments and my silence about this matter gave a false impression.

I misled people, including even my wife. I deeply regret that.

I can only tell you I was motivated by many factors. First by a desire to protect myself from the embarrassment of my own conduct. I was also very concerned about protecting my family. The fact that these questions were being asked in a politically inspired lawsuit, which has since been dismissed, was a consideration, too.

In addition, I had real and serious concerns about an independent counsel investigation that began with private business dealings twenty years ago, dealings, I might add, about which an independent federal agency found no evidence of any wrongdoing by me or my wife over two years ago.

The independent counsel investigation moved on to my staff and friends, then into my private life. And now the investigation itself is under investigation. This has gone on too long, cost too much and hurt too many innocent people.

Now, this matter is between me, the two people I love most – my wife and our daughter – and our God.

I must put it right, and I am prepared to do whatever it takes to do so. Nothing is more important to me personally.

But it is private, and I intend to reclaim my family life for my family. It's nobody's business but ours.

Even presidents have private lives. It is time to stop the pursuit of personal destruction and the prying into private lives and get on with our national life.

Our country has been distracted by this matter for too long, and I take my responsibility for my part in all of this. That is all I can do. Now it is time – in fact, it is past time – to move on. We have important work to do, real opportunities to seize, real problems to solve, real security matters to face.

And so tonight, I ask you to turn away from the spectacle of the past seven months, to repair the fabric of our national discourse and to return our attention to all the challenges and all the promise of the next American century. Thank you for watching. And good night.

## BILL CLINTON
### Washington, DC, 11 September 1998

*'I have sinned'*

*Less than a month later President Clinton had to admit that his speech of 17 August had not been sufficiently contrite. He delivered this speech, written in his own hand, at the annual White House prayer breakfast to an audience of more than 100 ministers, priests and other religious leaders, which also included Hillary Clinton.*

*It was the day that the first report to Congress by Independent Counsel Ken Starr was published, setting out the grounds for possible impeachment of the President and accusing him of perjury, obstruction of justice and other offences, chiefly resulting from his desire to conceal a relationship with Monica Lewinsky.*

This is always an important day for our country. It is an unusual and, I think, unusually important day today. I may not be quite as easy with my words today as I have been in years past, and I was up rather late last night thinking about and praying about what I ought to say today. And rather unusual for me, I actually tried to write it down. So if you will forgive me, I will do my best to say what it is I want to say to you – and I may have to take my glasses out to read my own writing.

First, I want to say to all of you that, as you might imagine, I have been on quite a journey these last few weeks to get to the end of this, to the rock bottom truth of where I am and where we all are.

I agree with those who have said that in my first statement after I testified I was not contrite enough. I don't think there is a fancy way to say that I have sinned.

It is important to me that everybody who has been hurt know that the sorrow I feel is genuine: first and most important, my family; also my friends, my staff, my Cabinet, Monica Lewinsky and her family, and the American people. I have asked all for their forgiveness.

But I believe that to be forgiven, more than sorrow is required – at least two more things. First, genuine repentance – a determination to change and to repair breaches of my own making. I have repented.

Second, what my Bible calls a 'broken spirit'; an understanding that I must have God's help to be the person that I want to be; a willingness to give the very forgiveness I seek; a renunciation of the pride and the anger which cloud judgement, lead people to excuse and compare and to blame and complain.

Now, what does all this mean for me and for us? First, I will instruct my lawyers to mount a vigorous defence, using all available appropriate arguments. But legal language must not obscure the fact that I have done wrong. Second, I will continue on the path of repentance, seeking pastoral support and that of other caring people so that they can hold me accountable for my own commitment.

Third, I will intensify my efforts to lead our country and the world toward peace and freedom, prosperity and harmony, in the hope that with a broken spirit and a still strong heart I can be used for greater good, for we have many blessings and many challenges and so much work to do.

In this, I ask for your prayers and for your help in healing our nation. And though I cannot move beyond or forget this – indeed, I must always keep it as a caution light in my life – it is very important that our nation move forward.

I am very grateful for the many, many people – clergy and ordinary citizens alike – who have written me with wise counsel. I am profoundly grateful for the support of so many Americans who somehow through it all seem to still know that I care about them a great deal, that I care about their problems and their dreams. I am grateful for those who have stood by me and who say that in this case and many others, the bounds of privacy have been excessively and unwisely invaded. That may be. Nevertheless, in this case, it may be a blessing, because I still sinned. And if my repentance is genuine and sustained, and if I can maintain both a broken spirit and a strong heart, then good can come of this for our country as well as for me and my family. (*Applause.*)

The children of this country can learn in a profound way that integrity is important and selfishness is wrong, but God can change us and make us strong at the broken places. I want to embody those lessons for the children of this country – for that little boy in Florida who came up to me and said that he wanted to grow up and be President and to be just like me. I want the parents of all the children in America to be able to say that to their children.

A couple of days ago when I was in Florida a Jewish friend of mine gave me this liturgy book called *Gates of Repentance*. And there was this incredible passage from the Yom Kippur liturgy. I would like to read it to you:

Now is the time for turning. The leaves are beginning to turn from green to red to orange. The birds are beginning to turn and are heading once more toward the south. The animals are beginning to turn to storing their food for the winter. For leaves, birds and animals, turning comes instinctively. But for us, turning does not come so easily. It takes an act of will for us to make a turn. It means breaking old habits. It means admitting that we have been wrong, and this is never easy. It means losing face. It means starting all over again. And this is always painful. It means saying I am sorry. It means recognizing that we have the ability to change. These things are terribly hard to do. But unless we turn, we will be trapped forever in yesterday's ways. Lord help us to turn, from callousness to sensitivity, from hostility to love, from pettiness to purpose, from envy to contentment, from carelessness to discipline, from fear to faith. Turn us around, O Lord, and bring us back toward you. Revive our lives as at the beginning, and turn us toward each other, Lord, for in isolation there is no life.

I thank my friend for that. I thank you for being here. I ask you to share my prayer that God will search me and know my heart, try me and know my anxious thoughts, see if there is any hurtfulness in me, and lead me toward the life everlasting. I ask that God give me a clean heart, let me walk by faith and not sight.

I ask once again to be able to love my neighbour – all my neighbours – as my self, to be an instrument of God's peace; to let the words of my mouth and the meditations of my heart and, in the end, the work of my hands, be pleasing. This is what I wanted to say to you today.

Thank you. God bless you.

•

## BILL CLINTON
### Washington, DC, 11 December 1998

### *'I am profoundly sorry'*

*Only minutes before the House Judiciary Committee voted to pass its first article of impeachment, President Clinton gave this speech — his third on the subject — to reporters in the Rose Garden of the White House. The impeachment proceedings marked the culmination of a long chain of legal entanglements resulting from a sweeping investigation of the President by Independent Counsel Ken Starr as well as a private lawsuit concerning alleged sexual harassment committed by Clinton before he became President.*

*Clinton had strongly denied, then later reluctantly admitted a relationship 'that was not appropriate' with Monica Lewinsky, a young White House intern. The President's initial denial had been staunchly defended by First Lady Hillary Clinton, White House staff and various friends and supporters of the President — all of whom knew by now they had been duped.*

Good afternoon.

As anyone close to me knows, for months I have been grappling with how best to reconcile myself to the American people, to acknowledge my own wrongdoing and still to maintain my focus on the work of the presidency.

Others are presenting my defence on the facts, the law and the Constitution. Nothing I can say now can add to that.

What I want the American people to know, what I want the Congress to know is that I am profoundly sorry for all I have done wrong in words and deeds.

I never should have misled the country, the Congress, my friends or my family. Quite simply, I gave in to my shame. I have been condemned by my accusers with harsh words.

And while it's hard to hear yourself called deceitful and manipulative, I remember Ben Franklin's admonition that our critics are our friends, for they do show us our faults.

Mere words cannot fully express the profound remorse I feel for what our country is going through and for what members of both parties in Congress are now forced to deal with. These past months have been a torturous process of coming to terms with what I did. I understand that accountability demands consequences, and I'm prepared to accept them.

Painful as the condemnation of the Congress would be, it would pale in comparison to the consequences of the pain I have caused my family. There is no greater agony.

Like anyone who honestly faces the shame of wrongful conduct, I would give anything to go back and undo what I did.

But one of the painful truths I have to live with is the reality that that is simply not possible. An old and dear friend of mine recently sent me the wisdom of a poet who wrote, 'The moving finger writes and having writ, moves on. Nor all your piety nor wit shall lure it back to cancel half a line. Nor all your tears wash out a word of it.'

So nothing, not piety, nor tears, nor wit, nor torment can alter what I have done. I must make my peace with that.

I must also be at peace with the fact that the public consequences of my actions are in the hands of the American people and their representatives in the Congress.

Should they determine that my errors of word and deed require their rebuke and censure, I am ready to accept that.

Meanwhile, I will continue to do all I can to reclaim the trust of the American people and to serve them well.

We must all return to the work, the vital work, of strengthening our nation for the new century. Our country has wonderful opportunities and daunting challenges ahead. I intend to seize those opportunities and meet those challenges with all the energy and ability and strength God has given me.

That is simply all I can do – the work of the American people. Thank you very much.

•

## TONY BLAIR
### Brighton, 2 October 2001

*'The kaleidoscope has been shaken'*

*In his autobiography, Tony Blair says that he wrote this speech (of which what follows is the beginning and the end), virtually straight out, only weeks after 9/11, the al-Qaeda terrorist attack on New York and the Pentagon, which claimed nearly 3,000 victims, on September 11 2001. 'There was none of the usual agonizing. The redrafts were minimal. I sat in Chequers in the study overlooking the Rose Garden, as the first autumn colours began to appear and wrote . . . I felt we were on the eve of a mighty decision about the world's future. I wrote easily because I wrote what I thought.'*

In retrospect, the Millennium marked only a moment in time. It was the events of September 11 that marked a turning point in history, where we confront the dangers of the future and assess the choices facing humankind.

It was a tragedy. An act of evil. From this nation goes our deepest sympathy and prayers for the victims and our profound solidarity with the American people.

We were with you at the first. We will stay with you to the last.

Just two weeks ago, in New York, after the church service I met some of the families of the British victims.

It was in many ways a very British occasion. Tea and biscuits. It was raining outside. Around the edge of the room, strangers making small talk, trying to be normal people in an abnormal situation.

And as you crossed the room, you felt the longing and sadness; hands clutching photos of sons and daughters, wives and husbands;

imploring you to believe them when they said there was still an outside chance of their loved ones being found alive, when you knew in truth that all hope was gone.

And then a middle-aged mother looks you in the eyes and tells you her only son has died, and asks you: why?

I tell you: you do not feel like the most powerful person in the country at times like that.

Because there is no answer. There is no justification for their pain. Their son did nothing wrong. The woman, seven months pregnant, whose child will never know its father, did nothing wrong.

They don't want revenge. They want something better in memory of their loved ones.

I believe their memorial can and should be greater than simply the punishment of the guilty. It is that out of the shadow of this evil should emerge lasting good: destruction of the machinery of terrorism wherever it is found; hope amongst all nations of a new beginning where we seek to resolve differences in a calm and ordered way; greater understanding between nations and between faiths; and above all justice and prosperity for the poor and dispossessed, so that people everywhere can see the chance of a better future through the hard work and creative power of the free citizen, not the violence and savagery of the fanatic.

I know that here in Britain people are anxious, even a little frightened. I understand that. People know we must act but they worry what might follow.

They worry about the economy and talk of recession.

And, of course there are dangers; it is a new situation.

But the fundamentals of the US, British and European economies are strong.

Every reasonable measure of internal security is being undertaken.

Our way of life is a great deal stronger and will last a great deal longer than the actions of fanatics, small in number and now facing a unified world against them.

People should have confidence.

This is a battle with only one outcome: our victory not theirs.

What happened on 11 September was without parallel in the bloody history of terrorism.

Within a few hours, up to 7,000 people were annihilated, the commercial centre of New York was reduced to rubble and in Washington and Pennsylvania further death and horror on an unimaginable scale. Let no one say this was a blow for Islam when the blood of innocent Muslims was shed along with those of the Christian, Jewish and other faiths around the world.

We know those responsible. In Afghanistan are scores of training camps for the export of terror. Chief amongst the sponsors and organizers is Osama Bin Laden.

He is supported, shielded and given succour by the Taliban regime.

Two days before the 11 September attacks, Masood, the leader of the opposition Northern Alliance, was assassinated by two suicide bombers. Both were linked to Bin Laden. Some may call that coincidence. I call it payment – payment in the currency these people deal in: blood.

Be in no doubt: Bin Laden and his people organized this atrocity. The Taliban aid and abet him. He will not desist from further acts of terror. They will not stop helping him.

Whatever the dangers of the action we take, the dangers of inaction are far, far greater.

Look for a moment at the Taliban regime. It is undemocratic. That goes without saying.

There is no sport allowed, or television or photography. No art or culture is permitted. All other faiths, all other interpretations of Islam are ruthlessly suppressed. Those who practise their faith are imprisoned. Women are treated in a way almost too revolting to be credible. First driven out of university; girls not allowed to go to school; no legal rights; unable to go out of doors without a man. Those that disobey are stoned.

There is now no contact permitted with western agencies, even those delivering food. The people live in abject poverty. It is a regime founded on fear and funded on the drugs trade. The biggest drugs hoard in the world is in Afghanistan, controlled by the Taliban. Ninety per cent of the heroin on British streets originates in Afghanistan.

The arms the Taliban are buying today are paid for with the lives of young British people buying their drugs on British streets.

That is another part of their regime that we should seek to destroy. So what do we do?

Don't overreact some say. We aren't.

We haven't lashed out. No missiles on the first night just for effect.

Don't kill innocent people. We are not the ones who waged war on the innocent. We seek the guilty.

Look for a diplomatic solution. There is no diplomacy with Bin Laden or the Taliban regime.

State an ultimatum and get their response. We stated the ultimatum; they haven't responded.

Understand the causes of terror. Yes, we should try, but let there be no moral ambiguity about this: nothing could ever justify the events of 11 September, and it is to turn justice on its head to pretend it could.

The action we take will be proportionate; targeted; we will do all we humanly can to avoid civilian casualties. But understand what we are dealing with. Listen to the calls of those passengers on the planes. Think of the children on them, told they were going to die.

Think of the cruelty beyond our comprehension as amongst the screams and the anguish of the innocent, those hijackers drove at full throttle planes laden with fuel into buildings where tens of thousands worked.

They have no moral inhibition on the slaughter of the innocent. If they could have murdered not 7,000 but 70,000 does anyone doubt they would have done so and rejoiced in it?

There is no compromise possible with such people, no meeting of minds, no point of understanding with such terror.

Just a choice: defeat it or be defeated by it. And defeat it we must.

Any action taken will be against the terrorist network of Bin Laden.

As for the Taliban, they can surrender the terrorists; or face the consequences and again in any action the aim will be to eliminate their military hardware, cut off their finances, disrupt their supplies, target their troops, not civilians. We will put a trap around the regime.

I say to the Taliban: surrender the terrorists; or surrender power. It's your choice.

We will take action at every level, national and international, in the UN, in G8, in the EU, in NATO, in every regional grouping in the world, to strike at international terrorism wherever it exists.

For the first time, the UN Security Council has imposed mandatory obligations on all UN members to cut off terrorist financing and end safe havens for terrorists.

Those that finance terror, those who launder their money, those that cover their tracks are every bit as guilty as the fanatic who commits the final act.

Here in this country and in other nations round the world, laws will be changed, not to deny basic liberties but to prevent their abuse and protect the most basic liberty of all: freedom from terror. New extradition laws will be introduced; new rules to ensure asylum is not a front for terrorist entry. This country is proud of its tradition in giving asylum to those fleeing tyranny. We will always do so. But we have a duty to protect the system from abuse.

It must be overhauled radically so that from now on, those who abide by the rules get help and those that don't can no longer play the system to gain unfair advantage over others.

Round the world, 11 September is bringing governments and people to reflect, consider and change. And in this process, amidst all the talk of war and action, there is another dimension appearing.

There is a coming together. The power of community is asserting itself. We are realizing how fragile are our frontiers in the face of the world's new challenges.

Today conflicts rarely stay within national boundaries.

Today a tremor in one financial market is repeated in the markets of the world.

Today confidence is global; either its presence or its absence.

Today the threat is chaos; because for people with work to do, family life to balance, mortgages to pay, careers to further, pensions to provide, the yearning is for order and stability and if it doesn't exist elsewhere, it is unlikely to exist here.

I have long believed this interdependence defines the new world we live in.

People say: we are only acting because it's the USA that was attacked. Double standards, they say. But when Milosevič embarked on the ethnic cleansing of Muslims in Kosovo, we acted.

The sceptics said it was pointless, we'd make matters worse, we'd make Milosevič stronger and look what happened, we won, the refugees went home, the policies of ethnic cleansing were reversed and one of the great dictators of the last century will see justice in this century.

And I tell you, if Rwanda happened again today as it did in 1993, when a million people were slaughtered in cold blood, we would have a moral duty to act there also. We were there in Sierra Leone when a murderous group of gangsters threatened its democratically elected government and people.

And we as a country should, and I as Prime Minister do, give thanks for the brilliance, dedication and sheer professionalism of the British Armed Forces . . .

When we act to bring to account those that committed the atrocity of September 11, we do so not out of bloodlust.

We do so because it is just. We do not act against Islam. The true followers of Islam are our brothers and sisters in this struggle. Bin Laden is no more obedient to the proper teaching of the Koran than those Crusaders of the twelfth century who pillaged and murdered, represented the teaching of the Gospel.

It is time the west confronted its ignorance of Islam. Jews, Muslims and Christians are all children of Abraham.

This is the moment to bring the faiths closer together in understanding of our common values and heritage, a source of unity and strength.

It is time also for parts of Islam to confront prejudice against America and not only Islam but parts of western societies too.

America has its faults as a society, as we have ours.

But I think of the Union of America born out of the defeat of slavery.

I think of its Constitution, with its inalienable rights granted to every citizen, still a model for the world.

I think of a black man born in poverty, who became chief of their armed forces and is now secretary of state – Colin Powell – and I wonder frankly whether such a thing could have happened here.

I think of the Statue of Liberty and how many refugees, migrants and the impoverished passed its light and felt that if not for them, for their children, a new world could indeed be theirs.

I think of a country where people who do well don't have questions asked about their accent, their class, their beginnings but have admiration for what they have done and the success they've achieved.

I think of those New Yorkers I met, still in shock, but resolute; the firefighters and police, mourning their comrades but still head held high.

I think of all this and I reflect: yes, America has its faults, but it is a free country, a democracy, it is our ally and some of the reaction to September 11 betrays a hatred of America that shames those that feel it.

So I believe this is a fight for freedom. And I want to make it a fight for justice too. Justice not only to punish the guilty. But justice to bring those same values of democracy and freedom to people round the world.

And I mean freedom, not only in the narrow sense of personal liberty but in the broader sense of each individual having the economic and social freedom to develop their potential to the full. That is what community means, founded on the equal worth of all.

The starving, the wretched, the dispossessed, the ignorant, those living in want and squalor from the deserts of Northern Africa to the slums of Gaza, to the mountain ranges of Afghanistan: they too are our cause.

This is a moment to seize. The kaleidoscope has been shaken. The pieces are in flux. Soon they will settle again. Before they do, let us re-order this world around us.

Today, humankind has the science and technology to destroy

itself or to provide prosperity to all. Yet science can't make that choice for us. Only the moral power of a world acting as a community can.

'By the strength of our common endeavour we achieve more together than we can alone.'

For those people who lost their lives on September 11 and those that mourn them; now is the time for the strength to build that community. Let that be their memorial.

•

## GEORGE W. BUSH
Washington, DC, 29 January 2002

### *'An axis of evil'*

*When President George W. Bush made his State of the Union address four months after 9/11, he used the most memorable and notorious phrase of his presidency. He accused three countries of forming an 'axis of evil' by helping terrorism and seeking weapons of mass destruction – Iran, Iraq and North Korea. Libya, Syria and Cuba were added to the list later by John R. Bolton, the American ambassador to the United Nations. The speech made the case for the subsequent invasion of Iraq. Speechwriter David Frum wrote the speech at the request of head White House speechwriter Mike Gerson, who substituted 'evil' for Frum's 'hatred' in the final text. Frum's assignment was to make the case for dislodging the government of Saddam Hussein in only a few sentences.*

As we gather tonight, our nation is at war, our economy is in recession, and the civilized world faces unprecedented dangers. Yet the state of our Union has never been stronger.

We last met in an hour of shock and suffering. In four short months, our nation has comforted the victims, begun to rebuild New York and the Pentagon, rallied a great coalition, captured, arrested, and rid the world of thousands of terrorists, destroyed Afghanistan's terrorist training camps, saved a people from starvation, and freed a country from brutal oppression.

The American flag flies again over our embassy in Kabul. Terrorists who once occupied Afghanistan now occupy cells at Guantanamo Bay. And terrorist leaders who urged followers to sacrifice their lives are running for their own.

America and Afghanistan are now allies against terror. We'll be partners in rebuilding that country.

The last time we met in this chamber, the mothers and daughters of Afghanistan were captives in their own homes, forbidden from working or going to school. Today women are free, and are part of Afghanistan's new government. Our progress is a tribute to the spirit of the Afghan people, to the resolve of our coalition, and to the might of the United States military. When I called our troops into action, I did so with complete confidence in their courage and skill. And tonight, thanks to them, we are winning the war on terror. The men and women of our Armed Forces have delivered a message now clear to every enemy of the United States: even 7,000 miles away, across oceans and continents, on mountaintops and in caves – you will not escape the justice of this nation.

For many Americans, these four months have brought sorrow, and pain that will never completely go away. Every day a retired firefighter returns to Ground Zero, to feel closer to his two sons who died there. At a memorial in New York, a little boy left his football with a note for his lost father: 'Dear Daddy, please take this to heaven. I don't want to play football until I can play with you again some day.'

Last month, at the grave of her husband, Michael, a CIA officer and Marine who died in Mazur-e-Sharif, Shannon Spann said these words of farewell: 'Semper Fi, my love.' Shannon is with us tonight.

Shannon, I assure you and all who have lost a loved one that our cause is just, and our country will never forget the debt we owe Michael and all who gave their lives for freedom.

Our cause is just, and it continues. Our discoveries in Afghanistan confirmed our worst fears, and showed us the true scope of the task ahead. We have seen the depth of our enemies' hatred in videos, where they laugh about the loss of innocent life. And the depth of their hatred is equalled by the madness of the destruction they design. We have found diagrams of American nuclear power plants and public water facilities, detailed instructions for making chemical weapons, surveillance maps of American cities, and thorough descriptions of landmarks in America and throughout the world.

What we have found in Afghanistan confirms that, far from ending there, our war against terror is only beginning. Most of the nineteen men who hijacked planes on September the 11th were trained in Afghanistan's camps, and so were tens of thousands of others. Thousands of dangerous killers, schooled in the methods of murder, often supported by outlaw regimes, are now spread throughout the world like ticking time bombs, set to go off without warning.

Thanks to the work of our law enforcement officials and coalition partners, hundreds of terrorists have been arrested. Yet, tens of thousands of trained terrorists are still at large.

These enemies view the entire world as a battlefield, and we must pursue them wherever they are. So long as training camps operate, so long as nations harbour terrorists, freedom is at risk. And America and our allies must not, and will not, allow it.

Our nation will continue to be steadfast and patient and persistent in the pursuit of two great objectives. First, we will shut down terrorist camps, disrupt terrorist plans, and bring terrorists to justice. And, second, we must prevent the terrorists and regimes who seek chemical, biological or nuclear weapons from threatening the United States and the world.

Our military has put the terror training camps of Afghanistan out of business, yet camps still exist in at least a dozen countries. A terrorist underworld – including groups like Hamas, Hezbollah, Islamic Jihad, Jaish-i-Mohammed – operates in remote jungles and deserts, and hides in the centres of large cities.

While the most visible military action is in Afghanistan, America is acting elsewhere. We now have troops in the Philippines, helping to train that country's armed forces to go after terrorist cells that have executed an American, and still hold hostages. Our soldiers, working with the Bosnian government, seized terrorists who were plotting to bomb our embassy. Our Navy is patrolling the coast of Africa to block the shipment of weapons and the establishment of terrorist camps in Somalia.

My hope is that all nations will heed our call, and eliminate the terrorist parasites who threaten their countries and our own. Many nations are acting forcefully. Pakistan is now cracking down on terror, and I admire the strong leadership of President Musharraf.

But some governments will be timid in the face of terror. And make no mistake about it: If they do not act, America will.

Our second goal is to prevent regimes that sponsor terror from threatening America or our friends and allies with weapons of mass destruction. Some of these regimes have been pretty quiet since September the 11th. But we know their true nature. North Korea is a regime arming with missiles and weapons of mass destruction, while starving its citizens.

Iran aggressively pursues these weapons and exports terror, while an unelected few repress the Iranian people's hope for freedom.

Iraq continues to flaunt its hostility toward America and to support terror. The Iraqi regime has plotted to develop anthrax, and nerve gas, and nuclear weapons for over a decade. This is a regime that has already used poison gas to murder thousands of its own citizens – leaving the bodies of mothers huddled over their dead children. This is a regime that agreed to international inspections – then kicked out the inspectors. This is a regime that has something to hide from the civilized world.

States like these, and their terrorist allies, constitute an axis of evil, arming to threaten the peace of the world. By seeking weapons of mass destruction, these regimes pose a grave and growing danger. They could provide these arms to terrorists, giving them the means to match their hatred. They could attack our allies or attempt to blackmail the United States. In any of these cases, the price of indifference would be catastrophic.

We will work closely with our coalition to deny terrorists and their state sponsors the materials, technology, and expertise to make and deliver weapons of mass destruction. We will develop and deploy effective missile defences to protect America and our allies from sudden attack. And all nations should know: America will do what is necessary to ensure our nation's security.

We'll be deliberate, yet time is not on our side. I will not wait on events, while dangers gather. I will not stand by, as peril draws closer and closer. The United States of America will not permit the world's most dangerous regimes to threaten us with the world's most destructive weapons.

Our war on terror is well begun, but it is only begun. This campaign may not be finished on our watch – yet it must be and it will be waged on our watch.

We can't stop short. If we stop now – leaving terror camps intact and terror states unchecked – our sense of security would be false and temporary. History has called America and our allies to action, and it is both our responsibility and our privilege to fight freedom's fight . . .

During these last few months, I've been humbled and privileged to see the true character of this country in a time of testing. Our enemies believed America was weak and materialistic, that we would splinter in fear and selfishness. They were as wrong as they are evil.

The American people have responded magnificently, with courage and compassion, strength and resolve. As I have met the heroes, hugged the families, and looked into the tired faces of rescuers, I have stood in awe of the American people.

None of us would ever wish the evil that was done on September the 11th. Yet after America was attacked, it was as if our entire country looked into a mirror and saw our better selves. We were reminded that we are citizens, with obligations to each other, to our country, and to history. We began to think less of the goods we can accumulate, and more about the good we can do . . .

For too long our culture has said, 'If it feels good, do it.' Now America is embracing a new ethic and a new creed: 'Let's roll.' In the sacrifice of soldiers, the fierce brotherhood of firefighters, and the bravery and generosity of ordinary citizens, we have glimpsed what a new culture of responsibility could look like. We want to be a nation that serves goals larger than self. We've been offered a unique opportunity, and we must not let this moment pass . . .

This time of adversity offers a unique moment of opportunity – a moment we must seize to change our culture. Through the gathering momentum of millions of acts of service and decency and kindness, I know we can overcome evil with greater good. And we have a great opportunity during this time of war to lead the world toward the values that will bring lasting peace.

All fathers and mothers, in all societies, want their children to be educated, and live free from poverty and violence. No people on Earth yearn to be oppressed, or aspire to servitude, or eagerly await the midnight knock of the secret police.

If anyone doubts this, let them look to Afghanistan, where the Islamic 'street' greeted the fall of tyranny with song and celebration. Let the sceptics look to Islam's own rich history, with its centuries of learning, and tolerance and progress. America will lead by defending liberty and justice because they are right and true and unchanging for all people everywhere.

No nation owns these aspirations, and no nation is exempt from them. We have no intention of imposing our culture. But America will always stand firm for the non-negotiable demands of human dignity: the rule of law; limits on the power of the state; respect for women; private property; free speech; equal justice; and religious tolerance.

America will take the side of brave men and women who advocate these values around the world, including the Islamic world, because we have a greater objective than eliminating threats and containing resentment. We seek a just and peaceful world beyond the war on terror.

In this moment of opportunity, a common danger is erasing old rivalries. America is working with Russia and China and India, in ways we have never before, to achieve peace and prosperity. In every region, free markets and free trade and free societies are proving their power to lift lives. Together with friends and allies from Europe to Asia, and Africa to Latin America, we will demonstrate that the forces of terror cannot stop the momentum of freedom.

The last time I spoke here, I expressed the hope that life would return to normal. In some ways, it has. In others, it never will. Those of us who have lived through these challenging times have been changed by them. We've come to know truths that we will never question: evil is real, and it must be opposed. Beyond all differences of race or creed, we are one country, mourning together and facing danger together. Deep in the American character, there is honour, and it is stronger than cynicism. And many have discovered again that even in tragedy – especially in tragedy – God is near.

In a single instant, we realized that this will be a decisive decade in the history of liberty, that we've been called to a unique role in human events. Rarely has the world faced a choice more clear or consequential.

Our enemies send other people's children on missions of suicide and murder. They embrace tyranny and death as a cause and a creed. We stand for a different choice, made long ago, on the day of our founding. We affirm it again today. We choose freedom and the dignity of every life.

Steadfast in our purpose, we now press on. We have known freedom's price. We have shown freedom's power. And in this great conflict, my fellow Americans, we will see freedom's victory.

Thank you all. May God bless.

•

## TONY BLAIR
### Blackpool, 1 October 2002

*'At our best when at our boldest'*

*On the night before this speech, Alastair Campbell, Tony Blair's director of communications and strategy, Blair's pollster Phillip Gould and policy adviser Liz Lloyd were up until 3 a.m. going through the speech line by line and trying to get in more 'colour and texture'. They thought that it was in good shape. Blair was up at around six. Campbell saw him at seven and the prime minister 'was pretty happy with it. He felt it was the most rounded intellectual speech of the lot'. This was the final section. Note the verbless sentences which mark some modern speeches.*

Up to 1997, do you know how many years of the twentieth century Labour was in power with a substantial majority?

Nine. By the end of this Parliament, we will have doubled it.

We learnt the hard way.

But now we have to show that we have the capacity not only to learn but to transform, to show what a liberated modern social democracy can do.

We can do it. I'm an optimist.

Why?

Because there is change happening.

Ten years ago people asked would Labour ever win again.

Now, they ask it of the Tories.

Ten years ago, they asked if we were fit to manage the economy.

Now, thanks to the vision and brilliance of Gordon Brown, we have succeeded beyond any previous Labour or Tory government. Not by chance.

Every part of it – from the first years of discipline, through to Bank of England independence through to reform of tax and benefits to make work pay – was a bold choice.

The right wing never deserved their reputation for economic competence.

And we've made sure they'll never have exclusive rights to it again.

Ten years ago, claims that the minimum wage would cost a million jobs were the centrepiece of John Major's election campaign: now it's the law, business and trade unions agree it, and the Tories have to pretend they were in favour of it all along.

At our best when at our boldest.

For four elections, anyone who said investment before tax cuts was brave but doomed.

In 2001, we did it and it is those who oppose the investment who are on the run.

The New Deal was savaged by the Tories, challenged politically, challenged legally, challenged by business.

Now it's in its sixth year, over a million people have been helped by it and not one Tory candidate dares to stand up and say we should abolish it.

At our best when at our boldest.

Remember how devolution would break up Britain?

And now there is a Scottish Parliament and a Welsh Assembly, the nationalists are running from their separatism and not a single party in Britain proposes going back. And in Northern Ireland, for all the difficulties, Republicans and Unionists sit in government together and the principle of consent is accepted North and South on the island of Ireland for the first time in eighty years.

At our best when at our boldest.

And remember how for 100 years we tried to reform the House of Lords and now the reform is happening, the hereditary peers are leaving and the attack is that it doesn't go far enough?

The equal age of consent passed massively in the House of Commons.

The first black Cabinet minister. Record numbers of women Cabinet ministers.

Record numbers of women MPs.

From progress here to life and death, abroad, it is happening.

A month ago I visited Beira District Hospital in Mozambique. There are as many doctors in the whole of Mozambique as there are in Oldham. I saw four children to a bed, sick with malaria. Nurses dying of AIDS faster than others can be recruited. Tens of thousands of children dying in that country needlessly every year.

I asked a doctor: What hope is there? Britain is our hope, he said. Thanks to you we have debt relief. Thanks to you we have new programmes to fight AIDS and malaria. Thanks to you the docks at Maputo are being rebuilt and we can sell our goods abroad.

When you tire of knocking on the door, putting the leaflet in the envelope, wonder what it's all about and what it's all for, reflect on that doctor, feel proud of what you do, and understand that's what we elect a Labour government for.

We haven't just nailed the myths about Labour of old; we've created some legend of achievement about New Labour too.

We've been at our best when we've been at our boldest.

And now we need to be again.

And all it takes is for us to do what we believe in.

We believe in a school system of equal opportunity for all. But we don't yet have it.

We believe in an NHS with equal access for all; but not all get it.

We believe in punishing the guilty and acquitting the innocent but it's not what happens.

We believe in ridding Britain of child poverty but children are still poor.

We believe in Europe but we're not yet at the centre of it.

There's nothing wrong with the old principles but if the old ways worked, they'd have worked by now.

If you believe in social justice, in solidarity, in equality of opportunity and responsibility, then believe in the reforms to get us there.

Now is the time.

To quicken the march of progress not mark time.

What started with the renewal of the Labour Party only ends with the renewal of Britain.

Pessimism or hope

Despair or confidence

Decline or renewal

At our best when at our boldest.

This is not the time to abandon our journey of modernization but to see it through.

•

### ROBIN COOK
London, 17 March 2003

*'With a heavy heart I resign from the government'*

*The stakes were high when the House of Commons debated whether to back Tony Blair in joining the United States in invading Iraq with the aim of toppling Saddam Hussein, its dictator president. Blair knew that if the vote was lost, he would be forced to resign. There were two outstanding performers – Blair and Robin Cook, who as Foreign Secretary and then Leader of the House of Commons, was one of the big beasts of Blair's New Labour government. A swelling wave of applause greeted Cook as he sat down and he was given a standing ova-tion. Blair won the vote by 412 to 149 – 139 Labour MPs voted against Blair, a record revolt in modern times.*

I have chosen to address the House on why I cannot support a war without international agreement or domestic support. The present Prime Minister is the most successful leader of the Labour Party in my lifetime. I hope that he will continue to be the leader of our party, and I hope that he will continue to be successful. I have no sympathy with, and I will give no comfort to, those who want to use this crisis to displace him. I applaud the heroic efforts that the prime minister has made in trying to secure a second resolution. I do not think that anybody could have done better than the foreign secretary [Jack Straw] in working to get support for a second resolution within the Security Council. But the very intensity of those attempts underlines how important it was to succeed. Now that those attempts have failed, we cannot pretend that getting a second resolution was of no importance.

France has been at the receiving end of bucket loads of commen-tary in recent days. It is not France alone that wants more time for inspections. Germany wants more time for inspections; Russia wants more time for inspections; indeed, at no time have we signed up even the minimum necessary to carry a second resolution. We delude ourselves if we think that the degree of international hostility is all the result of President Chirac. The reality is that Britain is being asked to embark on a war without agreement in any of the inter-national bodies of which we are a leading partner – not NATO, not the European Union and, now, not the Security Council.

To end up in such diplomatic weakness is a serious reverse. Only a year ago, we and the United States were part of a coalition against terrorism that was wider and more diverse than I would ever have imagined possible. History will be astonished at the diplomatic mis-calculations that led so quickly to the disintegration of that powerful coalition. The US can afford to go it alone, but Britain is not a super-power. Our interests are best protected not by unilateral action but by multilateral agreement and a world order governed by rules. Yet tonight the international partnerships most important to us are weakened: the European Union is divided; the Security Council is in stalemate.

Those are heavy casulaties of a war in which a shot has yet to be fired. I have heard some parallels between military action in these circumstances and the military action that we took in Kosovo. There was no doubt about the multilateral support that we had for the action that we took in Kosovo. It was supported by NATO; it was supported by the European Union; it was supported by every single one of the seven neighbours in the region. France and Germany were our active allies. It is precisely because we have none of that support in this case that it was all the more important to get agreement in the Security Council as the last hope of demonstrating international agreement.

The legal basis for our action in Kosovo was the need to respond to an urgent and compelling humanitarian crisis. Our difficulty in getting support this time is that neither the international community nor the British public is persuaded that there is an urgent and compelling reason for this military action in Iraq.

The threshold for war should always be high. None of us can predict the death toll of civilians from the forthcoming bombardment of Iraq, but the US warning of a bombing campaign that will 'shock and awe' makes it likely that casualties will be numbered at least in the thousands. I am confident that British servicemen and women will acquit themselves with professionalism and with courage. I hope that they all come back.

I hope that Saddam, even now, will quit Baghdad and avert war, but it is false to argue that only those who support war support our troops. It is entirely legitimate to support our troops while seeking an alternative to the conflict that will put those troops at risk. Nor is it fair to accuse those of us who want longer for inspections of not having an alternative strategy.

For four years as foreign secretary I was partly responsible for the Western strategy of containment. Over the past decade that strategy destroyed more weapons than in the Gulf War, dismantled Iraq's nuclear weapons programme and halted Saddam's medium- and long-range missiles programmes. Iraq's military strength is now less than half its size at the time of the last Gulf War. Ironically, it is only because Iraq's military forces are so weak that we can even contemplate its invasion. Some advocates of conflict claim that Saddam's forces are so weak, so demoralized and so badly equipped that the war will be over in a few days.

We cannot base our military strategy on the assumption that Saddam is weak and at the same time justify pre-emptive action on the claim that he is a threat. Iraq probably has no weapons of mass destruction in the commonly understood sense of the term – namely a credible device capable of being delivered against a strategic city target. It probably still has biological toxins and battlefield chemical munitions, but it has had them since the 1980s when US companies sold Saddam anthrax agents and the then British Government approved chemical and munitions factories.

Why is it now so urgent that we should take military action to disarm a military capacity that has been there for twenty years, and which we helped to create? Why is it necessary to resort to war this week, while Saddam's ambition to complete his weapons programme is blocked by the presence of UN inspectors? Only a couple of weeks ago, Hans Blix told the Security Council that the key remaining disarmament tasks could be completed within months.

I have heard it said that Iraq has had not months but twelve years in which to complete disarmament, and that our patience is exhausted. Yet it is more than thirty years since resolution 242 called on Israel to withdraw from the occupied territories. We do not express the same impatience with the persistent refusal of Israel to comply. I welcome the strong personal commitment that the prime minister has given to Middle East peace, but Britain's positive role in the Middle East does not redress the strong sense of injustice throughout the Muslim world at what it sees as one rule for the allies of the US and another rule for the rest.

Nor is our credibility helped by the appearance that our partners in Washington are less interested in disarmament than they are in regime change in Iraq. That explains why any evidence that inspections may be showing progress is greeted in Washington not with satisfaction but with consternation: it reduces the case for war. What has come to trouble me most over past weeks is the suspicion that if the hanging chads in Florida had gone the other way and Al Gore had been elected, we would not now be about to commit British troops.

The longer that I have served in this place, the greater the respect I have for the good sense and collective wisdom of the British people. On Iraq, I believe that the prevailing mood of the British people is sound. They do not doubt that Saddam is a brutal dictator, but they are not persuaded that he is a clear and present danger to Britain. They want inspections to be given a chance, and they suspect that they are being pushed too quickly into conflict by a US Administration with an agenda of its own. Above all, they are uneasy at Britain going out on a limb on a military adventure without a broader international coalition and against the hostility of many of our traditional allies.

From the start of the present crisis, I have insisted, as Leader of the House, on the right of this place to vote on whether Britain should go to war. It has been a favourite theme of commentators that this House no longer occupies a central role in British politics. Nothing could better demonstrate that they are wrong than for this House to stop the commitment of troops in a war that has neither international agreement nor domestic support.

I intend to join those tomorrow night who will vote against military action now. It is for that reason, and for that reason alone, and with a heavy heart, that I resign from the government.

•

TONY BLAIR
London, 18 March 2003

*'The possibility . . . of terrorist groups in possession of WMD . . . is now, in my judgement, a real and present danger'*

*This was the most important speech that Tony Blair had ever made: he believed he would have to go if a majority of the Labour Party failed to support him. He told his three eldest children he might not be prime minister by the end of the*

*week. 'At times like this, I just put my head down and write,' he wrote in his*
*autobiography. 'The argument came easily.' This is mainly the edited version of*
*his speech that Blair used in his autobiography.*

It is right that this house debate this issue and pass judgement. That
is the democracy that is our right but that others struggle for in vain.

And again I say: I do not disrespect the views of those in opposition to mine.

This is a tough choice. But it is also a stark one: to stand British
troops down and turn back; or to hold firm to the course we have set.

I believe we must hold firm.

The question most often posed is not why does it matter? But
why does it matter so much? Here we are, the government with its
most serious test, its majority at risk, the first Cabinet resignation
over an issue of policy. The main parties divided.

People who agree on everything else, disagree on this and like-
wise, those who never agree on anything, finding common cause.
The country and parliament reflect each other, a debate that, as time
has gone on has become less bitter but not less grave.

So: why does it matter so much? Because the outcome of this
issue will now determine more than the fate of the Iraqi regime and
more than the future of the Iraqi people, for so long brutalized by
Saddam. It will determine the way Britain and the world confront the
central security threat of the twenty-first century; the development
of the UN; the relationship between Europe and the US; the relations within the EU and the way the US engages with the rest of the
world. It will determine the pattern of international politics for the
next generation ...

Let me tell the house what I know. I know that there are some
countries or groups within countries that are proliferating and trading in WMD, especially nuclear weapons technology.

I know there are companies, individuals, some former scientists
on nuclear weapons programmes, selling their equipment or expertise.

I know there are several countries – mostly dictatorships with
highly repressive regimes – desperately trying to acquire chemical

weapons, biological weapons or, in particular, nuclear weapons capability. Some of these countries are now a short time away from having a serviceable nuclear weapon. This activity is not diminishing. It is increasing.

We all know that there are terrorist cells now operating in most major countries. Just as in the last two years, around twenty different nations have suffered serious terrorist outrages. Thousands have died in them.

The purpose of terrorism lies not just in the violent act itself. It is in producing terror. It sets out to inflame, to divide, to produce consequences which they then use to justify further terror.

Round the world it now poisons the chances of political progress: in the Middle East; in Kashmir; in Chechnya; in Africa.

The removal of the Taliban in Afghanistan dealt it a blow. But it has not gone away.

And these two threats have different motives and different origins but they share one basic common view: they detest the freedom, democracy and tolerance that are the hallmarks of our way of life.

At the moment, I accept that association between them is loose. But it is hardening.

And the possibility of the two coming together – of terrorist groups in possession of WMD, even of a so-called dirty radiological bomb, is now, in my judgement, a real and present danger.

And let us recall: what was shocking about September 11 was not just the slaughter of the innocent, but the knowledge that had the terrorists been able to, there would have been not 3,000 innocent dead, but 30,000 or 300,000 and the more the suffering, the greater the terrorists' rejoicing.

Three kilograms of VX from a rocket launcher would contaminate a quarter of a square kilometre of a city.

Millions of lethal doses are contained in one litre of anthrax; 10,000 litres are unaccounted for; 11 September has changed the psychology of America. It should have changed the psychology of the world. Of course Iraq is not the only part of this threat. But it is the test of whether we treat the threat seriously.

Faced with it, the world should unite. The UN should be the

focus, both of diplomacy and of action. That is what 1441 said. That was the deal. And I say to you to break it now, to will the ends but not the means that would do more damage in the long term to the UN than any other course.

To fall back into the lassitude of the last twelve years, to talk, to discuss, to debate but never act; to declare our will but not enforce it; to combine strong language with weak intentions, a worse outcome than never speaking at all.

And then, when the threat returns from Iraq or elsewhere, who will believe us? What price our credibility with the next tyrant? . . .

What we have witnessed is indeed the consequence of Europe and the United States dividing from each other. Not all of Europe – Spain, Italy, Holland, Denmark, Portugal – have all strongly supported us. And not a majority of Europe if we include, as we should, Europe's new members who will accede next year, all ten of whom have been in our support.

But the paralysis of the UN has been born out of the division there is. And at the heart of it has been the concept of a world in which there are rival poles of power. The US and its allies in one corner. France, Germany, Russia and its allies in the other. I do not believe that all of these nations intend such an outcome. But that is what now faces us.

I believe such a vision to be misguided and profoundly dangerous. I know why it arises. There is resentment of US predominance.

There is fear of US unilateralism. People ask: do the US listen to us and our preoccupations? And there is perhaps a lack of full understanding of US preoccupations after 11th September. I know all of this. But the way to deal with it is not rivalry but partnership. Partners are not servants but neither are they rivals. I tell you what Europe should have said last September to the US. With one voice it should have said: we understand your strategic anxiety over terrorism and WMD and we will help you meet it.

We will mean what we say in any UN resolution we pass and will back it with action if Saddam fails to disarm voluntarily; but in return we ask two things of you: that the US should choose the UN path and you should recognize the fundamental overriding importance of re-starting the Middle East Peace Process, which we will hold you to . . .

I have never put our justification for action as regime change. We have to act within the terms set out in resolution 1441. That is our legal base.

But it is the reason, I say frankly, why if we do act we should do so with a clear conscience and strong heart.

I accept fully that those opposed to this course of action share my detestation of Saddam. Who could not? Iraq is a wealthy country that in 1978, the year before Saddam seized power, was richer than Portugal or Malaysia.

Today it is impoverished, sixty per cent of its population dependent on food aid.

Thousands of children die needlessly every year from lack of food and medicine.

Four million people out of a population of just over twenty million are in exile.

The brutality of the repression – the death and torture camps, the barbaric prisons for political opponents, the routine beatings for anyone or their families suspected of disloyalty are well documented.

Just last week, someone slandering Saddam was tied to a lamp post in a street in Baghdad, his tongue cut out, mutilated and left to bleed to death, as a warning to others.

I recall a few weeks ago talking to an Iraqi exile and saying to her that I understood how grim it must be under the lash of Saddam.

'But you don't,' she replied. 'You cannot. You do not know what it is like to live in perpetual fear.'

And she is right. We take our freedom for granted. But imagine not to be able to speak or discuss or debate or even question the society you live in. To see friends and family taken away and never daring to complain. To suffer the humility of failing courage in face of pitiless terror. That is how the Iraqi people live. Leave Saddam in place and that is how they will continue to be forced to live . . .

We must face the consequences of the actions we advocate. For me, that means all the dangers of war. But for others, opposed to this course, it means – let us be clear – that the Iraqi people, whose only true hope of liberation lies in the removal of Saddam, for them, the darkness will close back over them again; and he will be free to take his revenge upon those he must know wish him gone.

And if this house now demands that at this moment, faced with this threat from this regime, that British troops are pulled back, that we turn away at the point of reckoning, and that is what it means – what then?

What will Saddam feel? Strengthened beyond measure. What will the other states who tyrannize their people, the terrorists who threaten our existence, what will they take from that? That the will confronting them is decaying and feeble.

Who will celebrate and who will weep?

And if our plea is for America to work with others, to be good as well as powerful allies, will our retreat make them multilateralist? Or will it not rather be the biggest impulse to unilateralism there could ever be. And what of the UN and the future of Iraq and the Middle East peace plan, devoid of our influence, stripped of our insistence?

This house wanted this decision. Well it has it. Those are the choices. And in this dilemma, no choice is perfect, no cause ideal.

But on this decision hangs the fate of many things:

Of whether we summon the strength to recognize this global challenge of the twenty-first century and meet it.

Of the Iraqi people, groaning under years of dictatorship.

Of our armed forces – brave men and women of whom we can feel proud, whose morale is high and whose purpose is clear.

Of the institutions and alliances that will shape our world for years to come.

I can think of many things, of whether we summon the strength to recognize the global challenge of the twenty-first century and beat it, of the Iraqi people groaning under years of dictatorship, of our armed forces – brave men and women of whom we can feel proud, whose morale is high and whose purpose is clear – of the institutions and alliances that shape our world for years to come.

To retreat now, I believe, would put at hazard all that we hold dearest, turn the UN back into a talking shop, stifle the first steps of progress in the Middle East, leave the Iraqi people to the mercy of events on which we would have relinquished all power to influence for the better.

Tell our allies that at the very moment of action, at the very moment when they need our determination, that Britain faltered. I will not be party to such a course. This is not the time to falter. This is the time for this house, not just this government or indeed this prime minister, but for this house to give a lead, to show that we will stand up for what we know to be right, to show that we will confront the tyrannies and dictatorships and terrorists who put our way of life at risk, to show at the moment of decision that we have the courage to do the right thing.

*Blair won the motion by 412 votes to 149 (which included 129 of the 413 Labour MPs). It was a speech that would haunt him for the rest of his career. No weapons of mass destruction were found in Iraq – the premise for action – and 179 British troops and more than 100,000 Iraqi citizens were killed during the war and its bloody aftermath.*

•

## COLONEL TIM COLLINS
### Kuwaiti desert, 19 March 2003

*'There are some who are alive at this moment
who will not be alive shortly'*

*Colonel Tim Collins delivered this off-the-cuff speech to about 800 men of the battlegroup of the 1st Battalion of the Royal Irish Regiment when they were 20 miles from the Iraqi border before the invasion by the 16 Air Assault Brigade. Sarah Oliver of the* Mail on Sunday, *who recorded the speech, said that it grew and grew into something magnificent. 'It made you realize the true meaning of the term "rallying cry" . . . It was just after a sandstorm and the men were standing around him in a U-shape . . . He delivered the speech without a note . . . By the end everyone felt they were ready for whatever lay ahead.'*

We go to liberate, not to conquer. We will not fly our flags in their country. We are entering Iraq to free a people and the only flag which will be flown in that ancient land is their own. Show respect for them.

There are some who are alive at this moment who will not be alive shortly. Those who do not wish to go on that journey, we will not send. As for the others, I expect you to rock their world. Wipe them out if that is what they choose. But if you are ferocious in battle remember to be magnanimous in victory.

Iraq is steeped in history. It is the site of the Garden of Eden, of the Great Flood and the birthplace of Abraham. Tread lightly there. You will see things that no man could pay to see – and you will have to go a long way to find a more decent, generous and upright people than the Iraqis. You will be embarrassed by their hospitality even though they have nothing. Don't treat them as refugees for they are in their own country. Their children will be poor, in years to come they will know that the light of liberation in their lives was brought by you.

If there are casualties of war then remember that when they woke up and got dressed in the morning they did not plan to die this day. Allow them dignity in death. Bury them properly and mark their graves.

It is my foremost intention to bring every single one of you out alive. But there may be people among us who will not see the end of this campaign. We will put them in their sleeping bags and send them back. There will be no time for sorrow.

The enemy should be in no doubt that we are his nemesis and that we are bringing about his rightful destruction. There are many regional commanders who have stains on their souls and they are stoking the fires of hell for Saddam. He and his forces will be destroyed by this coalition for what they have done. As they die they will know their deeds have brought them to this place. Show them no pity.

It is a big step to take another human life. It is not to be done lightly. I know of men who have taken life needlessly in other conflicts. I can assure you they live with the mark of Cain upon them. If someone surrenders to you then remember they have that right in international law and ensure that one day they go home to their family.

The ones who wish to fight, well, we aim to please.

If you harm the regiment or its history by over-enthusiasm in killing or in cowardice, know it is your family who will suffer. You will be shunned unless your conduct is of the highest – for your deeds will follow you down through history. We will bring shame on neither our uniform or our nation.

(*On Saddam's chemical and biological weapons*) It is not a question of if, it's a question of when. We know he has already devolved the decision to lower commanders, and that means he has already taken the decision himself. If we survive the first strike we will survive the attack.

As for ourselves, let's bring everyone home and leave Iraq a better place for us having been there.

Our business now is north.

•

### DAVID GROSSMAN
### Tel Aviv, 4 November 2006

#### *'Turn to the Palestinian people'*

*The Israeli author David Grossman's books have been translated into more than thirty languages and won many prizes. He is an activist and critic of Israeli policy towards Palestinians. The Yellow Wind, his non-fiction study of the life of Palestinians in the Israeli-occupied West Bank and Gaza Strip, was applauded abroad but provoked controversy at home. Alongside Amos Oz, he has been one of the most prominent cultural advocates of a two-state solution to the Israeli–Palestinian conflict. When he made this speech at a rally attended by 100,000 people he was also a bereaved father. It generated responses across the world.*

The annual memorial ceremony for Yitzhak Rabin is the moment when we pause for a while to remember Rabin the man, the leader. And we also take a look at ourselves, at Israeli society, its leadership, the national mood, the state of the peace process, at ourselves as individuals in the face of national events.

It is not easy to take a look at ourselves this year. There was a war, and Israel flexed its massive military muscle, but also exposed Israel's fragility. We discovered that our military might ultimately cannot be the only guarantee of our existence. Primarily, we have found that the crisis Israel is experiencing is far deeper than we had feared, in almost every way.

I am speaking here tonight as a person whose love for the land is overwhelming and complex, and yet it is unequivocal, and as one whose continuous covenant with the land has turned his personal calamity into a covenant of blood.

I am totally secular, and yet in my eyes the establishment and the very existence of the State of Israel is a miracle of sorts that happened to us as a nation – a political, national, human miracle.

I do not forget this for a single moment. Even when many things in the reality of our lives enrage and depress me, even when the miracle is broken down to routine and wretchedness, to corruption and cynicism, even when reality seems like nothing but a poor parody of this miracle, I always remember. And with these feelings, I address you tonight.

'Behold land, for we hath squandered,' wrote the poet Saul Tchernikovsky in Tel Aviv in 1938. He lamented the burial of our young again and again in the soil of the Land of Israel. The death of young people is a horrible, ghastly waste.

But no less dreadful is the sense that for many years the State of Israel has been squandering, not only the lives of its sons, but also its miracle; that grand and rare opportunity that history bestowed upon it, the opportunity to establish here a state that is efficient, democratic, which abides by Jewish and universal values; a state that would be a national home and haven, but not only a haven, also a place that would offer a new meaning to Jewish existence; a state that holds as an integral and essential part of its Jewish identity and its Jewish ethos, the observance of full equality and respect for its non-Jewish citizens.

Look at what befell us. Look what befell the young, bold, passionate country we had here, and how, as if it had undergone a quickened ageing process, Israel lurched from infancy and youth to a perpetual state of gripe, weakness and sourness.

How did this happen? When did we lose even the hope that we

would eventually be able to live a different, better life? Moreover, how do we continue to watch from the side as though hypnotized by the insanity, rudeness, violence and racism that has overtaken our home?

And I ask you: How could it be that a people with such powers of creativity, renewal and vivacity as ours, a people that knew how to rise from the ashes time and again, finds itself today, despite its great military might, at such a state of laxity and inanity, a state where it is the victim once more, but this time its own victim, of its anxieties, its short-sightedness.

One of the most difficult outcomes of the recent war is the heightened realization that at this time there is no king in Israel, that our leadership is hollow. Our military and political leadership is hollow. I am not even talking about the obvious blunders in running the war, of the collapse of the home front, nor of the large-scale and small-time corruption.

I am talking about the fact that the people leading Israel today are unable to connect Israelis to their identity. Certainly not with the healthy, vitalizing and productive areas of this identity, with those areas of identity and memory and fundamental values that would give us hope and strength, that would be the antidote to the waning of mutual trust, of the bonds to the land, that would give some meaning to the exhausting and despairing struggle for existence.

The fundamental characteristics of the current Israeli leadership are primarily anxiety and intimidation, of the charade of power, the wink of the dirty deal, of selling out our most prized possessions. In this sense they are not true leaders, certainly they are not the leaders of a people in such a complicated position that has lost the way it so desperately needs. Sometimes it seems that the sound box of their self-importance, of their memories of history, of their vision, of what they really care for, exist only in the minuscule space between two headlines of a newspaper or between two investigations by the attorney general.

Look at those who lead us. Not all of them, of course, but many among them. Behold their petrified, suspicious, sweaty conduct. The conduct of advocates and scoundrels. It is preposterous to expect to hear wisdom emerge from them, that some vision or even just an original, truly creative, bold and ingenuous idea would emanate from them.

When was the last time a prime minister formulated or took a step that could open up a new horizon for Israelis, for a better future? When did he initiate a social or cultural or ideological move, instead of merely reacting feverishly to moves forced upon him by others?

Mr Prime Minister, I am not saying these words out of feelings of rage or revenge. I have waited long enough to avoid responding on impulse. You will not be able to dismiss my words tonight by saying a grieving man cannot be judged. Certainly I am grieving, but I am more pained than angry. This country and what you and your friends are doing to it pains me.

Trust me, your success is important to me, because the future of all of us depends on our ability to act. Yitzhak Rabin took the road of peace with the Palestinians, not because he possessed great affection for them or their leaders. Even then, as you recall, common belief was that we had no partner and we had nothing to discuss with them.

Rabin decided to act because he discerned very wisely that Israeli society would not be able to sustain itself endlessly in a state of unresolved conflict. He realized long before many others that life in a climate of violence, occupation, terror, anxiety and hopelessness extracts a price Israel cannot afford. This is all relevant today, even more so. We will soon talk about the partner that we do or do not have, but before that, let us take a look at ourselves.

We have been living in this struggle for more than 100 years. We, the citizens of this conflict, have been born into war and raised in it, and in a certain sense indoctrinated by it. Maybe this is why we sometimes think that this madness in which we live for over 100 years is the only real thing, the only life for us, and that we do not have the option or even the right to aspire for a different life.

By our sword we shall live and by our sword we shall die and the sword shall devour for ever. Maybe this would explain the indifference with which we accept the utter failure of the peace process, a failure that has lasted for years and claims more and more victims . . .

And these are partly the cause of Israel's quick descent into the heartless, essentially brutal treatment of its poor and suffering. This indifference to the fate of the hungry, the elderly, the sick and the disabled, all those who are weak, this equanimity of the State of Israel in the face of human trafficking or the appalling employment conditions of our foreign workers, which border on slavery, to the deeply ingrained institutionalized racism against the Arab minority.

When this takes place here so naturally, without shock, without protest, as though it were obvious that we would never be able to get the wheel back on track, when all of this takes place, I begin to fear that even if peace were to arrive tomorrow, and even if we ever regained some normalcy, we may have lost our chance for full recovery. The calamity that struck my family and myself with the falling of our son, Uri, does not grant me any additional rights in the public discourse, but I believe that the experience of facing death and loss brings with it a sobriety and lucidity, at least regarding the distinction between the important and the unimportant, between the attainable and the unattainable.

Any reasonable person in Israel, and I will say in Palestine too, knows exactly the outline of a possible solution to the conflict between the two peoples. Any reasonable person here and over there knows deep in their heart the difference between dreams and the heart's desire, between what is possible and what is not possible by the conclusion of negotiations. Anyone who does not know, who refuses to acknowledge this, is already not a partner, be he Jew or Arab, is entrapped in his hermetic fanaticism, and is therefore not a partner.

Let us take a look at those who are meant to be our partners. The Palestinians have elected Hamas to lead them, Hamas who refuses to negotiate with us, refuses even to recognize us. What can be done in such a position? Keep strangling them more and more, keep mowing down hundreds of Palestinians in Gaza, most of whom are innocent civilians like us? Kill them and get killed for all eternity?

Turn to the Palestinians, Mr Olmert, address them over the heads of Hamas, appeal to their moderates, those who like you and I oppose Hamas and its ways, turn to the Palestinian people, speak to their deep grief and wounds, acknowledge their ongoing suffering.

Nothing would be taken away from you or Israel's standing in future negotiations. Our hearts will only open up to one another slightly, and this has a tremendous power, the power of a *force majeure*. The power of simple human compassion, particularly in this state of deadlock and dread. Just once, look at them not through the sights of a gun, and not behind a closed roadblock. You will see there a people that is tortured no less than us. An oppressed, occupied people bereft of hope.

Certainly, the Palestinians are also to blame for the impasse, certainly they played their role in the failure of the peace process. But take a look at them from a different perspective, not only at the radicals in their midst, not only at those who share interests with our own radicals. Take a look at the overwhelming majority of this miserable people, whose fate is entangled with our own, whether we like it or not.

Go to the Palestinians, Mr Olmert, do not search all the time for reasons not to talk to them. You backed down on the unilateral convergence, and that's a good thing, but do not leave a vacuum. It will be occupied instantly with violence, destruction. Talk to them, make them an offer their moderates can accept. They argue among themselves far more than we are shown in the media. Make them an offer that will force them to choose between accepting it or preferring to remain hostage to fanatical Islam.

Approach them with the bravest and most serious plan Israel can offer. With the offer that any reasonable Palestinian and Israeli knows is the boundary of their refusal and our concession. There is no time. Should you delay, in a short while we will look back with longing at the amateur Palestinian terror. We will hit our heads and yell at our failure to exercise all of our mental flexibility, all of the Israeli ingenuity to uproot our enemies from their self-entrapment. We have no choice and they have no choice. And a peace of no choice should be approached with the same determination and creativity as one approaches a war of no choice. And those who believe we do have a choice, or that time is on our side, do not comprehend the deeply dangerous processes already in motion.

Maybe, Mr Prime Minister, you need to be reminded that if an

Arab leader is sending a peace signal, be it the slightest and most hesitant, you must accept it, you must test immediately its sincerity and seriousness. You do not have the moral right not to respond.

You owe it to those whom you would ask to sacrifice their lives should another war break out. Therefore, if President Assad says that Syria wants peace, even if you don't believe him, and we are all suspicious of him, you must offer to meet him that same day.

Don't wait a single day. When you launched the last war you did not even wait one hour. You charged with full force, with the complete arsenal, with the full power of destruction. Why, when a glimmer of peace surfaces, must you reject it immediately, dissolve it? What have you got to lose? Are you suspicious of it? Go and offer him such terms that would expose his schemes. Offer him a peace process that would last over several years, and only at its conclusion, and provided he meets all the conditions and restrictions, will he get back the Golan. Commit him to a prolonged process, act so that his people also become aware of this possibility. Help the moderates, who must exist there as well. Try to shape reality. Not only serve as its collaborator. This is what you were elected to do.

Certainly, not all depends on our actions. There are major powers active in our region and in the world. Some, like Iran, like radical Islam, seek our doom and despite that, so much depends on what we do, on what we become.

Disagreements today between right and left are not that significant. The vast majority of Israel's citizens understand this already, and know what the outline for the resolution of the conflict would look like. Most of us understand, therefore, that the land would be divided, that a Palestinian State would be established.

Why, then, do we keep exhausting ourselves with the internal bickering that has gone on for forty years? Why does our political leadership continue to reflect the position of the radicals and not that held by the majority of the public? It is better to reach national consensus before circumstances or, God forbid, another war force us to reach it. If we do it, we would save ourselves years of decline and error, years when we will cry time and again: 'Behold land, for we hath squandered.'

From where I stand right now, I beseech, I call on all those who listen, the young who came back from the war, who know they are the ones to be called upon to pay the price of the next war, on citizens, Jew and Arab, people on the right and the left, the secular, the religious, stop for a moment, take a look into the abyss. Think of how close we are to losing all that we have created here. Ask yourselves if this is not the time to get a grip, to break free of this paralysis, to finally claim the lives we deserve to live.

•

## BARACK OBAMA
### Philadelphia, 18 March 2008

### *'A more perfect union'*

*The Rev. Jeremiah Wright of Trinity United Church of Christ in Chicago embarrassed the Democrat candidate Barack Obama, who had regularly worshipped in his church during the 2008 presidential election campaign, by making strong criticisms of American policy — for instance, for putting Africans into slavery. He did not justify the 9/11 attacks but said that America's chickens were coming home to roost because 'the stuff we have done overseas has now been brought right back into our own front yards'. Obama's response in his 'race speech' has been compared to Martin Luther King's 'I Have A Dream' speech or the Gettysburg Address, exaggeratedly, according to the American commentator Garry Wills. But both Lincoln and Obama argued against the politics of fear, said Wills; each forged a moral position that rose above the occasions for their speaking. The* New York Times *columnist Maureen Dowd noted that only Barack Obama 'could alchemize a nuanced 40-minute speech on race into must-see YouTube viewing for 20-year-olds'.*

'We the people, in order to form a more perfect union.' Two hundred and twenty-one years ago, in a hall that still stands across the street, a group of men gathered and, with these simple words, launched America's improbable experiment in democracy. Farmers and scholars; statesmen and patriots who had travelled across an

ocean to escape tyranny and persecution finally made real their declaration of independence at a Philadelphia convention that lasted
through the spring of 1787.

The document they produced was eventually signed but ultimately unfinished. It was stained by this nation's original sin of slavery,
a question that divided the colonies and brought the convention to a
stalemate until the founders chose to allow the slave trade to continue for at least twenty more years, and to leave any final resolution
to future generations.

Of course, the answer to the slavery question was already embed-
ded within our Constitution – a Constitution that had at its very core
the ideal of equal citizenship under the law; a Constitution that
promised its people liberty, and justice, and a union that could be
and should be perfected over time.

And yet words on a parchment would not be enough to deliver
slaves from bondage, or provide men and women of every colour
and creed their full rights and obligations as citizens of the United
States. What would be needed were Americans in successive generations who were willing to do their part – through protests and
struggle, on the streets and in the courts, through a civil war and civil
disobedience and always at great risk – to narrow that gap between
the promise of our ideals and the reality of their time.

This was one of the tasks we set forth at the beginning of this
campaign – to continue the long march of those who came before
us, a march for a more just, more equal, more free, more caring and
more prosperous America. I chose to run for the presidency at this
moment in history because I believe deeply that we cannot solve the
challenges of our time unless we solve them together – unless we
perfect our union by understanding that we may have different stories, but we hold common hopes; that we may not look the same and
we may not have come from the same place, but we all want to move
in the same direction – towards a better future for our children and
our grandchildren.

This belief comes from my unyielding faith in the decency and
generosity of the American people. But it also comes from my own
American story.

I am the son of a black man from Kenya and a white woman from Kansas. I was raised with the help of a white grandfather who survived a Depression to serve in Patton's Army during World War II and a white grandmother who worked on a bomber assembly line at Fort Leavenworth while he was overseas. I've gone to some of the best schools in America and lived in one of the world's poorest nations. I am married to a black American who carries within her the blood of slaves and slave owners – an inheritance we pass on to our two precious daughters. I have brothers, sisters, nieces, nephews, uncles and cousins, of every race and every hue, scattered across three continents, and for as long as I live, I will never forget that in no other country on Earth is my story even possible.

It's a story that hasn't made me the most conventional candidate. But it is a story that has seared into my genetic makeup the idea that this nation is more than the sum of its parts – that out of many, we are truly one.

Throughout the first year of this campaign, against all predictions to the contrary, we saw how hungry the American people were for this message of unity. Despite the temptation to view my candidacy through a purely racial lens, we won commanding victories in states with some of the whitest populations in the country. In South Carolina, where the Confederate Flag still flies, we built a powerful coalition of African Americans and white Americans . . . it has only been in the last couple of weeks that the discussion of race in this campaign has taken a particularly divisive turn.

On one end of the spectrum, we've heard the implication that my candidacy is somehow an exercise in affirmative action; that it's based solely on the desire of wide-eyed liberals to purchase racial reconciliation on the cheap. On the other end, we've heard my former pastor, Reverend Jeremiah Wright, use incendiary language to express views that have the potential not only to widen the racial divide, but views that denigrate both the greatness and the goodness of our nation; that rightly offend white and black alike.

I have already condemned, in unequivocal terms, the statements of Reverend Wright that have caused such controversy. For some, nagging questions remain. Did I know him to be an occasionally fierce critic of American domestic and foreign policy? Of course. Did I ever hear him make remarks that could be considered controversial while I sat in church? Yes. Did I strongly disagree with many of his political views? Absolutely – just as I'm sure many of you have heard remarks from your pastors, priests or rabbis with which you strongly disagreed.

But the remarks that have caused this recent firestorm weren't simply controversial. They weren't simply a religious leader's effort to speak out against perceived injustice. Instead, they expressed a profoundly distorted view of this country – a view that sees white racism as endemic, and that elevates what is wrong with America above all that we know is right with America; a view that sees the conflicts in the Middle East as rooted primarily in the actions of stalwart allies like Israel, instead of emanating from the perverse and hateful ideologies of radical Islam.

As such, Reverend Wright's comments were not only wrong but divisive, divisive at a time when we need unity; racially charged at a time when we need to come together to solve a set of monumental problems – two wars, a terrorist threat, a falling economy, a chronic health care crisis and potentially devastating climate change; problems that are neither black or white or Latino or Asian, but rather problems that confront us all.

Given my background, my politics, and my professed values and ideals, there will no doubt be those for whom my statements of condemnation are not enough. Why associate myself with Reverend Wright in the first place, they may ask? Why not join another church? And I confess that if all that I knew of Reverend Wright were the snippets of those sermons that have run in an endless loop on the television and YouTube, or if Trinity United Church of Christ conformed to the caricatures being peddled by some commentators, there is no doubt that I would react in much the same way.

But the truth is, that isn't all that I know of the man. The man I met more than twenty years ago is a man who helped introduce me to my Christian faith, a man who spoke to me about our obligations to love one another; to care for the sick and lift up the poor. He is a man who served his country as a US Marine; who has studied and lectured at some of the finest universities and seminaries in the country, and who for over thirty years led a church that serves the community by doing God's work here on Earth – by housing the homeless, ministering to the needy, providing day care services and scholarships and prison ministries, and reaching out to those suffering from HIV/AIDS.

In my first book, *Dreams from My Father*, I described the experience of my first service at Trinity:

> People began to shout, to rise from their seats and clap and cry out, a forceful wind carrying the reverend's voice up into the rafters . . . And in that single note – hope! – I heard something else; at the foot of that cross, inside the thousands of churches across the city, I imagined the stories of ordinary black people merging with the stories of David and Goliath, Moses and Pharaoh, the Christians in the lion's den, Ezekiel's field of dry bones. Those stories – of survival, and freedom, and hope – became our story, my story; the blood that had spilled was our blood, the tears our tears; until this black church, on this bright day, seemed once more a vessel carrying the story of a people into future generations and into a larger world. Our trials and triumphs became at once unique and universal, black and more than black; in chronicling our journey, the stories and songs gave us a means to reclaim memories that we didn't need to feel shame about . . . memories that all people might study and cherish – and with which we could start to rebuild.

That has been my experience at Trinity. Like other predominantly black churches across the country, Trinity embodies the black community in its entirety – the doctor and the welfare mom, the model student and the former gang-banger. Like other black churches, Trinity's services are full of raucous laughter and sometimes bawdy humour. They are full of dancing, clapping, screaming and shouting that may seem jarring to the untrained ear. The church contains in full the kindness and cruelty, the fierce intelligence and the shocking ignorance, the struggles and successes, the love and yes, the bitterness and bias that make up the black experience in America.

And this helps explain, perhaps, my relationship with Reverend Wright. As imperfect as he may be, he has been like family to me. He strengthened my faith, officiated my wedding, and baptized my children. Not once in my conversations with him have I heard him talk about any ethnic group in derogatory terms, or treat whites with whom he interacted with anything but courtesy and respect. He contains within him the contradictions – the good and the bad – of the community that he has served diligently for so many years.

I can no more disown him than I can disown the black community. I can no more disown him than I can my white grandmother – a woman who helped raise me, a woman who sacrificed again and again for me, a woman who loves me as much as she loves anything in this world, but a woman who once confessed her fear of black men who passed by her on the street, and who on more than one occasion has uttered racial or ethnic stereotypes that made me cringe.

These people are a part of me. And they are a part of America, this country that I love. Some will see this as an attempt to justify or excuse comments that are simply inexcusable. I can assure you it is not. I suppose the politically safe thing would be to move on from this episode and just hope that it fades into the woodwork. We can dismiss Reverend Wright as a crank or a demagogue . . .

But race is an issue that I believe this nation cannot afford to ignore right now. We would be making the same mistake that Reverend Wright made in his offending sermons about America – to simplify and stereotype and amplify the negative to the point that it distorts reality.

The fact is that the comments that have been made and the issues that have surfaced over the last few weeks reflect the complexities of race in this country that we've never really worked through – a part of our union that we have yet to perfect. And if we walk away now, if we simply retreat into our respective corners, we will never be able to come together and solve challenges like health care, or education, or the need to find good jobs for every American.

Understanding this reality requires a reminder of how we arrived at this point. As William Faulkner once wrote, 'The past isn't dead and buried. In fact, it isn't even past.' We do not need to recite here the history of racial injustice in this country. But we do need to remind ourselves that so many of the disparities that exist in the African-American community today can be directly traced to inequalities passed on from an earlier generation that suffered under the brutal legacy of slavery and Jim Crow. Segregated schools were, and are, inferior schools; we still haven't fixed them, fifty years after Brown v. Board of Education, and the inferior education they provided, then and now, helps explain the pervasive achievement gap between today's black and white students.

Legalized discrimination – where blacks were prevented, often through violence, from owning property, or loans were not granted to African-American business owners, or black homeowners could not access FHA mortgages, or blacks were excluded from unions, or the police force, or fire departments – meant that black families could not amass any meaningful wealth to bequeath to future generations. That history helps explain the wealth and income gap between black and white, and the concentrated pockets of poverty that persist in so many of today's urban and rural communities.

A lack of economic opportunity among black men, and the shame and frustration that came from not being able to provide for one's family, contributed to the erosion of black families – a problem that welfare policies for many years may have worsened. And the lack of basic services in so many urban black neighbourhoods – parks for kids to play in, police walking the beat, regular garbage pick-up and building code enforcement – all helped create a cycle of violence, blight and neglect that continues to haunt us.

This is the reality in which Reverend Wright and other African-Americans of his generation grew up. They came of age in the late fifties and early sixties, a time when segregation was still the law of the land and opportunity was systematically constricted. What's remarkable is not how many failed in the face of discrimination, but rather how many men and women overcame the odds; how many were able to make a way out of no way for those like me who would come after them.

But for all those who scratched and clawed their way to get a piece of the American Dream, there were many who didn't make it – those

who were ultimately defeated, in one way or another, by discrimination. That legacy of defeat was passed on to future generations – those
young men and increasingly young women who we see standing on
street corners or languishing in our prisons, without hope or prospects for the future. Even for those blacks who did make it, questions
of race, and racism, continue to define their worldview in fundamental ways. For the men and women of Reverend Wright's
generation, the memories of humiliation and doubt and fear have
not gone away; nor has the anger and the bitterness of those years.
That anger may not get expressed in public, in front of white co-
workers or white friends. But it does find voice in the barbershop or
around the kitchen table. At times, that anger is exploited by politicians, to gin up votes along racial lines, or to make up for a politician's
own failings.

And occasionally it finds voice in the church on Sunday morning,
in the pulpit and in the pews. The fact that so many people are surprised to hear that anger in some of Reverend Wright's sermons
simply reminds us of the old truism that the most segregated hour
in American life occurs on Sunday morning. That anger is not always
productive; indeed, all too often it distracts attention from solving
real problems; it keeps us from squarely facing our own complicity
in our condition, and prevents the African-American community
from forging the alliances it needs to bring about real change. But
the anger is real; it is powerful; and to simply wish it away, to condemn it without understanding its roots, only serves to widen the
chasm of misunderstanding that exists between the races.

In fact, a similar anger exists within segments of the white community. Most working- and middle-class white Americans don't feel
that they have been particularly privileged by their race. Their experience is the immigrant experience – as far as they're concerned, no
one's handed them anything, they've built it from scratch. They've
worked hard all their lives, many times only to see their jobs shipped
overseas or their pension dumped after a lifetime of labour. They are
anxious about their futures, and feel their dreams slipping away; in
an era of stagnant wages and global competition, opportunity comes
to be seen as a zero sum game, in which your dreams come at my

expense. So when they are told to bus their children to a school across town; when they hear that an African-American is getting an advantage in landing a good job or a spot in a good college because of an injustice that they themselves never committed; when they're told that their fears about crime in urban neighbourhoods are somehow prejudiced, resentment builds over time.

Like the anger within the black community, these resentments aren't always expressed in polite company. But they have helped shape the political landscape for at least a generation. Anger over welfare and affirmative action helped forge the Reagan Coalition. Politicians routinely exploited fears of crime for their own electoral ends. Talk show hosts and conservative commentators built entire careers unmasking bogus claims of racism while dismissing legitimate discussions of racial injustice and inequality as mere political correctness or reverse racism.

Just as black anger often proved counterproductive, so have these white resentments distracted attention from the real culprits of the middle-class squeeze – a corporate culture rife with inside dealing, questionable accounting practices, and short-term greed; a Washington dominated by lobbyists and special interests; economic policies that favour the few over the many. And yet, to wish away the resentments of white Americans, to label them as misguided or even racist, without recognizing they are grounded in legitimate concerns – this too widens the racial divide, and blocks the path to understanding.

This is where we are right now. It's a racial stalemate we've been stuck in for years. Contrary to the claims of some of my critics, black and white, I have never been so naïve as to believe that we can get beyond our racial divisions in a single election cycle, or with a single candidacy – particularly a candidacy as imperfect as my own.

But I have asserted a firm conviction – a conviction rooted in my faith in God and my faith in the American people – that working together we can move beyond some of our old racial wounds, and that in fact we have no choice if we are to continue on the path of a more perfect union.

For the African-American community, that path means embracing the burdens of our past without becoming victims of our past.

It means continuing to insist on a full measure of justice in every aspect of American life. But it also means binding our particular grievances – for better health care, and better schools, and better jobs – to the larger aspirations of all Americans – the white woman struggling to break the glass ceiling, the white man who's been laid off, the immigrant trying to feed his family. And it means taking full responsibility for our own lives – by demanding more from our fathers, and spending more time with our children, and reading to them, and teaching them that while they may face challenges and discrimination in their own lives, they must never succumb to despair or cynicism; they must always believe that they can write their own destiny.

Ironically, this quintessentially American – and yes, conservative – notion of self-help found frequent expression in Reverend Wright's sermons. But what my former pastor too often failed to understand is that embarking on a programme of self-help also requires a belief that society can change.

The profound mistake of Reverend Wright's sermons is not that he spoke about racism in our society. It's that he spoke as if our society was static; as if no progress has been made; as if this country – a country that has made it possible for one of his own members to run for the highest office in the land and build a coalition of white and black, Latino and Asian, rich and poor, young and old – is still irrevocably bound to a tragic past. But what we know – what we have seen – is that America can change. That is true genius of this nation. What we have already achieved gives us hope – the audacity to hope – for what we can and must achieve tomorrow.

In the white community, the path to a more perfect union means acknowledging that what ails the African-American community does not just exist in the minds of black people; that the legacy of discrimination – and current incidents of discrimination, while less overt than in the past – are real and must be addressed. Not just with words, but with deeds – by investing in our schools and our communities; by enforcing our civil rights laws and ensuring fairness in our criminal justice system; by providing this generation with ladders of opportunity that were unavailable for previous generations. It requires all Americans to realize that your dreams do not have to come at the expense of my dreams; that investing in the health, welfare and education of black and brown and white children will ultimately help all of America prosper.

In the end, then, what is called for is nothing more, and nothing less, than what all the world's great religions demand – that we do unto others as we would have them do unto us. Let us be our brother's keeper, Scripture tells us. Let us be our sister's keeper. Let us find that common stake we all have in one another, and let our politics reflect that spirit as well.

For we have a choice in this country. We can accept a politics that breeds division, and conflict, and cynicism. We can tackle race only as spectacle, as we did in the OJ trial – or in the wake of tragedy, as we did in the aftermath of Katrina – or as fodder for the nightly news. We can play Reverend Wright's sermons on every channel, every day and talk about them from now until the election, and make the only question in this campaign whether or not the American people think that I somehow believe or sympathize with his most offensive words. We can pounce on some gaffe by a Hillary supporter as evidence that she's playing the race card, or we can speculate on whether white men will all flock to John McCain in the general election regardless of his policies.

We can do that.

But if we do, I can tell you that in the next election, we'll be talking about some other distraction. And then another one. And then another one. And nothing will change.

That is one option. Or, at this moment, in this election, we can come together and say, 'Not this time.' This time we want to talk about the crumbling schools that are stealing the future of black children and white children and Asian children and Hispanic children and Native American children. This time we want to reject the cynicism that tells us that these kids can't learn; that those kids who don't look like us are somebody else's problem. The children of America are not those kids, they are our kids, and we will not let them fall behind in a twenty-first century economy. Not this time.

This time we want to talk about how the lines in the Emergency

Room are filled with whites and blacks and Hispanics who do not have healthcare; who don't have the power on their own to overcome the special interests in Washington, but who can take them on if we do it together.

This time we want to talk about the shuttered mills that once provided a decent life for men and women of every race, and the homes for sale that once belonged to Americans from every religion, every region, every walk of life. This time we want to talk about the fact that the real problem is not that someone who doesn't look like you might take your job; it's that the corporation you work for will ship it overseas for nothing more than a profit.

This time we want to talk about the men and women of every colour and creed who serve together, and fight together, and bleed together under the same proud flag. We want to talk about how to bring them home from a war that never should've been authorized and never should've been waged, and we want to talk about how we'll show our patriotism by caring for them, and their families, and giving them the benefits they have earned.

I would not be running for President if I didn't believe with all my heart that this is what the vast majority of Americans want for this country. This union may never be perfect, but generation after generation has shown that it can always be perfected. And today, whenever I find myself feeling doubtful or cynical about this possibility, what gives me the most hope is the next generation – the young people whose attitudes and beliefs and openness to change have already made history in this election.

There is one story in particular that I'd like to leave you with today – a story I told when I had the great honour of speaking on Dr King's birthday at his home church, Ebenezer Baptist, in Atlanta.

There is a young, twenty-three-year-old white woman named Ashley Baia who organized for our campaign in Florence, South Carolina. She had been working to organize a mostly African-American community since the beginning of this campaign, and one day she was at a roundtable discussion where everyone went around telling their story and why they were there.

And Ashley said that when she was nine years old, her mother got cancer. And because she had to miss days of work, she was let go and lost her health care. They had to file for bankruptcy, and that's when Ashley decided that she had to do something to help her mom.

She knew that food was one of their most expensive costs, and so Ashley convinced her mother that what she really liked and really wanted to eat more than anything else was mustard and relish sandwiches. Because that was the cheapest way to eat.

She did this for a year until her mom got better, and she told everyone at the roundtable that the reason she joined our campaign was so that she could help the millions of other children in the country who want and need to help their parents too.

Now Ashley might have made a different choice. Perhaps somebody told her along the way that the source of her mother's problems were blacks who were on welfare and too lazy to work, or Hispanics who were coming into the country illegally. But she didn't. She sought out allies in her fight against injustice.

Anyway, Ashley finishes her story and then goes around the room and asks everyone else why they're supporting the campaign. They all have different stories and reasons. Many bring up a specific issue. And finally they come to this elderly black man who's been sitting there quietly the entire time. And Ashley asks him why he's there. And he does not bring up a specific issue. He does not say health care or the economy. He does not say education or the war. He does not say that he was there because of Barack Obama. He simply says to everyone in the room, 'I am here because of Ashley.'

'I'm here because of Ashley.' By itself, that single moment of recognition between that young white girl and that old black man is not enough. It is not enough to give healthcare to the sick, or jobs to the jobless, or education to our children.

But it is where we start. It is where our union grows stronger. And as so many generations have come to realize over the course of the two hundred and twenty-one years since a band of patriots signed that document in Philadelphia, that is where the perfection begins.

•

## BARACK OBAMA
### Chicago, 4 November 2008

#### 'Yes we can'

*There were tears on the faces of a vast Chicago crowd when Barack Obama, aged forty-seven, became the first black American to be elected to the presidency in 2008. Change had come to America, he proclaimed. The speech drew a line under the presidency of George W. Bush, who had led America into the disastrous invasion of Iraq (even though it toppled Saddam Hussein). After his speech Obama lingered on the stage with his wife, Michelle, in a striking black dress with red splashes, and their daughters, as well as his running mate, Joe Biden, now the vice president-elect. Note Obama's use of the rhetorical device, the tricolon, a series of three parallel words, phrases or clauses (used to great effect by President John F. Kennedy in his inaugural).*

Hello, Chicago.

If there is anyone out there who still doubts that America is a place where all things are possible, who still wonders if the dream of our founders is alive in our time, who still questions the power of our democracy, tonight is your answer.

It's the answer told by lines that stretched around schools and churches in numbers this nation has never seen, by people who waited three hours and four hours, many for the first time in their lives, because they believed that this time must be different, that their voices could be that difference.

It's the answer spoken by young and old, rich and poor, Democrat and Republican, black, white, Hispanic, Asian, Native American, gay, straight, disabled and not disabled. Americans who sent a message to the world that we have never been just a collection of individuals or a collection of red states and blue states. We are, and always will be, the United States of America.

It's the answer that led those who've been told for so long by so many to be cynical and fearful and doubtful about what we can achieve to put their hands on the arc of history and bend it once more toward the hope of a better day.

It's been a long time coming, but tonight, because of what we did on this date in this election at this defining moment change has come to America.

I will never forget who this victory truly belongs to. It belongs to you. It belongs to you.

I was never the likeliest candidate for this office. We didn't start with much money or many endorsements. Our campaign was not hatched in the halls of Washington. It began in the backyards of Des Moines and the living rooms of Concord and the front porches of Charleston.

It was built by working men and women who dug into what little savings they had. It grew strength from the young people who rejected the myth of their generation's apathy; who left their homes and their families for jobs that offered little pay and less sleep; from the not-so-young people who braved the bitter cold and scorching heat to knock on doors of perfect strangers, and from the millions of Americans who volunteered and organized and proved that more than two centuries later a government of the people, by the people, and for the people has not perished from the earth. This is your victory.

I know you didn't do this just to win an election. And I know you didn't do it for me. You did it because you understand the enormity of the task that lies ahead. For even as we celebrate tonight, we know the challenges that tomorrow will bring are the greatest of our lifetime — two wars, a planet in peril, the worst financial crisis in a century.

Even as we stand here tonight, we know there are brave Americans waking up in the deserts of Iraq and the mountains of Afghanistan to risk their lives for us.

There are mothers and fathers who will lie awake after the children fall asleep and wonder how they'll make the mortgage or pay their doctors' bills or save enough for their child's college education.

There's new energy to harness, new jobs to be created, new schools to build, and threats to meet, alliances to repair.

The road ahead will be long. Our climb will be steep. We may not get there in one year or even in one term. But, America, I have never been more hopeful than I am tonight that we will get there.

I promise you, we as a people will get there.

(*Audience: 'Yes we can! Yes we can! Yes we can!'*)

There will be setbacks and false starts. There are many who won't agree with every decision or policy I make as president. And we know the government can't solve every problem.

But I will always be honest with you about the challenges we face. I will listen to you, especially when we disagree. And, above all, I will ask you to join in the work of remaking this nation, the only way it's been done in America for 221 years – block by block, brick by brick, calloused hand by calloused hand.

What began twenty-one months ago in the depths of winter cannot end on this autumn night.

This victory alone is not the change we seek. It is only the chance for us to make that change. And that cannot happen if we go back to the way things were.

It can't happen without you, without a new spirit of service, a new spirit of sacrifice.

So let us summon a new spirit of patriotism, of responsibility, where each of us resolves to pitch in and work harder and look after not only ourselves but each other.

Let us remember that, if this financial crisis taught us anything, it's that we cannot have a thriving Wall Street while Main Street suffers.

In this country, we rise or fall as one nation, as one people. Let's resist the temptation to fall back on the same partisanship and pettiness and immaturity that has poisoned our politics for so long.

Let's remember that it was a man from this state who first carried the banner of the Republican Party to the White House, a party founded on the values of self-reliance and individual liberty and national unity.

Those are values that we all share. And while the Democratic Party has won a great victory tonight, we do so with a measure of humility and determination to heal the divides that have held back our progress.

As Lincoln said to a nation far more divided than ours, we are not enemies but friends. Though passion may have strained, it must not break our bonds of affection.

And to those Americans whose support I have yet to earn, I may not have won your vote tonight, but I hear your voices. I need your help. And I will be your president, too.

And to all those watching tonight from beyond our shores, from parliaments and palaces, to those who are huddled around radios in the forgotten corners of the world, our stories are singular, but our destiny is shared, and a new dawn of American leadership is at hand.

To those – to those who would tear the world down: we will defeat you. To those who seek peace and security: we support you. And to all those who have wondered if America's beacon still burns as bright: tonight we proved once more that the true strength of our nation comes not from the might of our arms or the scale of our wealth, but from the enduring power of our ideals: democracy, liberty, opportunity and unyielding hope.

That's the true genius of America: that America can change. Our union can be perfected. What we've already achieved gives us hope for what we can and must achieve tomorrow.

This election had many firsts and many stories that will be told for generations. But one that's on my mind tonight's about a woman who cast her ballot in Atlanta. She's a lot like the millions of others who stood in line to make their voice heard in this election except for one thing: Ann Nixon Cooper is 106 years old.

She was born just a generation past slavery; a time when there were no cars on the road or planes in the sky; when someone like her couldn't vote for two reasons – because she was a woman and because of the colour of her skin.

And tonight, I think about all that she's seen throughout her century in America – the heartache and the hope; the struggle and the progress; the times we were told that we can't, and the people who pressed on with that American creed: Yes we can.

At a time when women's voices were silenced and their hopes dismissed, she lived to see them stand up and speak out and reach for the ballot. Yes we can.

When there was despair in the dust bowl and depression across the land, she saw a nation conquer fear itself with a New Deal, new jobs, a new sense of common purpose. Yes we can.

(*Audience: 'Yes we can.'*)

When the bombs fell on our harbour and tyranny threatened the world, she was there to witness a generation rise to greatness and a democracy was saved. Yes we can.

(*Audience: 'Yes we can.'*)

She was there for the buses in Montgomery, the hoses in Birmingham, a bridge in Selma, and a preacher from Atlanta who told a people that We Shall Overcome. Yes we can.

(*Audience: 'Yes we can.'*)

A man touched down on the moon, a wall came down in Berlin, a world was connected by our own science and imagination.

And this year, in this election, she touched her finger to a screen, and cast her vote, because after 106 years in America, through the best of times and the darkest of hours, she knows how America can change.

Yes we can.

(*Audience: 'Yes we can.'*)

America, we have come so far. We have seen so much. But there is so much more to do. So tonight, let us ask ourselves – if our children should live to see the next century; if my daughters should be so lucky to live as long as Ann Nixon Cooper, what change will they see? What progress will we have made?

This is our chance to answer that call. This is our moment.

This is our time, to pur our people back to work and open doors of opportunity for our kids; to restore prosperity and promote the cause of peace; to reclaim the American dream and reaffirm that fundamental truth, that, out of many, we are one; that while we breathe, we hope. And where we are met with cynicism and doubts and those who tell us that we can't, we will respond with that timeless creed that sums up the spirit of a people: Yes, we can.

Thank you. God bless you. And may God bless the United States of America.

•

# DAVID CAMERON
## London, 15 June 2010

### 'A catastrophe for the people of Northern Ireland'

*In January 1972, thirteen civil rights demonstrators were shot dead in Londonderry, Northern Ireland, by British Army paratroopers in an event that became known as 'Bloody Sunday'. The protesters, all Northern Irish Catholics, were marching in protest at the British policy of internment of suspected Irish nationalists. British authorities had ordered the march banned, and sent troops to confront the demonstrators when it went ahead. The soldiers fired indiscriminately into the crowd of protesters, killing thirteen and wounding seventeen. The Bloody Sunday Inquiry, also known as the Saville Inquiry after its chairman, Lord Saville of Newdigate, was set up in 1998 by the British Prime Minister Tony Blair to establish a definitive version of the events of Sunday 30 January 1972, superseding the tribunal set up under Lord Widgery that had reported on 19 April 1972, eleven weeks after the events, and to resolve the accusations of a whitewash that had surrounded it. This is an edited extract from the Prime Minister David Cameron's speech to the House of Commons.*

Mr Speaker, I am deeply patriotic. I never want to believe anything bad about our country. I never want to call into question the behaviour of our soldiers and our army, who I believe to be the finest in the world.

And I have seen for myself the very difficult and dangerous circumstances in which we ask our soldiers to serve.

But the conclusions of this report are absolutely clear. There is no doubt, there is nothing equivocal, there are no ambiguities. What happened on Bloody Sunday was both unjustified and unjustifiable. It was wrong.

Lord Saville concludes that the soldiers of the support company who went into the Bogside did so as a result of an order which should not have been given by their commander.

He finds that, on balance, the first shot in the vicinity of the march was fired by the British Army.

He finds that none of the casualties shot by the soldiers of the support company was armed with a firearm.

He finds that there was some firing by Republican paramilitaries but none of this firing provided any justification for the shooting of civilian casualties.

And he finds that, in no case, was any warning given by soldiers before opening fire.

He also finds that the support company reacted by losing their self-control, forgetting or ignoring their instructions and training and with a serious and widespread loss of fire discipline.

He finds that despite the contrary evidence given by the soldiers, none of them fired in response to attacks or threatened attacks by nail or petrol bombers.

And he finds that many of the soldiers – and I quote knowingly – put forward false accounts to seek to justify their firing. Lord Saville says that some of those killed or injured were clearly fleeing or going to the assistance of others who were dying.

The report refers to one person who was shot while crawling away from the soldiers. Another was shot in all probability when he was lying mortally wounded on the ground.

The report refers to the father who was hit and injured by army gunfire after going to attend to his son.

For those looking for statements of innocence, Saville says that the immediate responsibility for the deaths and injuries on Bloody Sunday lies with those members of support company whose unjustifiable firing was the cause of those deaths and injuries.

Crucially, that, and I quote, none of the casualties was posing a threat of causing death or serious injury or indeed was doing anything else that could, on any view, have justified the shooting.

For those people who are looking for the report to use terms like murder and unlawful killing, I remind the House that these judgements are not matters for a tribunal or politicians to determine.

Mr Speaker, these are shocking conclusions to read and shocking words to have to say. But Mr Speaker, you do not defend the British Army by defending the indefensible.

We do not honour all those who have served with such distinction in keeping the peace and upholding the rule of law in Northern Ireland by hiding from the truth.

There is no point in trying to soften or equivocate what is in this report. It is clear from the tribunal's authoritative conclusions that the events of Bloody Sunday were in no way justified.

I know that some people wonder whether, nearly forty years on from an event, [if] a Prime Minister needs to issue an apology.

For someone of my generation, Bloody Sunday and the early 1970s are something we feel we have learned about rather than lived through.

But what happened should never, ever have happened. The families of those who died should not have had to live with the pain and the hurt of that day and with a lifetime of loss.

Some members of our armed forces acted wrongly. The government is ultimately responsible for the conduct of the armed forces and for that, on behalf of the government, indeed, on behalf of our country, I am deeply sorry.

Mr Speaker, just as this report is clear that the actions of that day were unjustifiable, so too is it clear in some of its other findings.

Those looking for premeditation, a plan, those even looking for a conspiracy involving senior politicians or senior members of the armed forces, they will not find it in this report.

Indeed, Lord Saville finds no evidence that the events of Bloody Sunday were premeditated, he concludes that the United Kingdom and Northern Ireland governments and the army neither tolerated nor encouraged the use of unjustified lethal force.

He makes no suggestion of a government cover-up.

No government I lead will ever put those who fight to defend democracy on an equal footing with those who contine to seek to destroy it.

But neither will we hide from the truth that confronts us today.

In the words of Lord Saville, what happened on Bloody Sunday strengthened the Provisional IRA, increased hostility towards the Army and exacerbated the violent conflict of the years that followed.

Bloody Sunday was a tragedy for the bereaved and the wounded and a catastrophe for the people of Northern Ireland.

•

# MALALA YOUSAFZAI
## UN General Assembly, New York, 12 July 2013

### 'The right of education for every child'

*Malala Yousafzai was born in Pakistan. She became an advocate for girls' educa-*
*tion, which resulted in the Taliban issuing a death threat against her. She was shot*
*while travelling home on the school bus in October 2012. She was taken to England*
*where it was eventually discovered that she had suffered no major brain damage. In*
*March 2013 she began attending school in Birmingham. This is the speech she gave*
*to the UN General Assembly on 12 July 2013.*

Dear friends, on 9 October 2012, the Taliban shot me on the left side
of my forehead. They shot my friends, too. They thought that the bullets would silence us, but they failed. And out of that silence came
thousands of voices. The terrorists thought they would change my
aims and stop my ambitions. But nothing changed in my life except
this: weakness, fear and hopelessness died. Strength, power and courage were born. I am the same Malala. My ambitions are the same. My
hopes are the same. And my dreams are the same. Dear sisters and
brothers, I am not against anyone. Neither am I here to speak in terms
of personal revenge against the Taliban or any other terrorist group. I
am here to speak for the right of education for every child. I want education for the sons and daughters of the Taliban and all the terrorists
and extremists. I do not even hate the Talib who shot me.

Even if there was a gun in my hand and he was standing in front
of me, I would not shoot him. This is the compassion I have learned
from Mohammed, the prophet of mercy, Jesus Christ and Lord
Buddha. This is the legacy of change I have inherited from Martin
Luther King, Nelson Mandela and Mohammed Ali Jinnah.

This is the philosophy of non-violence that I have learned from
Gandhi, Bacha Khan and Mother Theresa. And this is the forgiveness that I have learned from my father and from my mother. This is
what my soul is telling me: be peaceful and love everyone.

Dear sisters and brothers, we realize the importance of light when
we see darkness. We realize the importance of our voice when we are

silenced. In the same way, when we were in Swat, the north of Pakistan, we realized the importance of pens and books when we saw the guns. The wise saying, 'The pen is mightier than the sword'. It is true. The extremists are afraid of books and pens. The power of education frightens them. They are afraid of women. The power of the voice of women frightens them. This is why they killed fourteen innocent students in the recent attack in Quetta. And that is why they kill female teachers. That is why they are blasting schools every day because they were and they are afraid of change and equality that we will bring to our society. And I remember that there was a boy in our school who was asked by a journalist: 'Why are the Taliban against education?' He answered very simply by pointing to his book, he said: 'A Talib doesn't know what is written inside this book.'

They think that God is a tiny, little conservative being who would point guns at people's heads just for going to school. These terrorists are misusing the name of Islam for their own personal benefit. Pakistan is a peace-loving, democratic country. Pashtuns want education for their daughters and sons. Islam is a religion of peace, humanity and brotherhood. It is the duty and responsibility to get education for each child, that is what it says. Peace is a necessity for education. In many parts of the world, especially Pakistan and Afghanistan, terrorism, war and conflicts stop children from going to schools. We are really tired of these wars. Women and children are suffering in many ways in many parts of the world.

In India, innocent and poor children are victims of child labour. Many schools have been destroyed in Nigeria. People in Afghanistan have been affected by extremism. Young girls have to do domestic child labour and are forced to get married at an early age. Poverty, ignorance, injustice, racism and the deprivation of basic rights are the main problems, faced by both men and women.

Today, I am focusing on women's rights and girls' education because they are suffering the most. There was a time when women activists asked men to stand up for their rights. But this time we will do it by ourselves. I am not telling men to step away from speaking for women's rights, but I am focusing on women to be independent and fight for themselves. So dear sisters and brothers, now it's time to speak up. So today, we call upon the world leaders to change their strategic policies in favour of peace and prosperity. We call upon the world leaders that all of these deals must protect women and children's rights. A deal that goes against the rights of women is unacceptable.

We call upon all governments to ensure free, compulsory education all over the world for every child. We call upon all the governments to fight against terrorism and violence. To protect children from brutality and harm. We call upon the developed nations to support the expansion of education opportunities for girls in the developing world. We call upon all communities to be tolerant, to reject prejudice based on caste, creed, sect, colour, religion or agenda to ensure freedom and equality for women so they can flourish. We cannot all succeed when half of us are held back. We call upon our sisters around the world to be brave, to embrace the strength within themselves and realize their full potential.

Dear brothers and sisters, we want schools and education for every child's bright future. We will continue our journey to our destination of peace and education. No one can stop us. We will speak up for our rights and we will bring change through our voice. We believe in the power and the strength of our words. Our words can change the whole world because we are all together, united for the cause of education. And if we want to achieve our goal, then let us empower ourselves with the weapon of knowledge and let us shield ourselves with unity and togetherness.

Dear brothers and sisters, we must not forget that millions of people are suffering from poverty and injustice and ignorance. We must not forget that millions of children are out of their schools. We must not forget that our sisters and brothers are waiting for a bright, peaceful future.

So let us wage a glorious struggle against illiteracy, poverty and terrorism, let us pick up our books and our pens; they are the most powerful weapons. One child, one teacher, one book and one pen can change the world. Education is the only solution. Education first. Thank you.

•

# BARACK OBAMA
## Selma, 7 March 2015

*'A contest to determine the meaning of America'*

*President Obama delivered this speech before thousands on the fiftieth anniversary of 'Bloody Sunday', when 600 non-violent protesters were attacked by Alabama stormtroopers as they tried to march from Selma to Montgomery for voting rights. In the* Washington Post, *Greg Jaffe asked which of Obama's speeches would be read decades from now. 'Selma's true genius', he wrote, 'lies in its ability to speak to America's future. The Census Bureau projects that the US population will become "majority minority" in 2044. The shift has fuelled anxiety among whites and has probably given a boost to Republican nominee Donald Trump's "make America great again" campaign for the White House. It has spawned some of the backlash against Obama's presidency, along with questions about his legitimacy to serve, his love of country and his faith. Someday, though, this demographic shift will be seen as an inevitable part of the American story. Selma is the first, great presidential address to speak to that America and a speech only our first black president could give. Selma is the one.'*

It is a rare honour in this life to follow one of your heroes. And John Lewis is one of my heroes.

Now, I have to imagine that when a younger John Lewis woke up that morning fifty years ago and made his way to Brown Chapel, heroics were not on his mind. A day like this was not on his mind. Young folks with bedrolls and backpacks were milling about. Veterans of the movement trained newcomers in the tactics of non-violence; the right way to protect yourself when attacked. A doctor described what tear gas does to the body, while marchers scribbled down instructions for contacting their loved ones. The air was thick with doubt, anticipation, and fear. They comforted themselves with the final verse of the final hymn they sung:

No matter what may be the test, God will take care of you;
Lean, weary one, upon His breast, God will take care of you.

Then, his knapsack stocked with an apple, a toothbrush, a book on government – all you need for a night behind bars – John Lewis led them out of the church on a mission to change America.

President Bush and Mrs Bush, Governor Bentley, Members of Congress, Mayor Evans, Reverend Strong, friends and fellow Americans:

There are places, and moments in America, where this nation's destiny has been decided. Many are sites of war – Concord and Lexington, Appomattox and Gettysburg. Others are sites that symbolize the daring of America's character – Independence Hall and Seneca Falls, Kitty Hawk and Cape Canaveral.

Selma is such a place.

In one afternoon fifty years ago, so much of our turbulent history – the stain of slavery and anguish of civil war; the yoke of segregation and tyranny of Jim Crow; the death of four little girls in Birmingham, and the dream of a Baptist preacher – met on this bridge. It was not a clash of armies, but a clash of wills; a contest to determine the meaning of America.

And because of men and women like John Lewis, Joseph Lowery, Hosea Williams, Amelia Boynton, Diane Nash, Ralph Abernathy, C.T. Vivian, Andrew Young, Fred Shuttlesworth, Dr King, and so many more, the idea of a just America, a fair America, an inclusive America, a generous America – that idea ultimately triumphed.

As is true across the landscape of American history, we cannot examine this moment in isolation. The march on Selma was part of a broader campaign that spanned generations; the leaders that day part of a long line of heroes.

We gather here to celebrate them. We gather here to honour the courage of ordinary Americans willing to endure billy clubs and the chastening rod; tear gas and the trampling hoof; men and women who despite the gush of blood and splintered bone would stay true to their North Star and keep marching toward justice.

They did as Scripture instructed: 'Rejoice in hope, be patient in tribulation, be constant in prayer.' And in the days to come, they went back again and again. When the trumpet call sounded for more to join, the people came – black and white, young and old, Christian and Jew, waving the American flag and singing the same anthems full of faith and hope. A white newsman, Bill Plante, who covered the marches then and who is with us here today, quipped that the growing number of white people lowered the quality of the singing. To those who marched, though, those old gospel songs must have never sounded so sweet.

In time, their chorus would reach President Johnson. And he would send them protection, echoing their call for the nation and the world to hear:

'We shall overcome.'

What enormous faith these men and women had. Faith in God – but also faith in America.

The Americans who crossed this bridge were not physically imposing. But they gave courage to millions. They held no elected office. But they led a nation. They marched as Americans who had endured hundreds of years of brutal violence, and countless daily indignities – but they didn't seek special treatment, just the equal treatment promised to them almost a century before.

What they did here will reverberate through the ages. Not because the change they won was preordained; not because their victory was complete; but because they proved that non-violent change is possible; that love and hope can conquer hate.

As we commemorate their achievement, we are well-served to remember that at the time of the marches, many in power condemned rather than praised them. Back then, they were called Communists, half-breeds, outside agitators, sexual and moral degenerates, and worse – everything but the name their parents gave them. Their faith was questioned. Their lives were threatened. Their patriotism was challenged.

And yet, what could be more American than what happened in this place?

What could more profoundly vindicate the idea of America than plain and humble people – the unsung, the downtrodden, the dreamers not of high station, not born to wealth or privilege, not of one religious tradition but many – coming together to shape their country's course?

What greater expression of faith in the American experiment than this; what greater form of patriotism is there; than the belief that America is not yet finished, that we are strong enough to be self-critical, that each successive generation can look upon our imperfections and decide that it is in our power to remake this nation to more closely align with our highest ideals?

That's why Selma is not some outlier in the American experience. That's why it's not a museum or static monument to behold from a distance. It is instead the manifestation of a creed written into our founding documents:

'We the People . . . in order to form a more perfect union.'

'We hold these truths to be self-evident, that all men are created equal.'

These are not just words. They are a living thing, a call to action, a roadmap for citizenship and an insistence in the capacity of free men and women to shape our own destiny. For founders like Franklin and Jefferson, for leaders like Lincoln and FDR, the success of our experiment in self-government rested on engaging all our citizens in this work. That's what we celebrate here in Selma. That's what this movement was all about, one leg in our long journey toward freedom.

The American instinct that led these young men and women to pick up the torch and cross this bridge is the same instinct that moved patriots to choose revolution over tyranny. It's the same instinct that drew immigrants from across oceans and the Rio Grande; the same instinct that led women to reach for the ballot and workers to organize against an unjust status quo; the same instinct that led us to plant a flag at Iwo Jima and on the surface of the Moon.

It's the idea held by generations of citizens who believed that America is a constant work in progress; who believed that loving this country requires more than singing its praises or avoiding uncomfortable truths. It requires the occasional disruption, the willingness to speak out for what's right and shake up the status quo.

That's what makes us unique, and cements our reputation as a beacon of opportunity. Young people behind the Iron Curtain would see Selma and eventually tear down a wall. Young people in Soweto would hear Bobby Kennedy talk about ripples of hope and eventually banish the scourge of apartheid. Young people in Burma went to prison rather than submit to military rule. From the streets of Tunis to the Maidan in Ukraine, this generation of young people can draw strength from this place, where the powerless could change the world's greatest superpower, and push their leaders to expand the boundaries of freedom.

They saw that idea made real in Selma, Alabama. They saw it made real in America.

Because of campaigns like this, a Voting Rights Act was passed. Political, economic, and social barriers came down, and the change these men and women wrought is visible here today in the presence of African-Americans who run boardrooms, who sit on the bench, who serve in elected office from small towns to big cities; from the Congressional Black Caucus to the Oval Office.

Because of what they did, the doors of opportunity swung open not just for African-Americans, but for every American. Women marched through those doors. Latinos marched through those doors. Asian-Americans, gay Americans, and Americans with disabilities came through those doors. Their endeavours gave the entire South the chance to rise again, not by reasserting the past, but by transcending the past.

What a glorious thing, Dr King might say.

What a solemn debt we owe.

Which leads us to ask, just how might we repay that debt?

First and foremost, we have to recognize that one day's commemoration, no matter how special, is not enough. If Selma taught us anything, it's that our work is never done – the American experiment in self-government gives work and purpose to each generation.

Selma teaches us, too, that action requires that we shed our cynicism. For when it comes to the pursuit of justice, we can afford neither complacency nor despair.

Just this week, I was asked whether I thought the Department of Justice's Ferguson report shows that, with respect to race, little has changed in this country. I understand the question, for the report's narrative was woefully familiar. It evoked the kind of abuse and disregard for citizens that spawned the Civil Rights Movement. But I rejected the notion that nothing's changed. What happened in

Ferguson may not be unique, but it's no longer endemic, or sanctioned by law and custom; and before the Civil Rights Movement, it most surely was.

We do a disservice to the cause of justice by intimating that bias and discrimination are immutable, or that racial division is inherent to America. If you think nothing's changed in the past fifty years, ask somebody who lived through the Selma or Chicago or LA of the Fifties. Ask the female CEO who once might have been assigned to the secretarial pool if nothing's changed. Ask your gay friend if it's easier to be out and proud in America now than it was thirty years ago. To deny this progress – our progress – would be to rob us of our own agency; our responsibility to do what we can to make America better.

Of course, a more common mistake is to suggest that racism is banished, that the work that drew men and women to Selma is complete, and that whatever racial tensions remain are a consequence of those seeking to play the 'race card' for their own purposes. We don't need the Ferguson report to know that's not true. We just need to open our eyes, and ears, and hearts, to know that this nation's racial history still casts its long shadow upon us. We know the march is not yet over, the race is not yet won, and that reaching that blessed destination where we are judged by the content of our character – requires admitting as much.

'We are capable of bearing a great burden,' James Baldwin wrote, 'once we discover that the burden is reality and arrive where reality is.'

This is work for all Americans, and not just some. Not just whites. Not just blacks. If we want to honour the courage of those who marched that day, then all of us are called to possess their moral imagination. All of us will need to feel, as they did, the fierce urgency of now. All of us need to recognize, as they did, that change depends on our actions, our attitudes, the things we teach our children. And if we make such effort, no matter how hard it may seem, laws can be passed, and consciences can be stirred, and consensus can be built.

With such effort, we can make sure our criminal justice system serves all and not just some. Together, we can raise the level of mutual trust that policing is built on – the idea that police officers are members of the communities they risk their lives to protect, and citizens in Ferguson and New York and Cleveland just want the same thing young people here marched for – the protection of the law. Together, we can address unfair sentencing, and overcrowded prisons, and the stunted circumstances that rob too many boys of the chance to become men, and rob the nation of too many men who could be good dads, and workers, and neighbours.

With effort, we can roll back poverty and the roadblocks to opportunity. Americans don't accept a free ride for anyone, nor do we believe in equality of outcomes. But we do expect equal opportunity, and if we really mean it, if we're willing to sacrifice for it, then we can make sure every child gets an education suitable to this new century, one that expands imaginations and lifts their sights and gives them skills. We can make sure every person willing to work has the dignity of a job, and a fair wage, and a real voice, and sturdier rungs on that ladder into the middle class.

And with effort, we can protect the foundation stone of our democracy for which so many marched across this bridge – and that is the right to vote. Right now, in 2015, fifty years after Selma, there are laws across this country designed to make it harder for people to vote. As we speak, more of such laws are being proposed. Meanwhile, the Voting Rights Act, the culmination of so much blood and sweat and tears, the product of so much sacrifice in the face of wanton violence, stands weakened, its future subject to partisan rancour.

How can that be? The Voting Rights Act was one of the crowning achievements of our democracy, the result of Republican and Democratic effort. President Reagan signed its renewal when he was in office. President Bush signed its renewal when he was in office. One hundred Members of Congress have come here today to honour people who were willing to die for the right it protects. If we want to honour this day, let these hundred go back to Washington, and gather four hundred more, and together, pledge to make it their mission to restore the law this year.

Of course, our democracy is not the task of Congress alone, or the courts alone, or the President alone. If every new voter suppression law was struck down today, we'd still have one of the lowest voting rates among free peoples. Fifty years ago, registering to vote here in Selma and much of the South meant guessing the number of jellybeans in a jar or bubbles on a bar of soap. It meant risking your dignity, and sometimes, your life. What is our excuse today for not voting? How do we so casually discard the right for which so many fought? How do we so fully give away our power, our voice, in shaping America's future?

Fellow marchers, so much has changed in fifty years. We've endured war, and fashioned peace. We've seen technological wonders that touch every aspect of our lives, and take for granted convenience our parents might scarcely imagine. But what has not changed is the imperative of citizenship, that willingness of a twenty-six-year-old deacon, or a Unitarian minister, or a young mother of five, to decide they loved this country so much that they'd risk everything to realize its promise.

That's what it means to love America. That's what it means to believe in America. That's what it means when we say America is exceptional.

For we were born of change. We broke the old aristocracies, declaring ourselves entitled not by bloodline, but endowed by our Creator with certain inalienable rights. We secure our rights and responsibilities through a system of self-government, of and by and for the people. That's why we argue and fight with so much passion and conviction, because we know our efforts matter. We know America is what we make of it.

We are Lewis and Clark and Sacajawea – pioneers who braved the unfamiliar, followed by a stampede of farmers and miners, entrepreneurs and hucksters. That's our spirit.

We are Sojourner Truth and Fannie Lou Hamer, women who could do as much as any man and then some; and we're Susan B. Anthony, who shook the system until the law reflected that truth. That's our character.

We're the immigrants who stowed away on ships to reach these shores, the huddled masses yearning to breathe free – Holocaust survivors, Soviet defectors, the Lost Boys of Sudan. We are the hopeful strivers who cross the Rio Grande because they want their kids to know a better life. That's how we came to be.

We're the slaves who built the White House and the economy of the South. We're the ranch hands and cowboys who opened the West, and countless labourers who laid rail, and raised skyscrapers, and organized for workers' rights.

We're the fresh-faced GIs who fought to liberate a continent, and we're the Tuskeegee Airmen, Navajo code-talkers, and Japanese-Americans who fought for this country even as their own liberty had been denied. We're the firefighters who rushed into those buildings on 9/11, and the volunteers who signed up to fight in Afghanistan and Iraq.

We are the gay Americans whose blood ran on the streets of San Francisco and New York, just as blood ran down this bridge.

We are storytellers, writers, poets, and artists who abhor unfairness, and despise hypocrisy, and give voice to the voiceless, and tell truths that need to be told.

We are the inventors of gospel and jazz and the blues, bluegrass and country, hip-hop and rock and roll, our very own sounds with all the sweet sorrow and reckless joy of freedom.

We are Jackie Robinson, enduring scorn and spiked cleats and pitches coming straight to his head, and stealing home in the World Series anyway.

We are the people Langston Hughes wrote of, who 'build our temples for tomorrow, strong as we know how'.

We are the people Emerson wrote of, 'who for truth and honor's sake stand fast and suffer long'; who are 'never tired, so long as we can see far enough'.

That's what America is. Not stock photos or airbrushed history or feeble attempts to define some of us as more American then others. We respect the past, but we don't pine for it. We don't fear the future; we grab for it. America is not some fragile thing; we are large, in the words of Whitman, containing multitudes. We are boisterous and diverse and full of energy, perpetually young in spirit. That's why someone like John Lewis at the ripe age of twenty-five could lead a mighty march.

And that's what the young people here today and listening all across the country must take away from this day. You are America. Unconstrained by habits and convention. Unencumbered by what is, and ready to seize what ought to be. For everywhere in this country, there are first steps to be taken, and new ground to cover, and bridges

to be crossed. And it is you, the young and fearless at heart, the most
diverse and educated generation in our history, who the nation is
waiting to follow.

Because Selma shows us that America is not the project of any
one person.

Because the single most powerful word in our democracy is the
word 'We'. We The People. We Shall Overcome. Yes We Can. It is
owned by no one. It belongs to everyone. Oh, what a glorious task
we are given, to continually try to improve this great nation of ours.

Fifty years from Bloody Sunday, our march is not yet finished.
But we are getting closer. Two hundred and thirty-nine years after
this nation's founding, our union is not yet perfect. But we are getting closer. Our job's easier because somebody already got us through
that first mile. Somebody already got us over that bridge. When it
feels the road's too hard, when the torch we've been passed feels too
heavy, we will remember these early travellers, and draw strength
from their example, and hold firmly the words of the prophet Isaiah:

'Those who hope in the Lord will renew their strength. They will
soar on wings like eagles. They will run and not grow weary. They
will walk and not be faint.'

We honour those who walked so we could run. We must run so our
children soar. And we will not grow weary. For we believe in the power
of an awesome God, and we believe in this country's sacred promise.

May He bless those warriors of justice no longer with us, and
bless the United States of America.

•

## HILARY BENN
London, 3 December 2015

### *'The deadly serious threat from Daesh'*

*Hilary Benn, the younger son of Tony Benn, made this impassioned speech
winding up a Commons debate on Syria for the Labour Opposition. He asserted
Labour's claim to be the party of activist internationalism. He compared the*

*imperative to bomb ISIS (aka Daesh) in Syria to why the House of Commons stood up to Hitler and Mussolini in the 1930s. He subsequently resigned from the Shadow Cabinet.*

The question that confronts us in a very complex conflict is, at its heart, very simple. What should we do with others to confront this threat to our citizens, our nation, other nations and the people who suffer under the cruel yoke of Daesh? The carnage in Paris brought home to us the clear and present danger that we face from Daesh. It could just as easily have been London, Glasgow, Leeds, or Birmingham and it could still be. I believe that we have a moral and practical duty to extend the action that we are already taking in Iraq to Syria. I am also clear – and I say this to my colleagues – that the conditions set out in the emergency resolution passed at the Labour party conference in September have been met. We now have a clear and unambiguous UN Security Council resolution 2249, paragraph 5 of which specifically calls on member states 'to take all necessary measures . . . to redouble and coordinate their efforts to prevent and suppress terrorist acts committed specifically by ISIL . . . and to eradicate the safe haven they have established over significant parts of Iraq and Syria'.

The United Nations is asking us to do something; it is asking us to do something now; it is asking us to act in Syria as well as in Iraq. It was a Labour Government who helped to found the United Nations at the end of the Second World War. Why did we do so? It was because we wanted the nations of the world working together to deal with threats to international peace and security, and Daesh is unquestionably that. Given that the United Nations has passed this resolution, and that such action would be lawful under article 51 of the UN charter – because every state has the right to defend itself – why would we not uphold the settled will of the United Nations, particularly when there is such support from within the region, including from Iraq? We are part of a coalition of more than sixty countries, standing together shoulder to shoulder to oppose the ideology and brutality of Daesh.

We all understand the importance of bringing an end to the Syrian civil war, and there is now some progress on a peace plan because of the Vienna talks. Those are our best hope of achieving a ceasefire – now that would bring an end to Assad's bombing – leading to a transitional Government and elections. That is vital, both because it would help in the defeat of Daesh and because it would enable millions of Syrians who have been forced to flee to do what every refugee dreams of – they just want to be able to go home.

No one in the debate doubts the deadly serious threat that we face from Daesh and what it does, although we sometimes find it hard to live with the reality. In June, four gay men were thrown off the fifth storey of a building in the Syrian city of Deir ez-Zor. In August, the 82-year-old guardian of the antiquities of Palmyra, Professor Khaled al-Asaad, was beheaded, and his headless body was hung from a traffic light. In recent weeks, mass graves in Sinjar have been discovered, one said to contain the bodies of older Yazidi women murdered by Daesh because they were judged too old to be sold for sex. Daesh has killed 30 British tourists in Tunisia; 224 Russian holidaymakers on a plane; 178 people in suicide bombings in Beirut, Ankara and Suruç; 130 people in Paris, including those young people in the Bataclan, whom Daesh, in trying to justify its bloody slaughter, called apostates engaged in prostitution and vice. If it had happened here they could have been our children.

Daesh is plotting more attacks, so the question for each of us and for our national security is this: given that we know what it is doing, can we really stand aside and refuse to act fully in self-defence against those who are planning these attacks? Can we really leave to others the responsibility for defending our national security? If we do not act, what message will that send about our solidarity with those countries that have suffered so much, including Iraq and our ally, France?

It has been argued in the debate that airstrikes achieve nothing. Not so: the House should look at how Daesh's forward march has been halted in Iraq. It will remember that 14 months ago, people were saying that it was almost at the gates of Baghdad, which is why we voted to respond to the Iraqi Government's request for help to defeat it. Its military capacity and freedom of movement have been put under pressure. Ask the Kurds about Sinjar and Kobane. Of course, airstrikes alone will not defeat Daesh, but they make a difference, because they give it a hard time, making it more difficult for it to expand its territory. I share the concerns that have been expressed this evening about potential civilian casualties. However, unlike Daesh, none of us today acts with the intent to harm civilians. Rather, we act to protect civilians from Daesh, which targets innocent people.

On the subject of ground troops to defeat Daesh, there has been much debate about the figure of 70,000, and the Government must explain that better. But we know that most of those troops are engaged in fighting President Assad. I will tell Members what else we know: whatever the number – 70,000, 40,000, 80,000 – the current size of the opposition forces means that the longer we leave it to take action, the longer Daesh will have to decrease that number. So to suggest that airstrikes should not take place until the Syrian civil war has come to an end is to miss the urgency of the terrorist threat that Daesh poses to us and others, and to misunderstand the nature and objectives of the extension to airstrikes that is proposed.

Of course we should take action – there is no contradiction between the two – to cut off Daesh's support in the form of money, fighters and weapons, of course we should give humanitarian aid, of course we should offer shelter to more refugees, including in this country, and yes, we should commit to play our full part in helping to rebuild Syria when the war is over.

I accept that there are legitimate arguments, and we have heard them in the debate, for not taking this form of action now . . . But I say the threat is now and there are rarely, if ever, perfect circumstances in which to deploy military forces.

I hope the House will bear with me if I direct my closing remarks to my Labour friends and colleagues. As a party we have always been defined by our internationalism. We believe we have a responsibility one to another. We never have and we never should walk by on the other side of the road. We are faced by fascists – not just their calculated brutality, but their belief that they are superior to every single one of us in this Chamber tonight and all the people we represent. They hold us in contempt. They hold our values in contempt. They hold our belief in tolerance and decency in contempt. They hold our democracy – the means by which we will make our decision tonight – in contempt.

What we know about fascists is that they need to be defeated. It is why, as we have heard tonight, socialists, trade unionists and others joined the International Brigade in the 1930s to fight against Franco. It is why this entire House stood up against Hitler and Mussolini. It is why our party has always stood up against the denial of human rights and for justice. My view is that we must now confront this evil. It is now time for us to do our bit in Syria. That is why I ask my colleagues to vote for the motion tonight.

•

## BORIS JOHNSON
### London, 9 May 2016

*'Ever more centralizing, interfering and anti-democratic'*

*As first journalist and then Conservative MP and Mayor of London, Boris Johnson has perhaps become England's most charismatic politician. It was a major disappointment for Prime Minister David Cameron when Johnson finally decided to work for the Leave campaign during the 2016 referendum on the European Union. These are extracts from Johnson's first major speech.*

What was once the EEC has undergone a spectacular metamorphosis in the last thirty years, and the crucial point is that it is still becoming ever more centralizing, interfering and anti-democratic.

You only have to read the Lisbon Treaty – whose constitutional provisions were rejected by three EU populations, the French, the Dutch and the Irish – to see how far this thing has moved on from what we signed up for in 1972. Brussels now has exclusive or explicit competence for trade, customs, competition, agriculture, fisheries, environment, consumer protection, transport, trans-European networks, energy, the areas of freedom, security and justice, and new powers over culture, tourism, education and youth. The EU already has considerable powers to set rates of indirect taxation across the whole 28-nation territory, and of course it has total control of monetary policy for all 19 in the eurozone.

In recent years Brussels has acquired its own foreign minister, its own series of EU embassies around the world, and is continuing to develop its own defence policy. We have got to stop trying to kid the British people; we have got to stop saying one thing in Brussels, and another thing to the domestic audience; we have got to stop the systematic campaign of subterfuge – to conceal from the public the scale of the constitutional changes involved. We need to look at the legal reality, which is that this is a continuing and accelerating effort to build a country called Europe.

Look at that list of Lisbon competences – with 45 new fields of policy where Britain can be outvoted by a qualified majority – and you can see why the House of Commons Library has repeatedly confirmed that when you add primary and secondary legislation together the EU is now generating 60 per cent of the laws passing through parliament.

The independence of this country is being seriously compromised. It is this fundamental democratic problem    this erosion of democracy – that brings me into this fight.

People are surprised and alarmed to discover that our gross contributions to the EU budget are now running at about £20bn a year, and that the net contribution is £10 bn; and it is not just that we have no control over how that money is spent.

No one has any proper control – which is why EU spending is persistently associated with fraud. Of course the Remain campaign dismisses this UK contribution as a mere bagatelle – even though you could otherwise use it to pay for a new British hospital every week. But that expense is, in a sense, the least of the costs inflicted by the EU on this country.

It is deeply corrosive of popular trust in democracy that every year UK politicians tell the public that they can cut immigration to the tens of thousands – and then find that they miss their targets by hundreds of thousands, so that we add a population the size of Newcastle every year, with all the extra and unfunded pressure that puts on the NHS and other public services.

In our desperation to meet our hopeless so-called targets, we push away brilliant students from Commonwealth countries, who want to pay to come to our universities; we find ourselves hard pressed to recruit people who might work in our NHS, as opposed to make use of its services – because we have absolutely no power to control the numbers who are coming with no job offers and no qualifications from the 28 EU countries. I am in favour of immigration; but I am also in favour of control, and of politicians taking responsibility for what is happening; and I think it bewilders people to be told that this most basic power of a state – to decide who has the right to live and work in your country – has been taken away and now resides in Brussels.

And, as I say, that is only one aspect of a steady attrition of the rights of the people to decide their priorities, and to remove, at elections, those who take the decisions. It is sad that our powers of economic self-government have become so straitened that the Chancellor of the Exchequer has to go around personally asking other finance ministers to allow him to cut VAT on tampons, and as far as I can see we still have not secured consent.

It is very worrying that the European Court of Justice – Luxembourg, not Strasbourg – should now be freely adjudicating on human rights questions, and whether or not this country has the right to deport people the Home Office believes are a threat to our security; and it is peculiar that the government is now straining at the gnat of the Convention and the Strasbourg court, whose rulings are not actually binding on UK courts, while swallowing the camel of the 55-article charter of Fundamental rights, which is fully justiciable by the European Court in Luxembourg, when you consider that it is the rulings of this court that are binding and that must be applied by every court in this country, including parliament.

It is absurd that Britain – historically a great free-trading nation – has been unable for 42 years to do a free trade deal with Australia, New Zealand, China, India and America . . .

The answer to the problems of Europe today is not 'more Europe', if that means more forcible economic and political integration. The answer is reform, and devolution of powers back to nations and people, and a return to intergovernmentalism, at least for this country – and that means Vote Leave.

And of course there will be some in this country who are rightly troubled by a sense of neighbourly duty. There are Remainers who may agree with much of the above; that the economic advantages for Britain are either overstated or non-existent. But they feel uneasy about pulling out of the EU in its hour of need, when our neighbours are in distress; and at this point they deploy the so-called 'Peace in Europe' argument: that if Britain leaves the EU, there will be a return to slaughter on Flanders Fields.

I think this grossly underestimates the way Europe has changed, and the NATO guarantee that has really underpinned peace in Europe. I saw the disaster when the EU was charged with sorting out former Yugoslavia, and I saw how NATO sorted it out.

And it understates the sense in which it is the EU itself, and its anti-democratic tendencies that are now a force for instability and alienation.

Europe faces twin crises of mass migration, and a euro that has proved a disaster for some member states; and the grim truth is that the risks of staying in this unreformed EU are intensifying and not diminishing.

If we leave on June 23, we can still provide leadership in so many areas. We can help lead the discussions on security, on counter-terrorism, on foreign and defence policy, as we always have. But all those conversations can be conducted within an intergovernmental framework, and without the need for legal instruments enforced by the European Court of Justice. We will still be able to cooperate on the environment, on migration, on science and technology; we will still have exchanges of students.

We will trade as much as ever before, if not more. We will be able to love our fellow Europeans, marry them, live with them, share the joy of discovering our different cultures and languages – but we will not be subject to the jurisdiction of a single court and legal system that is proving increasingly erratic and that is imitated by no other trading group.

We will not lose influence in Europe or around the world – on the contrary, you could argue we will gain in clout. We are already drowned out around the table in Brussels; we are outvoted far more than any other country – 72 times in the last 20 years, and ever more regularly since 2010; and the Eurozone now has a built-in majority on all questions.

We will recapture or secure our voice – for the fifth biggest economy in the world – in international bodies such as the WTO or the IMF or the CITES, where the EU is increasingly replacing us and laying a claim to speak on our behalf. If you want final and conclusive proof of our inability to 'get our way' in Brussels – and the contempt with which we will be treated if we vote to Remain – look again at the UK deal and the total failure to secure any change of any significance.

Above all – to get to the third key point of the Remainers – if we leave the EU we will not, repeat not, be leaving Europe. Of all the arguments they make, this is the one that infuriates me the most. I am a child of Europe. I am a liberal cosmopolitan and my family is a genetic UN peacekeeping force.

I can read novels in French and I can sing the Ode to Joy in German, and if they keep accusing me of being a Little Englander, I will. Both as editor of the *Spectator* and Mayor of London I have promoted the teaching of modern European languages in our schools. I have dedicated much of my life to the study of the origins of our common – our common – European culture and civilization in ancient Greece and Rome.

So I find if offensive, insulting, irrelevant and positively cretinous to be told – sometimes by people who can barely speak a foreign language – that I belong to a group of small-minded xenophobes; because the truth is it is Brexit that is now the great project of European liberalism, and I am afraid that it is the European Union – for all the high ideals with which it began – that now represents the *ancien régime*.

It is we who are speaking up for the people, and it is they who are defending an obscurantist and universalist system of government that is now well past its sell-by date and which is ever more remote from ordinary voters.

It is we in the Leave Camp – not they – who stand in the tradition of the liberal cosmopolitan European enlightenment – not just of Locke and Wilkes, but of Rousseau and Voltaire; and though they are many, and though they are well-funded, and though we know that they can call on unlimited taxpayer funds for their leaflets, it is we few, we happy few who have the inestimable advantage of believing strongly in our cause, and that we will be vindicated by history; and we will win for exactly the same reason that the Greeks beat the Persians at Marathon – because they are fighting for an outdated absolutist ideology, and we are fighting for freedom.

That is the choice: It is between taking back control of our money – or giving a further £100bn to Brussels before the next election. Between deciding who we want to come here to live and work – or letting the EU decide between a dynamic liberal cosmopolitan open global free-trading prosperous Britain, or a Britain where we remain subject to a undemocratic system devised in the 1950s that is now actively responsible for low growth and in some cases economic despair, between believing in the possibility of hope and change in Europe – or accepting that we have no choice but to knuckle under.

It is a choice between getting dragged ever further into a federal superstate, or taking a stand now.

Vote Leave and take back control of our democracy.

•

## THERESA MAY
### Downing Street, London, 13 July 2016

*'You can just about manage but you worry about the cost of living'*

*In her first speech as Prime Minister and with her husband Philip standing beside her, Theresa May distanced herself from David Cameron's premiership and its aura of Etonian privilege and set out her vision as a One Nation Conservative. She appealed to the JAMs – the just about managing. It was the most radical speech by a Tory Prime Minister since John Major. She called a snap election in June 2017 expecting a landslide but was re-elected with fewer seats, now heading a minority government. It seemed unlikely that her ambitions would be realized.*

I have just been to Buckingham Palace, where Her Majesty the Queen has asked me to form a new government, and I accepted.

In David Cameron, I follow in the footsteps of a great, modern Prime Minister. Under David's leadership, the government stabilized the economy, reduced the budget deficit, and helped more people into work than ever before.

But David's true legacy is not about the economy but about social justice. From the introduction of same-sex marriage, to taking people on low wages out of income tax altogether; David Cameron has led a one-nation government, and it is in that spirit that I also plan to lead.

Because not everybody knows this, but the full title of my party is the Conservative and Unionist Party, and that word 'unionist' is very important to me.

It means we believe in the Union: the precious, precious bond between England, Scotland, Wales and Northern Ireland. But it means something else that is just as important; it means we believe in a union not just between the nations of the United Kingdom but between all of our citizens, every one of us, whoever we are and wherever we're from.

That means fighting against the burning injustice that, if you're born poor, you will die on average nine years earlier than others.

If you're black, you're treated more harshly by the criminal justice system than if you're white.

If you're a white, working-class boy, you're less likely than anybody else in Britain to go to university.

If you're at a state school, you're less likely to reach the top professions than if you're educated privately.

If you're a woman, you will earn less than a man.

If you suffer from mental health problems, there's not enough help to hand.

If you're young, you'll find it harder than ever before to own your own home.

But the mission to make Britain a country that works for everyone means more than fighting these injustices. If you're from an ordinary working class family, life is much harder than many people in Westminster realize. You have a job but you don't always have job security. You have your own home, but you worry about paying a mortgage. You can just about manage but you worry about the cost of living and getting your kids into a good school.

If you're one of those families, if you're just managing, I want to address you directly.

I know you're working around the clock, I know you're doing your best, and I know that sometimes life can be a struggle. The government I lead will be driven not by the interests of the privileged few, but by yours.

We will do everything we can to give you more control over your lives. When we make the big calls, we'll think not of the powerful, but you. When we pass new laws, we'll listen not to the mighty but to you. When it comes to taxes, we'll prioritize not the wealthy, but you. When it comes to opportunity, we won't entrench the advantages of the fortunate few. We will do everything we can to help anybody, whatever your background, to go as far as your talents will take you.

We are living through an important moment in our country's history. Following the referendum, we face a time of great national change.

And I know because we're Great Britain, that we will rise to the challenge. As we leave the European Union, we will forge a bold new positive role for ourselves in the world, and we will make Britain a country that works not for a privileged few, but for every one of us.

That will be the mission of the government I lead, and together we will build a better Britain.

•

## MICHELLE OBAMA
### New Hampshire, 14 October 2016

*'A candidate for president has bragged about sexually assaulting women'*

*One of the many controversies surrounding Donald Trump during the 2016 presidential election occurred after a report by the* Washington Post *which had obtained an 'extremely crass' recording on which Trump conversed with* Access Hollywood *host Billy Bush about women aboard a bus on the set of* Days of Our Lives. *Among the things Trump said were:* 'I moved on her like a bitch, but I couldn't get there, and she was married. Then all of a sudden I see her, she's now got the big phony tits and everything.' *(It's not clear who Trump was talking about.)* 'I'm automatically attracted to beautiful [women] – I just start kissing them. It's like a magnet. Just kiss. I don't even wait. And when you're a star they let you do it. You can do anything . . . Grab them by the pussy. You can do anything.' *It was this report and these comments which provoked Michelle Obama's speech. What follow are extracts.*

It has been a week of profound contrast. On Tuesday, at the White House, we celebrated the International Day of the Girl and Let Girls Learn, and it was a wonderful celebration. It was the last event that I'm going to be doing as First Lady for Let Girls Learn. And I had the pleasure of spending hours talking to some of the most amazing young women you will ever meet, young girls here in the US and all around the world. And we talked about their hopes and their dreams. We talked about their aspirations. See, because many of these girls have faced unthinkable obstacles just to attend school, jeopardizing their personal safety, their freedom, risking the rejection of their families and communities.

So I thought it would be important to remind these young women how valuable and precious they are. I wanted them to understand that the measure of any society is how it treats its women and girls. And I told them that they deserve to be treated with dignity and respect, and I told them that they should disregard anyone who demeans or devalues them, and that they should make their voices heard in the world. And I walked away feeling so inspired, just like I'm inspired by all the young people here – and I was so uplifted by these girls. That was Tuesday.

And now, here I am, out on the campaign trail in an election where we have consistently been hearing hurtful, hateful language about women – language that has been painful for so many of us, not just as women, but as parents trying to protect our children and raise them to be caring, respectful adults, and as citizens who think that our nation's leaders should meet basic standards of human decency.

The fact is that in this election, we have a candidate for president of the United States who, over the course of his lifetime and the course of this campaign, has said things about women that are so shocking, so demeaning that I simply will not repeat anything here today. And last week, we saw this candidate actually bragging about sexually assaulting women. And I can't believe that I'm saying that a candidate for president of the United States has bragged about sexually assaulting women.

And I have to tell you that I can't stop thinking about this. It has shaken me to my core in a way that I couldn't have predicted. So while I'd love nothing more than to pretend like this isn't happening, and to come out here and do my normal campaign speech, it would be dishonest and disingenuous of me to just move on to the next thing like this was all just a bad dream.

This is not something that we can ignore. It's not something we can just sweep under the rug as just another disturbing footnote in a sad election season. Because this was not just a 'lewd conversation'. This wasn't just locker-room banter. This was a powerful individual speaking freely and openly about sexually predatory behaviour, and actually bragging about kissing and groping women, using language so obscene that many of us were worried about our children hearing it when we turn on the TV.

And to make matters worse, it now seems very clear that this isn't an isolated incident. It's one of countless examples of how he has treated women his whole life. And I have to tell you that I listen to all of this and I feel it so personally, and I'm sure that many of you do too, particularly the women. The shameful comments about our bodies. The disrespect of our ambitions and intellect. The belief that you can do anything you want to a woman.

It is cruel. It's frightening. And the truth is, it hurts. It hurts. It's like that sick, sinking feeling you get when you're walking down the street minding your own business and some guy yells out vulgar words about your body. Or when you see that guy at work that stands just a little too close, stares a little too long, and makes you feel uncomfortable in your own skin.

It's that feeling of terror and violation that too many women have felt when someone has grabbed them, or forced himself on them and they've said no but he didn't listen – something that we know happens on college campuses and countless other places every single day. It reminds us of stories we heard from our mothers and grand-mothers about how, back in their day, the boss could say and do whatever he pleased to the women in the office, and even though they worked so hard, jumped over every hurdle to prove themselves, it was never enough.

We thought all of that was ancient history, didn't we? And so many have worked for so many years to end this kind of violence and abuse and disrespect, but here we are in 2016 and we're hearing these exact same things every day on the campaign trail. We are drowning in it. And all of us are doing what women have always done: we're trying to keep our heads above water, just trying to get through it, trying to pretend like this doesn't really bother us, maybe because we think that admitting how much it hurts makes us as women look weak.

Maybe we're afraid to be that vulnerable. Maybe we've grown accustomed to swallowing these emotions and staying quiet, because we've seen that people often won't take our word over his. Or maybe we don't want to believe that there are still people out there who think so little of us as women. Too many are treating this as just another day's headline, as if our outrage is overblown or unwar-ranted, as if this is normal, just politics as usual.

But, New Hampshire, be clear: this is not normal. This is not pol-itics as usual. This is disgraceful. It is intolerable. And it doesn't matter what party you belong to – Democrat, Republican, independ-ent – no woman deserves to be treated this way. None of us deserves this kind of abuse.

And I know it's a campaign, but this isn't about politics. It's about basic human decency. It's about right and wrong. And we simply cannot endure this, or expose our children to this any more – not for another minute, and let alone for four years. Now is the time for all of us to stand up and say enough is enough. This has got to stop right now.

•

## HILLARY CLINTON
### New York, 9 November 2017

*'We still have not shattered that highest and hardest glass ceiling, but someday someone will'*

*In the 2016 presidential election, Hillary Clinton, the Democrat candidate, beat Donald Trump by almost 2.9 million votes, with 65,844,954 (48.2per cent) to his 62,979,879 (46.1per cent). But Trump won the Electoral College with 304 votes compared to 227 votes for Clinton and became President. This is from Clinton's concession speech.*

Last night I congratulated Donald Trump and offered to work with him on behalf of our country.

I hope that he will be a successful president for all Americans. This is not the outcome we wanted or we worked so hard for, and I'm sorry we did not win this election for the values we share and the vision we hold for our country.

But I feel pride and gratitude for this wonderful campaign that we built together. This vast, diverse, creative, unruly, energized campaign. You represent the best of America, and being your candidate has been one of the greatest honours of my life.

I know how disappointed you feel, because I feel it too. And so do tens of millions of Americans who invested their hopes and dreams in this effort. This is painful, and it will be for a long time. But I want you to remember this.

Our campaign was never about one person, or even one election. It was about the country we love and building an America that is hopeful, inclusive, and big-hearted. We have seen that our nation is more deeply divided than we thought. But I still believe in America, and I always will. And if you do, then we must accept this result and then look to the future. Donald Trump is going to be our president. We owe him an open mind and the chance to lead. Our constitutional democracy enshrines the peaceful transfer of power.

We don't just respect that. We cherish it. It also enshrines the rule of law; the principle we are all equal in rights and dignity; freedom of worship and expression. We respect and cherish these values, too, and we must defend them. (*Applause.*)

Let me add: Our constitutional democracy demands our participation, not just every four years, but all the time. So let's do all we can to keep advancing the causes and values we all hold dear. Making our economy work for everyone, not just those at the top, protecting our country and protecting our planet.

And breaking down all the barriers that hold any American back from achieving their dreams. We spent a year and a half bringing together millions of people from every corner of our country to say with one voice that we believe that the American dream is big enough for everyone.

For people of all races, and religions, for men and women, for immigrants, for LGBT people, and people with disabilities. For you poured your hearts into this campaign. To some of you who are veterans, it was a campaign after you had done other campaigns. Some of you, it was your first campaign. I want each of you to know that you were the best campaign anybody could have ever expected or wanted.

And to the millions of volunteers, community leaders, activists and union organizers who knocked on doors, talked to their neighbours, posted on Facebook – even in secret private Facebook sites.

I want everybody coming out from behind that and make sure your voices are heard going forward. (*Cheers and applause.*)

To anyone that sent contributions, even as small as $5, that kept us going, thank you. To all of us, and to the young people in particular, I hope you will hear this – I have, as Tim[Kaine] said, I have spent my entire life fighting for what I believe in.

I've had successes and setbacks and sometimes painful ones. Many of you are at the beginning of your professional, public, and political careers – you will have successes and setbacks too.

This loss hurts, but please never stop believing that fighting for what's right is worth it.

It is, it is worth it. (*Cheers and applause.*)

And so we need – we need you to keep up these fights now and for the rest of your lives. And to all the women, and especially the young women, who put their faith in this campaign and in me: I want you to know that nothing has made me prouder than to be your champion.

Now, I know we have still not shattered that highest and hardest glass ceiling, but someday someone will – and hopefully sooner than we might think right now. (*Cheers and applause.*)

And to all of the little girls who are watching this, never doubt that you are valuable and powerful and deserving of every chance and opportunity in the world to pursue and achieve your own dreams. (*Cheers and applause.*)

Finally, finally, I am so grateful for our country and for all it has given to me.

I count my blessings every single day that I am an American, and I still believe, as deeply as I ever have, that if we stand together and work together with respect for our differences, strength in our convictions, and love for this nation, our best days are still ahead of us.

Because, you know, I believe we are stronger together and we will go forward together. And you should never, ever regret fighting for that. You know, scripture tells us, let us not grow weary of doing good, for in good season we shall reap. My friends, let us have faith in each other, let us not grow weary and lose heart, for there are more seasons to come and there is more work to do.

I am incredibly honoured and grateful to have had this chance to represent all of you in this consequential election. May God bless you and may God bless the United States of America.

∙

# KENNETH CLARKE
London, 31 January 2017

*'It is a very bad move, particularly for our children and grandchildren'*

*In 2017, after serving in parliament as a Conservative MP for forty-seven years, Kenneth Clarke became 'Father of the House'. As a former Chancellor of the Exchequer, Home Secretary, Lord Chancellor and Justice Secretary, Education Secretary and Health Secretary, he was a Big Beast who had been a fervent*

*Europhile throughout his career – which explains the passion in this speech made during the Brexit debate from which these are extracts.*

The Conservative Governments in which I served made very positive contributions to the development of the European Union. There were two areas in which we were the leading contender and made a big difference. The first was when the Thatcher Government led the way in the creation of the single market. The customs union – the so-called common market – had served its purpose, but regulatory barriers matter more than tariffs in the modern world. But for the Thatcher Government, the others would not have been induced to remove those barriers, and I think that the British benefited more from the single market than any other member state. It has contributed to our comparative economic success today.

We were always the leading Government after the fall of the Soviet Union in the process of enlargement to Eastern Europe, taking in the former Soviet states. That was an extremely important political contribution. After the surprising collapse of the Soviet Union, eastern and central Europe could have collapsed into its traditional anarchy, nationalist rivalry and military regimes that preceded the Second World War. We pressed the urgency of bringing in these new independent nations, giving them the goal of the European Union, which meant liberal democracy, free market trade and so forth. We made Europe a much more stable place.

That has been our role in the European Union, and I believe that it is a very bad move, particularly for our children and grandchildren, that we are all sitting here now saying that we are embarking on a new unknown future. I shall touch on that in a moment, because I think the position is simply baffling to every friend of the British and of the United Kingdom throughout the world. That is why I shall vote against the Bill.

Let me deal with the arguments that I should not vote in that way, that I am being undemocratic, that I am quite wrong, and that, as an elected Member of Parliament, I am under a duty to vote contrary to the views I have just given. I am told that this is because we held a referendum. First, I am in the happy situation that my opposition to referendums as an instrument of government is quite well known and has been frequently repeated throughout my political career. I have made no commitment to accept a referendum, and particularly this referendum, when such an enormous question, with hundreds of complex issues wrapped up within it, was to be decided by a simple yes/no answer on one day. That was particularly unsuitable for a plebiscite of that kind, and that point was reinforced by the nature of the debate.

Constitutionally, when the Government tried to stop the House from having a vote, they did not go to the Supreme Court arguing that a referendum bound the House and that that was why we should not have a vote. The referendum had always been described as advisory in everything that the Government put out. There is no constitutional standing for referendums in this country. No sensible country has referendums – the United States and Germany do not have them in their political systems. The Government went to the Supreme Court arguing for the archaic constitutional principle of the royal prerogative – that the Executive somehow had absolute power when it came to dealing with treaties. Not surprisingly, they lost.

Let me provide an analogy – a loose one but, I think, not totally loose – explaining the position of Members of Parliament after this referendum. I have fought Lord knows how many elections over the past fifty years, and I have always advocated voting Conservative. The British public, in their wisdom, have occasionally failed to take my advice and have by a majority voted Labour. I have thus found myself here facing a Labour Government, but I do not recall an occasion when I was told that it was my democratic duty to support Labour policies and the Labour Government on the other side of the House. That proposition, if put to Mr Skinner in opposition or myself, would have been treated with ridicule and scorn. Apparently, I am now being told that despite voting as I did in the referendum, I am somehow an enemy of the people for ignoring my instructions and for sticking to the opinions that I expressed rather strongly, at least in my meetings, when I urged people to vote the other way.

I have no intention of changing my opinion on the ground. Indeed, I am personally convinced that the hard-core Eurosceptics in my party, with whom I have enjoyed debating this issue for decades, would not have felt bound in the slightest by the outcome of the referendum to abandon their arguments – [Interruption.] I do not say that as criticism; I am actually on good terms with the hard-line Eurosceptics because I respect their sincerity and the passionate nature of their beliefs. If I ever live to see my Hon. Friend Sir William Cash turn up here and vote in favour of Britain remaining in the European Union, I will retract what I say, but hot tongs would not make him vote for membership of the EU.

I am a Conservative; I have been a decently loyal Conservative over the years. The last time I kicked over the traces was on the Lisbon treaty, when for some peculiar reason my party got itself on the wrong side of the argument, but we will pass over that. I would point out to those who say that I am somehow being disloyal to my party by not voting in favour of this Bill that I am merely propounding the official policy of the Conservative party for fifty years until 23 June 2016. I admire my colleagues who can suddenly become enthusiastic Brexiteers, having seen a light on the road to Damascus on the day that the vote was cast, but I am afraid that that light has been denied me.

There are very serious issues that were not addressed in the referendum: the single market and the customs union. They must be properly debated. It is absurd to say that every elector knew the difference between the customs union and the single market, and that they took a careful and studied view of the basis for our future trading relations with Europe.

The fact is that I admire the Prime Minister and her colleagues for their constant propounding of the principles of free trade. My party has not changed on that. We are believers in free trade and see it as a win-win situation. We were the leading advocate of liberal economic policies among the European powers for many years, so we are free traders. It seems to me unarguable that if we put between us and the biggest free market in the world new tariffs, new regulatory barriers, new customs procedures, certificates of origin and so on, we are bound to be weakening the economic position from what it would otherwise have been, other things being equal, in future. That is why it is important that this issue is addressed in particular.

I am told that that view is pessimistic, and that we are combining withdrawal from the single market and the customs union with a great new globalized future that offers tremendous opportunities for us.

Apparently, when we follow the rabbit down the hole, we will emerge in a wonderland where, suddenly, countries throughout the world are queuing up to give us trading advantages and access to their markets that we were never able to achieve as part of the European Union. Nice men like President Trump and President Erdogan are impatient to abandon their normal protectionism and give us access. Let me not be too cynical; I hope that that is right. I do want the best outcome for the United Kingdom from this process. No doubt somewhere a hatter is holding a tea party with a dormouse in the teapot.

We need success in these trade negotiations to recoup at least some of the losses that we will incur as a result of leaving the single market. If all is lost on the main principle, that is the big principle that the House must get control of and address seriously, in proper debates and votes, from now on.

I hope that I have adequately explained that my views on this issue have not been shaken very much over the decades – they have actually strengthened somewhat. Most Members, I trust, are familiar with Burke's address to the electors of Bristol. I have always firmly believed that every MP should vote on an issue of this importance according to their view of the best national interest. I never quote Burke, but I shall paraphrase him. He said to his constituents, 'If I no longer give you the benefit of my judgement and simply follow your orders, I am not serving you; I am betraying you.' I personally shall be voting with my conscience content, and when we see what unfolds hereafter as we leave the European Union, I hope that the consciences of other Members of Parliament will remain equally content.

•

# DONALD TRUMP
## Washington, 28 February 2017

*'A new chapter of American greatness is now beginning'*

*Ater his provocative speeches and tweets during the election campaign, President Trump struck a different note when he made his first address to Congress.*

*Speaking from the Speaker's Rostrum in the House of Representatives, Trump made a palpable effort to court voters who didn't support him with an offer to lay to rest the battles of the past. His address ticked almost all the boxes of a traditional State of the Union-style appearance. 'Trump adopted a statesmanlike cadence, hitting notes of inspiration,' said CNN. 'For once, this most unorthodox of politicians struck a conventional presidential posture as he sought to stabilize his administration after a tumultuous five weeks in office.'*

Each American generation passes the torch of truth, liberty and justice in an unbroken chain all the way down to the present. That torch is now in our hands. And we will use it to light up the world. I am here tonight to deliver a message of unity and strength, and it is a message deeply delivered from my heart. A new chapter – [*applause*] – of American Greatness is now beginning. A new national pride is sweeping across our nation. And a new surge of optimism is placing impossible dreams firmly within our grasp.

What we are witnessing today is the renewal of the American spirit. Our allies will find that America is once again ready to lead. (*Applause.*) All the nations of the world – friend or foe – will find that America is strong, America is proud, and America is free.

In nine years, the United States will celebrate the 250th anniversary of our founding – 250 years since the day we declared our independence. It will be one of the great milestones in the history of the world. But what will America look like as we reach our 250th year? What kind of country will we leave for our children?

I will not allow the mistakes of recent decades past to define the course of our future. For too long, we've watched our middle class shrink as we've exported our jobs and wealth to foreign countries. We've financed and built one global project after another, but ignored the fates of our children in the inner cities of Chicago, Baltimore, Detroit, and so many other places throughout our land.

We've defended the borders of other nations while leaving our own borders wide open for anyone to cross and for drugs to pour in at a now unprecedented rate. And we've spent trillions and trillions of dollars overseas, while our infrastructure at home has so badly crumbled.

Then, in 2016, the Earth shifted beneath our feet. The rebellion started as a quiet protest, spoken by families of all colours and creeds – families who just wanted a fair shot for their children and a fair hearing for their concerns.

But then the quiet voices became a loud chorus as thousands of citizens now spoke out together, from cities small and large, all across our country. Finally, the chorus became an earthquake, and the people turned out by the tens of millions, and they were all united by one very simple, but crucial demand: that America must put its own citizens first. Because only then can we truly make America great again. (*Applause.*)

Dying industries will come roaring back to life. Heroic veterans will get the care they so desperately need. Our military will be given the resources its brave warriors so richly deserve. Crumbling infrastructure will be replaced with new roads, bridges, tunnels, airports and railways gleaming across our very, very beautiful land. Our terrible drug epidemic will slow down and, ultimately, stop. And our neglected inner cities will see a rebirth of hope, safety and opportunity. Above all else, we will keep our promises to the American people. (*Applause.*)

It's been a little over a month since my inauguration, and I want to take this moment to update the nation on the progress I've made in keeping those promises.

Since my election, Ford, Fiat-Chrysler, General Motors, Sprint, Softbank, Lockheed, Intel, Walmart and many others have announced that they will invest billions and billions of dollars in the United States, and will create tens of thousands of new American jobs. (*Applause.*)

The stock market has gained almost $3 trillion in value since the election on November 8th, a record. We've saved taxpayers hundreds of millions of dollars by bringing down the price of a fantastic – and it is a fantastic – new F 35 jet fighter, and we'll be saving billions more on contracts all across our government. We have placed a hiring freeze on non-military and non-essential federal workers.

We have begun to drain the swamp of government corruption by imposing a five-year ban on lobbying by executive branch officials and a lifetime ban – [*applause*] – thank you – and a lifetime ban on becoming lobbyists for a foreign government.

We have undertaken a historic effort to massively reduce job-crushing regulations, creating a deregulation task force inside of every government agency. (*Applause.*) And we're imposing a new rule which mandates that for every one new regulation, two old regulations must be eliminated. (*Applause.*) We're going to stop the regulations that threaten the future and livelihood of our great coal miners. (*Applause.*)

We have cleared the way for the construction of the Keystone and Dakota Access Pipelines – [*applause*] – thereby creating tens of thousands of jobs. And I've issued a new directive that new American pipelines be made with American steel. (*Applause.*)

We have withdrawn the United States from the job-killing Trans-Pacific Partnership. (*Applause.*) And with the help of Prime Minister Justin Trudeau, we have formed a council with our neighbours in Canada to help ensure that women entrepreneurs have access to the networks, markets and capital they need to start a business and live out their financial dreams. (*Applause.*)

To protect our citizens, I have directed the Department of Justice to form a Task Force on Reducing Violent Crime. I have further ordered the Departments of Homeland Security and Justice, along with the Department of State and the Director of National Intelligence, to coordinate an aggressive strategy to dismantle the criminal cartels that have spread all across our nation. (*Applause.*) We will stop the drugs from pouring into our country and poisoning our youth, and we will expand treatment for those who have become so badly addicted. (*Applause.*)

At the same time, my administration has answered the pleas of the American people for immigration enforcement and border security. (*Applause.*) By finally enforcing our immigration laws, we will raise wages, help the unemployed, save billions and billions of dollars, and make our communities safer for everyone. (*Applause.*) We want all Americans to succeed, but that can't happen in an environment of lawless chaos. We must restore integrity and the rule of law at our borders. (*Applause.*)

For that reason, we will soon begin the construction of a great, great wall along our southern border. (*Applause.*) As we speak tonight, we are removing gang members, drug dealers, and criminals that threaten our communities and prey on our very innocent citizens. Bad ones are going out as I speak, and as I promised throughout the campaign.

To any in Congress who do not believe we should enforce our laws, I would ask you this one question: What would you say to the American family that loses their jobs, their income, or their loved one because America refused to uphold its laws and defend its borders? (*Applause.*)

Our obligation is to serve, protect, and defend the citizens of the United States. We are also taking strong measures to protect our nation from radical Islamic terrorism. (*Applause.*) According to data provided by the Department of Justice, the vast majority of individuals convicted of terrorism and terrorism-related offences since 9/11 came here from outside of our country. We have seen the attacks at home – from Boston to San Bernardino to the Pentagon, and, yes, even the World Trade Center.

We have seen the attacks in France, in Belgium, in Germany, and all over the world. It is not compassionate, but reckless to allow uncontrolled entry from places where proper vetting cannot occur. (*Applause.*) Those given the high honour of admission to the United States should support this country and love its people and its values. We cannot allow a beachhead of terrorism to form inside America. We cannot allow our nation to become a sanctuary for extremists. (*Applause.*)

That is why my administration has been working on improved vetting procedures, and we will shortly take new steps to keep our nation safe and to keep out those who will do us harm. (*Applause.*)

As promised, I directed the Department of Defense to develop a plan to demolish and destroy ISIS – a network of lawless savages that have slaughtered Muslims and Christians, and men, and women, and children of all faiths and all beliefs. We will work with our allies, including our friends and allies in the Muslim world, to extinguish this vile enemy from our planet. (*Applause.*)

I have also imposed new sanctions on entities and individuals who support Iran's ballistic missile program, and reaffirmed our unbreakable alliance with the State of Israel. (*Applause.*)

Finally, I have kept my promise to appoint a justice to the United States Supreme Court, from my list of twenty judges, who will defend our Constitution. (*Applause.*)

Tonight, as I outline the next steps we must take as a country, we must honestly acknowledge the circumstances we inherited. Ninety-four million Americans are out of the labour force. Over 43 million people are now living in poverty, and over 43 million Americans are on food stamps. More than one in five people in their prime working years are not working. We have the worst financial recovery in sixty-five years. In the last eight years, the past administration has put on more new debt than nearly all of the other Presidents combined.

We've lost more than one-fourth of our manufacturing jobs since NAFTA was approved, and we've lost 60,000 factories since China joined the World Trade Organization in 2001. Our trade deficit in goods with the world last year was nearly $800 billion dollars. And overseas we have inherited a series of tragic foreign policy disasters.

Solving these and so many other pressing problems will require us to work past the differences of party. It will require us to tap into the American spirit that has overcome every challenge throughout our long and storied history. But to accomplish our goals at home and abroad, we must restart the engine of the American economy – making it easier for companies to do business in the United States, and much, much harder for companies to leave our country. (*Applause.*)

Right now, American companies are taxed at one of the highest rates anywhere in the world. My economic team is developing historic tax reform that will reduce the tax rate on our companies so they can compete and thrive anywhere and with anyone. (*Applause.*) It will be a big, big cut.

At the same time, we will provide massive tax relief for the middle class. We must create a level playing field for American companies and our workers. We have to do it. (*Applause.*) Currently, when we ship products out of America, many other countries make us pay very high tariffs and taxes. But when foreign companies ship their products into America, we charge them nothing, or almost nothing.

I believe strongly in free trade but it also has to be fair trade. It's been a long time since we had fair trade. The first Republican President, Abraham Lincoln, warned that the 'abandonment of the protective policy by the American government . . . will produce want and ruin among our people'. Lincoln was right – and it's time we heeded his advice and his words. (*Applause.*) I am not going to let America and its great companies and workers be taken advantage of any longer. They have taken advantage of our country. No longer. (*Applause.*)

I am going to bring back millions of jobs. Protecting our workers also means reforming our system of legal immigration. (*Applause.*) The current, outdated system depresses wages for our poorest workers, and puts great pressure on taxpayers. Nations around the world, like Canada, Australia and many others, have a merit-based immigration system. (*Applause.*) It's a basic principle that those seeking to enter a country ought to be able to support themselves financially. Yet, in America, we do not enforce this rule, straining the very public resources that our poorest citizens rely upon. According to the National Academy of Sciences, our current immigration system costs American taxpayers many billions of dollars a year.

Switching away from this current system of lower-skilled immigration, and instead adopting a merit-based system, we will have so many more benefits. It will save countless dollars, raise workers' wages, and help struggling families – including immigrant families – enter the middle class. And they will do it quickly, and they will be very, very happy, indeed. (*Applause.*)

I believe that real and positive immigration reform is possible, as long as we focus on the following goals: To improve jobs and wages for Americans; to strengthen our nation's security; and to restore respect for our laws. If we are guided by the wellbeing of American citizens, then I believe Republicans and Democrats can work together to achieve an outcome that has eluded our country for decades. (*Applause.*)

Finally, to keep America safe, we must provide the men and women of the United States military with the tools they need to prevent war – if they must – they have to fight and they only have to win. (*Applause.*)

I am sending Congress a budget that rebuilds the military, eliminates the defence sequester – [*applause*] – and calls for one of the largest increases in national defence spending in American history. My budget will also increase funding for our veterans. Our veterans have delivered for this nation, and now we must deliver for them. (*Applause.*)

The challenges we face as a nation are great, but our people are even greater. And none are greater or braver than those who fight for America in uniform. (*Applause.*)

For as the Bible teaches us, 'There is no greater act of love than to lay down one's life for one's friends.' Ryan laid down his life for his friends, for his country, and for our freedom. And we will never forget Ryan. (*Applause.*)

To those allies who wonder what kind of a friend America will be, look no further than the heroes who wear our uniform. Our foreign policy calls for a direct, robust and meaningful engagement with the world. It is American leadership based on vital security interests that we share with our allies all across the globe.

We strongly support NATO, an alliance forged through the bonds of two world wars that dethroned fascism, and a Cold War, and defeated communism. (*Applause.*)

But our partners must meet their financial obligations. And now, based on our very strong and frank discussions, they are beginning to do just that. In fact, I can tell you, the money is pouring in. Very nice. (*Applause.*) We expect our partners – whether in NATO, the Middle East, or in the Pacific – to take a direct and meaningful role in both strategic and military operations, and pay their fair share of the cost. Have to do that.

We will respect historic institutions, but we will respect the foreign rights of all nations, and they have to respect our rights as a nation also. (*Applause.*) Free nations are the best vehicle for expressing the will of the people, and America respects the right of all nations to chart their own path. My job is not to represent the world. My job is to represent the United States of America. (*Applause.*)

But we know that America is better off when there is less conflict, not more. We must learn from the mistakes of the past. We have seen the war and the destruction that have ravaged and raged throughout the world – all across the world. The only long-term solution for these humanitarian disasters, in many cases, is to create the conditions where displaced persons can safely return home and begin the long, long process of rebuilding. (*Applause.*)

America is willing to find new friends, and to forge new partnerships, where shared interests align. We want harmony and stability, not war and conflict. We want peace, wherever peace can be found.

America is friends today with former enemies. Some of our closest allies, decades ago, fought on the opposite side of these terrible, terrible wars. This history should give us all faith in the possibilities for a better world. Hopefully, the 250th year for America will see a world that is more peaceful, more just, and more free.

On our 100th anniversary, in 1876, citizens from across our nation came to Philadelphia to celebrate America's centennial. At that celebration, the country's builders and artists and inventors showed off their wonderful creations. Alexander Graham Bell displayed his telephone for the first time. Remington unveiled the first typewriter. An early attempt was made at electric light. Thomas Edison showed an automatic telegraph and an electric pen. Imagine the wonders our country could know in America's 250th year. (*Applause.*)

Think of the marvels we can achieve if we simply set free the dreams of our people. Cures to the illnesses that have always plagued us are not too much to hope. American footprints on distant worlds are not too big a dream. Millions lifted from welfare to work is not too much to expect. And streets where mothers are safe from fear, schools where children learn in peace, and jobs where Americans prosper and grow are not too much to ask. (*Applause.*)

When we have all of this, we will have made America greater than ever before — for all Americans. This is our vision. This is our mission. But we can only get there together. We are one people, with one destiny. We all bleed the same blood. We all salute the same great American flag. And we all are made by the same God. (*Applause.*)

When we fulfil this vision, when we celebrate our 250 years of glorious freedom, we will look back on tonight as when this new chapter of American Greatness began. The time for small thinking is over. The time for trivial fights is behind us. We just need the courage to share the dreams that fill our hearts, the bravery to express the hopes that stir our souls, and the confidence to turn those hopes and those dreams into action.

From now on, America will be empowered by our aspirations, not burdened by our fears; inspired by the future, not bound by the failures of the past; and guided by our vision, not blinded by our doubts.

I am asking all citizens to embrace this renewal of the American spirit. I am asking all members of Congress to join me in dreaming big, and bold, and daring things for our country. I am asking everyone watching tonight to seize this moment. Believe in yourselves, believe in your future, and believe, once more, in America.

Thank you, God bless you, and God bless the United States. (*Applause.*)

# THE PENGUIN BOOK OF
# HISTORIC SPEECHES

**EDITED BY BRIAN MACARTHUR**

From Moses to Nelson Mandela, speeches have helped both change the way we see the world and the way the world is shaped. A great orator, however, has to have the right words and the right message to inspire his or her followers.

*The Penguin Book of Historic Speeches* gathers together the world's greatest speeches, bringing together the words of over one hundred men and women. These brilliant and passionate declarations by Disraeli, Lincoln, Gladstone, Churchill, Washington, Socrates, Pankhurst, Lenin, Gandhi and many others provide a vivid glimpse of history in the making while retaining their power to move and inspire today.

'Impeccable. MacArthur prefaces each address with a short but scholarly historical explanation that sets the scene perfectly. An attractive volume with a splendidly pithy introducton' *Sunday Times*